# Praise for the *Photoshop Bible* Books and Deke McClelland

*You're probably thinking that if someone has the gall to call his book a Bible, it had better be pretty good. If you're not thinking that, it's probably because you've already experienced the* Photoshop Bible *and you know it's good.*
— ***Los Angeles Times***

*Say goodbye to those dull and dusty step-by-step tutorials now that Deke McClelland, the Digital Guru of computer graphics, has updated his international bestseller, the* Macworld Photoshop 5 Bible.
— **Adobe.com**

*A great program deserves a great book. Photoshop has one in this mammoth paperback* (Photoshop Bible).
— ***Cincinnati Enquirer***

*I've been involved with Photoshop for over 7 years, and for as long as I can remember, I've had Deke looking over my shoulder. Deke takes you through Photoshop and covers a lot of areas with impressive depth.*
— **Mark Hamburg, Adobe principal scientist and architect for Photoshop, from the Foreword**

*It's always nice to see something that was very good become great — bigger and better than its predecessor (which was already quite good), the* Macworld Photoshop 5 Bible *kicks some serious butt: It's simply outstanding.*
— **PhotoBooks.com**

*The* Photoshop Bible *is a must-have encyclopedia of Photoshop info. It's a tribute to Deke's Photoshop knowledge that even the most veteran Photoshop users find the "Bible" required reading.*
— **Jeff Schewe, imaging artist and author**

*(The* Photoshop Bible *books) show you the ins and outs of this fascinating program, with step-by-step instructions for both everyday techniques and unusual but useful tricks.*
— ***Houston Chronicle***

*This is an excellent book. I believe you will use it for years.*
— ***Space Coast PC Journal***

*[In* Photoshop Studio Secrets*]McClelland takes you step by step through every stage of the design, from concept to execution. This is the book you need if you're more interested in the artwork than in the tools.*
— ***Los Angeles Times***

*With Photoshop expert Deke McClelland at the steering wheel, how can you go wrong?*
— **The Design & Publishing Center**

*The* Photoshop 5 Bible *by Deke McClelland sits proudly on my desk and is a constant source of information and assistance as I confidently create with Adobe Photoshop 5. McClelland's complete understanding of Adobe's suite of imaging software is only surpassed by his ability to teach. He may be my favorite author!*
**—Susanne York, Houston, TX**

*I gotta tell you—the* Photoshop Bible *has saved me many times. There is nothing more a designer needs (except for coffee) sitting beside his Mac than the* Photoshop Bible.
**—Jason K. Jennings, Nashville, TN**

*While it may theoretically be possible to use Photoshop without the* Photoshop Bible, *I can't imagine why anyone would want to try.*
**—Tim Wilson, Keys Entertainment**

*McClelland offers tons of tips, tricks and procedures. There are more insights than any one person will likely be able to digest, but even a few will prove invaluable for getting more out of the program. . . . One advantage of such a large book is that complicated subjects can be dealt with at length. McClelland takes full advantage of this in the special effects section, detailing how the different filters work, what the effects of the filters are, and how users can better control the results. . . . Macworld Photoshop Bible succeeds as a valuable tome for users of all levels. It will be helpful for beginners and relevant to advanced users.*
**—Communication Arts**

*This was the best computer book I've ever read.*
**—SM, Boulder, CO**

*This author's style is inviting and comfortable. He explains complex concepts in a very simple, familiar manner. Nothing else comes close.*
**—TG, North Hollywood, CA**

*I read this book on vacation—and still had a good time!*
**—DLG, Vanderbilt, Mississippi**

*This book has the most extensive coverage of Adobe Photoshop I've seen! Thanks for helping me realize the limitless potential of Photoshop!*
**—DG, Big Sandy, Texas**

*. . . this encyclopedic effort ought to help both new and experienced users unleash the power of this multidimensional program. Nearly every feature is explored in detail— in McClelland's conversational style. . . . One imaging topic of importance among Photoshop disciples—Unsharp Masking—gets no less than seven pages in the Bible. It's as clear an explanation of USM as has ever been published, backed up with examples showing the effects achieved by varying the Amount, Radius, and Threshold settings. In fact, if you're looking for only one comprehensive Photoshop book, this may be the one.*
**—Photo District News**

*It's a must-have for every professional Photoshop user.*
**—RC, London, England**

*I teach Photoshop; there would be no way for me to survive my first class without this book! Deke McClelland incorporates a funny way of explaining things, he's very thorough and tells you about "real-life" situations, not just what Adobe wants its customers to know.*
**—CD, Addison, Texas**

*I thought I was an expert Photoshop user, but you should see how many pages I've marked in this book. Deke's presentation is one of the clearest and most accurate I've seen.*
**—CS, Fullerton, California**

*This book puts the Photoshop user manual to shame!*
**—DB, Toronto, Ontario, Canada**

*Deke is humorous, not a self-righteous "know everything" author. This book cuts straight to the usable information, without the typical hype or fluff of the manufacturer manuals.*
**—EV, Somerset, New Jersey**

*I'm able to do more than I thought possible with Photoshop using this guide.*
**—DH, Lincoln, Nebraska**

*I like the clear, concise, and practical application of each process in Photoshop. Especially the use of layers! WOW!*
**—MRB, Langley, Washington**

*I have every Photoshop book and this one is the best. It is the one I go to when I need an answer.*
**—EF, Boulder Colorado**

*What I really like about the book is that Deke McClelland starts at the basics and takes you step by step as if you knew nothing about scanning or images. He takes nothing for granted, explaining in the introduction such fundamentals as when to use Photoshop and when to use a drawing program. . . . So what does Photoshop do and how does this book help you in doing it? Mr. McClelland will answer both questions and every other question you can think of within the confines of the Macintosh and Photoshop.*
**—Work Place, University College, Dublin, Ireland**

*No other book about Photoshop is as good as this one. It's the best!*
**—JO, Garsfontein, South Africa**

*A truly wonderful book, jam-packed with useful hints, tricks, and basic procedures in Photoshop.*
**—TW, Dubuque, Iowa**

*I had tough deadlines and had never used Photoshop before. This book added years to my life!*
**—RB, Green Bay, Wisconsin**

*Great job McClelland! Many books are dull, but this one made me laugh out loud. It was easy to read the whole thing.*
—**PM, Vallejo, California**

*I am laughing all day thinking about and reading this book.*
—**SA, Barcelona, Spain**

*Given the technical nature of the topic and the depth of coverage, you might expect the writing to be rather dry—somewhat less than inspiring. Fortunately, Deke McClelland is as accomplished a writer as he is a Photoshop guru. He has managed to keep a potentially heavy topic from becoming too great a burden on the reader, while maintaining a strong flow of information. His wit and style show through repeatedly in every chapter. I strongly recommend this book to anyone who uses Adobe Photoshop on the Mac or PC.*
—**Flash**

*It has an answer waiting for every question I could possibly have about Photoshop.*
—**TL, Corona, California**

*This "Bible" brings all the comfort that the King James Version no longer does—it's my new "Linus Blanket!" I have yet to go find a topic that I can think of that isn't covered by the book, and it is stuffed full of topics that wouldn't have occurred to me.*
—**NC, London, England**

*I learn something new every time I open it.*
—**SFJ, Billerica, Massachusetts**

*It's a great book . . . definitely every Photoshop user's dream.*
—**CT, Brisbane, Australia**

*I like Deke McClelland's sense of humor! Plus I loved all the information he poured forth about every feature of Photoshop. I just think this book is excellent!*
—**TC, Augusta, Georgia**

*I think I love you, Deke McClelland! Thank you for continuing my ongoing quest!*
—**KW, Ocoee, Florida**

*This is a great book. I know Photoshop, but I never realized you could do so much with it until I read this book.*
—**TLS, Whitestone, New York**

*It is easily understandable and very easy reading with as much information put together as I thought possible. It has everything!*
—**GKP, Eugene, Oregon**

*This book helped me to understand the thought processes the developers went through to build the program, which helps me to be a better user.*
—**JD, Arkansas City, Kansas**

# Photoshop® 5 Bible, Gold Edition

# Photoshop® 5 Bible, Gold Edition

**Deke McClelland**

IDG Books Worldwide, Inc.
An International Data Group Company

Foster City, CA ✦ Chicago, IL ✦ Indianapolis, IN ✦ New York, NY

**Photoshop® 5 Bible, Gold Edition**

Published by

**IDG Books Worldwide, Inc.**

An International Data Group Company

919 E. Hillsdale Blvd., Suite 400

Foster City, CA 94404

www.idgbooks.com (IDG Books Worldwide Web site)

Library of Congress Catalog Card Number: 99-62215

ISBN: 0-7645-3372-X

Printed in the United States of America

10 9 8 7 6 5 4 3 2 1

1P/QV/QV/ZZ/FC

Distributed in the United States by IDG Books Worldwide, Inc.

Distributed by Macmillan Canada for Canada; by Transworld Publishers Limited in the United Kingdom; by IDG Norge Books for Norway; by IDG Sweden Books for Sweden; by Woodslane Pty. Ltd. for Australia; by Woodslane (NZ) Ltd. for New Zealand; by Addison Wesley Longman Singapore Pte Ltd. for Singapore, Malaysia, Thailand, and Indonesia; by Norma Comunicaciones S.A. for Colombia; by Intersoft for South Africa; by International Thomson Publishing for Germany, Austria and Switzerland; by Distribuidora Cuspide for Argentina; by Livraria Cultura for Brazil; by Ediciencia S.A. for Ecuador; by Ediciones ZETA S.C.R. Ltda. for Peru; by WS Computer Publishing Corporation, Inc., for the Philippines; by Contemporanea de Ediciones for Venezuela; by Express Computer Distributors for the Caribbean and West Indies; by Micronesia Media Distributor, Inc. for Micronesia; by Grupo Editorial Norma S.A. for Guatemala; by Chips Computadoras S.A. de C.V. for Mexico; by Editorial Norma de Panama S.A. for Panama; by Wouters Import for Belgium; by American Bookshops for Finland. Authorized Sales Agent: Anthony Rudkin Associates for the Middle East and North Africa.

For general information on IDG Books Worldwide's books in the U.S., please call our Consumer Customer Service department at 800-762-2974. For reseller information, including discounts and premium sales, please call our Reseller Customer Service department at 800-434-3422.

For information on where to purchase IDG Books Worldwide's books outside the U.S., please contact our International Sales department at 317-596-5530 or fax 317-596-5692.

For information on foreign language translations, please contact our Foreign & Subsidiary Rights department at 650-655-3021 or fax 650-655-3281.

For sales inquiries and special prices for bulk quantities, please contact our Sales department at 650-655-3200 or write to the address above.

For information on using IDG Books Worldwide's books in the classroom or for ordering examination copies, please contact our Educational Sales department at 800-434-2086 or fax 317-596-5499.

For press review copies, author interviews, or other publicity information, please contact our Public Relations department at 650-655-3000 or fax 650-655-3299.

For authorization to photocopy items for corporate, personal, or educational use, please contact Copyright Clearance Center, 222 Rosewood Drive, Danvers, MA 01923, or fax 978-750-4470.

# ABOUT IDG BOOKS WORLDWIDE

Welcome to the world of IDG Books Worldwide.

IDG Books Worldwide, Inc., is a subsidiary of International Data Group, the world's largest publisher of computer-related information and the leading global provider of information services on information technology. IDG was founded more than 30 years ago by Patrick J. McGovern and now employs more than 9,000 people worldwide. IDG publishes more than 290 computer publications in over 75 countries. More than 90 million people read one or more IDG publications each month.

Launched in 1990, IDG Books Worldwide is today the #1 publisher of best-selling computer books in the United States. We are proud to have received eight awards from the Computer Press Association in recognition of editorial excellence and three from Computer Currents' First Annual Readers' Choice Awards. Our best-selling *...For Dummies*® series has more than 50 million copies in print with translations in 31 languages. IDG Books Worldwide, through a joint venture with IDG's Hi-Tech Beijing, became the first U.S. publisher to publish a computer book in the People's Republic of China. In record time, IDG Books Worldwide has become the first choice for millions of readers around the world who want to learn how to better manage their businesses.

Our mission is simple: Every one of our books is designed to bring extra value and skill-building instructions to the reader. Our books are written by experts who understand and care about our readers. The knowledge base of our editorial staff comes from years of experience in publishing, education, and journalism — experience we use to produce books to carry us into the new millennium. In short, we care about books, so we attract the best people. We devote special attention to details such as audience, interior design, use of icons, and illustrations. And because we use an efficient process of authoring, editing, and desktop publishing our books electronically, we can spend more time ensuring superior content and less time on the technicalities of making books.

You can count on our commitment to deliver high-quality books at competitive prices on topics you want to read about. At IDG Books Worldwide, we continue in the IDG tradition of delivering quality for more than 30 years. You'll find no better book on a subject than one from IDG Books Worldwide.

John Kilcullen
Chairman and CEO
IDG Books Worldwide, Inc.

Steven Berkowitz
President and Publisher
IDG Books Worldwide, Inc.

*Eighth Annual
Computer Press
Awards ≥1992*

*Ninth Annual
Computer Press
Awards ≥1993*

*Tenth Annual
Computer Press
Awards ≥1994*

*Eleventh Annual
Computer Press
Awards ≥1995*

IDG is the world's leading IT media, research and exposition company. Founded in 1964, IDG had 1997 revenues of $2.05 billion and has more than 9,000 employees worldwide. IDG offers the widest range of media options that reach IT buyers in 75 countries representing 95% of worldwide IT spending. IDG's diverse product and services portfolio spans six key areas including print publishing, online publishing, expositions and conferences, market research, education and training, and global marketing services. More than 90 million people read one or more of IDG's 290 magazines and newspapers, including IDG's leading global brands — Computerworld, PC World, Network World, Macworld and the Channel World family of publications. IDG Books Worldwide is one of the fastest-growing computer book publishers in the world, with more than 700 titles in 36 languages. The "...For Dummies®" series alone has more than 50 million copies in print. IDG offers online users the largest network of technology-specific Web sites around the world through IDG.net (http://www.idg.net), which comprises more than 225 targeted Web sites in 55 countries worldwide. International Data Corporation (IDC) is the world's largest provider of information technology data, analysis and consulting, with research centers in over 41 countries and more than 400 research analysts worldwide. IDG World Expo is a leading producer of more than 168 globally branded conferences and expositions in 35 countries including E3 (Electronic Entertainment Expo), Macworld Expo, ComNet, Windows World Expo, ICE (Internet Commerce Expo), Agenda, DEMO, and Spotlight. IDG's training subsidiary, ExecuTrain, is the world's largest computer training company, with more than 230 locations worldwide and 785 training courses. IDG Marketing Services helps industry-leading IT companies build international brand recognition by developing global integrated marketing programs via IDG's print, online and exposition products worldwide. Further information about the company can be found at www.idg.com.                                                                                                1/24/99

# Credits

**Acquisitions Editor**
Andy Cummings

**Development Editors**
Amy Thomas Buscaglia
Kenyon Brown

**Technical Editors**
Marc Pawliger
Amy Thomas Buscaglia

**Copy Editors**
Corey Cohen
Colleen Dowling
Ami Knox
Amanda Kaufmann

**Project Coordinator**
Susan Parini

**Cover Coordinator**
Constance Petros

**Graphics and Production Specialists**
Jude Levinson
Dina F Quan
Christopher Pimentel

**Quality Control Specialists**
Mick Arellano
Mark Schumann

**Proofreading and Indexing**
York Production Services

# About the Author

**Deke McClelland** is a contributing editor for *Macworld* and *Publish* magazines.
He has authored more than 50 books on electronic publishing and the Macintosh
computer, and his work has been translated into more than 20 languages. He
started his career as artistic director at the first service bureau in the United States.

Deke won a Society of Technical Communication Award in 1994, an American
Society for Business Press Editors Award in 1995, and the Ben Franklin Award
for Best Computer Book in 1989. He is also a five-time recipient of the prestigious
Computer Press Award.

Deke is the author of the following books published by IDG Books Worldwide, Inc.:
*Macworld Photoshop 5 Bible*, *Photoshop 5 for Windows Bible*, *Web Design Studio
Secrets*, and *Photoshop Studio Secrets, 2nd Edition*. He is also the author of *Real
World Illustrator 8* and *Real World Digital Photography* from Peachpit Press. The first
edition of *Photoshop Studio Secrets* won the Computer Press Award for the best
advanced how-to book of 1997.

*Though you are asleep and I am awake*
*there is this one matter of urgency*
*that demands your attention. Wake up, dear,*
*so I can tell you how much I love you.*

*Darling EP.*

# Foreword

If you are reading this foreword, it probably means that you've purchased a copy of Adobe Photoshop 5.0. For that, I and the rest of the Photoshop team at Adobe thank you.

If you own a previous edition of the *Photoshop Bible*, you probably know what to expect. If not, get ready for an interesting trip.

I have long felt that the best way to learn Photoshop is through exploration. Rather than just offering a set of canned effects, Photoshop offers a broad collection of tools for a wide range of imaging tasks. Becoming a skilled Photoshop user involves getting to know these tools, how they interact, and when to use them. The best way I've found to do that is through use, exploration, and play.

Photoshop 5.0 contains a number of features designed to allow you to change your mind repeatedly while working on an image. Those features should make it easier to explore the product without fear. On the other hand, because Photoshop allows one to do so much, it can be difficult to know where to begin. It's like opening a watch maker's tool chest: the screwdrivers are pretty obvious, but what about all these other strange and mysterious instruments?

This is where Deke McClelland comes in.

In Deke's hands, Photoshop goes from being just a toolbox to being a strange and wonderful land all its own. The *Photoshop Bible* is a guided tour through that land with a guide who has been over the territory many times. (I've been involved with Photoshop for seven years, and for essentially as long as I can remember, I've had Deke looking over my shoulder.)

Deke takes you through most of Photoshop and covers a lot of areas in impressive depth. Not only does he show you the features in Photoshop — after all, you've got the manual to do that — he shows you how to use them to solve issues that look almost like real-world problems. This is the *Photoshop Bible*, not the *Photoshop Encyclopedia*; it tells stories rather than just present information. Those stories take the form of looking at complex problems — like dealing with hair (believe me, it can be difficult in ways you've never imagined) — and showing how you can use Photoshop's tools to solve those problems.

A second thing you'll get from this book is a lot of commentary. Deke isn't shy about letting you know how he feels about various features. I don't always agree with Deke's opinions on these matters, but I think his openness about his opinions makes the book much richer. If you become a routine user of Photoshop, you will almost certainly develop your own opinions, some of which will probably match Deke's and some of which probably won't. It's valuable to get his opinions during the tour, however, because, even if you end up disagreeing with them, they give you more to think about.

Finally, the most invigorating aspect of this book is the enthusiasm Deke brings to the tour. You'll note that I included "play" in my list of strategies for coming to know Photoshop, and I think just having fun with the program is really one of the best things you can do when starting out. Deke almost relentlessly conveys that sense of excitement and fun, and for that I thank him.

So, fasten your seat belts, put on your pith helmets, and get ready. It's a fascinating trip ahead.

Mark Hamburg
Principal Scientist and Architect for Adobe Photoshop
Adobe Systems Incorporated

# Preface

Ihave no idea where you are as you read this. You might be sitting in front of your computer, lounging on a beach in Martinique, or curled up under the covers with a flashlight. But there's a chance you're standing in a bookstore with a clerk behind you asking if you need any help. If so, you're at what we in the book biz like to call the "point of purchase" (POP). From my perspective, the POP is a dangerous place, fraught with ambiguities and temptations. There's a chance — however infinitesimal — that you might put this book back where you found it and buy a competing title. I shudder to think of it.

So for the benefit of you POPers, I'm about to lay it on a bit thick.

First, let's talk lineage. Weighing in at about four pounds, eight ounces, this book is the colossal offspring of a proud and accomplished parent, the *Photoshop Bible*. Not only is the *Photoshop Bible* the number-one selling guide to Adobe Photoshop, but it's one of the two or three most successful books on any electronic publishing topic ever printed. You can find dozens of localized translations throughout the world. (The Dutch translation has even been known to come out before the English edition.) The *Photoshop Bible* is the most widely accepted textbook for college courses. It is the only book of its kind that has been edited for technical accuracy by members of Photoshop's programming team (for which I am duly grateful). And I'm told it's the first book new members of the Photoshop programming and support team are handed to introduce them to the product.

Now, we all know "bestseller" doesn't necessarily translate to "best" — I needn't remind you that Air Supply sold a lot of albums in its day. But the *Photoshop Bible* seems to have touched a chord. Based on the letters I've received over the years, most readers find the book informative, comprehensive, and entertaining. (Okay, one woman summed it up as "violent, satanic, and blasphemous" — cross my heart, it's true — but now that we've removed all the backward lyrics, I think that complaint has been addressed.) Knowing that people not only buy the book, but actually *read* it and find it pleasurable, gives me more satisfaction than I can say.

# Introducing the Gold Edition

Now that I've sufficiently boasted about this book's pedigree, let me introduce you to the newest addition to the *Photoshop Bible* family — the *Photoshop 5 Bible, Gold Edition*. The book you're holding in your hands is the most ambitious and exhaustive tome I've ever written. Simply put, it's nothing short of a Photoshop extravaganza. In addition to containing updated, cross-platform versions of every chapter from the standard edition (several of which are now located on the second CD-ROM at this back of the book), it includes 20 full-color chapters that are brand new to the *Photoshop Bible*. Fourteen of these chapters reveal proven techniques and approaches from some of the top artists working with Photoshop today. The other six color chapters walk you through essential techniques that I've written up specifically in response to the most common questions I've received from readers.

Whether revised or new, every chapter follows the simple driving philosophy that has governed the *Photoshop Bible* for years: Even the most intimidating topic can be made easy if it's explained properly. This goes double when the subject of the discussion is something as modest as a piece of software. Photoshop isn't some remarkable work of nature that defies our comprehension. It's nothing more than a commercial product designed by a bunch of regular people like you for the express purpose of being understood and put to use by a bunch of regular people like you. If I can't explain something that's inherently so straightforward, then shame on me.

I've made it my mission to address every topic head on — no cop-outs, no apologies. Everything's here, from the practical benefits of creating accurate masks to the theoretical wonders of designing your own custom filters. I wasn't born with this knowledge, and there are plenty of times when I'm learning with you. But if I don't know how something works, I do the research and figure it out, sometimes discussing features directly with the programmers, sometimes taking advantage of other sources. My job is to find out the answers, make sure those answers make sense, and pass them along to you as clearly as I can.

I also provide background, opinions, and humor. A dry listing of features followed by ponderous discussions of how they work doesn't mean squat unless I explain why the feature is there, where it fits into your workflow, and — on occasion — whether or not it's the best solution. I am alternatively cranky, excited, and just plain giddy as I explain Photoshop, and I make no effort to contain my criticisms or enthusiasm.

The color chapters in this book examine proven secrets from top artistic and photographic studios as related to me by the artists themselves, along with some techniques that I've discovered during my own work with Photoshop. Rather than focus exclusively on Photoshop's features, these chapters tackle broad artistic topics and examine the larger imaging process. Speaking purely personally, these are my favorite chapters in the book.

All told, the *Photoshop 5 Bible, Gold Edition* is me alternately walking you through the program as subjectively as I would explain it to a friend and sharing in your awe as we explore techniques and mysteries revealed to me by some of the best graphic artists at work today. I only hope you have as much fun reading the book as I had writing it.

## The Frisbees at the back of the book

At the back of this book, you'll find not one but *two* CD-ROMs containing Photoshop plug-ins; hundreds of pieces of original artwork; lots of stock photography in full, natural color; QuickTime movies from some of artists featured in the book's color chapters; artist interviews; and much, much more. CD #1 includes most of the pivotal images from this book so that you can follow along with my examples if you see fit. CD #2 contains several chapters (A–H) that I simply couldn't cram in the book — you probably agree that it's already heavy enough. Occasionally, I refer you to a chapter on the CD for further information about a topic. Both CDs are cross-platform, so you can open them on a Mac or on a PC equipped with Windows 95, 98, or NT.

**Cross-Reference**

Read the Appendix, "Using the CD-ROMs," for a complete listing of the contents of each CD.

# The Guts of the Book

I wrote *Photoshop 5 Bible, Gold Edition* to serve as the ultimate guide to retouching and enhancing scanned images in Photoshop. After you finish reading this book, it is my sincere hope not only that you will understand virtually every nook and cranny of Photoshop, but also that you will know how to apply your vast expanse of knowledge to real-world design situations.

Moderately experienced artists and designers as well as veteran imaging professionals are likely to benefit the most from this book. I endeavor to leave no stone unturned, I assume no prior knowledge, and I treat you with the respect a dedicated student deserves. In a few hours, you'll be fixing, enhancing, and printing images in style. (Hang in there, you can do it. Honest.)

Such an ambitious book requires an ambitious reader. To help make the reading process seem a little less like climbing Mount Everest and a little more like fun, I've divided these pages and pages of content into a total of 36 chapters organized into ten broad parts. Here's how the parts shape up:

**Part I: Photoshop 5 Fundamentals** — Here's all the basic stuff you need to know about Photoshop. I give you an overview of the low-level functions that have changed in Photoshop 5 and examine the core image editing process, taking you from composition and construction to color management and output. You learn how to change the size and resolution of an image, set up your monitor and color settings, navigate among color channels, and finally print the image to paper or film.

**Part II: Making a Living** — This part takes a look at the philosophies and techniques of three prominent artists to whom Photoshop is an essential tool of the trade. You learn how Glenn Mitsui approaches the commercial art process, how Gordon Studer uses Photoshop to turn stock photography into works of art, and how Karin Schminke mixes traditional and digital media to create fine art pieces — all complete with color illustrations.

**Part III: Painting and Retouching Images** — Every month or so, some fraudulent photo sparks a new flame of public scorn and scrutiny. Now it's your chance to give people something to talk about. The chapters in this part show you how to exchange fact with a modicum of fantasy.

**Part IV: Color and History Techniques** — See color and history techniques at work — and in color. Find out how illustrator Bud Peen enhances traditional watercolor illustrations using Photoshop. Learn how to colorize scanned line art and retouch vintage images with the history brush. And see how commercial artist Robert Bowen uses Photoshop to master the art of illusion.

**Part V: Selections, Layers, and Text** — Selections are Photoshop's most important capability. They permit you to limit the area that you edit, as well as lift foreground images and combine them with other backgrounds. You learn how layers work in Photoshop 5 and how to apply transformations. I also cover text in this section, because text in Photoshop is no more than character-shaped selection outlines.

**Part VI: Things Only Photoshop Can Do** — In this part, you learn how artist Greg Vander Houwen keeps his artistic process simple using layers and find out why Illustrator artist Ron Chan has begun using Photoshop to add textures and depth to his illustrations. You also experience Eric Reinfeld's special type effects and learn how to set up clipping paths for use with object-oriented programs.

**Part VII: Filters and Special Effects** — Making manual artistic enhancements is all very well and good, but it's easier to let your computer do the work. The chapters in this part show ways to produce highly entertaining and effective results using fully automated operations. You find out how to get the most out of Photoshop's most commonly used filters and learn about the wide range of special effects filters available to Photoshop 5.

**Part VIII: Special Effects Made Practical** — In this color part, you learn how to create raised type and use the new 3D Transform filter to wrap images around 3-D shapes. You also see how artists Jeff Schewe, Mark Moore, and Eric Chauvin create stunning special effects using distortions and other filters.

**Part IX: Corrections, Composites, and the Web** — Here's where you learn what you can do with Photoshop's most powerful color correction commands, how to composite images using overlay modes and channel operations, and how to create images specifically for the World Wide Web.

**Part X: New Frontiers** — Digital photography and Web design are two of the hottest and rapidly growing areas of digital imaging. In this part, you learn secrets about working with digital cameras from electronic photography pro Katrin Eismann. You also get tips on creating professional-quality Web images and buttons from Web artists Ben Benjamin and Michael Ninness.

Following the final chapter in Part X is an appendix that explains the expansive contents of the CD-ROMs at the back of the book. And last but not least is an astonishingly comprehensive index. It'll knock your socks off, should you happen to be wearing any.

# Conventions

Every computer book seems to conform to a logic all its own, and this one's no exception. Although I try to avoid pig latin — ellway, orfay hetay ostmay artpay — I do subscribe to a handful of conventions that you may not immediately recognize.

## Vocabulary

Call it computerese, call it technobabble, call it the synthetic jargon of propeller heads. The fact is, I can't explain Photoshop in graphic and gruesome detail without reverting to the specialized language of the trade. However, to help you keep up, I can and have italicized vocabulary words (as in *random-access memory*) with which you may not be familiar or which I use in an unusual context. An italicized term is followed by a definition.

If you come across a strange word that is not italicized (that bit of italics was for emphasis), look it up in the index to find the first reference to the word in the book.

## Commands and options

To distinguish the literal names of commands, dialog boxes, buttons, and so on, I capitalize the first letter in each word (for example, *click on the Cancel button*). The only exceptions are option names, which can be six or seven words long and filled with prepositions like *to* and *of*. Traditionally, prepositions and articles (*a, an, the*) don't appear in initial caps, and this book follows that time-honored rule, too.

When discussing menus and commands, I use an arrow symbol to indicate hierarchy. For example, Choose File ⇨ Open means to choose the Open command from the File menu. If you have to display a submenu to reach a command, I list the command used to display the submenu between the menu name and the final command. Choose Image ⇨ Adjust ⇨ Invert means to choose the Adjust command from the Image menu and then choose the Invert command from the Adjust submenu.

## About the whole platform thing

As I mentioned earlier, this is a cross-platform book, which is to say that it's written for both Macintosh and Windows users. If I write "⌘/Ctrl+K," for example, it means to press ⌘+K if you're working on a Mac or Ctrl+K if you're working on a PC. If I discuss a feature or topic that is specific to one platform or the other, I call it out in the section heading or in the text.

## Version numbers

A new piece of software comes out every 15 minutes. That's not a real statistic, mind you, but I bet I'm not far off. As I write this, Photoshop has advanced to Version 5.0.2. But by the time you read this, the version number may be seven hundredths of a percentage point higher. So know that when I write *Photoshop 5*, I mean any version of Photoshop short of 6.

Similarly, when I write *Photoshop 4*, I mean Versions 4.0 and 4.0.1; *Photoshop 3* means Versions 3.0, 3.0.1, 3.0.3, 3.0.4, and 3.0.5; *Photoshop 2.5* means 2.5 and 2.5.1 — you get the idea.

## Icons

Like just about every computer book currently available on your green grocer's shelves, this one includes alluring icons that focus your eyeballs smack dab on important information. The icons make it easy for folks who just like to skim books to figure out what the heck's going on. Icons serve as little insurance policies against short attention spans. On the whole, the icons are self-explanatory, but I'll explain them anyway.

The Caution icon warns you that a step you're about to take may produce disastrous results. Well, perhaps "disastrous" is an exaggeration. Inconvenient, then. Uncomfortable. For heaven's sake, use caution.

The Note icon highlights some little tidbit of information I've decided to share with you that seemed at the time to be remotely related to the topic at hand. I might tell you how an option came into existence, why a feature is implemented the way it is, or how things used to be better back in the old days.

The Photoshop 5 icon explains an option, command, or other feature that is brand spanking new to the program. If you're already familiar with previous versions of Photoshop, you might just want to plow through the book looking for Photoshop 5 icons and see what new stuff is out there.

This book is bursting with tips and techniques. If I were to highlight every one of them, whole pages would be gray with triangles popping out all over the place. The Tip icon calls attention to shortcuts that are specifically applicable to the Photoshop application. For the bigger, more useful power tips, I'm afraid you'll have to actually read the text.

The Cross-Reference icon tells you where to go for information related to the current topic. I included one a few pages back, and you probably read it without thinking twice. That means you're either sharp as a tack or an experienced computer-book user. Either way, you won't have any trouble with this icon.

# How to Bug Me

Even though this book was scrutinized intensely by me and my editors, I'll bet someone, somewhere will still manage to locate errors and oversights. If you notice those kinds of things and you have a few spare moments, please let me know what you think. I always appreciate readers' comments.

If you want to share your insights, comments, or corrections, please visit my Web site, the infamous *http://www.dekemc.com*. There you'll find news and excerpts about my books, tips for various graphics products, and other goofy online stuff. Let me know what you think. To e-mail me, click on the Contact Deke button. Don't fret if you don't hear from me for a few days, or months, or ever. I read every letter and try to implement nearly every constructive idea anyone bothers to send me. But because I receive hundreds of reader letters a week, I can respond to only a small percentage of them.

Please, do not write to ask me why your copy of Photoshop is misbehaving on your specific computer. I was not involved in developing Photoshop, I am not paid by Adobe, and I am not trained in product support. Adobe can answer your technical support questions way better than I can, so I leave it to the experts.

Now, without further ado, I urge you to turn the page and advance forward into the great untamed frontier of image editing. But remember, this book can be a dangerous tool if wielded unwisely. Don't set it on any creaky card tables or let your children play with it without the assistance of a stalwart adult, preferably an All-Star Wrestler or that guy who played the Incredible Hulk on TV. And no flower pressing. The little suckers would be pummeled to dust by this monstrously powerful colossus of a book.

# Acknowledgments

Thank you to the following people and companies for their assistance in providing me with the information and product loans that I needed to complete this book: Marc Pawliger, Christie Cameron, and Mark Hamburg at Adobe Systems; David Iglehart at Intergraph; Bruce Berkoff at Umax; Wynne Ahern at A&R Partners; William Hollingworth at Mitsubishi; Roger Kasten, Jack Putnam, and Eric Dahlinger at Newer Technology; Charles Smith at Digital Stock; Sophia McShea at PhotoDisc; Scott Signore at Agfa; Burton Holmes at Burton Holmes Associates; Scott Rawlings and Steve Sechrist at Wacom; Myke Ninness and Kevin Hurst at Extensis; Skip Elsheimer and JB Popplewell at Alien Skin Software; Barry Burns and Sumeet Pasricha at Andromeda; Chris Mills at Ulead Systems; Chuck Duff and Dawn Ginn at Digital Frontiers; Travis Anton and Cindy Johnson at BoxTop Software; Sid Fish and Carolyne Walton at Altamira Group; Michael Schumaker and Kirk Lyford at Vivid Details; Robin Shiverick at Chroma Graphics; Ted Cheney at ImageXpress; Mark Feldman at Xaos Tools; Renee Cooper at Miramar Systems; and Kris Atkins, Kristina Ross, and Steve Zahm at DigitalThink.

Additional kudos to the artists who contributed their work to this book: Ben Benjamin, Robert Bowen, Ron Chan, Eric Chauvin, Katrin Eismann, Janie Fitzgerald, Helen Golden, Wendy Grossman, Dorothy Krause, Bonny Lhotka, Kent Maske, Judith Moncrieff, Mark Moore, Myke Ninness, Bud Peen, Eric Reinfeld, Jeff Schewe, Karin Schminke, Gordon Studer, Richard Tuschman, Greg Vander Houwen, and Nanette Wylde.

Extra special thanks to fabulous editor Amy Thomas Buscaglia; the great overseers Andy Cummings and Walt Bruce; CD mistress Lisa Sontag; longtime image providers Mark Collen, Denise McClelland, and Russell McDougal; page layout supervisors Susan Parini and Laura Carpenter; and background champions Ted Padova, Katrin Eismann, Steve Roth, and Steve Broback. Thanks to John Kilcullen and Matt Wagner for getting this book up and running lo these many years ago.

Finally, thanks to you, the reader. You're what makes this big, thick, exhaustive tome possible.

# Contents at a Glance

# Contents

· · · · · · · · · · · · · · · · · · · · · · · · · · · · · · · · · · · · ·

## Part IV: Color and History Techniques            299

### Chapter 11: Integrating Natural Media into Digital Art .......300

### Chapter 12: Colorizing Scanned Line Art .................................314

### Chapter 13: Retouching with the History Brush .......................320

## Part VIII: Special Effects Made Practical     699

### Chapter 25: The Face-Melting Power of Distortions ...........................700

### Chapter 26: Popping Type Off the Page .........................................710

### Chapter 27: Wrapping Images Around 3-D Shapes ...........................714

### Chapter 28: Photographing for Photoshop ....................................720

# Photoshop 5 Fundamentals

# Getting to Know Photoshop

## What Is Photoshop?

Adobe Photoshop is the most popular image-editing application available for use on Macintosh and Windows-based computers. Despite hefty competition from programs such as Macromedia xRes, Live Picture, Wright Design, and others, Adobe Systems, Inc., reports that Photoshop's sales account for more than 80 percent of the image-editing market. (This estimate includes Painter from MetaCreations, an image-creation program that does not strictly compete with Photoshop.) This makes Photoshop four times more popular than all its competitors combined.

Photoshop's historically lopsided sales advantage provides Adobe with a clear incentive to reinvest in Photoshop and regularly enhance — even overhaul — its capabilities. Meanwhile, other vendors have had to devote smaller resources to playing catch-up. Although competitors provide interesting and sometimes amazing capabilities, the sums of their parts remain inferior to Photoshop.

As a result, Photoshop rides a self-perpetuating wave of industry predominance. It hasn't always been the best image editor, nor was it the earliest. But its deceptively straightforward interface combined with a few terrific core functions made it a hit from the moment of its first release. Nearly a decade later — thanks to substantial capital injections and highly creative programming on the part of Adobe's staff and Photoshop originator Thomas Knoll — it has evolved into the most popular program of its kind.

If you're already familiar with Photoshop and you just want to scope out its new capabilities, skip to the section "Fast Track to Version 5."

# Image-Editing Theory

Like any *image editor*, Photoshop enables you to alter photographs and other scanned artwork. You can retouch an image, apply special effects, swap details between photos, introduce text and logos, adjust color balance, and even add color to a grayscale scan. Photoshop also provides the tools you need to create images from scratch. These tools are fully compatible with pressure-sensitive tablets, so you can create naturalistic images that look for all the world like watercolors and oils.

## Bitmaps versus objects

Image editors fall into the larger software category of painting programs. In a painting program, you draw a line, and the application converts it to tiny square dots called pixels. The painting itself is called a bitmapped image, but bitmap and image are equally acceptable terms. Every program discussed so far is a painting program. Other examples include Corel Photo-Paint, Micrografx Picture Publisher, and Ulead PhotoImpact.

**Note**

Photoshop uses the term *bitmap* exclusively to mean a black-and-white image, the logic being that each pixel conforms to one *bit* of data, 0 or 1 (off or on). In order to avoid ad hoc syllabic mergers such as *pix-map*—and because forcing a distinction between a painting with exactly two colors and one with anywhere from 4 to 16 million colors is entirely arbitrary—I use the term bitmap more broadly to mean any image composed of a fixed number of pixels, regardless of the number of colors involved.

What about other graphics applications, such as Adobe Illustrator and Macromedia FreeHand? Illustrator, FreeHand, CorelDraw, and others fall into a different category of software called *drawing programs*. Drawings comprise *objects*, which are independent, mathematically-defined lines and shapes. For this reason, drawing programs are sometimes said to be *object-oriented*. Some folks prefer the term *vector-based*, but I really hate that one because *vector* implies the physical components direction and magnitude, which generally are associated with straight lines. Besides, my preference suggests an air of romance, as in, "Honey, I'm bound now for the Object Orient."

## The ups and downs of painting

Painting programs and drawing programs each have their strengths and weaknesses. One strength of a painting program is that it offers an extremely straightforward approach to creating images. For example, although many of Photoshop's features are complex—*exceedingly* complex on occasion—its core painting tools are as easy to use as a pencil. You alternately draw and erase until you reach a desired effect, just as you've been doing since grade school. (Of course, for all I know, you've been using computers since grade school. If you're pushing 20, you probably managed to log in many happy hours on paint programs in your formative years. Then again, if you're under 20, you're still in your formative years. Shucks, we're *all* in our formative years. Wrinkles, expanding tummies, receding hairlines . . . if that's not a new form, I don't know what is.)

In addition to being simple to use, each of Photoshop's core painting tools is fully customizable. It's as if you have access to an infinite variety of crayons, colored pencils, pastels, airbrushes, watercolors, and so on, all of which are entirely erasable. Doodling on the phone book was never so much fun.

The downside of a painting program is that it limits your *resolution* options. Because bitmaps contain a fixed number of pixels, the resolution of an image—the number of pixels per inch—is dependent upon the size at which the image is printed, as demonstrated in Figure 1-1. Print the image small, and the pixels become tiny, which increases resolution; print the image large, and the pixels grow, which decreases resolution. An image that fills up a standard 13-inch screen (640 × 480 pixels) prints with smooth color transitions when reduced to, say, half the size of a postcard. But if you print that same image without reducing it, you may be able to distinguish individual pixels, which means that you can see jagged edges and blocky transitions. The only way to remedy this problem is to increase the number of pixels in the image, which dramatically increases the size of the file on disk.

 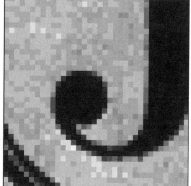

**Figure 1-1:** When printed small, a painting appears smooth (left). But when printed large, it appears jagged (right).

Bear in mind that this is a very simplified explanation of how images work. For a more complete description that includes techniques for maximizing image performance, refer to the "How Images Work" section of Chapter 2.

# The downs and ups of drawing

Painting programs provide tools reminiscent of traditional art tools. A drawing program, on the other hand, features tools that have no real-world counterparts. The process of drawing might more aptly be termed *constructing*, because you actually build lines and shapes point by point and stack them on top of each other to create a finished image. Each object is independently editable—one of the few structural advantages of an object-oriented approach—but you're still faced with the task of building your artwork one chunk at a time.

Nevertheless, because a drawing program defines lines, shapes, and text as mathematical equations, these objects automatically conform to the full resolution of the *output device*, whether it's a laser printer, imagesetter, or film recorder. The drawing program sends the math to the printer and the printer *renders* the math to paper or film. In other words, the printer converts the drawing program's equations to printer pixels. Your printer offers far more pixels than your screen—a 300 dots-per-inch (dpi) laser printer, for example, offers 300 pixels per inch (dots equal pixels), whereas most screens offer 72 pixels per inch. So the printed drawing appears smooth and sharply focused regardless of the size at which you print it, as shown in Figure 1-2.

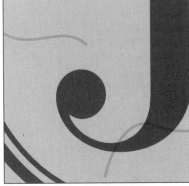

**Figure 1-2:** Small or large, a drawing prints smooth, but it's a pain to create. This one took more than an hour out of my day, and as you can see, I didn't even bother with the letters around the perimeter of the design.

Another advantage of drawings is that they take up relatively little room on disk. The file size of a drawing depends on the quantity and complexity of the objects the drawing contains. Thus, the file size has almost nothing to do with the size of the printed image, which is just the opposite of the way bitmapped images work. A thumbnail drawing of a garden that contains hundreds of leaves and petals consumes several times more disk space than a poster-sized drawing that contains three rectangles.

## When to use Photoshop

Thanks to their specialized methods, painting programs and drawing programs fulfill distinct and divergent purposes. Photoshop and other painting programs are best suited to creating and editing the following kinds of artwork:

✦ Scanned photos, including photographic collages and embellishments that originate from scans

✦ Images captured with any type of digital camera

✦ Realistic artwork that relies on the play between naturalistic highlights, midranges, and shadows

✦ Impressionistic-type artwork and other images created for purely personal or aesthetic purposes

✦ Logos and other display type featuring soft edges, reflections, or tapering shadows

✦ Special effects that require the use of filters and color enhancements you simply can't achieve in a drawing program

## When to use a drawing program

You're probably better off using Illustrator, FreeHand, or some other drawing program if you're interested in creating more stylized artwork, such as the following:

✦ Poster art and other high-contrast graphics that heighten the appearance of reality

✦ Architectural plans, product designs, or other precise line drawings

✦ Business graphics, such as charts and other "infographics" that reflect data or show how things work

✦ Traditional logos and text effects that require crisp, ultrasmooth edges

✦ Brochures, flyers, and other single-page documents that mingle artwork, logos, and standard-sized text (such as the text you're reading now)

If you're serious about computer graphics, you should own at least one painting program and one drawing program. If I had to rely exclusively on two graphics applications, I would probably choose Photoshop and Illustrator. Adobe has done a fine job of establishing symmetry between the two programs, so that they share common interface elements and keyboard shortcuts. Learn one and the other makes a lot more sense.

On the other hand, if you don't care if your drawing program and image editor share a common interface, then FreeHand is currently more powerful than

Illustrator. It offers a better realized collection of features, including better blending, tracing, and lens-effect tools. It also works remarkably well in combination with Photoshop. The only downside is that knowing Photoshop doesn't prepare you as well for FreeHand as it does for Illustrator.

**Cross-Reference**

For those who are interested, I write cradle-to-grave books on both FreeHand and Illustrator. I authored the *FreeHand Bible*—which comes from this same publisher, IDG Books Worldwide—and *Real World Illustrator*. (Occasionally a reader asks me why I didn't write IDG's *Illustrator Bible*, perhaps hoping for a salacious insight into the publishing world. Sadly, the reason is altogether mundane: I already had a signed contract to write the *Real World* book when IDG offered the *Bible* to me. Fortunately for IDG Books Worldwide and the industry at large, a talented first-time author named Ted Alspach stepped in. The result is a fine resource—which, to its credit, has made me work much harder.)

# The Computer Design Scheme

If your aspirations go beyond image editing into the larger world of computer-assisted design, you'll soon learn that Photoshop is just one cog in a mighty wheel of programs used to create artwork, printed documents, and presentations.

The natural-media paint program Fractal Design Painter emulates real-world tools such as charcoal, chalk, felt-tip markers, calligraphic pen nibs, and camel-hair brushes as deftly as a synthesizer mimics a thunderstorm. Three-dimensional drawing applications such as Infini-D, Strata StudioPro, Caligari trueSpace, and Ray Dream Designer enable you to create hyper-realistic objects with depth, lighting, shadows, surface textures, reflections, refractions—you name it. These applications can import images created in Photoshop as well as export images you can then enhance and adjust with Photoshop.

Page-layout programs such as Adobe PageMaker and QuarkXPress let you integrate images into newsletters, reports, books (such as this one), and just about any other kind of document you can imagine. If you prefer to transfer your message to slides, you can use Microsoft PowerPoint to add impact to your images through the use of charts and diagrams.

With Adobe Premiere and After Effects, you can merge images with video sequences recorded in the QuickTime format. You even can edit individual frames in Premiere movies with Photoshop. Macromedia Director makes it possible to combine images with animation, QuickTime movies, and sound to create multimedia presentations you can show on a screen or record on videotape.

Finally, you can publish your images over the World Wide Web. You can code HTML pages in any word processor, or mock up pages in a drag-and-drop editor, such as Adobe PageMill or Symantec Visual Page. (If you want my opinion, avoid Microsoft FrontPage like the plague.) You can even integrate images into simple GIF animations using any number of shareware programs available over the Internet. The Web is single-handedly breathing new life and respectability into low-resolution images, as I explore in Chapter 32.

# Photoshop Scenarios

All the programs I mentioned above are well-known industry standards. But they also cost money—sometimes lots of money—and they take time to learn. The number of programs you decide to purchase and how you use them is up to you. The following list outlines a few specific ways to use Photoshop alone and in tandem with other products:

✦ After scanning and adjusting an image inside Photoshop, use PageMaker or QuarkXPress to place the image into your monthly newsletter and then print the document from the page-layout program.

✦ After putting the finishing touches on a lovely tropical vista inside Photoshop, import the image for use as an eye-catching background inside PowerPoint. Then save the document as a self-running screen presentation or print it to overhead transparencies or slides from the presentation program.

✦ Capture an on-screen image by pressing ⌘+Shift+3 on a Mac, the Print Screen key on a PC, or using a screen capture utility. Then, if you're using a PC, create a new image in Photoshop and paste the screen image from the Clipboard. If you're using a Mac, simply open the image inside Photoshop. That's how the screens in this book were produced.

✦ If you want to annotate the image, import it into Illustrator or FreeHand, add arrows and labels as desired, and print it from the drawing program.

✦ Paint an original image inside Photoshop using a pressure-sensitive tablet. Use the image as artwork in a document created in a page-layout program or print it directly from Photoshop.

✦ Snap a photo with a digital photograph. As I write this, the best midrange cameras come from Kodak, Olympus, and Epson. Correct the focus and brightness in Photoshop (as explained in Chapters 23 and 30). Then add the photo to your personal Web site or print it out from a color printer.

✦ Scan a surface texture such as wood or marble into Photoshop and edit it to create a fluid repeating pattern (as explained in Chapter 10). Import the image for use as a texture map in a three-dimensional drawing program. Render the 3-D graphic to an image file, open the image inside Photoshop, and retouch as needed.

✦ Create a repeating pattern, save it as a BMP file, and apply it to the Windows desktop using the Display control panel.

✦ Take a problematic drawing that keeps generating errors and save it as an EPS file. Then open the file inside Photoshop to render it as a high-resolution bitmap. Place the image in a document created in a page-layout program or print it directly from Photoshop.

✦ Start an illustration in a drawing program and save it as an EPS file. Open the file in Photoshop and use the program's unique tools to add textures and tones that are difficult or impossible to create in a vector-based drawing program.

✦ Record a QuickTime movie in Premiere and export it to the FilmStrip format. Open the file inside Photoshop and edit it one frame at a time by drawing on the frame or applying filters. Finally, open the altered FilmStrip file in Premiere and convert it back to the QuickTime format.

Obviously, few folks have the money to buy all these products and even fewer have the energy or inclination to implement every one of these ideas. But quite honestly, these are just a handful of projects I can list off the top of my head. There must be hundreds of uses for Photoshop that involve no outside applications whatsoever. In fact, so far as I've been able to figure, there's no end to the number of design jobs you can handle in whole or in part using Photoshop.

Photoshop is a versatile and essential product for any designer or artist who owns a personal computer. Simply put, this is the software around which virtually every other computer graphics program revolves. I, for one, wouldn't remove Photoshop from my hard drive for a thousand bucks. (Of course, that's not to say I'm not willing to consider higher offers. For $1,500, I'd gladly swap it to a Jaz cartridge.)

# Fast Track to Version 5

**Photoshop 5.0**

If it seems like you've been using Photoshop for the better part of your professional career and you're itching to strap on the new version and ride, the following list explains all. Here I've compiled a few of the most prominent features that are new to Photoshop 5, in rough order of importance. I also point you to the chapter where you can rocket on to more information:

✦ **Multiple undos (Chapter 10):** They said it couldn't be done, but users kept on asking for it. Finally, Adobe gives the gift that keeps on undoing. Photoshop 5 keeps track of your most recent actions in the History palette. You can revert to any previous state in the list merely by clicking on it. Or if you prefer, you can paint back to a previous state with the new history brush. The implementation is nontraditional, but it amounts to the best implementation of multiple undos that I've ever seen. We're not just talking multiple undos, we're talking time travel.

✦ **Editable text layer (Chapter 18):** Text in Photoshop has remained virtually undisturbed since Version 1. You click with the tool, enter type into a dialog box, hit the Return/Enter key, and take what you get. Photoshop 5 still makes you edit type inside a dialog box, but now you can mix typefaces, sizes, and other formatting attributes within a single block. You can also adjust tracking and baseline shift and preview changes in the image window. But best of all, text remains forever editable until you rasterize it. It's a bold new day for type.

✦ **Revised RGB and CMYK color matching (Chapter 3):** Adobe has re-engineered much of the way that Photoshop makes conversions between the basic color spaces. You now identify an RGB source for matching foreign monitors (great for Web folks) and a CMYK destination for printing. These profiles then get embedded into an image when you save it. Color matching is always a tricky business, and the new methods are likely to cause considerable confusion. But if you take the time to calibrate your system properly—as documented at length in Chapter 3—Photoshop 5's new color matching capabilities rock. (I know, you may hate them now, but you'll come to love them.)

✦ **Spot-color separations (Chapter 4):** Yes, it's true, you can add Pantone and other spot colors to any image, not just duotones. Just add a channel to the image, specify the color and ink solidity, and fill the channel with whatever you deem appropriate. Photoshop 5 not only prints the channel onto a separate plate, but does a decent job of previewing the effect on screen. You can also convert duotones to multichannel images and edit the channels independently.

✦ **DCS 2.0 format support (Chapter 2):** If you can add spot channels to an image, you need to be able to save the result in the DCS 2.0 file for placement into PageMaker or QuarkXPress. True to form, Photoshop 5 does just that, giving you the option of saving a single large file or a separate file for each channel.

✦ **Layer effects (Chapter 17):** Everyone has a way of making drop shadows, but you don't need it anymore. Photoshop 5 automates the creation of a variety of stacking effects, including shadows, glows, and bevels. If you're considering scoffing, don't. These effects are not only well implemented, but they're fully editable from one session to the next. And if you apply one or more effects to a text layer, they update automatically when you edit the text.

✦ **3-D transformation filter (Chapter 24):** Photoshop 5 adds a new filter—Render ➪ 3D Transform—that wraps a selected image around a three-dimensional primitive, such as a cube or sphere. The bad news: You have no control over lighting and it doesn't render the image onto a new layer. The good news: It's fun and even moderately useful when matching 2-D images to 3-D environments.

✦ **Better scripts (Chapter E on CD-ROM #2):** Adobe has made a series of minor modifications to Photoshop's Actions palette. You can now organize scripts into groups, assign a wider range of keyboard shortcuts, and adjust playback speed. Photoshop 5 also lets you record more operations. It's virtually perfect.

✦ **Magnetic selection tools (Chapter 15):** Photoshop 5 offers two new selection tools that make it a little easier to select complicated images. The magnetic lasso and magnetic pen are designed to automatically snap to the contours of a foreground image. They take a little time to get used to—and they don't always work the way you might hope—but they're wonderful additions to the basic lasso and pen.

✦ **Less guesswork with GIFs (Chapter 32):** You can now preview the effects of the Indexed Color command! Adobe has also improved its color-reduction algorithms a little, but it's the preview that will make a difference in the quality of your Web pages.

✦ **New image saving options (Chapter 2):** Photoshop 5 introduces a handful of new saving options. You can choose whether to save upper or lowercase extensions at the end of file names, which is great for Web designers. When you choose Save a Copy, you can select to dump all nonimage data—including paths, guides, file info, and anything that might balloon the file size. If you're the cross-platform type, you can save Windows-compatible thumbnail previews with Mac files. And finally, Photoshop can open and save FlashPix files.

✦ **Improved Hue/Saturation command (Chapter 30):** You now have precise control over the range of colors you want to adjust inside the Hue/Saturation dialog box. You can add and subtract colors by clicking in the image window with an eyedropper, and adjust the "fuzziness" between modified and unmodified colors. Colorization is also handled better. All in all, it's a substantial improvement.

✦ **Freeform path tool (Chapter 15):** Hate drawing paths? Then Photoshop 5 brings glad tidings. The new freeform path tool lets you draw a path as simply as dragging your mouse across the screen.

✦ **Align layers (Chapter 17):** Attention Web designers, you can now align and distribute layers in Photoshop 5. Just link the layers you want to align or distribute and choose the desired command from the Layer menu. The active layer serves as the anchor for the alignment.

✦ **Transform paths and selection outlines (Chapter 15):** In the past, the only way to scale or rotate a path was to transform the entire image. To transform a selection outline independently of its pixels, you had to visit the quick mask mode. Now, you can access path-specific transformation functions under the Edit menu. To transform a selection outline, choose Select ⇨ Transform Selection.

✦ **Replay last transformation (Chapter 17):** After transforming a layer, selection, or path, you can apply that exact transformation to another element simply by pressing ⌘/Ctrl+Shift+T. Simple, useful, awesome.

✦ **Automated channel mixing (Chapter 3):** A new command under the Image⇨ Adjust submenu lets you merge the contents of color channels. It's great for fixing problem scans and creating custom RGB-to-grayscale conversions.

✦ **More gradient styles (Chapter 9):** For ages now, you've been able to select between two gradient patterns—linear and radial. Photoshop 5 adds three more—wrap-around, reflected, and diamond.

✦ **Measure tool (Chapter 17):** If you've been measuring images with the line tool set to a weight of 0, you can stop. The measuring tool does the same thing but better, even permitting you to move endpoints after setting the basic line.

✦ **Color sampler (Chapter C on CD-ROM #2):** Do you find the eyedropper too limiting? Wish you could sample and compare multiple colors at once? Now you can with the new color sample tool. Together with the Info palette you can examine the colors of five regions of an image at the same time.

✦ **Reselect (Chapter 15):** Photoshop now offers a separate undo buffer that holds the most recent selection outline. The upshot is that you can deselect an area, perform a variety of modifications, and then restore the selection several actions later by choosing Select⇨Reselect. Your selections are now safer than ever before.

✦ **Position the transformation origin (Chapter 17):** Previous versions of Photoshop rotated selections and layers around their centers. Now you can specify the precise origin of a rotation or any other transformation. It's a small precision thing, but some folks (myself included) will really appreciate it.

✦ **Toolbox reorganization (Chapter B on CD-ROM #2):** As with Photoshop 4, Version 5 is witness to yet another toolbox reorganization. Some tools have new keyboard equivalents. To access the alternative tools, you press Shift along with the key.

✦ **Revised rubber stamp (Chapter 10):** The hall-of-mirrors effect introduced in Photoshop 2.5 is a thing of the past. The rubber stamp now clones like it did in the good old days, which is infinitely better. Tell ya more in Chapter 10.

✦ **Page left, page right (Chapter B on CD-ROM #2):** It's a relatively little known fact that you can scroll up and down inside an image by pressing the Page Up and Page Down keys. But what about left and right? ⌘/Ctrl+Page Up goes left and ⌘/Ctrl+Page Down goes right.

Photoshop 5 also introduces a new breed of helper plug-in that automates certain kinds of operations and walks you step-by-step through others. Plug-ins that automate tasks appear as commands under the File⇨Automate submenu. Step-by-step Wizards appear under the Help menu. I discuss these plug-ins at different stages in the book. If you need help with a specific command, consult the index.

If you have access to a 48-bit drum scanner—which scans 65,000 brightness levels per color channel—then Photoshop 5 provides more reason to rejoice. You can now crop, resample, rotate, filter, and even clone inside 48-bit images with the rubber stamp tool. For most folks, 48-bit color is overkill. But for the very few who need it, Photoshop provides expanded support.

All in all, this is a meaty list of new features. In fact, I don't think I've seen an Adobe upgrade this dramatic since Photoshop 3, and there's *never* been one quite this thorough. Good job, Adobe!

Naturally, that makes my job all the more difficult. (Shame on you, Adobe!) Nonetheless, I've risen to the challenge, making every effort to document the new features with clarity and in their proper context. Just remember to keep an eye peeled for the Photoshop 5 icon and you'll be over the hump and back into the image-editing groove in no time.

✦   ✦   ✦

# Understanding Digital Images

## How Images Work

Think of a bitmapped image as a mosaic made from square tiles of various colors. When you view the mosaic up close, it looks like something you might use to decorate your bathroom. You see the individual tiles, not the image itself. But if you back a few feet away from the mosaic, the tiles lose their definition and merge together to create a recognizable work of art, presumably Medusa getting her head whacked off or some equally appetizing thematic classic.

Similarly, *images* are colored pixels pretending to be artwork. If you enlarge the pixels, they look like an unrelated collection of colored squares. Reduce the size of the pixels, and they blend together to form an image that looks to all the world like a standard photograph. Photoshop deceives the eye by borrowing from an artistic technique older than Mycenae or Pompeii.

Of course, differences exist between pixels and ancient mosaic tiles. Pixels come in 16 million distinct colors. Mosaic tiles of antiquity came in your basic granite and sandstone varieties, with an occasional chunk of lapis lazuli thrown in for good measure. Also, you can resample, color separate, and crop electronic images. We know from the time-worn scribblings of Dionysius of Halicarnassus that these processes were beyond the means of classical artisans.

But I'm getting ahead of myself. I won't be discussing resampling, cropping, or Halicarnassus for several pages. First, I'll address the inverse relationship between image size and resolution.

## Size versus resolution

If you haven't already guessed, the term *image size* describes the physical dimensions of an image. *Resolution* is the number of pixels per linear inch in the final printed image. I say linear because you measure pixels in a straight line. If the resolution of an image is 72 *ppi* — that is, pixels per inch — you get 5,184 pixels per square inch (72 pixels wide × 72 pixels tall = 5,184).

Assuming the number of pixels in an image is fixed, increasing the size of an image decreases its resolution and vice versa. An image that looks good when printed on a postage stamp, therefore, probably looks jagged when printed as an 11 × 17-inch poster.

Figure 2-1 shows a single image printed at three different sizes and resolutions. The smallest image is printed at twice the resolution of the medium-sized image; the medium-sized image is printed at twice the resolution of the largest image.

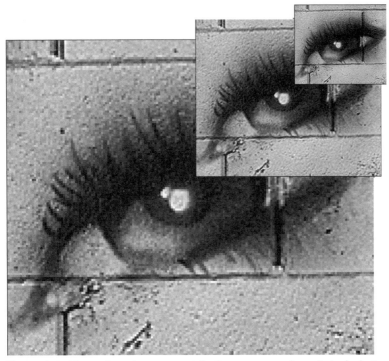

**Figure 2-1:** These three images contain the same number of pixels, but are printed at different resolutions. Doubling the resolution of an image reduces it to 25 percent of its original size.

One inch in the smallest image includes twice as many pixels vertically and twice as many pixels horizontally as an inch in the medium-sized image, for a total of four times as many pixels per square inch. Therefore, the smallest image covers ¼ the area of the medium-sized image.

The same relationships exist between the medium-sized image and the largest image. An inch in the medium-sized image comprises four times as many pixels as an inch in the largest image. Consequently, the medium-sized image consumes one-fourth the area of the largest image.

## Changing the printing resolution

When printing an image, a higher resolution translates to a sharper image with greater clarity. Photoshop lets you change the resolution of a printed image in one of two ways:

✦ Choose Image ⇨ Image Size to access the controls that enable you to change the pixel dimensions and resolution of an image. Then enter a value into the Resolution option box, either in pixels per inch or pixels per centimeter.

A good idea (although not essential) is to turn off the Resample Image check box, as demonstrated in Figure 2-2. If you leave it on, Photoshop may add or subtract pixels, as discussed in the "Resampling and Cropping" section later in this chapter. By turning it off, you instruct Photoshop to leave the pixels intact but merely change how many of them print per inch.

✦ Alternatively, you can ask Photoshop to scale an image during the print cycle. Choose File ⇨ Page Setup (⌘/Ctrl+Shift+P). If you're using a PC, click on the Properties button and then click on the Graphics tab. Enter a percentage value into the Reduce or Enlarge option box on a Mac or the Scaling option box on a PC. Lower values reduce the size of the printed image and thereby increase the resolution; higher values lower the resolution.

Both the Resolution and Reduce or Enlarge (or Scaling) settings are saved with an image. Together, the two determine the printed resolution. Photoshop divides the Resolution value in the Image Size dialog box by the Reduce or Enlarge (or Scaling) percentage from Page Setup. For example, if the image resolution is set to 72 ppi and you reduce the image to 48 percent, then the final printed image has a resolution of 150 ppi (72 divided by .48).

At the risk of boring some of you, I'll briefly remind the math haters in the audience that whenever you use a percentage in an equation, you first convert it to a decimal. For example, 100 percent is 1.0; 64 percent is .64; 5 percent is .05, and so on.

To avoid confusion, most folks rely exclusively on the Resolution value and leave Page Setup's Reduce or Enlarge (or Scaling) value set to 100 percent. The only exception is when printing tests and proofs. Because ink-jet and other consumer printers offer lower-resolution output than high-end commercial devices, you may find it helpful to proof images larger so you can see more pixels. Raising the Reduce or Enlarge (or Scaling) value lets you accomplish this without upsetting the Resolution value. Just be sure to restore the value to 100 percent after you make your test print.

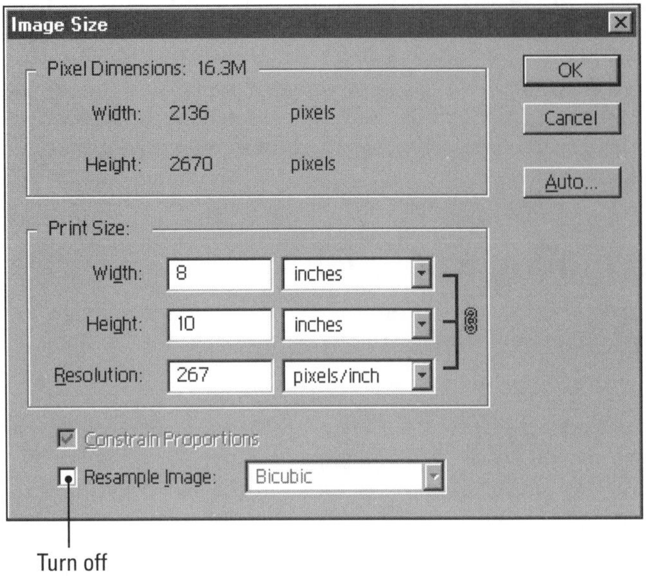

**Figure 2-2:** Turn off the Resample Image check box to maintain a constant number of pixels in an image and to change only the printed resolution.

## Changing the page-layout resolution

The Reduce or Enlarge (or Scaling) value has no effect on the size and resolution of an image imported into an object-oriented application, such as QuarkXPress or Illustrator. But these same applications do observe the Resolution setting from the Image Size dialog box.

Specifying the resolution in Photoshop is a handy way to avoid resizing operations and printing complications in your page-layout program. For example, I preset the resolution of all the images in this book so the production team had only to import the images and print away.

Always remember: Photoshop is as good or better at adjusting pixels than any other program you work with. So prepare an image as completely as possible in Photoshop before importing the image into another program. Ideally, you should never have to resize, rotate, or crop an image in any other program.

That tip is so important I'm going to repeat it: *Never* resize, rotate, or crop an image in Illustrator, FreeHand, CorelDraw, PageMaker, or QuarkXPress. Get your image fully ready to go in Photoshop, and then place it in the drawing or page-layout program, position it on the page, and leave it alone.

# So what's the perfect resolution?

After all this explanation of pixels and resolution, you might be thinking, "Okay, this is all very interesting, but what's my bottom line? What Resolution value should I use?" The answer is frustrating to some and freeing to others: Any darn resolution you like. It's true — there is no right answer; there is no wrong answer. The images in this book vary from 100 ppi for screen shots to 300 ppi for color plates. I've seen low-resolution art that looks great and high-resolution art that looks horrible. As with all things, quality counts for more than quantity. You take the pixels you're dealt and you make the best of them.

That said, there are a few guidelines, which I'll share only if you promise to take them with a grain of salt:

✦ Most experts recommend that you set the Resolution value to somewhere between 150 percent and 200 percent of the screen frequency of the final output device. The screen frequency is the number of halftone dots per linear inch, measured in lpi (short for lines per inch). So ask your commercial printer what screen frequency he uses — generally 120 lpi to 150 lpi — and multiply that times 1.5 or 2.

✦ Want to be more specific? For high-end photographic print work, it's hard to go wrong with a Resolution value of 267 ppi. That's 200 percent of 133 lpi, arguably the most popular screen frequency. When in doubt, most professionals aim for 267 ppi.

✦ What if you don't have enough pixels for 267 ppi? Say that you shoot a digital snapshot that measures 768  1,024 pixels and you want to print it at 6  8 inches. That works out to a relatively scant 128 ppi. Won't that look grainy? Probably. Should you add pixels with Image Size or some other command? No, that typically won't help. You have a finite number of pixels to work with, so you can print the image large and a little grainy, or sharp and small. The choice is yours.

✦ What if you have a photograph or slide and you can scan it at any resolution you want? Flat-bed scanners typically offer two maximum resolutions: a true optical maximum and an interpolated digital enhancement. The lower of the two values is invariably the true optical resolution. Scan at this lower maximum setting. Then use Image ➪ Image Size to resample the image down to the desired size and resolution, as explained in the "Resampling and Cropping" section near the end of this chapter.

Orson Welles claimed that he relied on his inexperience when creating *Citizen Kane*. He didn't know the rules of film making, so he couldn't be hampered by them. When his assistants and technicians told him, "You can't do that," he ignored them because he didn't know any better.

I feel the same about resolution. Take the pixels you have and try to make them look the best you can. Then print the image at the size you want it to appear. If you focus on the function of your image first and fret about resolution and other technical issues second, you'll produce better art.

# The Resolution of Screen Images

Regardless of the Resolution and Reduce or Enlarge (or Scaling) values, Photoshop displays each pixel on screen according to the zoom ratio (covered in Chapter B on CD-ROM #2). If the zoom ratio is 100 percent, for example, each image pixel takes up a single screen pixel. Zoom ratio and printer output are unrelated.

This same rule applies outside Photoshop as well. Other programs that display screen images — including multimedia development applications, presentation programs, and Web browsers — default to showing one image pixel for every screen pixel. This means when creating an image for the screen, the Resolution value has no affect whatsoever. I've seen some very bright people recommend that screen images should be set to 72 ppi on the Mac or 96 ppi for Windows, and while there's nothing wrong with doing this, there's no benefit either. When publishing for the screen, the Resolution value is ignored.

So all that counts is the 100-percent view. That means you want the image to fit inside the prospective monitor when you choose View ⇨ Actual Pixels (⌘/Ctrl+Option/Alt+zero) inside Photoshop. I say *prospective* monitor because although you may use a 17-inch monitor when you create the image, you most likely need the final image to fit on a 13-inch display. So even though your monitor probably displays as many as 1,024 × 768 pixels, most Web and screen artists prepare for the worst-case scenario, 640 × 480 pixels. This is the 13-inch VGA standard, shared by some of the first color Macs and PCs, most laptops, an endless array of defunct computers, and even televisions.

Of course, a 640 × 480-pixel image would consume an entire 13-inch screen. If you want the image to share the page with text and other elements, the image needs to be smaller than that. A typical screen image varies from as small as 16 × 16 pixels for icons and buttons to 320 × 240 pixels for a stand-alone photograph. Naturally, these are merely guidelines. You can create images at any size you like.

For more information on creating images specifically for the World Wide Web, read Chapter 32.

# How to Open, Duplicate, and Save Images

Before you can work on an image in Photoshop — whether you're creating a brand new document or opening an image from disk — you must first load the image into an image window. Here are the four basic ways to create an image window:

✦ **File ⇨ New**: Create a new window by choosing File ⇨ New (⌘/Ctrl+N). After you fill out the desired size and resolution specifications in the New dialog box, Photoshop confronts you with a stark, white, empty canvas. You then face the ultimate test of your artistic abilities — painting from scratch. Feel free to go nuts and cut off your ear.

✦ **File ⇨ Open**: Open an image saved to disk or CD-ROM by choosing File ⇨ Open (⌘/Ctrl+O), or in rare cases on your PC, File ⇨ Open As (Ctrl+Alt+O). Of the four ways to create an image window, this method is the one you'll probably use most often. You can open images scanned in other applications, images purchased from stock photo agencies, slides and transparencies digitized to a Kodak Photo CD, or an image you previously edited in Photoshop.

✦ **Edit ⇨ Paste**: Photoshop automatically adapts a new image window to the contents of the Clipboard (provided those contents are bitmapped). So if you copy an image inside a different application or in Photoshop, and then choose File ⇨ New, Photoshop enters the dimensions and resolution of the image into the New dialog box. All you must do is accept the settings and choose Edit ⇨ Paste (⌘/Ctrl+V) to introduce the image into a new window. This technique is useful for editing screen shots captured to the Clipboard or for testing effects on a sample of an image without harming the original.

**Tip**

This technique works great when pasting screen shots captured on a PC with a utility such as Corel Capture (bundled with CorelDraw) or the shareware Clipmate. But Photoshop can be fickle about importing images shot using Windows's built-in Print Screen and Alt+Print Screen functions. To make Photoshop more aware of the Windows Clipboard, do the following: Quit Photoshop. Open the Prefs folder and double-click on the Photos50.ini file to open it up in Notepad. Then add the line ALWAYSIMPORTCLIP=1 anywhere in the file. Now quit Notepad and save your changes. The next time you launch Photoshop, your Print Screen captures should paste without incident.

✦ Photoshop automatically pastes an image to a new layer, preventing you from saving the file in any but the native Photoshop format (as I explain later in this chapter). To flatten the pasted image so you can save it in some other format, choose Layer ⇨ Merge Down or press ⌘/Ctrl+E.

✦ **File ⇨ Import**: If you own a scanner or digital camera, it may include a plug-in module that lets you transfer an image directly into Photoshop. Just copy the module into Photoshop's Plug-Ins folder and then run or relaunch the Photoshop application. To initiate a scan or to load an image into Photoshop, choose the plug-in module from the File ⇨ Import submenu.

For example, to load an image from my Polaroid PDC-2000 — an aging but still very good camera under $2,000 — I cable the camera to my Mac's SCSI port or my Adaptec SCSI card. Then I turn the camera on and choose File ⇨ Import ⇨ PDC-2000. A dialog box appears showing thumbnails of all the images I've shot, as in Figure 2-3. I select the images I want to edit, click on the Transfer button, and the images open directly inside Photoshop.

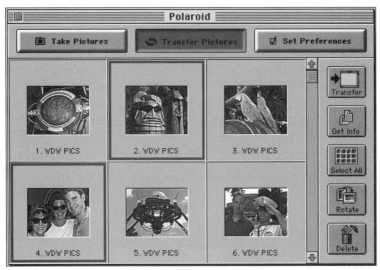

**Figure 2-3:** The Polaroid PDC-2000 module lets me view images stored in the camera's memory and open them up directly inside Photoshop.

## Creating a new image

Whether you're creating an image from scratch or transferring the contents of the Clipboard to a new image window, choose File ➪ New or press ⌘/Ctrl+N to bring up the New dialog box shown in Figure 2-4. If the Clipboard contains an image, the Width, Height, and Resolution option boxes show the size and resolution of this image. Otherwise, you can enter your own values in one of five units of measurement: pixels, inches, centimeters, picas, or points. If you're uncertain exactly what size image you want to create, enter a rough approximation. You can always change your settings later.

**Tip**

Although Photoshop matches the contents of the Clipboard by default, you can also match the size and resolution of other images:

✦ Press Option/Alt when choosing File ➪ New, or press ⌘/Ctrl+Option/Alt+N to override the contents of the Clipboard. Photoshop displays the size and resolution of the last image you created, whether it came from the Clipboard or not. Use this technique when creating many same-sized images in a row.

✦ You can also match the size and resolution of the new image to any other open image. While the New dialog box is open, choose the name of the image you want to match from the Window menu. It's that simple.

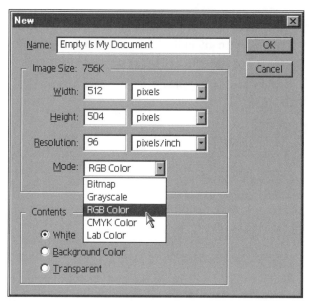

**Figure 2-4:** Use the New dialog box to specify the size, resolution, and color mode of your new image.

### Units of measure

The Width and Height pop-up menus contain the five common units of measure mentioned earlier: pixels, inches, centimeters, points, and picas. But the Width pop-up menu offers one more, called Columns. If you want to create an image that fits exactly within a certain number of columns when it's imported into a desktop publishing program, select this option. You can specify the width of a column and the gutter between columns by pressing ⌘/Ctrl+K and ⌘/Ctrl+5 for the Units & Rulers preferences. Then enter values into the Column Size option boxes.

The Gutter value affects multiple-column images. Suppose you accept the default setting of a 15-pica column width and a 1-pica gutter. If you specify a one-column image in the New dialog box, Photoshop makes it 15 picas wide. If you ask for a two-column image, Photoshop adds the width of the gutter to the width of the two columns and creates an image 31 picas wide.

The Height pop-up menu in the New dialog box lacks a Column option because vertical columns have nothing to do with an image's height.

**Tip** You can change the default unit of measure that appears in the Width and Height pop-up menus by pressing ⌘/Ctrl+K, ⌘/Ctrl+5, and selecting a different option from the Units pop-up menu. Easier still, bring up the Info palette by pressing the F8 key. Then click or drag on the little cross icon in the palette's lower-left corner. Up comes a pop-up menu of units, as demonstrated in Figure 2-5.

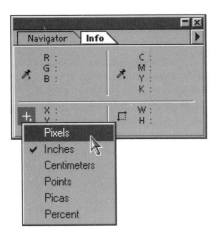

**Figure 2-5:** You can select a default unit of measure from the coordinates pop-up menu in the lower-left corner of the Info palette.

## New image size

In most cases, the on-screen dimensions of an image depend on your entries in the Width, Height, and Resolution option boxes. If you set both the Width and Height values to 10 inches and the Resolution to 72 ppi, the new image will measure 720 × 720 pixels. The exception occurs if you choose pixels as your unit of measurement, as in Figure 2-5. In this case, the on-screen dimensions depend solely on the Width and Height options, and the Resolution value determines the size at which the image prints.

## Color mode

Use the Mode pop-up menu to specify the number of colors that can appear in your image. Choose Bitmap to create a black-and-white image and choose Grayscale to access only gray values. RGB Color, CMYK Color, and Lab Color all provide access to the full range of 16 million colors, although their methods of doing so differ.

RGB stands for red, green, blue; CMYK for cyan, magenta, yellow, black, and Lab for luminosity and two abstract color variables: a and b. To learn how each of these color modes works, read the "Working in Different Color Modes" section of Chapter C on CD-ROM #2.

## Background color

The New dialog box also provides three Contents radio buttons that enable you to change the color of the background for the new image. You can fill the new image with white, with the current background color (assuming, of course, the background color is something other than white), or with no color at all. This last setting, Transparent, results in a floating layer with no background image whatsoever. This can be useful when editing one layer independently of the rest of an image, or when preparing a layer to be composited with an image. (For an in-depth examination of the more nitty-gritty aspects of layering, see Chapter 17.)

If you do select a transparent background, you must later flatten the layer by choosing Layer ➪ Flatten Image if you want to save the image to any format other than native Photoshop. The advantage of the Transparent setting, however, is that Photoshop doesn't create a new layer when you press ⌘/Ctrl+V to paste the contents of the Clipboard. In the long run, this doesn't make much difference—you still must flatten the image before you save it—but at least you needn't fuss around with two layers, one of which is completely empty.

Incidentally, just because you create an image with a transparent background doesn't mean you can automatically import a free-form image with transparency intact into an object-oriented program like Illustrator or QuarkXPress. In order to carve a transparent area out of the naturally rectangular boundaries of an image, you have to use the pen tool to create a clipping path. I explain how in the "Retaining transparent portions of an image" section of Chapter 15.

### Naming the new image

The New dialog box provides a Name option. If you know what you want to call your new image, enter the name now. Or don't. It doesn't matter. Either way, when you choose File ➪ Save, Photoshop asks you to specify the location of the file and confirm the file's name, just as in previous versions. So don't feel compelled to name your image anything. The only reason for this option is to help you keep your images organized on screen. Lots of folks create temporary images they never save; Photoshop offers a way to assign temporary images more meaningful names than *Untitled-4, Untitled-5, Untitled-6,* and so on.

Unlike some PC traditionalists, I whole-heartedly endorse using long file names under Windows 95, NT 4, and later. But naturally you should be aware of the implications. If you send a file to someone using Windows 3.1, DOS, or some other operating system, the long file name gets truncated to eight characters with a tilde symbol (~) and number. (You can view the truncated DOS-style name at the desktop by right-clicking on the file and choosing Properties.) This can also happen when exchanging files between PCs and Macs, depending on how you do it. If you swap files to a Mac using a PC-formatted floppy disk, Zip, or the like, the filenames get the ax when the disk is popped into the Mac. But if you network your PC to a Mac using Miramar Systems' (*www.miramarsys.com*) PC MacLAN or the like, then the long filenames come through swimmingly. In fact, this is precisely how I exchange files over my own cross-platform Ethernet LAN.

## Opening an existing image

If you want to open an image stored on disk, choose File ➪ Open or press ⌘/Ctrl+O to display the Open dialog box. The Open dialog box behaves just like the ones in other Macintosh and Windows applications, with a folder bar at top, a scrolling list of files, a Desktop button on a Mac or a pop-up menu of file formats on a PC, and the usual file management and navigation options. On a Mac, you can also use standard navigational shortcuts. Press ⌘+left and right arrow to change drives,

⌘+up and down arrow to exit and enter folders, and ⌘+D to switch to the desktop view. On a PC, you can also open multiple files at a time. Shift+click on a file name in the Open dialog box to select a range of files. Ctrl+click to add a single file to the group you want to open.

Photoshop's Open dialog box offers a few options that other Open dialog boxes lack. These options differ a bit between Macintosh and Windows machines, as I explain in the following sections.

### Viewing the thumbnail

On a Mac, turn on the Show Thumbnail check box to display a thumbnail preview of the selected image on the left side of the dialog box, as shown in Figure 2-6. If you deselect the option, the preview disappears and the Open dialog box collapses to save screen space. On a PC, Photoshop automatically displays a thumbnail preview of the selected file at the bottom of the dialog box.

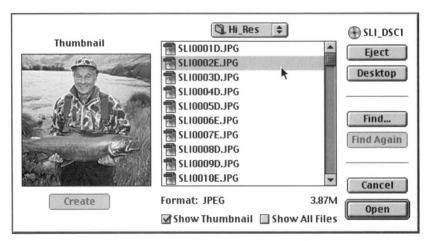

**Figure 2-6:** On a Mac, turn on the Show Thumbnail check box to see a preview of the image in the Open dialog box.

If the thumbnail space is empty, it means the file does not contain a Photoshop-compatible preview. The file may have been created by a piece of hardware or software that doesn't support thumbnails, or the thumbnail feature may have simply been turned off. To save thumbnails from Photoshop, press ⌘/Ctrl+K, ⌘/Ctrl+2 to display the Saving Files panel of the Preferences dialog box. On your Mac, turn on the Macintosh Thumbnail check box or set the Image Previews pop-up menu to Ask When Saving. On your PC, set the Image Previews pop-up menu to Always Save or Ask When Saving. If you select Ask When Saving, Photoshop gives you the option of adding a thumbnail to the image inside the Save dialog box.

If you're using a Mac, just because you don't see a thumbnail in the Open dialog box doesn't mean all chance of previewing is gone. Under the right circumstances, you can generate a thumbnail preview on the fly by clicking on the Create button. The QuickTime system extension must be running for this button to function, and even then, the button only applies to a few file formats including PICT, GIF, JPEG, and the native Photoshop format. If the image is saved in any other file format—notably TIFF or EPS—you can generate a preview only by opening the image and resaving it.

If you've swapped images between Mac OS and Windows machines, you might have wondered why the heck the thumbnail previews you saved with your images on your Mac weren't displaying on PCs. The problem was, your Mac thumbnails weren't surviving the journey to the other side. See, Photoshop for the Mac saves thumbnails in the so-called resource fork of the file, but Windows programs can't even see the resource fork, much less translate it. Fortunately for all, both versions of Photoshop 5 can save Windows thumbnails. On the Mac, the Saving Files panel of the Preferences dialog box contains a check box called Windows Thumbnail. When turned on, a thumbnail is added to the data fork of the file, which translates to Windows fully intact.

Sadly, thumbnails don't work in the other direction. Since Windows doesn't recognize the resource fork, Photoshop for Windows can't save a Macintosh-style thumbnail. And because Photoshop on the Mac relies on Apple's QuickTime to interpret thumbnails, it can't see data-fork thumbnails. Dang.

## Previewing outside Photoshop on a PC

Under Windows 95 and later, the Open dialog box isn't the only place you can preview an image before you open it. In fact, provided you save the image in the native Photoshop (.psd) format, you can peek at an image without even opening the program.

Right-click on a file with a *.psd* extension—either at the desktop, in a folder window, or in the Windows Explorer—and choose Properties from the pop-up menu. When the Properties dialog box opens, click on the Photoshop Image tab to look at your image, as shown in Figure 2-7. Again, you must have saved a thumbnail preview along with the image for this feature to work.

You can also see a tiny thumbnail in the General panel of the Properties dialog box. This same thumbnail appears at the desktop level, assuming that the folder is set to View ⇨ Large Icons. Using the other tabs in the Properties dialog box, you can view the caption, keywords, credits, and other information created using Photoshop's File ⇨ File Info command (covered at the end of Chapter B on CD-ROM #2).

Unfortunately, this trick works only for images saved in the native Photoshop format. TIFF, JPEG, GIF, and other images can only be previewed from inside Photoshop's Open dialog box. But even so, it's a heck of a trick.

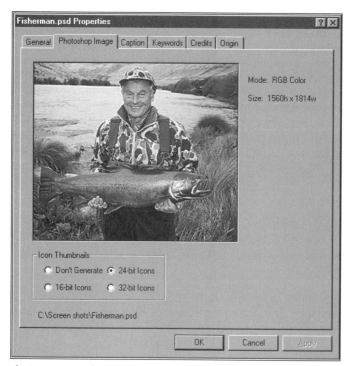

**Figure 2-7:** Under Windows 95 and later, you can preview files saved in the native .psd format from the Properties dialog box.

## Opening elusive files on a Mac

The scrolling list in the Open dialog box contains the names of just those documents that Photoshop recognizes it can open. If you can't find a desired document on your Mac, it may be because Photoshop doesn't recognize the document's four-character *type code*. The type code for a document created or last edited on a Macintosh computer corresponds to the file format under which the image was saved (as explained in the upcoming "File Format Roundup" section). For example, TIFF is the type code for a TIFF image, JPEG is the code for a JPEG image, GIFf is the code for a GIF image, and so on. However, if you transferred a document to your Mac from another platform, such as a Windows machine or Unix workstation, it probably lacks a type code. In the absence of a type code, Photoshop looks for a three-character extension at the end of the file name, such as *.tif* or *.jpg* or *.gif*. But if the extension is so much as a character off — *.tff* or *.jpe* or *.jif* — Photoshop won't know the file from Adam.

To see *all* documents regardless of type code or extension, select the Show All Files check box inside the Open dialog box. When you click on a document in the scrolling list, Photoshop displays the format that it thinks the file is saved in — if it has any thoughts to offer — in the Format option. If you disagree, click on the

Format option and select the correct file format from the pop-up menu, as demonstrated in Figure 2-8. Provided that the image conforms to the selected format option, Photoshop opens the image when you press Return. If Photoshop gives you an error message instead, you need to either select a different format or try to open the document in a different application.

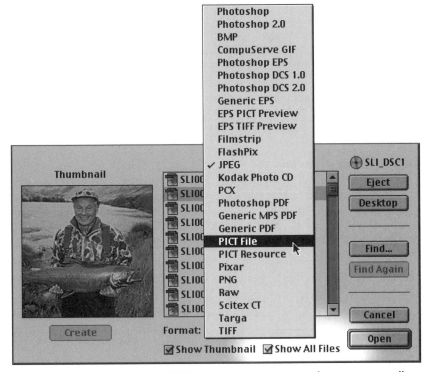

**Figure 2-8:** Select the Show All Files option to access any document regardless of its four-character type code.

Normally, you can't see a file's four-character type code because it's socked away inside the resource fork. Unless, that is, you're willing to purchase a special utility such as PrairieSoft's (*www.prgrsoft.com*) DiskTop or Apple's (*www.apple.com*) ResEdit. Both are great, but DiskTop is more convenient for the simple day-to-day tasks of viewing and modifying type codes and other invisible resources.

## Opening elusive files on a PC

If you can't find a desired document in the Open dialog box on your PC, it may be because the Files of Type pop-up menu is set to the wrong file format. To view all supported formats, either select All Formats from the Files of Type pop-up, or enter *.* into the File Name option box and press Enter.

If a file lacks any form of extension whatsoever, the Open dialog box won't be able to identify it. This unusual situation may arise in one of two ways. On rare occasions, a file transmitted electronically (via the Internet, for example) loses its extension en route. But more likely, the file comes from a Macintosh computer. The Mac doesn't need file extensions — the file type identification resides in that resource fork I was telling you about — therefore many Mac users never give a thought to three-character extensions.

You can solve this problem either by renaming the file and adding the proper extension, or by choosing File ➪ Open As (Ctrl+Alt+O). If you choose Open As, Photoshop shows you all documents in a directory, whether it supports them or not. Just click on the extension-less file and select the correct file format from the Open As pop-up menu. As long as the image conforms to the selected format option, Photoshop opens the image when you press Enter. If Photoshop gives you an error message, either select a different format or try to open the document in a different application.

### Finding lost files on a Mac

If you know the name of a file — or at least part of the name — but you can't remember where you put it, you can look for it using the Find button in the Open dialog box. Just click on the button or press ⌘+F, enter some text in the resulting option box, and press the Return key. Photoshop searches the disk in a fairly random fashion and takes you to the first file name that contains the exact characters you entered.

If the first file name isn't the one you're looking for, click on the Find Again button or press ⌘+G to find the next file name that contains your text. If you want to search for a different string of characters, press ⌘+F and enter some different text.

## Duplicating an image

Have you ever wanted to try an effect without permanently damaging an image? Photoshop 5 offers multiple undos, and you'll get a kick out of using the History palette to see before and after views of your image (as I explain in Chapter 10). But what if you want to apply a series of effects to an image independently and compare them side by side? And save the variations as separate files? Or perhaps even merge them? This is a job for image duplication.

To create a new window with an independent version of the foreground image, choose Image ➪ Duplicate. A dialog box appears, requesting a name for the new image. Just like the Name option in the New dialog box, the option is purely an organizational tool you can use or ignore. If your image contains multiple layers, Photoshop will, by default, retain all layers in the duplicate document. Or you can merge all visible layers into a single layer by selecting the Merged Layers Only check box. (Hidden layers remain independent.) Press Return/Enter to create your new, independent image. Bear in mind that this image is unsaved; you need to choose File ➪ Save to save any changes to disk.

**Tip**

If you're happy to let Photoshop automatically name your image and you don't care what it does with the layers, press Option/Alt while choosing Image ➪ Duplicate. This bypasses the Duplicate Image dialog box and immediately creates a new window.

## Saving an image to disk

The first rule of storing an image on disk is to save it frequently. If the foreground image is untitled, as it is when you work on a new image, choosing File ➪ Save (⌘/Ctrl+S) displays the Save dialog box, enabling you to name the image, specify its location on disk, and select a file format.

I recommend that you set the Image Previews option in the Saving Files preferences panel (⌘/Ctrl+K, ⌘/Ctrl+2) to Ask When Saving. If you do, then the Save dialog box on your Mac offers a slew of Image Previews check boxes. On your PC, it offers a Save Thumbnail check box. For print work, I generally select both the Macintosh and Windows Thumbnail options on my Mac or the Save Thumbnail option on my PC. Previews consume extra disk space, but it's well worth it in exchange for being able to see the file before opening it. Why save a Windows thumbnail on a Mac? If you ever swap files between platforms, it will come in handy.

The only reason *not* to save a thumbnail with an image is if you plan to post it on the Web. In that case, the file has to be as streamlined as possible, and that means shaving away the preview.

After you save the image once, choosing the Save command updates the file on disk without bringing up the Save dialog box. Choose File ➪ Save As or press ⌘/Ctrl+ Shift+S to change the name, location, or format of the image stored on disk. By the way, if your only reason for choosing the Save As command is to change the file format, it's perfectly acceptable to overwrite (save over) the original document, assuming you no longer need the previous copy of the image. Granted, your computer could crash during the Save As operation, but because Photoshop actually creates a new file during any save operation, your original document should survive the accident. Besides, the chance of crashing during a Save As is extremely remote — no more likely than crashing during any other save operation.

**Tip**

To speed the save process, I usually save an image in Photoshop's native format until I'm finished working on it. Then, when the file is all ready to go, I choose File ➪ Save As and save the image in the compressed TIFF or JPEG format. This way, I compress each image only once during the time I work on it.

### Adding an extension to Mac files

On a Mac, the Preferences dialog box includes an option that lets you append a three-character file extension to the end of your files. (Again, this option is located in the Saving Files panel, so press ⌘+K, ⌘+2 to get to it.) Here I have two recommendations. First, leave the Use Lower Case check box turned on. It ensures fewer conflicts if and when you post your images on the Web. Second, go ahead and append extensions to your file names.

Why add PC file extensions on a Mac? Obviously, it makes life easier when sharing images with PCs. But more importantly, it's another form of insurance. If you're a Mac user and ever find yourself using a PC, you're going to have tons and tons of old Macintosh image files that you'd like to open and reuse. With file extensions, you'll have no problem. Without them, good luck. The file extension is the only way a Windows application has to identify the file format. If there's no file extension, you'll have to tell the application which format to use. And while I don't question the basic record-keeping capabilities of your brain, you probably have better things to remember than what file format you used five years ago.

You can automatically append an extension from the Save dialog box regardless of your preference settings. Press the Option key, choose an option from the Format pop-up menu, and there it is.

### Saving a copy

The final save command — File ⇨ Save a Copy (⌘/Ctrl+Option/Alt+S) — lets you save a copy of the current image without changing that special relationship between the image and its original on disk. This is like duplicating the image, saving it, and closing the duplicate all in one step.

The whole purpose of the Save a Copy command is to save a flattened version of a layered image or to dump the extra channels in an image that contains masks. Just select the file format you want to use and let Photoshop do the flattening and dumping automatically.

When you choose the Save a Copy command, Photoshop offers three extra check boxes at the bottom of the standard Save dialog box, as shown in Figure 2-9.

✦ **Flatten Image**: Photoshop activates this check box whenever you select a format other than the native Photoshop format. Because no other format supports layers, the check box must turn on to show that the layers will fuse together when the image is saved.

✦ **Exclude Alpha Channels**: "Alpha channel" is Photoshop's techy name for an extra channel, such as a mask (discussed in Chapter 16) or spot color (Chapter 4). But only a few formats — notably Photoshop, TIFF, and DCS 2.0 — support extra channels. Most other formats abandon them. Again, Photoshop automatically activates this check box when you select a no-mask, no-spot color format.

Exclude Non-Image Data: Select this option to jettison everything except the pixels in an attempt to get your file down to the smallest size possible. When turned on, this option excludes guides, paths, text entered into the File Info dialog box, color samples, and color profiles. It also excludes thumbnails, which is why the Image Previews check boxes on a Mac and the Save Thumbnail check box on a PC dims when you select Exclude Non-Image Data. Select this check box when creating graphics for the Web.

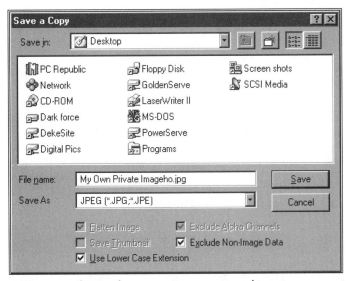

**Figure 2-9:** Choose the Save a Copy command to save a separate, flattened copy of a layered image. This way, you can continue to adjust the layers in the future.

The Save a Copy command is perfect for when you want to export a layered image for use in another program. A page-layout application such as QuarkXPress doesn't support Photoshop's native format, but you don't want to flatten the image and permanently lose your layers. So here's your compromise: Keep one copy with layers in the Photoshop format and create a flattened copy for QuarkXPress.

# File Format Roundup

Photoshop 5 supports more than 20 file formats from inside its Open and Save dialog boxes. It can support even more through the addition of plug-in modules, which attach commands to the File ➪ Save As, File ➪ Import and File ➪ Export submenus.

*File formats* represent different ways to save a file to disk. Some formats provide unique image-compression schemes, which save an image in a manner that consumes less space on disk. Other formats enable Photoshop to trade images with different applications running on the Mac, under Windows, or on some other platform.

## The native format

Like most programs, Photoshop offers its own native format — that is, a format optimized for Photoshop's particular capabilities and functions. This (.psd) format saves every attribute that you can apply in Photoshop — including layers, extra channels, file info, and so on — and is compatible with Versions 3 and later of the program.

Tip

Perhaps not surprisingly, Photoshop can open and save in its native format more quickly than in any other format. The native format also offers image compression. Like TIFF's compression, the Photoshop compression scheme does not result in any loss of data. But Photoshop can compress and decompress its native format much more quickly than TIFF, and the compression scheme is better able to minimize the size of mask channels (as explained in Chapter 16).

The downside of the Photoshop format is that relatively few applications other than Photoshop support it, and those that do don't always do a great job. Some applications such as CorelPhoto-Paint and Adobe After Effects can open a layered Photoshop image and interpret each layer independently. But most of the others limit their support to flat Photoshop files. To accommodate these programs, you can either 1) use File ➪ Save a Copy to save the image in the flat Photoshop 2.0 format, or 2) activate the Include Composited Image with Layered Files check box in the Preferences dialog box.

But in point of fact, I intensely dislike either of these options. (In fact, you should be sure to turn off Include Composited Image with Layered Files.) The native *.psd* format was never intended to function as an interapplication standard; it was meant for Photoshop alone. So use it that way. If you want to trade a flattened image with some other program, use TIFF, JPEG, or one of the other universal formats explained over the course of this chapter.

One exception: If you're creating a grayscale image for use with Filter ➪ Distort ➪ Displace, you have to create a 2.0-compatible file. The best bet is to save the image in the Photoshop 2.0 format. Otherwise the Displace filter won't see the grayscale image. I tell more about this filter in Chapter D on CD-ROM #2.

## The mainstream formats

Two formats — JPEG and TIFF — are the all-stars of digital imagery. You'll use these formats the most because of their outstanding compression capabilities and almost universal support among graphics applications.

### JPEG

The JPEG format is named after the folks who designed it, the Joint Photographic Experts Group. JPEG is the most efficient and essential compression format currently available and is likely to be the compression standard for years to come. JPEG is a lossy compression scheme, which means it sacrifices image quality to conserve space on disk. You can control how much data is lost during the save operation, however.

When you save an image in the JPEG format, Photoshop displays the dialog box in Figure 2-10, which offers a total of 11 compression settings. Just select an option from the Quality pop-up menu or drag the slider triangle from 0 to 10 to specify the quality setting. Of the named options, Low takes the least space on disk, but distorts the image rather severely; Maximum retains the highest amount of image quality, but consumes more disk space. Of the numbered options, 0 is the most severe compressor and 10 does the least damage.

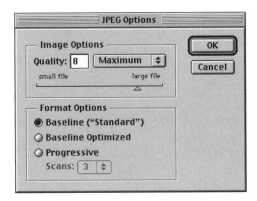

**Figure 2-10:** The new JPEG Options dialog box provides a total of 11 compression settings, ranging from 0 (heaviest compression) to 10 (best quality).

**Note**

JPEG evaluates an image in 8 × 8-pixel blocks, using a technique called *Adaptive Discrete Cosine Transform* (or ADCT, as in "Yes, I'm an acronym ADCT"). It averages the 24-bit value of every pixel in the block (or 8-bit value of every pixel in the case of a grayscale image). ADCT then stores the average color in the upper-left pixel in the block and assigns the remaining 63 pixels smaller values relative to the average.

Next, JPEG divides the block by an 8 × 8 block of its own called the *quantization matrix,* which homogenizes the pixels' values by changing as many as possible to zero. This process saves the majority of disk space and loses data. When Photoshop opens a JPEG image, it can't recover the original distinction between the zero pixels, so the pixels become the same, or similar, colors. Finally, JPEG applies lossless Huffman encoding to translate repeating values to a single symbol.

In most instances, I recommend you use JPEG only at the Maximum quality setting (8 or higher), at least until you gain some experience with it. The smallest amount of JPEG compression saves more space on disk than any non-JPEG compression format and still retains the most essential detail from the original image. Figure 2-11 shows a grayscale image saved at each of the four compression settings.

The samples are arranged in rows from highest image quality (upper left) to lowest quality (lower right). Below each sample is the size of the compressed document on disk. Saved in the only moderately compressed native Photoshop format, the image consumes 116K on disk. From 116K to 28K — the result of the lowest-quality JPEG setting — is a remarkable savings, but it comes at a price.

I've taken the liberty of sharpening the focus of strips in each image so you can see more easily how JPEG averages neighboring pixels to achieve smaller file sizes. The first strip in each image appears in normal focus, the second strip is sharpened once by choosing Filter ➪ Sharpen ➪ Sharpen More, and the third strip is sharpened twice. I also adjusted the gray levels to make the differences even more pronounced. You can see that although the lower-image quality setting leads to a dramatic saving in file size, it also excessively gums up the image. The effect, incidentally, is more obvious on screen. And believe me, after you familiarize yourself with JPEG compression, you can spot other people's overly compressed JPEG images a mile away. This isn't something you want to exaggerate in your images.

Maximum                    66K    High                    50K

Medium                     33K    Low                     28K

**Figure 2-11:** Four JPEG settings applied to a single image, with the highest image quality setting illustrated at the upper left and the lowest at the bottom right.

Cross-Reference

To see the impact of JPEG compression on a full-color image, check out Color Plate 2-1. The original image consumes 693K in the native Photoshop format, but 116K when compressed at the JPEG module's Maximum setting. To demonstrate the differences between different settings better, I enlarged one portion of the image and oversharpened another.

Caution

JPEG is a *cumulative compression scheme,* meaning Photoshop recompresses an image every time you save it in the JPEG format. There's no disadvantage to saving an image to disk repeatedly during a single session, because JPEG always works from the on-screen version. But if you close an image, reopen it, and save it in the JPEG format, you inflict a small amount of damage. Use JPEG sparingly. In the best of all possible worlds, you should only save to the JPEG format after you finish all work on an image. Even in a pinch, you should apply all filtering effects before saving to JPEG, because these have a habit of exacerbating imperfections in image quality.

JPEG is best used when compressing continuous-tone images (images in which the distinction between immediately neighboring pixels is slight). Any image that includes gradual color transitions, as in a photograph, qualifies for JPEG compression. JPEG is not the best choice for saving screen shots, line drawings (especially those converted from EPS graphics), and other high-contrast images. These are better served by a lossless compression scheme such as TIFF with LZW. The JPEG format is available when you are saving grayscale, RGB, and CMYK images.

Occupying the bottom half of the JPEG Options dialog box are three radio buttons, designed primarily to optimize JPEG images for the Web. Progressive isn't applicable to print images, and the Baseline options don't affect print images enough to make any difference. For now, just select the first option, Baseline ("Standard"), and be done with it. If you want to learn more about the remaining options, read the "Saving JPEG Images" section of Chapter 32.

## TIFF

Developed by Aldus in the early days of the Mac to standardize an ever-growing population of scanned images, TIFF (*Tag Image File Format*) is the most widely supported image printing format across both the Macintosh and PC platforms. Unlike EPS, it can't handle object-oriented artwork, and it doesn't support lossy compression like JPEG. But, otherwise, it's unrestricted. In fact, TIFF offers a few tricks of its own that make it very special.

When you save an image in the TIFF format, Photoshop displays the TIFF Options dialog box (see Figure 2-12), which offers these options:

✦ **Byte Order:** Every once in a while, Photoshop chooses to name a straightforward option in the most confusing way possible. Byte Order is a prime example. No, this option doesn't have anything to do with how you eat your food. Instead, there are two variations of TIFF, one for the PC and the other for the Mac. I'm sure this has something to do with the arrangement of 8-bit chunks of data, but who cares? You want PC or you want Mac? It's that simple.

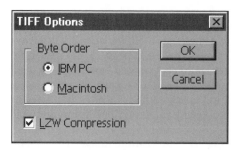

**Figure 2-12:** Photoshop enables you to save TIFF files in either the Mac or PC format and to compress the image using LZW.

✦ **LZW Compression:** Like Huffman encoding (previously described in the "Saving an EPS image" section), the LZW (Lempel-Ziv-Welch) compression scheme digs into the computer code that describes an image and substitutes frequently used codes with shorter equivalents. But instead of substituting characters, as Huffman does, LZW substitutes strings of data. Because LZW doesn't so much as touch a pixel in your image, it's entirely lossless. Most image editors and desktop publishing applications — including Illustrator, FreeHand, PageMaker, and QuarkXPress — import LZW-compressed TIFF images, but a few still have yet to catch on.

If names like Huffman and LZW ring a faint bell, it may be because these are the same compression schemes used by StuffIt, Compact Pro, PKZIP, WinZip, and other compression utilities. For this reason, using an additional utility to compress a TIFF image that you've already compressed using LZW makes no sense. Neither do you want to compress a JPEG image, because JPEG takes advantage of Huffman encoding. You may shave off a few K, but this isn't enough space to make it worth your time and effort.

In Photoshop, the TIFF format supports up to 24 channels, the maximum number permitted in any image. In fact, TIFF is the only format other than DCS 2.0, "raw," and the native Photoshop format that can save more than four channels. To save a TIFF file without extra mask channels, choose File ➪ Save a Copy and select the Don't Include Alpha Channels check box. (For an educational introduction to channels, read Chapter 3.)

If you have limited RAM, or you're working with a very large TIFF image, you can open an isolated detail of the image using File ➪ Import ➪ Quick Edit. (If this command does not appear in your menu, install the optional plug-in off your original Photoshop CD.) Photoshop displays a small preview of the image. Drag in the preview to select the area you want to open and press Return/Enter. Photoshop opens only that isolated portion of the file. To save the detail back into the larger TIFF image, choose File ➪ Export ➪ Quick Edit.

I must admit, I have a love/hate thing going with Quick Edit. I appreciate that Quick Edit lets you open small chunks of an image at a time. But I hate that you can open uncompressed TIFF images only, and that Quick Edit doesn't support any format other than TIFF. It doesn't even support the native Photoshop format. What a drag.

## Special-purpose formats

With 20 file formats to choose from, you can imagine that most of them are not the kinds of things you'll be using on a regular basis. In fact, apart from the native Photoshop format, you'll probably want to stick with TIFF, JPEG, and GIF for Web images, and EPS when preparing images for placement into QuarkXPress, PageMaker, and others.

Many of the other formats are provided simply so you can open an image created on another platform, saved from some antiquated paint program, or downloaded from the Web. In this section, I cover these special-purpose formats.

You'll notice that I lump Web standards GIF and PNG in with the special-purpose formats. The reason is simple — if you don't design for the Web, you rarely need them. On the other hand, if you do design for the Web, the formats take on special significance, which is why I cover them in depth in Chapter 32.

### Amiga's IFF

The Amiga was a failed experiment in desktop computers pioneered by Commodore. One of the first computers to ship with a color monitor, it never caught on with mainstream developers. But despite the fact that Commodore bowed out of the computer market more than two years ago now, Amiga fans are adamant that their systems live on — as I can attest from personal experience with several angry Amiga owners responding to previous editions of this paragraph.

Still, even a sensible Amiga user of the past who has gone on to bigger and better things may have several hundred Amiga files sitting around. To this end, Photoshop lets you open and save IFF (*Interchange File Format*) files. IFF is the Amiga's all-around graphics format, serving much the same function as PICT on the Mac. IFF is even supported by a few antiquated DOS applications, most notably DeluxePaint from Electronic Arts.

### Microsoft Paint's BMP

*Windows Bitmap* (BMP) is the native format for Microsoft Paint (included with Windows) and is supported by a variety of Windows and DOS applications. Photoshop supports BMP images with up to 16 million colors. You also can use *Run-Length Encoding* (RLE), a lossless compression scheme specifically applicable to the BMP format.

The term *lossless* refers to compression schemes such as BMP's RLE and TIFF's *Lempel-Ziv-Welch* (LZW) that conserve space on disk without sacrificing any data in the image. The only reasons not to use lossless compression are that it slows down the open and save operations and it may prevent less-sophisticated applications from opening an image. (Lossy compression routines, such as JPEG, sacrifice a user-defined amount of data to conserve even more disk space, as I explained earlier.)

The most common use for BMP is to create images for use in help files and Windows wallpaper. In fact, rolling your own wallpaper is a fun way to show off your Photoshop skills, which is exactly what I did in Color Plate 2-2. For the best results, make sure your image is set to exactly the same pixel dimensions as your screen (which you can check from the Settings panel in the Display control panel). To conserve memory, you may want to reduce the number of colors in your wallpaper image to 256 using Image ➪ Mode ➪ Indexed Color. Though Color Plate 2-2 may look quite colorful, I did in fact reduce the palette to a bare-bones 256 colors. See Chapter 32 for the complete lowdown on indexed color.

When you save the wallpaper image, Photoshop displays the options shown in Figure 2-13. Generally, you'll want to select the Windows option, but it really doesn't matter when creating wallpaper. But be sure to turn off Compress (RLE), and don't mess with the Depth options. Either you reduced the bit depth using the Indexed Color command as I directed above or you didn't. There's no sense in changing the colors during the save process.

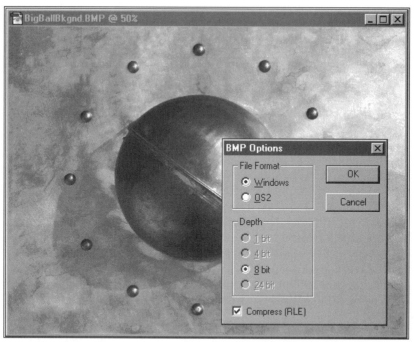

**Figure 2-13:** Select the options shown here when saving a BMP image for use as a desktop background. Leave the Depth setting alone.

To load the wallpaper onto your PC desktop, right-click on anywhere on the desktop and choose the Properties command. This brings up the Display Properties dialog box shown in Figure 2-14. Click the Browse button and locate your BMP image on disk. Then click on the Apply button to see how it looks.

### CompuServe's GIF

In the old days, the CompuServe online service championed GIF (short for *Graphics Interchange Format*) as a means of compressing files so you could quickly transfer photographs over your modem. Like TIFF, GIF uses LZW compression; but unlike TIFF, GIF is limited to just 256 colors.

With the advent of the World Wide Web, the GIF format has grown slightly more sophisticated. Two varieties of GIF currently exist, known by the helpful codes 87a and 89a. GIF87a supports strictly opaque pixels, while GIF89a permits some pixels to be transparent. You can open either kind of image using File ➪ Open. You can save an image to the GIF87a format by choosing File ➪ Save and selecting CompuServe GIF from the Format pop-up menu (or Save As pop-up menu on a PC). To save a GIF89a file with transparent pixels, choose File ➪ Export ➪ GIF89a Export.

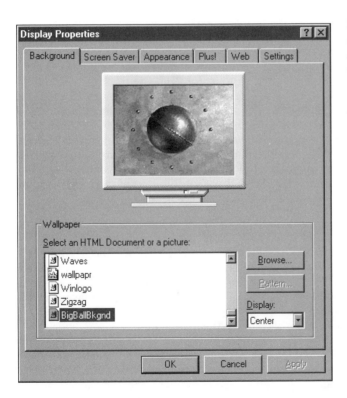

**Figure 2-14:** You can load a BMP file as desktop wallpaper using the Display control panel provided with Windows 95 and later.

**Cross-Reference**

Before saving a GIF image, use Image ➪ Mode ➪ Indexed Color to lower the number of colors to 256 or fewer. In fact, the GIF format doesn't appear in the Format (or Save As) pop-up menu if your image has more than 256 colors. For complete information about creating and saving GIF images for the Web, see Chapter 32.

## PC Paintbrush's PCX

PCX doesn't stand for anything. Rather, it's the extension PC Paintbrush assigns to images saved in its native file format. Although the format is losing favor, many PCX images are still in use today, largely because PC Paintbrush is the oldest painting program for DOS. Photoshop supports PCX images with up to 16 million colors. You can find an enormous amount of art, usually clip art, in this format. But don't save files to PCX unless a client specifically demands it. Other formats are better.

## Adobe's paperless PDF

The *Portable Document Format* (PDF) is a variation on the PostScript printing language that enables you to view electronically produced documents on screen. This means you can create a publication in QuarkXPress or PageMaker, export it to PDF, and distribute it without worrying about color separations, binding, and other printing costs. Using a program called Adobe Acrobat, you can open PDF documents, zoom in and out of them, and follow hypertext links by clicking on highlighted words. Adobe distributes Mac, Windows, and UNIX versions of the Acrobat Reader free, so about anyone with a computer can view your stuff in full, natural color.

Where Photoshop 4 offered limited support for PDF — permitting you to open Photoshop-created PDF files only — Version 5 can open arbitrary PDF files created with any application. When you open a PDF file, Photoshop lets you browse through thumbnail page previews — provided that previews were saved with the file — and select the exact page you want to open. You can even print a contact sheet showing every page in a PDF file by choosing File ➪ Automate ➪ Multi-Page PDF to PSD. Unless you create a lot of documents with Acrobat Exchange — which limits its image support to PDF files — there's not much reason to save an image in PDF. But the enhanced opening functions are great.

## Apple's PICT

PICT (*Macintosh Picture*) is the Macintosh system software's native graphics format. Based on the QuickDraw display language the system software uses to convey images on screen, PICT is one of the few file formats that handles object-oriented artwork and bitmapped images with equal aplomb. It supports images in any bit depth, size, or resolution. PICT even supports 32-bit images, so you can save a fourth masking channel when working in the RGB mode.

On a Mac, if you've installed QuickTime, you can subject PICT images to JPEG compression. But while PICT's compression options may look similar to JPEG's, they are actually significantly inferior. The differences become especially noticeable if you open an image, make a change, and again save it to disk, effectively reapplying the compression.

In most cases, you'll want to use the JPEG format instead of PICT when compressing images on a Mac. JPEG images are compatible with the Web; PICT images are not. Also, more Windows applications recognize JPEG than PICT, and it's extremely difficult to find a Windows program that can handle PICT files with QuickTime compression.

In fact, the only reason to use PICT is low-end compatibility. If you're trying to save an image in a format that your mom can open on her Mac, for example, PICT is a better choice than JPEG. Heck, you can open PICT files inside a word processor, including everything from SimpleText to Microsoft Word. Just be sure mom has QuickTime loaded on her machine.

When you save a PICT image, Photoshop also lets you set the bit depth. You should always stick with the default option, which is the highest setting available for the particular image. Don't mess around with these options; they apply automatic pattern dithering, which is a bad thing.

If you're using a PC, you may need to open a PICT file a Mac friend sends you. Photoshop can do this, but one thing may trip you up: On the Mac, you have the option of saving PICT files with a variety of JPEG compression supplied by Apple's QuickTime, as I mentioned above. Unless you have QuickTime installed on your PC — which you might if you do a lot of surfing on the Web — you won't be able to open compressed PICT images.

## PICT resource #1, the startup screen

PICT resources are images contained in the resource fork of a Mac file. (As I mentioned earlier, Windows programs can't recognize resource forks, so this and the following section are only relevant to Mac folks.) The only reason to save a PICT resource is to create a startup screen for your Mac, and the most likely reason to open one is to extract images from the Scrapbook.

The startup screen is that message that welcomes you to the great big wonderful Macintosh experience when you boot your computer. If you like to customize your system, you can create your own startup screen by saving an image in the PICT Resource file format under the name *StartupScreen* in the root directory of your System Folder. My own personal startup screen appears in Color Plate 2-3.

To save an image as a startup screen, first make sure that the image is set to exactly the same pixel dimensions as your screen (which you can check in the Monitors or Monitors & Sound control panel). And set the Resolution value in the Image Size dialog box to 72 ppi. Then choose File ⇨ Save, select PICT Resource from the Format pop-up menu, name the image *StartupScreen*, and save it in your System Folder. The PICT Resources Options dialog box appears (as in Figure 2-15), asking you to enter a four-character Name code. The secret code is *SCRN*.

If you're saving a 24-bit startup screen, the PICT Resources Options dialog box offers a bunch of QuickTime compression options. *Don't select any of them!* Because QuickTime isn't built into the ROM of your computer, it won't be available when the startup screen appears, and therefore a weird-looking, stretched error message will appear on-screen instead. To avoid this, select None from the Compression options.

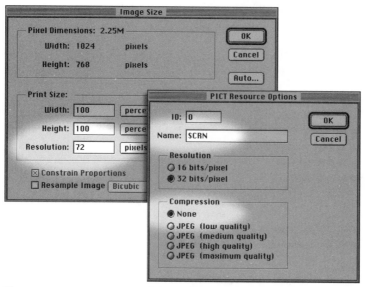

**Figure 2-15:** Be sure to set the Resolution to 72, the Name to SCRN, and the Compression to None when saving a custom startup screen.

## PICT resource #2, the Scrapbook

To open a PICT resource other than the startup screen file, you bypass the Open command in favor of File ➪ Import ➪ PICT Resource. This command lets you open an application or other non-image file on disk and browse through any PICT resources it may contain. Figure 2-16 shows the dialog box that appears after you select a file to open. You use the double arrow symbols to advance from one PICT image to the next. Click on the Preview button to display the image in the preview box.

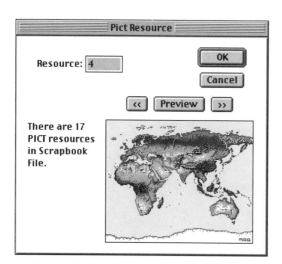

**Figure 2-16:** Choose File ➪ Import ➪ PICT Resource to browse through the PICT images inside the Scrapbook.

The best use of File ➪ Import ➪ PICT Resource is to open images directly from the Scrapbook. In fact, this function becomes phenomenally practical if you use a commercial or shareware screen-capture utility (such as Mainstay's Capture) that can store screen shots in the Scrapbook. You can process your screen shots *en masse* at your leisure. In fact, this is how I created most of the Mac screen shots in this book.

### Pixar workstations

Pixar has created some of the most memorable computer-animated movies and commercials in recent memory. Examples include the desk lamps playing with a beach ball from *Luxo, Jr.,* the run-amok toddler from the Oscar-winning *Tin Toy*, and the commercial adventures of a Listerine bottle that boxes gingivitis one day and swings Tarzan-like through a spearmint forest the next. But Pixar really made the grade with the feature-length *Toy Story*, which provided Disney with enough merchandising options to last a lifetime.

Pixar works its 3-D magic using mondo-expensive workstations. Photoshop enables you to open a still image created on a Pixar machine or to save an image to the Pixar format so you can integrate it into a 3-D rendering. The Pixar format supports grayscale and RGB images.

### PNG for the Web

Pronounced *ping*, the PNG format enables you to save 16 million color images without compression for use on the Web. As I write this, neither Netscape Navigator nor Microsoft Internet Explorer support PNG without the help of a special plug-in. But for those folks who want full-color images without the pesky visual compression artifacts you get with JPEG, PNG may well be a big player in the future. (Of course, I wrote this exact same paragraph two years ago, so there's always the chance PNG will never gain acceptance.)

PNG was invented for the Web and I've never seen anyone use it for a purpose other than the Web. So, like all things Webby, you'll find more information about PNG in Chapter 32.

### Scitex image-processors

Some high-end commercial printers use Scitex printing devices to generate color separations of images and other documents. Photoshop can open images digitized with Scitex scanners and save the edited images to the *Scitex CT* (Continuous Tone) format. Because you need special hardware to transfer images from the PC to a Scitex drive, you'll probably want to consult with your local Scitex service bureau technician before saving to the CT format. The technician may prefer that you submit images in the native Photoshop, TIFF, or JPEG format. The Scitex CT format supports grayscale, RGB, and CMYK images.

### TrueVision's TGA

TrueVision's Targa and NuVista video boards enable you to overlay computer graphics and animation onto live video. The effect is called *chroma keying* because, typically, a key color is set aside to let the live video show through. TrueVision designed the TGA (*Targa*) format to support 32-bit images that include 8-bit alpha channels capable of displaying the live video. Support for TGA is widely implemented among professional-level color and video applications on the PC.

## Interapplication formats

In the name of interapplication harmony, Photoshop supports a few software-specific formats that permit you to trade files with popular object-oriented programs such as Illustrator and QuarkXPress. Every one of these formats is a variation on EPS (*Encapsulated PostScript*), which is based in turn on Adobe's industry-standard PostScript printing language. You can use Photoshop to edit frames from a QuickTime movie created with Adobe Premiere.

### Rasterizing an Illustrator or FreeHand file

Photoshop supports object-oriented files saved in the EPS format. EPS is specifically designed to save object-oriented graphics that you intend to print to a PostScript output device. Just about every drawing and page-layout program on the planet (and a few on Mars) can save EPS documents.

Prior to Version 4, Photoshop could interpret only a small subset of EPS operations supported by Illustrator (including the native .ai format). But then Photoshop 4 came along and offered a full-blown EPS translation engine, capable of interpreting EPS illustrations created in FreeHand, CorelDraw, Deneba's Canvas, and more. You can even open EPS drawings that contain imported images, something else Version 3 could not do.

When you open an EPS or native Illustrator document, Photoshop *rasterizes* (or *renders*) the artwork—that is, it converts the artwork from a collection of objects to a bitmapped image. During the open operation, Photoshop presents the Rasterize Generic EPS Format dialog box (see Figure 2-17), which allows you to specify the size and resolution of the image, just as you can in the New dialog box. Assuming the illustration contains no imported images, you can render it as large or as small as you want without any loss of image quality.

**Tip**

If the EPS illustration does contain an imported image or two, you need to know the resolution of the images and factor this information into the Rasterize Generic EPS Format dialog box. Select anything but Pixels from both the Width and Height pop-up menus, and leave the suggested values unchanged. Then enter the setting for the highest-resolution imported image into the Resolution option box. (If all the images are low-rez, you may want to double or triple the Resolution value to ensure the objects render smoothly.)

You should always select the Anti-aliased check box unless you're rendering a very large image—say, 300 ppi or higher. *Anti-aliasing* blurs pixels to soften the edges of the objects so they don't appear jagged. When you're rendering a very large image, the difference between image and printer resolution is less noticeable, so anti-aliasing is unwarranted.

Photoshop renders the illustration to a single layer against a transparent background. Before you can save the rasterized image to a format other than native Photoshop, you must eliminate the transparency by choosing Layer ⇨ Flatten Image. Or save a flattened version of the image to a separate file by choosing File ⇨ Save a Copy.

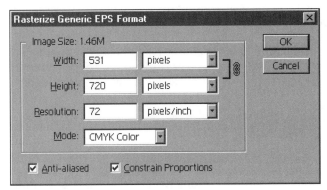

**Figure 2-17:** You can specify the size and resolution at which Photoshop renders an EPS illustration.

**Tip**

Rendering an EPS illustration is an extremely useful technique for resolving printing problems. If you regularly work in Illustrator or FreeHand, you no doubt have encountered *limitcheck errors*, which occur when an illustration is too complex for an imagesetter or other high-end output device to print. If you're frustrated with the printer and tired of wasting your evening trying to figure out what's wrong (sound familiar?), use Photoshop to render the illustration at 300 ppi and print it. Nine times out of ten, this technique works flawlessly.

If Photoshop can't *parse* the EPS file — a techy way of saying Photoshop can't break down the individual objects — it attempts to open the PICT (Mac) or TIFF (Windows) preview. This exercise is usually futile, but occasionally you may wish to take a quick look at an illustration in order to, say, match the placement of elements in an image to those in the drawing.

### Placing an EPS illustration

If you want to introduce an EPS graphic into the foreground image rather than to render it into a new image window of its own, choose File ⇨ Place. Unlike other File menu commands, Place supports only EPS illustrations.

After you import the EPS graphic, it appears inside a box with a great big X across it. Then you can move, scale, and rotate the illustration into position before rasterizing it to pixels. Drag a corner handle to resize the image, drag outside the image to rotate it. You can also nudge the graphic into position by pressing the arrow keys. When everything is the way you want it, press Return/Enter or double-click inside the box to rasterize the illustration. If the placement isn't perfect, not to worry. The graphic appears on a separate layer, so you can move it with complete freedom. To cancel the Place operation, press Escape instead of Return/Enter.

## Saving an EPS image

When preparing an image for placement inside a drawing or page-layout document that you plan on printing to a PostScript output device, many artists prefer to save the image in the EPS format. First, by converting the image to PostScript up front, you prevent the drawing or page-layout program from having to do the work. The result is an image that prints more quickly and with less chance of problems. (Note that an image does not *look* any different when saved in EPS. The idea that the EPS format somehow blesses an image with better resolution is pure nonsense.)

The second point in the EPS format's favor is clipping paths. As explained graphically at the end of Chapter 15, a clipping path defines a free-form boundary around an image. When you place the image into an object-oriented program, everything outside the clipping path becomes transparent. While some programs — notably PageMaker — recognize clipping paths saved with a TIFF image, most programs — Illustrator and QuarkXPress among them — acknowledge a clipping path only when saved in the EPS format.

Third, although Illustrator has remedied the problems it had importing TIFF images, it still likes EPS best, especially where screen display is concerned. Thanks to the EPS file's fixed preview, Illustrator can display an EPS image on screen very quickly compared with other file formats. And Illustrator can display an EPS image both in the preview mode and in the super-fast artwork mode.

So if you want to import an image into Illustrator, QuarkXPress, or another object-oriented program, your best bet is EPS. On the downside, EPS is an inefficient format for saving images thanks to the laborious way that it describes pixels. An EPS image may be three to four times larger than the same image saved to the TIFF format with LZW compression. But this is the price we pay for reliable printing.

Absolutely avoid the EPS format if you plan on printing your final pages to a non-PostScript printer. This defeats the entire purpose of EPS, which is meant to avoid printing problems, not cause them. When printing without PostScript, use TIFF or JPEG instead.

To save an image in the EPS format, choose Photoshop EPS from the Format (or Save As) pop-up menu in the Save dialog box. After you press Return/Enter, Photoshop displays the dialog box shown in Figure 2-18. The options in this dialog box work as follows:

> ✦ **Preview:** Technically, an EPS document comprises two parts: a pure PostScript-language description of the graphic for the printer and a bitmapped preview so you can see the graphic on screen. On a Mac, select the Macintosh (8 Bits/Pixel)

option from the Preview pop-up menu to save a 256-color PICT preview of the image. Or select the Macintosh (JPEG) option for a 24-bit preview (which in most cases takes up less room on disk, thanks to the JPEG compression). If you plan on passing off the image to a Windows colleague, select TIFF (8 Bits/Pixel). On a PC, select the TIFF (8 Bits/Pixel) option from the Preview pop-up menu to save a 256-color TIFF preview of the image. The 1-bit options provide black-and-white previews only, which are useful if you want to save a little room on disk. Select None to include no preview and save even more disk space.

✦ **Encoding:** If you're saving an image for import into Illustrator, QuarkXPress, or some other established program, select the Binary encoding option (also known as Huffman encoding), which compresses an EPS document by substituting shorter codes for frequently used characters. The letter a, for example, receives the 3-bit code 010, rather than its standard 8-bit ASCII code, 01100001 (the binary equivalent of what we humans call 97).

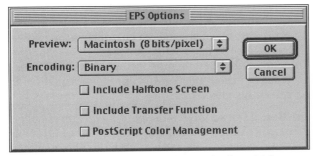

**Figure 2-18:** When you save an image in the EPS format, you can specify the type of preview and tack on some printing attributes.

Sadly, some programs and printers don't recognize Huffman encoding, in which case you must select the less efficient ASCII option. ASCII stands for *American Standard Code for Information Interchange*, which is fancy jargon for text-only. In other words, you can open and edit an ASCII EPS document in a word processor, provided you know how to read and write PostScript.

**Tip**

Actually, this can be a useful technique if you have a Mac file that won't open on a PC, especially if the file was sent to you electronically. Chances are that a Mac-specific header got into the works. Open the file in a word processor and look at the beginning. You should see the four characters %!PS. Anything that comes before this line is the Macintosh header. Delete the garbage before %!PS, save the file in text format, and try again to open the file in Photoshop.

**Caution**

The remaining Encoding options are JPEG settings. JPEG compression not only results in smaller files on disk, but it also degrades the quality of the image. Select JPEG (Maximum Quality) to invoke the least degradation. Better yet, avoid the JPEG settings altogether. These options work only if you plan to print your final artwork to a PostScript Level 2 or Level 3 device. Earlier PostScript printers do not support EPS artwork with JPEG compression and will choke on the code.

So, to recap, ASCII results in really big files that will work with virtually any printer or application. Binary creates smaller files which work with most mainstream applications but may choke some older-model printers. And the JPEG settings are compatible exclusively with Level 2 and later PostScript printers.

✦ **Clipping Path**: I mention this option because it no longer exists in Photoshop 5. You used to be able to specify a clipping path when saving an EPS file, now you have to specify the clipping path in advance using the Clipping Path command. To learn how, read the final section in Chapter 15.

✦ **Include Halftone Screen**: Another advantage of EPS over other formats is that it can retain printing attributes. If you specified a custom halftone screen using the Screens button inside the Page Setup dialog box, you can save this setting with the EPS document by selecting the Include Halftone Screen check box. But be careful — you can just as easily ruin your image as help it. Read Chapter 4 before you select this check box.

✦ **Include Transfer Function**: As described in Chapter 4, you can change the brightness and contrast of a printed image using the Transfer button inside the Page Setup dialog box. To save these settings with the EPS document, select the Include Transfer Function check box. Again, this option can be dangerous when used casually. See Chapter 4 for more details.

✦ **PostScript Color Management**: Like JPEG compression, this check box is compatible with Level 2 and 3 printers only. It embeds a color profile which helps the printer to massage the image during the printing cycle in order to generate more accurate colors. Unless you plan on printing to a Level 2 or later device, leave the option off. (For more information about color profiles, read Chapter 3.)

✦ **Transparent Whites**: When saving black-and-white EPS images in Photoshop, the two check boxes previously discussed drop away, replaced by Transparent Whites. Select this option to make all white pixels in the image transparent.

Although Photoshop EPS is the only format that offers the Transparent Whites option, many programs — including Illustrator — treat white pixels in black-and-white TIFF images as transparent as well.

## QuarkXPress DCS

Quark developed a variation on the EPS format called *Desktop Color Separation* (DCS). When you work in QuarkXPress, PageMaker, and other programs that support the format, DCS facilitates the printing of color separations. Before you can use DCS, you have to convert your image to the CMYK color space using Image ⇨ Mode ⇨ CMYK Color. (DCS 2.0 also supports grayscale images with spot-color channels.) Then bring up the Save dialog box and select Photoshop DCS 1.0 or 2.0 from the Format (or Save As) pop-up menu.

Photoshop 5 introduced support for DCS 2.0 to accommodate images that contain extra spot-color channels, as explained in Chapter 4. If you add a Pantone channel to an image, DCS 2.0 is the only PostScript format you can use. If your image doesn't contain any extra channels beyond the basic four required for CMYK, then DCS 1.0 is the safer and simpler option.

After you press Return/Enter, Photoshop displays an additional pop-up menu of DCS options, which vary depending on whether you've selected DCS 1.0 or 2.0, as shown in Figure 2-19. The DCS 1.0 format invariably saves a total of five files: one master document (which is the file that you import into XPress) plus one file each for the cyan, magenta, yellow, and black color channels (which are the files that get printed). The DCS 2.0 format can be expressed as a single file (tidier) or five separate files (better compatibility).

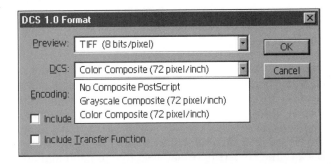

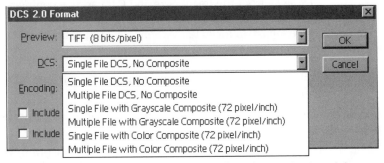

**Figure 2-19:** The extra options for the DCS 1.0 format (top) and those for the DCS 2.0 format (bottom).

Either way, the DCS pop-up menu gives you the option of saving a 72-ppi PostScript composite of the image inside the master document. Independent from the bitmapped preview—which you specify as usual by selecting a Preview option—the PostScript composite makes it possible to print a low-resolution version of a DCS image to a consumer-quality printer. If you're using a black-and-white printer, select the 72 pixel/inch grayscale option; if you're using a color printer, select the final option. Be forewarned, however, that the composite image significantly increases the size of the master document on disk.

## Premiere Filmstrip

Adobe Premiere is a popular QuickTime movie-editing application for both Macs and PCs. The program is a wonder when it comes to fades, frame merges, and special effects, but it offers no frame-by-frame editing capabilities. For example, you can neither draw a mustache on a person in the movie nor can you make brightly colored brush strokes swirl about in the background—at least, not inside Premiere.

You can export the movie to the Filmstrip format, though, which is a file-swapping option exclusive to Photoshop and Premiere. A Filmstrip document organizes frames in a long vertical strip, as shown on the left side of Figure 2-20. The right side of the figure shows the movie after I edited each individual frame in ways not permitted by Premiere. A boring movie of a cat stuck in a bag becomes an exciting movie of a cat-stuck-in-a-bag flying. If that doesn't sum up the miracle of digital imaging, I don't know what does.

A gray bar separates each frame. The number of each frame appears on the right; the *Society of Motion Picture and Television Engineers* (SMPTE) time code appears on the left. The structure of the three-number time code is minutes:seconds:frames, with 30 frames per second.

If you change the size of a Filmstrip document inside Photoshop in any way, you cannot save the image back to the Filmstrip format. Feel free to paint and apply effects, but stay the heck away from the Image Size and Canvas Size commands.

I don't really delve into the Filmstrip format anywhere else in this book, so I want to pass along a few quick Filmstrip tips right here and now:

✦ First, you can scroll up and down exactly one frame at a time by pressing Shift+Page Up or Shift+Page Down, respectively.

✦ Second, you can move a selection exactly one frame up or down by pressing ⌘/Ctrl+Shift+up arrow or ⌘/Ctrl+Shift+down arrow.

✦ If you want to clone the selection as you move it, ⌘/Ctrl+Shift+Option/Alt+up arrow or ⌘/Ctrl+Shift+Option/Alt+down arrow.

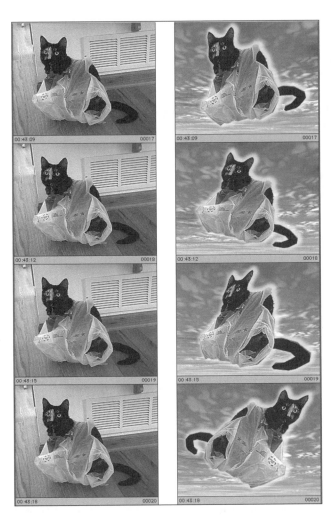

**Figure 2-20:** Four frames from a QuickTime movie as they appear in the Filmstrip format before (left) and after (right) editing the frames in Photoshop.

## Steps: Selecting Sequential Frames in a Movie

1. **Select the first frame you want to edit.** Select the rectangular marquee tool by pressing the M key. Then drag around the area you want to edit in the movie. (This is the only step that takes any degree of care or coordination whatsoever.)

2. **Switch to the quick mask mode by pressing the Q key.** The areas around the selected frame are overlaid with pink.

3. **Set the magic wand Tolerance value to 0.** Double-click on the magic wand tool icon in the Toolbox to display the Magic Wand Options palette. Enter 0 for the Tolerance value and deselect the Anti-aliased check box.

4. **Click inside the selected frame (the one that's not pink) with the magic wand tool.** This selects the unmasked area inside the frame.

5. **Press ⌘/Ctrl+Shift+Option/Alt+down arrow to clone the unmasked area to the next frame in the movie.** When you exit the quick mask mode, both this frame and the one above it will be selected.

6. **Repeat several times.** Keep ⌘/Ctrl+Shift+Option/Alt+down-arrowing until you're rid of the pink stuff on all the frames you want to select.

7. **Exit the quick mask mode by pressing the Q key again.** All frames appear selected.

8. **Edit the frames to your heart's content.**

If you're new to Photoshop, half of these steps, if not all of them, probably sailed over your head like so many low-flying cats stuck in bags. If you want to learn more about selections and cloning, see Chapter 15. In Chapter 16, I explore the quick mask mode and other masking techniques. After you finish reading those chapters, return to this section to see if it doesn't make a little more sense. Or don't. It's entirely up to you.

The process of editing individual frames as just described is sometimes called *rotoscoping*, named after the traditional technique of combining live-action film with animated sequences. You also can try out some scratch-and-doodle techniques, which is where an artist scratches and draws directly on frames of film. If this isn't enough, you can emulate *xerography*, in which an animator makes Xerox copies of photographs, enhances the copies using markers or whatever else is convenient, and shoots the finished artwork, frame by frame, on film. In a nutshell, Photoshop extends Premiere's functionality by adding animation to its standard supply of video-editing capabilities.

You can save an image in the Filmstrip format only if you opened the image as a Filmstrip document and did not change the size of the image. To do so, press ⌘/Ctrl+S.

## The oddball formats

Can you believe it? After plowing through a half-million formats, I still haven't covered them all. The last three are the odd men out. One format has a purpose so specific that Photoshop can open files saved in the format but it can't save to the format. The second is a new format that, while moderately promising, is not implemented thoroughly enough inside Photoshop to provide much benefit. And the last is less a format than a manual can opener that may come in handy for jimmying open a file from an unknown source.

## Photo CD YCC images

Photoshop can open Eastman Kodak's Photo CD and Pro Photo CD formats directly. A Photo CD contains compressed versions of every image in each of the five scan sizes provided on Photo CDs—from 128 × 192 pixels (72K) to 2,048 × 3,072 pixels (18MB).

The Pro Photo CD format can accommodate each of the five sizes included in the regular Photo CD format, plus one additional size—4,096 × 6,144 pixels (72MB)—that's four times as large as the largest image on a regular Photo CD. As a result, Pro Photo CDs hold only 25 scans; standard Photo CDs hold 100. Like their standard Photo CD counterparts, Pro Photo CD scanners can accommodate 35mm film and slides. But they can also handle 70mm film and 4 × 5-inch negatives and transparencies. The cost might knock you out, though. While scanning an image to a standard Photo CD costs between $1 and $2, scanning it to a Pro Photo CD costs about $10. It goes to show you, once you gravitate beyond consumerland, everyone expects you to start coughing up the big bucks.

Both Photo CD and Pro Photo CD use the YCC color model, a variation on the CIE (Commission Internationale de l'Eclairage) color space, which I discuss in the next chapter. YCC provides a broader range of color—theoretically, every color your eye can see. By opening Photo CD files directly, you can translate the YCC images directly to Photoshop's Lab color mode, another variation on CIE color space that ensures no color loss.

Photoshop includes the latest Kodak Color Management Software (CMS), which tweaks colors in Photo CD images based on the kind of film from which they were scanned. When you open a Photo CD image, Photoshop displays the dialog box shown in Figure 2-21.

**Note**

Finding your photos on a Photo CD is a little harder than it should be. Look inside the Images folder in the Photo_CD folder. The files have friendly names like Img0017.pcd.

The friendlier Photos folder you'll see on your Mac contains PICT versions of the images generated by the operating system. While there's nothing precisely wrong with them, they don't offer the same degree of color control as the real files that are buried in the Images folder.

The Photo CD dialog box lets you specify the image size you want to use by selecting an option from the Resolution pop-up menu. The dialog box even shows you a preview of the image. But the options that make a difference are the Source and Destination buttons:

✦ **Source**: Click on this button to select the kind of film from which the original photographs were scanned. You can select from two specific Kodak brands—Ektachrome and Kodachrome—or settle for the generic Color Negative Film option. Stock Photo CD vendors such as Digital Stock ensure a precise match by providing source profiles of their own, as I've selected in Figure 2-21. Your selection determines the method Photoshop uses to transform the colors in the image.

✦ **Destination**: After clicking on this button, select an option from the Device pop-up menu to specify the color model you want to use. Select Adobe Photoshop RGB to open the image in the RGB mode; select Adobe Photoshop CIELAB to open the image in the Lab mode.

**Figure 2-21:** Use these options to select a resolution and to calibrate the colors in the Photo CD image.

A CMYK profile can be purchased separately from Kodak. Some stock photo agencies also include special color profiles. For example, Digital Stock currently provides its excellent image library on Photo CDs. The company offers a source profile for its particular drum-scanning technology, as well as CMYK destination profiles.

Photoshop cannot save to the Photo CD format. And, frankly, there's little reason you'd want to do so. Photo CD is strictly a means for transferring slides and film negatives onto the world's most ubiquitous and indestructible storage medium, the CD-ROM.

## Kodak's FlashPix

Photoshop 5 supports the new FlashPix format. Developed by Kodak, Live Picture, and a few other companies eager to get into the imaging game (notice Adobe is not on this list), FlashPix is a kind of Photo CD format without the CD. And Photoshop can both open and save images in the FlashPix format. The question is, will you ever want to? The answer is, wait and see.

The purpose of FlashPix is to turn every image editor into a kind of Live Picture. In case you're not familiar with this program, Live Picture is a Macintosh image editor that processes high-resolution images very quickly by performing its edits on a screen-resolution proxy. The program records its edits as a sequence of mathematical operations, but waits until you save the image out as a TIFF file before actually applying the edits to the image pixels.

In this same vein, the FlashPix format saves an image in multiple resolutions — first at full resolution, then at half resolution, then at quarter resolution, and so on. It keeps saving until it gets down to a width or height of less than 100 pixels and then it stops. With a high enough resolution file, you can end up with seven or eight iterations of the image. This kind of file structure is called a *pyramid* because each iteration of the file sits below the last. (It's really an inverted pyramid, but why split hairs?) FlashPix also subdivides each iteration into a bunch of 64 × 64-pixel tiles.

The point of all this iterating and subdividing is to give the image editor lots of little image chunks to work with. That way, the program can load a chunk, apply an edit to that little chunk (and thereby fool the user into thinking the entire image has been edited), record the edits to a file as it goes along, and then apply all the edits at once during the saving process while the user goes to the candy machine and gets a snack.

Luckily, Photoshop doesn't work that way. Version 5 remains the plodding pixel-by-pixel editor that we've all come to know and love. As a result, Photoshop doesn't take full advantage of the FlashPix format. (Kodak actually suggests that applications should do away with their native formats and gratefully embrace FlashPix instead. Again, count yourself lucky.)

## Saving and opening FlashPix images

So, now that you understand FlashPix, what it was meant to do, and how Photoshop doesn't do that, let's see what Photoshop *does* do. When you save an image in the FlashPix (*.fpx*) format, you are greeted by the dialog box shown in Figure 2-22. Your options are to apply no compression, or apply JPEG compression. You have 10 quality settings, just like Photoshop's standard JPEG. Photoshop save the iterations and tiles in the background without bothering you with the details. What could be easier?

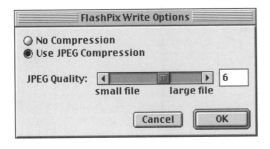

**Figure 2-22:** You can save a FlashPix image with or without JPEG compression.

Opening the file is twice as easy. Photoshop simply opens the largest iteration from the pyramid. End of story. (Interestingly, early in the beat cycle, Photoshop 5 let you select the exact iteration you wanted to open, but this idea was scrapped. Too bad.)

So when all is said and done, Photoshop's support for FlashPix serves two purposes: First, it allows Photoshop to open FlashPix images if and when you come upon them; second, it allows you to save images so that programs that rely on the FlashPix format can open them. Look for Photoshop's support for FlashPix to develop over time — particularly if the format becomes a more prominent force in the industry.

## Opening a raw document

A *raw document* is a plain binary file stripped of all extraneous information. It contains no compression scheme, specifies no bit depth or image size, and offers no color mode. Each byte of data indicates a brightness value on a single color channel, and that's it. Photoshop offers this function specifically so you can open images created in undocumented formats, such as those created on mainframe computers.

To open an image of unknown origin on a Mac, choose File ⇨ Open and select the Show All Files check box. On a PC, just choose File ⇨ Open As. Then select the desired image from the scrolling list and choose Raw from the Format pop-up menu on a Mac or choose Raw (*.raw) from the Open As pop-up menu on a PC. After you press Return/Enter, the dialog box shown in Figure 2-23 appears, featuring these options:

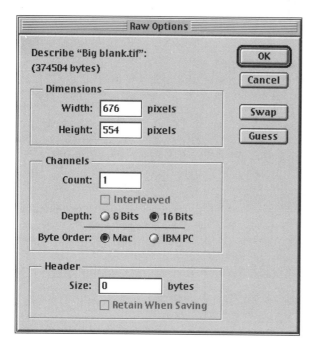

**Figure 2-23:** Photoshop requires you to specify the size of an image and the number of color channels when you open an image that does not conform to a standardized file format.

✦ **Width, Height**: If you know the dimensions of the image in pixels, enter the values in these option boxes.

✦ **Swap**: Click on this button to swap the Width value with the Height value.

✦ **Count**: Enter the number of color channels in this option box. If the document is an RGB image, enter 3; if it is a CMYK image, enter 4.

✦ **Interleaved**: Select this value if the color values are stored sequentially by pixels. In an RGB image, the first byte represents the red value for the first pixel, the second byte represents the green value for that pixel, the third the blue value, and so on. If you turn this check box off, the first byte represents the red value for the first pixel, the second value represents the red value for the second pixel, and so on. When Photoshop finishes describing the red channel, it describes the green channel and then the blue channel.

✦ **Depth**: Select the number of bits per color channel. Most images contain 8 bits per channel, but scientific scans from mainframe computers may contain 16.

✦ **Byte Order**: If you specify 16 bits per channel, you must tell Photoshop whether the image comes from a Mac or a PC.

✦ **Header**: This value tells Photoshop how many bytes of data at the beginning of the file comprise header information it can ignore.

✦ **Retain Header When Saving**: If the Header value is greater than zero, you can instruct Photoshop to retain this data when you save the image in a different format.

✦ **Guess**: If you know the Width and Height values, but you don't know the number of bytes in the header — or vice versa — you can ask Photoshop for help. Fill in either the Dimensions or Header information and then click on the Guess button to ask Photoshop to take a stab at the unknown value. Photoshop estimates all this information when the Raw Options dialog box first appears. Generally speaking, if it doesn't estimate correctly the first time around, you're on your own. But, hey, the Guess button is worth a shot.

**Tip**

If a raw document is a CMYK image, it opens as an RGB image with an extra masking channel. To display the image correctly, choose Image ➪ Mode ➪ Multichannel to free the four channels from their incorrect relationship. Then recombine them by choosing Image ➪ Mode ➪ CMYK Color.

## Saving a raw document

Photoshop also enables you to save to the raw document format. This capability is useful when you create files you want to transfer to mainframe systems or output to devices that don't support other formats, such as the Kodak XL7700.

**Caution**

Do not save 256-color indexed images to the raw format or you lose the color lookup table and, therefore, lose all color information. Be sure to convert such images first to RGB or one of the other full-color modes before saving.

When you save an image in the raw document format, Photoshop presents the dialog box shown in Figure 2-24. The dialog box options work as follows:

✦ **File Type:** This option defines information for the resource fork, so it's only pertinent to Mac folks. (On Windows, the option is always dimmed. Feel free to ignore.) Enter the four-character file type code (TIFF, PICT, and so on) in this option box. (You should check the documentation for the application you plan to use to open the raw document.) If you plan to use this file on a computer other than a Mac, you can enter any four characters you like; only Macs use this code.

✦ **File Creator:** Again, this option is only relevant on a Mac. Enter the four-character *creator code,* which tells the system software which application created the file. By default, the creator code is 8BIM, Photoshop's code. Ignore this option unless you have a specific reason for changing it — for example, to open the image in a particular Macintosh application. (You won't hurt anything by changing the code, but you will prevent Photoshop from opening the image when you double-click on the document icon at the Finder desktop.) On Windows machines, the default code 8BIM is selected for you and the option is dimmed.

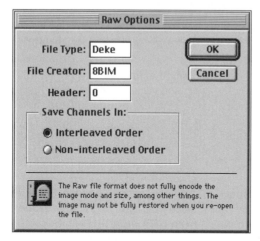

**Figure 2-24:** When saving a raw document on a Mac, enter the file type and creator codes and specify the order of data in the file.

✦ **Header**: Enter the size of the header in bytes. If you enter any value but zero, you must fill in the header using a data editor such as Norton Disk Editor.

✦ **Save Channels In**: Select the Interleaved Order option to arrange data sequentially by pixels, as described earlier. To group data by color channel, select Non-interleaved Order.

## Still can't get that file open?

File format specs are continually evolving. As a result, programs that provide support for a particular format may not support the specific version of the format used to save the file you're trying to open. For example, JPEG is notorious for causing problems because there were several private implementations in the early days. As a result, some JPEG files can only be read by the originating application.

If you can't open a file in Photoshop, you may have another program that can read and write the problem format. Try the problem file in every program you have — and every program your friends have. After all, what are friends for?

You may also want to try a program like DeBabelizer Toolbox, HiJaak, TransverterPro, or DeBabelizer Pro from Equilibrium (*www.equilibrium.com*). Absolutely the best format converter bar none, DeBabelizer handles every format Photoshop handles, as well as Dr. Halo's CUT, Fractal Design Painter's RIFF, the animation formats PICS, FLI, and ANM, as well as UNIX workstation formats for Silicon Graphics, Sun Microsystems, and others.

Still out of it? Go online and check out such forums as ADOBEAPPS on CompuServe. The Usenet newsgroups *comp.graphics.apps.photoshop* and *rec.photo.digital* are other good resources. Post a question about your problem; chances are good someone may have an answer for you.

# Resampling and Cropping

After you bring up an image — whether you created it from scratch or opened an existing image stored in one of the five billion formats discussed in the preceding pages — its size and resolution are established. Neither size nor resolution is set in stone, however. Photoshop provides two methods for changing the number of pixels in an image: resampling and cropping.

## Resizing versus resampling

Typically, when folks talk about *resizing* an image, they mean enlarging or reducing it without changing the number of pixels in the image, as demonstrated back in Figure 2-1. By contrast, *resampling* an image means scaling it so the image contains a larger or smaller number of pixels. With resizing, an inverse relationship exists between size and resolution — size increases when resolution decreases, and vice versa. But resampling affects either size or resolution independently. Figure 2-25 shows an image resized and resampled to 50 percent of its original dimensions. The resampled and original images have identical resolutions, while the resized image has twice the resolution of its companions.

## Resizing an image

To resize an image, use one of the techniques discussed in the "Changing the printing resolution" section near the beginning of this chapter. To recap briefly, the best method is to choose Image ➪ Image Size, turn off the Resample Image check box, and enter a value into the Resolution option box. See Figure 2-2 to refresh your memory.

Original

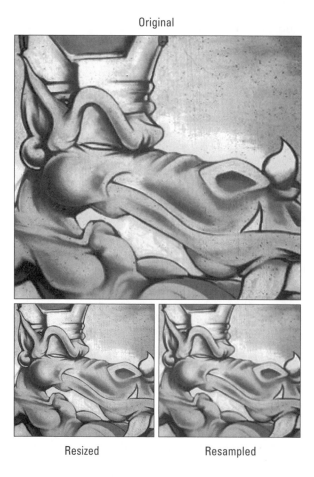

Resized                    Resampled

**Figure 2-25:** An image (top) resized (bottom left) and resampled (bottom right) down to 50 percent. The resized image sports a higher resolution; the resampled one contains fewer pixels.

## Resampling an image

You also use Image ➪ Image Size to resample an image. The difference is you leave the Resample Image check box turned on, as shown in Figure 2-26. As its name implies, the Resample Image check box is the key to resampling.

When Resample Image is selected, the Resolution value is independent of both sets of Width and Height values. (The only difference between the two sets of options is the top options work in pixels and the bottom options work in relative units of measure like percent and inches.) You can increase the number of pixels in an image by increasing any of the five values in the dialog box; you can decrease the number of pixels by decreasing any value. Photoshop stretches or shrinks the image according to the new size specifications.

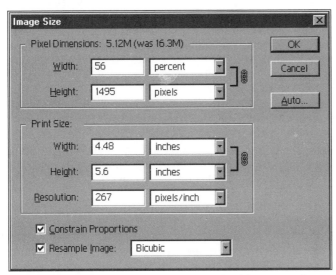

**Figure 2-26:** With the Resample Image check box turned on, you can modify the number of pixels in your image.

At all times, you can see the new number of pixels Photoshop will assign to the image, as well as the increased or decreased file size. In Figure 2-26, for example, I've changed the first Width value to 56 percent. The Pixel Dimensions value at the top of the dialog box reflects my change by reading *5.12M (was 16.3M)*, which shows that the file size has decreased.

To calculate the pixels in the resampled image, Photoshop must use its powers of interpolation, as explained in the "General preferences" section of Chapter B on CD-ROM #2. The interpolation setting defaults to the one chosen in the Preferences dialog box. But you can also change the setting right inside the Image Size dialog box. Simply select the desired method from the Resample Image pop-up menu. Bicubic results in the smoothest effects. Bilinear is faster. And Nearest Neighbor turns off interpolation so Photoshop merely throws away the pixels it doesn't need or duplicates pixels to resample up.

Here are a few more random items you should know about resampling with the Image Size dialog box:

✦ This may sound odd, but you generally want to avoid adding pixels. When you resample up, you're asking Photoshop to make up details from thin air, and the program isn't that smart. Simply put, an enlarged image almost never looks better than the original; it merely takes up more disk space and prints slower.

Resampling down, on the other hand, is a useful technique. It enables you to smooth away photo grain, halftone patterns, and other scanning artifacts. One of the most tried-and-true rules is to scan at the maximum resolution permitted by your scanner, and then resample the scan down to, say, 72 or 46 percent (with the interpolation set to Bicubic, naturally). By selecting a round value other than 50 percent, you force Photoshop to jumble the pixels into a regular, homogenous soup. You're left with fewer pixels, but these remaining pixels are better. And you have the added benefit that the image takes up less space on disk.

✦ To make an image tall and thin or short and fat, you must first turn off the Constrain Proportions check box. This enables you to edit the two Width values entirely independently of the two Height values.

You can resample an image to match precisely the size and resolution of any other open image. While the Image Size dialog box is open, choose the name of the image you want to match from the Window menu.

If you need help resampling an image to the proper size for a print job, choose Help ➪ Resize Image to bring up the Resize Image Wizard. The dialog box walks you through the process of resampling step by step. It's really for rank beginners, but you might find it helpful when you want to turn the old brain off and set Photoshop to autopilot. (Note that Adobe uses the word "resize" simply because it's friendlier than "resample." Whatever it's called, this command does indeed resample.)

If you ever get confused inside the Image Size dialog box, and you want to return to the original size and resolution settings, press the Option/Alt key to change the Cancel button to Reset. Then click the Reset button to start from the beginning.

Photoshop remembers the setting of the Resample Image check box and uses this same setting the next time you open the Image Size dialog box. This can trip you up if you record a script for the Actions palette, as discussed in Chapter E on CD-ROM #2. Suppose you create a script to resize images, turning Resample Image off. If you later resample an image—turning on Resample Image—the check box stays selected when you close the dialog box. The next time you run the script, you end up resampling instead of resizing. Always check the status of the check box before you apply the Image Size command or run any scripts containing the command.

## Cropping

Another way to change the number of pixels in an image is to crop it, which means to clip away pixels around the edges of an image without harming the remaining pixels. (The one exception occurs when you rotate a cropped image, in which case Photoshop has to interpolate pixels to account for the rotation.)

Cropping enables you to focus on an element in your image. For example, Figure 2-27 shows a bit of urban graffiti from a Digital Stock CD. I like this fellow's face — good chiaroscuro — but I can't quite figure out what's going on with this guy. I mean, what's with the screw? And is that a clown hat or what? That's the problem with graffiti — no art direction. Luckily, I can crop around the guy's head to delete all the extraneous image elements and hone in on his sleepy features, as shown in Figure 2-28.

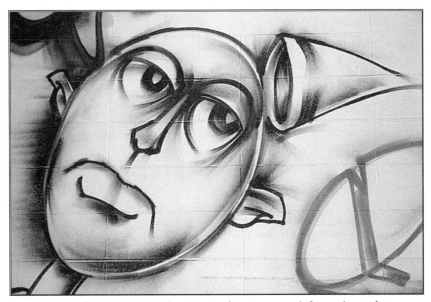

**Figure 2-27:** This image contains too much extraneous information. Where should my eye go? I'm so confused.

**Figure 2-28:** Cropping enables you to clean up the background junk and focus on the essential foreground image.

## Changing the canvas size

One way to crop an image is to choose Image ⇨ Canvas Size, which displays the Canvas Size dialog box shown in Figure 2-29. The options in this dialog box enable you to scale the imaginary canvas on which the image rests separately from the image itself.

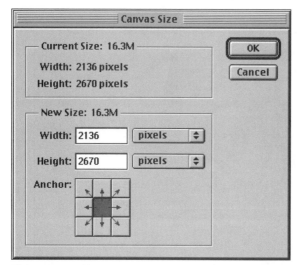

**Figure 2-29:** Choose Image ⇨ Canvas Size to crop an image or to add empty space around the perimeter of an image.

If you enlarge the canvas, Photoshop surrounds the image with a white background (assuming the background color is white). If you reduce the canvas, you crop the image.

Click inside the Anchor grid to specify the placement of the image on the new canvas. For example, if you want to add space to the bottom of an image, enlarge the canvas size and then click inside the upper-middle square. If you want to crop away the upper left corner of an image, create a smaller canvas size and then click on the lower-right square. The Anchor grid offers little arrows to show how the canvas will shrink or grow.

## Using the crop tool

Generally speaking, the Canvas Size command is most useful for enlarging the canvas or shaving a few pixels off the edge of an image. If you want to crop away a large portion of an image, using the crop tool is a better choice.

To crop the image, select the crop tool by pressing the C key. (Selecting the tool manually is quite inconvenient thanks to the long marquee-tool pop-up menu, so get used to pressing the C key.) Then drag with the crop tool to create a rectangular marquee that surrounds the portion of the image you want to retain.

As you drag, you can press the spacebar to move the crop boundary temporarily on the fly. To stop moving the boundary and return to resizing it, release the spacebar.

If you don't get the crop marquee right the first time, you can move, scale, or rotate it at will. Here's what you do:

✦ Drag inside the crop marquee to move it.

✦ Drag one of the square handles to resize the marquee. You can Shift+drag a handle to scale the marquee proportionally (the same percentage vertically and horizontally).

In Photoshop 5, you can drag a corner handle beyond the perimeter of the codument boundaries. It's just the ticket for cropping layers that exceed the image dimensions.

✦ Drag outside the crop marquee to rotate it, as shown in Figure 2-30. This may strike you as weird at first, but it works wonderfully.

✦ Drag the origin point (labeled in Figure 2-30) to change the center of a rotation.

When the marquee surrounds the exact portion of the image you want to keep, press Return/Enter or double-click inside the marquee. Photoshop clips away all pixels except those that lie inside and along the border of the crop marquee.

If you change your mind about cropping, you can cancel the crop marquee by pressing Escape.

Origin point   Crop marquee   Handles   Rotate cursor

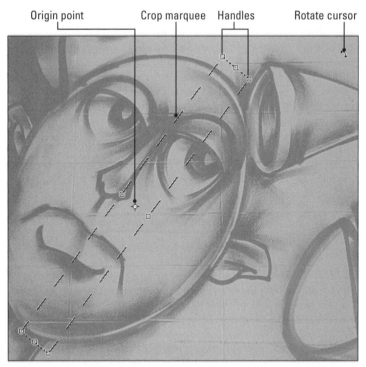

**Figure 2-30:** Align the crop marquee with an obvious axis in your image to determine the proper angle of rotation.

### Rotating the crop marquee

As I said, you can rotate an image by dragging outside the crop marquee. Straightening out a crooked image can be a little tricky, however. I wish I had a certified check for every time I thought I had the marquee rotated properly, only to find the image was still crooked after I pressed Enter. If this happens to you, choose Edit ➪ Undo (⌘/Ctrl+Z) and try again. Do not try using the crop tool a second time to rotate the already rotated image. If you do, Photoshop sets about interpolating between already interpolated pixels, resulting in more lost data. Every rotation gets farther away from the original image.

A better solution is to do it right the first time. Locate a line or general axis in your image that should be straight up and down. Rotate the crop marquee so it aligns exactly with this axis. In Figure 2-30, I rotated my crop marquee so one edge bisects the graffiti guy's egg-shaped head. Don't worry because this isn't how you want to crop the image — you're just using the line as a reference. After you arrive at the correct angle for the marquee, drag the handles to size and position the boundary properly. As long as you don't drag outside the marquee, its angle remains fixed throughout.

Yet another solution is to use the new measure tool. Just drag with the tool along the axis you want to make vertical and note the angle (A:) value in the Info palette. I don't like this technique as much because it requires you to do some unnatural math — depending on how you drag, you may have to subtract 90 degrees from the A: value or subtract the A: value from 90 degrees. Then you keep an eye on the Info palette and rotate until you get an A: value that matches the answer to the previous equation. If you like math, great. If not, it's much simpler to use the technique I suggested in the previous paragraph.

## Cropping an image to match another

There are two ways to crop an image so it matches the size and resolution of another:

&#10070; Bring the image you want to crop forward and choose Image ➪ Canvas Size. Then, while inside the Canvas Size dialog box, select the name of the image you want to match from the Window menu.

**Tip**

This method doesn't give you much control when cropping an image, but it's a great way to enlarge the canvas and add empty space around an image.

&#10070; Better yet, use the crop tool. First, bring the image you want to match to the front. Then select the crop tool and press Return/Enter to display the Crop Options palette, pictured in Figure 2-31. Select the Fixed Target Size check box and click the Front Image button. Photoshop loads the size and resolution values into the palette's option boxes.

Now bring the image you want to crop to the front and drag with the crop tool as normal. Photoshop constrains the crop marquee to the proportions of the targeted image. After you press Return/Enter, Photoshop crops, resamples, and rotates the image as necessary.

## Cropping a selection

Another way to crop an image is to create a rectangular selection and then choose Image ➪ Crop. One advantage of this technique is you needn't switch back and forth between the marquee and crop tools. One tool is all you need to select and crop. (If you're as lazy as I am, the mere act of selecting a tool can prove more effort than it's worth.) And, as with the crop tool, you can now press the spacebar while you draw a marquee to move it on the fly. It's no trick to get the placement and size exactly right — the only thing you can't do is rotate.

Another advantage of the Crop command is flexibility. You can draw a selection, switch windows, apply commands, and generally use any function you like prior to choosing Image ➪ Crop. The crop tool, by contrast, is much more limiting. After drawing a cropping marquee, you can't do anything but adjust the marquee until you press Return/Enter to accept the crop or Escape to dismiss it.

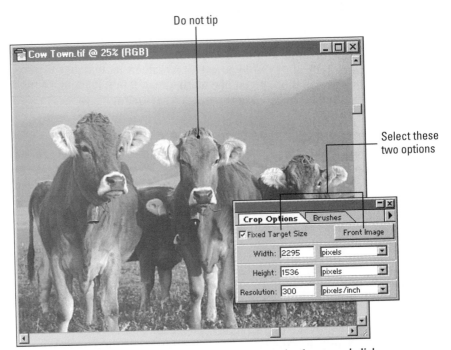

**Figure 2-31:** Bring the image you want to target to the front, and click each of the two options at the top of the Cropping Tool Options palette.

And finally, Image ➪ Crop lets you crop the canvas to the boundaries of an image pasted from the Clipboard or dragged and dropped from another image window. As long as the boundaries of the pasted image are rectangular, as in the case of an image copied from a different application, you can choose Edit ➪ Paste, ⌘/Ctrl+ click the new layer in the Layers palette to regain the selection outline, and then choose Image ➪ Crop. Photoshop replaces the former image and crops the window to fit the new image.

✦          ✦          ✦

# Basic Color Management

**N**ow that we've waded through the fundamentals of working with images, it's time to don scuba gear and immerse ourselves in the world of color under Photoshop 5. We'll immediately dive to 20 feet and take an elementary test run through Photoshop's color-space conversion capabilities. At 50 feet down, we'll stop and examine a school of exotic Profile Setup options. Then we'll risk nitrogen narcosis and drop to 100 feet where we'll find the Channels palette, the entryway to Photoshop's vital and mesmerizing color caverns.

I use this diving metaphor not merely to invoke a sense of wonder, but because, to most artists, color management is every bit as mysterious as the contours of the ocean floor. It's no exaggeration to say that color management is perhaps the least understood topic in all of computer imaging. From my experience with talking to Photoshop users, most folks expect to calibrate their monitors to achieve reliable if not perfect color, but in point of fact, there's no such thing. So called *device-dependent color*—that is, synthetic color produced by a piece of hardware—is a moving target. Photoshop's role is to convert from one target to the next.

For what it's worth, most consumer monitors (and video boards, for that matter) are beyond calibration, in the strict sense of the word. You can try your hand at using a hardware calibrator—one of those devices where you plop a little suction cup onto your screen, such as the cross-platform OptiCal from The Color Partnership (*www.colorpar.com*). But calibrators often have less to do with changing screen colors than identifying them, a process known as characterization.

Even if your monitor permits prepress-quality calibration—as in the case of the $4,000 PressView 21SR from Radius (*www.radius.com*)—it's not enough to simply correct the colors on screen, you also have to tell Photoshop what you've done.

Therefore, color management is first and foremost about identifying your monitor. You have to explain your screen's foibles to Photoshop so that it can make every attempt to account for them. In the old days, Photoshop used the screen data to calculate CMYK conversions and that was it. But with Version 5, Photoshop goes two steps farther, embedding *International Color Consortium* (ICC) *profiles* that identify the source of the image and using this information to translate colors from one monitor to another. The new Color Settings commands are both wonderful and bewildering. They can just as easily mess up colors as fix them. But if you read this chapter, you and your colors should be able to ride the currents safely from one digital destination to the next.

# The Color Settings Commands

In Photoshop 5, the File ⇨ Color Settings pop-up menu includes the following four commands:

- ✦ RGB Setup: Your RGB environment is what you see on screen. This command lets you confirm that you've correctly identified your monitor. But its primary purpose is to specify the RGB space that you want Photoshop to simulate.

- ✦ CMYK Setup: In Version 4 and earlier, Photoshop provided three commands for setting up your final CMYK output device. Now there's just one. I touch very lightly on this command in this chapter, but because it applies only to CMYK printing, I save most of the information for Chapter 4.

- ✦ Grayscale Setup: This command defines how Photoshop displays a grayscale image. You can see either an untreated RGB version of your image, or preview it the way it will print complete with dot gain (as defined by the Dot Gain value in the CMYK Setup dialog box).

- ✦ Profile Setup: This is the command that makes it all happen. Here you specify whether you want to save source profiles with an image and how to handle color conversions when you open images created on other computers. If there is one hinge pin in Photoshop's color matching functions, Profile Setup is it (which is why it gets its own section later in this chapter).

Like the Preferences commands, you only need to visit the Color Settings commands once and then forget about them. Photoshop even has the courtesy to save your settings in an independent file called Color Settings (or Color Settings.psp on a PC) in the Adobe Photoshop Settings folder.

After getting everything set up the way you like, it's a good idea to copy the Color Settings (or Color Settings.psp) file to a safe backup location. This way, if the settings file ever becomes corrupt, you can reinstate your careful color choices as easily as copying the backed up file.

# A Typical Color-Matching Scenario

The easiest way to understand the Color Settings commands is to see them in action. In this basic scenario, I'll take an RGB image I've created on my Mac and open it up on my PC. The Mac is equipped with a top-of-the-line PressView 21SR and the PC is hooked up to a generic Sony Trinitron screen, so I've got both extremes pretty well covered. Yet despite the change of platforms and the even more dramatic change in monitors, Photoshop maintains a high degree of consistency so the image looks the same on both sides of the divide. While the specifics of setting up your system will obviously vary, this walk-through should give you an idea of how the strange and intricate Color Settings commands work.

If you've installed the Photoshop 5.0.2 update, you might recall that a Color Management wizard appeared on screen the first time you launched Photoshop. (Don't worry if you just pressed Cancel and moved on. I'll discuss how to get back to it later in this chapter.) This wizard walks you through many of the settings covered in the following sections. Read on to learn how the Color Settings commands work. Then see "The Color Management wizard in Photoshop 5.0.2" section later in this chapter for details on using the wizard.

## Setting up the source monitor

If you own a monitor with calibration capabilities, I recommend that you start off by calibrating it. In the case of the PressView, I launch a utility called ProSense that works with the hardware calibrator to both adjust screen colors and save screen profiles in a variety of formats. For purposes of Photoshop for the Mac, the most important format is ColorSync, which is Apple's system-wide color management extension. I also save a Photoshop Monitor File version of the profile, as shown in Figure 3-1.

The next step is to open the profile in ColorSync. I choose Apple ➪ Control Panels ➪ ColorSync System Profile. Then I click on the Set Profile button to display the scrolling list of options shown in Figure 3-2. At the end of the list is the item PressView 21sr, which turns out to be the profile I just created with the ProSense utility. I select it and move on.

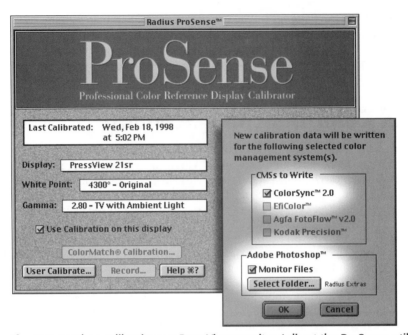

**Figure 3-1:** When calibrating my PressView monitor, I direct the ProSense utility to save a ColorSync and Photoshop Monitor File version of the screen profile.

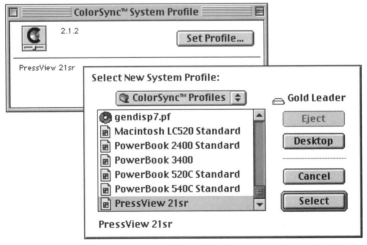

**Figure 3-2:** On the Mac, you use the ColorSync control panel to load monitor profiles that will automatically work with Photoshop.

## The Gamma wizard

"Swell," I can hear you say, "But what do those of us with more down-to-earth monitors do?" For everyday people, Photoshop 5.0 ships with a nicely improved version of the Gamma control panel. Inside the folder that contains Photoshop, open the Goodies folder and then the Calibration folder on your Mac, or the Calibrat folder on your PC. Inside is a utility called Adobe Gamma (or Adobe Gamma.cpl on a PC). If you're using a PC, you need to move the utility to your startup drive in order for it to perform properly. Under Windows 95, move the file to the System folder inside the Windows directory. Under Windows NT, move Adobe Gamma.cpl to the System32 folder inside the WinNT directory.

On a Mac, double-click on the Adobe Gamma icon to bring up the introductory screen shown in Figure 3-3. Select the Step by Step option to walk through the setup process one step at a time. On a PC, bring up the Control Panel window (Start ➪ Settings ➪ Control Panel) and double-click on the Adobe Gamma icon to display the screen shown in Figure 3-4. If the control panel displays a warning that your video card doesn't support system-wide color management, don't sweat it. Most video cards don't.

If you're using Photoshop 5.0.2, accessing the Adobe Gamma utility is much easier. See "The Color Management wizard in Photoshop 5.0.2" section later in this chapter for more details.

Then all you have to do is answer questions and click on the Next button to advance from one screen to another. Occasionally, you'll be asked to make some tricky choices. (The white point defines the general color cast of your screen, from 5000 degrees for slightly red to 9300 degrees for slightly blue; 6500 degrees is a happy "daylight" medium.) But most of the questions are pretty cut and dry. If you aren't sure about an answer to a setting—such as Phosphors (or Phosphor Type on a PC)—consult your monitor's documentation or call the vendor. (If the screen bows out slightly horizontally but is absolutely flat vertically, the answer is Trinitron.)

When you click on the Finish button, the Gamma utility generates a custom monitor profile and automatically alerts Photoshop to the change, even if the program is already running. You don't even have to bring up the ColorSync control panel on your Mac (though you may want to just to confirm). Your screen may not look any different than it did before you opened Gamma, but you can rest assured that Photoshop is now officially aware of your monitor's capabilities and limitations.

Just so you know, Gamma places the monitor profile in the ColorSync Profiles folder inside the Preference folder in the System Folder on your Mac or in the Color folder in Windows\System or WinNT\System32, depending on your operating system, on your PC.

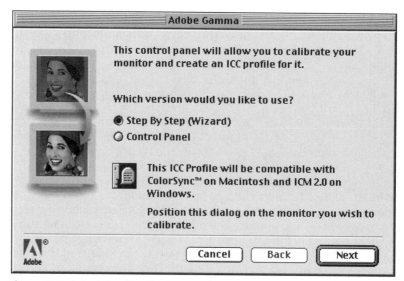

**Figure 3-3:** Select the Step By Step option to advance one step at a time through the monitor setup process.

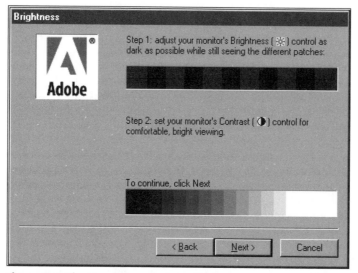

**Figure 3-4:** The Gamma control panel asks you to answer questions and even make occasional adjustments to the brightness and contrast of your monitor.

**Note**

Incidentally, the term *gamma* refers to the amount of correction required to convert the color signal generated inside the monitor (let's call it x) to the color display that you see on screen (y). Imagine a simple graph with the input signal x along the bottom and the output y along the side. A gamma of 1.0 would result in a diagonal line from bottom left to upper right corner. A higher gamma value tugs at the center of that line and curves it upward. As you tug, more and more of the curve is taken up by darker values, resulting in a darker display. So a typical Mac screen with default gamma of 1.8 is lighter than a typical PC screen with a default gamma of 2.2. (For a real-time display of gamma in action, check out the discussion of the Curve dialog box included in Chapter 30.)

## Inventing your ideal RGB environment

Now that I've identified my monitor, I need to explain my ideal RGB environment to Photoshop. This is the strangest step and it requires a little bit of imagination to fully understand.

I start by choosing File ⇨ Color Settings ⇨ RGB Setup inside Photoshop on my Mac. Photoshop displays the dialog box shown in Figure 3-5. Notice that the Monitor item is automatically set to PressView 21sr, thanks to the fact that I chose this profile with ColorSync. (If you used Adobe Gamma, your profile will appear here as well.) This shows that my monitor is recognized and accounted for.

But I still have to specify the larger RGB environment using the RGB pop-up menu. There are two purposes to this option:

✦ First, it allows you to preview how an RGB image will look on another screen when no color correction is applied. For example, to see how an image you created on a PC will look on a typical Mac screen, you could select Apple RGB. This is a fantastic feature for Web designers, as I explain more in Chapter 32.

✦ Second and more important, this is Adobe's attempt to create the perfect RGB environment, one that doesn't depend on a specific piece of hardware. As I said, some imagination is in order.

My recommendation here is to select the SMPTE-240M option from the RGB pop-up menu and be done with it. SMPTE-240M includes a wide range of theoretical RGB colors, whether they can truly be displayed on a monitor or not. You may see some *clipping* on screen — that is, two distinct colors in the SMPTE-240M space may appear as one on your screen — but Photoshop has greater latitude when interpolating and calculating colors.

The RGB Setup dialog box includes two check boxes. Preview just permits you to see the results of your changes on screen. But Display Using Monitor Compensation creates a monitor-to-ideal RGB conversion on the fly. In my case, Photoshop converts all colors from the PressView 21sr gamut to the unfettered SMPTE-240M. The result is that my colors brighten up considerably.

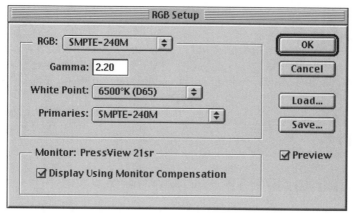

**Figure 3-5:** The SMPTE-240M option provides access to a large theoretical RGB spectrum.

## Embedding the profiles

The final step on the Mac side is to embed my profiles into a test image. (The word *embed* simply means that Photoshop adds a little bit of code to the beginning of the file stating where it was last edited.) For this, I choose File ➪ Color Settings ➪ Profile Setup, which displays the big dialog box in Figure 3-6. By default, all of the check boxes across the top of the dialog box are selected. This means Photoshop will embed profiles for the four main color spaces into the image. The RGB check box tells Photoshop to embed my ideal RGB setting — SMPTE-240M — into the test image. I click on the OK button to confirm that this is indeed what I want.

Next, I save my test image using the standard Save command. Thanks to my settings in the Profile Setup dialog box, Photoshop automatically saves my RGB environment along with the image.

Tip

If you had already saved the image before changing the RGB settings, the Save command will appear dimmed. Photoshop does not recognize RGB Setup as a significant modification to the image. You can either choose File ➪ Save As and write over the last saved version of the image, or make a minor adjustment — click on a pixel with the pencil tool — and then choose File ➪ Save.

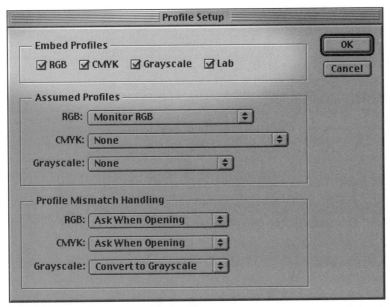

**Figure 3-6:** Select the check boxes across the top of this dialog box to append profiles into all saved images.

## Setting up the destination monitor

After saving the test image with RGB profile embedded, I network the image from my Mac over to my PC (via Miramar's PC MacLAN). No translation occurs here; this is a simple file copy from one computer to another.

Now before I can open this image and have it display properly on my PC, I have to set up my RGB colors. I start by setting up my monitor. This time, I'm using a no-frills Sony Multiscan monitor, so I have to perform the calibration using the Adobe Gamma control panel, as discussed previously in the "The Gamma wizard" section.

After I finish with Adobe Gamma, I go into Photoshop and choose File ➪ Color Settings ➪ RGB Setup, just as I did on the Mac. Behold, Photoshop has automatically instated my Gamma settings, as I can see by the message "Monitor: Sony Multiscan.icm" (see Figure 3-7).

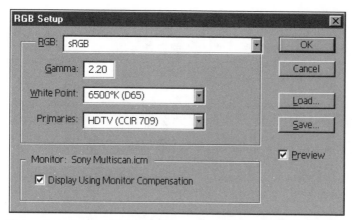

**Figure 3-7:** On the Windows side, I select sRGB as my ideal RGB environment to force Photoshop to make a conversion. (Nevertheless, I recommend you select SMPTE-240M, just as I did on the Mac.)

Now if I were really trying to calibrate my systems to match up, I would select SMPTE-240M from the RGB pop-up menu, just as I did on the Mac. But for purposes of this demonstration, I want to force Photoshop to perform a conversion, and a good conversion requires a little dissension. So this time around, I select sRGB — short for *standard RGB*, the universal monitor space presently touted by Microsoft, Pantone, Hewlett-Packard, and a host of others. This just so happens to be Photoshop's default setting, the reason being that many users will never visit this dialog box and, for better or worse, sRGB is fast becoming a cross-platform standard. (For the reasons I mentioned earlier, I and most inside Adobe believe SMPTE-240M is the better solution for savvy users who dare to change their defaults.)

## Converting the color space

The Profile Setup command determines not only how Photoshop embeds profiles but also how it reads embedded profiles. So I choose File ➪ Color Settings ➪ Profile Setup to display the dialog box shown in Figure 3-8, this time concentrating on the lower options. The three Profile Mismatch Handling pop-up menus determine how Photoshop reacts when it tries to open an image whose embedded profiles don't match the active color settings. By default, the RGB pop-up menu is set to Convert to RGB, which converts the colors in the image from the embedded RGB space to the current RGB space. But I'm not a big fan of having my images change automatically without warning or consent, so I set the RGB pop-up menu to Ask When Opening, as in Figure 3-8.

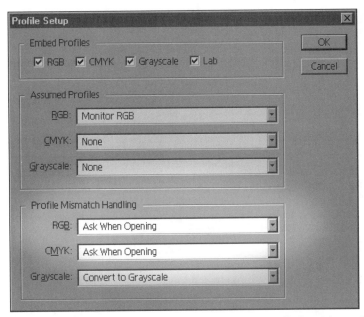

**Figure 3-8:** The Profile Mismatch Handling options tell Photoshop what to do when it opens an image created on a different computer.

Now I'm ready to open the test image. I choose File ⇨ Open just as I normally would. As Photoshop for Windows opens the test image, it detects that the embedded SMPTE-240M profile doesn't match the active sRGB profile. Justly troubled by this development, Photoshop displays the alert box shown in Figure 3-9. You have several conversion options — you can even choose to have an external color management system such as Kodak's ICC CMS step in and perform the conversion — but there are really just two choices that matter — Convert or Don't Convert. The Convert button converts the colors in the image from the SMPTE-240M space to the sRGB space. The Don't Convert button opens the image as is, without making any changes.

Obviously, I choose Convert. Photoshop spends a few seconds mulling it over and then displays the converted image on screen. The result is an almost perfect match. Granted the blues demonstrate a slight propensity toward green, as illustrated in Color Plate 3-1. And while I imagine I could address this by finessing the profile for my Sony Multiscan slightly on my PC, the match is frankly amazing, much better than the sort of results you could achieve with Photoshop 4.

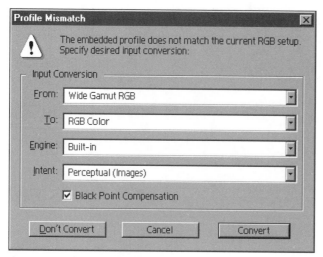

**Figure 3-9:** The alert box gives you the option of converting the colors from the foreign image or opening the image as is.

# Color Conversion Central

As I mentioned near the outset of this chapter, the Profile Setup command is the feature that puts Photoshop's color conversion functions in play. RGB Setup, CMYK Setup, and Grayscale Setup define the parameters, but File ➪ Color Settings ➪ Profile Setup makes the color conversions happen.

Now that you've seen Profile Setup in action, I'd like to take a few moments and run through the specific features according to the way they're grouped inside the Profile Setup dialog box.

## Embed profiles

When you save an image using the Save or Save As commands, Photoshop 5 saves color profiles with the image according to the Embed Profiles settings in the Profile Setup dialog box:

✦ **RGB** embeds the device-independent RGB profile (for example, SMPTE-240M) defined in the RGB Setup dialog box. This is very important — it does not embed the monitor profile. The conversion from monitor space to RGB space is handled internally by RGB Setup without Profile Setup's help. So if we all agree on SMPTE-240M, no color conversions will ever be necessary and all our images will display consistently on any machine in this best of all possible worlds. Amen.

One exception to this rule: Images saved in Photoshop 4 and earlier use the monitor setup as the profile because this is how Adobe used to deal with color spaces in the days before the RBG Setup command.

✦ **CMYK** embeds the profile defined in the CMYK Setup dialog box (which I discuss at length in the next chapter).

✦ **Grayscale** embeds the active Grayscale Setup setting. If RGB is the active setting in the Grayscale Setup dialog box (as by default), Photoshop also embeds the Gamma setting from the RGB Setup dialog box (2.2 in the case of SMPTE-240M). If you set the Grayscale Setup option to Black Ink, Photoshop jettisons Gamma and instead embeds the Dot Gain setting from the CMYK Setup dialog box.

✦ **Lab** appends Photoshop's CIE Lab profile to the image. There's no way to change this; it's simply a way for Photoshop to identify its native device-independent color space to the image.

Notice that you don't see Indexed Color on that list. So if you save an image as a GIF file—which is always indexed—Photoshop doesn't include any profile. The same goes for duotones and black-and-white bitmaps.

Thanks to a Macintosh file's resource fork, on a Mac Photoshop can save profiles with any file format. (Actually, this goes for GIF as well—Photoshop *can* save a profile with GIF, it simply chooses not to.) If you swap files with Windows machines, the resource fork dries up. This leaves just five color-savvy file formats—native Photoshop, EPS, PDF, JPEG, and TIFF. The others don't permit extra data to be saved with the image.

**Tip**

For typical prepress work, there's really no reason not to embed profiles. They add very little to the size of a file. However, if you're creating a JPEG image for the Web, you might want to dump the profiles to keep the file size at its lowest. No need to visit Profile Setup and turn off all the Embed Profiles check boxes just for one file. Instead, choose File ➭ Save a Copy (⌘/Ctrl+Option/Alt+S) and select the Exclude Non-Image Data check box.

But don't assume that you should always bail on color profiles for Web images. There's a big push right now to build profile support into browsers so that image colors will automatically adapt to a viewer's screen. (Pantone already distributes Netscape Navigator plug-ins that read and interpret profiles for JPEG and TIFF images.) While this technology is still in its infancy, it's very probable that it will find mainstream acceptance in the near future.

**Note**

When you elect not to embed a profile, Photoshop adds a little marker that tells the program the file was saved explicitly without a profile. When you open that file in the future, Photoshop will skip the conversion profile process, regardless of any other settings selected inside the Profile Setup dialog box.

## Assumed profiles

Given that this is the first version of Photoshop to embed profiles, you can imagine that most other applications don't either. So most of the files you open will be utterly profile-less. Photoshop has to invent a family tree for these motherless images. You specify this ancestry using the Assumed Profiles pop-up menus.

By default, the RGB option is set to Monitor RGB and the CMYK and Grayscale options are set to None. To maintain consistent colors from no-profile images — particularly from images created in previous versions of Photoshop — it's essential that Monitor RGB be active. Photoshop then makes a conversion from the monitor space to the device-independent RGB space, thus preventing the sort of wild color shifts that might happen without conversion. For example, if the RGB space is set to SMPTE-240M, the color saturation will go through the roof without proper conversion.

Having CMYK and Grayscale set to None ensures that no conversion occurs. Again, these are very sound defaults. CMYK images are typically designed for specific printing environments and unthinkingly converting them to another space could ruin them. (That said, if you know for a fact that you want to take a CMYK image designed for a Tektronix Phaser 220i and instead print it from a SWOP proofing device, conversion can be a very good thing. It's the difference between making a deliberate choice and having the choice made for you.) Grayscale images are likewise designed to be printed, so arbitrary conversion can be hazardous.

## Profile mismatch handling

The final set of pop-up menus control how Photoshop reacts when an image contains a profile (or an assumed profile) that doesn't match the parameters established by the RGB, CMYK, and Grayscale Setup commands. Personally, I set every one of them to Ask When Opening. I am not a fan of having color conversions occur without my permission — as they do by default — even when the converter is a trusted application like Photoshop. So long as Ask When Opening is active, an alert box appears and asks your permission to perform the conversion. You are always made aware of current events.

Ask When Opening also gives you the opportunity to try out different color scenarios. If you accept a color conversion and it ends up looking unusually garish, you can simply close the image and open it up again using different conversion settings or no conversion at all.

One case where I almost invariably decline conversion is when processing screen shots. Photoshop offers to convert every screen shot that I swap between my Mac and my PC, but because screen elements are designed for any monitor, they work best when I turn conversion off. I also advise that you refrain from converting CMYK and grayscale images unless you have a specific purpose in mind.

# The Color Management wizard in Photoshop 5.0.2

As I mentioned earlier, the Photoshop 5.0.2 update includes a Color Management wizard that walks you through the process of setting up your monitor and configuring color settings. The wizard appears automatically the first time you launch Photoshop 5.0.2 or you can choose Help ➪ Color Management to display the introductory screen shown in Figure 3-10. First, you need to create a profile for your monitor. The process is nearly identical to the one I discussed earlier in "The Gamma wizard" section. Click on the Open Adobe Gamma button and select the Step by Step option from the resulting screen. Then simply follow the directions and click on the Next button to advance through the screens. When you click on the Finish button, Photoshop saves your new monitor profile and returns to the initial Color Management wizard screen.

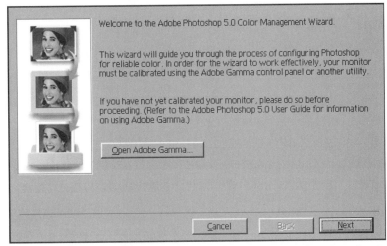

**Figure 3-10:** The Color Management wizard in Photoshop 5.0.2 makes it easy to set up your monitor and color settings.

The next step is to specify color settings. Click on the Next button to display the screen shown in Figure 3-11. This screen allows you to choose one of Photoshop's preset color configurations. Generally, you should ignore the first four options, although you may want to select Optimize for Web Use if you're preparing images exclusively for use on the Web. I recommend that you select Customize for Prepress and Other Uses and click on the Next button.

Click on the Next button again to display the screen shown in Figure 3-12. This is where you choose your RGB environment. Earlier in this chapter, I recommended selecting the SMPTE-240M RGB setting, but this option isn't available in the pop-up menu on this screen. That's because in Version 5.0.2 Adobe has given SMPTE-240M a friendlier name: Adobe RGB. Select Adobe RGB (1998) from the pop-up menu and click on the Next button. The screen that appears offers options that determine what Photoshop does when it tries to open an image whose embedded profiles don't match the active color settings. By default, the Ask Me What to Do With Mismatched Files option is selected. As I just explained in the "Profile mismatch handling" section, this is the best option, so click on the Next button to move on. The next screen lets you tell Photoshop what to do when opening an image with no profile embedded. By default, the Never Convert Untagged Files option is selected. Again, this is the best option, so click on the Next button to accept this setting. Finally, click on the Finish button to put your new RGB color settings into effect.

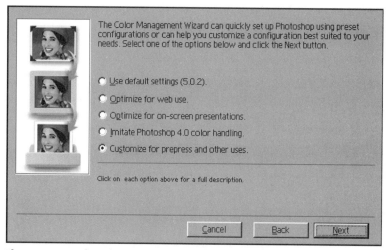

**Figure 3-11:** Select the Customize for Prepress and Other Uses option to walk through configuring Photoshop's color settings.

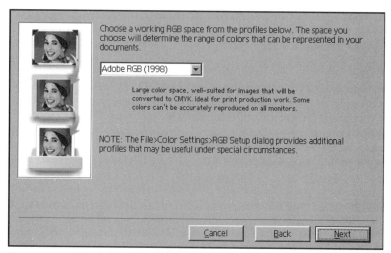

**Figure 3-12:** The SMPTE-240M RGB space is renamed Adobe RGB in Photoshop 5.0.2.

# Introducing Color Channels

After a chapter and a half of me droning on about color in Photoshop, it might surprise you when I say that Photoshop is at its heart a grayscale editor. Oh sure, it offers an array of color conversion features and it displays and prints spectacular full-color images. But when it comes to editing the image, everything happens in grayscale.

This is because Photoshop approaches every full-color image not as a single collection of 24-bit pixels, but as three or four bands of 8-bit (grayscale) pixels. An RGB file contains a band of red, a band of green, and a band of blue, each of which functions as a separate grayscale image. A Lab image likewise contains three bands, one corresponding to luminosity and the others to the variables *a* and *b*. A CMYK file contains four bands, one for each of the process-color inks. These bands are known as *channels*.

Channels frequently correspond to the structure of an input or output device. Each channel in a CMYK image, for example, corresponds to a different printer's plate when the document goes to press. The cyan plate is inked with cyan, the magenta plate is inked with magenta, and so on. Each channel in an RGB image corresponds to a pass of the red, green, or blue scanner sensor over the original photograph or artwork. Only the Lab mode is device independent, so its channels don't correspond to any piece of hardware.

## Why you should care

But so what, right? Who cares how many planes of color an image comprises? You want to edit the photograph, not dissect it. "Dammit, Jim, I'm an artist, not a doctor!" Well, even if you don't like to rebuild car engines or poke preserved frog entrails with sharp knives, you'll get a charge out of editing channels. The fact is, channels provide you with yet another degree of selective control over an image.

Consider this example: Your client scanned a photograph of his gap-toothed daughter that he wants you to integrate into some goofy ad campaign for his car dealership. Unfortunately, the scan is downright rotten. You don't want to offend the guy, so you praise him on his fine offspring and say something to the effect of, "No problem, boss." But after you take it back to your office and load it into Photoshop, you break out in a cold sweat. You try swabbing at it with the edit tools, applying a few filters, and even attempting some scary-looking color correction commands, but the image continues to look like the inside of a garbage disposal. (Not that I've ever seen the inside of a garbage disposal, but it can't be attractive.)

Suddenly, it occurs to you to look at the channels. What the heck, it can't hurt. With very little effort, you discover that the red and green channels look okay, but the blue channel looks like it's melting. Her mouth is sort of mixed in with her teeth, her eyes look like an experiment in expressionism, and her hair has taken on a slightly geometric appearance. (If you think that this is a big exaggeration, take a look at a few blue channels from a low-end scanner or digital camera. They're frequently rife with tattered edges, random blocks of color, stray pixels, and other so-called *digital artifacts*.)

The point is, you've located the cancer. You don't have to waste your time trying to perform surgery on the entire image; in fact, doing so may very well harm the channels that are in good shape. You merely have to fix this one channel. A wave of the Gaussian Blur filter here, an application of the Levels command there, and some selective rebuilding of missing detail borrowed from the other channels — all of which I'll get to in future sections and chapters — result in an image that resembles a living, breathing human being. Granted, she still needs braces, but you're an artist, not an orthodontist.

## How channels work

Photoshop devotes 8 bits of data to each pixel in each channel, thus permitting 256 brightness values, from 0 (black) to 255 (white). Therefore, each channel is actually an independent grayscale image. At first, you may be thrown off by this. If an RGB image is made up of red, green, and blue channels, why do all the channels look gray?

Photoshop provides an option in the Display & Cursors panel of the Preferences dialog box (⌘/Ctrl+K, ⌘/Ctrl+3) called Color Channels in Color. When selected, this function displays each channel in its corresponding primary color. But Option/Although this feature can be reassuring — particularly to novices — it's equally counterproductive.

When you view an 8-bit image composed exclusively of shades of red, for example, it's easy to miss subtle variations in detail that may appear obvious when you print the image. You may have problems accurately gauging the impact of filters and tonal adjustments. I mean, face it, red isn't a friendly shade to stare at for a half hour of intense editing. So leave the Color Channels in Color option off and temporarily suspend your biological urge for on-screen color. With a little experience, you'll be able to better monitor your adjustments and predict the outcome of your edits in plain old grayscale.

Images that include 256 or fewer colors can be expressed in a single channel and therefore do not include multiple channels that you can edit independently. A grayscale image, for example, is just one channel. A black-and-white bitmap permits only one bit of data per pixel, so a single channel is more than enough to express it.

**Cross-Reference**

You can add channels above and beyond those required to represent a color or grayscale image for the purpose of storing masks, as described in Chapter 16. But even then, each channel is typically limited to 8 bits of data per pixel — meaning that it's just another grayscale image. Mask channels do not affect the appearance of the image on-screen or when it is printed. Rather, they serve to save selection outlines, as Chapter 16 explains.

# How to switch and view channels

To access channels in Photoshop, display the Channels palette by choosing Window ⇨ Show Channels. Every channel in the image appears in the palette — including any mask channels — as shown in Figure 3-13. Photoshop even shows little thumbnail views of each channel so that you can see what it looks like.

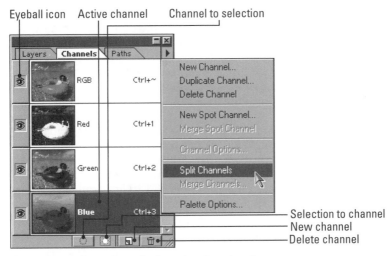

**Figure 3-13:** Photoshop displays tiny thumbnails of each color channel in the Channels palette.

To switch to a different channel, click on a channel name in the Channels palette. The channel name becomes gray — like the Blue channel in Figure 3-13 — showing that you can now edit it independently of other channels in the image.

To edit more than one channel at a time, click on one channel name and then Shift+click on another. You can also Shift+click on an active channel to deactivate it independently of any others.

When you select a single channel, Photoshop displays just that one channel on screen. However, you can view additional channels beyond those that you want to edit. To specify which channels appear and which remain invisible, click in the far left column of the Channels palette. Click on an eyeball icon to make it disappear and hence hide that channel. Click where there is no eyeball to create one and thus display the channel.

When only one channel is visible, that channel appears as a grayscale picture in the image window (possibly colorized in accordance with the Color Channels in Color check box in the Preferences dialog box). However, when more than one channel is visible, you always see color. If both the blue and green channels are visible, for example, the image appears blue-green. If the red and green channels are visible, the image has a yellow cast, and so on.

In addition to the individual channels, Photoshop provides access to a composite view that displays all colors in an RGB, CMYK, or Lab image at once. (The composite view does not show mask channels; you have to specify their display separately.) The composite view is listed first in the Channel palette and is displayed by default. Notice that when you select the composite view, all the names of the individual color channels in the Channels palette turn gray along with the composite channel. This shows that all the channels are active. The composite view is the one in which you will perform the majority of your image editing.

Press ⌘/Ctrl plus a number key to switch between color channels. Depending on the color mode you're working in, ⌘/Ctrl+1 takes you to the red (RGB), cyan (CMYK), or luminosity (Lab) channel; ⌘/Ctrl+2 takes you to the green, magenta, or *a* channel; and ⌘/Ctrl+3 takes you to the blue, yellow, or *b* channel. In the CMYK mode, ⌘/Ctrl+4 displays the black channel. Other ⌘/Ctrl-key equivalents — up to ⌘/Ctrl+9 — take you to mask or spot-color channels (if there are any). To go to the composite view, press ⌘/Ctrl+tilde (~). Tilde is typically the key to the left of 1, or on some keyboards, to the right of the spacebar.

**Tip**

When editing a single channel, you may find it helpful to monitor the results in both grayscale and full-color views. Choose View ⇨ New View to create a new window for the image, automatically set to the color composite view. Then return to the first window and edit away on the individual channel. One of the amazing benefits to creating multiple views in Photoshop is that the views may show entirely different channels, layers, and other image elements.

The shortcuts are slightly different when you're working on a grayscale image. You access the image itself by pressing ⌘/Ctrl+1. ⌘/Ctrl+2 and higher take you to extra spot-color and mask channels.

# Trying Channels on for Size

Feeling a little mystified? Need some examples? Fair enough. Color Plate 3-2 shows a woman in a bright yellow swim suit on a bright red floatation device set against a bright green ocean beneath a bright blue sky. These colors — yellow, red, green, and blue — cover the four corners of the color spectrum. Therefore, you can expect to see a lot of variation between the images in the independent color channels.

## RGB channels

Suppose that the sunbathing woman is an RGB image. Figure 3-14 compares a grayscale composite of this same image (created by choosing Image ⇨ Mode ⇨

Grayscale) compared with the contents of the red, green, and blue color channels from the original color image. The green channel is quite similar to the grayscale composite because green is an ingredient in all colors in the image, except for the red of the raft. The red and blue channels differ more significantly. The pixels in the red channel are lightest in the swimsuit and raft because they contain the highest concentrations of red. The pixels in the blue channel are lightest in the sky and water because — you guessed it — the sky and water are rich with blue.

Notice how the channels in Figure 3-14 make interesting grayscale images in and of themselves? The red channel, for example, looks like the sky darkening above our bather, even though the sun is blazing down.

When converting a color image to grayscale, you have the option of calculating a grayscale composite or simply retaining the image exactly as it appears in one of the channels. To create a grayscale composite, choose Image ➪ Mode ➪ Grayscale when viewing all colors in the image in the composite view, as usual. To retain a single channel only, switch to that channel and then choose Image ➪ Mode ➪ Grayscale. Instead of the usual *Discard color information?* message, Photoshop displays the message *Discard other channels?* If you click on the OK button, Photoshop chucks the other channels into the electronic abyss.

Grayscale composite        Red

Green        Blue

**Figure 3-14:** A grayscale composite of the image from Color Plate 3-2 followed by the contents of the red, green, and blue color channels.

## CMYK channels

In the name of fair and unbiased coverage, Figures 3-15 and 3-16 show the channels from the image after it was converted to other color modes. In Figure 3-15, I converted the image to the CMYK mode and examined its channels. Here, the predominant colors are cyan (sky and water) and yellow (in the swimsuit and raft). Because this color mode relies on pigments rather than light, dark areas in the channels represent high color intensity. For that reason, the sky in the cyan channel is dark, whereas it's light in the blue channel back in Figure 3-14.

Notice how similar the cyan channel in Figure 3-15 to its red counterpart in Figure 3-14. Same with the magenta and green channels, and the yellow and blue channels. The CMY channels have more contrast than the RGB pals, but the basic brightness distribution is the same. Here's another graphic demonstration of color theory. In a perfect world, the CMY channels would be identical to the RGB channels — one color model would simply be the other turned on its head. But because this is not a perfect world (you might have noticed that as you've traveled life's bitter highway), Photoshop has to boost the contrast of the CMY channels and throw in black to punch up those shadows.

Cyan

Magenta

Yellow

Black

**Figure 3-15:** The contents of the cyan, magenta, yellow, and black channels from the image shown in Color Plate 3-2.

# Lab channels

To create Figure 3-16, I converted the image in Color Plate 3-2 to the Lab mode. The image in the luminosity channel looks very similar to the grayscale composite because it contains the lightness and darkness values for the image. The *a* channel maps the greens and magentas, while the *b* channel maps the yellows and blues, so both channels are working hard to provide color information for this photograph. Certainly there are differences — the *a* channel is hotter in the raft, while the *b* channel offers more cloud detail — but the two channels carry roughly equivalent amounts of color information.

Grayscale composite                Luminosity

*a* (black is green, white is magenta)      *b* (black is blue, white is yellow)

**Figure 3-16:** The grayscale composite followed by the contents of the luminosity channel and the a and b color channels after converting the image shown in Color Plate 3-2 to the Lab mode.

You can achieve some entertaining effects by applying commands from the Image ⇨ Adjust submenu to the *a* and *b* color channels. For example, if I go to the *a* channel in Figure 3-16 and reverse the brightness values by choosing Image ⇨ Adjust ⇨ Invert (⌘/Ctrl+I), the water turns a sort of salmon red and the raft turns green, as demonstrated in the first example of Color Plate 3-3. If I apply Image ⇨ Adjust ⇨ Auto Levels (⌘/Ctrl+Shift+L) to the *b* channel, the sky lights up with brilliant blue without altering so much as a color in the woman or her raft, as in the second example. The third example in Color Plate 3-3 shows what happens when I apply both Invert and Auto Levels to both the *a* and *b* channels. Now there's the way I want to vacation — on a different planet!

# Other Channel Functions

In addition to viewing and editing channels using any of the techniques discussed in future chapters of this book, you can choose commands from the Channels palette menu and select icons along the bottom of the palette (labeled back in Figure 3-13). The following items explain how the commands and icons work.

You'll notice that I say "see Chapter 16" every so often when explaining these options, because many of them are specifically designed to accommodate masks. This list is designed to introduce you to *all* the options in the Channels palette, even if you'll need more background to use a few of them. After I introduce the options, we'll revisit the ones that have a direct affect on managing the colors in your image.

✦ **Palette Options:** Even though this is the last command in the menu, it's the easiest, so I'll start with it. When you choose Palette Options, Photoshop displays four Thumbnail Size radio buttons, enabling you to change the size of the thumbnail previews that appear along the left side of the Channels palette. Figure 3-17 shows the four thumbnail settings — nonexistent, small, medium, and large.

Have you ever wondered what those thumbnail icons in the Palette Options dialog box are supposed to show? They're silhouettes of tiny Merlins on a painter's palette. How do I know that? Switch to the Layers palette and choose Palette Options and you'll see them in color. But how do I know they're specifically Merlins? Press Option/Alt when choosing Palette Options to see the magician up close. We're talking vintage Easter egg, here — circa Photoshop 2.5.

✦ **New Channel:** Choose this command to add a mask channel to the current image. The Channel Options dialog box appears, requesting that you name the channel. You also can specify the color and translucency that Photoshop applies to the channel when you view it with other channels. I explain how these options work in the "Changing the red coating" section of Chapter 16. An image can contain up to 24 total channels, regardless of color mode.

You can also create a new channel by clicking on the new channel icon at the bottom of the Channels palette. (It's the one that looks like a little page.) Photoshop creates the channel without displaying the dialog box. To force the dialog box to appear on-screen, Option/Alt+click on the page icon.

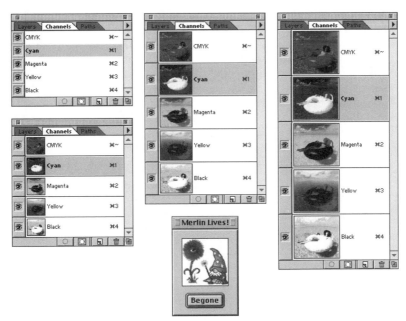

**Figure 3-17:** The Palette Options command lets you select between four thumbnail preview options and a Merlin.

✦ **Duplicate Channel:** Choose this command to create a duplicate of the selected channel, either inside the same document or as part of a new document. (If the composite view is active, the Duplicate Channel command is dimmed, because you can only duplicate one channel at a time.) The most common reason to use this command is to convert a channel into a mask. Again, you can find real-life applications in Chapter 16.

You can also duplicate a channel by dragging the channel name onto the new channel icon. No dialog box appears; Photoshop merely names the channel automatically. To copy a channel to a different document, drag the channel name and drop it into an open image window. Photoshop automatically creates a new channel for the duplicate.

✦ **Delete Channel:** To delete a channel from an image, click on the channel name in the palette and choose this command. You can delete only one channel at a time. The Delete Channel command is dimmed when any essential color channel is active, or when more than one channel is selected.

If choosing a command is too much effort, just drag the channel onto the delete channel icon (which is the little trash icon in the lower right corner of the Channels palette). Or you can just click on the trash icon, in which case Photoshop asks you if you really want to delete the channel. To bypass this warning, Option/Alt+click on the trash icon.

✦ **New Spot Channel:** Photoshop 5 lets you add spot color channels to an image. Each spot color channel prints to a separate plate, just like spot colors in Illustrator or QuarkXPress. When you choose the New Spot Color command, Photoshop asks you to specify a color and a Solidity. Click on the color square to bring up the Custom Colors dialog box, from which you can select a Pantone or other spot color (see Figure 3-18). The Solidity option lets you increase the opacity of the ink, perfect for Day-Glo fluorescents and metallic inks.

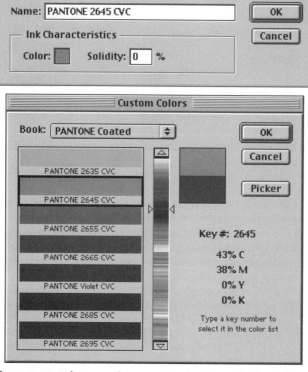

**Figure 3-18:** When creating a spot-color channel, Photoshop asks you to select a color and specify the degree to which the spot color will cover up other inks in the printed image.

**Tip**

To create a spot color channel without choosing a command, ⌘/Ctrl+click on the page icon at the bottom of the Channels palette. For more information on spot-color channels, read the "Spot-Color Separations" section at the end of Chapter 4.

✦ **Merge Spot Channel:** Select a spot-color channel and choose this command to merge the spot color in with the RGB, Lab, or CMYK colors in the image. Most spot colors don't have precise RGB or CMYK equivalents, so you will lose some color fidelity in the merge. Adobe includes this command to allow you to proof an image to a typical midrange color printer.

✦ **Channel Options:** Choose this command or double-click on the channel name in the palette's scrolling list to change the settings assigned to a spot-color or mask channel. The Channel Options command is dimmed when a regular, everyday color channels is active.

✦ **Split Channels:** When you choose this command, Photoshop splits off each channel in an image to its own independent grayscale image window. As demonstrated in Figure 3-19, Photoshop automatically appends the channel color to the end of the window name. The Split Channels command is useful as a first step in redistributing channels in an image prior to choosing Merge Channels, as I will demonstrate later in this same chapter.

**Figure 3-19:** When you choose the Split Channels command, Photoshop relocates each channel to an independent image window.

✦ **Merge Channels:** Choose this command to merge several images into a single multichannel image. The images you want to merge must be open, they must be grayscale, and they must be absolutely equal in size—the same number of pixels horizontally and vertically. When you choose Merge Channels, Photoshop displays the Merge Channels dialog box, shown in Figure 3-20. It then assigns a color mode for the new image based on the number of open grayscale images that contain the same number of pixels as the foreground image.

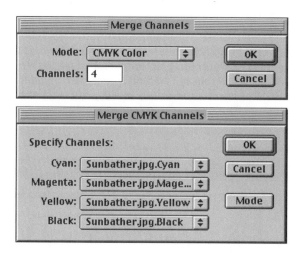

**Figure 3-20:** The two dialog boxes that appear after you choose Merge Channels enable you to select a color mode for the merged image (top) and to associate images with color channels (bottom).

You can override Photoshop's choice by selecting a different option from the Mode pop-up menu. (Generally, you won't want to change the value in the Channels option box because doing so causes Photoshop to automatically select Multichannel from the Mode pop-up menu. I explain multichannel images in the upcoming "Using multichannel techniques" section.)

After you press Return/Enter, Photoshop displays a second dialog box, which also appears in Figure 3-20. In this dialog box, you can specify which grayscale image goes with which channel by choosing options from pop-up menus. When working from an image split with the Split Channels command, Photoshop automatically organizes each window into a pop-up menu according to the color appended to the window's name. For example, Photoshop associates the window Sunbather.jpg.cyan (or Sunbat_C.jpg on a PC) with the Cyan pop-up menu.

# Color Channel Effects

Now that you know how to navigate among channels and apply commands, permit me to suggest a few reasons for doing so. The most pragmatic applications for channel effects involve the restoration of bad color scans. If you use a color scanner, know someone who uses a color scanner, or just have a bunch of color scans lying around, you can be sure that some of them look like dog meat. (Nothing against dog meat, mind you. I'm sure that Purina has some very lovely dog meat scans in their advertising archives.) With Photoshop's help, you can turn those scans into filet mignon — or at the very least, into an acceptable Sunday roast.

## Improving the appearance of color scans

The following are a few channel editing techniques you can use to improve the appearance of poorly scanned full-color images. Keep in mind that these techniques don't work miracles, but they can retrieve an image from the brink of absolute ugliness into the realm of tolerability.

**Note**

Don't forget that you can choose View ➪ New View to maintain a constant composite view. Or you can click on the eyeball icon in front of the composite view in the Channels palette to view the full-color image, even when editing a single channel.

✦ **Aligning channels:** Every so often, a scan may appear out of focus even after you use Photoshop's sharpening commands to try to correct the problem, as discussed in Chapter 23. If, on closer inspection, you can see slight shadows or halos around colored areas, one of the color channels probably is out of alignment. To remedy the problem, switch to the color channel that corresponds to the color of the halos. Then select the move tool (by pressing the V key) and use the arrow keys to nudge the contents of the channel into alignment. Use the separate composite view (created by choosing View ➪ New View) or click on the eyeball in front of the composite channel to monitor your changes.

✦ **Channel focusing:** If all channels seem to be in alignment (or, at least, as aligned as they're going to get), one of your channels may be poorly focused. Use the ⌘/Ctrl+key equivalents to search for the responsible channel. When and if you find it, use the Unsharp Mask filter to sharpen it as desired. You may also find it helpful to blur a channel, as when trying to eliminate moiré patterns in a scanned halftone. (For a specific application of these techniques, see the "Cleaning up Scanned Halftones" section in Chapter 23.)

✦ **Bad channels:** In your color channel tour, if you discover that a channel is not so much poorly focused as simply rotten to the core — complete with harsh transitions, jagged edges, and random brightness variations — you may be able to improve the appearance of the channel by mixing other channels with it.

Suppose that the blue channel is awful, but the red and green channels are in fairly decent shape. Photoshop 5's new Channel Mixer command lets you mix channels together, whether to repair a bad channel or achieve an interesting effect. Choose Image ➪ Adjust ➪ Channel Mixer and press ⌘/Ctrl+3 to switch to the blue channel. Then raise the Red and Green values and lower the Blue value to mix the three channels together to create a better blue. To maintain consistent brightness levels, it's generally a good idea to use a combination of Red, Green, and Blue values that adds up to 100 percent, as in Figure 3-21. If you can live with the inevitable color changes, the appearance of the image should improve dramatically.

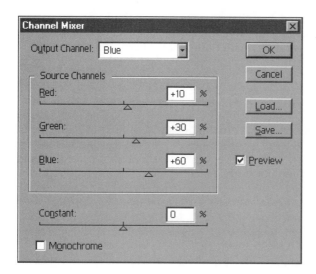

**Figure 3-21:** Here I use the Channel Mixer command to repair the blue channel by mixing in 10 percent of the red channel and 30 percent of the green channel. The red and green channels remain unaffected.

Note that Channel Mixer is also a great command for creating custom grayscale images. Rather than choosing Image ➭ Mode ➭ Grayscale command and select the Monochrome check box. Then adjust the Red, Green, and Blue values to mix your own grayscale variation.

Incidentally, the Constant slider simply brightens or darkens the image across the board. Usually, you'll want to leave it set to 0. But if you're having problems getting the color balance right, give it a tweak.

**Note**

Although Image ➭ Adjust ➭ Channel Mixer is new to Photoshop 5, I've been including my own channel mixing filter with the *Photoshop Bible* for better than three years now. Created in Photoshop's Filter Factory (see Chapter D on CD-ROM #2), this filter coincidentally went by the name . . . *Channel Mixer!* I submit Figure 3-22 as Exhibit A. "But Deke," you say, "your filter doesn't look anything like Adobe's Channel Mixer, and your sliders don't make nearly as much sense." Yes, I imagine that's precisely what they want you to think. Perhaps now you're beginning to understand how diabolically crafty these Photoshop programmers can be.

## Using multichannel techniques

The one channel function I've so far ignored is Image ➭ Mode ➭ Multichannel. When you choose this command, Photoshop changes your image so that channels no longer have a specific relationship to one another. They don't mix to create a full-color image; instead, they exist independently within the confines of a single image. The multichannel mode is generally an intermediary step for converting between different color modes without recalculating the contents of the channels.

For example, normally when you convert between the RGB and CMYK modes, Photoshop maps RGB colors to the CMYK color model, changing the contents of each channel as demonstrated back in Figures 3-14 and 3-15. But suppose, just as an experiment, that you want to bypass the color mapping and instead transfer the exact contents of the red channel to the cyan channel, the contents of the green channel to the magenta channel, and so on. You convert from RGB to the multichannel mode and then from multichannel to CMYK as described in the steps below.

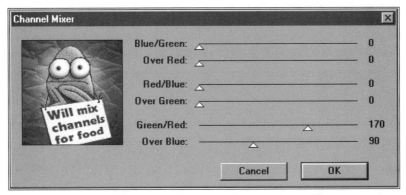

**Figure 3-22:** An early version of the Channel Mixer invented by yours truly. Has Adobe gone and swiped my visionary idea? You be the judge.

## Steps: Using the Multichannel Mode as an Intermediary Step

1. **Open an RGB image.** If the image is already open, make sure that it is saved to disk.

2. **Choose Image ⇨ Mode ⇨ Multichannel.** This eliminates any relationship between the formerly red, green, and blue color channels.

3. **Click on the new channel icon at the bottom of the Channels palette.** Or choose the New Channel command from the palette menu and press Return to accept the default settings. Either way, you add a mask channel to the image. This empty channel will serve as the black channel in the CMYK image. (Photoshop won't let you convert from the multichannel mode to CMYK with less than four channels.)

4. **Press ⌘/Ctrl+I.** Unfortunately, the new channel comes up black, which would make the entire image black. To change it to white, press ⌘/Ctrl+I or choose Image ⇨ Adjust ⇨ Invert.

5. **Choose Mode ⇨ CMYK.** The image looks washed out and a tad bit dark compared to its original RGB counterpart, but the overall color scheme of the image remains more or less intact. This is because the red, green, and blue color channels each have a respective opposite in the cyan, magenta, and yellow channels.

*Continued*

6. **Press ⌘/Ctrl+Shift+L.** Or choose Image ➪ Adjust ➪ Auto Levels. This punches up the color a bit by automatically correcting the brightness and contrast.

7. **Convert the image to RGB, and then back to CMYK again.** The problem with the image is that it lacks any information in the black channel. So Option/Although it may look okay on-screen, it will lose much of its definition when printed. To fill in the black channel, choose Image ➪ Mode ➪ RGB Color, then choose Image ➪ Mode ➪ CMYK Color. Photoshop automatically generates an image in the black channel in keeping with the standards of color separations (as explained in Chapter 4).

Keep in mind that these steps are by no means a recommended procedure for converting an RGB image to a CMYK image. Rather, they are merely intended to suggest one way to experiment with channel conversions to create a halfway decent image. You can likewise experiment with converting between the Lab, multichannel, and RGB modes, or Lab, multichannel, and CMYK.

## Replacing and swapping color channels

If you truly want to abuse the colors in an RGB or CMYK image, there's nothing like replacing one color channel with another to produce spectacular effects. Color Plate 3-4 shows a few examples applied to an RGB image.

✦ In the first example, I used the Channel Mixer to replace the red channel with the blue. I did this by setting the Output Channel to Red, changing the Red value to 0 percent and the Blue value to 100 percent. The result is a green woman floating in a green sea under a purple sky.

✦ To achieve the next example, I again started from the original RGB image and used Channel Mixer to replace the green channel with the red. The result this time is a yellow woman against a deep blue background.

✦ To create the purple woman in a green world on the right side of Color Plate 3-4, I replaced the blue channel with the red.

You can create more interesting effects by using Color Mixer to swap the contents of color channels. For example, in the lower left example of Color Plate 3-4, I swapped the contents of the red and blue channels to create a blue woman on a green sea under an orange sky. To accomplish this, I set the Output Channel to Red, set the Red value to 0 and the Blue to 100. Then I switched to the Blue channel (⌘/Ctrl+3) and set the Red value to 100 and the Blue to 0.

The next two examples along the bottom of Color Plate 3-4 show the results of swapping the red and green channels (for a bright green woman) and the green and blue channels. Because the green and blue channels contain relatively similar data, this produces the most subtle effect, chiefly switching the sea and sky colors and turning the swimsuit pink.

✦          ✦          ✦

# Printing Images

## Welcome to Printing

On one hand, printing can be a straightforward topic. You choose the Print command, press Return/Enter, wait for something to come out of your printer, and admire yet another piece of forestry that you've destroyed. On the other hand, printing can be a ridiculously complicated subject, involving dot gain compensation, hardware calibration, under color removal, toxic processor chemicals, separation table generation, and so many infinitesimal color parameters, you're liable to spend half your life trying to figure out what's happening.

This chapter is about finding a middle ground. Although it is in no way intended to cover every possible facet of printing digitized images, this chapter walks you through the process of preparing and printing the three major categories of output: composites, color separations, and duotones. By the end of the chapter, you'll be familiar with all of Photoshop's printing options. You'll also be prepared to communicate with professionals at your service bureau or commercial printer, if need be, and to learn from their input and expertise.

PC users should be aware that although most printer manufacturers now offer Windows 95 drivers, those drivers aren't always perfected. Sometimes you must get seriously down and dirty by using an older printer DLL (dynamic link library, a basic component of Windows) with a later printer driver.

If you encounter a Windows-related printing problem, your first cry for help should be to your printer manufacturer. If the manufacturer's tech support staff can't solve the problem, check online forums and newsgroups. Your service bureau can also be an excellent source for technical advice. Chances are, you're not the first person to experience the problem and someone, somewhere should have a fix for you.

# Understanding Printing Terminology

I'm not a big believer in glossaries. Generally, they contain glib, jargony, out-of-context definitions — about as helpful in gaining understanding of a concept as a seminar in which all the presenters speak pig latin. But before I delve into the inner recesses of printing, I want to introduce, in a semilogical, sort of random order, a smattering of the printing terms you'll encounter. Ood-gay uck-lay:

✦ **Service bureau:** A *service bureau* is a shop filled with earnest young graphic artists (at least they were young and earnest when *I* worked there), printer operators, and about a billion dollars' worth of hardware. A small service bureau is usually outfitted with a few laser printers, photocopiers, and self-service computers. Big service bureaus offer scanners, imagesetters, film recorders, and other varieties of professional-quality input and output equipment.

Service bureaus once relied exclusively on the Macintosh. This has changed, but a substantial number of Mac-based service bureaus remain. Most service bureaus are equally ready to help Photoshoppers on both PC and Mac platforms, but many will take a Windows Photoshop file and run it through a Mac. Nothing is wrong with this — Photoshop is nearly identical on the two platforms — but cross-platform problems may crop up. If you're a PC user, try to be sure your service bureau knows how to address cross-platform incompatibilities and has a general working knowledge of Windows.

✦ **Commercial printer:** Generally speaking, a *commercial printer* takes up where the service bureau leaves off. Commercial printers reproduce black-and-white and color pages using offset presses, Web presses, and a whole bunch of other age-old technology I don't cover in this miniglossary (or anywhere else in this book, for that matter). The process is less expensive than photocopying when you're dealing with large quantities, say, more than 100 copies, and it delivers professional-quality reproductions.

✦ **Output device:** This is just another way to say *printer*. Rather than writing *Print your image from the printer*, which sounds repetitive and a trifle obvious, I write *Print your image from the output device*. *Output devices* also include laser printers, imagesetters, film recorders, and a whole bunch of other machines.

✦ **Laser printer:** A *laser printer* works much like a photocopier. First, it applies an electric charge to a cylinder, called a *drum*, inside the printer. The charged areas, which correspond to the black portions of the image being printed, attract fine, petroleum-based dust particles called *toner*. The drum transfers the toner to the page, and a heating mechanism fixes the toner in place. Most laser printers have resolutions of at least 300 dots (or *printer pixels*) per inch. The newer printers offer higher resolutions, such as 600 and 1,200 dots per inch (*dpi*).

✦ **Color printers:** *Color printers* fall into three categories. Generally speaking, ink-jet and thermal-wax printers are at the low end, and dye-sublimation printers occupy the high end. *Ink-jet printers* deliver colored dots from disposable ink cartridges. *Thermal-wax printers* apply wax-based pigments to a page in multiple passes. Both kinds of printers mix cyan, magenta, yellow, and, depending on the specific printer, black dots to produce full-color output. If you want photographic quality prints — the kind you'd be proud to hang on your wall — you must migrate up the price ladder to *dye-sublimation printers*. Dye-sub inks permeate the surface of the paper, literally dying it different colors. Furthermore, the cyan, magenta, yellow, and black pigments mix in varying opacities from one dot to the next, resulting in a continuous-tone image that appears nearly as smooth on the page as it does on screen.

✦ **Imagesetter:** A typesetter equipped with a graphics page-description language (most often PostScript) is called an *imagesetter*. Unlike a laser printer, an imagesetter prints photosensitive paper or film by exposing the portions of the paper or film that correspond to the black areas of the image. The process is like exposing film with a camera, but an imagesetter only knows two colors: black and white. The exposed paper or film collects in a light-proof canister. In a separate step, the printer operator develops the film in a processor. Developed paper looks like a typical glossy black-and-white page. Developed film is black where the image is white and transparent where the image is black. Imagesetters typically offer resolutions between 1,200 and 3,600 dpi. But the real beauty of imageset pages is blacks are absolutely black (or transparent), as opposed to the irregular gray you get with laser-printed pages.

✦ **Film recorder:** The *film recorder* transfers images to full-color 35mm and 45 slides perfect for professional presentations. Slides also can be useful to provide images to publications and commercial printers. Many publications can scan from slides, and commercial printers can use slides to create color separations. So, if you're nervous a color separation printed from Photoshop won't turn out well, ask your service bureau to output the image to a 35mm slide. Then have your commercial printer reproduce the image from the slide.

✦ **PostScript:** The *PostScript* page-description language was the first project developed by Adobe — the same folks who sell Photoshop — and is now a staple of hundreds of brands of laser printers, imagesetters, and film recorders. A *page-description language* is a programming language for defining text and graphics on a page. PostScript specifies the locations of points, draws line segments between them, and fills in areas with solid blacks or *halftone cells* (dot patterns that simulate grays).

✦ **Spooling:** Printer *spooling* allows you to work on an image while another image prints. Rather than communicating directly with the output device, Photoshop describes the image to the system software. Under Mac System 7 and OS 8, this function is performed by a program called PrintMonitor. Under Windows 3.1, the Print Manager controls this. Under Windows 95, you set spooling options via the Printer control panel. Choose Settings ➪ Printers, right-click on the icon for your specific printer, and choose Properties from the pop-up menu. Inside the printer's Properties dialog box, switch to the Details panel and click on the Spool Settings button. When Photoshop finishes describing the image — a relatively quick process — you are free to resume working while the system software prints the image in the background.

✦ **Calibration:** Traditionally, *calibrating* a system means synchronizing the machinery. In the context of Photoshop, however, calibrating means to adjust or compensate for the color displays of the scanner, monitor, and printer so what you scan is what you see on screen, which in turn is what you get from the printer. Colors match from one device to the next. Empirically speaking, this is impossible; a yellow image in a photograph won't look exactly like the on-screen yellow or the yellow printed from a set of color separations. But calibrating is designed to make the images look as much alike as possible, taking into account the fundamental differences in hardware technology. Expensive hardware calibration solutions seek to change the configuration of scanner, monitor, and printer. Less expensive software solutions, including those provided by Photoshop, manipulate the image to account for the differences between devices.

✦ **Brightness values/shades:** A fundamental difference exists between the way your screen and printer create gray values and colors. Your monitor shows colors by lightening an otherwise black screen; the printed page shows colors by darkening an otherwise white piece of paper. On-screen colors, therefore, are measured in terms of *brightness values*. High values equate to light colors; low values equate to dark colors. On the printed page, colors are measured in percentage values called *shades* or, if you prefer, *tints*. High-percentage values result in dark colors, and low-percentage values result in light colors.

✦ **Composite:** A *composite* is a page that shows an image in its entirety. A black-and-white composite printed from a standard laser printer or imagesetter translates all colors in an image to gray values. A color composite printed from a color printer or film recorder shows the colors as they actually appear. Composites are useful any time you want to proof an image or print a final grayscale image from an imagesetter, an overhead projection from a color printer, or a full-color image from a film recorder.

✦ **Proofing:** To *proof* an image is to see how it looks on paper before the final printing. Consumer proofing devices include laser printers and color printers, which provide quality and resolution sufficient only to vaguely predict the appearance of your final output. Professional-level proofing devices include the 3M Rainbow dye-sublimation printer, which prints images of photographic quality, and the IRIS, which uses a special variety of ink-jet technology to create arguably the most accurate electronic proofs in the business.

✦ **Bleeds:** Simply put, a *bleed* is an area that can be printed outside the perimeter of a page. You use a bleed to reproduce an image all the way to the edge of a page, as in a slick magazine ad. For example, this book includes bleeds. Most of the pages — like the page you're reading — are encircled by a uniform 2-pica margin of white space. This margin keeps the text and figures from spilling off into oblivion. A few pages, however — including the parts pages and the color plates in the middle of the book — print all the way to the edges. In fact, the original artwork goes 2 picas beyond the edges of the paper. This ensures that if the paper shifts when printing — as it invariably does — you won't see any thin white edges around the artwork. This 2 picas of extra artwork is the bleed. In Photoshop, you create a bleed by clicking on the Bleed button in the Page Setup dialog box.

✦ **Color separations:** To output color reproductions, commercial printers require *color separations* (or slides, which they can convert to color separations for a fee). A color-separated image comprises four printouts, one each for the cyan, magenta, yellow, and black primary printing colors. The commercial printer transfers each printout to a *plate*, which is used in the actual reproduction process.

✦ **Duotone:** A grayscale image in Photoshop can contain as many as 256 brightness values, from white on up to black. A printer can convey significantly fewer shades. A laser printer, for example, provides anywhere from 26 to 65 shades. An imagesetter provides from 150 to 200 shades, depending on resolution and screen frequency. And this assumes perfect printing conditions. You can count on at least 30 percent of those shades to get lost in the reproduction process. A *duotone* helps to retain the depth and clarity of detail in a grayscale image by printing with two inks. The number of shades available to you suddenly jumps from 150 to a few thousand. Photoshop also lets you create *tritones* (three inks) and *quadtones* (four inks). Note, using more inks translates to higher printing costs.

✦ **Spot color:** Most color images are printed as a combination of four process color inks — cyan, magenta, yellow, and black. But Photoshop also lets you add premixed inks called *spot colors*. The most popular purveyor of spot-colors in the United States is Pantone, which provides a library with hundreds of mixings. But many large corporations use custom spot colors for logos and other proprietary emblems. Most spot colors fall outside the CMYK gamut and thus increase the number of colors available to you. In addition to using spot colors in duotone, Photoshop 5 lets you add a spot color channel to any image.

# Printing Composites

Now that you've picked up some printer's jargon, you're ready to learn how to put it all together. This section explores the labyrinth of options available for printing composite images. Later in this chapter, I cover color separations and duotones.

Like any Macintosh or Windows application, Photoshop can print composite images to nearly any output device you can hook up to your computer. Assuming your printer is turned on, properly attached, and in working order, printing a composite image from Photoshop is a five-step process, as outlined below. The sections that follow describe each of these steps in detail.

## Steps: Printing a Composite Image

1. **Choose your printer.** Use the Chooser on your Mac or the Printers control panel on your PC to select the output device to which you want to print. If your computer is not part of a network, you probably rely on a single output device, in which case you can skip this step.

2. **Choose File Page Setup (⌘/Ctrl+Shift+P).** This command permits you to specify the page size and the orientation of the image on the page. Depending on your printer, you may also be able to access specialized output functions via an Options button on your Mac or a Properties button on your PC.

3. **Adjust the halftone screens, if needed.** Click on the Screens button to change the size, angle, and shape of the halftone screen dots. This step is purely optional, useful mostly for creating special effects.

4. **Adjust the transfer function again, if needed.** Click on the Transfer button to map brightness values in an image to different shades when printed. This step is also optional, though frequently useful.

5. **Choose File ➪ Print (⌘/Ctrl+P).** Photoshop prints the image according to your specifications.

If you already have your printer set up to your satisfaction, you may be thinking about drag-and-drop printing, where you can drag a file and drop it onto the printer icon at the desktop. Don't. While this approach may seem more convenient, drag-and-drop printing has to launch Photoshop and access the same functions as the manual process. And in the worst-case scenario, the operating system may print your image from the wrong application. Drag-and-drop printing is great for making quick copies of text files, but when printing photographs and other artwork, don't look for shortcuts.

## Choosing a printer on a Mac

If you are connected to more than one network, you may need to choose the AppleTalk control panel to select the connection that you want to use. After that, select the Chooser desk accessory from the Apple menu to bring up the dialog box shown in Figure 4-1. The dialog box is split in two, with the left half devoted to a scrolling list of printer driver icons and/or network zones and the right half to specific printer options.

Select the printer driver icon that matches your model of printer. *Printer drivers* help the Macintosh hardware, system software, and Photoshop translate the contents of an image to the printer hardware and the page-description language it uses. You'll generally want to select the driver for your specific model of printer.

But you can, if necessary, prepare an image for output to a printer that isn't currently hooked up to your computer. For example, you can use this technique prior to submitting a document to be output on an imagesetter at a service bureau.

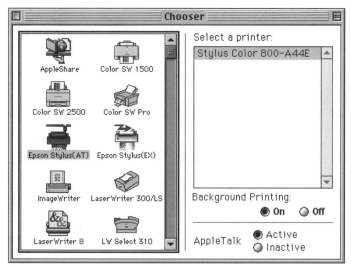

**Figure 4-1:** Use the Chooser desk accessory to select the desired output device.

Any PostScript printer driver beyond LaserWriter 8 includes support for *PostScript printer description (PPD)* files. A single driver can't account for the myriad differences between different models of PostScript printers, so each PPD serves as a little guidance file, customizing the driver to accommodate a specific printer model. After selecting a printer from the right-hand scrolling list, you can access the proper PPD by clicking on the Setup button. (Or just double-click on the printer name in the list.) Then click on the Auto Setup button to instruct the system software to automatically select the correct PPD for your printer.

If you select a networked printer, you may see a Background Printing option in the bottom right corner of the dialog box. When on, this option lets you print an image in the background while you continue to work in Photoshop or some other application. This enables you to take advantage of spooling, as defined earlier in this chapter. Normally, spooling works fine. But if you encounter printing problems, this is the first option you want to turn off.

If you use the Macintosh control strip, you may be able to bypass the Chooser when switching printers. Just click on the printer icon in the control strip and select the desired printer from the pop-up menu. Not all printers support this function, however, so you may have to visit the Chooser whether you like it or not.

## Choosing a printer on a PC

To select a printer, choose Start ⇨ Settings ⇨ Printers. Right-click on your printer of choice and select Set As Default on the resulting pop-up menu, as shown in Figure 4-2. If you want to add a printer, double-click on the Add Printer icon, and be sure to have either your Windows CD-ROM or a drivers disk from your printer manufacturer.

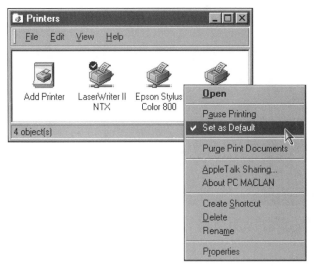

**Figure 4-2:** Specify your default printer from inside the Printers window.

Most of the time, you'll want to select the driver for your specific model of printer, but you can use this technique to prepare an image for output to a printer that isn't currently hooked up to your computer.

Starting with Windows 3.1, certain applications (such as PageMaker) could take advantage of PPD files. Windows 95 and later let you attach a PPD file globally to your PostScript printer, for which you need both the PPD file and the INF file to tell Windows 95 what to install. (Adobe offers its own printer driver called AdobePS — available via *www.adobe.com* — which doesn't require INF files. The setup program works only for Adobe-licensed PostScript printers, however.)

**Tip**

Windows 95 and later also let you switch printers from inside an application. Just choose File ⇨ Page Setup (Ctrl+Shift+P) inside Photoshop and select the printer you want to use from the Name pop-up menu.

# Setting up the page

The next step is to define the relationship between the current image and the page on which it prints. Choosing File ⇨ Page Setup (or pressing ⌘/Ctrl+Shift+P) displays the Page Setup dialog box. The Page Setup dialog box varies depending on what kind of printer you use. I usually show the Page Setup dialog box for a standard PostScript printer. But this time around, I reckoned a color ink-jet printer might be more in keeping with the current state of the art. Therefore, Figure 4-3 shows the Page Setup options for Epson's Color Stylus 800.

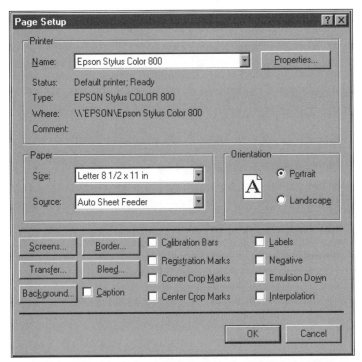

**Figure 4-3:** Use this dialog box to specify the relationship between the printed image and the page on which it appears.

Even though different printers offer different options, they all offer the following (or their equivalents):

✦ **Paper Size:** Select the size of the paper loaded into your printer's paper tray. The paper size you select determines the *imageable area* of a page — that is, the amount of the page that Photoshop can use to print the current image. For example, the US Letter option calls for a page that measures 8.5 11 inches, but only about 7.5 10 inches is imageable.

✦ **Source (Windows only):** Virtually all printers include paper cartridges, but some permit you to manually feed pages or switch between cartridges. Use this option to decide where your paper is coming from.

✦ **Orientation:** You can specify whether an image prints upright on a page (Portrait) or on its side (Landscape) by selecting the corresponding Orientation icon. Use the landscape setting when an image is wider than it is tall.

✦ **Reduce or Enlarge (Mac only):** Enter a percentage value into this option box to enlarge or reduce the size of the image when printed. Usually, you want to leave this option set to 100 percent. If you change the value, just know that your new setting gets saved with the file.

These aren't all the options available to your printer, just the most common ones. If you want to explore other printing settings, click on the Properties button (or Options button on a Mac) to display a dialog box of additional choices. In the case of the Color Stylus 800, for example, clicking on the Properties button on my PC displays the dialog box shown in Figure 4-4. Here I can modify the print quality, select whether to print in black-and-white or color, and specify the type of paper I'm using.

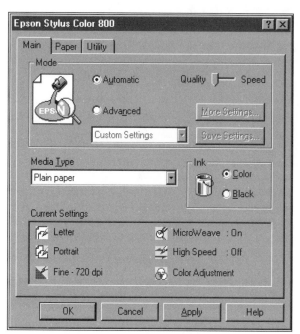

**Figure 4-4:** Click on the Properties button to access still more settings that are specific to the kind of printer you're using.

## Photoshop's special printing options

All of the options I've described so far are constant regardless of what application you're using. However, it's a different story when you descend to the bottom of the Page Setup dialog box. The options from the Screen button on down are unique to Photoshop. (If you're using a Mac and don't see a Screen button, then you should see a pop-up menu near the top of the Page Setup dialog box. Select Adobe Photoshop 5.0 from this pop-up menu to make Screen and the other options come into view.)

Here's how the buttons work:

✦ **Screens:** Click on this button to enter a dialog box that enables you to change the size, angle, and shape of the printed halftone cells, as described in the upcoming "Changing the halftone screen" section.

✦ **Transfer:** The dialog box that appears when you click on this button enables you to redistribute shades in the printed image, as explained in the upcoming section, "Specifying a transfer function."

✦ **Background:** To assign a color to the area around the printed image, click on this button and select a color from the Color Picker dialog box. This button and the one that follows (Border) are designed specifically to accommodate slides printed from a film recorder.

✦ **Border:** To print a border around the current image, click on this button and enter the thickness of the border into the Width option box. The border automatically appears in black.

✦ **Bleed:** This button lets you print outside the imageable area of the page when outputting to an imagesetter. (Imagesetters print to huge rolls of paper or film, so you can print far outside the confines of standard page sizes. Most other printers use regular old sheets of paper; any bleed — were the printer to acknowledge it — would print off the edge of the page.) Click on the Bleed button and enter the thickness of the bleed into the Width option box. Two picas (24 points) is generally a good bet. (Bleeds are defined in the "Understanding Printing Terminology" glossary at the beginning of this chapter.)

## The image-annotation check boxes

Most of the check boxes — all except Negative, Emulsion Down, and Interpolation — append special labels and printer marks to the printed version of the image. Figure 4-5 illustrates how these labels and marks look when printed.

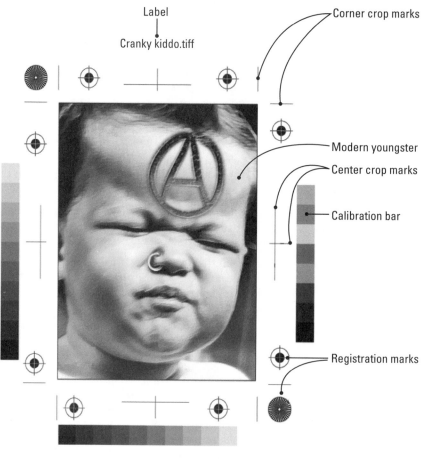

**Figure 4-5:** An image printed with nearly all the Page Setup check boxes turned on.

Here's how the check boxes work:

✦ **Caption:** To print a caption beneath the image, select this option. Then press Return/Enter to exit this dialog box, choose File ➪ File Info, and enter a caption into the File Info dialog box. The caption prints in 9-point Helvetica. This is strictly an image-annotation feature, something to help you 17 years down the road, when your brain starts to deteriorate and you can't remember why you printed the darn thing. (You might also use the caption to keep images straight in a busy office where hundreds of folks have access to the same images, but I don't like this alternative as much because I can't make fun of it.)

✦ **Calibration Bars:** A calibration bar is a 10-step grayscale gradation beginning at 10 percent black and ending at 100 percent black. The function of the calibration bar is to ensure all shades are distinct and on target. If not, the output device isn't properly calibrated, which is a fancy way of saying the printer's colors are out of whack and need realignment by a trained professional armed with a hammer and hacksaw. When you print color separations, the Calibration Bars check box instructs Photoshop to print a gradient tint bar and progressive color bar, also useful to printing professionals.

✦ **Registration Marks:** Select this option to print eight crosshairs and two star targets near the four corners of the image. Registration marks are imperative when you print color separations; they provide the only reliable means to ensure exact registration of the cyan, magenta, yellow, and black printing plates. When printing a composite image, however, you can ignore this option.

✦ **Corner Crop Marks:** Select this option to print eight hairline crop marks — two in each of the image's four corners — which indicate how to trim the image in case you anticipate engaging in a little traditional paste-up work.

✦ **Center Crop Marks:** Select this option to print four pairs of hairlines that mark the center of the image. Each pair forms a cross. Two pairs are located on the sides of the image, the third pair is above it, and the fourth pair is below the image.

✦ **Labels:** When you select this check box, Photoshop prints the name of the image and the name of the printed color channel in 9-point Helvetica. If you process many images, you'll find this option extremely useful for associating printouts with documents on disk.

✦ **Negative:** When you select this option, Photoshop prints all blacks as white and all whites as black. In-between colors switch accordingly. For example, 20 percent black becomes 80 percent black. Imagesetter operators use this option to print composites and color separations to film negatives.

✦ **Emulsion Down:** The emulsion is the side of a piece of film on which an image is printed. When the Emulsion Down check box is turned off, film prints from an imagesetter emulsion side up; when the check box is turned on, Photoshop flips the image so the emulsion side is down. Like the Negative option, this option is useful only when you print film from an imagesetter and should be set in accordance with the preferences of your commercial printer.

✦ **Interpolation:** If you own an output device equipped with PostScript Level 2 or later, you can instruct Photoshop to antialias the printed appearance of a low-resolution image by selecting this option. The output device resamples the image up to 200 percent, and then reduces the image to its original size using bicubic interpolation (as described in the "General preferences" section of Chapter B on CD-ROM #2), thereby creating a less-jagged image. This option has no effect on older-model PostScript devices.

**Note**

Incidentally, Figure 4-5 shows the actual labels and marks exactly as they print. I started by printing the Photoshop image to disk as an EPS file (as I describe later in the "Printing pages" section). Then I used Illustrator to open the EPS file and assign the callouts. This may not sound like much, but in the old days this would have been impossible. Figure 4-5 represents a practical benefit to Illustrator's (and Photoshop's) ability to open just about any EPS file on the planet.

## Changing the halftone screen

Before I proceed, I need to explain a bit more about how printing works. To keep costs down, commercial printers use as few inks as possible to create the appearance of a wide variety of colors. Suppose you want to print an image of a pink flamingo wearing a red bow tie. Your commercial printer could print the flamingos in one pass using pink ink, let that color dry, and then load the red ink and print all the bow ties. But why go to all this trouble? After all, pink is only a lighter shade of red. Why not imitate the pink by lightening the red ink?

Unfortunately, with the exception of dye-sublimation printers, high-end ink-jets, and film recorders, output devices can't print lighter shades of colors. They recognize only solid ink and the absence of ink. So how do you print the lighter shade of red necessary to represent pink?

The answer is *halftoning*. The output device organizes printer pixels into spots called halftone cells. Because the cells are so small, your eyes cannot quite focus on them. Instead, the cells appear to blend with the white background of the page to create a lighter shade of an ink. Figure 4-6 shows a detail of an image enlarged to display the individual halftone cells.

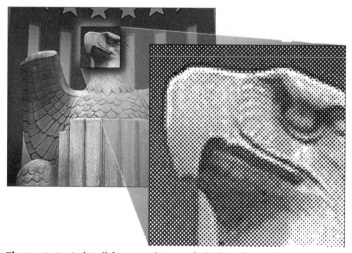

**Figure 4-6:** A detail from an image (left) is enlarged so you can see the individual halftone cells (right).

The cells grow and shrink to emulate different shades of color. Large cells result in dark shades; small cells result in light shades. Cell size is measured in printer pixels. The maximum size of any cell is a function of the number of cells in an inch, called the screen frequency.

For example, suppose the default frequency of your printer is 60 halftone cells per linear inch and the resolution is 300 printer pixels per linear inch. Each halftone cell must, therefore, measure 5 pixels wide ( 5 pixels tall (300(60 = 5), for a total of 25 pixels per cell ($5^2$). When all pixels in a cell are turned off, the cell appears white; when all pixels are turned on, you get solid ink. By turning on different numbers of pixels — from 0 up to 25 — the printer can create a total of 26 shades, as demonstrated in Figure 4-7.

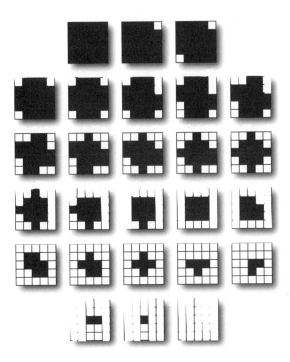

**Figure 4-7:** 5(5-pixel halftone cells with different numbers of pixels activated, ranging from 25 (top left) to 0 (bottom right). Each cell represents a unique shade from 100 to 0 percent black.

Photoshop enables you to change the size, angle, and shape of the individual halftone cells used to represent an image on the printed page. To do so, click on the Screens button in the Page Setup dialog box. The Halftone Screens dialog box shown in Figure 4-8 appears.

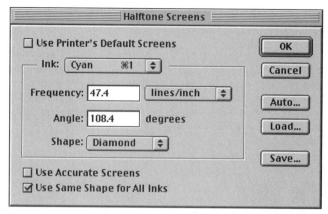

**Figure 4-8:** Use the Halftone Screens dialog box to edit the size, angle, and shape of the halftone cells or any one ink.

In the dialog box, you can manipulate the following options:

✦ **Use Printer's Default Screens:** Select this check box to accept the default size, angle, and shape settings built into your printer's ROM. All other options in the Halftone Screens dialog box automatically become dimmed to show they are no longer in force.

✦ **Ink:** If the current image is in color, you can select the specific ink you want to adjust from the Ink pop-up menu. When you work with a grayscale image, no pop-up menu is available.

✦ **Frequency:** Enter a new value into this option box to change the number of halftone cells that print per linear inch. A higher value translates to a larger quantity of smaller cells; a smaller value creates fewer, larger cells. Frequency is traditionally measured in *lines-per-inch*, or *lpi* (as in lines of halftone cells), but you can change the measurement to lines per centimeter by selecting Lines/cm from the pop-up menu to the right of the option box.

**Tip**

Higher screen frequencies result in smoother-looking printouts. Raising the Frequency value, however, also decreases the number of shades an output device can print because it decreases the size of each halftone cell and, likewise, decreases the number of printer pixels per cell. Fewer printer pixels means fewer shades. You can calculate the precise number of printable shades using the following formula:

*Number of shades = (printer resolution ÷ frequency)$^2$ + 1*

✦ **Angle:** To change the orientation of the lines of halftone cells, enter a new value into the Angle option box. In the name of accuracy, Photoshop accepts any value between negative and positive 180 degrees.

When printing color composites to ink-jet and thermal-wax printers, and when printing color separations, Photoshop calculates the optimum Frequency and Angle values required to print seamless colors. In such a case, you should change these values only if you know exactly what you're doing. Otherwise, your printout may exhibit weird patterning effects. When printing grayscale images, though, you can edit these values to your heart's content.

✦ **Shape:** By default, most PostScript printers rely on roundish halftone cells. You can change the appearance of all cells for an ink by selecting one of six alternate shapes from the Shape pop-up menu. For a demonstration of four of these shapes, see Figure C-8 in the "Black and white (bitmap)" section of Chapter C on CD-ROM #2. If you know how to write PostScript code, you can select the Custom option to display a text-entry dialog box and code away.

✦ **Use Accurate Screens:** If your output device is equipped with PostScript Level 2 or later, select this option to subscribe to the updated screen angles for full-color output. Otherwise, don't worry about this option.

✦ **Use Same Shape for All Inks:** Select this option if you want to apply a single set of size, angle, and shape options to the halftone cells for all inks used to represent the current image. Unless you want to create some sort of special effect, leave this check box deselected. The option is unavailable when you are printing a grayscale image.

✦ **Auto:** Click on this button to display the Auto Screens dialog box, which automates the halftone editing process. Enter the resolution of your output device in the Printer option box. Then enter the screen frequency you want to use in the Screen option box. After you press Return/Enter to confirm your change, Photoshop automatically calculates the optimum screen frequencies for all inks. This technique is most useful when you print full-color images — because Photoshop does the work for you, you can't make a mess of things.

✦ **Load/Save:** You can load and save settings to disk in case you want to reapply the options to other images. These buttons are useful if you find a magic combination of halftone settings that results in a really spectacular printout.

You can change the default size, angle, and shape settings Photoshop applies to all future images by Option/Alt+clicking on the Save button. When you press Option/Alt, the Save button changes to read >-Default. To restore the default screen settings at any time, Option/Alt+click on the Load button (<-Default).

The Halftone Screens dialog box settings don't apply only to printing images directly from Photoshop. You can export these settings along with the image for placement in QuarkXPress or some other application by saving the image in the Photoshop EPS format. Make sure you turn on the "Include Halftone Screen" check box in the EPS Format dialog box, as discussed in the "Saving an EPS image" section of Chapter 2. This also applies to transfer function settings, explained in the following section.

**Caution**

If you do decide to include the halftone screen information with your EPS file, be sure the settings are compatible with your intended output device. You don't want to specify a low Frequency value such as 60 lpi when printing to a state-of-the-art 3,600-dpi imagesetter, for example. If you have any questions, make certain to call your service bureau or printer before saving the image. You don't want both a last-minute surprise and a hefty bill to boot.

## Specifying a transfer function

A *transfer function* enables you to change the way on-screen brightness values translate — or *map* — to printed shades. By default, brightness values print to their nearest shade percentages. A 30 percent gray pixel on screen (which equates to a brightness value of roughly 180) prints as a 30 percent gray value.

Problems arise, however, when your output device prints lighter or darker than it should. For example, in the course of using a LaserWriter NTX over the past seven years or so — I know it's going to die one day but, until then, it keeps chugging along — I've discovered all gray values print overly dark. Dark values fill in and become black; light values appear a dismal gray, muddying up any highlights. The problem increases if I try to reproduce the image on a photocopier.

To compensate for this overdarkening effect, I click on the Transfer button in the Page Setup dialog box and enter the values shown in Figure 4-9. Notice I lighten 20 percent on screen grays to 10 percent printer grays. I also lighten 90 percent screen grays to 80 percent printer grays. The result is a smooth, continuous curve that maps each gray value in an image to a lighter value on paper.

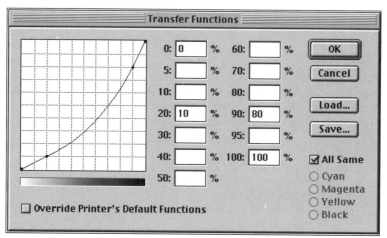

**Figure 4-9:** The transfer function curve enables you to map on-screen brightness values to specific shades on paper.

The options in the Transfer Functions dialog box work as follows:

✦ **Transfer graph:** The *transfer graph* is where you map on screen brightness values to their printed equivalents. The horizontal axis of the graph represents on screen brightness values; the vertical axis represents printed shades. The *transfer curve* charts the relationship between on screen and printed colors. The lower-left corner is the origin of the graph — the point at which both on screen brightness value and printed shade are white. Move to the right in the graph for darker on screen values; move up for darker printed shades. Click in the graph to add points to the line. Drag up on a point to darken the output; drag down to lighten the output.

For a more comprehensive explanation of how to graph colors on a curve, read about the incredibly powerful Curves command, covered in Chapter 30.

✦ **Percentage option boxes:** The option boxes are labeled according to the on-screen brightness values. To lighten or darken the printed brightness values, enter higher or lower percentage values in the option boxes. Note: There is a direct correlation between changes made to the transfer graph and the option boxes. For example, if you enter a value in the 50 percent option box, a new point appears along the middle line of the graph.

✦ **Override Printer's Default Functions:** As an effect of printer calibration, some printers have custom transfer functions built into their ROM. If you have problems making your settings take effect, select this check box to instruct Photoshop to apply the transfer function you specify, regardless of the output device's built-in transfer function.

✦ **Load/Save:** Use these buttons to load and save settings to disk. Option/Alt+click on the buttons to retrieve and save default settings.

✦ **Ink controls:** When you print a full-color image, five options appear in the lower-right corner of the Transfer Functions dialog box. These options enable you to apply different transfer functions to different inks. Select the All Same check box to apply a single transfer function to all inks. To apply a different function to each ink, deselect the check box, and then select one of the radio buttons and edit the points in the transfer graph as desired.

## Printing pages

When you finish slogging your way through the Page Setup options, you can initiate the printing process by choosing File ➪ Print (⌘/Ctrl+P). The Print dialog box appears, shown in its RGB and CMYK forms in Figure 4-10.

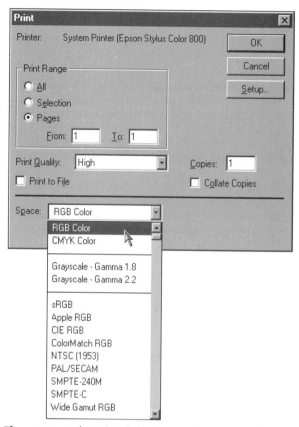

**Figure 4-10:** The Print dialog box as it appears when printing a color image.

Many of the options in this dialog box are a function of the Windows system software, but a few at the bottom of the dialog box are exclusive to Photoshop. The options work as follows:

✦ **Copies:** Enter the number of copies you want to print in this option box. You can print up to 999 copies of a single image, although why you would want to do so is beyond me.

✦ **Print Range (or Pages on a Mac):** No such thing as a multipage document exists in Photoshop, so you can ignore these options for the most part. If you're using a PC and you've selected an image area with the rectangular marquee tool, however, you can print just the selected area by choosing the Selection radio button. You may want to use this option to divide an image into pieces when it's too large to fit on a single page. (For information on printing a selected area on a Mac, see the upcoming bullet "Print Selected Area.")

✦ **Print to File (or Destination on a Mac):** Exclusively applicable to PostScript printing, this option lets you save a PostScript-language version of the file on disk rather than printing it directly to your printer. Deselect the Print to File option (or select the Printer option on a Mac) to print the image to an output device as usual. Select Print to File (or File on a Mac) to write a PostScript-language version of the image to disk.

Because Photoshop offers its own EPS option via the Save dialog box, you'll probably want to ignore this option. In fact, the only reason to select Print to File (or Destination on a Mac) is to capture printer's marks, as I did back in Figure 4-5. If you do, a second dialog box appears, asking where you want to save the PostScript file. You can navigate just as in the Open and Save dialog boxes. For the best results, select the Binary radio button.

✦ **Print Selected Area (Mac only):** Select this option to print the portion of an image that is selected with the rectangular marquee tool. You can use this option to divide an image into pieces when it's too large to fit on a single page. (Note that some printers make you select Adobe Photoshop 5.0 from a pop-up menu to see this and the next option.)

✦ **Space:** Back in Photoshop 4 and earlier, you could select whether to print in a few rudimentary color spaces—grayscale, RGB, and CMYK—but that was it. Thanks to Version 5's improved color management scheme, now you can convert to any color space offered by Photoshop, Apple's ColorSync, or Kodak's ICC CMS, as illustrated by the pop-up menu in Figure 4-10. Ideally, you want to select the specific profile for your brand of printer. If you can't find such a profile, you'll probably want to stick with the RGB Color space (specified with File ➪ Color Settings ➪ RGB Setup). Another option is to choose CMYK Color which prints the image just as if you had converted it to the CMYK color space. Unfortunately, most consumer printers are designed to accommodate RGB images and fair pretty badly when printing artwork converted to CMYK. (This is precisely the reason I frequently select RGB Color even when printing a CMYK image—it flat out produces better results.)

But you don't have to stop there. If you own a color printer, I encourage you to take an hour out of your day and conduct a few tests with the other Space options. For example, if you select Apple RGB, your printed image will darken several shades. This might throw you. Because the Apple RGB profile features the lightest of the monitor gammas—1.8—you might expect the image to print lighter. But what Photoshop is really doing is converting the colors as if the printer was as naturally light as an Apple RGB monitor. In order to maintain consistent color, the conversion therefore darkens the image to account for this unusually light device. Select the Wide Gamut setting and the colors appears lighter and washed out, again accounting for this hyper-saturated Space setting. So think opposite.

Yet another alternative is to convert an RGB image to the grayscale color space during printing. But it's generally a bad alternative. Asking Photoshop to convert colors on the fly dramatically increases the output time as well as the likelihood of printing errors. It's better and much faster to simply convert the image to the grayscale mode (Image ⇨ Mode ⇨ Grayscale) and then print it.

✦ **Encoding:** If your network doesn't support binary encoding (highly unlikely in this day and age) or your printer is attached through the local parallel printer port, instead of the network, select the ASCII option to transfer PostScript data in the text-only format. The printing process takes much longer to complete, but at least it's possible. If your printer supports PostScript Level 2 or later, you can also choose to use JPEG compression to reduce the amount of data sent to the printer. (This option is applicable to PostScript printers only.)

✦ **Setup (Windows only):** This button takes you to the Page Setup dialog box, discussed previously.

Press Return/Enter inside the Print dialog box to start the printing process on its merry way. To cancel a print in progress, click on the Cancel button or press the Escape key on your Mac. If you neglect to cancel before Photoshop spools the print job, don't worry, you can still cancel. Here's what you do if you're using a Mac: If your printer driver installed an icon on the desktop, double-click on it. Then select the print job and click on the pause button to interrupt it or click on the trash can to cancel. If there is no desktop icon, check the Extensions folder in the System Folder to see if there's a Monitor utility for your printer. It may even be running as it spools, in which case you can locate it in the Applications menu on the far right side of the screen. If you're using a PC, choose Settings ⇨ Printers from the Windows Start menu to display the Printers dialog box. Right-click on the icon for the printer you're using and then select Open. Or you can double-click on that tiny printer icon that appears on the far right side of the taskbar. Either way, Windows shows you a window listing the current print jobs in progress. You can pause or cancel the selected print job by choosing a command from the Document menu.

## Creating Color Separations

It's rare that you'll ever have to print color separations directly from Photoshop. You'll more likely import the image into QuarkXPress, PageMaker, or a similar application before printing separations. It's even more likely that you'll take the image or page-layout file to a commercial printer and have a qualified technician take care of it.

So why discuss this process? Two reasons. First, it's always a good idea to at least peripherally understand all phases of the computer imaging process, even if you have no intention of becoming directly involved. This way, if something goes wrong on the printer's end, you can decipher the crux of the problem and either propose a solution or strike a compromise that still works in your favor.

Second, before you import your image into another program or submit it to a commercial printer, you'll want to convert the RGB image to the CMYK color space. (You don't absolutely *have* to do this — with Photoshop 5's improved color matching functions, you can exchange RGB images with greater confidence — but it's always a good idea to prepare your images down to the last detail, and CMYK is invariably the final destination for printed imagery.) Accurately converting to CMYK is the trickiest part of printing color separations; the other steps require barely any effort at all.

So without further ado, here's how you convert an image to the CMYK color space and print separations. Many of the steps are the same as when printing a grayscale or color composite, others are new and different.

## Steps: Printing CMYK Color Separations

1. **Calibrate your monitor and specify the desired RGB environment.** Use the Gamma utility and File ➪ Color Settings ➪ RGB Setup as discussed at length in Chapter 3.

2. **Identify the final output device.** Use File ➪ Color Settings ➪ CMYK Setup to tell Photoshop what kind of printer you intend to use. If you're lucky, your commercial printer may provide a CMYK table that you can load and avoid the hassle. Otherwise, you'll have to grapple with some weird settings. The good news is that you only need to complete this step once for each time you switch hardware. If you always use the same commercial printer, then you can set it up and forget about it.

3. **Convert the image to the CMYK color space.** Choose Image ➪ Mode ➪ CMYK Color to convert the image from its present color mode to CMYK.

4. **Adjust the individual color channels.** Switching color modes can dramatically affect the colors in an image. To compensate for color and focus loss, you can edit the individual color channels as described in the "Color Channel Effects" section of Chapter 3.

5. **Trap your image, if necessary.** If your image features lots of high-contrast elements and you're concerned your printer might not do the best job of registering the cyan, magenta, yellow, and black color plates, you can apply Image ➪ Trap to prevent your final printout from looking like the color funnies. (When working with typical "continuous-tone" photographs, you can skip this step.)

6. **Choose your printer.** Select the printer you want to use, as described previously in the "Choosing a printer on a Mac" and "Choosing a printer on a PC" sections.

7. **Turn on a few essential printer marks.** Choose File ➪ Page Setup (⌘/Ctrl+Shift+P) to specify the size of the pages and the size and orientation of the image on the pages, as described earlier in this chapter. Also be sure to select — at the very least — the Calibration Bars, Registration Marks, and Labels check boxes.

*Continued*

8. **Adjust the halftone and transfer functions as needed.** Click on the Screen and Transfer buttons to modify the halftone screen dots and map brightness values for each of the CMYK color channels, as described earlier in the "Changing the halftone screen" and "Specifying a transfer function" sections. This step is entirely optional.

9. **Choose File ➪ Print (⌘/Ctrl+P).** Then choose the Separations option from the Space pop-up menu. This tells Photoshop to print each color channel to a separate piece of paper or film.

**Note**

You also can create color separations by importing an image into a page-layout or drawing program. Instead of choosing your printer in Step 6, you'd save the image in the DCS format, as described in the "QuarkXPress DCS" section of Chapter 2.

Steps 6 through 9 are repeats of concepts explained in previous sections of this chapter. Steps 1, 3, and 4 are covered at length in Chapters C (on CD-ROM #2) and 6. This leaves Steps 2 and 5 — CMYK Setup and trapping — which I explain in the following sections.

## Printer calibration

To prepare an image for reproduction on a commercial offset or web press, choose File ➪ Color Settings ➪ CMYK Setup. Shown in Figure 4-11, the CMYK Setup dialog box determines both how Photoshop converts images from the RGB to CMYK color spaces, and how CMYK images appear on screen (that is, the conversion from CMYK to RGB).

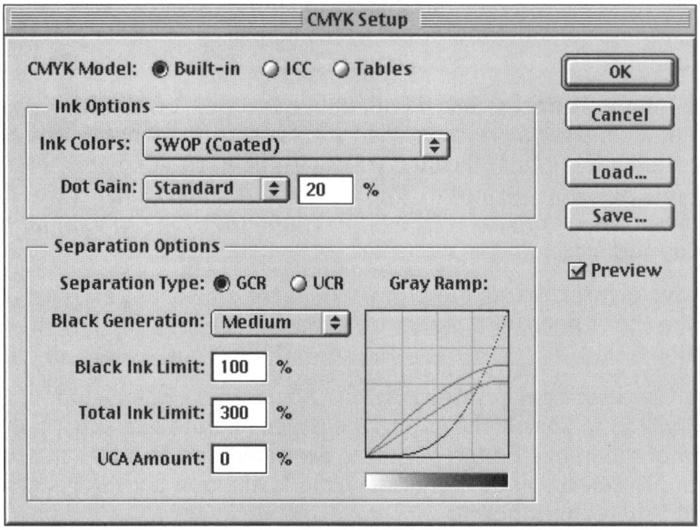

**Figure 4-11:** Use the options in the CMYK Setup dialog box to prepare an image for printing on a commercial offset or web press.

If you're familiar with previous versions of Photoshop, the CMYK Setup dialog box combines options from the old Printing Inks Setup, Separation Setup, and Separation Tables dialog boxes. Although this makes for a more complicated dialog box, it eliminates a lot of confusion; some of the options in the old dialog boxes overlapped and canceled each other out.

The following list explains each and every option in the CMYK Setup dialog box. If you're not a print professional, some of these descriptions may seem a little abstruse. After reading this section, you may want to talk with your commercial printer and find out what options, if any, he recommends.

✦ **Ink Colors:** This pop-up menu offers access to a handful of common press inks and paper stocks. Select the option that most closely matches your printing environment. (Your commercial printer can easily help you with this one.) The default setting, SWOP (Coated), represents the most common press type and paper stock used in the U.S. for magazine and high-end display work. Regardless of which setting you choose, Photoshop automatically changes the Dot Gain value to the most suitable setting.

✦ **Dot Gain:** Enter any value from −10 to 40 percent to specify the amount by which you can expect halftone cells to shrink or expand during the printing process, a variable known as *dot gain*. When printing to uncoated stock, for example, you can expect halftone cells to bleed into the page and expand by about 25 to 30 percent. For newsprint, it varies from 30 to 40 percent. If the dot gain varies between plates, choose Curves from the pop-up menu to display a transfer graph that works just like the one in the Transfer Functions dialog box. Whether you enter a percentage value or use the graph, Photoshop automatically adjusts the brightness of CMYK colors to compensate, lightening the image for high values and darkening it for low values.

✦ **Separation Type:** When the densities of cyan, magenta, and yellow inks reach a certain level, they mix to form a muddy brown. The GCR (*gray component replacement*) option avoids this unpleasant effect by overprinting these colors with black to the extent specified with the Black Generation option. If you select the UCR (*under color removal*) option, Photoshop removes cyan, magenta, and yellow inks where they overlap black ink. GCR is almost always the setting of choice except when printing on newsprint.

✦ **Black Generation:** Available only when the GCR option is active, the Black Generation pop-up menu determines how dark the cyan, magenta, and yellow concentrations must be before Photoshop adds black ink. Select Light to use black ink sparingly; select Heavy to apply it liberally. The None option prints no black ink whatsoever, while the Maximum option prints black ink over everything. You may want to use the UCA Amount option to restore cyan, magenta, and yellow ink if you select the Heavy or Maximum option.

✦ **Black Ink Limit:** Enter the maximum amount of black ink that can be applied to the page. By default, this value is 100 percent, which is solid ink coverage. If you raise the UCA Amount value, you'll probably want to lower this value by a similar percentage to prevent the image from overdarkening.

✦ **Total Ink Limit:** This value represents the maximum amount of all four inks permitted on the page. For example, assuming you use the default Black Ink Limit and Total Ink Limit values of 100 and 300 percent, respectively, the darkest printable color contains 100 percent black ink. The sum total of cyan, magenta, and yellow inks, therefore, is the difference between these values, 200 percent. A typical *saturated black* — a mix of inks that results in an absolute pitch-black pigment — is 70 percent cyan, 63 percent magenta, 67 percent yellow, and 100 percent black. And 70 + 63 + 67 + 100 =, you guessed it, 300.

✦ **UCA Amount:** The opposite of UCR, UCA stands for *under color addition*, which enables you to add cyan, magenta, and yellow inks to areas where the concentration of black ink is highest. For example, a value of 20 percent raises the amount of cyan, magenta, and yellow inks applied with black concentrations between 80 and 100 percent. This option is dimmed when the UCR radio button is active.

✦ **Gray Ramp:** The Gray Ramp graph shows the effects of your changes. Four lines — one in each color — represent the four inks. Although you can't edit the colored lines in this graph by clicking and dragging them, you can observe the lines to gauge the results of your settings. If you have an urge to grab a curve and yank on it, choose Custom from the Black Generation pop-up menu. The ensuing dialog box lets you edit the black curve directly while you preview its effect on the C, M, and Y curves in the background.

✦ **Preview:** Turn this option on to see how your changes affect any open CMYK images. RGB, Lab, and grayscale images remain unchanged.

If you prefer not to mess around with these complicated settings, you can rely on one of two kinds of predefined printer profiles. To load an ICC profile provided by ColorSync or Kodak ICC CMS, select ICC from the CMYK Model radio buttons (along the top of the CMYK Setup dialog box). Then select a printer from the Profile pop-up menu. Keep in mind, however, that these represent color printers and high-end printing devices, not commercial presses.

If you have access to Photoshop separation tables — such as the ColorMatch 3.0 profiles from Radius (included with the company's PressView monitor series) — you can load the table into Photoshop without further fanfare. Just select Tables from the CMYK Model radio buttons. Then click on the Load button, select Separation Table (*.AST*) from the Files of Type pop-up menu, if you're using a PC, and open up the desired table. (If you're using a Mac and you want to use a ColorMatch file or other separation table on the Windows side, be sure to give it the extension *.AST.*)

As shown in Figure 4-12, a separation file includes two tables — the From CMYK Table and the To CMYK Table. The first describes how CMYK colors should be displayed on screen. The second determines how Photoshop converts an RGB image to the CMYK color space. You don't have to worry about this — it's all handled automatically and you load just the one file — but as always it's good to know what's going on in the background.

In Photoshop 5, you can create a table of CMYK instructions using the built-in CMYK Setup options and then save the settings as an ICC profile. To do so, select the Built-In radio button at the top of the dialog box and fill out the desired options for your printer. Then select Tables from the CMYK Model options and click on the Save button. Photoshop saves an ICC table which you can use with any other ICC-compliant application.

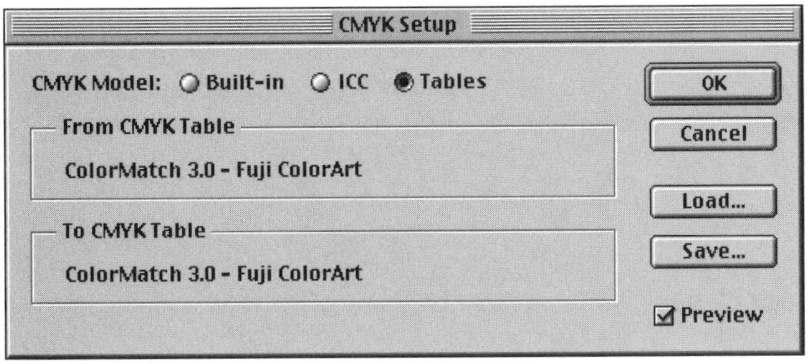

**Figure 4-12:** You can load a ColorMatch or other predefined separation table by selecting the Tables option and clicking on the Load button.

## Color trapping

If color separations misalign slightly during the reproduction process (a problem called *misregistration*), the final image can exhibit slight gaps between colors. Suppose an image features a 100 percent cyan chicken against a 100 percent magenta background. (Pretty attractive image idea, huh? Go ahead, you can use it if you like.) If the cyan and magenta plates don't line up exactly, you're left with a chicken with a white halo around it. Yuck.

A *trap* is a little extra bit of color that fills in the gap. For example, if you choose Image ➪ Trap and enter 4 into the Width option box, Photoshop outlines the chicken with an extra 4 pixels of cyan and the background with an extra 4 pixels of magenta. Now the registration can be off a full 8 pixels without any halo occurring.

Continuous-tone images, such as photographs and natural-media painting, don't need trapping because no harsh color transitions occur. In fact, trapping will actually harm such images by thickening up the borders and edges, smudging detail, and generally dulling the focus.

One of the primary reasons to use the Trap command, therefore, is to trap rasterized drawings from Illustrator or FreeHand. Some state-of-the-art prepress systems trap documents by first rasterizing them to pixels and then modifying the pixels. Together, Photoshop and Illustrator (or FreeHand) constitute a more rudimentary but, nonetheless, functional trapping system. When you open an illustration in Photoshop, the program converts it into an image according to your size and resolution specifications, as described in the "Rasterizing an Illustrator or

FreeHand file" section of Chapter 2. Once the illustration is rasterized, you can apply Image ➪ Trap to the image as a whole. Despite the command's simplicity, it handles nearly all trapping scenarios, even going so far as to reduce the width of the trap incrementally as the colors of neighboring areas grow more similar.

**Caution**    If you plan on having a service bureau trap your files for you, do not apply Photoshop's Trap command. You don't want to see what happens when someone traps an image that's already been trapped. If you're paying the extra bucks for professional trapping, leave it to the pros.

# Printing Duotones

It's been a few pages since the "Understanding Printing Terminology" section, so here's a quick recap: A *duotone* is a grayscale image printed with two inks. This technique expands the depth of the image by allowing additional shades for highlights, shadows, and midtones. If you've seen a glossy magazine ad for perfume, designer clothing, a car, or just about any other overpriced commodity, you've seen a duotone. Words like *rich*, *luxurious*, and *palpable* come to mind.

Photoshop also enables you to add a third ink to create a tritone and a fourth ink to create a quadtone. Color Plate 4-1 shows an example of an image printed as a quadtone. Figure 4-13 shows a detail from the image printed in its original grayscale form. See the difference?

**Figure 4-13:** This salute to all-around athlete Jim Thorpe by artist Mark Collen looks pretty good, but if you want to see great, check out the quadtone in Color Plate 4-1.

# Creating a duotone

To convert a grayscale image to a duotone, tritone, or quadtone, choose Image ➪ Mode ➪ Duotone. Photoshop displays the Duotone Options dialog box shown in Figure 4-14. By default, Monotone is the active Type option, and the Ink 2, Ink 3, and Ink 4 options are dimmed. To access the Ink 3 option, select Tritone from the Type pop-up menu; to access both Ink 3 and Ink 4, select Quadtone from the pop-up menu.

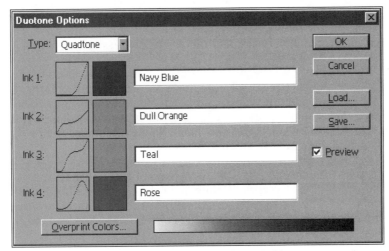

**Figure 4-14:** The Duotone Options dialog box enables you to apply multiple inks to a grayscale image.

You specify the color of each ink you want to use by clicking on the color box associated with the desired ink option. The first time you define colors, Photoshop displays the Color Picker dialog box. You can either define colors in the Color Picker or click on Custom Colors to select a color from the Custom Colors dialog box, as described in the "Predefined colors" section of Chapter C on CD-ROM #2).

Photoshop 5 takes the guesswork out of creating a duotone by previewing your settings in the image window so long as the Preview check box is turned on. Keep in mind, the preview may not exactly match your output when using certain Pantone inks. (This is a common problem when previewing Pantone inks in any program, but it's always a good idea to keep in mind, particularly since Photoshop mixes inks to create its dutone effects.)

The next time you create a duotone, Photoshop displays the same colors you defined in your last visit to the Duotone Options dialog box. If you previously defined colors in the Custom Colors dialog box, clicking on a color box brings up that same dialog box (click on Picker to get to the Color Picker dialog box).

When creating duotones, tritones, and quadtones, prioritize your inks in order — from darkest at the top to lightest at the bottom — when you specify them in the Duotone Options dialog box. Because Photoshop prints inks in the order they appear in the dialog box, the inks will print from darkest to lightest. This ensures rich highlights and shadows and a uniform color range.

After selecting a color, you can use either of two methods to specify how the differently colored inks blend. The first and more dependable way is to click on the transfer function box associated with the desired ink option. Photoshop then displays the Transfer Functions dialog box, described back in the "Specifying a transfer function" section of this chapter. This permits you to emphasize specific inks in different portions of the image according to brightness values.

For example, Figure 4-14 shows the inks and transfer functions assigned to the quadtone in Color Plate 4-1. The Navy Blue color is associated only with the darkest brightness values in the image; Rose peaks at about 80 percent gray and then descends; Teal covers the midtones in the image; Dull Orange is strongest in the light values. The four colors mix to form an image whose brightness values progress from light orange to olive green to brick red to black.

The second method for controlling the blending of colors is to click on the Overprint Colors button. An Overprint Colors dialog box appears, showing how each pair of colors will mix when printed. Other color swatches show how three and four colors mix, if applicable. To change the color swatch, click on it to display the Color Picker dialog box.

The problem with this second method is it complicates the editing process. Photoshop doesn't actually change the ink colors or transfer functions in keeping with your new specifications; it just applies the new overprint colors without any logical basis. And you lose all changes made with the Overprint Colors dialog box when you adjust any of the ink colors or any of the transfer functions.

To return and change the colors or transfer functions, choose Image ⇨ Mode ⇨ Duotone again. Instead of reconverting the image, the command now lets you edit the existing duotone, tritone, or quadtone.

## Reproducing a duotone

If you want a commercial printer to reproduce a duotone, tritone, or quadtone, you must print the image to color separations, just like a CMYK image. Because you already specified which inks to use and how much of each ink to apply, however, you needn't mess around with all those commands in the File ⇨ Color Settings submenu. Just take the following familiar steps:

## Steps: Printing a Duotone, Tritone, or Quadtone

1. **Choose the printer you want to use.** Select a printer as described previously in the "Choosing a printer on a Mac" and "Choosing a printer on a PC" sections.

2. **Turn on the printer marks.** Choose File ⇨ Page Setup (⌘/Ctrl+Shift+P) to specify the size of the pages and the size and orientation of the image on the pages, as described earlier in this chapter in the "Setting up the page" section. Be sure to select the Registration Marks option.

3. **Adjust the halftone screens, if desired.** If you're feeling inventive, click on the Screens button to change the size, angle, and shape of the halftone screen dots for the individual color plates, as described previously in the "Changing the halftone screen" section.

4. **Choose File ⇨ Print (⌘/Ctrl+P).** Select the Separations option from the Space pop-up menu to print each ink to a separate sheet of paper or film.

To prepare a duotone to be imported into QuarkXPress, Illustrator, or some other application, save the image in the EPS format, as described in the "Saving an EPS image" section of Chapter 2. As listed in Table C-1 of Chapter C on CD-ROM #2, EPS is the only file format other than the native Photoshop format that supports duotones, tritones, and quadtones.

## Editing individual duotone plates

If you'll be printing your duotone using CMYK colors and you can't quite get the effect you want inside the Duotone Options dialog box, you can convert the duotone to the CMYK mode by choosing Image ⇨ Mode ⇨ CMYK. Not only will all the duotone shades remain intact, but you'll also have the added advantage of being able to tweak colors and to add color using Photoshop's standard _color-correction commands and editing tools. You can even edit individual color channels, as described in Chapter 3.

If your duotone includes Pantone or other spot colors, converting to CMYK is not an option. But you can still access and edit the individual color channels. To separate the duotone inks into channels, choose Image ⇨ Mode ⇨ Multichannel. Each ink appears as a separate spot color inside the Channels palette, as shown in Figure 4-15. You can experiment with different color combinations by turning eyeball icons on and off. In Color Plate 4-2, for example, I turned off one channel in the top row and two channels in the bottom. You can even switch out one spot color for another by double-clicking on the channel name and then clicking on the color swatch.

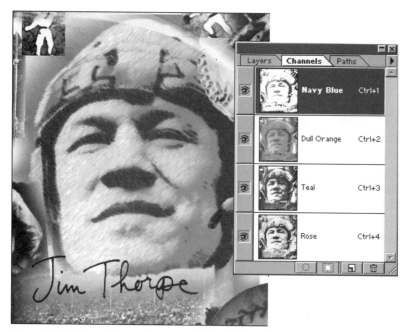

**Figure 4-15:** Here I chose Image ⇨ Mode ⇨ Multichannel to separate my quadtone into four independent spot-color channels.

To save a duotone converted to the multichannel mode, you have just two options: native Photoshop (as always) and DCS 2.0. For complete information on the latter, read the "QuarkXPress DCS" section in Chapter 2.

# Spot-Color Separations

Photoshop 5 now permits you to add spot colors to your images. While it's unlikely that you'll use spot colors to widen the gamut of your photographs — after all, scanners can't scan spot colors and Photoshop can't automatically lift them out of, say, the RGB color space — you may want to toss in a spot color to highlight a logo, a line of type, and some other special element.

For example, suppose you have a full-color image of a jet ski. The logo along the side of the boat is fully visible, just as the client wants it, but the color is off. Normally, the logo appears in Pantone 265 purple. But the CMYK equivalent for this color looks about three shades darker, four shades redder, and several times muddier. The only solution is to assign the proper spot color — Pantone 265 — to the logo. The following steps tell how:

## Steps: Adding a Spot Color to an Image

1. **Select the logo.** You can use the magic wand tool or some more exacting method, as described in Chapters 15 and 16.

2. **Fill the selection with white.** Press the D key to get the default foreground and background colors, then press ⌘/Ctrl+Delete/Backspace. It's important that you erase the old logo so that it appears in pure spot color without any mixing with the CMYK inks. But do not deselect your selection! It must remain active for Step 5 to work.

3. **Create a new spot channel.** As explained in Chapter 3, the easiest way to do this is to ⌘/Ctrl+click on the page icon at the bottom of the Channels palette. But you can also choose New Spot Channel from the Channels palette menu if you prefer.

4. **Set the color to Pantone 265.** Click on the Color swatch in the New Spot Channel dialog box. Then select Pantone 265 from the Custom Colors dialog box. (If the Color Picker comes up instead, click on the Custom button.)

5. **Press Return/Enter or click OK twice.** Photoshop adds the new spot color to the Channels palette and automatically fills the selection. Your logo automatically appears in the spot color. (Cool, huh?)

6. **Choose Image ➪ Trap.** It's a good idea to trap the spot color so that it covers up any gaps that may result from misregistration. Enter a value of 1 or 2 pixels and hit Return/Enter. Photoshop spreads the logo but leaves the CMYK image alone. Very intelligent program, that Photoshop.

7. **Save the image.** You have two choices of formats, native Photoshop or DCS 2.0. If you want to import the image into a different program, use the latter.

Naturally, you don't want to trust Photoshop's on-screen representation of the spot color any more than you would in Illustrator, QuarkXPress, or any other program. The screen version is an approximation, nothing more. So it's a good idea to have a Pantone swatch book on hand so that you know exactly what the color should look like when printed. (If the printed logo doesn't match the swatch book, it's the printer's fault, not Photoshop's.)

# Printing Contact Sheets

Photoshop's final printing feature is a representative from the new Actions plug-ins. This means that the command performs a series of automated operations — much like a script created in the Actions palette — but with the interface of a filter or other plug-in.

The purpose of File ⇨ Automated ⇨ Contact Sheet is to print a folder-full of images as thumbnails on a contact sheet. This way, you can quickly peruse the images in that folder and decide whether or not any of them would make good candidates for editing. It's sort of a do-it-yourself cataloging feature.

This command shows off both the strengths and weaknesses of Actions plug-ins. On the up side, it lets you do something you couldn't do before without requiring the programmer to invent a completely new feature. This means Actions plug-ins are easy to create and you'll probably see lots of them in the future years. On the down side, the plug-in is limited in its capabilities and slow.

In fact, the down side is sufficiently awful that I considered ignoring this command entirely. But contact sheets are extremely useful, so what the heck? Just bear in mind, you're going to have to be patient and resourceful to get predictable results out of this sucker.

## Steps: Creating a Contact Sheet

1. **Choose File ⇨ Automated ⇨ Contact Sheet.** This displays the dialog box shown in Figure 4-16. This is the interface for the script.

2. **Click on the Choose button.** Then locate the folder of images that you want to print on the contact sheet. Pay attention to how many images the folder contains. Photoshop will assemble only as many as will fit on a single page. The Contact Sheet plug-in is not smart enough to continue assembling images onto a second page.

3. **Enter the size and resolution of the contact sheet file.** The Contact Sheet command is unable to resample images as it brings them in — probably its greatest oversight — so be sure to make your contact sheet very large. To hold 30 digital snapshots, I had to set mine to 810 inches at 300 ppi.

4. **Specify a color mode.** This isn't something you're going to color separate, so RGB should do fine.

5. **Set the number of Columns and Rows of thumbnails.** The total number of thumbnails should match or exceed the number of images in the folder you selected with the Choose button. Excess images will be ignored.

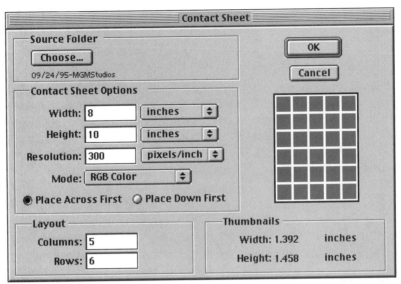

**Figure 4-16:** The Contact Sheet dialog box invokes a series of operations that open images from a folder and assemble them together on a single page.

6. **Press Return/Enter and watch the fireworks.** Photoshop creates a new contact sheet image, opens the first image from the folder, copies and pastes it into the contact sheet image, moves it into position, flattens the file, and then moves onto the next image. It takes several minutes to open, copy, paste, and position 30 or more images, so a break is definitely in order. When the command finishes, you should get something on the order of Figure 4-17. It looks pretty hodgepodge, but then it's not supposed to be a work of art.

7. **Resample the image down to a more reasonable size.** You can skip this step if you like, but a 20MB file seems excessive for what is ostensibly a quick reference of thumbnails. I'd take the image down to 50 percent at least, maybe more.

8. **Save the contact sheet and print it.** Then repeat for all your other images. At about 10 minutes per collection of 30, it should take me, oh, about 5 days to get through my digital snapshots. Yet another project to put off until my dotage.

*(continued)*

**Figure 4-17:** A sample contact sheet of images I shot with a Kodak DC40 at MGM Studios in Disney World. That was a couple of years ago now, so naturally I completely forget what I shot. This contact sheet should come in handy.

All in all, Contact Sheet reminds me of the kind of 75 percent-baked filters that found their way into Illustrator 5 for the Mac. (The original Create Star filter is a far cry from Illustrator 7's fully realized star tool.) It's useful in theory but clumsy in practice. Still, Contact Sheet gives you an idea of what Actions plug-ins are all about and the wonders that they hold in store. My guess (or should I say, my hope) is that we can expect better things from this command in the future.

✦        ✦        ✦

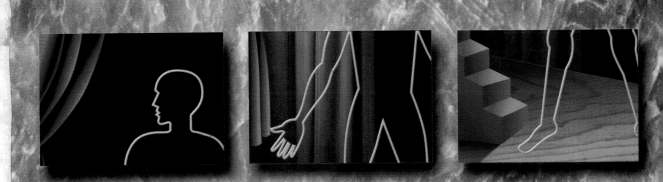

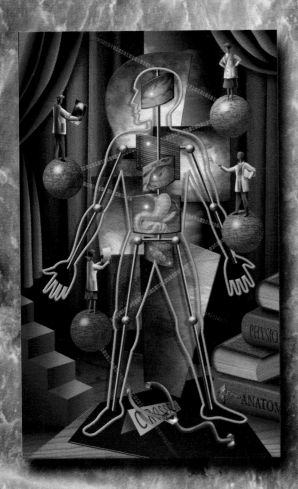

# PART II
# MAKING A LIVING

**Sketch to Execution:**
    **The Commercial Art Process**
**Working Stock Photography**
    **into Graphic Art**
**Fine Art Printing**

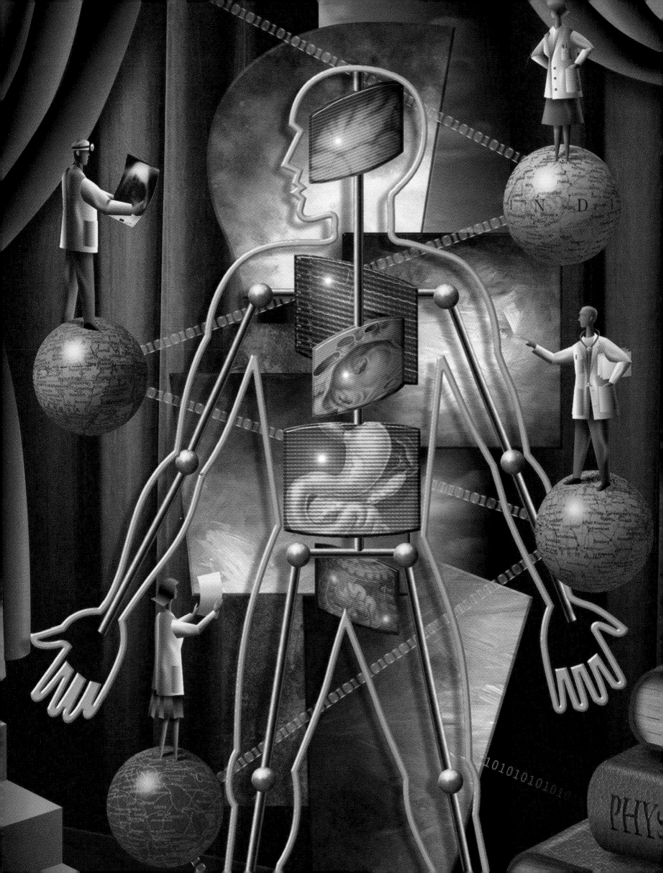

# CHAPTER 5
# SKETCH TO EXECUTION:
# THE COMMERCIAL ART PROCESS

Photoshop is, by most accounts, a powerful and well-constructed program, arguably the staple application of the professional graphics industry. But it's the program's price that really forces you to treat it with reverence. Unless you're a highly paid professional type who gets a kick out of image editing in your spare time, Photoshop is too expensive to purchase as a lark. After sinking $500 into the software, and who knows how much into learning it, the best way to recoup your costs is to make money with the program.

I'm not proposing to share with you some magic formula for breaking into the computer graphics market. Nor do I have a secret list of art directors who are looking for fresh talent. (If I did, I'd be filming infomercials and setting up 900 numbers instead of writing this book.) Having only a vague recollection of the random turn of events that got me where I am today, I'm hardly in a position to coach.

But with the help of veteran computer artist Glenn Mitsui, I can paint a picture of what it's like to create a commercial project from start to finish. If you've never sold a piece of artwork to a high-end client, then this little tour is the next best thing to serving six months as a studio apprentice. And if you already make a tidy living with Photoshop, I think you'll find Mitsui's approach uniquely insightful. This chapter shows Mitsui at work, from initial client contact to final product.

## WHO IS GLENN TO TALK?

Before I launch into what Mitsui does, it might help to know a little bit about who he is and what makes

*With different styles, you can handle a wide variety of jobs and you're never in a position of having to hammer a round peg in a square hole.*

GLENN MITSUI

him an expert on this particular topic. Art directors and colleagues recognize him as a rare chameleon of an artist who can shift styles to accommodate the interests and personalities of his clients. While just about every artist feels compelled to periodically modify his or her style to remain commercially viable, Mitsui seems capable of balancing multiple styles simultaneously.

"If you maintain a single particular style, it's not always possible to force that style into different subject matters. For example, my brightly colored architectural style probably wouldn't work as editorial art for a story about psychology. With different styles, you can handle a wide variety of jobs and you're never in a position of having to hammer a round peg in a square hole. I'm not saying it never works against you — you may find that your identity isn't as strong in one style as in another. And I always have to ask my clients which piece of mine led them to me so I can figure out which style they're looking for. But the mental advantages are well worth it. I don't get bored."

For A'cino, an emerging cosmetics company, Mitsui employed his sleek photo collage style (5.1). "A'cino wanted to create a series of postcards and placards for retail stores. They wanted chic, but they didn't want to look too high tech. So, I tried to create something that was crisp and elegant. And of course, I've always been intrigued by fish swimming beside birds with long legs."

Mitsui used a softer, more traditional style for a poster he did for the Seattle Repertory Theater (5.2).

5.2

5.1

**ARTIST:**
Glenn Mitsui

**ORGANIZATION:**
Studio M D
1512 Alaskan Way
Seattle, WA 98101
206/682-6221
glenn@studiomd.com

**SYSTEM:**
Power Mac 7100/66
1GB storage

**RAM:**
106MB total
70MB assigned to Photoshop

**MONITOR:**
Radius 17-inch

**EXTRAS:**
Hewlett-Packard ScanJet IIcx

**VERSION USED:**
Photoshop 5.0

**OTHER APPLICATIONS:**
Macromedia FreeHand, FractalDesign
Painter, Adobe After Effects

"I'm a big fan of playwright Philip Gotanda, so when they asked me to do a poster for one of his plays, I was very excited. The play's about a 17-year-old girl who grew up on the island of Kauai in the early 1900s. Part of the story is about how she becomes an apprentice for a bitter but very talented pottery artist, and later becomes romantically involved with him. So, I wanted to integrate the elements of natural art, with natural brushstrokes, pottery shards, and the fire from the kiln."

Folks in the computer industry are likely to see a starkly different side of Mitsui. "Resolution Technology asked me to create an ad for a 3-D program of theirs that allows artists to create realistic fly-throughs and landscapes. My approach to it was to build a volumetric person made up of various inter-active elements (5.3). It resembles a 3-D rendering, but I created everything using layers and gradients in Photoshop."

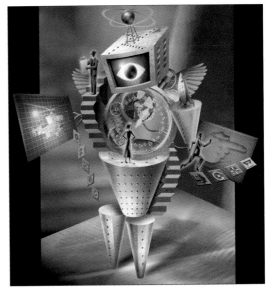

5.3

**WORK HISTORY:**

<u>1982</u> — Worked as technical illustrator on graveyard shift at Boeing; discovered that women's bathroom had a nap couch.

<u>1987</u> — Created corporate presentation slides on Genigraphics system for Magicmation.

<u>1990</u> — Started Studio M D with Jesse Doquilo and Randy Lim; purchased first Macintosh system.

<u>1992</u> — Started creating full-page fea-ture artwork for *Macworld* magazine.

<u>1995</u> — Became board member and speaker for American Institute of Graphics Arts; served as panel judge for SIGGRAPH fine arts competition.

**FAVORITE '70s TV SHOWS:**

"Green Hornet" (because Bruce Lee played Kato) and "Long Street" (because Bruce Lee played Kung Fu instructor)

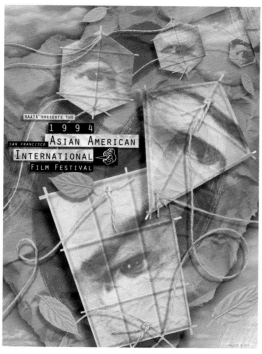

5.4

Mitsui used the theme of paper kites to symbolize the different nationalities represented at San Francisco's Asian American International Film Festival (5.4). "The Festival includes Chinese films, Japanese films, Korean, Thai, Indonesian, and all kinds of other contributions. I wanted to show that although we're all different in a lot of ways, we're blown by the same wind. Here I tried to emphasize the printed quality of the paper by exaggerating the creases and wrinkles and keeping the halftone dots in the eyes."

One of Mitsui's most recent stylistic developments is what he calls his "big hurkin' icons with Spirograph" approach. "The image of the two hands (5.5) was one of the illustrations I proposed to demonstrate compatibility issues for a new chip from Fujitsu. I feel like this style really emphasizes the power of the line. It lets me elicit humor, anger, and other raw emotions using quick icons. It's like a logo — it either succeeds or fails on first glance."

**THE CLIENT AND YOU**

Initial contact with a client usually starts with a phone call or e-mail from an art director. "By the time you hear from an art director, the client has probably already seen your work." Does the art director already

5.5

have a sketch or visual idea in mind? "Sometimes, but mostly not. If I'm doing magazine art, I probably get a copy of the article. If it's an ad, I might get the ad copy or they might send me the product. But the client usually relies on me to come up with a visual concept that relates to what they do."

## DEVELOPING QUALITY CONCEPTS

The art director is the client's one and only representative. To satisfy the client, you have to include the art director fully in the decision-making process. "Most problems occur when you don't involve the client enough. The last thing you want to do is surprise your client, like so many digital artists do. That usually happens when you take a concept and run with it on the computer before anybody but you has seen it.

"You can't just tie together a bunch of special effects and expect your artwork to sell. A good illustration is 90 percent concept and 10 percent execution. The concept has got to be strong. If you go to the computer right away, without completely developing the idea, you get 90 percent technique and 10 percent concept. That's simply not going to fly with high-end clients.

"It's really easy to take an idea too far, too fast, when you're working in a program like Photoshop. That's why I develop the concept with traditional pencil sketches. If I'm on a deadline, I sit down and force the sketches to work. If I have a week to come up with a concept, I sketch when I'm feeling creative. But as a rule, I avoid the computer altogether until the art director has signed off on the concept."

## THE IMPORTANCE OF COMMUNICATION

Much as we might like to hope that talent always wins, commercial art is a business like any other. The most successful artists are generally the ones who take the most care in securing and maturing personal relationships. Your ability to get work hinges on effective communication. "If you exclude art directors from the creative process, it can be a big strike against you, particularly if you've never worked with them before. You can almost guarantee that they're going to find things wrong. Whereas, if you get their input at the very beginning and you maintain good relationships, then you avoid surprises and get more

jobs in the future. Talk about the project up front. If you don't understand something at the beginning, feel free to ask dumb questions until you know who your client is and what he wants. Don't be nervous, don't feel like you have to apologize. Just patiently feel him out. Now you're working with the art director to get something that he can be comfortable with bringing to his client, and will fight for."

But accommodating your client doesn't mean you have to behave like a wimp. Mitsui advocates that you agree to a reasonable fee up front and stick to it. "The client signs a job estimate before I put pencil to paper for the first sketch. It's a standard contract that I and the others at Studio M D put together a few years back. The estimate is pretty much the exact fee, unless some special circumstances come along. I usually allow for a couple of rounds of revisions before I start charging hourly for anything beyond that. If you do good stuff, and you're predictable and reliable, then you'll always be in demand."

## ART ON THE MARCH

Mitsui's work for Advanced Medical Ventures probably illustrates the trials and rewards of creating computer art as well as any piece he's created. "It was an interesting job, all right." The assignment was to create a cover for a medical conference brochure. "The conference was about disorders of the upper stomach. The panelists at this conference were all leading experts in the field of digestive disorders. A bunch of other doctors who treat this illness were invited to come and participate in the audience. Everybody had a keyboard. They posed all questions and received consensus answers from the panelists. There was even going to be a satellite link to show operations beforehand. I can honestly say, it was unlike anything I had done before."

**Objective #1:** Define dyspepsia, appreciate its epidemiology and clinical significance, and understand the importance of dysomitility in its pathogenesis.

**Objective #2:** Understand the natural history of gastro-esphageal reflux disease (GERD), the importance of erosive compared to non-erosive esophagitis, and the complications of GERD.

5.6

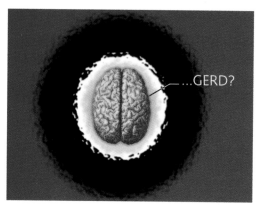

5.7

## MEDICAL OBJECTIVES AND INTESTINAL DIAGRAMS

"I didn't know anything about stomach disorders — you know, my stomach seems to be working okay — but I agreed to do the job because it sounded like it would be different. Then, the art director faxed me these two objectives that he wanted me to cover in the artwork (5.6). I don't usually get a list of objectives from a client — not like this, anyway. I looked them over, but for all I could tell, they were written in Greek."

Did the objectives imply that Mitsui should show GERD in action? Was he supposed to highlight the importance of understanding GERD? Or was his mission to produce the artwork while suffering the complications of GERD? Mitsui responds, "I see you have a sense of some of the questions that were going through my head (5.7). Part of the excitement and challenge of being an artist is that you learn so much. Even when you don't want to learn, you get to. It's quite thrilling."

So, how does Mitsui gain a clear understanding of a job when he embarks into such incredibly alien territory? Does he go to the library and search through a few medical encyclopedias? "No way. That might help me understand GERD, but it doesn't get me any closer to knowing the client. The only thing to do is talk and talk and talk to the art director. I ask every dumb question I can think of until I come across something I can work with. It's better to look like a dope up front than create an illustration that doesn't suit the client's needs."

To make things more interesting, the art director asked Mitsui to integrate some existing diagrams into his artwork. "He said, 'I'm going to totally leave the creative aspects up to you. But I have a couple of images that I want you to include in your illustration.' And then these intestinal tracts come through (5.8). I thought, whoa, these are pretty. I mean, what is that yellow thing back there? Did this guy swallow a whole cob of corn or something? What in the world am I going to do with this stuff?"

But the client is always right. Who knows, a couple of intestinal diagrams might provide the creative spark that Mitsui is looking for. "Whenever I have something weird like this, I always leave it until the last. That way, I can sit around and worry about it the whole time I'm working on the illustration. It provides motivation."

## SKETCH AND CONCEPT

"My personal objective in this project is to come up with a piece of artwork that looks cool and doesn't gross people out. In my first sketch (5.9), I had a little trouble focusing. I think it's Abe Lincoln in a lab coat surrounded by some fire. Even though I didn't use any of this, it was an important part of the process. When you're under a deadline, you don't have any choice. You have to work it out until you hit something that really works for you. For me, sketching is the best way to develop a concept.

"Then, I started brainstorming a little. I looked around the room, paged through books. At some point, I saw some clothes on a hanger, and it reminded me of this petroglyph (5.10). I read the petroglyph as a wire structure with these deelee-boppers hanging down from it, kind of like pots and pans. That's when the basic concept clicked. The body would be the frame, and the organs would hang inside it, like a primitive Visible Man."

With this concept in mind, Mitsui began to sketch in earnest. He quickly settled on a frontal view of the body with the head turned in profile. Then, he arranged a series of globes around the body (5.11). "The conference includes speakers and doctors from all over the world. So the globes demonstrate the international feel of the event.

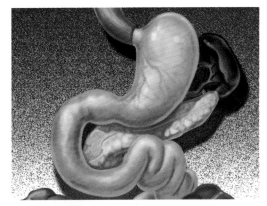

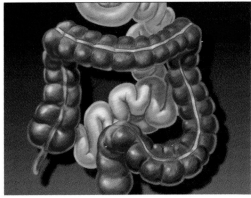

**5.8**

*Reprinted with permission from Advanced Medical Ventures. Artwork by Linda Nye.*

**5.9**

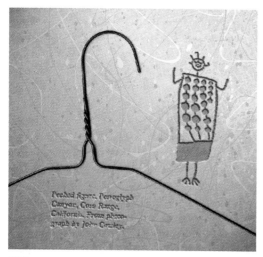

5.10

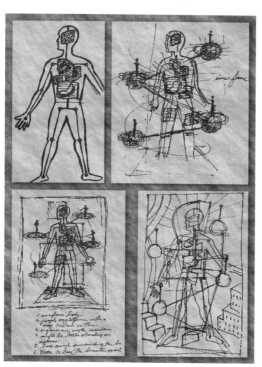

5.11

"As I sketch, I write myself little notes in the margins. These include little comments and ideas I want to remember, things I need clarification on, and questions that I have to ask the client. You have to make a real effort to stay on top of the client's needs. By keeping notes, I make sure I don't forget something that could gum up the works."

Mitsui's final sketch adds structure to the illustration (5.12). "The wireframe could look a little flimsy if I just stuck it against a neutral background. By adding some simple, block-like objects — the steps, the curtains, the books — I could convey depth without distracting attention from the primary element. It makes the sketch feel like a more substantial piece of artwork."

At this point, Glenn faxed his sketch to the art director for approval. "He signed off on it right away." Did the quick approval surprise Mitsui? "No, it was a solid concept. After working this long, I think I have a pretty good sense of whether I've nailed it or not. If I don't think I have it, I don't send it."

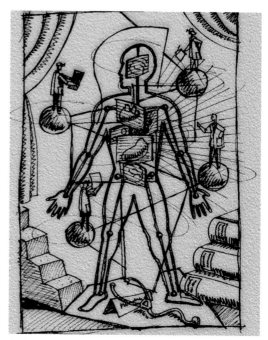

5.12

## TRACING THE SKETCH IN FREEHAND

After getting the sketch approved, Mitsui scanned it into Photoshop and scaled it to get the proper width and height dimensions. Then, he saved the sketch as a TIFF image and imported it into FreeHand. Inside FreeHand, Mitsui used the pen tool to trace the main outlines. As we'll see, these paths later served as template elements and selection outlines in Photoshop.

Mitsui likes FreeHand for its simplicity. "It's the 7-Eleven of graphics programs. If you need a Twinkie, you go to 7-Eleven, get in and get out. No one gets hurt. FreeHand is the same way. You get in, trace your paths, get out. No thinking necessary. I don't expect much from it, and it gives me very little in return."

I should mention that Mitsui is still using FreeHand 3.1, a program that was last seen in stores about four years ago. "Sure, it's old, but it's easy to use and it does everything I need it to. I can fly around and trace all the paths I need in 15 minutes or so. I don't think I even have the colors loaded anymore; I just use it in black and white."

## RASTERIZING AND TRACING IN PHOTOSHOP

"I saved the illustration in the Illustrator 3 format, because that's the best FreeHand 3.1 can do. Then, in Photoshop, I rasterized it at 300 pixels per inch. Since all the paths were black, I opened it as a grayscale image so it came up as fast as possible."

Mitsui had no intention of integrating the FreeHand drawing directly into his final artwork; it was merely an architectural template, cleaner and more precise than the original pencil sketch. And in Photoshop, the best place to put a template is in a separate channel. "I went to the Channels palette. Because it was a grayscale image, there was only one channel there. I duplicated it to a second channel and inverted it so it appeared white against black (5.13)."

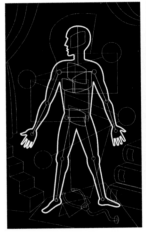   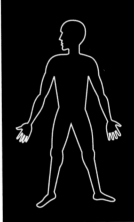

5.13                          5.14

Mitsui converted the file to the RGB mode and filled the RGB image with black to clear out the rasterized drawing. (The inverted template remained safe in the alpha channel.) He then returned to the alpha channel, now the fourth channel, and traced most of the template outlines with Photoshop's pen tool. "One of the things about using FreeHand 3.1 is that you can't bring the paths over directly. But that's okay. Tracing them again gives me the opportunity to further refine the drawing."

### MAKING THE BEVELED BODY OUTLINE

So Mitsui redraws every single path? "Not all of them. The outline of the body is something I used as is. I went back to the FreeHand file and copied the body path and pasted it into a file all by itself. Then, I brought that over as a fifth channel in my Photoshop image (5.14). This outline was thick enough to use as a mask all by itself."

The body outline was the first image element that Mitsui added to his illustration. He started by ⌘/Ctrl-clicking the fifth channel in the Channels palette to convert it into a selection outline. Then, he filled the selection with yellow (5.15). To add a beveled edge to the body outline (5.16), Mitsui relied

on the third-party Inner Bevel filter, which is part of the Eye Candy plug-in collection from Alien Skin Software. But he could have just as easily applied an Inner Bevel layer effect in Photoshop 5.0.

### ADDING THE BACKGROUND STUFF

Mitsui blocked in his background objects on separate layers using gradient fills and stock images. He started by creating red drapes in the upper left corner of the illustration (5.17). Each fold of the drapery is the result of converting one of his paths to a selection and then filling it with a red-to-black gradation. To make the soft blue drapes at the rear of his virtual auditorium (5.18), he imported a stock photo from the PhotoDisc image library. The floor of the stage (5.19) is a wood pattern that Mitsui shot himself. Like the red drapes, Mitsui created the green steps by converting paths to selection outlines and filling the selections with gradations.

No one can accuse Mitsui of being stingy with his gradient shadows. "My motto is simple. No shadow bad; plenty shadow good." But the astute viewer will notice that Mitsui plays fast and loose with his imaginary light source. "When my students tell me, 'Mr. Mitsui, your light source is inconsistent,' I just say, 'So?' Then they say, 'Your perspective is all screwy,' and I say, 'Yup.' I had my fill of paying attention to that kind of thing when I worked as a draftsman at

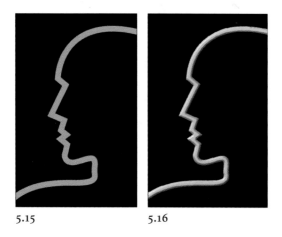

5.15                          5.16

5.17

Boeing. This is my world, darn it. Everybody else is just a nut trying to get a squirrel."

Was it possible Mitsui was inspired by French post-impressionist Paul Cézanne, who purposely violated perspective in order to focus on abstracted details in his artwork? "Oh, yeah, I'm big on violating stuff. But seriously, people don't come to me to create technically accurate illustrations. They're looking to me to create a mood and a feel and a dynamic."

## BINDING THE BOOKS

To highlight the scholarly nature of the conference, Mitsui's sketch called for books in the lower right corner of the artwork. He created the basic book shapes by reshaping and cloning elements from real books (5.20). But the bindings were generic hardcover fabric with no markings to identify them as medical volumes (5.21). The challenge was to take

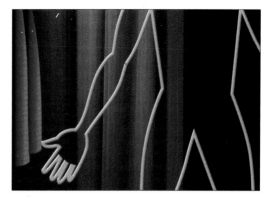

5.18

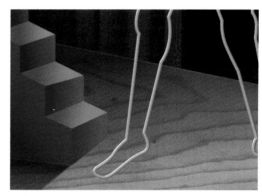

5.19

5.20

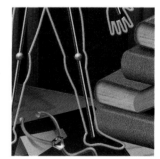

5.21

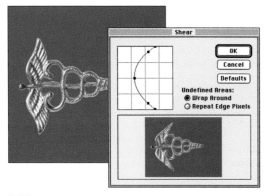

**5.22**

**5.23**

**5.24**

**5.25**

words such as Anatomy and Physiology and wrap them onto the curved spines of the books.

"Filter ➤ Distort ➤ Shear is great for faking 3-D effects. Here, I used the Shear filter to distort the text and medical emblem horizontally (5.22) so they appeared to bend around the sides of the books. Then, I just rotated the elements to match the angle of the spines (5.23). I used to do this kind of stuff in Ray Dream Designer, but now I totally avoid 3-D programs. I never did enjoy working in Ray Dream or any of them."

### CREATING THE GLOBES

For each of his four globes, Mitsui started with a small, square scrap from a scanned map (5.24). Then he applied the Glass Lens Bright filter from Kai's Power Tools 2 to wrap a circular area of the map around a 3-D sphere (5.25). "I bet I could've come up with something similar using the Spherize filter that's included with Photoshop, and layering on a couple of radial gradations. But some of those simple KPT filters are really useful."

Mitsui wanted to colorize each globe with a different hue, so he converted the globe to a grayscale image. Then, he indexed the color palette using Image ➤ Mode ➤ Indexed Color. This permitted him to modify the palette using Image ➤ Mode ➤ Color Table. "When you choose the Color Table command, Photoshop lets you edit all 256 colors in the indexed palette (5.26). I just dragged across all the colors in the palette. Then, Photoshop asked me to specify the darkest color in the table and the lightest color. I set them both to shades of blue. Then, Photoshop automatically blended between them (5.27)."

Why not use the Hue/Saturation command? "I don't feel like I have enough control over the process with that command. The ramping between light and dark colors is uneven. As a result, the colors tend to get too hot, and an image like this might start to band. With the Color Table command, I can precisely control the tonal range of colors in one fell swoop." After colorizing each globe, Mitsui selected it with the elliptical marquee tool and dragged it over into his composition (5.28).

## HANGING THE INTERNAL ORGANS

"So here I am, almost done with the job. One of the last things I have to do is insert the organs into the artwork. I've put it off as long as I can (5.29).

"By now, I've already decided that I'm going to frame the organs inside slanted viewing screens which will hang from the frame that I've set up inside the body. But I'm still a little nervous about integrating the client's images. These doctors are used to seeing internal organs. But it's up to me to make the artwork palatable to a general audience. I don't want some older couple to walk by the conference room and run away screaming when they see the artwork."

To get a feel for how the organs were going to work, Mitsui started with one of the more enlightened representatives, the brain (5.30). "The brain is another PhotoDisc image. This is one of those cases where I really have to rely on a stock image. I can't walk outside and say, 'Excuse me, could I, uh, saw your head open? It'll only be for a minute. I have some twine here to tie things back up when we're through.' That's just not going to cut it."

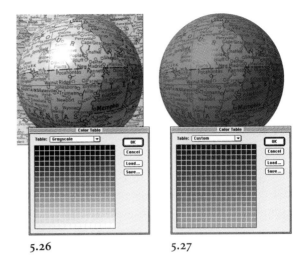

5.26          5.27

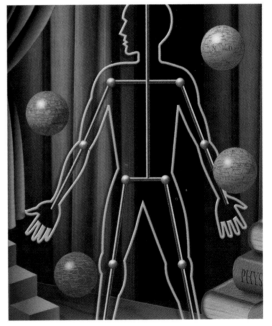

5.28

5.29

Reprinted with permission from Advanced Medical Ventures. Artwork by Linda Nye.

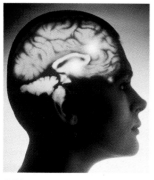

5.30

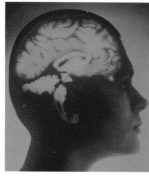

5.31

5.32

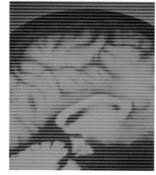

5.33

Mitsui converted the brain to grayscale and colored it green using the Color Table trick described earlier (5.31). "I wanted to simulate the look of those old-style green-and-black monitors." To create the effect of interlaced screen lines, Mitsui opened the green brain inside Fractal Design Painter, which offers better texturing capabilities than Photoshop. He selected a horizontal line pattern included in Painter's Art Materials palette (5.32). Then, he applied it to the brain as a paper texture (5.33). (This effect is not impossible to perform in Photoshop, it's just harder. You'd have to load the pattern into a separate alpha channel and apply it as a texture map using the Lighting Effects filter.)

After saving the brain out of Painter, Mitsui opened it up again in Photoshop and copied it to the Clipboard. Then, he returned to his medical composition and selected the path that traced around the outline of the monitor inside the head. He converted the path to a selection and chose Edit ➢ Paste Into to paste the green brain inside. Then, he slanted the brain to match the angle of the monitor using Edit ➢ Transform ➢ Skew (5.34).

"To give the monitors some depth, I beveled the edges with the Alien Skin filter. That didn't always produce the effect I was looking for, so I hand-brushed in a couple of highlights and shadows along the edges of the paths. Then, I hit each monitor with the Lens Flare filter to create a little reflection on the screen (5.35)."

5.34

5.35

Mitsui performed the same steps on the other organs with one exception. "I colored the main stomach image orange to set it off from the others (5.36)." Did the client have any problem with Mitsui de-emphasizing the organs by framing them inside monitors? "No, they loved it. I think they understood that it was a modern treatment of the subject that tied in well to the conference angle. You have these little doctor figures analyzing the big body and commenting on the screens. It's like he's their virtual patient."

We imagine the conference organizers were proud indeed to display this piece on the cover of their handouts. It establishes a bold and authoritative mood for the event from the outset, before a word is spoken on stage. The illustration tastefully introduces the topic at hand, explains the relationship between the experts and international attendees, highlights the role of technology at the event, and delivers the scene inside a lush and palpable diorama. Every need satisfied according to plan. This is one conference where the artist will get invited back.

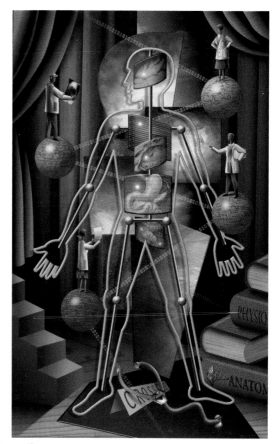

5.36

# CHAPTER 6
# WORKING STOCK PHOTOGRAPHY INTO GRAPHIC ART

There's a certain tiresome machismo associated with owning big, expensive computer gadgetry. When guys brag about their big disk arrays and their monster memory upgrades, I have to excuse myself and visit the little boy's room. Like everybody else out there, I fully admit that I personally have far too much capital sunk into my machinery, but it's because I can't manage to get by on less, not because I derive any pleasure from owning excessive equipment. I'm one of those crusty old codgers who still remembers fondly how I wrote, designed, and laid out my first book on a Mac 512Ke with two 400K floppy drives and no hard disk. Sure, I lived in a state of perpetual digital torment, but I was too young and stupid to know any better. The fact is, computers are like a sick addiction; we can't seem to live without them, but it's unbecoming to take pride in our depraved predicaments.

Refreshingly, professional illustrator Gordon Studer represents the other extreme. He proves that you can make a living with Photoshop without making the slightest attempt to keep up with the Joneses. Until recently, Studer got by with a Quadra — roughly equivalent to a 486 PC — equipped with 16MB of RAM and a 200MB hard drive. When I first wrote this several months after the release of Photoshop 4, Studer was making due with Version 2.5, which, as veteran devotees may recall, lacks layers. He even used a Zip cartridge as a scratch disk. Studer admitted this might not be the wisest solution in the world. "An Adobe representative came up to me once and said, 'You can't tell people that. They're going to

*The idea is to strip the forms down to their bare minimum and play with unrelated abstractions inside the forms. If the photograph wasn't there to identify the image, it would break down into a bunch of concentric squares.*

GORDON STUDER

destroy their computers!' But I've been doing it for about two years and I haven't had any problems."

What was Studer doing with his wee system? Creating illustrations that blend his primitive, whimsical style with volumes of royalty-free stock photography and occasional 35mm snapshots. Therefore, Studer's economical system matched his economical approach. "The funny thing is, I get nearly all my images from maybe a dozen PhotoDisc and Adobe CDs. I get my faces from 'Retro Americana' and 'Beyond Retro' (6.1) and my hands from a collection called 'Just Hands.' The 'Retro' collections are wildly popular, but the way I use the photos, no one even recognizes where they come from. I combine a man's head with a woman's eye and another guy's mouth. Then I carve them into simple geometric shapes (6.2). I use the same photos over and over again, but no one tells me, 'Man, I'm getting tired of that image.' All they see is the artwork."

6.1

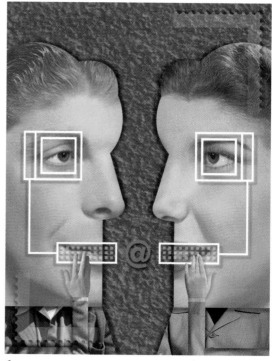

6.2

**ARTIST:**
Gordon Studer

**STUDIO:**
1576 62nd Street
Emeryville, California 94608
510/655-4256
gstuder363@aol.com

**SYSTEM:**
*When this chapter was first written:*
Quadra 840AV
200MB storage
*Now:*
Power Mac G3/266
6GB storage

**RAM:**
*When this chapter was first written:*
16MB total
8MB assigned to Photoshop
*Now:*
96MB total
60MB assigned to Photoshop

**MONITOR:**
Apple 17-inch

**EXTRAS:**
Microtek 300-dpi scanner, PhotoDisc and
Adobe Image Library royalty-free images

**VERSION USED:**
*When this chapter was first written:*
Photoshop 2.5.1
*Now:*
Photoshop 5.0

You can test Studer's hypothesis by trying to spot a separate illustration printed later in this chapter that repeats one of the stock photographs shown here. As you'll discover, the simple act of modifying the shape of the face lends the revised subject its own distinct appearance.

## IS IT ETHICAL?

Some might take exception to an artist who makes a living off repurposing a small collection of photographs. Setting aside the fact that the illustrations in this chapter are stylistically unique — being both compositionally and creatively independent of the photographs that populate them — Studer makes ethical use of what is generally accepted to be an ethical system of distribution. A reputable multiuse image dealer such as PhotoDisc or Digital Stock pays its photographers royalties based on how many copies of a CD it sells. Digital Stock estimates that its photographers earn on average $50,000 in the first year for a collection of 100 images — a figure that exceeds the average per-person royalties paid out by traditional stock agencies.

As an artist who likewise relies on royalties for a chunk of my income, I would argue that Studer's repeated use of an image is no less scrupulous than you making repeated use of a technique that you learn in this book. It is exceedingly important to observe codes of professional behavior, but it is equally important to evaluate new practices with an open mind. Otherwise, digital manipulation makes pirates and scalawags of us all.

## THE TREND TOWARD STOCK PHOTOGRAPHY

Studer's reliance on stock photography is a fairly recent phenomenon. "I made a whole style change about three years ago. Prior to that, I was doing really graphic stuff with sharp lines and abstract forms (6.3). But I grew tired of the fact that everything was so flat. So I started to experiment with textured patterns and designs. To avoid the computer look, I scanned in photographic textures and dropped them inside my basic shapes. It was like I had wrapped my artwork in a series of fabric coatings, giving the shapes a richness they didn't have before (6.4).

**OTHER APPLICATIONS:**
Adobe Illustrator, Adobe After Effects

**WORK HISTORY:**
1978 — After deciding football wasn't going to pan out, took up fine arts at Penn State.

1983 — Studied at Corchrain School of Arts; got job as paste-up artist and spot illustrator for Red Tree Associates.

1988 — Left *Oakland Tribune* for *San Francisco Examiner*; was introduced to Illustrator and computer design.

1990 — Created first piece for *MacWeek* "MacInTouch" column, which continued every week for seven years.

1994 — Shifted artistic style from high-contrast graphics to stock photo collage.

1998 — Took up After Effects, illustrated children's book about cats.

**FAVORITE WORKING WARDROBE:**
Bathrobe ("I got a new one and I just love it.")

6.3

6.4

6.5                                          6.6

"About this same time, I was playing around with deconstructing my artwork, reducing it to stark 'circle-head' characters (6.5). It was successful with my editorial clients, but the corporate and ad people were turned off. It was just too weird for them. Then I hit on something that really surprised me. If that same weird shape was filled with a photograph (6.6), no one seemed to have a problem with it. The client was able to make the jump. It was like the photograph identified the face as a person instead of a space alien. Then I was free to do whatever I wanted with the outline.

"To keep things interesting, I believe in making a stylistic shift every three or four years. Right now, I'm working on another shift. I'm trying to push the geometry of the shapes even further. For example, I have this one image that's cut out into completely abstract forms that don't even vaguely resemble a head outline (6.7). The idea is to strip the forms down to their bare minimum and play with unrelated abstractions inside the forms. If the photograph wasn't there to identify the image, it would break down into a bunch of concentric squares." From Studer's work of simple abstraction, the photo extends a fragile thread that touches the real world.

## GORDONIAN GEOMETRY

"I have two ways I work. One is really geometric — all right angles and circles. Another is more free-form with random cutouts. The illustration I made for Coca-Cola (6.8) is an example of the geometric look. Normally, when you think geometry, you think precision and order. But here, it's a complete abstraction. Nothing in real life is this exact, so the geometry takes you farther away from the real world."

6.7

6.8

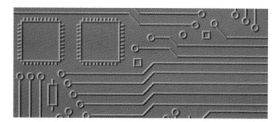

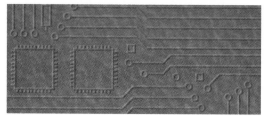

**6.9** (TOP), **6.10** (MIDDLE), **6.11** (BOTTOM)

6.12

6.13

## MIXING STATIC BACKDROPS

"Because I'm working without layers, I have to start at the back of the image and work my way forward. So I always lay in the background first." For the Coca-Cola illustration, Studer rendered a circuit board pattern he created in Illustrator and applied the Emboss filter inside Photoshop (6.9). Then he opened a cork texture (6.10), copied the circuit board, and pasted it on top. To merge the two images, he applied the Luminosity blend mode and set the Opacity to 50 percent (6.11).

Studer frequently wallpapers his artwork with static, textured backgrounds. "The cork and chip patterns are good examples. I use these backgrounds, or slight variations on them, in a lot of my work. Like I might colorize the cork brown in one image (6.12) and blue in another (6.13). The idea is to set up similar worlds, so each illustration feels like a room inside the same home."

## THE CENTRAL STOCK SUBJECT

"After the background, I lay in the big forms. Usually that's the face, because I like to work everything off the main head in the image (6.14). I always start with a grayscale image. Even if it's in color, I make it

### ALIGNING VECTOR ART WITH IMAGERY

Aligning an object-oriented pattern such as Studer's circuit board with a face (6.13) or other image can be a tricky matter. Except for scaling, rotating, and the like, you can't edit the pattern in Photoshop, so it's important to nail the alignment in Illustrator or FreeHand. "Before I create the pattern, I save a 72-ppi version of the Photoshop image as an EPS file. Then in Illustrator, I choose Place Art, which gives me a template for how the photographic part is laying out. I can draw the circle exactly around the eyeball or the chip around the mouth. I even have a little circle around the nostril. Then I delete the template, save the illustration, and import it into Photoshop."

grayscale. Then I convert the image to RGB and colorize it, as opposed to trying to make it look realistic (6.15). The colorizing reminds me of the way I used to work — with pure flat-color fills. Sometimes I add stylized highlights like rosy cheeks, but only to reaffirm the retro look. The images don't seem like photographs to me; they're more like scraps of color. I like to think of a face as just a big piece of yellow."

Studer's colorizing isn't the vanilla Hue/Saturation type. It's really more of a duotone effect, with hues ranging from yellow to red. "I use the Variations command to saturate the image with yellows and reds. In this case, I selected the Midtones radio button and nudged the slider bar toward Coarse. Then I clicked twice on the Yellow thumbnail and twice on Red (6.16). It's way easier than creating a real duotone, and it gets me the hyper-saturated colors I'm looking for. Awhile back, Glenn Mitsui showed me a trick where he gets a similar effect by indexing the image and modifying the color table (see Chapter 5). But I don't know — that seems like more work."

6.14 (TOP), 6.15 (BOTTOM)

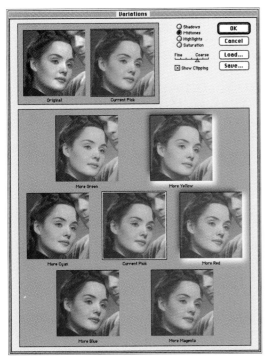

6.16

6.17                          6.18

To define the shape of the head, Studer superimposed a globe illustration he created in Illustrator. He filled the artwork with white (⌘/Ctrl+Shift+Delete in Photoshop 5) and dropped it on the woman's face (6.17). Then he lowered the Opacity to 50 percent to merge globe and face into one element (6.18).

### ADDING THE COMPUTER

"I have a small collection of computer pictures that I use over and over (6.19). All of them come from photos I shot myself. For a really brief period of time, I had a $20,000 Kodak digital camera on loan. I just went hog wild with it — I tried to photograph as many things as I could. Then I cut and pasted pieces of the monitors and computers to get a more stylized look. There's a geometric monitor, an orthogonal one, and another that's really irregular. I also colorized the images, airbrushed in shadows, and did whatever it took to convert the computers from photographs to graphics."

### COMPOSITION AND DROP SHADOWS

After selecting the least dimensional of his monitors, Studer copied the head and monitor and pasted each one at a time against his background (6.20). "You can see even in the early composition how I'm using simple geometry. The head's a circle, the monitor comes in at 90 degrees. The head is vertically centered on the background, and the green screen of the monitor is exactly centered with respect to the head.

"As each element goes in, I give it a drop shadow. Everyone has a method for making shadows, and whatever yours is, I'm sure it's as good as mine. I'm just going for the basics — feathered edges, black fill. When I add a shadow, it's not intended to convey perspective. I want it to look like I cut out a bunch of photographs and laid them on top of the background (6.21)."

6.19

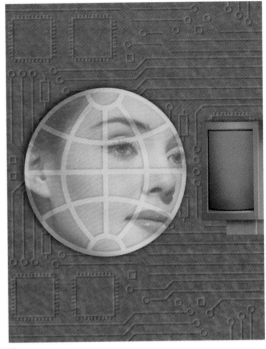

6.20

6.21

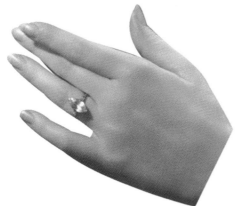

6.22 (TOP), 6.23 (MIDDLE), 6.24 (BOTTOM)

## THE ANATOMICALLY PRECISE HAND

Second only to faces in Studer's stock photo library are hands. For the Coca-Cola illustration, Studer wanted to add a single hand operating the keyboard. After finding a stock hand that fit his needs (6.22), he colorized it with the Variations command. "I can basically replay the last colorization I applied by pressing the Option/Alt key when I choose the Variations command. If the lighting isn't quite the same, I might have to tweak the settings a little, but usually it only takes a couple of seconds to get it dead on."

Instead of cutting the hand into an abstract shape, Studer carefully selects each and every finger (6.23). "You can't abstract hands the way you can faces. Fingers make hands what they are. Besides, I like the way the detailed treatment of the hands plays off the simple geometry of the head." Studer retouched away the ring by cloning from the third finger. Then he flipped and rotated the hand so it rested on top of the keyboard, detached from the body without even a hint of arm. "Again, the hand sits at a right angle (6.24). Despite the detailing, I have to make it conform to the geometry of the overall illustration."

## THE FINAL ADJUSTMENTS

"To make that alternating yellow/black accent across the top of the art (6.25), I just create a black square, a yellow square, and clone them over and over again. Of course, I never hit it right on, so I leave a big gap at the end and fill it with red." What is the purpose of this accent? "I've used that pattern since day one, and I have no idea why. No sense questioning it — it just is."

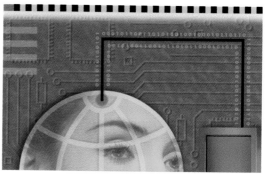

6.25

At this point, the image was ready to send off to the client. But as any working artist knows, the job doesn't necessarily end when you turn in the artwork. "The first image (6.8) is the one I submitted. But the art director had me make a bunch of last-minute changes. He had me change the body — it was too pointy — and he had me flip-flop the entire image. He also wanted me to add a little Coke bottle cap at the top of the forehead (6.26)."

Whenever a client dictates modifications to an illustration, there's a chance for damage. The smallest changes can upset a hearty aesthetic balance and send it teetering headlong into a pile of digital goop. "My biggest concern was the flip. I've had so many images where you flip them and they don't look right at all; everything seems off. But because this one was so geometric, it survived pretty well." I guess if your face can tolerate the occasional mirror image as you comb your hair in the morning, a face in a circle can hold up to reflection as well.

## FREE-FORM IMAGE CHOPPING

Not all of Studer's images adhere to strict geometric guidelines. Many of his illustrations deliberately shun order in favor of chaos, with carefully clipped cutouts jockeying for attention inside crowded compositions. In an image he did for *CIO* magazine, the assignment was to show a cat working at a computer while his previous lives look on (6.27). "I had to take this one cat and create a bunch of different variations on him. It gave me the opportunity to focus on one element at a time, completely out of context with the others." Studer carved his subjects into human forms, some resembling cartoon skulls, others suggestive of Jimmy Durante in profile.

6.26

6.27

"The cats are mine. I just shot them with my camera, went down to a one-hour delivery place, and scanned them (6.28). In Photoshop, I cut and paste the cats into basic arrangements of faces and fur. Then I used the pen tool to shave the cats into the cartoon shapes (6.29)."

**ROUGH PIXELS INSIDE SMOOTH OUTLINES**

"The resolution of my original photographs was more or less awful. I had to sample them up and sharpen them to get them the way they look in the finished artwork." Is increasing the resolution a wise idea? "If I was working with a flat photograph, probably not. But I've got all kinds of elements coming in at different resolutions. Maybe I'm more cavalier than I ought to be, but I just scale things as I need them. I know I can always deal with any softness or graininess later.

"Besides, I don't think people read a piece of artwork one element at a time; they see the whole piece together, even when it's an obvious composition. The fact that the pen tool edges are nice and sharp makes the entire image look in focus. I've never had a client complain about the resolution or softness of my art."

**CACOPHONY OF KITTIES**

As before, Studer built his composition off a single image. This time, it was the computer-capable cat in the lower right corner (6.30). But with no layers at his disposal, Studer was cautious not to go too far too quickly. "I put the bodies in first, because the placement was so tricky. After I got the bodies arranged the way I wanted them, I put in the arms and tails (6.31).

"It was a challenge to get all those cats arranged properly. As I positioned each cat body, I just had to hope that I was making the right decisions. Squeezing that last cat in there was the toughest. I specified in my rough that I was going to do nine cats — for each of the nine lives — but it didn't quite fit. I had to call the art director and say, 'Is it okay if he still has a life left? He's still alive; there he is working. I'd hate to think he could get, like, electrocuted and then drop off for good.' I don't think anyone quite bought my argument, but they gave me a break. So eight cats it is."

**HAS PHOTOSHOP 5 RUINED GORDON?**

Since this chapter was first published, Studer's world has transformed dramatically. He now uses a G3 Power Mac equipped with a 6GB hard drive and 96MB of RAM. He's taken up digital video editing with After Effects. And, yes, he's using Photoshop 5.

6.28

6.29

**6.30**                              **6.31**

**6.32**

The blame must be laid at the feet of Russell Brown, one of Adobe's creative directors and a member of the Photoshop development team. "Russell invited me to an Adobe training event in Santa Fe  and talked me into buying a new computer and getting Photoshop 5. I still own my old machine, and I still use Photoshop 2.5 occasionally. But I spend most of my time now in Version 5."

Is that a good thing? "You know, I think it is. It's made a huge difference in the way I work. I used to have to be so organized. I had to dissect the image from back to front and figure out exactly how it was going to lay out. Now, I just start dumping in images — 40 or 50 layers — and then clean it up from there. I used to work with 8MB images, now they grow to 150MB. You'd think that would slow me down, but it doesn't. I'm working faster than ever."

Layers have also permitted Studer to experiment with new techniques. "Instead of cutting just one face into a shape, now I can merge multiple faces into one (6.32). I might take the eyes from one image and the nose from another. I also have more flexibility when experimenting with color and positioning. I feel like I'm much more versatile. I can throw stuff together that before would have been a nightmare."

What about multiple undos? Do they come in handy? "The undos really help. I talk to artists who have been upgrading Photoshop all along, and they act like they've come up with ways to avoid any need for multiple undos by using layers. But since I came across layers and multiple undos at the same time, I use them both. Constantly."

6.33

Such a huge leap forward must be downright life-changing. "You wouldn't believe it. I have so much less stress, I feel like I sleep better. When my clients want changes, it's no problem. I don't have to save a million versions of my artwork to Zip files. I can keep it all together in one file."

After so much modernization, does Studer have any plans to abandon the retro images in favor of newer material? "Oh, no. If anything, I'm getting more retro than ever. Right now, I'm using After Effects to create movies featuring these '40s and '50s characters (6.33). I still use the abstracted forms, but now they're moving. It carries the abstraction one step farther. It adds another layer of realism and depth, where all I really have are these simple shapes."

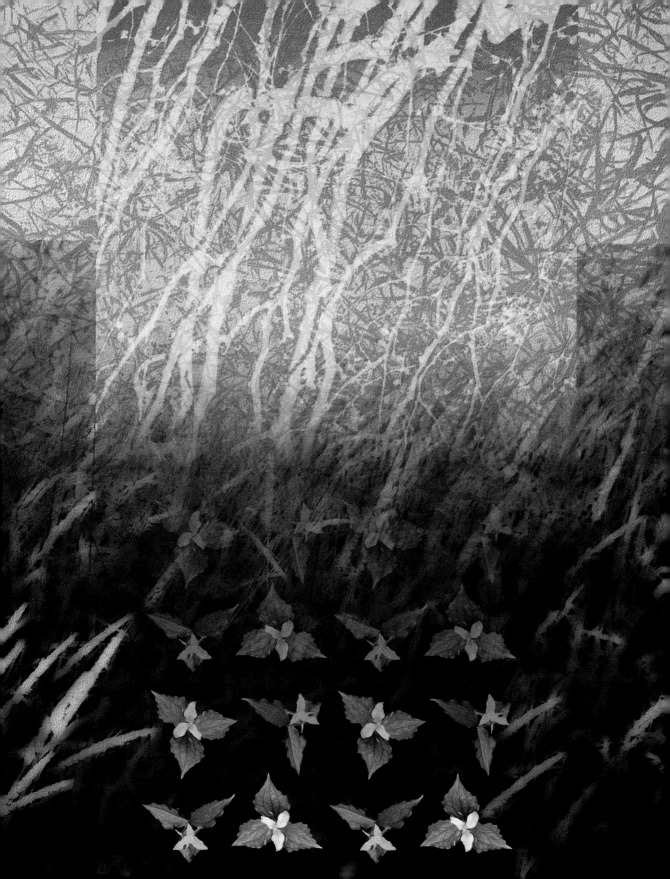

# CHAPTER 7
# FINE ART PRINTING

For a typical commercial artist working in print media, the goal is to create a piece of artwork that the client can reproduce hundreds, thousands, or even millions of times. Computers are perfect for this purpose, because they permit you to create camera-ready files that include lots of different elements and layers, eliminating the need for fragile mechanicals and expensive stat-camera composites. When the artist hands off the finished Photoshop file to an art director or client, the file includes all elements fully intact. All the production designer has to do is convert the image to CMYK, slap it on a page, and send it to the printer.

But not all artists design for mass-market output. Consider the case of fine artist Karin Schminke, a cofounder of the loose-knit Unique Editions. ("We're really just five independent artists who have come together to form a support group.") As the name of the organization implies, Schminke and her colleagues create one-of-a-kind artwork, suitable for framing and hanging on the wall. For Schminke, the electronic files are just approximations of the effect she wants to achieve. The final physical, tangible paper output is the stuff that really counts.

In Schminke's world, a color ink-jet printer is just another tool in her paint box, one that she can mix freely with other media. Obviously, she can't paint onto the paper while she's printing, nor can she attach a brush to the printer head, so she does the next best thing — she applies her elements in passes. She frequently starts with a layer of acrylics or other media, prints a lightened version of an image over the dried acrylic, paints in a few areas, prints over a few

*With Photoshop, you can bring together elements of printmaking, painting, and photography in ways that you couldn't have before.*

KARIN SCHMINKE

other areas, and so on until the artwork takes on the look of a finished piece.

"Before I started printing my own art, I looked at what I was getting on the monitor and made decisions based on that. The screen was the determining factor. But once I got involved in the output process, it started to reflect back on the decisions that I made while I was working in the image. There's no longer a break where I'm done creating the artwork and it's time to print. It all blends together. Now the printing reflects on everything I do — down to the way I shoot the original photo. And obviously, everything I do affects the print." For Schminke, the printer is a full-fledged element in the creative process, not just a machine that churns out the finished piece. The result is an interactive continuum that weaves Photoshop so tightly into the fabric of the fine art tradition that it's often impossible to tell a computer was involved at all (7.1).

7.1

**ARTIST:**
Karin Schminke

**ORGANIZATION:**
Unique Editions
425/402-8606
*http://www.schminke.com*
kschminke@schminke.com

**SYSTEM:**
Intergraph ExtremeZ
13GB storage

**RAM:**
535MB total
50 percent assigned to Photoshop

**MONITOR:**
Intergraph 21-inch

**EXTRAS:**
CalComp Drawing Slate tablet
Epson Expression 836 scanner
CalComp TechJet 175i MX wide-format
printer, Encad NovaJet Pro50

**VERSION USED:**
Photoshop 5.0

**OTHER APPLICATIONS:**
Fractal Design Painter, Macromedia xRes,
Adobe Illustrator

## THE MESSY WORLD OF MIXED MEDIA

At this moment in time, Schminke's digital tools are an Epson Expression 836 scanner, an Olympus D-600L camera, Photoshop, and a 36-inch-wide CalComp TechJet 175i ink-jet printer. Her printing stock includes watercolor paper, specially prepared ink-jet canvas, and Stonehenge cotton rag paper — all available commercially. She paints with just about any media she can get her hands on, including acrylics, pastels, diluted glue for sizing, and photo-sensitive pigments (7.2).

Schminke contends that by mixing digital and traditional media, she can expand her color gamut and achieve subtle variations in hue and saturation that you simply can't achieve with CMYK inks on their own. She achieves her effects by printing on top of painted media, painting on top of printed ink, and even double-striking — that is, printing the same image twice in a row to burn in the inks and give them greater depth and range.

Obviously, it's a tricky and unscientific process; one that requires repeated inspection, testing, reflection, and a fair amount of old-fashioned creative brooding. Because she's working with traditional media, it's possible to reach a point of no return. Schminke freely admits that she's failed — or at least dead-ended — at an effect that isn't altogether successful and had to start over. It's a risk you take when you work in the real world bereft of an Undo command, but it offers its share of unique rewards. And Schminke for one wouldn't have it any other way.

7.2

**WORK HISTORY:**

<u>1979</u> — Learned BASIC computer language in University of Iowa graduate MFA program.

<u>1985</u> — Developed and taught first computer graphics course at University of Wisconsin, Eau Claire.

<u>1987</u> — First exhibition of digital artwork at Wisconsin ArtsWest, a juried fine art exhibition.

<u>1994</u> — Switched emphasis to fine art and cofounded Unique Editions.

<u>1997</u> — Participated as artist in residence at Smithsonian's National Museum of American Art.

**FAVORITE U.S. NATIONAL PARK:**
Olympic National Forest, west of Seattle. ("It's got everything.")

7.3                    7.4                    7.5

7.6

7.7

## PAINTING AND PRINTING, PRINTING AND PAINTING

The best way to get a feel for what Schminke is up to is to watch her work. Through electronic files, process snapshots, and finished artwork, we'll observe Schminke in her studio creating a piece from beginning to end.

### CREATING THE SUBIMAGE

For starters, Schminke created the *subimage*, which is the underlying photographic composition that serves as a backdrop and foundation for her piece *Mountain Meadow*. After scanning two of her photographic images to Photo CD — mountains (7.3) and sea foam (7.4) — she layered the second image on top of the first. Then she inverted the sea layer and applied the Overlay blend mode from the Layers palette. Finally, she duplicated the sea layer and reduced the Opacity to exaggerate the color and bring out additional details (7.5). As you can see, the

mountains and trees from the bottom layer are clearer in the composite than they are in the original.

### PRINTING THE SUBIMAGE

Schminke decided to create her artwork on rag paper with deckled edges. "It's a rough, natural edge that comes from pulling the paper off the screen during the paper-making process." To bleed all the way beyond the last fibers in the deckled edges, Schminke taped an acetate strip to either side. "I used double-stick tape to paste the acetate to the bottom of the paper. The printer can only print so close to the edges of the media. So the acetate exaggerates the width of the page and allows me to print over the edges."

Schminke ran the 30 × 42 inch paper through the CalComp printer (7.6) to output the completed subimage (7.7). It's interesting to notice the difference in color between the Photoshop file (7.5) and the printed image (7.7). Likely the result of calibration issues, the inherent gamut of the printer, and the off-white color of the paper, these are conditions to which every artist has to adapt and work around. "Unexpected color shifts in the prints are just a part of the process. I calibrate enough to control them within an acceptable range, then I make the most of the results."

After stripping the acetate away from the deckled edges (7.8), Schminke applied a layer of protective fixative. "I usually go ahead and apply some kind of spray-on fixative, although I'm not entirely convinced that it works. I put on several coats hoping they'll retard the bleeding of the inks into other media. It helps a little, but it doesn't altogether stop the problem."

## CREATING THE INSET IMAGE

Now for the next layer in the traditional media stack — the inset superimage. Schminke created a square composition in Photoshop that features two elks (7.9) layered on top of a leafless tree (7.10). To make the branches work as a framing device, she swapped the left and right halves of the tree. When viewed on its own (7.11), the composition is rather crude, with an obvious seam down the middle. But the seam will disappear when printed onto the final artwork. "With enough experience, you learn what will output and what won't."

## A GOLD BACKGROUND FOR THE INSET IMAGE

Schminke wanted the inset image to occupy a square area in the center of the artwork. But if she had simply overprinted the image, it would have blotted out the artwork below it and turned it into a muddy mess. So Schminke applied an underpainting to distinguish the inset image from its background.

After laying down masking tape to block out a square in the artwork, Schminke applied a coating of gold acrylic paint (7.12). "The paint isn't entirely even or opaque. It's kind of a shimmering gold — just enough to set off the inset image from the subimage, so the two mix together while remaining independently identifiable."

7.8

7.9 (TOP), 7.10 (MIDDLE), 7.11 (BOTTOM)

## TESTING THE OVERPRINT WITH ACETATE

"By the time I invest all this effort in the background, I get a little paranoid about printing directly onto the artwork and messing it up. So I'll print onto acetate and use that to mock up the image (7.13). Even though the colors are a lot different than they'll appear in the final artwork, the acetate helps me to determine scale, positioning, and get at least a feel for the color."

The acetate was also helpful for determining the amount of ink to apply to the final overprinting. "I wanted the elk to appear somewhat 'illusionistic.' You have to look just right to see them — look away and they're gone, just like real wildlife." Schminke ended up lightening the image a few notches with the Curves command to get the desired effect.

## OVERPRINTING THE INSET IMAGE

When overprinting one image onto another — particularly when a shimmering gold acrylic square is involved — registration has to be right on. Naturally, Schminke uses Photoshop's Canvas Size command to make sure that the images are the same physical size and resolution. But she also has to be careful that the paper is registered properly as it feeds through the printer.

7.12

"Every printer has something that you can use as an alignment marker. On my CalComp, it's the clamps that hold the paper in place. When I put the paper in for the first time, I make sure to draw little pencil marks on the sides of the artwork by the edges of the clamps. Then when I reinsert the paper for a second or third pass, I can make sure that the paper is properly aligned.

"In the case of *Mountain Meadow*, I also had to make sure the inset image filled the gold square. In Photoshop, I sized the inset image so it was about a half-inch taller and wider than the square. And I left the masking tape in place as I printed the image. When I stripped off the masking tape, the registration was perfect (7.14)."

7.14

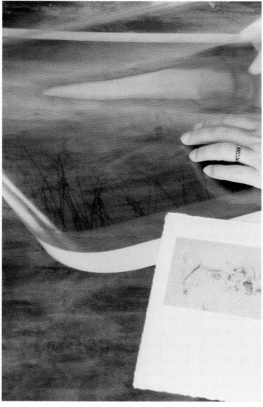

7.13

7.15

7.16

Doesn't Schminke run the risk of peeling off paint and ink as she removes the tape? "I'm pretty careful, so it's not usually a problem. But if I do get a little crack or something, I'm mixing so many media that it's easy to go in and touch up the mistakes." Clearly, there are advantages to having traditional tools lying around.

### PRINTING ON BLACK

The vast majority of commercial art is printed on white paper. Every once in a while, you might come across a flier output on some fluorescent parchment, but most designers regard colored stock with about as much enthusiasm as a school teacher grading a writing assignment on purple notebook paper.

Again, fine artists buck the trend. "Recently, I got this idea that I wanted to print on black paper." Offhand, this sounds like a formula for disappointment, particularly given that ink-jet printers apply translucent colors. In other words, the printer can darken the paper, but it can never lighten it. The solution, then, is to create an opaque underpainting and print on top of that.

**PAINTING ONTO A PRINTED TEMPLATE**

"I started with a photograph of some lily pads that I brushed and combined with two other photos inside Macromedia xRes (7.15). Then I increased the contrast of the image inside Photoshop and printed it onto black rag paper (7.16). The printout wasn't super colorful, of course, but I could see it well enough to use it as a template. Then I painted over the image with acrylics to create the color underpainting (7.17).

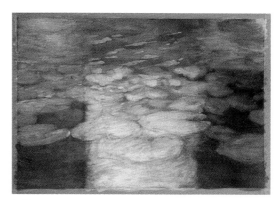

**PRINTING ONTO ACRYLIC**

"Now, at this point, I should say that if you're going to print on top of acrylic, you need to put some sort of coating over it. A company called StellaColor makes a precoat that you can paint onto anything, and it provides a surface to accept the ink-jet dot. Without it, the ink would simply smear across the acrylic."

After applying the coating, Schminke ran the paper through the printer again, overprinting the same image she had applied before (7.18). "Painting an image over itself and then printing on top of that — it's obviously a lot of work. But I was able to come up with a much different image while at the same time maintaining a consistent theme. It's a good demonstration of how you can take an image and greatly alter it by experimenting with the output. Better still, I sold the piece immediately, and I was asked to submit another version of the lilies to that same gallery."

7.17

7.18

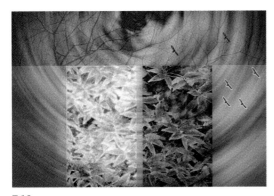

7.19

## PRINTING ONTO LIQUID PHOTO EMULSION

"Another media that I use a lot these days is KwikPrint." KwikPrint is a special brand of photosensitive emulsion that you can apply with a paintbrush. Where the emulsion is exposed to light, it adheres to the paper. Where it isn't exposed, the KwikPrint washes away.

What good is it? "I use it for backgrounds. For example, *Night Vortex* (7.19) is a piece that I created in Photoshop a while back. I really liked the image, but I had never managed to get an exciting print from it. But when I printed it against the KwikPrint background, it just came together (7.20)." It's easiest to see the light blue KwikPrint in the border around the artwork.

Schminke started by creating the wavy grass-like texture for the KwikPrint layer as a grayscale image inside

7.20

Photoshop. Then she inverted the texture to create a negative (7.21) and printed the negative onto acetate. "Actually, I double-struck the negative. Before I took the acetate out of the printer, I had the printer reload it (a special function of the CalComp). The acetate automatically went right back to where it started, and then ran through again. This made the inks denser, so they would completely block out the light."

Next, Schminke pretreated a sheet of paper with iridescent gold acrylic, and then applied the light blue KwikPrint. She laid the acetate on top of the KwikPrint-coated paper, exposed it for a few minutes to photographic flood lights, removed the acetate, and rinsed off the unexposed emulsion.

"When you apply paint with a brush, the brushstrokes have an inherent texture. But digital output is generally pretty flat, so sometimes it helps to build up a texture with different kinds of paints. The wavy KwikPrint substrate gave this image exactly the kind of texture I had been looking for. It also helps to enhance the color gamut. In *Night Vortex*, I'm getting colors that are brand new to the digital print world."

## PROTECTING YOUR INK-JET ARTWORK

High-end color output is notoriously fragile. The ultra-violet (UV) radiation in common sunlight can cause visible bleaching in a matter of months. Schminke recommends, "You should always varnish your ink-jet artwork to protect it. The best product that I know of right now is called MSA Varnish from Golden Artist Colors. It's a mineral spirit-based varnish with high UV protection that comes in three finishes — gloss, satin, and matte. You have to thin it with mineral spirits, not the odorless variety, and you have to apply four coats. The first two have to be the gloss because it absorbs into the paper the best. The next two can be anything, depending on what kind of finish you want. If you apply the matte varnish on top of the gloss, for example, the artwork has a flat finish that's virtually clear."

According to Schminke, the varnish is designed to last. "A guy from Golden varnished pieces we gave him from several different printers. Then he took some untreated watercolors and acrylics, and put them all under the lights. He kept them there for two weeks, long enough to simulate 30 years of museum conditions. The treated ink-jet prints held up as well as the untreated conventional watercolor. It also protects your prints from water — without the varnish, the ink is water soluble.

"Now, this was a company rep, so you have to take his results with a grain of salt. But it goes to show that you should definitely apply some kind of coating. Or hire it out. I've found a local company that applies the varnish for me, because you need good ventilation to use this stuff."

What about UV-protective glass? "When you're shipping art around the country, you can't use glass at all. It breaks too easily and it adds to your shipping costs. But if somebody wants to put UV glass on top of the artwork after they buy it, that's great. They're just adding another layer of protection."

## SHOPPING FOR A FINE-ART PRINTER

For the fine artist on a tight budget, is owning a high-quality ink-jet printer a realistic option? "The industry is just now at the point where an independent artist can afford to purchase a high-end color printer. Right now, I have a wide-format CalComp printer that costs about $10,000. But the prices are falling rapidly. The next generation of that printer will cost more like $8,000, making it accessible for schools and groups of artists. The smaller 1,440-dpi Epson StylusColor 3000 is less than $2,000. It's looking very close in quality to an Iris," the $40,000 color proofing device from Scitex.

7.21

7.22

If you happen to be in the market for a high-resolution color printer, one of the most important things to look at is the paper path. "You want the most straight-through paper path you can get, so the paper doesn't have to curl around a lot of rollers. You should be able to feed a stiff paper stock — like an off-the-shelf watercolor paper — without it getting bent or mangled or hitting up against the head. You might even be able to build a collage and feed it through the printer."

As an exservice bureau hack, the idea of printing on a collage struck me as a recipe for disaster. "Oh, no, I've cut up paper and put it through several times. Of course, I make sure I don't pile on too many layers. But something like rice paper against a thicker background — that works fine." While technically not a collage, Schminke has also experimented with printing on coarse and inconsistent surface textures. "I've painted on pumice mixed in with acrylic and then printed on top of that (7.22)." The straighter the paper path, the less likelihood the paint and pumice will flake off.

"The second issue is the head clearance. How much room is there between the print head and the surface that you're printing on? All printer manufacturers have approved substrates — papers that they've tested that they know will work. But artists are going to immediately start putting their own paper in." Too little clearance causes paper jams and can damage the print head; too much clearance lowers the clarity. "The ideal solution would be an adjustable clearance. But these printers are just starting to come out.

"Finally, you also want to be able to adjust the position of the paper after you've loaded it into the printer. This facilitates overprinting and other alignment tasks."

As when making any major purchase, it's a good idea to test the printer firsthand. Schminke recommends that you experiment not only with different paper stocks, but also with different artist materials. "In one test, I laid down a layer of oil pastels and then ran it through a Hewlett-Packard 560c (7.23). The girl, the shadow, and the triangle come from a Photoshop file; the background strokes I applied traditionally."

## WHY MIX DIGITAL WITH TRADITIONAL

Some digital purists might venture to suggest that Schminke spends so much time outside Photoshop that she might as well not use the program at all. After all, one of the big reasons that artists turn to computers is to get away from the limitations and sheer messiness of conventional tools. What's to be gained by mixing the digital and traditional worlds?

"Photoshop is an extremely enabling tool. It allows you to try out a lot of different ideas and put artwork together in ways that were very difficult before. Superimposing a photograph on top of a painting — there's an example of something that I simply could not have accomplished without a computer. With Photoshop, you can bring together elements of print-making, painting, and photography in ways that you couldn't have before.

"It's such a natural mix that one of the artists in my group, Judith Moncrieff, came up with a name for it. We tell people we create 'tradigital' artwork. It fits, don't you think?"

7.23

# Painting and Retouching Images

# Painting and Editing

## Paint and Edit Tool Basics

Here it is, Chapter 8, and I'm finally getting around to explaining how to use Photoshop's painting tools. You must feel like you're attending some kind of martial arts ritual where you have to learn to run away, cry, beg, and attempt bribery before you get to start karate-chopping bricks and kicking your instructor. "The wise person journeys through the fundamentals of image editing before painting a single brushstroke, Grasshoppa." *Wang, wang, wang.* (That's a musical embellishment, in case you didn't recognize it. Man, I hate to have to explain my jokes. Especially when they're so measly.) Now that you've earned your first belt or tassel or scouting patch or whatever it is you're supposed to receive for slogging this far through the book, you're as prepared as you'll ever be to dive into the world of painting and retouching images.

You may think these tools require artistic talent. In truth, each tool provides options for about any level of proficiency or experience. Photoshop offers get-by measures for novices who want to make a quick edit and put the tool down before they make a mess of things. If you have a few hours of experience with other painting programs, you'll find Photoshop's tools provide at least as much functionality and, in many cases, more. (The one exception is Painter, which is several times more capable than Photoshop in the painting department.) And if you're a professional artist — well, come on now — you'll have no problems learning how to make Photoshop sing. No matter who you are, you'll find electronic painting and editing tools more flexible, less messy, and more forgiving than their traditional counterparts.

**Cross-Reference**

If you screw something up in the course of painting your image, stop and choose Edit ➪ Undo (or press ⌘/Ctrl+Z). If this doesn't work, press ⌘/Ctrl+Option/Alt+Z to step back through your paint strokes. Or you can select a previous state in the History palette, as explained in Chapter 10. The History palette lists brushstrokes and other changes according to the tool you used to create them.

# Meet your tools

Photoshop provides three paint tools: the pencil, the paintbrush, and the airbrush. You also get six edit tools: smudge, blur, sharpen, burn, dodge, and sponge. Figure 8-1 shows these tools. The keyboard equivalent for each tool appears in parentheses.

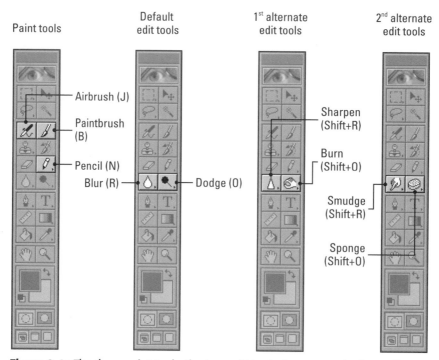

**Figure 8-1:** The three paint tools, the two edit tools that appear in the toolbox by default, and the four alternative edit tools.

In case you're wondering about all the other tools, Figure 8-2 segregates tools by category and lists the chapter in which you can find more information.

## The paint tools

The paint tools apply paint in the foreground color. In this and other respects, they work like their counterparts in other painting programs, but there are a few exceptions:

✦ **Pencil:** Unlike pencil tools found in most other painting programs — which paint lines 1-pixel thick — Photoshop's pencil paints a hard-edged line of any thickness. Figure 8-3 compares the default single-pixel pencil line with a fatter pencil line, a paintbrush line, and an airbrush line.

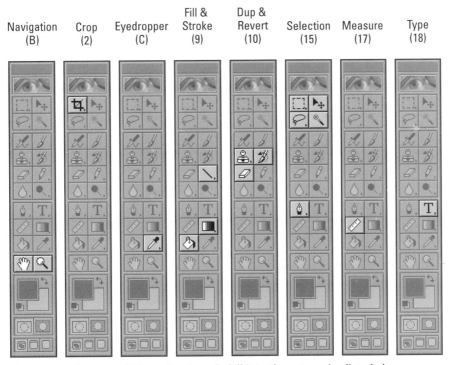

| Navigation (B) | Crop (2) | Eyedropper (C) | Fill & Stroke (9) | Dup & Revert (10) | Selection (15) | Measure (17) | Type (18) |

**Figure 8-2:** The rest of Photoshop's tools fall into the categories listed above each toolbox. The chapter in which I discuss each category of tools appears in parentheses.

**Photoshop 5.0**

If you're used to selecting the pencil tool by pressing the P key (as in Photoshop 3) or the Y key (as in Version 4), prepare for yet another change. You now select the pencil by pressing N, the old shortcut for the line tool.

✦ **Paintbrush:** The paintbrush works like the pencil tool, except it paints an antialiased line that blends in with its background.

The paintbrush offers a Wet Edges option. (Double-click on the paintbrush tool icon in the toolbox and you'll see the Wet Edges check box in the bottom left corner of the Paintbrush Options palette.) When this option is turned on, the paintbrush creates a translucent line with darkened edges, much as if you were painting with watercolors. Soft brush shapes produce more naturalistic effects. An example of this effect is shown in Figure 8-3.

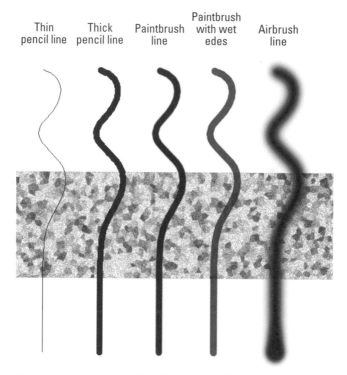

**Figure 8-3:** Five lines painted in black with the pencil, paintbrush, and airbrush tools. The Wet Edges option (second from right) causes the line to appear translucent. Notice I held the airbrush tool in place for a few moments at the end of the rightmost line.

✦ **Airbrush:** Dismissing Photoshop's airbrush tool as a softer version of the paintbrush is tempting because it uses a softer brush shape by default. Photoshop's default settings also call for a lighter pressure, so the airbrush paints a translucent line. But unlike the paintbrush, which applies a continuous stream of color and stops applying paint when you stop dragging, the airbrush applies a series of colored dollops and continues to apply these dollops as long as you press the mouse button. Figure 8-3 shows the dark glob of paint that results from pressing the mouse button while holding the mouse motionless at the end of the drag.

Like the pencil, the shortcut for the airbrush has changed. Now that the A key has been traded to the direct selection tool (used to edit paths), the airbrush has been assigned the one previously unused alphabetic key, J.

## The edit tools

The edit tools don't apply color; rather, they influence existing colors in an image. Figure 8-4 shows each of the six edit tools applied to a randomized background. The tools work as follows:

✦ **Blur:** The first of the two focus tools, the blur tool blurs an image by lessening the amount of color contrast between neighboring pixels.

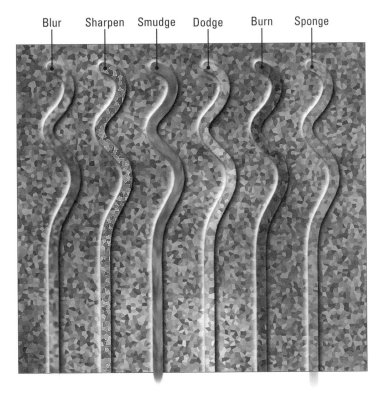

**Figure 8-4:** These are the effects of dragging with each of Photoshop's edit tools. The boundaries of each line are highlighted so you can clearly see the distinctions between line and background.

✦ **Sharpen:** The second focus tool selectively sharpens by increasing the contrast between neighboring pixels. Generally speaking, both the blur and sharpen tools are less useful than their command counterparts in the Filters menu. They provide less control and usually require scrubbing at an image. Maybe I've been using a computer too long, but my wrist starts to ache when I use these tools. If, unlike me, you like the basic principle behind the tools, but you want to avoid carpal tunnel syndrome, you can achieve consistent, predictable results without scrubbing by using the tools in combination with the Shift key, as described in the next section.

✦ **Smudge:** The smudge tool smears colors in an image. The effect is much like dragging your finger across wet paint. In Photoshop 5, the smudge tool has been demoted to an alternative to the focus tools. Otherwise, it's the same old tool.

✦ **Dodge:** The first of three toning tools, the dodge tool, enables you to lighten a portion of an image by dragging across it. Named after a traditional film exposure technique, the dodge tool is supposed to look like a little paddle thingie — you know, like one of those spoons you put over your eye at the optometrist's — that you wave over photographic paper to cast a shadow and thereby lighten the exposure. Thank golly we no longer have to wave little paddle thingies in our modern age.

✦ **Burn:** The burn tool lets you darken a portion of an image by dragging over it. The effect is similar to burning a film negative, which you apparently do by holding your hand in a kind of O shape in an effort to focus the light, kind of like frying a worker ant using a magnifying glass (except not quite so smelly). At least, that's what they tell me. Sadly, I've never had the pleasure of trying it.

**Tip**

If you're like most folks, you have difficulty remembering which tool lightens and which one darkens. So here's a little tip: That little hand icon looks like it could be holding a piece of toast, and when you burn toast, it gets darker. Hand, toast, burn, darker. That other tool, eye doctor paddle, not holding toast, must lighten. You'll never have problems again.

✦ **Sponge:** The final toning tool, the sponge tool, robs an image of both saturation and contrast. Or you can set the tool so it boosts saturation and adds contrast. For more information, stay tuned for the upcoming section "Mopping up with the sponge tool."

To access the sharpen tool temporarily when the blur tool is selected, press and hold the Option/Alt key while using the tool. The sharpen tool remains available only as long as you press the Option/Alt key. You also can press Option/Alt to access the blur tool when the sharpen tool is selected, to access the burn tool when the dodge tool is selected, and to access the dodge tool when the burn tool is selected. (If the sponge tool is active, pressing the Option/Alt key has no effect, except maybe to give your finger a cramp.)

**Tip**

You can replace the blur tool with the sharpen tool in the toolbox by Option/Alt+clicking on the tool's icon. Option/Alt+click again to select the smudge tool and yet again to cycle back to the blur tool. Likewise, you can Option/Alt+click on the dodge tool icon to cycle between the dodge, burn, and sponge tools.

As explained in Chapter E on CD #2, the keyboard equivalents also toggle between the tools. When the blur tool is selected, press Shift+R to toggle to the sharpen tool.

Repeated pressings of Shift+R take you to the smudge tool and back to the blur tool. When the dodge tool is selected, press Shift+O to toggle to the burn tool; press Shift+O again to get the sponge.

**Tip**

To modify the performance of a tool, double-click on its icon in the toolbox to display the customized Options palette. Or you can simply press Return/Enter while the tool is selected. I discuss the options inside the various Options palettes throughout the remainder of this chapter.

## Basic techniques

I know several people who claim they can't paint, and yet they create beautiful work in Photoshop. Even though they don't have sufficient hand-eye coordination to write their names on screen, they have unique and powerful artistic sensibilities and they know lots of tricks that enable them to make judicious use of the paint and edit tools. I can't help you in the sensibilities department, but I can show you a few tricks to boost your ability and inclination to use the paint and edit tools.

### Painting a straight line

You're probably already aware you can draw a straight line with the line tool. If not, try it. The line tool is the alternative tool for the pencil. (Press N then Shift+N to get to it quickly.) After selecting the tool, drag with it inside the image window to create a line. Pretty hot stuff, huh? Well, no, it's actually pretty dull, not to mention limited. In fact, the only reason I ever use this tool is to draw arrows, like those in Figure 8-6. (I explain how in the "Applying Strokes and Arrowheads" section of Chapter 9.) If you don't want to draw an arrow, you're better off using Photoshop's other means for creating straight lines: the Shift key.

To draw a straight line with any of the paint or edit tools, click at one point in the image and then press Shift and click at another point. Using the current tool, Photoshop draws a straight line between the two points.

To create free-form polygons, continue to Shift+click with the tool. Figure 8-5 features a photograph and a tracing I made on a separate layer (covered in Chapter 17) exclusively by Shift+clicking with the paintbrush tool. As an academic exercise, I never dragged with the tool, I never altered the brush size, and I used just two colors: black and gray.

**Tip**

The Shift key makes the blur and sharpen tools halfway useful. Suppose you want to edit the perimeter of the car shown in Figure 8-6. The arrows in the figure illustrate the path your Shift+clicks should follow. Figure 8-7 shows the effect of Shift+clicking with the blur tool; Figure 8-8 demonstrates the effect of Shift+clicking with the sharpen tool.

**Figure 8-5:** Starting from an image by photographer Barbara Penoyar (left), I created a stylized tracing (right) by clicking and Shift+clicking with the paintbrush tool on a separate layer.

**Figure 8-6:** It takes one click and 24 Shift+clicks to soften or accentuate the edges around this car using the blur or sharpen tool.

**Figure 8-7:** These are the results of blurring the car's perimeter with the pressure set to 50 percent (top) and 100 percent (bottom). You set the pressure using the slider bar in the Blur Options palette.

**Figure 8-8:** The results of sharpening the car with the pressure set to 50 percent (top) and 100 percent (bottom).

## Painting a perpendicular line

To draw a perpendicular line—either a vertical or a horizontal line—with any of the paint or edit tools, press and hold the mouse button, press the Shift key, and begin dragging in a vertical or horizontal direction. Don't release the Shift key until you finish dragging or until you want to change the direction of the line, as shown in Figure 8-9. Notice, pressing the Shift key in mid-drag snaps the line back into perpendicular alignment.

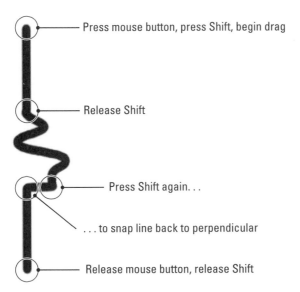

Press mouse button, press Shift, begin drag

Release Shift

Press Shift again. . .

. . . to snap line back to perpendicular

Release mouse button, release Shift

**Figure 8-9:** Pressing the Shift key after you
start to drag with a paint or edit tool results in a
perpendicular line for as long as the key is pressed.

One way to exploit the Shift key's penchant to snap to the perpendicular is to
draw "ribbed" structures. Being left-handed, I dragged from right to left with the
paintbrush to create both of the central outlines around the skeleton that appears
at the top of Figure 8-10. I painted each rib by pressing and releasing the Shift key
as I dragged with the paintbrush tool. Pressing Shift snapped the line to the
horizontal axis, whose location was established by the beginning of the drag.

In this figure, I represented the axis for each line in gray. After establishing the
basic skeletal form, I added some free-form details with the paintbrush and pencil
tools, as shown in the middle image in Figure 8-10. I then selected a general area
around the image and chose Filter ⇨ Stylize ⇨ Emboss to create the finished fossil
image. Nobody's going to confuse my painting with a bona fide fossil, but it's not
bad for a cartoon.

It's no accident Figure 8-10 features a swordfish instead of your everyday round-
nosed carp. To snap to the horizontal axis, I had to establish the direction of my
drag as being more horizontal than vertical. If I had, instead, dragged in a fish-faced
convex arc, Photoshop would have interpreted my drag as vertical and snapped to
the vertical axis.

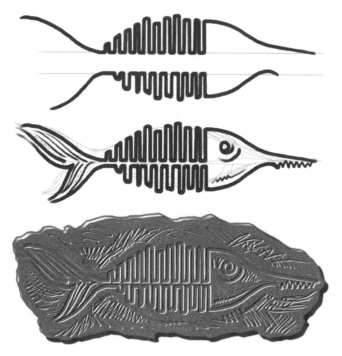

**Figure 8-10:** To create the basic structure for our bony pal, I periodically pressed and released the Shift key while dragging with the paintbrush (top). Then I embellished the fish using the paintbrush and pencil (middle). Finally, I applied the Emboss filter to transform fish into fossil (bottom).

## Painting with the smudge tool

Many first-time Photoshop artists misuse the smudge tool to soften color transitions. In fact, softening is the purpose of the blur tool. The smudge tool *smears* colors by shoving them into each other. The process bears more resemblance to the finger painting you did in grade school than to any traditional photographic-editing technique.

In Photoshop, the performance of the smudge tool depends in part on the settings of the Pressure and Finger Painting options. Both reside in the Smudge Tool Options palette (see Figure 8-11), which you access by pressing Return/Enter when the smudge tool is active. These two options work as follows:

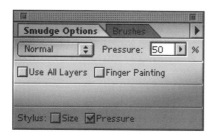

**Figure 8-11:** Combined with brush shape, the Pressure and Finger Painting options are the most important considerations when using the smudge tool.

✦ **Pressure:** Measured as a percentage of the brush shape, this option determines the distance the smudge tool drags a color. Higher percentages and larger brush shapes drag colors farthest. A Pressure setting of 100 percent equates to infinity, meaning the smudge tool drags a color from the beginning of your drag until the end of your drag, regardless of how far you drag. Cosmic, Daddy-O.

✦ **Finger Painting:** The folks at Adobe used to call this effect *dipping*, which I think more accurately expressed how the effect works. When you select this option, the smudge tool begins by applying a smidgen of foreground color, which it eventually blends in with the colors in the image. It's as if you dipped your finger in a color and then dragged it through an oil painting. Use the Pressure setting to specify the amount of foreground color applied. If you turn on Finger Painting and set the Pressure to 100 percent, the smudge tool behaves exactly like the paintbrush tool.

**Tip**

You can reverse the Finger Painting setting by Option/Alt+dragging. If the option is off, Option/Alt+dragging dips the tool into the foreground color. If Finger Painting is turned on, Option/Alt+dragging smudges normally.

For some examples of the smudge tool in action, see Figure 8-12. This figure shows the effects of using the smudge tool set to four different Pressure percentages and with the Finger Painting option both off and on. In each instance, the brush shape is 13 pixels in diameter and the foreground color is set to black.

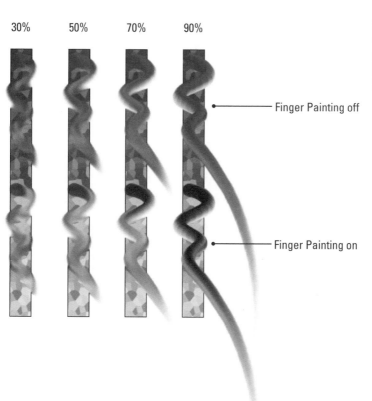

30%  50%  70%  90%

Finger Painting off

Finger Painting on

**Figure 8-12:** Eight drags with the smudge tool subject to different Pressure and Finger Painting settings.

The third option highlighted in Figure 8-11 — Use All Layers (previously called Sample Merged) — instructs the smudge tool to grab colors in all visible layers and smudge them into the current layer. Whether the option is on or off, only the current layer is affected; the background and other layers remain intact.

For example, suppose the inverted eyes of the woman at the top of Figure 8-13 are on a different layer than the rest of the face. If I use the smudge tools on the eyes layer with Use All Layers turned off, Photoshop ignores the face layer when smudging the eyes. As a result, details like the nose and teeth remain unsmudged, as you can see in the lower left example. If I turn Use All Layers on, Photoshop lifts colors from the face layer and mixes them in with the eyes layer, as shown in the lower right example.

Note that all this activity occurs exclusively on the eyes layer. To give you a better look, the two lower examples on the eyes layer are shown independently of those on the face layer in Figure 8-14. You can now clearly see the proliferation of face details mixed into the eyes in the right example. Meanwhile, the face layer remains absolutely unaffected.

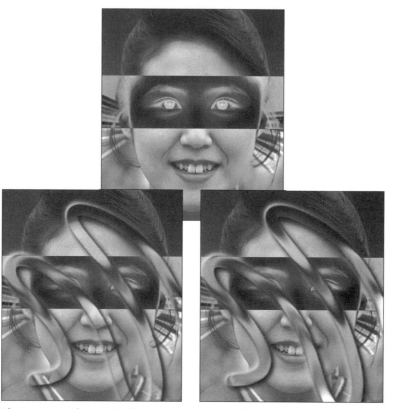

**Figure 8-13:** The original image (top) features inverted eyes on a layer above the rest of the face. I first smudged the eyes with Use All Layers turned off (lower left) and then with the option turned on (lower right).

**Figure 8-14:** The eyes layer from the previous figure shown by itself.

## Mopping up with the sponge tool

The sponge tool is actually a pretty darn straightforward tool, hardly worth expending valuable space in a book as tiny as this one. But I'm a compulsive explainer, so here's the deal: Press Return/Enter when the sponge tool is active to gain access to the Sponge Options palette. In the upper left corner of the palette is a pop-up menu that offers two options: Desaturate and Saturate.

✦ When set to Desaturate, the tool reduces the saturation of the colors over which you drag. When editing a grayscale image, the tool reduces the contrast.

✦ If you select the Saturate option, the sponge tool increases the saturation of the colors over which you drag or increases contrast in a grayscale image. Higher Pressure settings produce more dramatic results.

In Photoshop 5, you can switch between the Desaturate and Saturate modes from the keyboard. Press Shift+Option/Alt+J to select the Desaturate option. Press Shift+Option/Alt+A for Saturate.

Consider Color Plate 8-1. The upper left example shows the original PhotoDisc image. The upper right example shows the result of applying the sponge tool set to Desaturate. I dragged with the tool inside the pepper and around in the corner area. The Pressure was set to 100 percent. Notice the affected colors are on the wane, sliding toward gray. In the lower right example, the effect is even more pronounced. I applied the sponge tools here with great vim and vigor two additional times. Hardly any hint of color is left in these areas now.

To create the lower left example in Color Plate 8-1, I applied the sponge tool set to Saturate. This is where things get a little tricky. If you boost saturation levels with the sponge tool in the RGB or Lab color modes, you can achieve colors of absolutely neon intensity. However, these high-saturation colors don't stand a snowball's chance in a microwave of printing in CMYK. So I recommend you choose View ➪ Preview ➪

CMYK (⌘/Ctrl+Y) before boosting saturation levels with the sponge tool. This way, you can accurately view the results of your edits. After you're finished, choose View ➪ Preview ➪ CMYK to turn off the CMYK preview and return to the RGB view.

Figure 8-15 shows the yellow channel from each of the images in Color Plate 8-1. Because yellow is the most prevalent primary color in the image, it is the most sensitive to saturation adjustments. When I boosted the saturation in the lower left example, the yellow brightness values deepened, adding yellow ink to the CMYK image. When I lessened the saturation in the two right examples, the amount of ink diminished.

One of Adobe's recommended purposes of the sponge tool is to reduce the saturation levels of out-of-gamut RGB colors before converting an image to the CMYK mode. I'm not too crazy about this use of the tool because it requires a lot of scrubbing. Generally, selecting the out-of-gamut area and reducing the colors using more automated controls is easier (as discussed in Chapter 24). You might prefer, instead, to use the sponge tool when a more selective, personal touch is required, as when curbing a distracting color that seems to leap a little too vigorously off the screen or boosting the saturation of a detail in the CMYK mode.

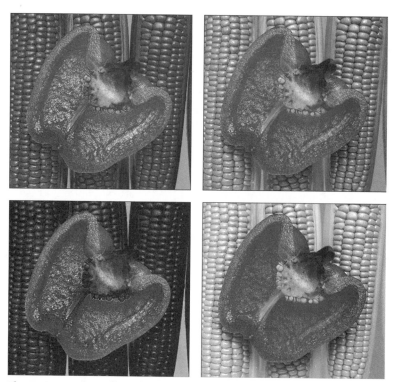

**Figure 8-15:** The yellow channel from Color Plate 8-1 shows the greatest amount of variation when reducing and boosting the saturation with the sponge tool.

# Brush Shape and Opacity

So far, I mentioned the words *brush shape* several times and I have yet to explain what the Sam Hill I'm talking about. Luckily, it's simple. The brush shape is the size and shape of the tip of your cursor when you use a paint or edit tool. A big, round brush shape paints or edits in broad strokes. A small, elliptical brush shape is useful for performing hairline adjustments.

Although Photoshop is not set up this way by default, it is capable of displaying a cursor whose outline reflects the selected brush shape. To access this incredibly useful cursor, press ⌘/Ctrl+K to bring up the Preferences dialog box and press ⌘/Ctrl+3 for the Display & Cursors panel. Then select Brush Size from the Painting Cursors radio buttons.

Unlike previous versions of Photoshop, Version 5 is not limited to displaying brush sizes of 300 pixels. You can now fill an entire 21-inch monitor with one big huge brush. (The actual brush size limit is 2,000 pixels, which is larger than any screen currently on the market.) Granted, a 21-inch brush is a bit excessive, but the point is, all limits are gone.

When using very small brushes, as when using the single-pixel pencil to do precise retouching, the cursor includes four dots around its perimeter, making the cursor easier to locate. If you need a little more help, press the Caps Lock key to access the more obvious crosshair cursor.

## The Brushes palette

You access brush shapes by choosing Window ⇨ Palettes ⇨ Show Brushes to display the Brushes palette. Or you can press the F5 key. Figure 8-16 shows the Brushes palette with its pop-up menu wide open for your viewing pleasure.

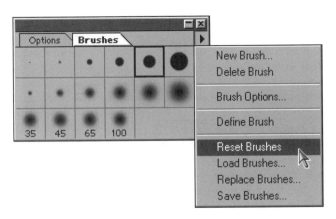

**Figure 8-16:** Photoshop's Brushes palette enables you to select a predefined brush shape or create one of your own.

**Tip**

You can switch brush shapes from the keyboard without displaying the Brushes palette. Press the left-bracket key, [, to select the previous brush shape in the palette; press the right-bracket key, ], to select the next brush shape. You can also press Shift+[ to select the first brush shape in the palette and Shift+] to select the last shape.

## Editing a brush shape

To edit a brush shape in the Brushes palette, select the brush you want to change and choose Brush Options from the palette menu. To create a new brush shape, choose New Brush. Either way, the dialog box shown in Figure 8-17 appears. (If you choose the New Brush command, the Title bar is different, but the options are the same.)

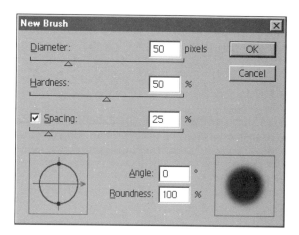

**Figure 8-17:** The Brush Options dialog box enables you to change the size, shape, and hardness of the brush shape.

**Tip**

If you hate menus — and who doesn't? — you can more conveniently edit a brush shape by simply double-clicking on it. To create a new brush shape, click once on an empty brush slot, as shown in the first example in Figure 8-18. (Incidentally, you can also delete a brush from the palette. To do so, press ⌘/Ctrl to display the scissors cursor — as in the second example in Figure 8-18 — then click. It's a great little housekeeping tip.)

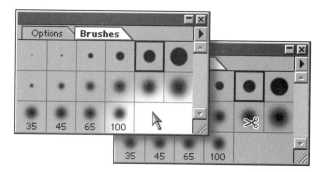

**Figure 8-18:** Clicking on an empty brush slot (left) brings up the New Brush dialog box so you can create a new brush shape. ⌘/Ctrl+clicking on a brush shape (right) deletes it from the palette.

Whether you're editing an existing brush or creating a new one, you have the following options at your disposal:

✦ **Diameter:** This option determines the width of the brush shape. If the brush shape is elliptical instead of circular, the Diameter value determines the longest dimension. You can enter any value from 1 to 999 pixels. Brush shapes with diameters of 30 pixels or higher are too large to display accurately in the Brushes palette and instead appear as circles with inset Diameter values.

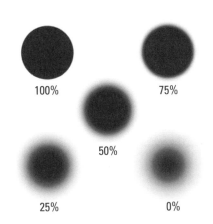

**Figure 8-19:** A 100-pixel diameter brush shown as it appears when set to a variety of Hardness percentages. I changed the background pixels below from white to black, so you can see the actual diameter of each brush shape. The tick marks indicate 10-pixel increments.

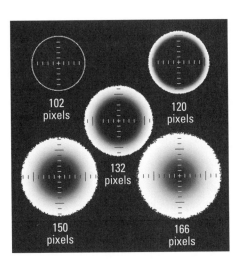

✦ **Hardness:** Except when you use the pencil tool, brush shapes are always antialiased. You can further soften the edges of a brush, however, by dragging the Hardness slider bar away from 100 percent. The softest setting, 0 percent, gradually tapers the brush from a single solid color pixel at its center to a ring of transparent pixels around the brush's perimeter. Figure 8-19 demonstrates how low Hardness percentages expand the size of a 100-pixel brush beyond the Diameter value (as demonstrated by the examples set against black). Even a 100-percent hard brush shape expands slightly because it is antialiased. The Hardness setting is ignored when you use the pencil tool.

✦ **Spacing:** The Spacing option controls how frequently a tool affects an image as you drag, measured as a percentage of the brush shape. Suppose the Diameter of a brush shape is 12 pixels and the Spacing is set to 25 percent (the setting for all default brush shapes). For every 3 pixels (25 percent of 12 pixels) you drag with the paintbrush tool, Photoshop lays down a 12-pixel wide spot of color. A Spacing of 1 percent provides the most coverage, but may also slow down the performance of the tool. If you deselect the Spacing check box, the effect of the tool is wholly dependent on the speed at which you drag; this can be useful for creating splotchy or oscillating lines. Figure 8-20 shows examples.

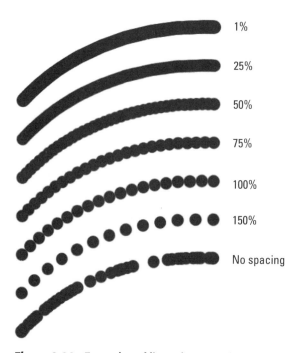

1%

25%

50%

75%

100%

150%

No spacing

**Figure 8-20:** Examples of lines drawn with different Spacing values in the Brush Options dialog box. Gaps or ridges generally begin to appear when the Spacing value exceeds 30 percent. The final line was created by turning off the Spacing option.

✦ **Angle:** This option enables you to pivot a brush shape on its axes. Unless the brush is elliptical, though, this won't make a difference in the appearance of the brush shape.

✦ **Roundness:** Enter a value of less than 100 percent into the Roundness option to create an elliptical brush shape. The value measures the width of the brush as a percentage of its height, so a Roundness value of 5 percent results in a long, skinny brush shape.

**Tip**

You can adjust the angle of the brush dynamically by dragging the gray arrow inside the box to the left of the Angle and Roundness options. Drag the handles on either side of the black circle to make the brush shape elliptical, as demonstrated in Figure 8-21.

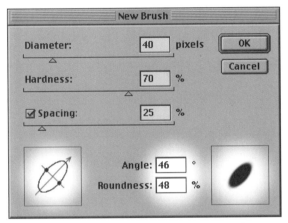

**Figure 8-21:** Drag the gray arrow or the black handles to change the angle or roundness of a brush, respectively. The Angle and Roundness values update automatically, as does the preview of the brush in the lower right corner of the dialog box.

I heartily recommend you take a few moments soon to experiment at length with the Brush Options dialog box. By combining paint and edit tools with one or more specialized brush shapes, you can achieve artistic effects unlike anything permitted via traditional techniques. Starting with a PhotoDisc image lightened and filtered to serve as a template, I painted Figure 8-22 using the flat, 45-pixel brush shape shown in the dialog box. No other brush shape or special effect was applied. Think of what you can accomplish if you don't limit yourself as ridiculously as I did.

## Creating and using custom brushes

You can define a custom brush shape by selecting a portion of your image that you want to change to a brush and choosing the Define Brush command from the Brushes palette pop-up menu.

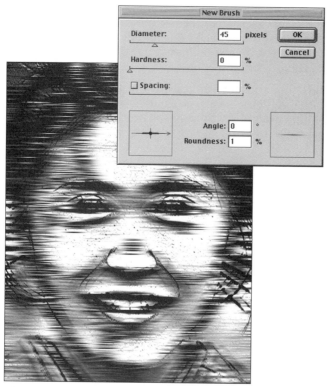

**Figure 8-22:** Just to show off, I painted over a scanned image with the paintbrush tool, using the brush shape shown in the dialog box at the top.

In addition to giving you the flexibility to create a brush from some element in your image, Photoshop ships with a file called Assorted Brushes, which contains all kinds of little symbols and doodads you can assign as custom brush shapes. You can load the contents of the Assorted Brushes file into the Brushes palette by choosing the Replace Brushes command from the palette menu (or Load Brushes if you don't want to lose the brush shapes that currently occupy the palette). You'll find Assorted Brushes in the Brushes folder inside the main Photoshop folder. Figure 8-23 shows an inspirational image I created using Photoshop's predefined custom brushes.

To return to the original default brush shapes, choose Reset Brushes from the palette menu. You then have the option of either replacing the existing brushes with the default brushes or simply adding the default brushes to the end of the palette.

**Figure 8-23:** Yes, it's Boris, the sleeping custom-brush guy. If you suspect this image is meant to suggest custom brushes are more amusing than utilitarian, you're right. The brushes from the Assorted Brushes file appear on the right.

In Photoshop, you can adjust the performance of a custom brush in the following ways:

✦ **Brush options:** Choose the Brush Options command from the palette menu or double-click on the custom brush in the Brushes palette to bring up the dialog box shown in Figure 8-24. Here you can adjust the spacing of the brush shape and specify whether Photoshop *antialiases* (softens) the edges or leaves them as is. If the brush is sufficiently large, the Anti-aliased check box appears dimmed. All custom brushes are hard-edged when you use the pencil tool.

**Figure 8-24:** The dialog box that appears when you double-click on a custom brush.

✦ **Brush color:** The foreground color affects a custom brush just as it does a standard brush shape. To erase with the brush, select white as the foreground color. To paint in color, select a color.

✦ **Opacity and brush modes:** The setting of the Opacity slider bar and the brush modes pop-up menu also affect the application of custom brushes. For more information on these options, keep reading this chapter.

You can achieve some unusual and, sometimes, interesting effects by activating the smudge tool's Finger Painting option and painting in the image window with a custom brush. At high Pressure settings, say 80 to 90 percent, the effect is rather like applying oil paint with a hairy paintbrush, as illustrated in Figure 8-25.

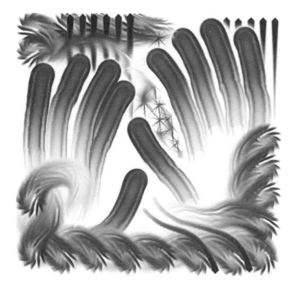

**Figure 8-25:** I created this organic, expressive image by combining the smudge tool's dipping capability with four custom brushes. I don't know what those finger-like growths are, but they'd probably feel right at home in an aquarium.

## Opacity, pressure, and exposure

Another way to change the performance of a paint or edit tool is to modify the amount of color or pressure that Photoshop applies to the canvas. You modify this behavior by entering a value into the option box in the upper right corner of the Options palette. Photoshop assigns one of three labels to this option box, as illustrated in Figure 8-26.

✦ **Opacity:** The Opacity value determines the translucency of colors applied with the paint bucket, gradient, line, pencil, paintbrush, eraser, or rubber stamp tool. At 100 percent, the applied colors appear opaque, completely covering the image behind them. (The one exception is the paintbrush with Wet Edges active, which is always translucent.) At lower settings, the applied colors mix with the existing colors in the image.

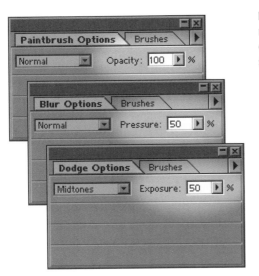

**Figure 8-26:** The option boxes in the upper right corner of the Options palette assumes one of these functions, depending on the selected paint or edit tool.

✦ **Pressure:** The Pressure value affects different tools in different ways. When you use the airbrush tool, the Pressure value controls the opacity of each spot of color the tool delivers. The effect appears unique because the airbrush lays each spot of color onto the previous spot, mixing them together. This results in a progressive effect. Meanwhile, the paintbrush and pencil tools are not progressive, so their spots blend to form smooth lines.

When you use the smudge tool, the Pressure value controls the distance the tool drags colors in the image. And in the case of the blur, sharpen, or sponge tool, the value determines the degree to which the tool changes the focus or saturation of the image, 1 percent being the minimum and 100 percent being the maximum.

✦ **Exposure:** If you select the dodge or burn tool, the title of this particular option box changes to Exposure. A setting of 100 percent applies the maximum amount of lightening or darkening to an image, which is still far short of either absolute white or black.

The factory default setting for all Exposure and Pressure values is 50 percent; the default setting for all Opacity values is 100 percent.

Tip

As long as one of the tools listed in this section is selected, you can change the Opacity, Pressure, or Exposure setting in 10 percent increments by pressing a number key on the keyboard or keypad. Press 1 to change the setting to 10 percent, press 2 for 20 percent, and so on, all the way up to 0 for 100 percent.

Want to change the Opacity, Pressure, or Exposure setting in 1 percent increments? No problem—just press two keys in a row. Press 4 twice for 44 percent, 0 and 7 for 7 percent, and so on. This tip and the previous one work whether or not the Options palette is visible. Get in the habit of using the number keys and you'll thank yourself later.

# Tapered Lines

Photoshop provides two ways to create tapering lines reminiscent of brushstrokes created using traditional techniques. You can specify the length over which a line fades by entering a value into the Fade option box, as described in the next section. Or, if you own a pressure-sensitive drawing tablet, you can draw brushstrokes that fade in and out automatically according to the amount of pressure you apply to the stylus. Both techniques enable you to introduce an element of spontaneity into what, otherwise, seems at times like an absolute world of computer graphics.

## Fading the paint

All three paint tools offer Fade check boxes in their respective Options palettes, which enable you to create lines that gradually fade away as you drag. Figure 8-27 shows the Fade option as it appears in the Paintbrush Options palette, along with some examples of the effect.

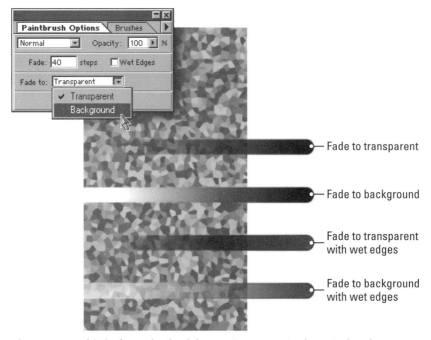

**Figure 8-27:** This is the Fade check box as it appears in the Paintbrush Options palette, along with four examples.

After selecting the Fade check box, enter a value into the option box to specify the distance over which the color fading should occur. The fading begins at the start of your drag and is measured in brush shapes.

For example, assume the foreground color is black. If you enter 40 into the Fade option box—as in Figure 8-27—Photoshop paints 40 brush shapes, the first in black and the remaining 39 in increasingly lighter shades of gray.

In Photoshop, you can paint gradient lines by selecting the To Background radio button. Photoshop fades the line from the foreground color to the background color, much the same way the gradient tool fades the interior of a selection. For more information on the gradient tool, see the "Applying Gradient Fills" section of Chapter 9.

### Fading and spacing

The physical length of a fading line is dependent both on the Fade value and on the value entered into the Spacing option box in the Brush Options dialog box, discussed back in the "Editing a brush shape" section earlier in this chapter.

To recap, the Spacing value determines the frequency with which Photoshop lays down brush shapes, and the Fade value determines the number of brush shapes laid down. Therefore, as demonstrated in Figure 8-28, a high Fade value combined with a high Spacing value creates the longest line.

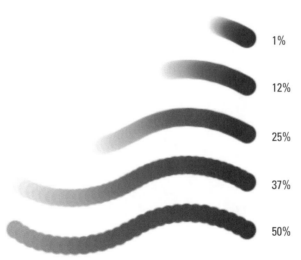

1%

12%

25%

37%

50%

**Figure 8-28:** Here are five fading lines drawn with the paintbrush tool. In each case, the Fade option is set to 36 brush shapes. I changed the Spacing value incrementally from 1 to 50 percent, as labeled.

### Creating sparkles and comets

Fading lines may strike you as pretty ho-hum, but they enable you to create some no-brainer, cool-mandoo effects, especially when combined with the Shift key techniques discussed earlier, in the "Painting a straight line" section.

Figures 8-29 and 8-30 demonstrate two of the most obvious uses for fading straight lines: creating sparkles and comets. The top image in Figure 8-29 features two sets of sparkles, each made up of 16 straight lines emanating from the sparkle's center. To create the smaller sparkle on the right, I set the Fade value to 60 and drew each of the four perpendicular lines with the paintbrush tool. I changed the Fade value to 36 before drawing the four 45-degree diagonal lines. The eight very short lines that occur between the perpendicular and diagonal lines were drawn with a Fade value of 20. I, likewise, created the larger sparkle on the left by periodically adjusting the Fade value, this time from 90 to 60 to 42.

For comparison's sake, I used different techniques to add a few more sparkles to the bottom image in Figure 8-29. To achieve the reflection in the upper left corner of the image, I chose Filter ➪ Render ➪ Lens Flare and selected 50-300mm Zoom from the Lens Type options. (Lens Flare works exclusively in the RGB mode, so I had to switch to RGB to apply the filter, even though Figure 8-29 is a grayscale image.)

**Figure 8-29:** I drew the sparkles in the top image using the paintbrush tool. The second image features a reflection applied with the Lens Flare filter (upper left corner) and two dabs of a custom brush shape (right edge of the bumper).

I created the two tiny sparkles on the right edge of the bumper using a custom brush shape. I merely selected the custom brush, set the foreground color to white, and clicked once with the paintbrush tool in each location. So many sparkles make for a tremendously shiny image.

In Figure 8-30 — a nostalgic tribute to the days when gas was cheap and the whole family would pile in the Plymouth for a Sunday drive through space — I copied the car and pasted it on top of a NASA photograph of Jupiter. I then went nuts clicking and Shift+clicking with the paintbrush tool to create the comets — well, if you must know, they're actually cosmic rays — you see shooting through and around the car. It's so real, you can practically hear the in-dash servo unit warning, "Duck and cover!"

**Figure 8-30:** To create the threatening cosmic rays, I set the Fade option to 110 and then clicked and Shift+clicked on opposite sides of the image with the paintbrush tool.

After masking portions of the image (a process described at length in Chapter 16), I drew rays behind the car and even one ray that shoots up through the car and out the spare tire. The three bright lights in the image — above the left fin, above the roof, and next to the right-turn signal — are more products of the Lens Flare filter in the RGB mode.

**Note**

I drew all the fading lines in Figures 8-29 and 8-30 with the paintbrush tool, using a variety of default brush shapes. Because I didn't edit any brush shape, the Spacing value for all lines was a constant 25 percent.

## Setting up pressure-sensitive tablets

The pressure-sensitive tablet may be the single most useful piece of optional hardware available to computer artists. Not only can you draw with a pen-like *stylus* instead of a clunky mouse, you also can dynamically adjust the thickness of lines and the opacity of colors by changing the amount of pressure you apply to the stylus. Several vendors currently manufacture pressure-sensitive tablets, but the most dynamic vendor — and the one with the best products — continues to be Wacom (*www.wacom.com*).

Of these, the best introductory all-purpose tablet is Wacom's $200 ArtPad II. Measuring a diminutive $7 \times 7.25$ inches (with an active area of $4 \times 5$ inches), this thing is smaller than a standard mouse pad. The tablet offers 256 levels of pressure and a resolution of thousands of lines per inch. (Like any digital tracking device, a tablet uses pixels to communicate the location of your stylus. The higher the resolution, the smoother your mouse movements.)

Wacom's cordless stylus comes in several different varieties — illustrated in Figure 8-31 — each of which weighs less than an ounce. All of them feature both a pressure-sensitive nib and at least one side switch for double-clicking or choosing macros. Many offer erasers at the opposite end from the nib. When you use the eraser, Photoshop automatically switches to the eraser tool. Then there's the WideBody series, where the nib includes real pencil lead or ink. This way, you can see what you're drawing both on paper and on screen. Oh, what miracles the modern age brings!

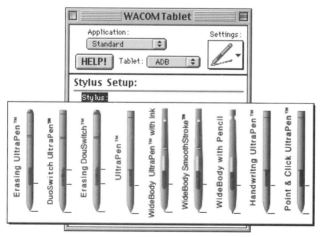

**Figure 8-31:** Wacom boasts the largest pressure-sensitive stylus library of any tablet vendor. You can customize the settings for your particular stylus from a pop-up menu in the central control panel.

Wacom's most recent miracle is the PL-300. Pictured in Figure 8-32, this tablet combines a drawing tablet with a fully functioning color LCD screen. If your computer includes an extra monitor port or video card, you can connect the PL-300 as a second screen. Then you can paint directly on the screen, just as you used to back in those ancient days when you used pencil and paper. It's nothing short of a computerized canvas. As I write this, the price ($2,700) is high enough to dissuade all but the most serious few. But it certainly fires the imagination — the day they combine a PressView and tablet all into one, I'm all over it.

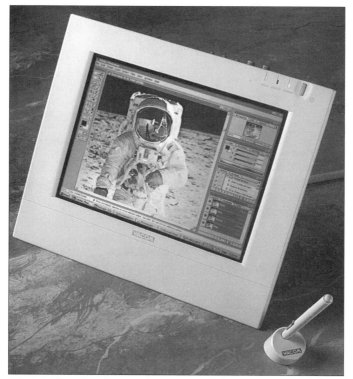

**Figure 8-32:** The PL-300 includes an LCD monitor so that you can draw directly on the screen.

If you're an artist and you've never experimented with a pressure-sensitive tablet — whether LCD-equipped or not — I recommend you do so soon. You'll be amazed at how much it increases your range of artistic options. Thirty minutes after I installed my first tablet back in 1990, I had executed the cartoon you see in Figure 8-33. Whether you like the image or not — I'll admit there's a certain troglodyte quality to the slope of his forehead, and that jaw could bust a coconut — it shows off the tablet's capability to paint tapering lines and accommodate artistic expression.

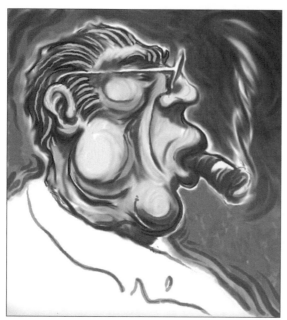

**Figure 8-33:** Although I painted this caricature years ago, it still demonstrates the range of artistic freedom provided by a pressure-sensitive tablet.

If you do own a Wacom tablet, you're in luck. Wacom offers a collection of pressure-sensitive painting and editing filters called PenTools. The filters are fun, easy to use, and best of all, free. You can check them out on CD #1 at the back of this book. The only caveat is that you need a Wacom-brand tablet to use them.

### Undoing pressure-sensitive lines

In the old days, pressure-sensitive lines were a pain to undo. Because a stylus is so sensitive to gradual pressure, you can unwittingly let up and repress the stylus during what you perceive as a single drag. If, after doing so, you decide you don't like the line and press ⌘/Ctrl+Z (Edit ⇨ Undo), Photoshop deletes only the last portion of the line, because it detected a release midway.

This is why it's a good idea to get in the habit of using ⌘/Ctrl+Option/Alt+Z, if you haven't already. Each time you press this shortcut, you take another step back in the history of your image, permitting you to eliminate every bit of a line regardless of how many times you let up on the stylus. (See Chapter 10 for more information on Photoshop 5's multiple undos.)

Tip

Better yet, crate a new layer before you paint with or without a stylus. Then you can refine your lines and erase them without harming the original appearance of your image. (You can do this without layers using the history brush, again explained in Chapter 10, but a relatively old-fashioned layer tends to be less hassle.)

## Pressure-sensitive options

All paint and edit tools, as well as the eraser and rubber stamp, provide three check boxes for controlling Photoshop's reaction to stylus pressure (see Figure 8-34). Available from the Options palette only when a pressure-sensitive tablet is hooked up to your computer, these options include the following:

✦ **Size:** If you select the Size check box, Photoshop varies the thickness of the line. The more pressure you apply, the thicker the line. The Size check box is selected by default. Figure 8-35 shows three paintbrush lines drawn with the Size option selected. I drew the first line using a hard brush, the second with a soft brush, and the third with a hard brush and with the Wet Edges check box selected.

**Figure 8-34:** Photoshop provides three check boxes for interpreting the signals from a pressure-sensitive tablet.

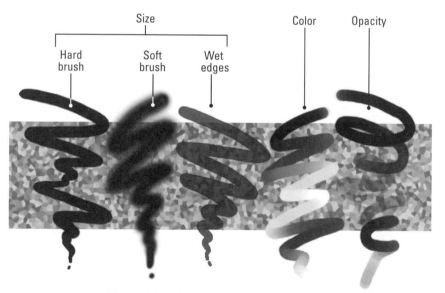

**Figure 8-35:** The effects of the Size, Color, and Opacity options on lines drawn with the paintbrush tool and a pressure-sensitive tablet.

✦ **Opacity:** This option paints an opaque coat of foreground color at full pressure that dwindles to transparency at slight pressure.

✦ **Color:** Select this option to create custom gradient lines. Full pressure paints in the foreground color, slight pressure paints in the background color, medium pressure paints a mix of the two.

Because Photoshop presents its pressure options as check boxes, you can select more than one option at a time. For example, you can select both Size and Color to instruct Photoshop to change both the thickness and color of a line as you bear down or lift up on the stylus.

# Brush Modes

When a painting or editing tool is active, the pop-up menu in the Options palettes provides access to Photoshop's brush modes, which control how the colors applied by the tools affect existing colors in the image. Figure 8-36 shows which brush modes are available when you select various tools.

With the exception of the specialized brush modes provided for the dodge, burn, and sponge tools, brush modes are merely variations on the blend modes described in Chapter 31. Read this section to get a brief glimpse of brush modes; read Chapter 31 for a more detailed account that should appeal to brush-mode aficionados.

You can now change brush modes from the keyboard by pressing Shift+plus (+) or Shift+minus (–). Shift+plus takes you to the next brush mode listed in the pop-up menu, Shift+minus selects the previous blend mode. It's a great way to cycle through the brush modes without losing your place in the image.

## The 19 paint tool modes

Photoshop offers 19 possible brush modes when you use the pencil, paintbrush, airbrush, or any of the other tools shown along the left side of Figure 8-36. (The one mode missing from the figure is Threshold, which is an alternative to Normal in certain color modes.) To show you what these brush modes look like when applied to an image, Color Plates 8-2, 8-3, and 8-4 illustrate all 18. In each case, I used the paintbrush tool to apply a bit of green graffiti to a work of fourteenth-century religious iconography. Who among us hasn't been tempted with the primal urge to paint "Kilroy" on something old and priceless? Now, thanks to the miracle of digital imagery, you need resist this temptation no longer.

Just as you can cycle from one brush mode to the next from the keyboard, you can jump directly to a specific brush mode as well. Just press Shift+Option/Alt and a letter key. For example, Shift+Option/Alt+N selects the Normal mode, Shift+Option/Alt+C selects the Color mode. I list the letter key for each brush mode in parentheses along with its description below:

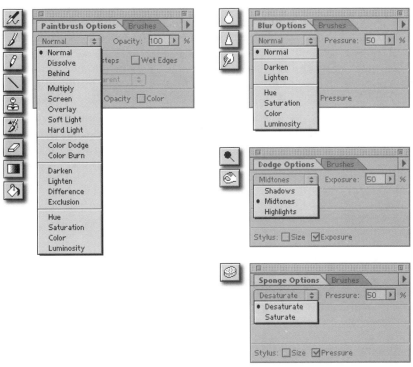

**Figure 8-36:** The number of options in the brush modes pop-up menu varies depending on whether you select a paint tool (left), an edit tool (top right), the dodge or burn tool (middle right), or the sponge tool (bottom right).

✦ **Normal (N):** Choose this mode to paint or edit an image normally. A paint tool coats the image with the foreground color, and an edit tool manipulates the existing colors in an image according to the Opacity or Pressure value.

✦ **Threshold (L):** Two color modes prevent Photoshop from rendering soft or translucent edges. The black-and-white and indexed modes (Image ⇨ Mode ⇨ Bitmap and Image ⇨ Mode ⇨ Indexed Color) simply don't have enough colors to go around. When painting in such a low-color image, Photoshop replaces the Normal brush mode with Threshold, which results in harsh, jagged edges, just like a stroke painted with the pencil tool. You can alternatively dither the soft edges by selecting the Dissolve mode, as described next.

✦ **Dissolve (I):** This mode and the six that follow are not applicable to the edit tools (though I wonder why — the Dissolve mode would be especially useful with the smudge tool). Dissolve scatters colors along the edge of a brushstroke randomly throughout the course of your drag. The Dissolve mode produces the most pronounced effects when used with soft brushes and the airbrush tool.

✦ **Behind (Q):** This one is applicable exclusively to layers with transparent backgrounds. When Behind is selected, the paint tool applies color behind the image on the active layer, showing through only in the transparent and translucent areas. In Color Plate 8-2, for example, I painted over the Madonna's head, and yet the brushstroke appears behind her head because she is positioned on an independent layer. When you're working on an image without layers or on the background layer of a multilayered image, the Behind mode is dimmed.

✦ **Multiply (M):** The Multiply mode combines the foreground color with an existing color in an image to create a third color, darker than the other two. Using the multiply analogy, red times white is red, red times yellow is orange, red times green is brown, red times blue is violet, and so on. As discussed in Chapter 5, this is subtractive (CMYK) color theory at work. The effect is almost exactly like drawing with felt-tipped markers, except the colors don't bleed. Check out the first Kilroy in Color Plate 8-3 to see the Multiply mode in action.

The multiply mode has no effect on the paintbrush when it's set to Wet Edges; the Wet Edges brush already multiplies.

✦ **Screen (S):** The inverse of the Multiply mode, Screen combines the foreground color with each colored pixel you paint over to create a third color, lighter than the other two. Red on white is white, red on yellow is off-white, red on green is yellow, and red on blue is pink. The Screen mode uses additive (RGB) color theory. If the effect has a traditional counterpart, it's like some impossibly bright, radioactive Uranium-238 highlighter, hitherto used only by G-Men to mark the pants' cuffs of Communist sympathizers.

Because the Wet Edges option always multiplies, combining it with the Screen mode must render the brush invisible. If the paintbrush tool isn't working, this could be your problem.

✦ **Overlay (O):** Overlay, Soft Light, and Hard Light are cousins. Each mode multiplies the dark pixels in an image and screens the light pixels as you lay down color with a paint tool. But although related, the three modes are not variations on an identical theme. In other words, you can't emulate the Soft Light mode by simply applying the Hard Light mode at 70 percent or some similar opacity.

Of the three modes, Overlay is the kindest. Overlay always enhances contrast and boosts the saturation of colors in an image. In fact, Overlay works rather like a colored version of the sponge tool set to Saturate. It mixes the colors in the image with the foreground color to come up with a vivid blend that is almost always visually pleasing. Overlay may be the most interesting and downright useful brush mode of the bunch.

✦ **Soft Light (F):** This mode applies a subtle glazing of color to an image. In fact, Soft Light is remarkably similar to painting a diluted acrylic wash to a canvas. Soft Light never completely covers the underlying detail—even black or white applied at 100 percent Opacity does no more than darken or lighten the image—but it does slightly diminish contrast.

✦ **Hard Light (H):** This mode might better be named *Obfuscate*. It's as if you were applying a thicker, more opaque wash to the image. You might think of Hard Light as Normal with a whisper of underlying detail mixed in.

For examples of Overlay, Soft Light, and Hard Light, check out the middle brushstrokes in Color Plate 8-3.

✦ **Color Dodge (D):** This brush mode lightens the pixels in an image according to the lightness or darkness of the foreground color. Color Dodge produces a harsher, chalkier effect than the Screen mode and is designed to act like a dodge tool that also adds color. At 100 percent Opacity, even painting with black has a lightening effect.

✦ **Color Burn (B):** If Color Dodge is like drawing with chalk, Color Burn is like drawing with coal. It darkens pixels according to the lightness or darkness of the foreground color and is designed to simulate a colored version of the burn tool. For examples of Color Dodge and Color Burn, look to the last two Kilroys in Color Plate 8-3.

✦ **Darken (K):** Ah, back to the old familiars. If you choose the Darken mode, Photoshop applies a new color to a pixel only if that color is darker than the present color of the pixel. Otherwise, the pixel is left unchanged. The mode works on a channel-by-channel basis, so it might change a pixel in the green channel, for example, without changing the pixel in the red or blue channel. I used this mode to create the first brushstroke of Color Plate 8-4.

✦ **Lighten (G):** The opposite of the previous mode, Lighten ensures that Photoshop applies a new color to a pixel only if the color is lighter than the present color of the pixel. Otherwise, the pixel is left unchanged. On or off — either you see the color or you don't.

✦ **Difference (E):** When a paint tool is set to the Difference mode, Photoshop subtracts the brightness value of the foreground color from the brightness value of the pixels in the image. If the result is a negative number, Photoshop simply makes it positive. The result of this complex-sounding operation is an inverted effect. Black has no effect on an image; white inverts it completely. Colors in between create psychedelic effects. In the third example of Color Plate 8-4, for example, the Difference mode inverts the green paint to create a red brushstroke.

**Tip**

Because the Difference mode inverts an image, it results in an outline around the brushstroke. You can make this outline thicker by using a softer brush shape. For a really trippy effect, select the paintbrush tool, turn on Wet Edges, and apply the Difference mode with a soft brush shape.

✦ **Exclusion (X):** When I first asked Mark Hamburg, lead programmer for Photoshop, for his definition of Exclusion, he kindly explained, "Exclusion applies a probabilistic, fuzzy-set-theoretic, symmetric difference to each channel." Don't think about it too long — your frontal lobe will turn to boiled squash. After Mark remembered he was communicating with a lower life form, he told me (very slowly) that Exclusion inverts an image in much the same way as Difference, except colors in the middle of the spectrum mix to form medium gray. Exclusion typically results in high-contrast effects with less color saturation than Difference. My suggestion is you try the Difference mode first. If you're looking for something a little different, press ⌘/Ctrl+Z and try Exclusion instead. (Both Difference and Exclusion brushstrokes appear in Color Plate 8-4.)

✦ **Hue (U):** Understanding the next few modes requires a color theory recap. Remember how the HSL color model calls for three color channels? One is for hue, the value that explains the colors in an image; the second is for saturation, which represents the intensity of the colors; and the third is for luminosity, which explains the lightness and darkness of colors. If you choose the Hue brush mode, therefore, Photoshop applies the hue from the foreground color without changing any saturation or luminosity values in the existing image.

None of the HSL brush modes — Hue, Saturation, Color, or Luminosity — is available when painting within grayscale images.

✦ **Saturation (T):** If you choose this mode, Photoshop changes the intensity of the colors in an image without changing the colors themselves or the lightness and darkness of individual pixels. In Color Plate 8-4, Saturation has the effect of breathing new life into those ancient egg-tempura colors.

✦ **Color (C):** Color mode might be more appropriately titled *Hue and Saturation*. Color enables you to change the colors in an image and the intensity of those colors without changing the lightness and darkness of individual pixels.

The Color mode is most often used to colorize grayscale photographs. Open a grayscale image and then choose Image ➪ Mode ➪ RGB Color to convert the image to the RGB mode. Then select the colors you want to use and start painting. The Color mode ensures the details in the image remain completely intact.

✦ **Luminosity (Y):** The opposite of the Color mode, Luminosity changes the lightness and darkness of pixels, but leaves the hue and saturation values unaffected. Frankly, this mode is rarely useful. But its counterpart — the Luminosity blend mode — is exceptionally useful when applied to layers. Read Chapter 31 to find out more.

## The three dodge and burn modes

Phew, that takes care of the brush modes available to the paint tools, the smudge tool, and the two focus tools. I already explained the Desaturate and Saturate modes available to the sponge tool (in the "Mopping up with the sponge tool" section of this chapter). That leaves us with the three brush modes available to the dodge and burn tools.

As with other brush modes, you can select the dodge and burn modes from the keyboard. Just press Shift+Option/Alt and the letter in parentheses below.

✦ **Shadows (W):** Along with the Midtones and Highlights modes (described next), Shadows is unique to the dodge and burn tools. When you select this mode, the dodge and burn tools affect dark pixels in an image more dramatically than they affect light pixels and shades in between.

✦ **Midtones (V):** Select this mode to apply the dodge or burn tools equally to all but the very lightest or darkest pixels in an image.

✦ **Highlights (Z):** When you select this option, the dodge and burn tools affect light pixels in an image more dramatically than they affect dark pixels and shades in between.

Selecting Shadows when using the dodge tool or selecting Highlights when using the burn tool has an equalizing effect on an image. Figure 8-37 shows how using either of these functions and setting the Exposure slider bar to 100 percent lightens or darkens pixels in an image to nearly identical brightness values.

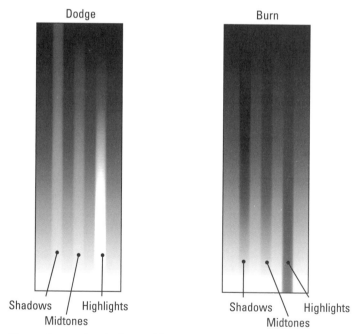

**Figure 8-37:** The dodge and burn tool applied at 100 percent Exposure settings subject to each of the three applicable brush modes.

✦     ✦     ✦

# Filling and Stroking

## Filling Portions of an Image

No explanation of filling and stroking would be complete without a definition, so here goes: To *fill* a selection or layer is to put color inside it; to *stroke* a selection or layer is to put color around it. Some folks prefer the term "outline" to "stroke," but I defer to PostScript terminology because that's where this whole desktop graphics thing started. Besides, when I think outline, I think perimeter, boundary, enclosure, prison, let me out of here. Stroke is more like brush, caress, pet, puppy, warm fire, glad heart. I'm a joker, I'm a smoker, I'm a midnight stroker. I'd rather be stroking. Stop me before I stroke again. And, that timeless favorite, keep on strokin'. So you see, people who prefer the word "outline" have no soul.

But whatever you call them, Photoshop's fill and stroke functions are so straightforward that you may have long since dismissed them as wimpy little tools with remarkably limited potential. But the truth is, you can do a world of stuff with them. In this chapter, for example, I'll show you how to fill selections using nifty keyboard shortcuts, how to create an antique framing effect, how to make the most of Photoshop's new gradient tools, and how to add an arrowhead to a curving line, all in addition to the really basic stuff every Photoshop user needs to know.

As the poet said, "Teacher don't you *fill* me up with your rules, I know *strokin's* not allowed in school." I'd love to share the entire transcript from "Strokin' in the Boy's Room," but this is, after all, a family book.

### In This Chapter

Applying color with the paint bucket tool and Fill command

Having fun with the Delete/Backspace key

Creating an antique framing effect with the paint bucket

Using the new gradient tools in Photoshop 5

Compensating for banding in printed gradations

Designing your own multicolor gradation

Using the gradient tool with the Dissolve brush mode

Creating outlines and borders

Attaching an arrowhead to any stroke

# Filling an Area with Color

You can fill an area of an image with color in four ways:

✦ **The paint bucket tool:** You can apply the foreground color or a repeating pattern to areas of related color in an image by clicking in the image window with the paint bucket tool (known in some circles as the fill tool). For example, if you want to turn all midnight blue pixels in an image into red pixels, set the foreground color to red and then click on one of the blue pixels.

✦ **The Fill command:** Select the portion of the image you want to color and then fill the entire selection with the foreground color or a repeating pattern by choosing Edit ➪ Fill.

To choose the Fill command without so much as moving the mouse, press Shift+Delete/Backspace.

✦ **Delete/Backspace key techniques:** After selecting part of a single-layer image — or part of the Background layer in a multi-layered image — you can fill the selection with the background color by pressing the Delete/Backspace key. On any other layer, press ⌘/Ctrl+Delete/Backspace. To fill the selection with the foreground color, press Option/Alt+Delete/Backspace.

✦ **The gradient tool:** Drag across a selection with a gradient tool to fill it with a multi-color gradation. In Photoshop 5, you can choose between five styles of gradation by pressing Shift+G to cycle between gradient tools.

The following sections discuss each of these options in depth.

## The paint bucket tool

Unlike remedial paint bucket tools in other painting programs, which apply paint exclusively within outlined areas or areas of solid color, the Photoshop paint bucket tool offers several useful adjustment options. To explore them, double-click on the paint bucket icon in the toolbox to display the Paint Bucket Options palette, shown in Figure 9-1. (Or you can press the K key to select the paint bucket tool and then press Return/Enter to display the Options palette.)

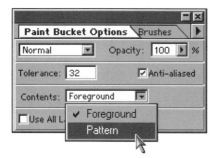

**Figure 9-1:** The Paint Bucket Options palette governs the performance of the paint bucket tool.

The brush mode pop-up menu and the Opacity value work like their counterparts in the Paintbrush Options palette, which I covered at length in Chapter 8. But in case you need a recap, here's how these and other options work, in the order they appear in the palette:

✦ **Brush modes:** Select an option from the brush mode pop-up menu to specify how and when color is applied. For example, if you select Darken (Shift+Option/Alt+K), the paint bucket tool affects a pixel in the image only if the foreground color is darker than that pixel. If you select Color (Shift+Option/Alt+C), the paint bucket colorizes the image without changing the brightness value of the pixels.

✦ In Color Plate 9-1, for example, I used the Color mode to change a few oranges to blue and the background to green, all by clicking on five different spots with the paint bucket tool. I then touched up the stray pixels the paint bucket didn't catch with the paintbrush and airbrush tools.

✦ **Opacity:** Enter a new value or press a number key to change the translucency of a color applied with the paint bucket.

✦ **Tolerance:** You can raise or lower the Tolerance value to increase or decrease the number of pixels affected by the paint bucket tool. The Tolerance value represents a range in brightness values, as measured from the pixel which you click on with the paint bucket.

Immediately after you click on a pixel, Photoshop reads the brightness value of that pixel from each color channel. Next, the program calculates a color range based on the Tolerance value — which can vary from 0 to 255. The program adds the Tolerance to the brightness value of the pixel on which you clicked to determine the top of the range, and subtracts the Tolerance from the pixel's brightness value to determine the bottom of the range. For example, if the pixel's brightness value is 100 and the Tolerance value is 32, the top of the range is 132, and the bottom is 68.

After establishing a Tolerance range, Photoshop applies the foreground color to any pixel that both falls inside the range and touches some other affected pixel. (This way, the paint bucket fills an isolated area, rather than seeping out into every similarly colored pixel in the image.)

Figure 9-2 shows the result of clicking on the same pixel three separate times, each time using a different Tolerance value. In Color Plate 9-1, I raised the Tolerance to 120. But even with this high setting, I had to click several times to recolor all the nooks and crannies of the oranges. The moral is, don't get too hung up on getting the Tolerance exactly right — no matter how you paint it, the bucket is not a precise tool.

Paint bucket cursor

**Figure 9-2:** The results of applying the paint bucket tool to the exact pixel after setting the Tolerance value to 16 (top), 32 (middle), and 64 (bottom). In each case, the foreground color is light gray.

✦ **Anti-aliased:** Select this option to soften the effect of the paint bucket tool. As demonstrated in the left-hand example of Figure 9-3, Photoshop creates a border of translucent color between the filled pixels and their unaffected neighbors. If you don't want to soften the transition, turn off the Anti-aliased check box. Photoshop then fills only those pixels that fall inside the Tolerance range, as demonstrated in the right example of the figure.

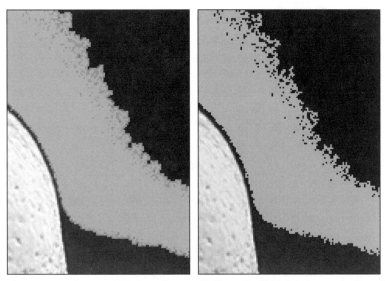

**Figure 9-3:** The results of turning on (left) and off (right) the Anti-aliased check box prior to using the paint bucket tool. It all depends on whether you want cottage cheese or little spiky coral edges.

✦ **Contents:** In this pop-up menu, you can choose whether you want to apply the foreground color or a repeating pattern created using Edit ➪ Define Pattern. The Define Pattern command is covered in the "Applying Repeating Patterns" section of Chapter 10.

✦ **Use All Layers:** Select this option to make the paint bucket see beyond the current layer. When the option is selected, the tool takes all visible layers into account when calculating the area to fill. Mind you, it only fills the active layer, but the way it fills an area is dictated by all layers.

For an example of Use All Layers, look no further than Figure 9-4. The dog sits on one layer and the fire hydrant rests on another layer directly below it. If I were to click on the fire hydrant when the dog layer was active and the Use All Layers check box was turned off, I'd fill everything around the dog. The paint bucket couldn't see the hydrant; all the paint bucket could see would be the transparent area of the dog layer, so it would try to fill that area. To avoid this, I selected Use All Layers and then clicked on the hydrant. With Use All Layers on, the paint bucket could see all layers, so it contained its fill within the hydrant, as in the second example of the figure.

**Figure 9-4:** Although dog and hydrant are on separate layers (top), I can mix them together with Use All Layers. This option enables me to fill an area of the hydrant (middle), even though the dog layer is active. Then I paint in front of and behind the fill without harming the hydrant (bottom).

Because the fill and hydrant were on separate layers, I could edit the two independently of each other. I used the airbrush to paint inside and behind the fill alternatively (using the Behind brush mode, discussed in the previous chapter). I painted the teeth and eyes with the paintbrush and used the smudge tool to mix colors around the white fill. (Naturally, I had to turn on the Use All Layers check box inside the Smudge Tool Options palette as well.) As a result, all the bizarre alterations you see in the bottom example of Figure 9-4 were applied to the dog layer. I didn't change a single pixel in the hydrant layer (which is a good thing — in light of my changes, I might like to get that hydrant back).

To limit the area affected by the paint bucket, select a portion of the image before using the tool. As when using a paint or edit tool, the region outside the selection outline is protected from the paint bucket. To see an interesting application of this, skip ahead to the "Using the paint bucket inside a selection" section later in this chapter.

When working on a layer, you can, likewise, protect pixels by turning on the Preserve Transparency check box in the Layers palette. Like all layering issues, I cover Preserve Transparency in Chapter 17.

Here's one more paint bucket tip for good measure: You can use the paint bucket to color the empty window area around your image. First, make your image window larger than your image, so you can see some gray canvas area around the image. Now Shift+click with the paint bucket to fill the canvas area with the foreground color. This technique can come in handy if you're creating a presentation or you simply don't care for the default shade of gray.

## The Fill command

The one problem with the paint bucket tool is its lack of precision. Although undeniably convenient, the effects of the Tolerance value are so difficult to predict, you typically have to click with the tool, choose Edit ⇨ Undo when you don't like the result, adjust the Tolerance value, and reclick with the tool several times more before you fill the image as desired. For my part, I rarely use the paint bucket for any purpose other than filling same-colored areas. On my machine, the Tolerance option is nearly always set to 0 and Anti-alias is generally off, which puts me right back in the all-the-subtlety-of-dumping-paint-out-of-a-bucket camp.

A better option is to select the area you want to fill and choose Edit ⇨ Fill or press Shift+Delete/Backspace. (If you prefer function keys, try Shift+F5.) In this way, you can define the exact area of the image you want to color using the entire range of Photoshop's selection tools, which are so extensive they consume all four chapters in Part V. For example, instead of putting your faith in the paint bucket tool's Anti-aliased option, you can draw a selection outline that features hard edges in one area, anti-aliased edges elsewhere, and downright blurry edges in between.

When you press Shift+Delete/Backspace, Photoshop displays the Fill dialog box shown in Figure 9-5. In this dialog box, you can apply a translucent color or pattern by entering a value into the Opacity option box. You can also choose a brush mode option from the Mode pop-up menu. In addition to its inherent precision, the Fill command maintains all the functionality of the paint bucket tool—and then some.

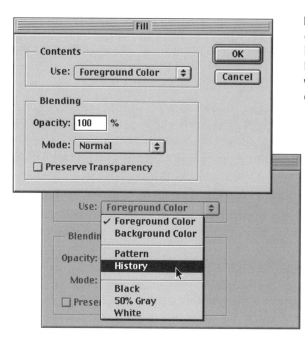

**Figure 9-5:** The Fill dialog box combines the Opacity and brush mode options from the Paint Bucket Options palette with an expanded collection of Contents options.

If you display the Contents pop-up menu, as shown in the lower example in Figure 9-5, you'll see a collection of things you can use to fill the selected area. Foreground Color and Pattern perform the same functions they do with the paint bucket tool. You can also fill a selection with the Background Color and such monochrome options as Black, White, and 50% Gray. Black and White are useful if the foreground and background colors have been changed from their defaults; 50% Gray fills the selection with the absolute medium color without having to mess around with the Color palette. History enables you to revert the selected area to a previous appearance, as I discuss at length in Chapter 10.

The Preserve Transparency check box works exactly like the identically named option in the Layers palette (discussed in Chapter 17). When the option is turned on, you can't fill the transparent pixels in the active layer. When Preserve Transparency is turned off, you can fill the selection outline uniformly. (The option is dimmed when you're working on the background layer or when the Preserve Transparency check box in the Layers palette is already turned on.)

## Delete/Backspace-key techniques

Of all the fill techniques, the Delete key (or Backspace key on Windows machines) is by far the most convenient and, in most respects, every bit as capable as the

others. The key's only failing is that it can neither fill a selection with a repeating pattern nor revert a selection
to a previous state. But with the exception of those two items, you can rely on the Delete/Backspace key for the overwhelming majority of your fill needs.

Here's how to get a ton of functionality out of Delete/Backspace:

✦ **Background color, method 1:** To fill a selection on the background layer with solid background color, press Delete/Backspace. The selection outline remains intact.

✦ **Background color, method 2:** The problem with pressing Delete/Backspace is it's unreliable. If the selection is floating, as I explain in Chapter 15, the Delete/Backspace key deletes it. The Delete/Backspace key also erases pixels on a layer. So there's no time like the present to get into a new habit — press ⌘/Ctrl+Delete/Backspace instead. ⌘/Ctrl+Delete/Backspace fills the selection with the background color, no matter where it is.

✦ **Foreground color:** To fill a selection or layer with solid foreground color, press Option/Alt+Delete/Backspace. This works when filling floating and nonfloating selections alike.

✦ **Black or white:** To fill an area with black, press D to get the default foreground and background colors and then press Option/Alt+Delete/Backspace. To fill it with white, press D for the defaults and then ⌘/Ctrl+Delete/Backspace.

✦ **Preserve transparency:** Add the Shift key and you get two more key tricks that will make more sense when you read Chapter 17. (Don't worry, I'll repeat the tricks then.) You can fill only the opaque pixels in a layer — whether or not Preserve Transparency is turned on — by pressing Shift. Press Shift+ Option/Alt+Delete/Backspace to fill a selection with the foreground color while preserving transparency. Press ⌘/Ctrl+Shift+Delete/Backspace to fill the opaque pixels with the background color.

## Using the paint bucket inside a selection

So far, I've come up with two astounding generalizations: The paint bucket tool is mostly useless, and you can fill anything with the Delete/Backspace key. Well, just to prove you shouldn't believe everything I say — some might even suggest you dismiss everything I say — the following steps explain how to create an effect you can perform only with the paint bucket tool. Doubtless, it's the only such example you'll ever discover using Photoshop — after all, the paint bucket is mostly useless and you can fill anything with the Delete/Backspace key — but I'm man enough to eat my rules this once.

The following steps explain how to create an antique photographic frame effect like the one shown in Figure 9-6.

## Steps: Creating an Antique Framing Effect

1. **Use the rectangular marquee tool to select the portion of the image you want to frame.** Make certain the image extends at least 20 pixels outside the boundaries of the selection outline. And be sure to use a photo — this effect won't look right against a plain white background.

2. **Choose Select ⇨ Feather (⌘/Ctrl+Option/Alt+D).** Then specify a Radius value somewhere in the neighborhood of 6 to12 pixels. I've found these values work for nearly any resolution of image. (If you enter too high a value, the color you'll add in a moment with the paint bucket will run out into the image.)

**Figure 9-6:** I created this antique frame effect by filling a feathered selection with the paint bucket tool.

3. **Choose Select ⇨ Inverse (⌘/Ctrl+Shift+I).** This exchanges the selected and deselected portions of the image.

4. **Press the D key to make certain the background color is white.** Then press ⌘/Ctrl+Delete/Backspace to fill the selected area with the background color.

5. **Select the paint bucket tool and press Return/Enter to display the Paint Bucket Options palette.** Enter 20 to 30 in the Tolerance option box and turn on the Anti-aliased check box. (You can also experiment with turning off this option.)

6. **Click inside the feathered selection to fill it with black.** The result is an image fading into white and then into black, like the edges of a worn slide or photograph, as shown in Figure 9-6.

Figure 9-7 shows a variation on this effect you can create using the Dissolve brush mode. Rather than setting the Tolerance value to 20, raise it to around 60. Then select the Dissolve option from the brush mode pop-up menu in the Paint Bucket Options palette. When you click inside the feathered selection with the paint bucket tool, you create a frame of random pixels, as illustrated in the figure.

**Figure 9-7:** Select Dissolve from the Brushes palette pop-up menu to achieve a speckled frame effect.

# Applying Gradient Fills

The last two versions of Photoshop have witnessed great strides in the gradation department. Version 4 introduced the Edit button into the Gradient Options palette. This one button made it possible to create a gradient with as many as 32 colors, name gradients and save them to disk, and adjust the transparency of colors so they fade in and out over the course of the fill.

Version 5 goes a step better, widening the range of gradient styles to include angled (conical), reflected, and diamond patterns. You can also reverse the foreground and background colors from within the Gradient Options palette, a nice convenience feature when applying radial and diamond fills. You still can't apply a gradation along a path, but that seems to be the only remaining omission.

If you're used to using gradients in a drawing program — such as Illustrator or FreeHand — Photoshop is better. Because Photoshop is a pixel editor, it lets you blur and mix colors in a gradation if they start *banding* — banding being when you can see a hard edge between one color and the next when you print the image. And Photoshop's gradations will never choke the printer or slow it down, no matter how many colors you add. While each band of color in an object-oriented gradation is expressed as a separate shape — so one gradation can contain hundreds, or even thousands, of objects — gradations in Photoshop are plain old colored pixels, the kind we've been editing for eight and a half chapters.

## Using the gradient tools

First, the basics. A *gradation* (also called a *gradient fill*) is a progression of colors that fade gradually into one another, as demonstrated in Figure 9-8. You specify a few key colors in the gradation, and Photoshop automatically generates the hundred or so colors in between to create a smooth transition.

You apply gradations using one of the five gradient tools, located just above the eyedropper in the toolbox. Unlike the paint bucket, which fills areas of similar color according to the Tolerance setting, the gradient tool affects all colors within a selection. If you don't select a portion of your image, Photoshop applies the gradation to the entire layer.

To select the default linear gradient tool, press the G key. To use the tool, drag inside the selection, as shown in the left example of Figure 9-8. The point at which you begin dragging (upper left corner in the figure) defines the location of the first color in the gradation. The point at which you release (lower right corner) defines the location of the last color. If multiple portions of the image are selected, the gradation fills all selections continuously, as demonstrated by the right example of Figure 9-8.

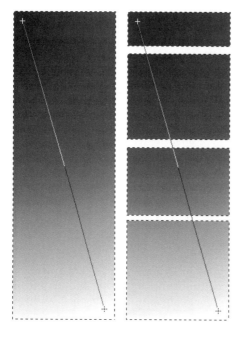

**Figure 9-8:** Dragging with the gradient tool within a single selection (left) and across multiple selections (right) of the gradation.

# Gradient styles

In Photoshop 5, switching to a different gradient tool changes the style of gradation. In previous versions, you could select between two styles — linear and radial — by selecting a Type option from the Gradient Options palette. Now, you switch styles either by Option/Alt+clicking on the gradient tool icon in the toolbox or by pressing Shift+G.

Shown in Figure 9-9, the five styles are as follows:

✦ **Linear:** A linear gradation progresses in bands of color in a straight line between the beginning and end of your drag. The top two examples in Figure 9-9 show linear gradations created from black to white, and from white to black. The point labeled B marks the beginning of the drag; E marks the end.

✦ **Radial:** A radial gradation progresses outward from a central point in concentric circles, as in the second row of examples in Figure 9-9. The point at which you begin dragging defines the center of the gradation, and the point at which you release defines the outermost circle. This means the first color in the gradation appears in the center of the fill. So to create the gradation on the right side of Figure 9-9, you must set white to the foreground color and black to the background color (or select the Reverse check box in the Gradient Options palette).

✦ **Angle:** The angle gradient tool creates a fountain of colors flowing in a counterclockwise direction with respect to your drag, as demonstrated by the middle two examples of Figure 9-9. This type of gradient is known more commonly as a conical gradation, because it looks like the bird's eye view of the top of a cone.

Of course, a real cone doesn't have the sharp edge between black and white that you see in Photoshop's angle gradient. To eliminate this edge, create a custom gradation from black to white to black again, as I explain in the "Adding and deleting color stops" section later in this chapter. (Take a peek at Figure 9-16 if you're not sure what I'm talking about.)

✦ **Reflected:** Drag with the fourth gradient tool to create a linear gradation that reflects back on itself. Photoshop positions the foreground color at the beginning of your drag and the background color at the end, as when using the linear gradient tool. But it also repeats the gradient in the opposite direction of your drag, as demonstrated in Figure 9-9. It's great for creating natural shadows or highlights that fade in two directions.

✦ **Diamond:** The last gradient tool creates a series of concentric diamonds (if you drag at a 90-degree angle) or squares (if you drag at a 45-degree angle, as in Figure 9-9). Otherwise, it works exactly like the radial gradient tool.

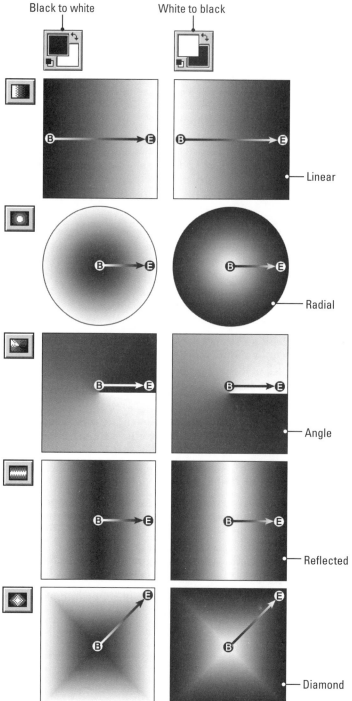

**Figure 9-9:** Examples of each of the five gradient styles created using the default foreground and background colors (left column) and with the foreground and background colors reversed (right column). B marks the beginning of the drag, E marks the end.

# Gradient options

To master any of the gradient tools, you must understand how to modify its performance. Press Return/Enter when a gradient tool is active to display the Gradient Options palette, shown in Figure 9-10. (This happens to be the Linear Gradient Options palette, but they all look the same.) This palette lets you specify the colors in a gradation, as well as the arrangement of those colors, using the following options:

✦ **Brush mode and Opacity:** These options work the same way they do in the paint and edit tool Options palettes, in the Paint Bucket Options palette, in the Fill dialog box, and everywhere else they pop up. Select a different brush mode to change how colors are applied; lower the Opacity value to make a gradation translucent. In both cases — as with all the other options in this palette — you must adjust the options before using the gradient tool. They do not affect existing gradations.

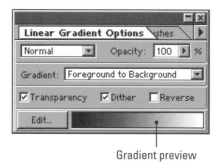

Gradient preview

**Figure 9-10:** The Gradient Options palette provides access to the all-important Edit button, which enables you to create custom gradations.

✦ **Gradient:** The Gradient pop-up menu provides access to gobs of factory-predefined gradations. When you select a gradation, Photoshop displays it in the gradient preview (labeled in Figure 9-10). The first three factory gradations are dependent on the current foreground and background colors. The others contain specific colors bearing no relationship to the colors in the toolbox. If you create and name your own custom gradations, they will also show up in this menu.

✦ **Transparency:** You can specify different levels of opacity throughout a gradation. For example, the Transparent Stripes effect (available from the Gradient pop-up menu) lays down a series of alternately black and transparent stripes. But you needn't use this transparency information. If you prefer to apply a series of black and white stripes instead, you can make all portions of the gradation equally opaque by turning off the Transparency check box.

✦ **Dither:** In the old days, Photoshop drew its gradients one band at a time. Each band was filled with an incrementally different shade of color. The potential result was banding, in which you could clearly distinguish the transition between two or more bands of color. The Dither check box helps to eliminate this problem by mixing up the pixels between bands (much as Photoshop dithers pixels when converting a grayscale image to black and white). You should leave this option turned on unless you want to use the banding to create a special effect.

 ✦ **Reverse:** When active, this simple check box begins the gradation with the background color and ends it with the foreground color. Use this option when you want to start a radial or other style of gradation with white, but you want to keep the foreground and background colors set to their defaults.

## Eliminating gradient banding

Adobe assures me that banding problems have been all but eliminated in Photoshop 5. And while gradations are certainly smoother in the new version, I'm not sure I'd go so far as to assure you that banding is altogether a thing of the past. After all, banding has as much to do with the capabilities of your printer as with Photoshop's ability to generate properly colored pixels. If you never once see any banding in your output, excellent. Skip this section and have a nice day. But if you do experience banding, this section describes how to eliminate it.

As explained in Chapter 23, the Add Noise filter randomizes pixels in a selection. So when you apply Filter ➪ Noise ➪ Add Noise to a gradation, it randomly mixes the bands of color, very much like a variable dithering function. In fact, it enables you to outdither the Dither check box.

The first column in Figure 9-11 shows linear and radial gradations. In the second column, I applied the Add Noise filter three times in a row to both gradations. To make the effect as subtle as possible — you don't want the noise to be obvious — I specified an Amount value of 8 and selected the Uniform radio button inside the Add Noise dialog box. Multiple repetitions of a subtle noise effect are preferable to a single application of a more radical effect.

If noise isn't enough or if the noise appears a little too obvious, you can further mix the colors in a gradation by applying a directional blur filter. To blur a linear or reflected gradation, apply the Motion Blur filter in the direction of the gradation. In the top-right example of Figure 9-11, I applied Filter ➪ Blur ➪ Motion Blur with an Angle value of 90 degrees (straight up and down) and a Distance value of 3 pixels.

To blur a radial, angle, or diamond gradation, apply the Radial Blur filter (Filter ➪ Blur ➪ Radial Blur). To mix the noise around the center of the gradation, select the Spin option in the Radial Blur dialog box. To blend color in the bands, select the Zoom option. The lower right example in Figure 9-11 is divided into two halves. To create the top half, I applied the Spin option with an Amount value of 10; to create the bottom half, I applied Zoom with an Amount value of 20. (If you can barely see any difference between the two — that's the idea when it comes to gradations — look closely at the perimeter of the gradients. The top one, created with the Spin option, is smooth; the bottom one, created with the Zoom option, is rougher.)

**Cross-Reference**

You can get a sense of what the Add Noise, Motion Blur, and Radial Blur filters do by experimenting with them for a few minutes. If you want to learn even more, I discuss all four in Chapter 23.

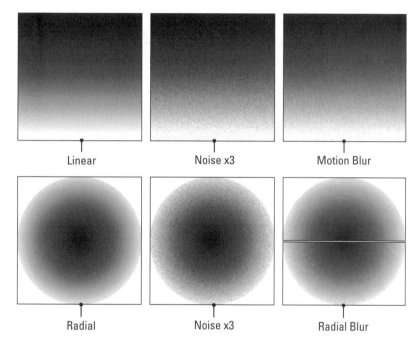

Linear          Noise x3          Motion Blur

Radial          Noise x3          Radial Blur

**Figure 9-11:** The results of applying noise (middle column) and directional blur effects (right column) to linear and radial gradations.

## Creating custom gradations

The only remaining option in the Gradient Options palette is the Edit button. Click on this button to create your own custom gradation or to edit one of the factory presets. Photoshop answers your request with the Gradient Editor dialog box, pictured in Figure 9-12. Because this dialog box has so much going on in it, I've lifted the most essential options and labeled them in Figure 9-13.

Select a named gradation that interests you from the scrolling list. Then click on the Duplicate button to design a new gradation based on the selected one. Photoshop asks you to name the new gradient. Do so and then press Return/Enter.

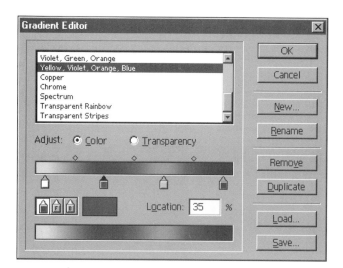

**Figure 9-12:** Click on the Edit button in the Gradient Options palette to bring up this dialog box, which allows you to design your own custom gradations.

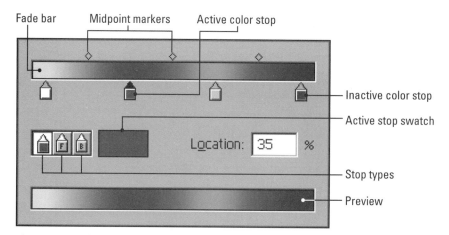

**Figure 9-13:** These few small options are quite powerful. Despite the array of buttons available in the Gradient Editor dialog box, these controls are where it's happening.

## Positioning colors and midpoint markers

Below the scrolling list is the *fade bar* (labeled in Figure 9-13). The starting color appears as a house-shaped *color stop* on the left; the ending color appears on the far right. Positioned between each pair of color stops along the top of the fade bar is a diamond-shaped *midpoint marker*, which represents the spot where the two colors mix in exactly equal amounts. You can change the location of any stop or marker by dragging it. Or you can click on a stop or marker to select it and then enter a value into the Location option box below the fade bar. The selected stop or marker appears black.

✦ When numerically positioning a selected color stop, a value of 0 percent indicates the left end of the fade bar; 100 percent indicates the right end. Even if you add more color stops to the gradation, the values represent absolute positions along the fade bar.

✦ When repositioning a midpoint marker, the initial setting of 50 percent is smack dab between the two color stops; 0 percent is all the way over to the left stop; and 100 percent is all the way over to the right. Midpoint values are, therefore, measured relative to color stop positions. In fact, when you move a color stop, Photoshop moves the midpoint marker along with it to maintain the same relative positioning. Figure 9-14 shows four radial gradations subjected to different midpoint settings.

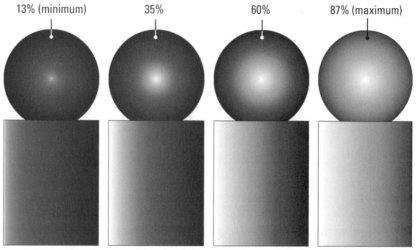

**Figure 9-14:** Four sets of white-to-black gradations — radial on top and linear at bottom — subject to different midpoint settings.

Pressing Return/Enter after you enter a value into the Location option box is tempting, but don't do it. If you do, Photoshop will dump you out of the Gradient Editor dialog box. Instead, press the Tab key. Tab advances you from one marker to the next — from color stop to midpoint marker to the next color stop and so on. Press Shift+Tab to move to the previous marker.

## Adjusting the colors in a gradation

You can change the colors in a gradation by selecting a color stop and clicking on the active stop swatch (immediately to the left of the Location option box). Photoshop displays the familiar Color Picker dialog box. Select the desired color and press Return/Enter.

That's the hard way. The easy way is to lift a color from the image window. When you move the cursor outside the dialog box into the image window, it changes to an eyedropper. Just click on the color in the image you want to use. You can also click on the Color palette's color bar or in the Swatches palette.

If you want a color stop to vary with the active foreground color, select the color stop and click on the little F icon in the stop types area (on the left side of the dialog box, labeled back in Figure 9-13). To use the background color, select a stop and click on the little B icon.

### Adding and deleting color stops

Here are three last items you should know about color stops:

✦ Photoshop 4 was limited to 32 colors per gradient, but Version 5 lets you add as many colors as you like. To add a color stop, click anywhere along the bottom of the fade bar. A new stop appears right where you click. Photoshop also adds a midpoint marker between the new color stop and its neighbor.

✦ To duplicate a color stop, Option/Alt+drag it to a new location along the fade bar. One great use for this to create a reflecting gradation.

For example, select Foreground to Background from the scrolling list of gradients and click on the Duplicate button. After naming your new gradient — something like Fore to Back to Fore — click on the B stop and change the Location value to 50. Then Option/Alt+drag the F stop all the way to the right. This new gradient is perfect for making true conical gradations with the angle gradient tool, as demonstrated in Figure 9-15.

✦ To remove a color stop, drag the stop away from the fade bar. The stop icon vanishes and the fade bar automatically adjusts as defined by the remaining color stops.

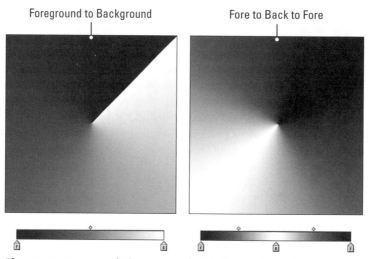

**Figure 9-15:** Two gradations created with the angle gradient tool, one using the standard Foreground to Background gradient (left) and the other with my reflected Fore to Back to Fore style (right). Which looks better to you?

## Adjusting the transparency mask

If you like, you can include a *transparency mask* with each gradation. The mask determines where the colors are opaque and where they fade into translucency or even transparency. You create and edit this mask independently of the colors in the gradation, and you can turn it on and off using the Transparency check box in the Gradient Options palette (as explained earlier).

To create a transparency mask, click on the Transparency radio button in the Gradient Editor dialog box. The fade bar changes to reflect the transparency settings (if any), as shown in Figure 9-16. As when editing colors, you click under the fade bar to add *transparency stops*, drag the stops to move them, and to edit the Location value to position a selected stop numerically.

The difference is, instead of changing the color of the stops, you modify their opacity. By default, each new stop is 100 percent opaque. You can modify the transparency by selecting a stop and changing the Opacity value. The preview along the bottom of the dialog box updates to reflect your changes. A checkerboard pattern represents the underlying image.

Color Plate 9-2 demonstrates the effect of applying a three-color gradation to a photograph. The gradation fades from red to transparency to green to transparency and, finally, to blue. In the first example in the color plate, I dragged over a standard checkerboard pattern with the gradient tool, from the lower left corner to the upper right corner. The second example shows the photograph prior to applying the gradation. In the last example, I applied the gradient — again from lower left to upper right — using the Overlay brush mode.

**Figure 9-16:** Click on the Transparency radio button to switch to a different fade bar that controls how the gradation fades in and out of sight.

### Saving gradients

Photoshop automatically saves your custom gradients to the Adobe Photoshop 5 Prefs file. But as we all know, Prefs can go bad. Clicking on the Save button in the Gradient Editor dialog box gives you the option of saving the selected gradients to a more secure, less volatile location.

Note that Photoshop 5 saves only those gradients that you select from the list. (Version 4 saved all gradients, whether selected or not.) This gives you more control, so you don't go saving the same gradient to multiple files—unless, of course, you want to.

To save a range of gradients, click on one and then Shift+click on another before clicking on the Save button. To select multiple non-sequential gradients, ⌘/Ctrl+ click on them.

## Gradations and brush modes

Overlay isn't the only brush mode you can use with gradations. All 18 of the standard brush modes are available and they make a tremendous impression on the performance of the gradient tool. This section examines yet another way to apply a brush mode in conjunction with the tool. Naturally, it barely scrapes the surface of what's possible, but it may inspire you to experiment and discover additional effects on your own.

The following steps tell you how to use the Dissolve mode in combination with a radial gradation to create a supernova explosion. (At least, it looks like a supernova to me—not that I've ever seen one up close, mind you.) Figures 9-17 through 9-19 show the nova in progress. The steps offer you the opportunity to experiment with a brush mode setting and some general insight into creating radial gradations.

These steps involve the use of the elliptical marquee tool. Generally speaking, it's an easy tool to use. But if you find you have problems making it work according to my instructions, you may want to read the "Geometric selection outlines" section of Chapter 15. It's only a few pages long.

### Steps: Creating a Gradient Supernova

1. **Create a new image window.** Make it 500×500 pixels. A grayscale image is fine for this exercise.

2. **Click with the pencil tool at the apparent center of the image.** Don't worry if it's not the exact center. This point is merely intended to serve as a guide. If a single point is not large enough for you to identify easily, draw a small cross.

*Continued*

3. **Option/Alt+drag from the point with the elliptical marquee tool to draw the marquee outward from the center.** You can select the elliptical marquee tool by pressing the M key twice in a row. While dragging with the tool, press and hold the Shift key to constrain the marquee to a circle. Release Shift after you release the mouse button. Draw a marquee that fills about ¾ of the window.

4. **Choose Image ➪ Adjust ➪ Invert (⌘/Ctrl+I).** This fills the marquee with black and makes the center point white.

5. **Choose Select ➪ Deselect (⌘/Ctrl+D).** As the command name suggests, this deselects the circle.

6. **Again, Option/Alt+drag from the center point with the elliptical marquee tool.** And, again, press Shift to constrain the shape to a circle. Create a marquee roughly 20 pixels larger than the black circle.

7. **Option/Alt+drag from the center point with the elliptical marquee tool.** This subtracts a hole from the selection. After you begin dragging, release the Option/Alt key (but keep that mouse button down). Then press and hold both Shift and Option/Alt together and keep them down. Draw a marquee roughly 20 pixels smaller than the black circle. Release the mouse button and finally release the keys. The result is a doughnut-shaped selection — a large circle with a smaller circular hole — as shown in Figure 9-17.

8. **Choose Select ➪ Feather (⌘/Ctrl+Option/Alt+D) and enter 10 for the Radius value.** Then press Return/Enter to feather the section outline.

9. **Press the D key, and then press X.** This makes the foreground color white and the background color black.

10. **Select the radial gradient tool.** Assuming default settings, you can get to it by pressing G and then Shift+G. Otherwise, just keep pressing Shift+G until it comes up.

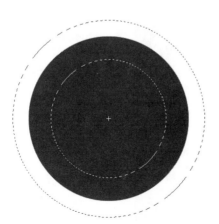

**Figure 9-17:** The result of creating a black circle and two circular marquees, all centered about a single point.

11. **Press Return/Enter to display the Options palette.** Then select Foreground to Background from the Gradient pop-up menu.

12. **Select Dissolve from the brush mode pop-up menu.** It's the one on the left side of the Gradient Options palette.

13. **Drag from the center point in the image window to anywhere along the outer rim of the largest marquee.** The result is the fuzzy gradation shown in Figure 9-18.

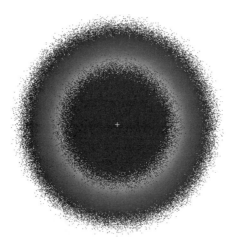

**Figure 9-18:** The Dissolve brush mode option randomizes the pixels around the feathered edges of the selection outlines.

14. **Choose Select ➪ Deselect (⌘/Ctrl+D) to deselect the image.**

15. **Choose Image ➪ Adjust ➪ Invert (⌘/Ctrl+I) to invert the entire image.**

16. **Press the D key to restore black and white as foreground and background colors, respectively.** Then use the eraser tool to erase the center point. The finished supernova appears in Figure 9-19.

**Figure 9-19:** By inverting the image from the previous figure and erasing the center point, you create an expanding series of progressively lighter rings dissolving into the black void of space, an effect better known to its friends as a supernova.

# Applying Strokes and Arrowheads

Photoshop is nearly as adept at drawing lines and outlines as it is at filling selections. The following sections discuss how to apply a border around a selection outline — which is practical, if not terribly exciting — and how to create arrowheads — which can yield more interesting results than you might think.

## Stroking a selection outline

Stroking is useful for creating frames and outlines. Generally speaking, you can stroke an image in Photoshop in three ways:

✦ **The Stroke command:** Select the portion of the image you want to stroke and choose Edit ➪ Stroke to display the Stroke dialog box shown in Figure 9-20. Enter the thickness of the stroke in pixels into the Width option box. Select a Location radio button to specify the position of the stroke with respect to the selection outline. The Stroke dialog box also includes Opacity, Mode, and Preserve Transparency options that work like those in the Fill dialog box.

Tip

When in doubt, select Inside from the Location radio buttons. This setting ensures the stroke is entirely inside the selection outline in case you decide to move the selection. If you select Center or Outside, Photoshop may apply part or all of the stroke to the deselected area around the selection outline.

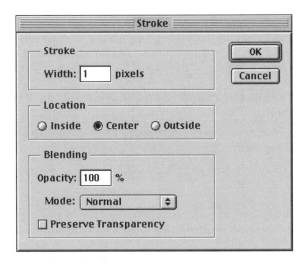

**Figure 9-20:** Use the options in the Stroke dialog box to specify the thickness of a stroke and its location with respect to the selection outline.

✦ **The Border command:** Select a portion of the image and choose Select ➪ Modify ➪ Border to retain only the outline of the selection. Specify the size of the border by entering a value in pixels into the Width option box and press Return/Enter. To fill the border with the background color, press ⌘/Ctrl+ Delete/Backspace. To fill the border with the foreground color, press

Option/Alt+Delete/Backspace. To apply a repeating pattern to the border, choose Edit ➪ Fill and select the Pattern option from the Use pop-up menu. You can even apply a command under the Filter menu or some other special effect.

✦ **The Canvas Size trick:** Okay, so this one is a throwaway, but I use it all the time. To create an outline around the entire image, change the background color (yes, the background color) to the color you want to apply to the outline. Then choose Image ➪ Canvas Size and add twice the desired border thickness to the Width and Height options in pixels.

For example, to create a 1-pixel border all the way around, add 2 pixels to the Width value (1 for the left side and 1 for the right) and 2 pixels to the Height value (1 for the top and 1 for the bottom). Leave the Anchor option set to the center tile. When you press Return/Enter, Photoshop enlarges the canvas size according to your specifications and fills the new pixels around the perimeter of the image with the background color. Simplicity at its best.

## Applying arrowheads

The one function missing from all the operations in the previous list is applying arrowheads. The fact is, in Photoshop, you can apply arrowheads only to straight lines drawn with the line tool.

To get to the line tool in Photoshop 5, you have to Option/Alt+click on the pencil tool icon in the toolbox. Or press N to select the pencil tool slot then Shift+N to switch to the line tool.

Double-click on the line tool icon in the toolbox (or press Return/Enter when the line tool is active) to display the Line Options palette shown in Figure 9-21. Enter a value into the Weight option box to specify the thickness of the line and then use the Arrowheads options as follows:

✦ **Start:** Select this check box to append an arrowhead to the beginning of a line drawn with the line tool.

✦ **End:** Select this check box to append an arrowhead to the end of a line. (Like you needed me to tell you this.)

✦ **Shape:** Click on the Shape button to display the Arrowhead Shape dialog box, which also appears in Figure 9-21.

The Arrowhead Shape dialog box contains three options, which enable you to specify the size and shape of the arrowhead as a function of the line weight:

✦ **Width:** Enter the width of the arrowhead into this option box. The width is measured as a percentage of the line weight, so if the Weight is set to 6 pixels and the Width value is 500 percent, then the width of the arrowhead will be 30 pixels. Math in action.

✦ **Length:** Enter the length of the arrowhead, measured from the base of the arrowhead to its tip, again as a percentage of the line weight.

✦ **Concavity:** You can specify the shape of the arrowhead by entering a value between negative and positive 50 percent into the Concavity option box. Figure 9-22 shows examples of a few Concavity settings applied to an arrowhead 50 pixels wide and 100 pixels long.

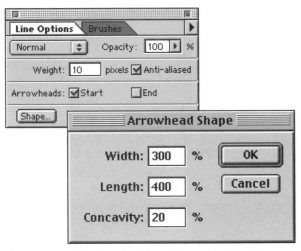

**Figure 9-21:** Click on the Shape button in the Line Options palette (top) to display the Arrowhead Shape box (bottom). The line tool remains the only way to create arrowheads in Photoshop.

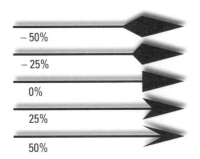

**Figure 9-22:** Examples of a 50×100-pixel arrowhead subject to five different Concavity values.

## Appending arrowheads to curved lines

Applying arrowheads to straight lines is a simple matter. Double-click on the line tool icon, select a few choice options, and draw a line. Applying an arrowhead to a stroked selection outline is a little trickier, but still possible. The following steps explain the process.

## Steps: Adding an Arrowhead to a Free-form Stroke

1. **Create a new layer.** Display the Layers palette by pressing the F7 key. Then click on the little page icon at the bottom of the palette to create a new layer.

2. **Draw and stroke a selection.** Draw any selection outline you like. Stroke it by choosing Edit ➪ Stroke and applying whatever settings strike your fancy. Remember the value you enter into the Width option. In Figure 9-23, I drew a wiggly line with the lasso tool and applied a 4-pixel black stroke set to 30 percent Opacity.

3. **Press ⌘/Ctrl+D.** This deselects all portions of the image.

4. **Erase the portions of the stroke you don't need.** Select the eraser tool by pressing the E key. Then drag to erase through the stroke layer without harming the layer below. Erase away the areas of the stroke at which you want to add arrowheads. I wanted to add an arrowhead behind the fly, so I erased around the fly.

5. **Select the line tool and press Return/Enter.** Up comes the Line Options palette.

**Figure 9-23:** Here, I created a new layer, drew a free-form shape with the lasso tool, and stroked it with a 4-pixel black outline at 30 percent Opacity.

6. **Specify the arrowhead settings.** Enter the line weight you used when stroking the selection outline into the Weight option box (in my case, 4 pixels). Then select the End check box and deselect the Start check box. Click on the Shape button and specify the width, length, and concavity of the arrowhead as desired.

7. **Set the foreground color as needed.** I applied a black stroke at 30 percent Opacity, so I set the foreground color to 30 percent gray. (Click on the stroke with the eyedropper to change the foreground color to the stroke color.)

8. **Zoom in on the point in the image at which you want to add the arrowhead.** You have to get in close enough to see what you're doing, as in Figure 9-24.

9. **Draw a very short line exactly the length of the arrowhead at the tip of the stroke.** Figure 9-24 illustrates what I mean. This may take some practice to accomplish. Start the line a few pixels in from the end of the stroke to make sure the base of the arrowhead fits snugly. If you mess up the first time, choose Edit ➪ Undo (⌘/Ctrl+Z) and try again.

**Figure 9-24:** Use the line tool to draw a line no longer than the arrowhead. This appends the arrow to the end of the stroke. The view size of this image is magnified to 300 percent.

That's all there is to it. From there on, you can continue to edit the stroke as you see fit. In Figure 9-25, for example, I erased a series of scratches across the stroke to create a dashed-line effect, all the rage for representing cartoon fly trails. I then set the eraser brush size to the largest, fuzziest setting and erased the end of the stroke (above the dog's head) to create a gradual trailing off. That crazy fly is now officially distracting our hero from his appointed rounds.

**Figure 9-25:** I finished by erasing dashes into the line and softening the end of the trail with a large, fuzzy eraser.

✦    ✦    ✦

# Retouching, Repeating, and Restoring

## Three of the Best

So far in Part III, we've looked at more than a dozen tools covering a host of editing disciplines — smearing and sponging, focus and color adjustment, filling and stroking, and plain old painting. But while most of these tools perform as well as can be expected, they don't add up to a hill of beans compared with Photoshop's foremost retouchers — the rubber stamp, the eraser, and the history brush. These remarkable three permit you to repair damaged images, create and apply repeating patterns, erase away mistakes, and restore operations from your recent past. Together, they permit you to perform the sorts of miracles that simply weren't possible in the days before computer imaging, all without the slightest fear of damaging your image.

Very briefly, here's how each tool works:

✦ **Rubber stamp:** Use the rubber stamp to replicate pixels from one area in an image to another. This one feature makes the rubber stamp the perfect tool for removing dust and scratches, repairing defects, and eliminating distracting background elements. Option/Alt+click on the rubber stamp icon in the toolbox or press Shift+S to switch to the pattern stamp tool, which paints with a repeating image fragment defined using Edit ➪ Define Pattern.

If you're wondering what happened to the rubber stamp's From Saved, From Snapshot, and Impressionist functions, they've been transferred to the history brush.

Photoshop **5.0**

✦ **Eraser:** When used in a single-layer image or on the Background layer, the eraser paints in the background color. When applied to a layer, it erases pixels to reveal the layers below. You can change the performance of the eraser either by Option/Alt+clicking on the eraser icon in the toolbox or by pressing Shift+E. This cycles through the four brush settings shown in Figure 10-1.

✦ **History brush:** The new history brush selectively reverts to any of several previous states listed in the History palette. To select the "source state" that you want to paint with, click in the first column of the History palette. A brush icon identifies the source state, as illustrated by the Duplicate item in Figure 10-1.

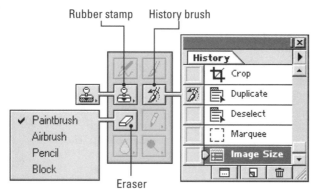

**Figure 10-1:** The three image restoration tools shown with the primary options for modifying their performance.

(If Photoshop displays a little not-allowed cursor when you try to use the history brush, it means you can't paint from the selected state. Click on another state in the History palette and try again.)

Obviously, these are but the skimpiest of all possible introductions, every bit as stingy with information as a nineteenth-century headmaster might have been with his Christmas gruel and treacle. But fear not, my hungry one. This chapter doles out so many courses of meaty facts, fibrous techniques, and sweet, buttery insights that you'll need a whole box of toothpicks to dislodge the excess tips from your incisors.

# Cloning Image Elements

In previous versions of Photoshop, the rubber stamp tools did everything but mop the floor, iron your socks, and call the kids for dinner. It had become a clearing house for every misfit function that didn't seem to fit anywhere else. Thankfully, the new history brush has appropriated and improved upon the most extreme of the superfluous functions, leaving the rubber stamp to do what it does best — clone image elements.

Personally, I've always found the name "rubber stamp" misleading. First, no tree sap is involved — let's get that sticky issue resolved right off the bat. Second, you don't use the tool to stamp an image. When I think of rubber stamps, I think of those things you see in stationery stores that plunk down smiley faces and Pooh bears. Elementary school teachers and little girls use rubber stamps. I've never seen a professional image editor walking around with a rubber stamp in my life.

A better name for the rubber stamp is the clone tool, because that's precisely what it does — it duplicates portions of an image. After selecting the tool (by pressing the S key), Option/Alt+click in the image window to specify the portion of the image you want to clone. Then paint with the tool to clone the Option/Alt+clicked area of the image.

If this is your first experience with a clone tool, it might sound peculiar. Sheep, cows, dinosaurs — these are things you might want to clone. Pixels, never. But as any dyed-in-the-wool Photoshop user will tell you, the rubber stamp is nothing short of invaluable for touching up images. You can remove dust fragments, hairs, and other impurities; rebuild creased or torn photographs, and even eliminate elements that wandered into your picture when you weren't looking. So get set for what is undoubtedly the best retouching tool of them all.

**Note**

You also can use the rubber stamp to duplicate specific elements in an image, such as petals in a flower or umbrellas on a beach (actual suggestions from previous editions of Photoshop's manual). But this is rarely an efficient use of the tool. If you want to duplicate an element, you'll have better luck if you select it and clone it, as explained in Chapter 15. Selection tools let you specify the exact boundaries of the element, the softness of the edges, and the precise location of the clone. Because of its reliance on a brush metaphor — that is, you drag across the image window to paint with it — the rubber stamp is better suited to buffing away defects and filling in missing details.

## The cloning process

To clone part of an image, Option/Alt+click in the image window to specify a point of reference in the portion of the image you want to clone. Then click or drag with the tool in some other region of the image to paint a cloned spot or line.

In Figure 10-2, for example, I Option/Alt+clicked above and to the right of the bird's head, as demonstrated by the appearance of the stamp pickup cursor. I then painted the line shown inside the white rectangle. The rubber stamp cursor shows the end of my drag; the clone reference crosshair shows the corresponding point in the original image.

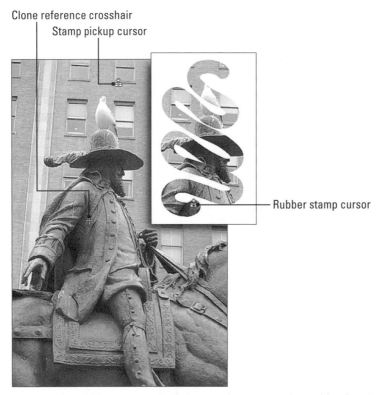

Clone reference crosshair
Stamp pickup cursor

Rubber stamp cursor

**Figure 10-2:** After Option/Alt+clicking at the point indicated by the stamp pickup cursor, I dragged with the rubber stamp tool to paint with the image. (The only reason I painted inside the white rectangle was to set off the line so you can see it better.)

**Tip**

Photoshop lets you clone not only from within the image you're working on, but also from an entirely separate image window. This technique makes it possible to merge two different images together, as demonstrated in Figure 10-3. To achieve this effect, Option/Alt+click in one image, bring a second image to the foreground, and then drag with the rubber stamp tool to clone from the first image. You can also clone between layers. Option/Alt+click on one layer, then switch to a different layer and drag.

## Aligned and not-aligned cloning

The Rubber Stamp Options palette features the standard brush mode, Opacity, and Use All Layers options that I covered in Chapter 8. The only unique item is the Aligned check box. To understand how this option works, think of the locations where you Option/Alt+click and begin dragging with the rubber stamp tool as opposite ends of an imaginary straight line, as illustrated in the top half of Figure 10-4. When Aligned is turned on, the length and angle of this imaginary line remains fixed until the next time you Option/Alt+click. As you drag, Photoshop moves the line, cloning pixels from one end of the line and laying them down at the other. The upshot is that regardless of how many times you start and stop dragging with the stamp tool, all brushstrokes match up as seamlessly as pieces in a puzzle.

**Figure 10-3:** I merged the area around the horse and rider with a water image from another open window (see the upcoming Figure 10-6). The translucent effects were created by periodically adjusting the Opacity value to settings ranging from 50 to 80 percent.

If you want to clone from a single portion of an image repeatedly, turn off the Aligned check box. The second example in Figure 10-4 shows how Photoshop clones from the same point every time you paint a new line with the rubber stamp tool. As a result, each of the four brushstrokes features part of the bird and none line up with each other.

## Stamp differences

After nearly five years of incessant complaining from yours truly, Photoshop 5 reinstates the performance of the original rubber stamp tool. As in Version 2 and earlier, the rubber stamp clones the image as it existed before you began using the tool. Even when you drag over an area containing a clone, the tool references the original appearance of the image. This prevents you from creating more than one clone during a single drag and produces the entirely predictable effect pictured in the first example of Figure 10-5.

Aligned

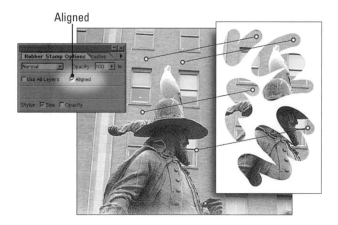

Not aligned

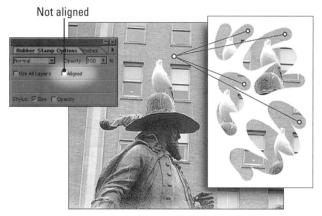

**Figure 10-4:** Turn on the Aligned check box to instruct Photoshop to clone an image continuously, no matter how many lines you paint (top). If you turn the option off, Photoshop clones each new line from the point at which you Option/Alt+click.

In the dim days from Photoshop 2.5 to 4.0, the rubber stamp tool suffered from what at least one programmer at Adobe characterized as the "hall of mirrors" syndrome. Any changes you made to the image affected the tool as you used it, which resulted in the repeating patterns such as those shown in the second example in Figure 10-5. Although you could achieve some interesting effects, the hall of mirrors was a real pain in the neck when retouching, frequently creating obvious patterns that betrayed your adjustments.

Single replication (Photoshops 1, 2, and 5)

Hall of Mirrors (Photoshops 3 and 4)

**Figure 10-5:** Photoshop 5 reinstates the behavior of the rubber stamp tool from the good old days, when it cloned the image as it existed before you started using the tool (top). In Version 4, the tool cloned and recloned images during a single drag (bottom).

Not everyone is in agreement with this vintage setup, so you never know what the future will bring. One day we might get a Hall of Mirrors check box in the Rubber Stamp Options palette. But for now, the stamp clones from one and only one source, just as God intended it. Life is good again.

## Touching up blemishes

One of the best uses of the rubber stamp tool is to touch up a scanned photo. Figure 10-6 shows a Photo CD image desperately in need of the stamp tool's attention. Normally, Kodak's Photo CD process delivers some of the best consumer-quality scans money can buy. But this particular medium-resolution image looks like the folks at the lab got together and blew their respective noses on it. It's too late to return to the service bureau and demand they rescan the photo, so my only choice is to touch it up myself.

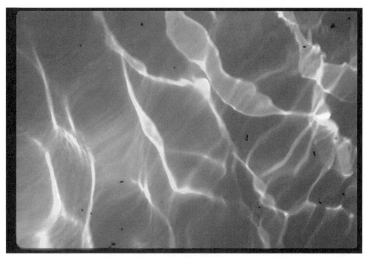

**Figure 10-6:** This appallingly bad Photo CD image is riddled with blotches and big hurky wads of dust that didn't exist on the original 35mm slide.

The best way to fix this image — or any image like it — is to use the rubber stamp over and over again, repeatedly Option/Alt+clicking at one location and then clicking at another. Begin by selecting a brush shape slightly larger than the largest blotch. Of the default brushes, the hard-edged varieties with diameters of 5 and 9 pixels generally work best. (The soft-edged brush shapes have a tendency to only partially hide the blemishes and leave ghosted versions behind.)

Option/Alt+click with the stamp tool at a location that features similarly colored pixels to the blemished area. Be sure to Option/Alt+click far enough away from the blemish that you don't run the risk of duplicating the blemish as you clone. Then click — do not drag — directly on the blemish to clone over it. The idea is to change as few pixels as possible.

If the retouched area doesn't look quite right, press ⌘/Ctrl+Z to undo it, Option/Alt+click at a different location, and try again. If your touchup appears seamless — *absolutely* seamless, there's no reason to settle for less — move on to the next blemish. Repeat the Option/Alt+click and click routine for every dust mark on the photo.

This process isn't necessarily time-consuming, but it does require patience. For example, although it took more than 40 Option/Alt+click and click combinations (not counting 10 or so undos) to arrive at the image shown in Figure 10-7, the process itself took less than 15 minutes. Boring, but fast.

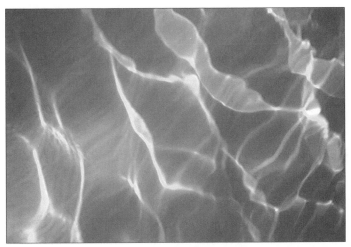

**Figure 10-7:** The result of Option/Alt+clicking and clicking more than 40 times on the photo shown in Figure 10-6. Notice I also cropped the image and added a border.

Retouching hairs is a little trickier than dust and other blobs. This is because a hair, although very thin, can be surprisingly long. The retouching process is the same, though. Rather than dragging over the entire length of the hair, Option/Alt+ click and click your way through it, bit by little bit. The one difference is brush shape. Because you'll be clicking so many times in succession, and because the hair is so thin, you'll probably achieve the least-conspicuous effects if you use a soft brush shape, such as the default 9-pixel model in the second row of the Brushes palette.

Caution

At this point you might wonder, "Why go to all this work to remove dust and scratches when Photoshop provides the automated feature Filter ➪ Noise ➪ Dust & Scratches?" The reason is — and I'm going to be painfully blunt here — the Dust & Scratches filter stinks. No offense to the designers of this filter: They're wonderful people, every one of them, but the filter simply doesn't produce the effect it advertises. It mucks up the detail in your image by averaging neighboring pixels, and this simply isn't an acceptable solution. Do your photograph a favor — fix its flaws manually (not to mention lovingly) with the rubber stamp tool.

## Restoring an old photograph

Dust, hairs, gloops, and other blemishes are introduced during the scanning process. But what about more severe problems that trace back to the original image? Figure 10-8 is a prime example. This photograph of my wife's grandmother was shot sometime prior to 1910. It's a wonderful photo, but 90 years is a long time for something as fragile and transient as a scrap of paper. It's torn, faded, stained, creased, and flaking. The normally simple act of extracting it from its photo album took every bit as long as scanning it.

**Figure 10-8:** This photo's seen better days. Then again, I hope to look so good when I'm 90 years old.

But despite it's rough condition, it was quite possible to restore the image in Photoshop, as evidenced by Figure 10-9. (For a full-color view of the before and after images, see Color Plate 10-1.) As in the case of the pool image (Figure 10-7), I used the rubber stamp to do most of the work. And as before, the process was tedious but straightforward. After about an hour and a few hundred brushstrokes, I had the image well in hand.

**Note**

If an hour sounds like a long time to fix a few rips and scrapes, then wake up and smell the coffee. This is not one-button editing. Photographic restoration is a labor-intensive activity that depends heavily on your talents and your mastery of Photoshop. The rubber stamp tool goes a long way toward making your edits believable, but it does little to automate the process. Retouching calls for a human touch, and that's where you come in.

**Figure 10-9:** The same image after about an hour of work with the rubber stamp tool.

I considered documenting every single one of my brushstrokes, but I value your time (yes, and my own) too highly. Suffice it to say that the general approach was the same as it was for the pool image. Option/Alt+click in an area that looks like it'd do a good job of covering up the blemish, then drag over the blemish. And repeat about 250 times.

That said, I do have some advice to offer that specifically addresses the art of photo restoration:

✦ Most images in this kind of condition are black-and-white. Scan them in color and then peruse the color channels to see which grayscale version of the image looks best. As you can see in Color Plate 10-1, the original image had lots of yellow stains around the tears. So when I viewed at the individual color channels (Figure 10-10), I was hardly surprised to see dark blotches in the blue channel. (Blue is the opposite of yellow, so where yellow is prominent, the blue channel was dark.) In my case, the red channel was in the best shape, so I switched to the red channel and disposed of the other two by choosing Image ➪ Mode ➪ Grayscale. The simple act of trashing the green and blue channels went a long way toward getting rid of the splotches.

Red        Green        Blue

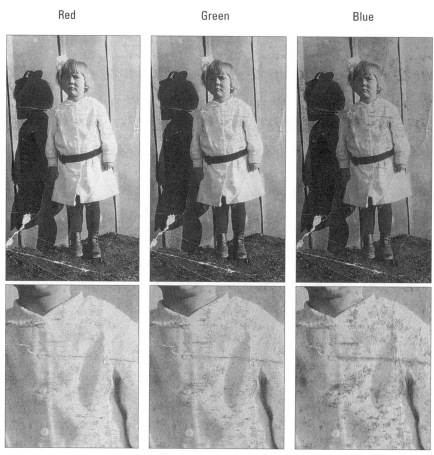

**Figure 10-10:** A quick peek through the color channels shows the red channel to be my best choice. The blotches are most evident in the girl's blouse, enlarged along the bottom.

✦ Work at 100 percent view size (⌘/Ctrl+Option/Alt+0) or larger. It's impossible to judge scratches and other defects accurately at smaller zoom ratios.

✦ Keep the original photo next to you as you work. What looks like a scratch on screen may actually be a photographic element, and what looks like an element may be a scratch. Only by referring to the original image can you be sure.

✦ Don't crop until you're finished retouching the image. You'd be surprised how useful that extra garbage around the perimeter is when it comes to covering up really big tears.

✦ Use hard brush shapes against sharp edges. But when working in general areas like the shadow, the ground, and the wall, mix it up between hard and soft brushes. Staying random is the best way to avoid harsh transitions, repeating patterns, and other digital giveaways.

✦ Paint in short strokes. This helps keep things random, but it also means you don't have to redraw a big long brushstroke if you make a mistake.

✦ When you *do* make a mistake, don't press ⌘/Ctrl+Z. Instead, use the history brush to paint back the image as it appeared before the last rubber stamp operation. (I explain more about the history brush later in this chapter.)

✦ Another way to stay random is to change the source of your clone frequently. That means Option/Alt+clicking after every second or third brushstroke. And keep the Aligned check box turned off — an aligned clone is not a random one.

✦ Feel free to experiment with the brush modes and the Opacity setting. For example, as shown magnified in Figure 10-11, the girl has a scratch over the left eye (her right). I corrected this by cloning the right eye, but the cloned eye was so much lighter that it gave the girl a possessed look. To fix this, I set the brush mode to Multiply and changed the Opacity to 30 percent. Then I cloned a bit of the shadowed flesh over the eye to get the finished effect.

✦ Don't attempt to smooth out the general appearance of grain in the image. Grain is integral to an old photo and hiding it usually makes the image look faked. If things get too smooth, or if your cloning results in irregular patterns, select the problem area and apply Filter ➪ Noise ➪ Add Noise. Enter very small Amount values (4 to 8); if necessary, press ⌘/Ctrl+F to reapply the filter one or more times. Remember, grain is good.

With Photoshop's history brush at your side, there's really no way to permanently harm an image. You can even let four or five little mistakes go and then correct them *en masse* with the history brush. Just click to the left of the state in the History palette that directly precedes your first screw-up, and then drag with the history brush. It's easy, satisfying, and incredibly freeing. To paint back to the original scanned image, click in front of the very top item in the History palette. For more information, check out "An Entirely New Reversion Metaphor" later in this chapter.

**Figure 10-11:** The left eye in the original image is scratched (top). I clone the right eye (middle), but it's too bright. So I set the brush mode to Multiply, lower the Opacity to 30 percent, and clone a little flesh over the eye (bottom).

## Eliminating distracting background elements

Another way to apply the stamp tool's cloning capabilities is to eliminate background action that competes with the central elements in an image. For example, Figure 10-12 shows a nifty news photo shot by Michael Probst for the Reuters image library. Although the image is well photographed and historic and all that good stuff, that rear workman doesn't contribute anything to the scene; in fact, he draws your attention away from the foreground drama. I mean, hail to the worker and everything, but the image would be better off without him. The following steps explain how I eradicated the offending workman from the scene.

**Note**

Remember as you read the following steps that deleting an image element with the rubber stamp tool is something of an inexact science; it requires considerable patience and a dash of trial and error. So regard the following steps as an example of how to approach the process of editing your image rather than as a specific procedure that works for all images. You may need to adapt the process slightly depending upon your image.

On the other hand, any approach that eliminates an element as big as the workman can also correct the most egregious of photographic flaws, including mold, holes, and fire damage. You can even restore photos that have been ripped into pieces, a particular problem for pictures of ex-boyfriends and the like. These steps qualify as major reconstructive surgery.

**Figure 10-12:** You have to love that old Soviet state-endorsed art. So bold, so angular, so politically intolerant. But you also have to lose that rear workman.

## Steps: Eliminating Distracting Elements from an Image

1. **I began by cloning the area around the neck of the statue with a soft brush shape.** Abandoning the controlled clicks I recommended in the last section, I allowed myself to drag with the tool because I needed to cover relatively large portions of the image. The apartment building (or whatever that structure is) behind the floating head is magnificently out of focus, just the thing for hiding any incongruous transitions I might create with the rubber stamp. So I warmed up to the image by retouching this area first. Figure 10-13 shows my progress.

   Notice, I covered the workman's body by cloning pixels from both his left and right sides. I also added a vertical bar where the workman's right arm used to be to maintain the rhythm of the building. Remember, variety is the key to using the rubber stamp tool: If you consistently clone from one portion of the image, you create an obvious repetition the viewer can't help but notice.

**Figure 10-13:** Cloning over the background worker's upper torso was fairly easy because the background building is so regular and out of focus, it provides a wealth of material from which to clone.

2. **The next step was to eliminate the workman's head.** This was a little tricky because it involved rubbing up against the focused perimeter of Lenin's neck. I had to clone some of the more intricate areas using a hard-edged brush. I also ended up duplicating some of the neck edges to maintain continuity. In addition, I touched up the left side of the neck (your left, not Lenin's) and removed a few of the white spots from his face. You see my progress in Figure 10-14.

3. **Now for the hard part: eliminating the worker's legs and lower torso.** See that fragment of metal that the foreground worker is holding? What a pain. Its edges were so irregular, there was no way I could restore it with the rubber stamp tool on the off chance that I messed up while trying to eradicate the background worker's limbs. So I lassoed around the fragment to select it and chose Select ⇨ Inverse (⌘/Ctrl+Shift+I) to protect it. I also chose Select ⇨ Feather (⌘/Ctrl+Option/Alt+D) and gave it a Radius value of 1 to soften its edges slightly. This prevented me from messing up the metal no matter what edits I made to the background worker's remaining body parts.

**Figure 10-14:** I eliminated the workman's head and touched up details around the perimeter of his neck.

4. **From here on, it was just more cloning.** Unfortunately, I barely had anything from which to clone. See the little bit of black edging between the two "legs" of the metal fragment? That's it. This was all I had to draw the strip of edging to the right of the fragment that eventually appears in Figure 10-15. To pull off this feat, I made sure that the Aligned check box was turned off in the Rubber Stamp Options palette. Then I Option/Alt+clicked on the tiny bit of edging and click, click, clicked my way down the street.

5. **Unfortunately, the strip I laid down in Step 4 appeared noticeably blobular — it looked for all the world like I clicked a bunch of times.** Darn. To fix this problem, I clicked and Shift+clicked with the smudge tool set to about 30 percent pressure. This smeared the blobs into a continuous strip but, again, the effect was noticeable. It looked as if I had smeared the strip. So I went back and cloned some more, this time with the Opacity value set to 50 percent.

6. **To polish the image off, I chose Select ➪ Deselect (⌘/Ctrl+D) and ran the sharpen tool along the edges of the metal fragment.** This helped to hide that I'd retouched around it and further distinguished the fragment from the unfocused background. I also cropped away 20 or so pixels from the right side of the image to correct the balance of the image.

**Figure 10-15:** After about 45 minutes of monkeying around with the rubber stamp tool — a practice declared illegal during Stalin's reign — the rear workman is gone, leaving us with an unfettered view of the dubious V. I. Lenin himself.

What I hope I demonstrated in these steps is this: Cloning with the rubber stamp tool requires you to alternate between patching and whittling away. There are no rights and wrongs, no hard and fast rules. Anything you can find to clone is fair game. As long as you avoid mucking up the foreground image, you can't go wrong (so I guess there is *one* hard and fast rule). If you're careful and diligent, no one but you is going to notice your alterations.

**Caution**

Any time you edit the contents of a photograph, you tread on sensitive ground. Although some have convincingly argued that electronically retouching an image is, theoretically, no different than cropping a photograph — a technique available and in use since the first daguerreotype — photographers have certain rights under copyright law that cannot be ignored. A photographer may have a reason for including an element you wish to eliminate. So, before you edit any photograph, be sure to get permission either from the original photographer or from the copyright holder (as I did for this photo).

# Applying Repeating Patterns

The rubber stamp tool's alternate is the pattern stamp tool, which paints with a rectangular pattern tile. You can use the pattern stamp to create frames, paint wallpaper-type patterns, or retouch textured patches of grass, dirt, or sky. To switch to the pattern stamp tool, press Shift+S or Option/Alt+click on the stamp tool icon in the toolbox.

The pattern stamp doesn't require you to Option/Alt+click to set a source. Instead, you must first define a pattern by selecting a portion of the image with the rectangular marquee tool and choosing Edit ➪ Define Pattern. Note that you have to use the rectangular marquee — no other selection tool will do. Also, the selection cannot be feathered, smoothed, expanded, or in any other way altered. If the selection is anything but rectangular, the command is dimmed.

Figure 10-16 shows an example of how you can apply repeating patterns. I selected the single apartment window (labeled in the figure) and chose Edit ➪ Define Pattern. I then painted with the pattern stamp tool at 80 percent opacity over the horse and rider statue.

**Caution**

As with an image in the Clipboard, Photoshop can retain only one pattern at a time and it remembers the pattern throughout a single session. Any time you choose Edit ➪ Define Pattern, you delete the previous pattern as you create a new one. Photoshop also deletes the pattern when you choose Edit ➪ Purge ➪ Pattern or quit the program.

## Aligning patterns (or not)

Like the Rubber Stamp Options palette, the Pattern Stamp Options palette provides an Aligned check box. When active, Photoshop aligns all patterns you apply with the stamp tool, regardless of how many times you start and stop dragging. The two left examples in Figure 10-17 show the effects of selecting this option. The elements in the pattern remain exactly aligned throughout all the brushstrokes. I painted the top image with the Opacity value set to 50 percent, which is why the strokes darken when they meet.

To allow patterns in different brushstrokes to start and end at different locations, turn the Aligned option off. The position of the pattern within each stroke is determined by the point at which you begin dragging. I dragged from right to left to paint the horizontal strokes and from top to bottom to paint the vertical strokes. The two right examples in Figure 10-17 show how nonaligned patterns overlap.

**Note**

As discussed in Chapter 9, you can also apply a pattern to a selected portion of an image by choosing Edit ➪ Fill and selecting the Pattern option from the Use pop-up menu. If you have an old grayscale image saved in the Photoshop 2 format sitting around, you can alternatively choose Filter ➪ Render ➪ Texture Fill to open the image and repeat it as many times as it takes to fill the selection. (Texture Fill is intended primarily for preparing textures and bump maps for a three-dimensional drawing program, so most folks never touch this filter.)

**Figure 10-16:** After marqueeing a single window (top) and choosing Edit ⇨ Define Pattern, I painted a translucent coat of the pattern over the statue with the pattern stamp tool (bottom).

## Creating patterns and textures

The biggest difficulty with painting patterns is not figuring out the pattern stamp tool, but creating the patterns in the first place. Ideally, your pattern should repeat continuously, without vertical and horizontal seams. Here are some ways to create repeating, continuous patterns:

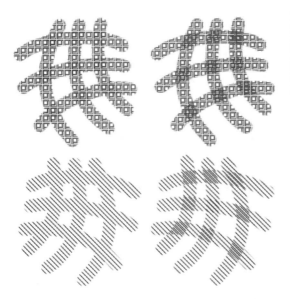

**Figure 10-17:** Select the Aligned check box to align the patterns in all brushstrokes so that they match up perfectly (left). If you turn the option off, Photoshop starts each pattern with the beginning of the brushstroke (right).

✦ **Load a displacement map:** Photoshop offers a Displacement Maps folder (or DispMaps on Windows) inside the Plug-Ins folder (or Filters\Plug-Ins directory on Windows). This folder contains several images, each of which represents a different repeating pattern, as illustrated in Figure 10-18. To use one of these patterns, open the image, choose Select ➪ All (⌘/Ctrl+A), and choose Edit ➪ Define Pattern. (For more information on displacement maps, see Chapter D on CD #2.)

✦ **Illustrator patterns:** Inside the Photoshop/Patterns folder are Illustrator EPS files that contain repeating object patterns. The patterns, some of which appear in Figure 10-19, are all seamless repeaters. You can open them and rasterize them to any size you like. Then press ⌘/Ctrl+A, choose Edit ➪ Define Pattern, and you have your pattern.

✦ **Using filters:** As luck would have it, you can create your own custom textures without painting a single line. In fact, you can create a nearly infinite variety of textures by applying several filters to a blank document. To create the texture shown in the top row of Figure 10-20, for example, I created a new 200 × 200-pixel image. I then chose Filter ➪ Noise ➪ Add Noise, entered a value of 64, and selected the Gaussian radio button. I pressed Ctrl+F twice to apply the noise filter two more times. Finally, I chose Filter ➪ Stylize ➪ Emboss and entered 45 into the Angle option box, 2 into the Height option box, and 100 percent into the Amount option box. The result is a bumpy surface that looks like stucco.

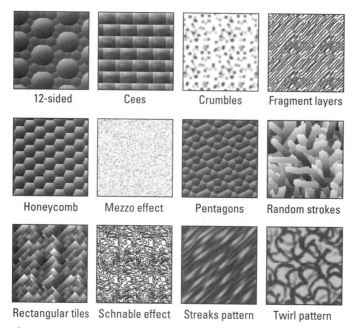

**Figure 10-18:** The 12 patterns contained in the Displacement Maps folder (or DispMaps on Windows) included with Photoshop.

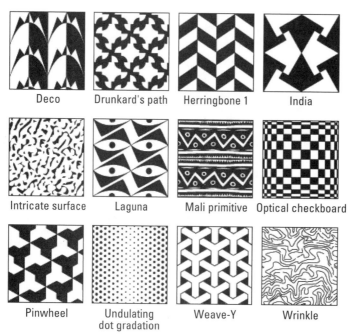

**Figure 10-19:** A random sampling of the illustrations contained in the PostScript Patterns folder inside the Patterns folder.

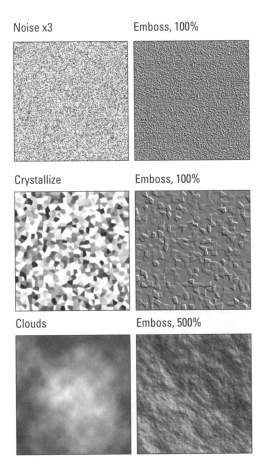

Noise x3    Emboss, 100%

Crystallize    Emboss, 100%

Clouds    Emboss, 500%

**Figure 10-20:** Three examples of filtered effects before (left) and after (right) applying the Emboss command.

To get the second row effects in Figure 10-20, I started with the noise pattern and applied Filter ➪ Pixelate ➪ Crystallize with a Cell Size of 10 pixels. Then I again applied the Emboss filter with the same settings as before. To create the third row of textures, I started with a blank image and chose Filter ➪ Render ➪ Clouds. Then I applied the Emboss filter with an Amount value of 500 percent. To punch up the contrast, I choose Image ➪ Adjust ➪ Auto Levels (⌘/Ctrl+Shift+L).

**Cross-Reference**

Naturally, I could go on like this for days. To learn more about filters so you can make up your own textures, read Chapters 23 and 24. Chapter 23 covers Add Noise; Chapter 24 explains Emboss, Crystallize, and Clouds.

✦ **Marquee and clone:** You can use the rectangular marquee and pattern stamp tools to transform a scanned image into a custom pattern. Because this technique is more complicated as well as more rewarding than the others, I explain it in the following section.

## Building your own seamless pattern

The following steps describe how to change a scanned image into a seamless, repeating pattern. To illustrate how this process works, Figures 10-21 through 10-24 show various stages in a project I completed. You need only two tools to carry out these steps: the rectangular marquee tool and the rubber stamp tool.

Even so, those of you reading sequentially will notice that these steps involve a few selection and layering techniques I haven't yet discussed. If you become confused, you can find out more about selecting, moving, and cloning images in Chapter 15.

### Steps: Building a Repeating Pattern from a Scanned Image

1. **Open the image that you want to convert into a pattern.** I started with an image from the PhotoDisc image library.

2. **Select the rectangular marquee tool, then press Return/Enter.** Photoshop displays the Marquee Options palette. Select Fixed Size from the Style pop-up menu and enter specific values into the Width and Height option boxes. This way, you can easily reselect a portion of the pattern in the steps that follow, as well as use the fixed-size marquee to define the pattern when you finish. To create the patterns shown in the figures, I set the marquee to 128 × 128 pixels.

3. **Select the portion of the image you want to feature in the pattern.** Because you've specified an exact marquee size, Photoshop selects a fixed area whenever you click. You also can drag to move the marquee around in the window.

4. **Press ⌘/Ctrl+C. This copies the image to the Clipboard.**

5. **Choose File ➪ New (⌘/Ctrl+N) and triple the Width and Height values.** In my case, Photoshop suggested a new image size of 128 × 128 pixels, which matches the size of the image I copied to the Clipboard. By tripling these values, I arrived at a new image size of 384 × 384 pixels.

6. **Press ⌘/Ctrl+V. Photoshop pastes the copied image smack dab in the center of the window, which is exactly where you want it.** This image will serve as the central tile of your repeating pattern.

7. **⌘/Ctrl+click on the item labeled Layer 1 in the Layers palette. Photoshop pastes the image on a new layer.** But in order to duplicate the image and convert it into a pattern, you need to select the image and flatten it. ⌘/Ctrl+clicking on the layer name does the selecting.

8. **Press ⌘/Ctrl+E.** This merges the layer with the background, thereby flattening it. Or you can choose Layer ➪ Flatten Image. Either way, the selection outline remains intact.

9. **Choose Edit ⇨ Define Pattern.** This establishes the selected image as a pattern tile.

10. **Press ⌘/Ctrl+D to deselect the image.** You neither need nor want the selection outline any more. You'll need to be able to fill and clone freely without a selection outline getting in the way.

11. **Press Shift+Delete/Backspace or choose Edit ⇨ Fill.** Then select Pattern from the Use pop-up menu and press Return/Enter. This fills the window with a 3 × 3-tile grid, as shown in Figure 10-21.

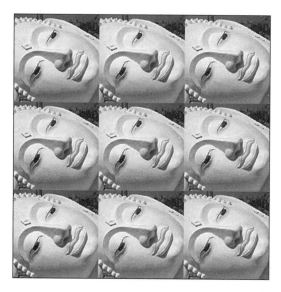

**Figure 10-21:** To build the repeating pattern shown in Figure 10-24, I started by creating a grid of nine image tiles. As you can see, the seams between the tiles in this grid are harsh and unacceptable.

12. **Drag the title bar of the new image window to position it so you can see the portion of the image you copied in the original image window.** If necessary, drag the title bar of the original image window to reposition it, as well. After you have your windows arranged, click on the title bar of the new image to make it the active window.

13. **Select the rubber stamp.** Press the S key.

14. **Turn off the Aligned check box in the Rubber Stamp Options palette.** Ironic as it may sound, it's easier to get the alignment between clone-from and clone-to points established with Aligned turned off.

*(continued)*

15. **Specify the image you want to clone by Option/Alt+clicking in the original image window.** No need to switch out of the new window. Option/Alt+click on an easily identifiable pixel that belongs to the portion of the image you copied. The exact pixel you click on is very important. If you press the Caps Lock key, you get the crosshair cursor, which makes it easier to narrow in on a pixel. In my case, I clicked on the corner of the Buddha's mouth. (At least, I assume that's Buddha. Then again, I'm a Western-bred ignoramus, so what do I know?)

16. **Now click with the stamp tool on the matching pixel in the central tile of the new window.** If you clicked the correct pixel, the tile should not change one iota. If it shifts at all, press ⌘/Ctrl+Z and try again. Because Aligned is turned off, you can keep undoing and clicking over and over again without resetting the clone-from point in the original image.

17. **Turn the Aligned check box on.** Once you click in the image without seeing any shift, select the Aligned option in the Rubber Stamp Options palette to lock in the alignment between the clone-from and clone-to points.

18. **Use the stamp tool to fill in portions of the central tile.** For example, in Figure 10-22, I extended the Buddha's cheek and neck down into the lower row of tiles. I also extended the central forehead to meet the Buddha on the left.

**Figure 10-22:** I used the rubber stamp's cloning capability to extend the features in the central face toward the left and downward.

19. **Select a portion of the modified image.** After you establish one continuous transition between two tiles in any direction — up, down, left, or right — click with the rectangular marquee tool to select an area that includes the transition. In my case, I managed to create a smooth transition between the central and bottom tiles. Therefore, I selected a region that includes half the central tile and half the tile below it.

20. **Repeat Steps 9 through 11.** That is, choose Edit ➪ Define Pattern, press
    ⌘/Ctrl+D, choose Edit ➪ Fill, and press Return/Enter. This fills the image with
    your new transition. Don't worry if the tiles shift around a bit — that's to be
    expected.

    If you plan on creating a lot of patterns, you might want to record Steps 9
    through 11 as a script in the Actions palette. Then you can replay the script
    after each time you clone away a seam.

21. **If you started by creating a horizontal transition, use the rubber stamp
    tool to create a vertical transition.** Likewise, if you started vertically, now
    go horizontally. You may need to turn off the Aligned check box again to
    establish the proper alignment between clone-from and clone-to points. In
    my case, I shifted the clone-to point several times — alternatively building
    on the central Buddha, the right-hand one, and the middle one in the
    bottom row. Each time you get the clone-to point properly positioned, turn
    the Aligned check box back on to lock in the alignment. Then clone away.

    As long as you get the clone-from and clone-to points properly aligned, you
    can't make a mistake. If you change your mind, realign the clone points and
    try again. In my case, I cloned the long droopy earlobe down into the face
    of the Buddha below. (I guess our young Buddha didn't stop to think that
    once the droopy-ear fad passed, he would be stuck with it for the rest of
    his life.) I also cloned the god's chin onto the forehead of the one to the
    right, ultimately achieving the effect shown in Figure 10-23.

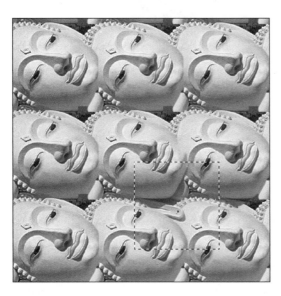

**Figure 10-23:** After
completing a smooth
transition between the
central tile and the tiles
below and to the right of
it, I selected a portion of
the image and chose
Edit ➪ Define Pattern.

*(continued)*

22. **After you build up one set of both horizontal and vertical transitions, click with the rectangular marquee tool to select the transitions.** Figure 10-23 shows where I positioned my 128 × 128-pixel selection boundary. This includes parts of each of four neighboring heads, including the all-important droopy ear. Don't worry if the image doesn't appear centered inside the selection outline. What counts is that the image flows seamlessly inside the selection outline.

23. **Repeat Steps 9 through 11.** Or play that script I suggested in Step 20 if you bothered to record it. If the tiles blend together seamlessly, as in Figure 10-24, then you're finished. If not, clone some more with the rubber stamp tool and try again.

**Figure 10-24:** This Eastern montage is the result of applying the Buddha pattern. Buddha sure looks serene and comfortable, especially considering he's resting on his own head.

# An Entirely New Reversion Metaphor

Since roughly the dawn of recorded time, folks have been begging, pleading, and screaming at the top of their lungs for multiple undos in Photoshop. But every time I witnessed an Adobe representative respond on the subject, the company line seemed to be the same: Multiple undos and pixels just don't mix. Photoshop is already caching enough data in RAM without asking it to keep track of 10 or 20 previous operations. If you want to backstep through editing history, buy a time machine.

In fact, my expectations had been sufficiently whittled down that I held out little hope of anything productive on the undo front. *If* Photoshop ever got around to adding multiple undos to its feature list, it'd be a partial implementation that would require the user to tag significant operations, or it would turn out to be smoke and mirrors *a la* Live Picture, xRes, and a host of others. The entire population of Roswell stood a better chance of being beamed aboard the Heaven's Gate spaceship than you and I stood of being able to undo the second-to-last operation in Photoshop.

Well, I just hope there's room on Hale-Bopp's tail for 40,000 New Mexicans, because Photoshop 5 has multiple undos. You can revisit as many as 100 consecutive operations from your past, just as in Illustrator, FreeHand, and virtually every other program that doesn't involve pixels.

But it gets better than that. Rather than settling for simple backstepping, Version 5 invents the best implementation of multiple undos that I've ever seen. The History palette takes the whole reversion metaphor into *Slaughterhouse Five* territory. If you've never read the novel (or you've somehow forgotten), Kurt Vonnegut, Jr. suggested that humans live from one moment to the next like a person strapped to a boxcar, unable to change the speed or direction of the train as it hurtles through time. With multiple undos, you can make the train stop and back up, but you're still strapped to it. The History palette is the first tool that lets you get off the train and transport to any point on the track — instantaneously. In short, we now have a digital version of time travel.

Here are just a few of the marvelous innovations of the History palette:

✦ **Undo-independent stepping.** Step backward by pressing ⌘/Ctrl+Option/Alt+Z; step forward by pressing ⌘/Ctrl+Shift+Z. Every program with multiple undos does this, but Photoshop's keyboard equivalents are different. Why? Because you can backstep independently of the Undo command, so that even backstepping is undoable.

✦ **Before and after.** Revert to a point in history to see a "before" view of your image, then fly forward to see the "after" view. From then on, ⌘/Ctrl+Z becomes a super-undo, toggling between the before and after views. The opportunities for comparing states and changing your mind are truly colossal.

✦ **Dynamic time travel.** If before and after isn't enough, how about animated history? You can drag a control to slide dynamically forward and backward through operations. It's like you recorded the operations to videotape, and now you're rewinding and fast-forwarding through them.

✦ **Sweeping away the mistakes.** Select a point in the history of your image and paint back to it using the history brush. You can let the mistakes pile up and then brush them away. This brush isn't a paintbrush, it's a hand broom.

✦ **Take a picture, it'll last longer.** You can save any point in the History palette as a snapshot. That way, even several hundred operations after that point in history is long gone, you can revisit the snapshot.

✦ **This is your life, Image A.** Each and every image has its own history. So after performing a few hundred operations on Image A, you can still go back to Image B and backstep through operations you performed hours ago. The caveat is that the history remains available only so long as an image is open. Close the image, and its history goes away.

The only thing you can't do is travel forward into the future — say, to about three days from now when you've finished your grueling project, submitted it to your client, and received your big fat paycheck. Believe it or not, that's actually good news. The day Adobe can figure out how to do your work for you, your clients will hire Photoshop and stop hiring you.

So I ask you — Photoshop 5, *Slaughterhouse Five*, just a coincidence? Well, yes, I suppose it is. But the fact remains, you now have the option of getting off the boxcar. How you make use of your new found freedom is up to you.

## Using the traditional undo functions

Before I dive into the History palette, I should take a moment to summarize Photoshop's more traditional reversion functions. (If you already know about this stuff, skip to the next section.)

✦ **Undo:** To restore an image to the way it looked before the last operation, choose Edit ➪ Undo (⌘/Ctrl+Z). You can undo the effect of a paint or edit tool, a change made to a selection outline, or a special-effect or color-correction command. You can't undo disk operations, such as opening or saving. Photoshop does enable you to undo an edit after printing an image, though. You can test out an effect, print it, and then undo it if you think the effect looks awful.

✦ **Revert:** Choose File ➪ Revert (or press the F12 key) to reload an image from disk. This is generally the last-resort function, the command you choose after everything else has failed.

To restore the image back to the way it looked when you originally opened it — which may precede the last-saved state — scroll to the top of the History palette and click on the topmost item. (This assumes that you haven't gone and turned off the Automatically Create First Snapshot check box in the History Options dialog box.)

✦ **Selective reversion:** To revert a selected area to the way it appeared when it was first opened — or some other source state identified in the History palette — choose Edit ➪ Fill (Shift+Delete/Backspace). Then select History from the Use pop-up menu and press Return/Enter.

Better yet, just press ⌘/Ctrl+Option/Alt+Delete/Backspace. This one keystroke fills the selection with the source state in a jiffy. (You set the source state by clicking in the left column of the History palette, as I explain in the very next section.)

✦ **The eraser tool:** Drag in the Background layer with the eraser tool to paint in white or some other background color. You're essentially erasing the image back to bare canvas. Or apply the eraser to a layer to delete pixels and expose underlying layers.

You also can Option/Alt+drag with the eraser to revert back to the targeted state in the History palette. But you're better off using the history brush for this purpose.

The history brush offers more capabilities — notably brush modes — and you don't have to press Option/Alt.

Where warranted, I explain these functions in greater detail in the following sections. But first, let's look at the central headquarters for the new reversion metaphor...

## The History palette

Choose Window ➪ Show History to view the History palette, annotated with the palette menu in full view in Figure 10-25. The History palette records each significant operation — everything other than settings and preferences (for example, selecting a new foreground color) — and adds it to a list. The oldest operations appear at the top of the list with the most recent operations at the bottom.

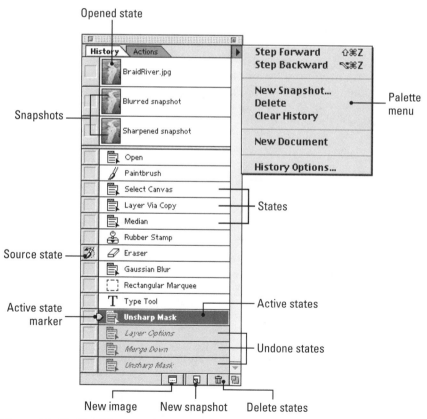

**Figure 10-25:** The History palette records each significant event as an independent state. To return to a state, just click on it.

Each item in the list is called a *state*. That's not my word, it's Adobe's, and several have voiced the opinion that the term is too stiff and formal. But I think it's dead on. Each item in the palette represents a stepping stone in the progression of the image, a condition at a moment in time — in other words, a state.

Photoshop automatically names each item according to the tool, command, or operation used to arrive at the state. The icon next to the name helps to identify the state further. But the best way to find out what a state is like is to click on it. Photoshop instantaneously undoes all operations performed after that state and returns you to the state so that you can inspect it in detail. To redo all the operations you just did in one fell swoop, press ⌘/Ctrl+Z or choose Edit ➪ Undo State Change.

That one action — clicking on a state — is the gist of what you need to know to travel forward and backward through time in Photoshop. If that's all you ever learn, you'll find yourself working with greater speed, freedom, and security than is possible in virtually any other graphics application. But this represents only the first in a long list of the History palette's capabilities. Here's the rest of what you might want to know:

✦ **Changing the number of undos:** By default, Photoshop records the last 20 operations in the History palette. When you perform the 21st operation, the first state is shoved off the list. To change this behavior, choose the History Option command from the palette menu and enter a new Maximum History Items value (see Figure 10-26). If your computer is equipped with 32MB or less of RAM, you might want to lower the value to 5 or 10 to maintain greater efficiency. On the other hand, if you become a time-traveling freak (like me) and you have plenty of RAM, then turn it up, baby, all the way up!

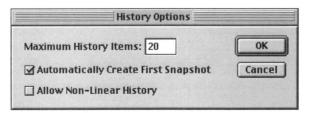

**Figure 10-26:** Choose the History Options command to change the number of undos and permit Photoshop to record states out of order.

✦ **Undone states:** When you revert to a state by clicking on it, every subsequent state turns gray to show that it's been undone. You can redo a grayed state simply by clicking on it. But if you perform a new operation, all grayed states disappear. You have one opportunity to bring them back by pressing ⌘/Ctrl+Z, but if you perform another new operation, the once grayed states are gone for good.

✦ **Working with non-sequential states:** If you don't like the idea of losing your undone states — every state is sacred, after all — then choose the History Options command and select the Allow Non-Linear History check box (see Figure 10-26). Undone states no longer drop off the list when you perform a new operation. They remain available on the off chance that you might want to revisit them. It's like having multiple possible time trails.

The Allow Non-Linear History check box does not permit you to undo a single state without affecting the subsequent states. For example, let's say you paint with the airbrush, smear with the smudge tool, and then clone with the rubber stamp. You can revert back to the airbrush state and then apply other operations without losing the option of restoring the smudge and clone. But you can't undo the smudge and leave the clone intact. Operations can only occur in the sequence they were applied.

✦ **Stepping through states:** As I mentioned earlier, you can press ⌘/Ctrl+Option/Alt+Z to undo the active step or ⌘/Ctrl+Shift+Z to redo the next step in the list. Backstepping goes up the list of states in the History palette, forward stepping goes down. Keep in mind that if the Allow Non-Linear History check box is active, backstepping may take you to a state that was previously inactive.

✦ **Flying through states:** Drag the right-pointing active step marker (labeled in Figure 10-25) up and down the list to rewind and fast-forward through time. If the screen image doesn't appear to change as you fly by certain states, it most likely means those states involve small brushstrokes or changes to selection outlines. Otherwise, the changes are quite apparent.

✦ **Taking a snapshot:** Every once in a while, a state comes along that's so great, you don't want it to fall by the wayside 20 operations from now. To set a state aside, choose New Snapshot or click on the little page icon at the bottom of the History palette. Photoshop asks you if you want to save all layers (as by default), flatten the image, or retain just the active layer. The new *snapshot* — as it's called — then appears in the top portion of the palette.

To create a snapshot without going through the New Snapshot dialog box, Option/Alt+click on the page icon. (The state has to be active to convert it to a snapshot, so you can't drag a state and drop it onto the page icon, as you can drag-and-drop elements in other palettes.)

Photoshop 5 lets you store as many snapshots as your computer's RAM will permit. Also worth noting, the program automatically creates a snapshot of the image as it appears when it's first opened. If you don't like this opening snapshot, you can turn it off using the History Options command.

✦ **Saving the state permanently:** The problem with snapshots is that they only last as long as the current session. If you quit Photoshop or the program crashes, you lose the entire history list, snapshots included. To save a state so you can refer to it several days from now, choose the New Document command from the History palette menu or click on the leftmost icon at the bottom of the History palette. You can also drag and drop a state onto the icon. Either way, Photoshop duplicates the state to a new image window. Then you can save the state to the format of your choice.

✦ **Setting the source:** Click to the left of a state to identify it as the *source state*. The history brush icon appears where you click. The source state affects the performance of the history brush, the magic eraser, and the Fill command. The keystroke ⌘/Ctrl+Option/Alt+Delete/Backspace fills the selection with the source state.

✦ **Trashing states:** If your machine is equipped with little RAM or you're working on a particularly large image, Photoshop may slow down as the states accumulate. If things get too slow, you may want to purge. You can delete every state from the active state forward by clicking on the trash can icon at the bottom of the palette. (Option/Alt+click the icon to bypass the warning.) If the Allow Non-Linear History check box is on, clicking on the trash can deletes just the active state.

To clear all states from the History palette, choose the Clear History command from the palette menu. (You can also choose Edit ⇨ Purge ⇨ Histories, but the advantage of Clear Histories is that you can undo it if you change your mind.)

## Painting away the past

The History palette represents the regimental way to revert images inside Photoshop. You can retreat, march forward, proceed in linear or non-linear formation, capture states, and retire them. Every state plays backward in the same way it played forward. It's precise, predictable, and positively by the book.

But what if you want to get free-form? What if you want to brush away the present and paint in the past? In that case, a palette isn't going to do you any good. What you need is a pliable, emancipated, free-wheeling tool.

As luck would have it, Photoshop offers two candidates — the eraser and the history brush. The eraser washes away pixels to reveal underlying pixels or exposed canvas. The history brush takes you back to a kinder, simpler state. Although the two overlap slightly, they each have a very specific purpose, as will become clear in the following sections.

### The eraser tool

Select the eraser tool by pressing the E key. Then press Return/Enter to display the Eraser Options palette, shown in Figure 10-27. The palette offers a pop-up menu of four eraser styles: Paintbrush, Airbrush, Pencil, and Block. *Block* is the old 16 × 16-pixel square eraser that's great for hard-edged touch-ups. The other options work exactly like the tools for which they're named.

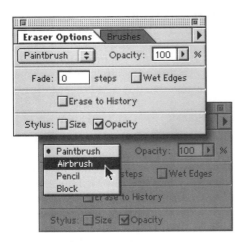

**Figure 10-27:** The eraser tool can paint like the paintbrush, the airbrush, the pencil, or the vintage Photoshop 2.5 eraser (Block).

**Tip**

You needn't go to the trouble of selecting the options from the pop-up menu. When the eraser tool is active, press Shift+E to cycle through the different styles.

As if this weren't enough, the eraser is pressure sensitive, it responds to Opacity settings, and you can create fading eraser strokes. When the Paintbrush option is active, you even have access to the Wet Edges check box described in Chapter 8. The only thing missing is the brush modes menu.

While the eraser tool is pretty straightforward, there's no sense in leaving any stone unturned. So here's everything you ever wanted to know about the art of erasing:

✦ **Erasing on a layer:** When working on the Background layer, the eraser merely paints in the background color. Big whoop. What distinguishes the eraser tool from the other brushes is layers. When working on a layer (with the Preserve Transparency check box turned off), the eraser tool actually removes paint and exposes portions of the underlying image. The eraser tool suddenly performs like a real eraser.

**Cross-Reference**

If the Layer palette's Preserve Transparency check box is turned on, Photoshop won't let the eraser bore holes in the layer. Instead, it paints in the background color. For more information on Preserve Transparency and its other pals in the Layers palette, read Chapter 17.

✦ **Erasing lightly:** Change the Opacity setting in the Eraser Options palette to make portions of a layer translucent in inverse proportion to the Opacity value. For example, if you set the Opacity to 90 percent, you remove 90 percent of the opacity from the layer and, therefore, leave 10 percent of the opacity behind. The result is a nearly transparent stroke through the layer.

✦ **The eraser compared with layer masks:** As described in the "Creating layer-specific masks" section of Chapter 17, you can also erase holes in a layer using a layer mask. But unlike the eraser—which eliminates pixels for good—a layer mask doesn't do any permanent damage. On the other hand, using the eraser tool doesn't increase the size of your image as much as a layer mask does. (One can argue *any* operation—even a deletion—increases the size of the image in RAM because the History palette has to track it. But the eraser is still more memory-efficient than a layer mask.) So it's a trade-off.

✦ **Erasing with the pencil:** If you double-click on the pencil icon in the toolbox and select the Auto Erase check box in the Pencil Options palette, the pencil draws in the background color any time you click or drag on a pixel colored in the foreground color. This can be useful when you're drawing a line against a plain background. Set the foreground color to the color of the line; set the background color to the color of the background. Then use the pencil tool to draw and erase the line until you get it just right. I use this feature all the time when preparing screen shots. Adobe engineers call the Auto Erase check box their "ode to Fatbits," from the ancient MacPaint zoom function.

Note

Unlike the eraser, the pencil always draws either in the foreground or background color, even when used on a layer.

✦ **The magic eraser:** Press the Option/Alt key to access the "magic" eraser. Option/Alt+dragging paints with the source state identified by the history brush icon in the History palette. (By default, Photoshop sets the source state to the image as it appeared when first opened.) It's like scraping away the paint laid down by the operations following the source state, as demonstrated quite graphically in Figure 10-28.

Or, you can also select the Erase to History check box in the Eraser Options palette. In this case, dragging with the eraser reverts and Option/Alt+dragging paints in the background color.

**Figure 10-28:** After making a dreadful mistake (left), I Option/Alt+dragged with the eraser tool to restore the image to the way it looked in the source state (right).

## The history brush

The history brush tool works like the magic eraser, except without the Option/Alt key. Just drag with the tool to paint down to the source state targeted in the History palette.

But the history brush offers three advantages over the magic eraser:

✦ **Brush modes:** First, you can take advantage of brush modes. By choosing a different brush mode from the pop-up menu in the upper left corner of the History Brush Options palette, you can mix pixels from the changed and saved images to achieve interesting and, sometimes, surprising effects.

✦ **Impressionist**: The other advantage is the Impressionist check box, highlighted in Figure 10-29. This option retrieves the source state and sort of smears it around to create a gooey, unfocused effect. You can achieve some mildly interesting effects by combining Impressionist with the Overlay, Hard Light, or Soft Light brush modes, but it's clearly a special effects function.

✦ **Fewer keystrokes:** You don't have to cycle through brush styles as with the eraser tool. Just press the Y key to select the history brush and start painting.

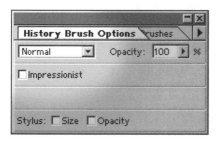

**Figure 10-29:** The history brush offers two advantages over the magic eraser—the brush modes pop-up menu and the Impressionist check box—both highlighted here.

Personally, I advise you to get in the habit of using the history brush instead of the magic eraser. Granted, the eraser gives you different cursors—pencil style and block—but when weighed against brush modes, this hardly seems much of an advantage at all. All things considered, the history brush is superior and it doesn't require you to press Option/Alt. The history brush is also more intuitive, because its icon matches the source state icon in the History palette.

## Merging alternative realities

The history brush is a great tool for erasing away mistakes. But you don't have to limit yourself to painting into the past. Just as the History palette lets you skip back and forth along the train track of time, the history brush lets you paint to any point in time.

The following steps provide an example of how you can use the History palette to establish an alternative reality and then follow up with the history brush to merge that reality with the present. It's trippy stuff, I realize, but I'm confident that with a little effort, you can give that post-modern brain of yours a half twist and wrap it around these steps like a big, mushy Mobius Strip.

## Steps: Brushing to a Parallel Time Line

1. **Open the image you want to warp into the fourth dimension.** I begin with a map of Japan (Figure 10-30). Japan is a wacky combination of seventeenth-century cultural uniformity, 1950s innocence, and twenty-first century corporate imperialism, so it strikes me as a perfect subject for my compound-time experiment.

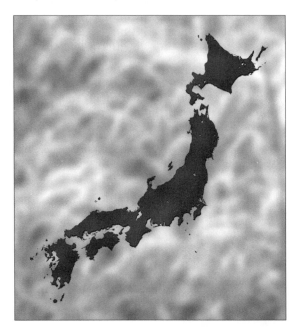

**Figure 10-30:** This map of Japan comes from the Digital Stock image library.

2. **Apply a couple of filters.** I choose Filter ➪ Pixelate ➪ Mosaic and set the Cell Size value to 20 pixels. Then I apply Filter ➪ Stylize ➪ Emboss with a Height of 5 pixels and an Amount of 200 percent. Figure 10-31 shows the results.

3. **Choose the History Options command from the History palette menu.** Then turn on the Allow Non-Linear History check box and press Return/Enter.

4. **Click on the Open item in the History palette.** This reverts the image to the state at which it existed when you first opened it. But thanks to non-linear history, Photoshop retains the alternate filtered versions of the image just in case you'd like to revisit this timeline in the future.

5. **Click in front of the first filter effect in the History palette to make it the source state.** In my case, I click in front of the Mosaic item.

6. **Select the history brush and start painting.** As you do, you'll paint with the filtered version of the image. For my part, I set the blend mode to Darken and painted around the island country to give it a digital edge, as in the first example of Figure 10-32.

7. **Switch the source state by clicking in front of the second filter effect.** Naturally, I clicked in front of the Emboss item.

8. **Paint again with the history brush.** This time, I changed the brush mode to Overlay and painted randomly over Japan and the surrounding ocean. The result appears in the second example of Figure 10-32.

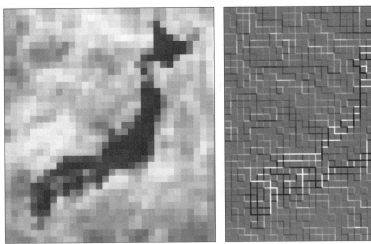

**Figure 10-31:** The results of applying the Mosaic (left) and Emboss (right) filters. Both of these effects are overstated, so I'll undo them and then paint them back in with the history brush.

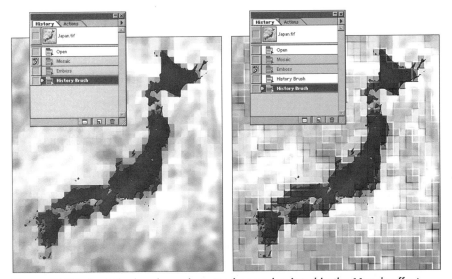

**Figure 10-32:** I set the brush mode to Darken and painted in the Mosaic effect with the history brush (left). Then I changed the brush mode to Overlay and brushed in the Emboss effect (right).

Once you finish, you can toss the filtered states. This alternate timeline has served its purpose. Or keep it around as a snapshot to come back to later.

### Source state limitations

Sadly, there are some minor limitations to history brushing. Photoshop won't let you paint with either the history brush or magic eraser if the source state is a different width or height than the current image. One pixel different and the source state is a moot point. (This also goes for Edit ⇨ Fill and ⌘/Ctrl+Option/Alt+Delete/Backspace.)

If Photoshop displays the not-allowed cursor (the circle with a slash through it) when you try to use the history brush, then move the source state icon in the History palette to a point after you modified the width or the height of the image. Commands that can mix up the history brush include Image ⇨ Image Size, Canvas Size, Rotate Canvas, and Crop, as well as the crop tool. If you applied one of these operations in the very last state, then you either have to backstep before that operation or find some alternative to the history brush.

It's not a big deal, though. Give it some time and you'll learn to anticipate this problem. In the case of my experiment with Japan, for example, I made sure to resample and crop the image before I began my experiment. Get the dimensions ironed out, and then start laying down your time trails.

To learn how to use the history brush to retouch a vintage image, read Chapter 13.

✦     ✦     ✦

# PART IV
# COLOR AND
# HISTORY
# TECHNIQUES

**Integrating Natural Media into
    Digital Art**
**Colorizing Scanned Line Art**
**Retouching with the
    History Brush**
**High-Resolution Imaging for
    Advertising**

# CHAPTER 11
# INTEGRATING NATURAL MEDIA
# INTO DIGITAL ART

This book devotes a lot of space to ways that a computer, together with Photoshop, can broaden your creative range and make you more productive. But I'd be lying if I characterized any computer — Mac, PC, or otherwise — as the ultimate achievement in artistic machinery.

Probably the most irritating aspect of a typical computer is that it doesn't begin to give you the same tactile feedback as a 25¢ pencil against a nickel sheet of paper. You move your mouse or stylus on a horizontal surface and observe the results a foot or more away on a vertical screen. Meanwhile, the screen provides you with a relatively tiny window into your artwork. As a result, it can be extremely difficult to sketch in, say, Photoshop and accurately gauge issues such as form and composition.

Simply put, you can expend less effort and create better artwork if you draw or paint directly to paper and then scan your artwork into Photoshop for further processing.

## BUD'S NATURAL MEDIA EPIPHANY

Veteran freelance illustrator Bud Peen learned this lesson the hard way. "I struggled for weeks trying to create simple watercolors in Fractal Design Painter. I came to hate that program. I really hate it with a passion. It's just so awkward and annoying to work with. Finally, it occurred to me, why am I doing this? Why don't I just paint with real watercolors, then scan in the artwork and modify it in Photoshop? It was like an anvil dropped on my head.

*The key is to recognize the inherent purpose and limitations of your tools.*

BUD PEEN

"It seems so obvious now. But I think the reason I never really considered it before is that there's a stigma associated with working outside the computer. It started when magazines like *Macworld* required that their artists work on a Macintosh. It built a dividing wall between traditional and nontraditional materials. Nowadays, it's almost like there's this religion where everything has to be created digitally."

If such a religion does exist, Peen has plainly left the fold. In fact, looking at Peen's playful, perspective-irreverent artwork (11.1), you'd swear he'd never touched a computer in his life. The watercolor effects were obviously created using real brushes dipped into real water-soluble pigments and dabbed onto real pieces of paper. (Shocking, really — I can hardly believe my editor lets me relate such appalling news.) But in truth, these are layered Photoshop files scanned in multiple passes and finished with the airbrush tool. As you'll discover in this chapter, Peen could not have achieved these effects without the aid of a computer.

11.1

**ARTIST:**
Bud Peen

**COMPANY:**
Bud Peen Illustration
2720 Madeline Street
Oakland, CA 94602
510/482-8302
*http://www.budpeen.com*
bud@budpeen.com

**SYSTEM:**
PowerWave 604/150 (Power Computing)
1GB storage

**RAM:**
80MB total
12MB to 30MB assigned to Photoshop

**MONITOR:**
Old Radius 19-inch (planning on getting professional Sony model)

**EXTRAS:**
Epson 1200e scanner with transparency adapter

**VERSION USED:**
Photoshop 5.0

"The key is to recognize the inherent purpose and limitations of your tools." Photoshop, for example, easily outperforms the $30,000 stat camera, but doesn't hold a candle to the $3 pen nib. By contrast, conventional illustration tools permit you to quickly create elements, but compositing and production are nothing short of tortuous. By merging natural media with digital tools, Peen has learned to command both ends of the process. The result is a style that favors efficiency and control without wearing its method on its sleeve.

## PART I: A CONVENTIONAL BEGINNING

Peen's illustrations typically comprise a series of calligraphic outlines laid against a brightly colored watercolor background. After getting the client's approval for his rough pencil sketch — which he draws meticulously on ledger paper — he traces the sketch onto five-ply bristol using graphite paper (it's like carbon paper except with graphite on it). "It's a very primitive method, but I don't know of any better way." He then paints the watercolors over the graphite lines on the bristol board (11.2).

Isn't it a little unusual to apply the watercolors before the line work? "Yeah, it's completely opposite the way most people do it. But I found that most artists are a little sloppy with the watercolors if they apply them second. The background becomes an afterthought. By painting the watercolor first, it makes me spend more time and get the colors just right. For me, the watercolor is the most important part of the illustration."

After the watercolors dry, Peen draws to registration dots on the bristol board. He then places a sheet of translucent Duralene on top of the bristol and copies the registration dots to ensure proper alignment. Finally, Peen traces along the graphite lines using a Gillot Extra Fine quill pen. "Once the line work dries, I'll go in with a single-edged razor and scrape away mistakes and sharpen up some of the lines.

"At this point the line work is all black (11.3). Now, in the old days, I would submit the bristol and Duralene as a composite mechanical and specify a flat process color for the line work. But the lines just sat there like lumps on top of this very expressive watercolor background. I was never really happy with that."

**OTHER APPLICATIONS:**
Adobe Illustrator, Adobe Streamline, Macromedia Director, QuarkXPress, Strata StudioPro (still learning)

**WORK HISTORY:**
1977 — After graduating from college, set up silk screening department in Santa Rosa print shop.
1979 — Worked for New York advertising agency.
1983 — Spent a year in Paris studying fine art and sculpture.

1989 — Commissioned by *PC World* to create five illustrations in CorelDraw; work came out flat and lifeless.
1995 — Gave up trying to create natural effects on computer and purchased scanner to integrate traditional media into digital workflow.

**FAVORITE MOVIE GENRE:**
Submarine flicks ("I often shout 'Dive! Dive!' when the phone is ringing off the hook and work is piling up.")

11.2                         11.3

11.4

## PART II: SHIFTING INTO DIGITAL

This sounds like a job for Photoshop. "There's something liberating about having a scanner hooked up to a computer. Once I crossed that threshold and decided that I could create things outside the computer and bring them in, everything started falling into place. I discovered I could do things that I never could before."

To prepare the watercolor and Duralene for scanning, Peen carefully aligns the registration dots and slices a common straight edge along the tops of both sheets. "This way, I can place the top of each page flush with the edge of the scanner to ensure vertical alignment inside Photoshop." He scans the watercolor in 24-bit color at 300 pixels per inch. Then he scans the line art in black and white at the same resolution.

### COMBINING THE ARTWORK

Peen opens both images in Photoshop. Using the Canvas Size command, Peen crops the taller of the two images to match the shorter one, making sure to crop away from the bottom. Then he drags the line art and Shift-drops it into the watercolor image, resulting in a new layer. Pressing the Shift key during the drop confirms that the two images are aligned vertically.

As things stand, the black-and-white line layer hides the watercolor background. To get rid of the white pixels, Peen goes to the Channels palette and ⌘/Ctrl-clicks the RGB composite channel. This selects the white pixels and leaves the black lines deselected. Pressing the Delete key makes the white go away. Then Peen deselects the image (⌘/Ctrl+D) and ⌘/Ctrl+Shift drags the lines into horizontal alignment with the watercolor background (11.4).

**11.5**

**11.6**

### COLORING THE LINES

Now for the fun part. Peen turns on the Preserve Transparency check box in the Layers palette so he can paint exclusively inside the quill lines. Then he uses the airbrush to add colors at will (11.5). "I'll use the eyedropper to lift colors from the watercolor layer. Then I'll adjust the color to darken it up in the Colors palette. The colors in the lines are always related to the colors in the background (11.6).

"If I wanted colored lines before Photoshop, I had to resort to dipping a brush into as many as 20 colored inks. It was incredibly complicated. Now it's not only easier and less messy, but I have much more control." One look at Peen's colored lines by themselves (11.7) illustrates just how much better Photoshop handles coloring functions than traditional media. "And I can go back and change colors with complete flexibility."

**11.7**

Does Peen experiment much with the Layer palette's blend modes before flattening the line art into the watercolor? "If the line work is really defining, I'll leave the blend mode set to Normal to make the lines opaque. But if I'm doing more subtle work, I'll apply the Multiply mode to burn the lines into the watercolor."

**WHEN YOU FIND A GOOD THING . . .**

Just for the sheer heck of it, I've included two additional examples of Peen's artwork showing the progression from scanned watercolors (11.8) to black line art overlay (11.9) and final airbrush-colored lines (11.10). "What I love about this technique is that I can place the lines on the watercolor work and see right away how the lines react to the watercolors. There's a degree of immediacy that you simply can't get with conventional mechanicals."

**VECTOR VARIATIONS**

Although flexible, Peen's watercolor approach isn't right for every job. Sometimes Peen wants a more synthetic look; other times the Photoshop approach simply isn't practical. "I originally wanted to create the Antiquarian Book Fair poster (11.11) using watercolor and quill pen. But it was such a large piece — over 30 inches tall — that I simply couldn't make it work inside Photoshop. I tried to airbrush one of the lines and it took like five minutes. So I was forced to turn to Illustrator instead."

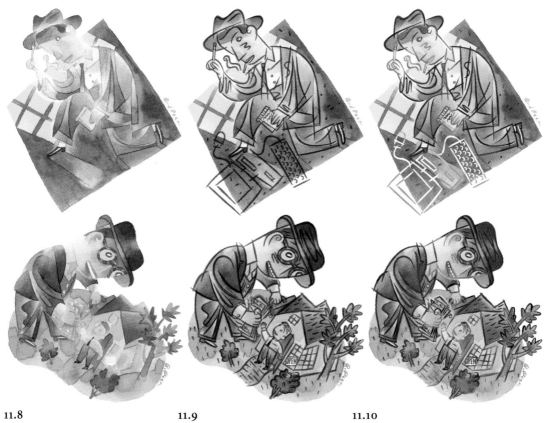

11.8                              11.9                              11.10

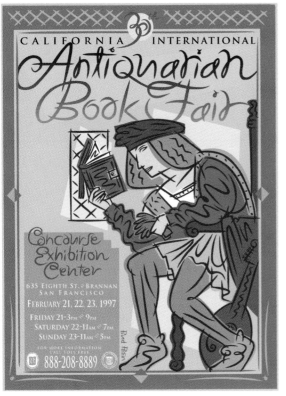

**11.11**

In this case, Peen scanned his quill-pen illustrations — one for the title, another for the reading minstrel — and converted it to vector objects using automatic tracing program Adobe Streamline. Peen then positioned the quill paths on a layer inside Illustrator and created the color paths on a separate layer in the background.

### PATHS INSTEAD OF WATERCOLOR

Why discuss a piece of Illustrator artwork inside a Photoshop book? Because this poster was a step in discovering additional ways to color lines inside Photoshop. "I began to experiment using Illustrator paths as a background element instead of watercolor."

For instance, in the case of the Emale graphic (11.12), Peen started as usual by inking in the line art, scanning it, and converting the lines to paths with Streamline. Then he used Illustrator's brush tool to paint in color on a separate layer behind the line art. "Generally, I don't like Illustrator's brush tool. But it came in handy here."

After saving the background paths and line art as independent files, Peen opened the background paths in Photoshop and airbrushed in a few dollops of color to add a hint of depth to the flat fills (11.13). He then opened the line art and dragged it over as a separate layer. And finally, he turned on the Preserve Transparency check box and painted color inside the lines (11.14).

In case you're wondering what font Peen used for Emale, the answer is none. "The type was a piece of quill pen artwork. I introduced it as a separate layer inside Photoshop."

## EMBRACING SYNTHETIC MEDIA

"I think the *Predicting Doom* piece I did for *InfoWorld* (11.15) is a really nice one because it allowed me to really push the synthetic aspect of the artwork. I used Illustrator blends to feather the sky and ground. You can even see the banding — it doesn't even remotely resemble watercolors, which is the way I wanted it."

**11.12 (TOP), 11.13 (MIDDLE), 11.14 (BOTTOM)**

**11.15**

**11.16**

**11.17**

As usual, Peen brought in the line art through Streamline. But when processing more complicated artwork like this, Streamline has something of a problem. "The program traces paths from the outside in. It actually stacks on top of each other areas of black and white. This means the white areas are opaque, which prevents the colored fills from showing through.

"To fix this in Illustrator, I go ahead and slip a dark box behind the traced paths so I can see which areas are opaque (11.16). Then I start selecting paths from the outside in and convert them into compound paths until all the interiors become transparent (11.17). It sounds like a lot of work, but it usually ends up being only about eight or nine paths that have to be converted."

### YOU USE *WHAT*-PEG?

Peen's colors are so vivid, you might think he spends a lot of time worrying about CMYK conversions and color matching. "I stick with RGB for the sake of e-mail. My colors are bright, but I'm not that concerned about specific color palettes. I just want small file sizes."

And with commercial printers urging their clients to submit printer-ready EPS files, what format does Peen use? "JPEG, actually. I've been using JPEG files for years without any problems. And they take far less time to e-mail to my clients." Chalk up another one for the independent-minded artist.

## SO MUCH MEDIA, SO LITTLE TIME

"Illustrating is all about solving problems within a framework of equations that you use on a regular basis. That's why I like the computer; it gives you so many different chances to exercise your options. With traditional art, the closer you get to the end, the fewer options you have. But with a computer, you never reach a dead end. You can always strip out elements or undo steps. You have this incredible freedom to experiment, from the beginning all the way to the end."

## THE WORLD OF THE TACTILE

Lately, Peen's artistic interests have been leading him into still other traditional and nontraditional media. "I'm a sculptor by training. So in addition to my illustrations, I've been dabbling in furniture design (11.18). It started a couple of years ago when I sent off a few drawings of lamps and clocks to a Dallas-

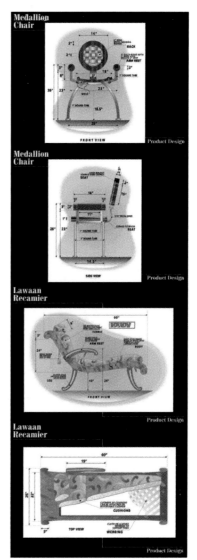

11.18

11.19 (TOP), 11.20 (BOTTOM)

based furniture artist named Lam Lee. I didn't expect much, but he just went nuts. He told me, 'Your work fills my heart with great joy.' It was wonderful! I've never had a client tell me that before. So he asked me to design a whole line of furniture. I use Photoshop to prepare the mechanical sketches for the factories, which lets me integrate different colors and materials very quickly. The frames are made of wood, then they cover it with these little tiles of beautiful stone. It looks great, but it's incredibly heavy."

### THE WORLD OF THE SCREEN

If you're more interested in something that you can bring into your house without the help of three hardy workmen, then you can find Peen's illustrations in the *National Geographic* online Fantastic Forest project (11.19). Designed by multimedia artist Brad Johnson, this award-winning site is definitely worth a visit — especially if you have kids. In addition to Peen's forest elements — each created as an independent water-color — Fantastic Forest offers excellent examples of Shockwave sounds and objects. Of particular interest, you can build your own forest using a few of Peen's watercolors (11.20). To see it for yourself, go to *http://www.nationalgeographic.com/modules/forest.*

# CHAPTER 12
# COLORIZING SCANNED LINE ART

P hotoshop is just the ticket for manipulating scanned photographs, but did you know that Photoshop is also the most popular program for colorizing scanned line art? These days, lots of professionals use the program to add color to medical illustrations, maps, fine-art designs, cartoons, schematic drawings, and even old clip art.

Computer colorizing is popular because it exploits the best aspects of traditional and digital media. It's easier to draw on paper with a pencil and pen than it is to sketch onscreen; on the other hand, it's easier to add colors in Photoshop than to hassle with conventional paints or assemble fussy mechnicals.

How you colorize your line art depends on what kind of effect you want to achieve. In this chapter, I examine five related techniques, applied in stages, to a cartoon frog I call Shenbop (12.1). For the sake of clarity, I've kept Shenbop simple. However, you can start with any kind of line art you like — living or dead; simple or complex; comical or serious; pen-and-ink, pencil, or brushwork. Photoshop lets you color the lines, fill in the shapes, add depth, create digital textures, and even introduce photographic backgrounds, all while respecting every stroke in your original drawing (12.2). It really is the best of both worlds.

12.1

**12.2**

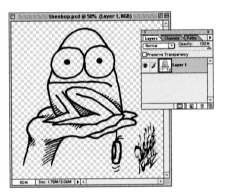

**12.3**

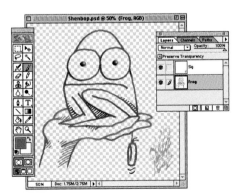

**12.4**

## COLORING THE LINES

I begin with a colorizing technique that I learned from Bud Peen, who you may remember as the featured artist in Chapter 11. (My only contribution is a slightly more efficient approach.) Bud draws his original art using a quill pen. Rather than directing the printer to assign one or more Pantone colors to the lines — as he did in the old days — he uses Photoshop to brush in RGB values. This way, he can see the colors as he applies them and achieve more subtle effects.

If you scanned your line art in color, convert it to grayscale by choosing Image ➤ Mode ➤ Grayscale. Clean up the artwork as necessary using Photoshop's eraser and paintbrush tools. Once the artwork is spotless, select the black lines in the image and send them to a separate layer. If you're thinking of using the magic wand, don't. The wand is clunky and involves too much work. The more precise solution requires just three keystrokes. Press ⌘/Ctrl+Option/Alt+1, press ⌘/Ctrl+Shift+I, and then press ⌘/Ctrl+J, in that order. The first keystroke selects all the white areas in the image, the second reverses the selection so the black lines are selected, and the third sends the black lines to a separate layer. Now you can delete the Background layer (12.3) or, if you prefer working against an opaque background, fill the entire Background layer with white. Either way, the black lines are relegated to their own layer.

To protect your scanned lines, press the slash (/) key to turn on the Preserve Transparency option in the Layers palette. Add colors willy-nilly with the paintbrush and airbrush tools (12.4). Feel free to go nuts. Thanks to the Preserve Transparency option, Photoshop keeps the paint inside the lines.

## FILLING AREAS WITH COLOR

To give your drawing substance, you need to fill the interiors of your shapes with color. You could use the paint bucket tool, but adding layers is easier and it expands your range of options later.

For maximum flexibility, you want to create a separate layer for each color. Start by adding an empty layer behind your colored lines. You can drag and drop layers directly in the palette to change the order. In this step, make sure the Preserve Transparency option is turned off. Choose a color and then use the lasso tool to select the basic area you want to fill. You don't have to be all that careful — the thickness of the lines should easily cover up small errors. Fill the selection with a flat color by pressing Option/Alt+Delete (12.5). Create a new layer for the next area of color, and so on (12.6). As long as you keep the layers in back of the line drawing layer, your fills will look great.

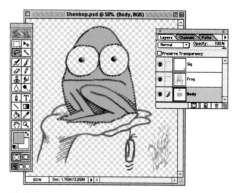

12.5

## AIRBRUSHING HIGHLIGHTS AND SHADOWS

The problem with flat colors is they don't convey depth. And what's the point of using Photoshop if you don't throw in a few highlights and shadows? Luckily, it's incredibly easy to add these now that you've set up your basic fill layers.

Go to the layer that you want to enhance (Shenbop's green body layer, in this case) and again press the slash (/) key to preseKrve transparency. Next, use the airbrush tool to paint in highlights and shadows. You can do this in one of two ways. The hard way is to select a light shade of your base fill color for painting highlights and a dark shade for painting shadows. The easy way (our way) is to use just one color and let blend modes do the work for you.

Here's how: Lift the base fill color with the eyedropper (green, in Shenbop's case). Set the blend mode in the Airbrush Options palette to Screen when painting highlights or Multiply when painting shadows (12.7).

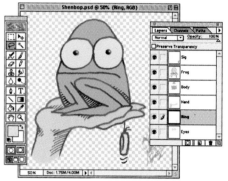

12.6

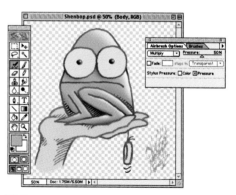

12.7

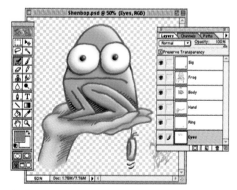

12.8

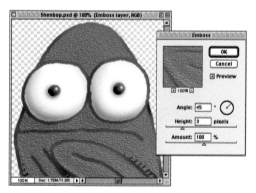

12.9

12.10

You can also use white for highlights, as I did for Shenbop's eyes (12.8), but steer clear of black — it just muddies things up. You can even restore areas of flat color by setting the blend mode to Normal. You never have to change the foreground color. And thanks to the Preserve Transparency option, you can't help but paint inside the lines.

## CREATING SYNTHETIC TEXTURES

A frog's skin is never smooth, even when he's a cartoon creature. To add a somewhat nubby texture, I take advantage of a few of Photoshop's filters. But first, it's a good idea to duplicate the green body layer as a precaution. (Incidentally, note that Photoshop turns off the Preserve Transparency option for the duplicate layer; press / to turn it on again.) Apply the Add Noise filter set to 64, to jumble up the pixels, and then run a slight Gaussian Blur with a Radius of 0.5. Apply the Emboss filter to etch the softened noise into nubs.

The problem with this technique is Emboss robs the layer of color, leaving it a dead gray (12.9). This will never do — dead though he may be, Shenbop is well preserved. To restore the color while retaining the nubs, merge the embossed layer with the underlying green body layer by selecting a blend mode from the Layers palette. The best mode for Shenbop turns out to be Hard Light (12.10). But if you run into a similar situation, I encourage you to experiment. Overlay, Luminosity, Multiply, Screen, and even Difference are splendiKd modes for merging an embossed texture with the colored layer below.

## INTRODUCING A NATURAL BACKGROUND

Emboss and other filters aren't the only way to introduce textures to a layer. You can use real-world scanned or stock-photo textures as well. And you can make them any color you want with the help of blend modes.

Start by creating a new layer in back of the others and filling it with a radial light-to-dark blue gradient (12.11). This new layer defines the colors of the photographic texture. Next, open a paper texture from any stock photo and drag it into your document. Note that the paper texture sits directly in front of the gradient layer — perfect for a blend mode. Select Multiply from the pop-up menu in the Layers palette and lower the opacity to 70 percent (12.12). The result is a deep-blue texture with a soft spotlight transition. Best of all, it took less than a minute to create.

## PRESERVE TRANSPARENCY
## AND BLEND MODES

As you can see, every one of these techniques relies on layers. The other big factors are Photoshop's blend modes and the Preserve Transparency option. Notice that I avoided using the standard color correction commands. Hue/Saturation, Variation, and others are extremely useful for adjusting colors, but when adding colors or colorizing black-and-white images, layers provide more flexibility and better control. Besides, you never know exactly what kind of effect you'll get when you start playing around with blend modes. The results can be both intriguing and inspirational — sometimes even amphibian.

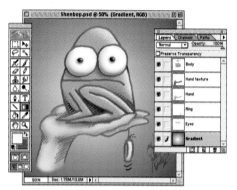

**12.11**

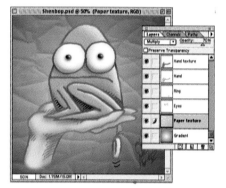

**12.12**

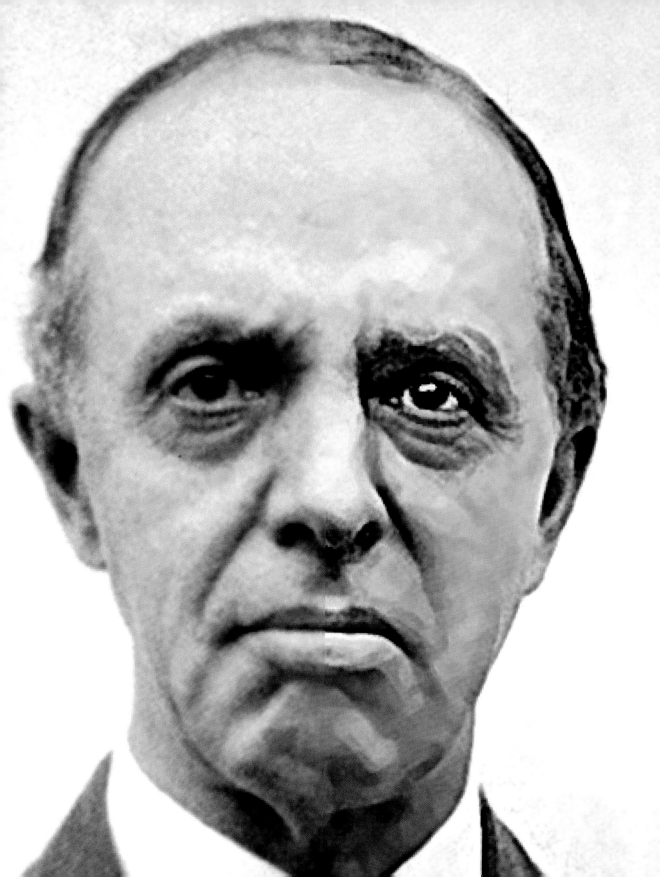

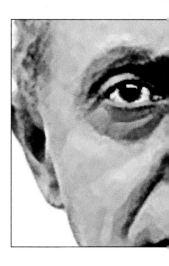

# CHAPTER 13
# RETOUCHING WITH THE HISTORY BRUSH

W hat's the best way to retouch an older image in Photoshop? I liken the process to washing a car — you can either do it well or do it fast. Buffing the image gently and meticulously with the rubber stamp tool yields excellent results, but it takes a lot of time. If you run the image through the Dust & Scratches filter — Photoshop's equivalent of an automatic car wash — you're done in a couple of minutes, but the result is hardly anything to be proud of.

So what do you do if you're on a deadline but you still want to do a good job? For folks in a moderate hurry, there's a compromise position. You can apply opposing filters such as Median and Unsharp Mask and then brush them in alternately to smooth over imperfections and sharpen edge details. The technique is hardly new — various approaches like this one have been floating around for years — but the Photoshop 5 history brush adds a new twist to it.

Rather than mixing images on separate layers or reverting from a snapshot — your only options in the past — you can now establish a collection of historical "states" and restore elements selectively from any one of them. The history brush and its partner, the History palette, take a little time to get used to. But once you figure them out, you can achieve effects that would have involved considerably more effort in the ancient days before History was invented.

**13.1**

*Image courtesy of Digital Stock*

**13.2**

## SHARPENING AND SMOOTHING

The problem with old photos is they're usually soft and grainy (13.1). This means you have to find some way to both sharpen the detail and smooth away the grain (13.2) — two contradictory operations. The solution is to perform both operations up front and worry about which specific areas need sharpening and smoothing later. Photoshop's history brush lets you do precisely that. You can create one sharpened version of an image, another smooth version, and then brush the two into the original as needed.

To start, apply the Unsharp Mask filter to your image. Because the sharpened state represents one extreme in this process, you'll want to apply the filter liberally. I recommend an Amount value of about 400 percent with a Radius value of 2.0. Leave the Threshold option set to 0; otherwise, you end up with harsh transitions between sharpened and soft areas, which looks pretty ratty.

As it does with all operations, Photoshop 5 automatically adds Unsharp Mask as a state in the History palette. This means the operation is just one possible state that you can keep or undo according to your whim. However, for purposes of this technique, Unsharp Mask is an important state that you'll need to come back to several times over the course of editing the image. To keep the state from cycling off the History palette (by default, the palette tracks the last 20 operations only), you can save it as a snapshot by clicking the little page icon at the bottom of the palette (13.3). (In this example, I wanted to give my image some extra color, so I also shifted the image to purple using Hue/Saturation.) The snapshot will remain available as long as the image is open.

Now click the state prior to Unsharp Mask in the History palette. (If Unsharp Mask was the first operation you applied after opening the image, you can click the default snapshot at the top of the palette.) This reverts the image to its pre–Unsharp Mask appearance. The undone states turn gray, but because you saved Unsharp Mask as a snapshot earlier, it remains available in the top portion of the palette.

To create the smooth version of the image, choose Filter ➤ Noise ➤ Median. Median smoothes out film grain by averaging the colors of neighboring pixels. (It's exactly like Dust & Scratches, except without the half-baked Threshold option.) Raise the Radius value until the grain disappears—probably somewhere in the 4 to 6 range. This will necessarily gum up the detail, but because the idea is to provide a smooth extreme, that's to be expected. Click OK to apply the filter.

As with Unsharp Mask, the Median operation becomes a new state in the History palette. You'll want to come back to it, so save it as a snapshot by clicking the page icon at the bottom of the palette (13.4). Next, undo the Median operation by clicking the state preceding it.

**13.3**

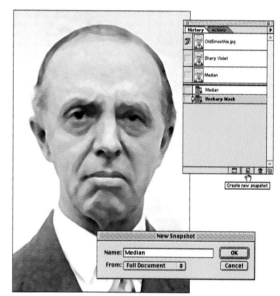

**13.4**

13.5

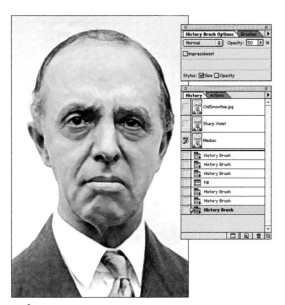

13.6

## PAINTING WITH THE SNAPSHOTS

You now have your original image onscreen with two snapshots waiting in memory: one that's too sharp and another that's too smooth. You are ready to paint the snapshots into the original with the history brush.

Select the history brush by pressing the Y key, and then click to the left of the Unsharp Mask item in the History palette. A brush icon appears in front of the snapshot, indicating that the snapshot is the "source state" for the history brush and other history operations. Trace around the important details in the image to apply the sharpened snapshot. If you're retouching a face, for example, you should paint around the eyes, mouth, and other features to improve their clarity and focus (13.5). To enhance the effect, select a brush mode such as Hard Light or Overlay from the History Brush Options palette. Don't worry if the effect is too garish or overdone; you can always temper it by painting from the Median snapshot or some other state later on.

After painting in all the sharpened areas, it's time to smooth away the film grain with the Median snapshot. Click in front of the Median snapshot in the History palette to make it the source state. I like to take the edge off the sharpened details by covering the entire image with a translucent coat of Median. The easiest way to do this is to press Shift+Delete/Backspace to bring up the Fill dialog box and then set the Use pop-up menu to History and the Opacity value to 50 percent. After applying the Fill command, paint with the history brush set to 50 percent to smooth out the film grain and other imperfections in the image (13.6).

From here on, it's just a matter of painting back and forth between the Unsharp Mask snapshot and the Median snapshot. Feel free to vary the brush size as you work. You might also want to experiment with the Opacity value and brush mode setting in the History Brush Options palette. The most effective brush modes tend to be Hard Light, Screen, Multiply, and Normal. In this example, I wasn't happy with the eyes, so I painted from the sharpened snapshot using the

Screen mode (13.7). I followed up by painting with the Median snapshot set to Multiply (13.8). In Photoshop 5, you can select the desired mode from the keyboard by pressing Shift+Option/Alt in combination with a letter key. For example, Shift+Option/Alt+H gets you the Hard Light mode, Shift+Option/Alt+S switches you to Screen mode, and Shift+Option/Alt+N returns to Normal.

## THE HISTORY LEGACY

When you achieve the effect you're looking for, save your image as you normally would. Bear in mind, however, that if you close the image, you throw away the snapshots along with the other contents of the History palette. Like any undo structure, the Photoshop history mechanism resides entirely in RAM; the program does not automatically save snapshots or other states to disk. However, if you think you might want to come back to the Unsharp Mask or Median snapshots, you can save the states manually. Drag the snapshot item onto the leftmost icon at the bottom of the History palette to open the state in a new window, and then save the state as you would any image.

If you're new to Photoshop 5, this little exercise may prove more challenging than most. The History palette is one of Photoshop's most powerful features — every bit as capable and complex as the Layers and Channels palettes — so don't be surprised if it takes you some time to master. In its simplest form, the History palette provides multiple undos (up to 100, actually). But as you become more familiar with it, you'll see that you can exploit history to mix and match any operations that you can perform in Photoshop, whether they involve brushstrokes, color corrections, or filters. Simply put: Gather your extremes, and then paint them into place on the fly. As they say on cable, learning history is time well spent.

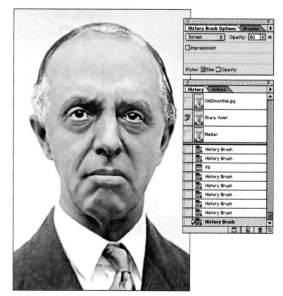

13.7

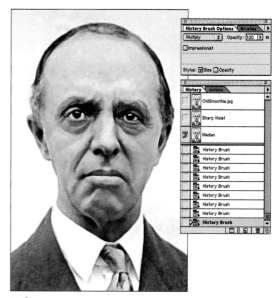

13.8

# CHAPTER 14
# HIGH-RESOLUTION IMAGING FOR ADVERTISING

The world of high-end advertising is a world of painstaking illusion and deliberate trickery. The companies who commission these ads are not simply trying to exaggerate the quality and performance of their products. If it were that simple, we'd all own Vegematics and Ronco would be king. A good advertisement misleads with the intent to entertain. It lures you inside it; offers a brief thrill, a smile, or a moment of glamour; and invites you to leave with the promise that more can be had for a price. Purchasing the product pays admission into the illusion. The fact that you receive a physical good in return is often little more than a nostalgic formality paying homage to the old barter-based society.

As one of Manhattan's most respected and admired commercial artists, Robert Bowen understands the role of illusion in advertising. "I've spent a fair amount of time looking at the history of art. I'm particularly interested in an approach called *trompe l'oeil* (pronounced *tromp-loy*) — which is French for 'trick the eye.' Trompe l'oeil images want to look real, like they were arranged and photographed exactly as you see them. But they're actually impossible."

Hollywood is the most conspicuous purveyor of the craft. "The intention of a typical movie — particularly an effects-oriented film — is to convey the look of realism without suggesting that what you're seeing actually happened. Everyone who goes to see a movie such as *Twister* or *Volcano* knows that it's not real. But if it has the appearance of realism, then they can suspend their disbelief and give themselves over to what they see. It's all based on an aesthetic of photorealism, as opposed to a more illustrative look that's grounded in the graphic tradition."

> *Trompe l'oeil images want to look real, like they were arranged and photographed exactly as you see them. But they're actually impossible.*
>
> ROBERT BOWEN

## BOB'S EXPLORATION INTO THE UNREAL

Bowen's art expresses roughly as much reverence for the laws of nature as a Lewis Carroll story. He grabs elements from the normal world, flings them down the rabbit's hole, and reassembles them on the other side. Curiously, the view from the bottom of the hole is often better than the one from above.

For example, we are all aware that young girls sometimes wear braces (14.1) and that cows as a rule do not (14.2). And yet, the appearance of a photorealistic cow undergoing dental adjustment is somehow extremely attractive. It amazes because it's peculiar; it amuses because it's so incredibly absurd. Without its accompanying ad copy, we may never understand why AT&T commissioned this artwork to target college students. But chances are good that the image of a "Cheshire Cow" will stick in your head. It's a smiling, ungulate, radioactive aberration.

The same goes for the mouse-headed man Bowen created for the high-tech company SDRC (14.3).

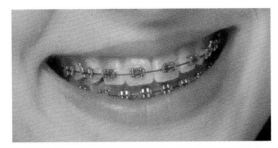

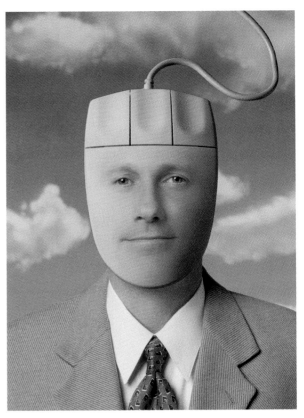

**14.1 (TOP), 14.2 (BOTTOM)**

*Photography by Dennis Gallante*

**14.3**

*Photography by Howard Berman*

**ARTIST:**
Robert Bowen

**ORGANIZATION:**
Robert Bowen Studio
New York City, NY
bowenbob@aol.com

**SYSTEMS:**
PowerWave 604/150 (Power Computing)
10GB storage
Silicon Graphics Indy 4400

**RAM:**
212MB total
190MB assigned to Photoshop

**MONITOR:**
Radius IntelliColor 20e

**EXTRAS:**
Adaptec Ultra-Wide controller with 2-drive
8GB Barracuda array

**VERSION USED:**
Photoshop 5.0

**OTHER APPLICATIONS:**
On Mac: Live Picture, Adobe Illustrator,
QuarkXPress
On SGI: Barco Creator, Alias Power Animator

This time, inspiration was close at hand. "I find this image kind of haunting. It reminds me of how I feel after a really bad day." But while the image looks a little painful, Bowen claims it was relatively easy to create. "I just painted the colorized mouse layer in and out with the face layer. I also threw in a few adjustment layers to match the highlights and colors."

Not all of Bowen's images are so outrageous. Sometimes he bends reality to soothe it. Several years ago, he worked with photographer Ryszard Horowitz on a series of images for Adobe that featured giant watery slabs hovering in space. "In this case, a slab of green universe pours water into the desert (14.4). It's kind of a pleasant idea — bringing life to a difficult world." Another image Bowen created for Adobe's introduction of Photoshop 5.0 is more fanciful (14.5). "I used lots of channel operations and adjustment layers to get the water ripples. The background was an invention created from chunks of photographic stuff that I shot during my teaching stint at CCI (the Center for Creative Imaging) in Maine."

In addition to his paid work for clients, Bowen devotes a modicum of time to creating stock images and purely personal art. Even then, he plays with what is real and what is not. "When I was in Italy, I took a lot of pictures of Roman ruins and came up with

**14.4**

*Photography by Ryszard Horowitz*

**WORK HISTORY:**

<u>1979</u> — Graduated from Pratt Institute with MFA, experimented with Polarized light projection.

<u>1984</u> — Studied computer science at Pratt and wrote simple 3-D wireframe animation program.

<u>1986</u> — Designed 3-D animation and TV commercials for Fantastic Animation Machine.

<u>1990</u> — Headed up print division at R/Greenberg Associates, worked on TV commercials and feature films (*Predator 2* and *Last Action Hero*).

<u>1994</u> — Started his own company aimed at creating final art for high-end ad campaigns.

**FAVORITE OLD MOVIE MAXIM:**

"Time flies like an arrow, fruit flies like a banana." (Courtesy of Groucho Marx)

**14.5**

*Photography by Howard Berman*

what amounts to a game of spaces (14.6). It's just something I did for myself, and this is the first time it's been printed. The whole foreground is tiled from a single arch that's about as tall as it is wide." Bowen cloned bits and pieces of the foreground texture to interrupt the repeating patterns. "If you look closely, you can still find a pattern, but I've worked it until it doesn't annoy me."

The most surprising elements in the image are found inside the archways. What initially appear to be rocky groves are actually distant views of the Roman Colosseum. "Everything about it is a contradiction. I repeated a small fragment to make it large and reduced the large elements to make them small. The overall image has a brooding interior quality, and yet it was all photographed outdoors." Last but not least, out of ruins, Bowen has created an inviolate structure.

"I'm trying to trick the eye without putting one over on anybody. I'm not seeking a photo-journalistic effect, but rather one that is obviously faked with all the hallmarks of realism. In a sense, I'm painting an impossible picture using stuff that you see every day." The most unlikely contradiction of all, however, may be Bowen himself. Soft-spoken and unassuming, widely regarded as one of the easiest people to work with east of the Mississippi, Bowen just so happens to occupy the exact point where reality hits the fan.

14.6

## MANAGING POPULATIONS OF A
## FEW MILLION PIXELS

Unfortunately, churning out elaborate visual fantasies is not all fun and games. Bowen has to deal with the same grim facts of Photoshop that confront every other professional image editor. Extreme resolutions and color space conversions take their toll.

"Typically, I work at very high resolutions. And much of what I do is poster art, so the images get very large." A piece of art commissioned by The New School, a New York City art school, is a case in point (14.7). Originally measuring 6561 × 4200 pixels (about 78MB), the image was large enough to double as both front and back cover for the summer course catalog and a poster-sized subway advertisement.

14.7

*Photography by Ryszard Horowitz*

**14.8**

"The clear blue Caribbean water against the backdrop of the Manhattan skyline made for a utopian view of New York harbor. Parsons also wanted me to push the concept of hats. Students have to try on different hats to decide what they want to be." In order to get the entire image — water, skyline, hats, and all — to fit on this page, I had to downsample the artwork to a paltry 30 percent of its original size. But never fear, I've also included a detail at full resolution (14.8). Regardless of size, the clarity is impeccable.

### WORKING WITH SUPER-HUGE FILES

Things must get miserably slow when editing such incredibly large images, particularly when you start slapping on the layers. But Bowen knows from experience that today's slowdowns have nothing on the past. "In the old days, we were working with images this size on IIfx machines. That was pitiful. I don't know how I survived. But with a Power Mac, lots of RAM, and a fast disk array, Photoshop is actually pretty fast, even when I'm working in poster-sized images with 10 or 12 layers. I love Barco on the SGI and Live Picture on the Mac, but I still spend most of my time in Photoshop because of the blend modes and other compositing advantages."

Bowen argues that speed buys you more than lost time; it gives you greater freedom to experiment. "Something big happened to me when the Power Macs came out. Suddenly, I could work in real time. Before then, I had to spend a lot of time planning and imagining what it was going to look like. But with faster machines, I can just do stuff and see it happen on screen. You wouldn't believe what a difference that makes in the way I work. The experience is becoming more and more immediate — almost like working with traditional tools, except that these tools are hundreds of times more powerful."

### CMYK FILES AND RGB TRANSPARENCIES

Some service bureau technicians will tell you that a guy like Bowen never ventures outside CMYK in his life. But like most Photoshop artists, Bowen spends his creative time in RGB with periodic visits to Photoshop's CMYK preview mode (⌘/Ctrl+Y). And for about half of his jobs, he never converts to CMYK at all. "When I deliver digital files, I always convert to CMYK. I never let anyone do an RGB to CMYK conversion of a Photoshop file on a different computer. That will always be bad. But lots of times, I give the client an RGB transparency. Then, they scan it with a Scitex or other high-end CMYK scanner. Different clients prefer one or the other."

But with transparencies, aren't you effectively printing a digital file, only to have it rescanned again? "Yes and no. When you record to film, you simply match its full resolution. Unlike printed separations, RGB film resolution is measured in pixels per millimeter, which is called 'rez.' Some film is rez-20, some is rez-40." That's 20 or 40 pixels per millimeter — or the equivalent of 500 to 1,000 pixels per inch — on film that measures 4 × 5 or 8 × 10 inches. "A rez-20 transparency is a little soft, a rez-40 transparency is sharper. I stick with rez-40 because I like to deliver a sharper product.

"After that, the transparency is treated like a resolution-independent source, just like photographic film. There's no attempt to scan one pixel in a CMYK file for each pixel in the RGB transparency. It can basically be projected to any size. It's sort of like the difference between 35mm and 70mm film. Both can be projected onto huge screens in a movie theater, but the 70mm film has less grain."

## CASE STUDIES AND NONEXISTENT WORLDS

Now that we have all the exposition and technical stuff out of the way, it's time to peek over Bowen's shoulder and see how he creates his artwork. Throughout the remainder of the chapter, I'll pull apart four jobs that have appeared in major magazine ads in recent years. With clients as varied as Panasonic and Johnnie Walker Black, this small collection represents a few of Bowen's best.

### STAGING AN ILLUSTRATION

In an ad for Adaptec (14.9), Bowen wanted to create the effect of sudden and dramatic color set against a drab background. "The Adaptec image is one of the best examples of my use of trompe l'oeil. I was inspired by a short story by Jorge Luis Borges called

**14.9**

*Photography by Robert Bowen and Howard Berman*

**14.10 (TOP), 14.11 (BOTTOM)**

**14.12**          **14.13**          **14.14**

'The Aleph.' The title refers to a place where you can literally see a whole universe from a single point of view. I turned this idea into a theatrical set. The stage is a loft roof somewhere in Brooklyn on a rainy, dismal day (14.10). But the roof scene is really just a backdrop. The color image of these buildings is leaning up against it, even casting a shadow (14.11). The result is a spatial play."

Bowen's construction is extremely simple. Each element — roof, shadow, color buildings, and vent (lower right corner) — appears on its own layer. The shadow required some layer masking, but that's it. "Of course, for this particular ad, the client wanted a lot of color. I started by adding some depth inside the buildings (14.11), but then I substituted the green space instead."

This was an unusual ad in that Bowen actually appeared inside it. Photographer Howard Berman shot Bowen against a plain white backdrop, with the base of his coat elevated to indicate a small breeze (14.12). After scanning himself, Bowen created a rough mask around his body, dragged and dropped the selection into the Adaptec composition, and scaled the layer to match its new surroundings (14.13). He finessed the edges with a layer mask and added a shadow by applying Levels adjustments to the background layers. To make the tie-dye pattern in the shirt, he applied a rainbow gradient to a separate layer, subject to the Color blend mode. He also added small color highlights to the function strip along the top of the Wacom tablet clutched in his right arm (14.14).

"There are three levels here, with the gray city interrupted by the color city which is interrupted by the green country. But the thing that interests me most is that the most drab element in the image — the grunge background — is presented as a total fake. Nothing about the entire image is real, except for me. Even my shirt is a forgery."

## DRINKING WITH DOLPHINS

"This next ad is part of a campaign that Johnnie Walker's been running for a couple of years. Each ad shows an individual involved in a creative pursuit set against a natural landscape. There's been a sculptor, an architect, a painter, a filmmaker. One golfer. A jazz bass player. This one is about a computer artist (14.15), a topic that's particularly near and dear to my heart.

**14.15**

*Photography by Eric Meola*

**14.16 (TOP), 14.17 (MIDDLE), 14.18 (BOTTOM)**

"We had lots of pictures for this ad. There were two background shots, both from the California coast." One photograph served as the main background (14.16), with additional waves brought in from the second image (14.17). "The deck and computer stand are both props that we shot inside the studio (14.18). We also had several shots of the computer artist. He's the product of two or three different photos.

## TEXTURING GRADIENT SKIES

"The sky in the Johnnie Walker ad is an all-digital creation. If you've ever tried to work with a flat gradient in Photoshop, you know there's always some degree of banding (14.19). The way to get around this is to put the gradient on a separate layer and then apply the Add Noise filter to each color channel independently. For this image, I think I applied an Amount of 8 in the Red channel and 4 in the other two (14.20). I also applied Gaussian Blur separately to each channel at very low values — 0.5 one time, 0.3 another (14.21). In the worst cases, I might create a couple of skies on different layers and then combine them at 50 percent Opacity or so." The inset boxes in the figures show magnified views.

**14.19** (TOP), **14.20** (MIDDLE), **14.21** (BOTTOM)

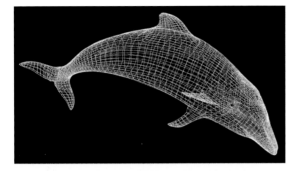

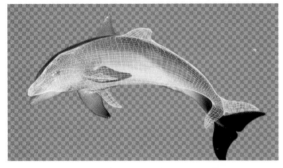

14.22 (TOP), 14.23 (MIDDLE), 14.24 (BOTTOM)

"The dolphin came from two pieces of stock art, including a photograph and a piece of 3-D clip art (14.22). Once we chose the stock image for the front part of the dolphin, I imported the image as a template layer into Alias Power Animator on the SGI machine. Then, I rotated and bent the model into the correct position until the wireframe matched the photo. Then, I anti-aliased the wireframe and imported it into Photoshop." After aligning the wireframe and dolphin on separate layers (14.23), Bowen brushed in layer masks to erase away the left side of the wireframe layer and the right side of the dolphin (14.24). The result was a graceful transition between the physical and digital worlds.

"The wireframe shown on the computer screen in the ad is the same 3-D dolphin model. But it had to be big enough so you could see it easily and make out what it was. So I rotated the model into a different position and magnified it so we see just the tail." The relationship between the onscreen tail and the leaping dolphin in digital transition questions the nature of creativity. Is the artist sketching what he sees, or is the dolphin a product of computer-aided manufacturing? Bowen consciously sprinkles these ambiguities throughout his artwork. "I don't know about you, but I've never seen anyone work with a computer on a pedestal. Where's the keyboard? What's it plugged in to? Little puzzles and contradictions like these invite the viewer to get involved in the artwork."

## CRAFTING A SPONTANEOUS SNAPSHOT

"The circus image comes from an ad for a warehouse management product by Computer Associates. The idea was, if your current warehouse management software is like this (14.25), then you need our product."

While the main subject of the image is based on a living, breathing elephant, she wasn't actually caught in the act of dancing the hula. "A trained elephant can manage to sit up, but it sits on a stool with both legs on the ground (14.26). It can also raise its legs up, but at most two at a time. The final elephant is close to an actual pose, but it's an amalgam of two or three pictures (14.27). Not including the hula skirt or the hat, of course."

**14.25**

*Photography by Howard Berman*

**14.26**          **14.27**

An off-center image is one thing, but a completely cockeyed composition is another. Isn't it? Bowen suggests that it rarely pays to work in small increments. "Let's say a client says to you, 'I want that elephant moved a little to the left.' If you're a little green, you'll do as you're told and move the elephant just the slightest amount. Then the client looks at it and decides that the elephant has nothing to do with it — some other piece of the artwork needs rethinking. All the while, the first impression was right. It was the elephant, you just didn't take it far enough. My advice is to take things too far. Then, evaluate and come back midway if you need to. But don't take baby steps. Take your risks up front and try to push it all the way out there."

One of Bowen's early drafts includes a parrot on the monkey's head and a second little dog on the left side of the weight (14.28). What made Bowen cut these elements out and submit such a strangely balanced composition (14.25)? "When you create these complex composites, you start off with the intention of building the whole world. But very often, after working for a few days and zooming in on a few details, you find that a slice of the image is far more dynamic than the whole. It happens so often that I made a decision up front to experiment with the framing on this image."

14.28

"I decided to capture the appearance of an instantaneous photograph. The final artwork is off center to suggest that it was captured with a 35mm camera. For one brief moment, all these animals were just in the right place at the right time. That's what I love about working in Photoshop. You can create a scene that says, 'Here's something ridiculous that happened for a split second. We were fortunate enough to record it on film.' But it's really just another trick."

## THE PHYSICS OF CLONING SHEEP

One of Bowen's most complex images called for a wolf rising up from a sea of sheep. And just to keep things interesting, the client, Panasonic, wanted to see every animal wearing headphones (14.29). "If you're a farmer, then your eyes are probably pretty accustomed to picking out sheep. You might recognize that there are just three sheep repeated over and over a hundred or so times."

Photographer Howard Berman shot the sheep in his studio, complete with headphones (14.30). But Bowen wasn't satisfied with the results. "There's something I call 'cartoon physics.' It applies to anything nonsensical, like the way headphones look on a sheep. The camera doesn't lie, so it shows headphones on a sheep the way they really are. But if they don't look right, then they don't conform to the laws of cartoon physics. You have no choice but to edit them."

**14.29**

*Photography by Howard Berman*

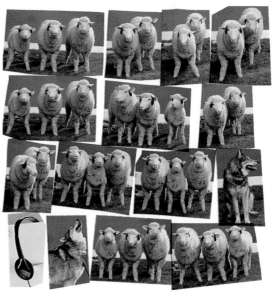

**14.30**

14.31

But the real fun came in duplicating the sheep into tidy and infinite rows. "For me, this was a fun perspective problem. Philosophically, we know that the sheep in front should be bigger than the ones in back. But what percentage do you scale down the sheep for each row? The solution of course is to apply some more cartoon physics. Maybe try reducing each row by 10 percent. That works for the first four rows, then you have to try something different. It was a matter of experimenting row by row.

"After I got the sheep arranged in rows, I had to deal with the focal issues. As you can see, there's a depth of field going on here — a nice sharp foreground, getting blurry as we move toward the back. I spent a lot of time applying the Gaussian Blur filter in incremental steps and then painting in shadows."

To me, this job in particular seems like a recipe for aggravation. Photographing sheep, outfitting them with headphones, cloning three sheep into 300, experimenting with depth and perspective, and grappling with some of the more difficult applications of cartoon physics — it takes a while to say, let alone do. "After I put together the rough comp (14.31), I knew right away it was going to be a learning experience. If you compare the rough to the finished piece (14.29), you can see that I had a lot of depth and perspective issues left to work out on the job. Still, I figured it would be interesting, so what the heck? Sure, I probably ended up spending a couple extra days on it, but it didn't kill me."

**14.32**

*Photography by Howard Berman*

## THE INFINITE DINER

Bowen used a combination of cartoon physics and straight perspective drawing to pull off an ad for IBM servers (14.32). "The idea was that one server could service an infinite number of people." The problem, of course, was rounding up an infinite number of people for a photo shoot. Even hiring 100 or so models — infinitely shy of infinite — is prohibitively expensive. So Bowen again turned to cloning.

"Howard Berman photographed a small group of people — about a dozen — in different locations in the diner (14.33, 14.34). We changed the colors of their clothing, experimented with different camera angles, changed the lighting.

**14.33**

**14.34**

**14.35**

"I finally committed to one camera angle, but we had to use a wide-angle lens, which really distorts space. The center seats had the least amount of distortion, so I built my perspective around them. I ended up repeating a series of seats over and over again, each time scaled to about 50 percent (14.35). I must confess, the finished effect still looks a little wonky, maybe impossible. But it has a consistent vanishing point, which is what you need to create a credible sense of depth.

"In the end, I spent a lot of time retouching the people and the ceiling. The hardest part was the checkered floor. Luckily, there was an overlay of black text in the final ad, which helped cover up some of the weirdness."

## AND NOW FOR SOMETHING COMPLETELY DIFFERENT

Before we said our good-byes, Bowen had the uncommon courtesy to walk me through an image that has nothing whatsoever to do with advertising (14.36). "If you have a pair of 3-D glasses lying around — the kind with the red and blue lenses — take a look at this image. It's called an anaglyph. You've probably seen this kind of effect printed in comic books, but I think you'll find that this might possibly be the best anaglyph you'll ever see. You can really feel the space of the great valley between the buildings. It stretches way, way back.

"As you probably know, a stereo picture is made from a left and right view, one for each eye. So I started by taking photos from the position of the left eye and the right eye — actually a little wider apart. In this case, I was shooting from the offices of Apple Computer here in New York.

"Then, I took the photos into Photoshop and converted them to grayscale. I copied the left-eye view, created a new RGB image, and pasted it into the Red channel. Then, I copied the right-eye view and pasted it into the Green and Blue channels of the new image. Switch back to the RGB view, and the two views converge.

"On top of all that, I've added a very simple warp inside Photoshop. I merely applied Filter ➢ Distort ➢ Shear, which is great for creating vertical waves. For me, it's the Shear filter that really makes the picture. You just don't see buildings roll back and forth like that in real life." Not in New York, anyway. Now, if this were San Francisco . . .

By the way, most 3-D glasses work better for viewing RGB light than printed CMYK colors. If you want to see the image without any ghosting, you can load Bowen's full-resolution original off CD #2 at the back of the book. "Open it up in Photoshop and zoom into it. Then, move it around. It'll blow your mind." Honestly, if you don't learn one thing from this book, playing around with this image will make it a worthwhile purchase.

*Sine Wave City 3-D*

**14.36**
*©1997 Robert Bowen*

# Selections, Layers, and Text

# Selections and Paths

## Selection Fundamentals

Selections direct and protect. If it weren't for Photoshop's selection capabilities, you and I would be flinging paint on the canvas for all we're worth, like so many Jackson Pollock and Vasily Kandinsky wannabes without any means to constrain, discriminate, or otherwise regulate the effects of our actions. Without selections, there'd be no filters, no color corrections, and no layers. In fact, we'd all be dangerously close to real life, that dreaded environment we've spent so much time and money to avoid.

No other program gives you so much control over the size and shape of selections. You can finesse selection outlines with unparalleled control, alternatively adding to selected areas, subtracting from them, and moving and rotating selections independently of the pixels inside them. You can even mix masks and selection outlines together, as covered in Chapter 16.

That's why this chapter and the one that follows are the most important chapters in this book.

**Note**

Pretty cool, huh? You put a provocative sentence like that on a line by itself and it resonates with authority. Granted, it's a little overstated, but can you blame me? I mean, I can't have a sentence like, "If you want my opinion, I think these are some pretty dog-gone important chapters — at least, that's the way it seems to me; certainly, you might have a different opinion," on a line by itself. The other paragraphs would laugh at it.

At any rate, I invite you to pay close attention to the fundamental concepts and approaches documented throughout this chapter. While I wouldn't characterize each and every technique as essential — lots of artists get by without paying much attention to paths, for example, while other artists swear by them — a working knowledge of selection outlines is key to using Photoshop successfully.

## How selections work

Before you can edit a portion of an image, you must first *select* it, which is computerese for indicating the boundaries of the area you want to edit. To select part of an image in a painting program, you must surround it with a selection outline or marquee; this tells Photoshop where to apply your editing instructions. The selection outline appears as a moving pattern of dash marks, lovingly termed marching ants by doughheads who've been using computers too long. (See Figure 15-1 for the inside story.)

**Figure 15-1:** A magnified view of a dash mark in a selection outline reveals a startling discovery.

Photoshop 5 provides 10 tools for drawing selection outlines — up three from Version 4 — all of which I describe briefly in the following list. You can access most of the tools from the keyboard, as noted in the parentheses:

✦ **Rectangular marquee (M)**: The rectangular marquee tool has long been a staple of painting programs. This tool enables you to select rectangular or square portions of an image.

✦ **Elliptical marquee (Shift+M)**: The elliptical marquee tool works like the rectangular marquee except it selects elliptical or circular portions of an image. (Pressing the M key switches between the rectangular and elliptical marquee tools.)

✦ **Single-row/single-column**: The single-row and single-column tools enable you to select a single row or column of pixels that stretches the entire width or height of the image. These are the only tools in all of Photoshop you can't access from the keyboard.

✦ **Lasso (L)**: The lasso tool enables you to select a free-form portion of an image. You simply drag with the lasso tool around the area you want to edit. Unlike the lasso tools in most painting programs, which shrink selection outlines to disqualify pixels in the background color, Photoshop's lasso tool selects the exact portion of the image you enclose in your drag.

✦ **Polygonal lasso (Shift+L)**: Click on different points in your image to set corners in a straight-sided selection outline. This is a great way to select free-form areas if you're not good at wielding the mouse or your wrists are a tad sore. (You can achieve this same effect by Alt+clicking with the lasso tool, but I'll explain this more in the "Free-form outlines" section later in this chapter.)

✦ **Magnetic lasso (Shift+L again)**: Click with the magnetic lasso along the edge of an image element that you want to select independently from its background. Then move the magnetic lasso (you don't have to drag) around the edge of the element. It's a tricky tool to use, so you can be sure I describe it in excruciating detail in the coming pages.

✦ **Magic wand (W)**: First introduced by Photoshop, the Magic wand tool lets you select a contiguous region of similarly colored pixels by clicking inside it. For example, you might click inside the boundaries of a face to isolate it from the hair and background elements. Novices tend to gravitate toward the magic wand because it seems like such a miracle tool but, in fact, it's the least predictable and ultimately the least useful of the bunch.

✦ **Pen (P)**: Now available in the main toolbox, the pen tool is both the most difficult to master and the most accurate and versatile of the selection tools. You use the pen tool to create a path, which is an object-oriented breed of selection outline. You click and drag to create individual points in the path. You can edit the path after the fact by moving, adding, and deleting points. You can even transfer a path by dragging and dropping between Photoshop and either Illustrator 8 or FreeHand 8. For a discussion of the pen tool, read the "How to Draw and Edit Paths" section later in this chapter.

✦ **Magnetic pen (Shift+P)**: The magnetic pen is basically an object-oriented version of the magnetic lasso tool. Click to set the first point, then move your mouse and watch Photoshop create the other points automatically. It's not a great tool, but it can prove handy when selecting image elements that stand out very clearly from their backgrounds.

✦ **Freeform pen (Shift+P again)**: If you hate setting points but you need to create a clipping path, this is the tool for you. You just drag with the tool as if you were selecting with the lasso tool and let Photoshop define the points automatically. Obviously, you can't expect the same level of accuracy that you get from the standard pen tool, but it's child's play to use.

Photoshop's two type mask tools (press Shift+T to get to them) are also technically selection tools because Photoshop converts each character of type to a selection outline. But type involves other issues that would merely confuse the contents of this chapter. So I've awarded type its own chapter (Chapter 18).

If this were all you needed to know to use the selection tools in Photoshop, the application would be on par with the average paint program. Part of what makes Photoshop exceptional, however, is that it provides literally hundreds of little tricks to increase the functionality of every selection tool.

Furthermore, all of Photoshop's selection tools work together in perfect harmony. You can exploit the specialized capabilities of all 11 tools (and the type mask tools) to create a single selection boundary. After you understand which tool best serves which purpose, you can isolate any element in an image, no matter how complex or how delicate its outline.

## Geometric selection outlines

The default tool in the upper left corner of the toolbox is the rectangular marquee tool. You can access the elliptical marquee tool by Option/Alt+clicking on the marquee tool icon or by pressing Shift+M when the rectangular marquee tool is already selected. Pressing Shift+M again returns you to the rectangular marquee tool. Option/Alt+clicking cycles through the single-row and single-column tools, as well.

The marquee tools are more versatile than they may appear at first glance. You can adjust the performance of each tool as follows:

✦ **Constraining to a square or circle**: Press and hold Shift after beginning your drag to draw a perfect square with the rectangular marquee tool or a perfect circle with the elliptical marquee tool. (Pressing Shift before dragging also works if no other selection is active; otherwise, this adds to a selection, as I explain later in the "Ways to Change Selection Outlines" section.)

✦ **Drawing a circular marquee**: When perusing an online forum a while back, someone asked how to create a perfect circular marquee. Despite more than a month of helpful suggestions — some highly imaginative — no one offered the easiest suggestion of all (well, I ultimately did, but I'm a know-it-all). So remember to press Shift after you begin to drag and you'll be one step ahead of the game.

✦ **Drawing out from the center**: Press and hold the Option/Alt key after you begin dragging to draw the marquee from the center outward instead of from corner to corner. (Again, pressing Option/Alt before dragging works if no selection outline is active; otherwise, this subtracts from the selection.) This technique is especially useful when you draw an elliptical marquee. Locating the center of the area you want to select is frequently easier than locating one of its corners — particularly because ellipses don't have corners.

✦ **Moving the marquee on the fly**: While drawing a marquee, press and hold the spacebar to move the marquee rather than resize it. When you get the marquee in place, release the spacebar and keep dragging to modify the size. The spacebar is most helpful when drawing elliptical selections or when drawing a marquee out from the center — this eliminates the guesswork, so you can position your marquees exactly on target.

✦ **Selecting a single-pixel line**: Use the single-row and single-column tools to select a single row or column of pixels. I use these tools to fix screw-ups such as a missing line of pixels in a screen shot, to delete random pixels around the perimeter of an image, or to create perpendicular lines within a fixed space.

✦ **Constraining the aspect ratio**: If you know you want to create an image that conforms to a certain height/width ratio — called an *aspect ratio* — you can constrain either a rectangular or an elliptical marquee so the ratio between height and width remains fixed, no matter how large or small a marquee you create. To accomplish this, press Return/Enter when the marquee tool is active to display the Marquee Options palette, shown in Figure 15-2. Then select Constrained Aspect Ratio from the Style pop-up menu. Enter the desired ratio values into the Width and Height option boxes.

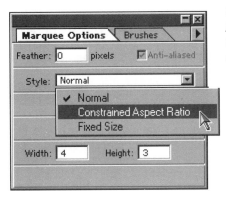

**Figure 15-2:** Select the Constrained Aspect Ratio option in the Marquee Options palette to constrain the width and height of a marquee.

For example, if you want to crop an image to the ratio of a 13-inch (640 × 480-pixel) screen, enter 4 and 3, respectively, into the Width and Height option boxes and press Return/Enter to confirm your changes. Then select the area of the image you want to retain and choose Image ⇨ Crop.

✦ **Sizing the marquee numerically**: If you're editing a screen shot or some other form of regular or schematic image, you may find specifying the size of a marquee numerically helpful. To do so, select the Fixed Size option from the Style pop-up menu and enter size values into the Width and Height option boxes. To match the selection to a 640 × 480-pixel screen, for example, just change the Width and Height values to 640 and 480.

✦ **Drawing feathered selections**: A Feather option box is available when you use either of the marquee tools. To feather a selection is to blur its edges beyond the automatic antialiasing afforded to most tools. For more information on feathering, refer to the "Softening selection outlines" section later in this chapter.

✦ **Creating jagged ellipses**: By default, elliptical selection outlines are antialiased. If you don't want antialiasing — you might prefer harsh edges when editing screen shots or designing screen interfaces — deselect the Anti-aliased check box. (This option is dimmed when you use the rectangular marquee because antialiasing is always on for this tool.)

**Tip**

Frequently, Photoshop's lack of geometric shape tools throws novices for a loop. In fact, such tools do exist—you simply don't recognize them. To draw a rectangle or ellipse in Photoshop, draw the shape as desired using the rectangular or elliptical marquee tool. Then choose Edit ➪ Fill or Edit ➪ Stroke, respectively, to color the interior or outline of the selection. You can also fill the selection using the Delete/Backspace-key techniques discussed in Chapter 9. It's that easy.

## Freeform outlines

In comparison to the rectangular and elliptical marquee tools, the lasso tool provides a rather limited range of options. Generally speaking, you drag in a freeform path around the image you want to select. The few special considerations are as follows:

✦ **Feathering and antialiasing**: To adjust the performance of the lasso tool, press Return/Enter while the lasso tool is selected to display the Lasso Options palette. The palette contains just two options, a Feather option box and an Anti-aliased check box. Just as you can feather rectangular and elliptical marquees, you can feather selections drawn with the lasso tool. You can also soften the edges of a lasso outline by selecting the Anti-aliased check box.

**Note**

Be aware that, although you can adjust the feathering of any selection after you draw it by choosing Select ➪ Feather, you must specify antialiasing before you draw a selection. Unless you have a specific reason for doing otherwise, leave the Anti-aliased check box turned on (as it is by default).

✦ **Drawing polygons**: If you press and hold the Option/Alt key, the lasso tool works like a free-form polygon tool. (*Polygon*, incidentally, means a shape with multiple straight sides.) With the Option/Alt key down, click to specify corners in a free-form polygon, as shown in Figure 15-3. If you want to add curves to the selection outline, drag with the tool while still pressing the Option/Alt key. Photoshop closes the selection outline the moment you release both the Option/Alt key and the mouse button.

**Tip**

You can extend a polygon selection outline to the absolute top, right, or bottom edges of an image. Just Option/Alt+click with the lasso tool outside the image window or, if the image window is larger than the image, on the background canvas surrounding the image. You can even click on the scroll bars. Figure 15-3 illustrates the idea.

✦ **The polygonal lasso tool**: If you don't want to bother with pressing the Option/Alt key, you can use the polygonal lasso tool. Press Shift+L when the lasso is active to switch to the polygonal lasso tool. Then click inside the image to set corners in the selection. Click on the first point in the selection or double-click with the tool to complete the selection outline.

**Tip**

If you make a mistake while creating a selection outline with the polygonal lasso, you can press Delete to eliminate the last segment you drew. Keep pressing Delete to eliminate more segments in the selection outline. This technique works until you close the selection outline and it turns into marching ants.

To create freeform curves with the polygonal lasso tool, press the Option/Alt key and drag.

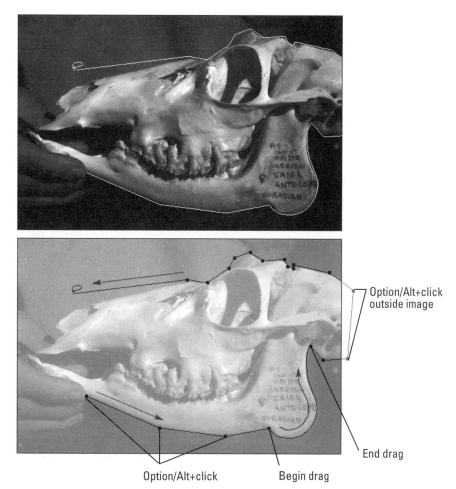

**Figure 15-3:** Option/Alt+click with the lasso tool to create corners in a selection outline, shown as black squares in the bottom image. Drag to create free-form curves. Surprisingly, you can Option/Alt+click outside the image to add corners outside the boundaries of the image window.

Adobe added the polygonal lasso for those times when Option/Alt+clicking isn't convenient. If no portion of the image is selected, it's no trick to Option/Alt+click with the standard lasso to draw a straight-sided selection. But if some area in the image is selected, pressing Option/Alt tells Photoshop that you want to subtract from the selection outline. For this reason, it's often easier to use the polygonal lasso (although you still can make it work by pressing Option/Alt *after* you click with the lasso tool, as I explain in the "Using Shift and Option/Alt like a pro" section later in this chapter).

## Magnetic selections

In the old days of black-and-white painting programs—most notably MacPaint on the Mac—black pixels were considered foreground elements and white pixels were the background. To select a black element, you have only to vaguely drag around it with the lasso tool and the program would automatically omit the white pixels and "shrink" the selection around the black ones.

The magnetic lasso tool is Adobe's attempt to transfer shrinking into the world of color. Under ideal conditions—very ideal conditions, I might add—a selection drawn with the magnetic lasso automatically shrinks around the foreground element and omits the background. Naturally, it rarely works this miraculously, but it does produce halfway decent selection outlines with very little effort—provided that you know what you're doing.

### Using the magnetic lasso tool

Typically, when people have a problem using the magnetic lasso tool, it's because they're trying to make the process too complex. Work less and it works smarter. Here are the basic steps for using this unusual tool:

### Steps: Making Sense of the Magnetic Lasso Tool

1. **Select an image with very definite contrast between the foreground image and its background.** The skull in Figure 15-4 is a good example. A light gray skull against a dark gray background. Here's something that Photoshop can really sink its teeth into.

2. **Select the magnetic lasso.** Press the L key to select the lasso tool, then press Shift+L a couple of times to cycle to the magnetic setting.

3. **Click anywhere along the edge of the foreground element.** I clicked at the top of the skull, as labeled in Figure 15-4.

4. **Move the cursor around the edge of the foreground element.** Move the mouse, don't drag it—that is, there's no need to press the mouse button. Dragging is more difficult to control, it's harder on our wrists, and it doesn't do any good. Move the cursor around the image and Photoshop will do the rest of the work for you.

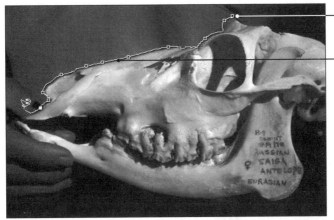

Click to
begin selection...

...then move cursor
along edge

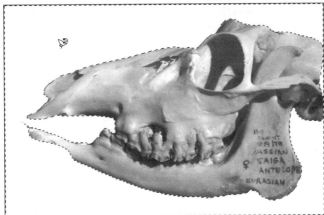

**Figure 15-4:** After clicking to set the start point (top), I moved
the magnetic lasso cursor along the edge of the skull. Then I
reversed the completed selection (C/Ctrl+Shift+I) and pressed
Delete/Backspace to fill it with white (bottom).

**Tip**

As you move, the magnetic lasso lays down a line along the edge of the
element, as Figure 15-4 shows. If you don't like where it puts a line, just
back up the cursor and try moving along the edge again. The magnetic
lasso also lays down anchor points at significant locations around the
image. If you don't like where it puts a point, press the Delete key. Each
time you press Delete, Photoshop gets rid of the most recent point along
the line. To set your own anchor points, just click.

5. **When you make it all the way around to the beginning of the shape,
   click on the first point in the outline to close the selection.** Or just
   double-click to close with a straight edge.

As I mentioned before, the magnetic lasso does not perform miracles. It will almost never select an image exactly the way you would like it to. After moving the cursor around the skull, I reversed the selection by choosing Select ⇨ Inverse (⌘/Ctrl+Shift+I); then I pressed the Delete/Backspace key to fill the background with white. The result appears in the second example in Figure 15-4. As you can see, the magnetic lasso did a very nice job of isolating the skull — much better than I could have done with the lasso alone — but the selection isn't perfect. Notice the gap on the right side of the skull and the clumsy treatment of the tip of the pointy lower jaw on left. Okay, no automated selection tool is perfect, but the magnetic lasso makes as few mistakes as any I've seen.

To create a straight segment while working with the magnetic lasso tool, press the Option/Alt key and click. Release the option key and drag momentarily to reset the tool to its normal magnetic self.

## Modifying the magnetic lasso options

You can modify the performance of the magnetic lasso tool by adjusting the values in the Magnetic Lasso Options palette, shown in Figure 15-5. The first two options — Feather and Anti-aliased — define the softness of the final selection outline, just as they do for the standard lasso tool. The others control how the magnetic lasso positions lines and lays down points:

✦ **Lasso Width**: I might have named this option Sloppiness Factor. It determines how close to an edge you have to move the cursor in order for Photoshop to accurately see the image element. Large values are great for smooth elements that stand out clearly from their backgrounds. If I raise the Lasso Width to 20 when selecting the top of the skull, for example, I can move the cursor 20 pixels away from the skull and Photoshop still shrinks the selection tight around the skull's edge. That's a lot of wiggle room and it makes my life quite a bit easier. But when selecting narrow passageways, the value needs to be low to keep Photoshop from veering off to the wrong edge. The location at which the pointy jaw meets with the snout is a good example of a place where I need to set a small Lasso Width and move very carefully around the edge.

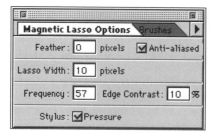

**Figure 15-5:** These options determine how the magnetic lasso tool draws lines and places points inside the image window.

The great thing about the Lasso Width value is that you can change it on the fly by pressing a bracket key as you work with the magnetic lasso. Press the [

key to lower the Lasso Width value; press the ] key to raise the value. Shift+[ lowers the value to its minimum, 1, and Shift+] raises it to the maximum, 40.

If you have a pressure-sensitive tablet, you can control the sloppiness factor dynamically according to how hard you press on the pen. Bear down to be careful, let up to be sloppy. Because this is the way you probably work naturally, the tool accommodates your movements pretty much without you even thinking about it.

✦ **Frequency**: This option tells the magnetic lasso when to lay down points. As you drag with the tool, the line around the image changes to keep up with your movements. When some point in the line stays still for a few moments, Photoshop decides it must be on target and anchors it down with a point. If you want Photoshop to anchor points more frequently, raise the value. For less frequent anchoring, lower the option. High values tend to do better for rough edges, lower values do better for smooth edges.

✦ **Edge Contrast**: This is the simplest of the options. It tells Photoshop how much contrast there has to be between the element you're trying to select and its background in order to even be recognized. If the foreground element stands out clearly, you might want to raise the Edge Contrast value to avoid selecting random flack around the edges. If the contrast between foreground and background is subtle, lower the value.

Most of the time, you can rely on the bracket keys to adjust the Lasso Width and leave the Frequency and Edge Contrast values set to their defaults. When dealing with a low-contrast image, lower the Edge Contrast value to 5 percent or so. And when selecting unusually rough edges, raise the Frequency to 70 or more. But careful movements with the magnetic lasso tool will go farther than adjusting any of these settings.

## The world of the wand

Using the magic wand tool is a no-brainer, right? You just click with the tool and it selects all the neighboring colors that fall within a selected range. The problem is getting the wand to recognize the same range of colors you see on screen. For example, if you're editing a photo of a red plate against a pink tablecloth, how do you tell the magic wand to select the plate and leave the tablecloth alone?

Sadly, adjusting the performance of the wand is pretty tricky and frequently unsatisfying. If you press Return/Enter when the magic wand is active, you'll see three options inside the Magic Wand Options palette:

✦ **Anti-aliased** softens the selection, just as it does for the lasso tool.

✦ **Tolerance** determines the range of colors the tool selects when you click with it in the image window.

✦ **Use All Layers** allows you to take all visible layers into account when defining a selection.

## Adjusting the tolerance

By now you already understand what's up with the Anti-aliased option, so I'll start with Tolerance. You may have heard the standard explanation for adjusting the Tolerance value: You can enter any number from 0 to 255 in the Tolerance option box. Enter a low number to select a small range of colors; increase the value to select a wider range of colors. Nothing is wrong with this explanation — in its own small way, the explanation is accurate — but it doesn't provide one iota of information you couldn't glean on your own. If you really want to understand this option, you have to dig a little deeper.

When you click on a pixel with the magic wand tool, Photoshop first reads the brightness value assigned to that pixel by each of the color channels. If you're working with a grayscale image, Photoshop reads a single brightness value from the one channel only; if you're working with an RGB image, it reads three brightness values, one each from the red, green, and blue channels; and so on. Because each color channel permits 8 bits of data, brightness values range from 0 to 255.

Next, Photoshop applies the Tolerance value, or simply *tolerance*, to the pixel. The tolerance describes a range that extends in both directions — lighter and darker — from each brightness value.

Suppose you're editing a standard RGB image. The tolerance is set to 32 (as it is by default); you click with the magic wand on a turquoise pixel, whose brightness values are 40 red, 210 green, and 170 blue. Photoshop adds and subtracts 32 from each brightness value to calculate the magic wand range that, in this case, is 8 to 72 red, 178 to 242 green, and 138 to 202 blue. Photoshop selects any pixel that both falls inside this range and can be traced back to the original pixel via an uninterrupted line of other pixels, which also fall within the range.

From this information, you can draw the following basic conclusions about the magic wand tool:

✦ **Creating a contiguous selection**: The magic wand selects a contiguous region of pixels emanating from the pixel on which you click. If you're trying to select land masses on a globe, for example, clicking on St. Louis selects everything from Juneau to Mexico City. It doesn't select London, though, because the cities are separated by an ocean of water that doesn't fall within the tolerance range.

✦ **Clicking on midtones maintains a higher range**: Because the tolerance range extends in two directions, you cut off the range when you click on a light or dark pixel, as demonstrated in Figure 15-6. Consider the two middle gradations: In both cases, the tolerance is set to 60. In the top gradation, I clicked on a pixel with a brightness of 140, so Photoshop calculated a range from 80 to 200. But when I clicked on a pixel with a brightness value of 10, as in the bottom gradation, the range shrank to 0 to 70. Clicking on a medium-brightness pixel, therefore, permits the most generous range.

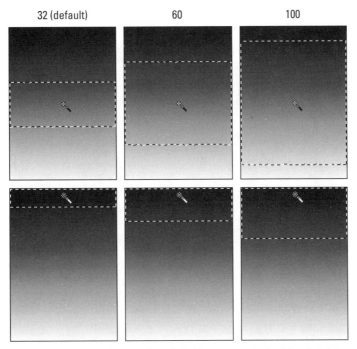

**Figure 15-6:** Note the results of clicking on a pixel with a brightness value of 140 (top row) and a brightness value of 10 (bottom row) with the tolerance set to three different values.

✦ **Selecting brightness ranges**: Many people have the impression the magic wand selects color ranges. The magic wand, in fact, selects brightness ranges within color channels. So if you want to select a flesh-colored region—regardless of shade—set against an orange or red background, roughly equivalent in terms of brightness values, you probably should use a different tool.

✦ **Selecting from a single channel**: If the magic wand repeatedly fails to select a region of color that appears unique from its background, try isolating that region inside a single-color channel. You'll probably have the most luck isolating a color on the channel that least resembles it. For example, to select the yellow Sasquatch Xing sign shown in Color Plate 15-1, I switched to the blue channel (⌘/Ctrl+3). Because yellow contains no blue, and the brambly background contains quite a bit of blue—as demonstrated in the last example of Figure 15-7—the magic wand can distinguish the two relatively easily. Experiment with this technique and it will prove even more useful over time.

**Figure 15-7:** Because the yellow Sasquatch sign contains almost no blue, it appears most clearly distinguished from its background in the blue channel. So the blue channel is the easiest channel in which to select the sign with the magic wand.

## Making the wand see beyond a single layer

The final option in the Magic Wand Options palette, the Use All Layers option, enables you to create a selection based on pixels from different layers (see Chapter 17). For example, returning to my previous land mass example, suppose you set Europe on one layer and North America on the layer behind it. The two continents overlap. Normally, if you clicked inside Europe with the magic wand tool, the wand would select an area inside Europe without extending out into the area occupied by North America. This is because the wand doesn't even see the contents of other layers; anything outside Europe is an empty void. We're talking pre-Columbus Europe here.

If you select the Use All Layers option, though, things change. Suddenly, the wand can see all the layers you can see. If you click on Europe, and if North America and Europe contain similar colors, the wand selects across both shapes.

Mind you, the Use All Layers option does not permit the wand to select images on two separate layers. Strange as this may sound, no selection tool can pull off this feat. Every one of the techniques explained in this chapter is applicable to only a single layer at a time. Use All Layers merely allows the wand to draw selection outlines that appear to encompass colors on many layers.

What good is this? Well, suppose you want to apply an effect to both Europe and North America. With the help of Use All Layers, you can draw a selection outline that encompasses both continents. After you apply the effect to Europe, you can switch to the North America layer — the selection outline remains intact — and then reapply the effect.

# Ways to Change Selection Outlines

If you don't draw a selection outline correctly the first time, you have two options. You can either draw it again from scratch, which is a real bore, or you can change your botched selection outline, which is likely to prove the more efficient solution. You can deselect a selection, add to a selection, subtract from a selection, and even select the stuff that's not selected and deselect the stuff that is. (If this sounds like a load of nonsense, keep reading.)

## Quick changes

Some methods of adjusting a selection outline are automatic: You choose a command and you're done. The following list explains how a few commands — all members of the Select menu — work:

✦ **Hide Edges (⌘/Ctrl+H)**: Get those marching ants out of my face! We're all grown-ups, right? Do we really need constant streams of marching ants to tell us what we've selected? We were there; we remember. My point is, although visible selection outlines can be helpful sometimes, they can as readily impede your view of an image. When they annoy you, press ⌘/Ctrl+H. Press ⌘/Ctrl+H again if you later need to see the selection outline.

✦ **Deselect (⌘/Ctrl+D)**: You can deselect the selected portion of an image in three ways. You can select a different portion of the image; click anywhere in the image window with the rectangular marquee tool, the elliptical marquee tool, or the lasso tool; or choose Select ➪ Deselect. Remember, though, when no part of an image is selected, the entire image is susceptible to your changes. If you apply a filter, choose a color-correction command, or use a paint tool, you affect every pixel of the foreground image.

✦ **Reselect (⌘/Ctrl+Shift+D)**: If you accidentally deselect an image, you can retrieve the most recent selection outline by choosing Select ➪ Reselect. It's a great function that operates entirely independently of the Undo command and History palette, and it works even after performing a long string of selection-unrelated operations. (You can restore older selections from the History palette, but that usually means undoing operations along the way.)

✦ **Inverse (⌘/Ctrl+Shift+I)**: Choose Select ➪ Inverse to reverse the selection. Photoshop deselects the portion of the image that was previously selected and selects the portion of the image that was not selected. This way, you can begin a selection by outlining the portion of the image you want to protect, rather than the portion you want to affect.

## Manually adding and subtracting

Ready for some riddles? When editing a portrait, how do you select both eyes without affecting any other portion of the face? Answer: By drawing one selection and then tacking on a second selection. How do you select a doughnut and leave the hole behind? Answer: Encircle the doughnut with the elliptical marquee tool, and then use the same tool to subtract the center.

Photoshop enables you to whittle away at a selection, add pieces on again, whittle away some more, ad infinitum, until you get it exactly right. Short of sheer laziness or frustration, no reason exists why you can't eventually create the selection outline of your dreams:

✦ **Adding to a selection outline**: To increase the area enclosed in an existing selection outline, Shift+drag with one of the marquee or lasso tools. You also can Shift+click with the magic wand tool or Shift+click with one of the marquee tools when the Fixed Size option is active (as described back in the "Geometric selection outlines" section earlier in this chapter).

✦ **Subtracting from a selection outline**: To take a bite from an existing selection outline, press the Option/Alt key while using one of the selection tools.

✦ **Intersecting one selection outline with another**: Another way to subtract from an existing selection outline is to Shift+Option/Alt+drag around the selection with the rectangular marquee, elliptical marquee, or lasso tool. You also can Shift+Option/Alt+click with the magic wand tool. Shift+Option/Alt+dragging instructs Photoshop to retain only the portion of an existing selection that also falls inside the new selection outline. I frequently use this technique to confine a selection within a rectangular or elliptical border.

To help you keep the various techniques straight, Photoshop presents you with special cursors that help explain what you're doing. Say that you've selected part of an image and the lasso tool is active. When you press the Shift key, Photoshop appends a little plus sign to the lasso cursor to show you're about to add. When you press Option/Alt, you see a little minus sign. Press Shift+Option/Alt to get an × for intersect. Watching your cursors will make the transition easier.

## Using Shift and Option/Alt like a pro

The roles of the Shift and Option/Alt keys in adding, subtracting, and intersecting selection outlines can interfere with your ability to take advantage of other functions of the selection tools. For example, when no portion of an image is selected, you can Shift+drag with the rectangular marquee tool to draw a square. But after a selection is active, Shift+dragging adds a rectangle — not a square — to the selection outline.

The trick is to learn when to press the Shift and Option/Alt keys. Sometimes you have to press the key before you begin your drag; other times you must press the key after you begin the drag, but before you release. For example, to add a square to a selection outline, Shift+drag, release Shift while keeping the mouse button pressed, and press Shift again to snap the rectangle to a square. The same goes for adding a circle with the elliptical marquee tool.

A few other techniques follow that you'll do well to master. They sound pretty elaborate, I admit, but with a little practice, they become second nature (so does tightrope walking, but don't let that worry you):

✦ To subtract a square or circle from a selection, Option/Alt+drag, release Option/Alt, press Shift, drag until you get it right, release the mouse button, and then release Shift.

✦ To add a rectangle or ellipse and draw from the center outward, Shift+drag, release Shift, press the Option/Alt key, and hold Option/Alt until after you release the mouse button. You can even press the spacebar during the drag to move the marquee around, if you like.

✦ To subtract a marquee drawn from the center outward, Option/Alt+drag, release Option/Alt, press Option/Alt again, and hold the key down until after you release.

✦ What about drawing a straight-sided selection with the lasso tool? To add a straight-sided area to an existing selection, Shift+drag with the tool for a short distance. With the mouse button still down, release Shift and press the Option/Alt key. Then click around as you normally would, while keeping the Option/Alt key down.

✦ To subtract a straight-sided area, Option/Alt+drag with the lasso, release Option/Alt, press Option/Alt again, and click around with the tool.

If you can't manage the last two lasso-tool techniques, then switch to the polygonal lasso instead. In fact, the reason Adobe provided the polygonal lasso tool was to accommodate folks who don't want to deal with pressing the Option/Alt key seven times during a single drag (which I strangely quite enjoy).

## Adding and subtracting by command

Photoshop provides several commands under the Select menu that automatically increase or decrease the number of selected pixels in an image according to numerical specifications. The commands in the Select ➪ Modify submenu work as follows:

✦ **Border**: This command selects an area of a specified thickness around the perimeter of the current selection outline and deselects the rest of the selection. For example, to select a 6-point-thick border around the current selection, choose Select ➪ Modify ➪ Border, enter 6 into the Width option box, and press Return/Enter. But what's the point? After all, if you want to create an outline around a selection, you can accomplish this in fewer steps by choosing Edit ➪ Stroke. The Border command, however, broadens your range of options. You can apply a special effect to the border, move the border to a new location, or even create a double-outline effect by first applying Select ➪ Modify ➪ Border and then Edit ➪ Stroke.

✦ **Smooth**: This command rounds off the sharp corners and weird anomalies in the outline of a selection. When you choose Select ➪ Modify ➪ Smooth, the program asks you to enter a Sample Radius value. Photoshop smoothes out corners by drawing little circles around them, and the Sample Radius value determines the radius of these circles. Larger values result in smoother corners.

The Smooth command is especially useful in combination with the magic wand. After you draw one of those weird, scraggly selection outlines with the wand tool, use Select ➪ Modify ➪ Smooth to smooth out the rough edges.

✦ **Expand and Contract**: Both of these commands do exactly what they say, either expanding or contracting the selected area by 1 to 16 pixels. For example, if you want an elliptical selection to grow by 8 pixels, choose Select ➪ Modify ➪ Expand, enter 8, and call it a day. These are extremely useful commands I'll refer to several times throughout the book.

Both Expand and Contract have a flattening effect on a selection. To round things off, apply the Smooth command with a Sample Radius value equal to the number you just entered into the Expand Selection or Contract Selection dialog box. You'll end up with a pretty vague selection outline, but what do you expect from automated commands?

In addition to the Expand command, Photoshop provides two older commands — Grow and Similar — that increase the area covered by a selection outline. Both commands resemble the magic wand tool because they measure the range of eligible pixels by way of a Tolerance value. In fact, the commands rely on the same Tolerance value found inside the Magic Wand Options palette. So if you want to adjust the impact of either command, you must first select the magic wand icon in the toolbox:

✦ **Grow**: Choose Select ➪ Grow to select all pixels that both neighbor an existing selection and resemble the colors included in the selection, in accordance with the Tolerance value. In other words, Select ➪ Grow is the command equivalent of the magic wand tool. If you feel constrained because you can only click on one pixel at a time with the magic wand tool, you may prefer to select a small group of representative pixels with a marquee tool, and then choose Select ➪ Grow to initiate the wand's magic.

✦ **Similar**: Another member of the Select menu, the Similar command works like the Grow command, except the pixels needn't be adjacent to one another. When you choose Select ➪ Similar, Photoshop selects any pixel that falls within the tolerance range, regardless of the location of the pixel in the foreground image.

One of the best applications for the Similar command is to isolate a complicated image set against a consistent background whose colors are significantly lighter or darker than the image. Consider Figure 15-8, which features a dark and ridiculously complex foreground image set against a continuous background of medium-to-light brightness values. Although the image features sufficient contrast to make it a candidate for the magic wand tool, I would never in a million years recommend using this tool; too many of the colors in the foreground image are discontinuous. The following steps explain how to separate this image using the Similar command in combination with a few other techniques I've described thus far.

## Steps: Isolating a Complex Image Set Against a Plain Background

1. **Use the rectangular marquee tool to select some representative portions of the background.** In Figure 15-8, I selected the lightest and darkest portions of the background along with some representative shades in between. Remember, you make multiple selections by Shift+dragging with the tool.

**Figure 15-8:** Before choosing Select ➪ Similar, select a few sample portions of the background, so Photoshop has something on which to base its selection range.

2. **Double-click on the magic wand tool icon to display the Tolerance option box.** For my image, I entered a Tolerance value of 16, a relatively low value, in keeping with the consistency of the background. If your background is less homogenous, you may want to enter a higher value. Make certain you turn on the Anti-aliased check box.

3. **Choose Select ➪ Similar.** Photoshop should select the entire background. If Photoshop fails to select all the background, choose Edit ➪ Undo (⌘/Ctrl+Z) and use the rectangular marquee tool to select more portions of the background. You may also want to increase the Tolerance value in the Magic Wand Options palette. If Photoshop's selection bleeds into the foreground image, try reducing the Tolerance value.

*(continued)*

4. **Choose Select ⇨ Inverse.** Or press ⌘/Ctrl+Shift+I. Photoshop selects the foreground image and deselects the background.

5. **Modify the selection as desired.** If the detail you want to select represents only a fraction of the entire image, Shift+Option/Alt+drag around the portion of the image you want to retain using the lasso tool. In Figure 15-9, I Shift+Option/Alt+dragged with the polygonal lasso tool to draw a straight-sided outline around the selection.

**Figure 15-9:** Shift+Option/Alt+drag with the polygonal lasso tool to intersect the area you want to select with a straight-sided outline.

6. **Congratulations, you've isolated your complex image.** Now you can filter your image, colorize it, or perform whatever operation inspired you to select this image in the first place. For myself, I wanted to super-impose the image onto a different background. To do so, I copied the image to the Clipboard (⌘/Ctrl+C), opened the desired background image, and then pasted the first image into place (⌘/Ctrl+V). The result, shown in Figure 15-10, still needs some touching up with the paint and edit tools, but it's not half bad for an automated selection process.

**Figure 15-10:** The completed selection superimposed onto a new background.

Whenever you introduce a selection into another image — by copying and pasting or by dragging the selection and dropping it into another image window — Photoshop automatically assigns the selection to a new layer. This is a great safety mechanism that prevents you from permanently affixing the selection to its new background. But it also means you can't save the image in a file format other than the native Photoshop format without first flattening the image. For the big story on layers, read Chapter 17.

## Softening selection outlines

You can soften a selection in two ways. The first method is antialiasing, introduced in the "Rasterizing an Illustrator or FreeHand file" section of Chapter 4. Antialiasing is an intelligent and automatic softening algorithm, which mimics the appearance of edges you'd expect to see in a sharply focused photograph.

**Note**

Where did the term *antialias* originate? Anytime you try to fit the digital equivalent of a square peg into a round hole — say, by printing a high-resolution image to a low-resolution printer — the data gets revised during the process. This revised data, called an *alias*, is frequently inaccurate and undesirable. Antialiasing is the act of revising the data ahead of time, essentially rounding off the square peg so it looks nice as it goes into the hole. According to a reader who spent time at MIT's Architecture Machine Group, "We did the first work with displaying smooth lines. We called the harsh transitions *jaggies* and the display process *dejaggying*. Somehow, this easy-to-understand term slid sideways into 'alias' (which it isn't, really, but it's too late to change)." Now you know.

When you draw an antialiased selection outline in Photoshop, the program calculates the hard-edged selection at twice its actual size. The program then shrinks the selection in half using bicubic interpolation (described in the "General preferences" section of Chapter B on CD-ROM #2). The result is a crisp image with no visible jagged edges.

The second softening method, feathering, is more dramatic. Feathering gradually dissipates the selection outline, giving it a blurry edge. Photoshop accommodates partially selected pixels; feathering fades the selection both inward and outward from the original edge.

You can specify the number of pixels affected either before or after drawing a selection. To feather a selection before you draw it, double-click on the marquee or lasso tool icon and enter a value into the Feather option box in the Options palette. To feather a selection after drawing it, choose Select ➪ Feather. Or press the new keyboard shortcut, ⌘/Ctrl+Option/Alt+D. (The old shortcut, ⌘/Ctrl+Option/Shift+D, was reassigned to the Reselect command.)

The Feather Radius value determines the approximate distance over which Photoshop fades a selection, measured in pixels in both directions from the original selection outline. Figure 15-11 shows three selections lifted from the image at the bottom of the figure. The first selection is antialiased only. I feathered the second and third selections, assigning Feather Radius values of 4 and 12, respectively. As you can see, a small feather radius makes a selection appear fuzzy; a larger radius makes it fade into view.

## The math behind the feather

A few eagle-eyed readers have written to ask me why feathering blurs a selection outline more than the number of pixels stated in the Feather Radius value. A radius of 4 pixels actually affects a total of 20 pixels: 10 inward and 10 outward. The reason revolves around Photoshop's use of a mathematical routine called the *Gaussian bell curve*, which exaggerates the distance over which the selection outline is blurred.

Figure 15-12 demonstrates the math visually. The top-left image shows a hard-edged elliptical selection filled with white against a black background. To its right is a side view of the ellipse, in which black pixels are short and white pixels are tall. (Okay, so it's really a graph, but I didn't want to scare you.) Because no gray pixels are in the ellipse, the side view has sharp vertical walls.

The bottom-left image shows what happens if I first feather the selection with a radius of 4 pixels and then fill it with white. The side view now graphs a range of gray values, which taper gradually from black to white. See those gray areas on the sides (each labeled *Diameter*)? Those are the pixels that fall into the 8-pixel diameter, measured 4 pixels in and out from the original selection outline. These gray areas slope in straight lines.

The rounded areas of the side view — painted black — are the Gaussian bell curves. These are appended onto the radius of the feather to ensure smooth transitions between the blurry edges and the selected and deselected pixels. Programs that do not include these extra Gaussian curves, such as Corel Photo-Paint for Windows, end up producing ugly feathered selections that appear to have sharp, incongruous edges.

**Figure 15-11:** Three clones selected with the elliptical marquee tool. The top image is antialiased and not feathered, the next is feathered with a radius of 4 pixels, and the third is feathered with a radius of 12 pixels.

**Tip**

If exact space is an issue, you can count on the Feather command affecting about 2.7 times as many pixels as you enter into the Feather Radius option box, both in and out from the selection. That's a total of 5.4 times as many pixels as the radius in all.

If this is more than you wanted to know, cast it from your mind. Feathering makes the edges of a selection fuzzy — 'nuff said.

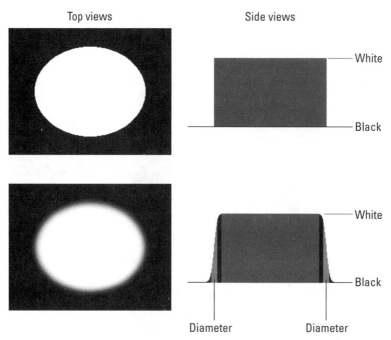

Figure 15-12: Here are some graphic demonstrations of what happens when you feather a selection. Photoshop tapers the ends of the feathered selections (shown by the black areas, bottom right) to prevent your eye from easily detecting where the feathering starts and stops.

## Putting feathering to use

You can use feathering to remove an element from an image while leaving the background intact, a process described in the following steps. The image described in these steps, shown in Figure 15-13, is a NASA photo of a satellite with the Earth in the background. I wanted to use this background with another image, but to do so I first had to eliminate that satellite. By feathering and cloning a selection outline, I covered the satellite with a patch so seamless you'd swear the satellite was never there.

## Steps: Removing an Element from an Image

1. **Draw a selection around the element using the lasso tool.** The selection needn't be an exact fit; in fact, you want it rather loose, so allow a buffer zone of at least six pixels between the edges of the image and the selection outline.

**Figure 15-13:** Your mission, if you choose to accept it, is to remove the satellite by covering it with selections cloned from the background.

2. **Drag the selection outline over a patch in the image.** Now that you've specified the element you want to remove, you must find a patch, that is, some portion of the image to cover the element in a manner that matches the surrounding background. In Figure 15-14, the best match seemed an area just below and to the right of the satellite. To select this area, move the selection outline independently of the image merely by dragging it with the lasso tool. (Dragging a selection with a selection tool moves the outline without affecting the pixels.) Make certain you allow some space between the selection outline and the element you're trying to cover.

3. **Choose Select ⇨ Feather.** Or press ⌘/Ctrl+Option/Alt+D. Enter a small value (8 or less) in the Feather Radius option box — just enough to make the edges fuzzy. (I entered 3.) Then press Return/Enter to initiate the operation.

4. **Clone the patch onto the area you want to cover.** Select the move tool by pressing the V key. Then Option/Alt+drag the feathered selection to clone the patch and position it over the element you want to cover, as shown in Figure 15-15. To align the patch correctly, choose Select ⇨ Hide Edges (⌘/Ctrl+H) to hide the marching ants and then nudge the patch into position with the arrow keys.

5. **Repeat as desired.** My patch was only partially successful. The upper-left corner of the selection matches clouds in the background, but the lower-right corner is dark and cloudless, an obvious rift in the visual continuity of the image. The solution: Try again. With the lasso tool, I drew a loose outline around the dark portion of the image and dragged it up and to the left as shown in Figure 15-16.

*(continued)*

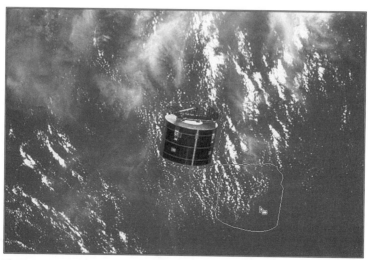

**Figure 15-14:** After drawing a loose outline around the satellite with the lasso tool, I dragged the outline to select a portion of the background.

**Figure 15-15:** Next, I used the move tool to Option/Alt+drag the feathered selection over the satellite. Sadly, the patch was imperfect and required further adjustments.

6. **It's all déjà vu from here.** I chose Select ⇨ Feather, entered 6 into the Feather Radius option box — thus allowing the clouds a sufficient range to taper off — and pressed Return/Enter. I then selected the move tool and

Option/Alt+dragged the feathered patch over the dark, cloudless rift. Finally, I nudged, nudged, nudged with the arrow keys, and voilà, no more satellite. Figure 15-17 shows $200 million worth of hardware vaporized in less than five minutes.

**Figure 15-16:** I used the lasso tool to draw a new outline around the dark, cloudless portion of the patch. Then I dragged the outline to a different spot in the background.

**Figure 15-17:** I selected a new bit of cloudy sky and placed it over the formerly cloudless portion of the patch. Satellite? What satellite?

# Moving and Duplicating Selections

The previous steps showed how you can move either the selected pixels or the empty selection outline to a new location. Now it's time to examine these techniques in greater depth.

## The role of the move tool

To move the selected pixels, you have to use the move tool. No longer is it acceptable merely to drag inside the selection with the marquee, lasso, or wand tool, as it was in Photoshop 3 and earlier. If you haven't gotten used to it yet, then now is as good a time as any. The move tool is here to stay.

You can select the move tool at any time by pressing the V key (for mooV). The advantage of the move tool is no chance exists of deselecting an image or harming the selection outline. Drag inside the selected area to move the selection; drag outside the selection to move the entire layer, selection included. I explain layers in more detail in Chapter 17.

To access the move tool on a temporary basis, press and hold the ⌘/Ctrl key. The move tool remains active as long as ⌘/Ctrl is pressed. This shortcut works when any tool except the hand or pen tool is active. Assign this shortcut to memory at your earliest convenience. Believe me, you spend a lot of time ⌘/Ctrl+dragging in Photoshop.

## Making precise movements

Photoshop provides three methods for moving selections in prescribed increments. In each case, the move tool is active, unless otherwise indicated:

✦ First, you can nudge a selection in 1-pixel increments by pressing an arrow key on the keyboard or nudge in 10-pixel increments by pressing Shift with an arrow key. This technique is useful for making precise adjustments to the position of an image.

To nudge a selected area when the move tool is not active, press ⌘/Ctrl with an arrow key. Press ⌘/Ctrl and Shift with an arrow key to move in 10-pixel increments. Once the selection is floating—that is, after your first nudge—you can let up on the ⌘/Ctrl key and use only the arrows (assuming a selection tool is active).

✦ Second, you can press Shift during a drag to constrain a move to some 45-degree direction—that is, horizontally, vertically, or diagonally.

✦ And third, you can use the Info palette to track your movements and to help locate a precise position in the image.

To display the Info palette, choose Window ➪ Show Info or press F8. Figure 15-18 shows the Info palette as it appears in Photoshop. The first section of the Info palette displays the color values of the image area beneath your cursor. When you move a selection, the other eight items in the palette monitor movement, as follows:

✦ **X, Y**: These values show the coordinate position of your cursor. The distance is measured from the upper-left corner of the image in the current unit of measure. The unit of measure in Figure 15-18 is pixels.

✦ **ΔX, ΔY**: These values indicate the distance of your move as measured horizontally and vertically.

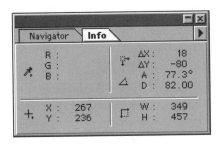

**Figure 15-18:** The Info palette provides a world of numerical feedback when you move a selection.

✦ **A, D**: The A and D values reflect the angle and direct distance of your drag.

✦ **W, H**: These values reflect the width and height of your selection.

## Cloning a selection

When you move a selection, you leave a hole in your image in the background color, as shown in the top half of Figure 15-19. If you prefer, instead, to leave the original in place during a move, you have to *clone* the selection — that is, create a copy of the selection without upsetting the contents of the Clipboard. Photoshop offers several different ways to clone a selection:

✦ **Option/Alt+dragging**: When the move tool is active, press the Option/Alt key and drag a selection to clone it. The bottom half of Figure 15-19 shows a selection I Option/Alt+dragged three times. (Between clonings, I changed the gray level of each selection to set them apart a little more clearly.)

✦ **⌘/Ctrl+Option/Alt+dragging**: If some tool other than the move tool is active, ⌘/Ctrl+Option/Alt+drag the selection to clone it. This is probably the technique you'll end up using most often.

✦ **Option/Alt+arrowing**: When the move tool is active, press Option/Alt in combination with one of the arrow keys to clone the selection and nudge it one pixel away from the original. If you want to move the image multiple pixels, press Option/Alt+arrow the first time only. Then nudge the clone using the arrow key alone. Otherwise, you'll create a bunch of clones which can be a pain in the neck to undo.

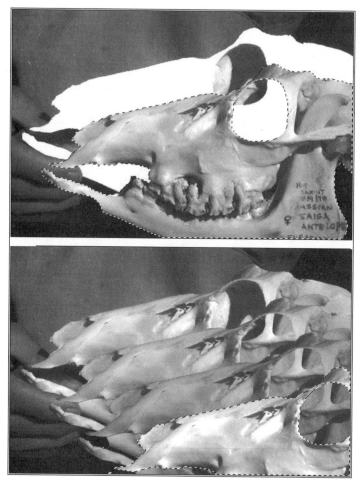

**Figure 15-19:** When you move a selection, you leave a gaping hole in the selection's wake (top). When you clone an image, you leave a copy of the selection behind. To make a point, I cloned the selection in the bottom image three times.

✦ **⌘/Ctrl+Option/Alt+arrowing**: If some other tool is active, press ⌘/Ctrl and Option/Alt with an arrow key. Again, press only the Option/Alt key the first time, unless you want to create a string of clones.

✦ **Drag-and-drop**: Like about every other program on the planet, Photoshop lets you clone a selection between documents by dragging it with the move tool from one open window and dropping it in another, as demonstrated in Figure 15-20. As long as you manage to drop into the second window, the original image remains intact and selected in the first window. My advice: Don't worry about exact positioning during a drag-and-drop; first get it into the second window and then worry about placement.

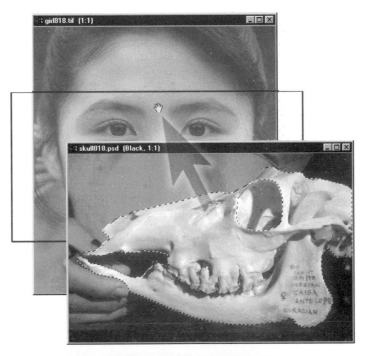

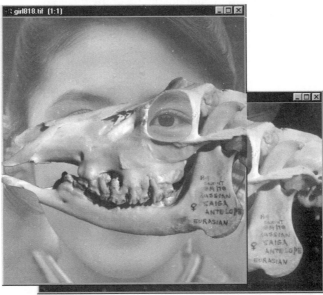

**Figure 15-20:** Use the move tool to drag a selection from one open window and drop it into another (top). This creates a clone of the selection in the receiving window (bottom).

You can drag-and-drop multiple layers if you link the layers first. For more information on this subject, see "Linking layers" in Chapter 17.

✦ **Shift+drop**: If the two images are exactly the same size — pixel for pixel — press the Shift key when dropping the selection to position it in the same spot from which it came in the original image. This is called *registering* the selection.

If an area is selected in the destination image, Shift+dropping positions the selection you're moving in the center of the selection in the destination image. This tip works regardless of whether or not the two images are the same size.

✦ **⌘/Ctrl+drag and drop**: Again, if some other tool than the move tool is selected, you must press the ⌘/Ctrl key when you drag to move the selected pixels from one window to the other.

## Moving a selection outline independently of its contents

After all this talk about the move tool and the ⌘/Ctrl key, you may wonder what happens if you drag a selection with the marquee, lasso, or wand. The answer is, you move the selection outline independently of the image. This technique serves as yet another means to manipulate inaccurate selection outlines. It also enables you to mimic one portion of an image inside another portion of the image or inside a completely different image window.

In the top image in Figure 15-21, I used the marquee tool to drag the skull outline down and to the right, so it only partially overlapped the skull. Note, the image itself remains unaltered. I then lightened the new selection, applied a few strokes to set it off from its background, and gave it stripes, as shown in the bottom image. For all I know, this is exactly what a female Russian Saiga antelope looks like.

You can nudge a selection outline independently of its contents by pressing an arrow key when a selection tool is active. Press Shift with an arrow key to move the outline in 10-pixel increments.

The great news about the revised role of the selection tools is you can drag-and-drop empty selection outlines between images. Just drag the selection from one image and drop it into another, as demonstrated in the first example of Figure 15-20. The only difference is just the selection outline gets cloned; the pixels remain behind. This is a great way to copy pixels back and forth between images. You can set up an exact selection in Image A, drag it into Image B with the marquee tool, move it over the pixels you want to clone, and ⌘/Ctrl+drag-and-drop the selection back into Image A. This is slick as hair grease, I'm telling you.

So remember, the selection tools now affect only the selection outline. The selection tools never affect the pixels themselves; that's the move tool's job.

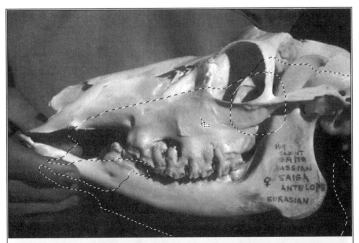

**Figure 15-21:**
Drag a selection with a selection tool to move the outline independently of its image (top). Wherever you drag the selection outline becomes the new selection (bottom).

## Scaling or rotating a selection outline

In Photoshop 5, you can also scale, rotate, skew, and otherwise transform selection outlines independently of the image. To transform a selection outline, choose Select ➪ Transform Selection. Photoshop displays a transformation boundary framed by eight handles. Here are the basic ways to use it:

✦ **Scale**: Drag any of the handles to scale the selection. Shift+drag to scale proportionally, Option/Alt+drag to scale with respect to the origin (labeled in Figure 15-22). You can move the origin just by dragging it.

✦ **Rotate**: Drag outside the transformation boundary to rotate the selection, as in the second example in Figure 15-22. The rotation always occurs with respect to the origin.

Drag a handle to scale          Transformation origin

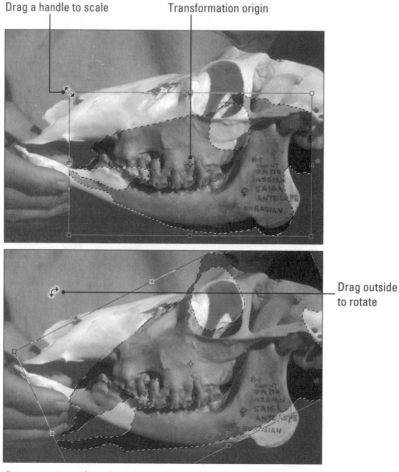

Drag outside
to rotate

**Figure 15-22:** After choosing Select ➪ Transform Selection, you
can scale the selection outline (top) and rotate it (bottom), all
without harming the image in the slightest.

✦ **Flip**: You can flip a selection outline by dragging one handle past its opposite
   handle. But this is a lot of work. The easier way is to Control/right-click inside
   the image window and choose Flip Horizontal or Flip Vertical from the pop-up
   menu.

✦ **Skew and distort**: To skew the selection outline, ⌘/Ctrl+drag a side, top, or
   bottom handle. To distort the selection, ⌘/Ctrl+drag a corner handle.

✦ **Do it by the numbers**: Control/right-click in the image window and choose
   Numeric to display the Numeric Transform dialog box. Here you can move,
   scale, rotate, and skew the selection by a specific numerical amount.

When you get the selection outline the way you want it, press Return/Enter or double-click inside the boundary. To cancel the transformation, press the Escape key.

If that felt like an awfully fast explanation of the Transform Selection command, that's because it's virtually identical to Edit ⇨ Free Transform which I discuss at length elsewhere in the book. To check out this more detailed explanation, read the "Transforming layers and selections" section of Chapter 17.

## The untimely demise of floating selections

One brief note before I move on to my long and glorious explanation of paths: It is with sad heart that I announce the near death of floating selections. As you may (or may not) recall, Photoshop 4 bludgeoned floating selections into a state of unconsciousness. While Version 5 has not entirely killed them, it has moved them to the critical list.

In case you're unsure of what I'm talking about, a *floating selection* is an element that hovers above the surface of the image. Any time you move a selection or clone it, Photoshop floats the selection onto a temporary layer. This way, you can move the selection or nudge it into position without harming the underlying image. And if you press the Delete/Backspace key, Photoshop deletes the floater rather than filling the selection with the background color.

But that's all there is to floating selections in Photoshop 5. The *Floating Selection* item that used to appear in the Layers palette is a thing of the past, so you don't even know when a selection is floating or not. And the only way to defloat a floater is to deselect it.

Quite unexpectedly, Photoshop 5 still lets you mix a floater with the image behind it by modifying the opacity and blend mode settings. After dragging a selection to float it, choose Filter ⇨ Fade (⌘/Ctrl+Shift+F). Then modify the settings inside the Fade dialog box to mix the floater with the background. It's incredibly nonintuitive, but it works.

# How to Draw and Edit Paths

Photoshop's path tools provide the most flexible and precise ways to define a selection short of masking. However, while a godsend to the experienced user, the path tools represent something of a chore to novices and intermediates. Most people take some time to grow comfortable with the pen tool because it requires you to draw a selection outline one point at a time.

If you're familiar with Illustrator's pen tool and other path-editing functions, you'll find Photoshop's tools are nearly identical. Photoshop doesn't provide the breadth of options available in Illustrator — you can't join paths or apply sophisticated path operations in Photoshop, for example — but the basic techniques are the same.

Photoshop 5 includes two additional pen tools designed to help smooth out the learning curve for inexperienced users. The freeform pen and magnetic pen work just like the lasso and magnetic lasso tools, automatically generating points as you drag. Neither tool is as precise as the traditional point-by-point pen tool, but nor are they as difficult to use.

The following pages are designed to get you up and running with paths. I'll explain how you approach drawing a path, how you edit it, how you convert it to a selection outline, and how you stroke it with a paint or edit tool. All in all, you'll learn more about paths than you ever wanted to know.

## Paths overview

Photoshop makes the path tools available in the toolbox. Meanwhile, the path management options — which enable you to convert paths to selections, fill and stroke paths, and save and delete them — reside in the Paths palette, as labeled in Figure 15-23. Together, tools and palette options make up a fully functioning path-drawing environment, which rivals (though does not equal) similar features provided by Illustrator or FreeHand.

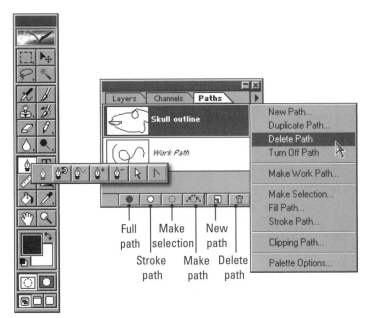

**Figure 15-23:** The toolbox provides access to every one of Photoshop's path-drawing tools. To save and organize your paths, display the Paths palette by choosing Window ➪ Show Paths.

## How paths work

Paths differ from normal selections because they exist on the equivalent of a distinct, object-oriented layer, which sits in front of the bitmapped image. After you draw a path, this setup enables you to edit it with point-by-point precision to make sure the path meets the exact requirements of your artwork. This also prevents you from accidentally messing up the image, as you can when you edit ordinary selection outlines. After you create the path, you convert it into a standard selection outline before you use it to edit the contents of the image, as explained in the section "Converting and saving paths," later in this chapter.

The following steps explain the basic process of drawing a selection outline with the path tools. I explain each step in more detail throughout the remainder of this chapter.

## Steps: Create a Selection with the Path Tools

1. **Draw the path.** Use the pen tool to draw the outline of your prospective selection. You can select the pen tool by pressing the P key. Or cycle to the magnetic or freeform pen by pressing Shift+P.

2. **Edit the path.** If the outline of the path requires some adjustment, reshape it using the other path tools. These tools have their own keyboard shortcuts, such as A for the arrow, + for the insert point tool, and − for the remove point tool.

3. **Save the path.** When you get the path exactly as you want it, save the path in Photoshop by choosing the Save Path command from the Paths palette menu. Or you can double-click on the *Work Path* item in the scrolling list.

4. **Convert the path to a selection.** You can make the path a selection outline by choosing the Make Selection command. Or press the Enter key on the numeric keypad when a path or selection tool is active.

That's it. After you convert the path to a selection, it works like any of the selection outlines described earlier. You can feather a selection, move it, copy it, clone it, or apply one of the special effects described in future chapters. The path remains intact in case you want to do further editing or to use it again.

## Using the Paths palette tools

Before I get into my long-winded description of how you draw and edit paths, here is a quick introduction to the seven path tools:

✦ **Pen**: Use the pen tool to draw paths in Photoshop one point at a time. Click to create a corner in a path, drag to make a smooth point which results in a continuous arc. (Never fear, I explain this tool *ad nauseum* in the "Drawing with the pen tools" section.) Press the P key to select the pen.

✦ **Magnetic pen**: Click on the edge of the foreground element you want to select, then move the cursor along the edge of the shape. Photoshop automatically assigns points as it deems appropriate.

✦ **Freeform pen**: Drag with this tool to create a path that automatically follows the twists and turns of your drag. Simplicity at its best, control at its lowest. Luckily, you can turn around and edit the path with any of the following tools.

✦ **Insert point**: Click on an existing path to add a point to it. To select the insert point tool from the keyboard, press the plus (+) key.

✦ **Remove point**: Click on an existing point in a path to delete the point without creating a break in the path's outline. Press the minus key (-) to select this tool.

✦ **Arrow**: The arrow (or direct selection) tool permits you to drag points and handles to reshape a path. You can access the arrow tool when any other path tool is active by pressing and holding the ⌘/Ctrl key. Or press the A key to make the tool permanently active.

✦ **Convert point**: Click or drag on a point to convert it to a corner or smooth point. You also can drag on a handle to convert the point. Press Option/Alt to access the convert point tool when the pen is active. Press ⌘/Ctrl and Option/Alt when the arrow tool is active.

**Note** The terms *anchor point, smooth point*, and others associated with drawing paths are explained in the upcoming section.

## Drawing with the pen tools

When drawing with the default point-by-point pen tool, you build a path by creating individual points. Photoshop automatically connects the points with segments, which are simply straight or curved lines.

**Note** Adobe prefers the term *anchor points* because the points anchor the path into place. But most folks just call 'em points. I mean, all points associated with paths are anchor points, so it's not like there's some potential for confusion.

All paths in Photoshop are *Bézier* (pronounced bay-zee-ay) paths, meaning they rely on the same mathematical curve definitions that make up the core of the PostScript printer language. The Bézier curve model allows for zero, one, or two levers to be associated with each point in a path. These levers, labeled in Figure

15-24, are called *Bézier control handles* or simply *handles*. You can move each handle in relation to a point, enabling you to bend and tug at a curved segment like a piece of soft wire.

Smooth points

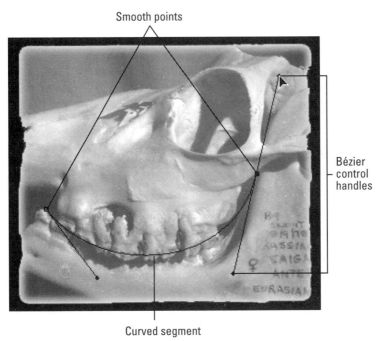

Bézier control handles

Curved segment

**Figure 15-24:** Drag with the pen tool to create a smooth point flanked by two Bézier control handles.

The following list summarizes how you can use the pen tool to build paths in Photoshop:

✦ **Adding segments**: To build a path, create one point after another until the path is the desired length and shape. Photoshop automatically draws a segment between each new point and its predecessor.

✦ **Closing the path**: If you eventually plan to convert the path to a selection outline, you need to complete the outline by clicking again on the first point in the path. Every point will then have one segment entering it and another segment exiting it. Such a path is called a *closed path* because it forms one continuous outline.

✦ **Leaving the path open**: If you plan to apply the Stroke Path command (explained later), you may not want to close a path. To leave the path open, so it has a specific beginning and ending, deactivate the path by saving it (choose the Save Paths command from the Paths palette menu). After you complete the save operation, you can click in the image window to begin a new path.

✦ **Extending an open path**: To reactivate an open path, click or drag one of its endpoints. Photoshop draws a segment between the endpoint and the next point you create.

✦ **Joining two open paths**: To join one open path with another open path, click or drag an endpoint in the first path, and then click or drag an endpoint in the second.

**Tip**

To get a better sense of how the pen tool works, press Return/Enter when the pen is active and turn on the Rubber Band check box in the Pen Options palette. This tells Photoshop to draw an animated segment between the last point drawn and the cursor. Unless you're an old pro and the connecting segment gets in your face, there's no reason not to select Rubber Band. (Besides, what with the '70s being so hot with the teenies, the Rubber Band check box makes the pen tool seem, well, kind of funky. Consider it another chance to bond with today's youth.)

## The anatomy of points and segments

Points in a Bézier path act as little road signs. Each point steers the path by specifying how a segment enters it and how another segment exits it. You specify the identity of each little road sign by clicking, dragging, or Option/Alt+dragging with the pen tool. The following items explain the specific kinds of points and segments you can create in Photoshop. See Figure 15-25 for examples.

✦ **Corner point**: Click with the pen tool to create a *corner point*, which represents the corner between two straight segments in a path.

✦ **Straight segment**: Click at two different locations to create a straight segment between two corner points. Shift+click to draw a 45-degree-angle segment between the new corner point and its predecessor.

✦ **Smooth point**: Drag to create a *smooth point* with two symmetrical Bézier control handles. A smooth point ensures that one segment meets with another in a continuous arc.

✦ **Curved segment**: Drag at two different locations to create a curved segment between two smooth points.

✦ **Curved segment followed by straight**: After drawing a curved segment, Option/Alt+click on the smooth point you just created to delete the forward Bézier control handle. This converts the smooth point to a corner point with one handle. Then click at a different location to append a straight segment to the end of the curved segment.

✦ **Straight segment followed by curved**: After drawing a straight segment, drag from the corner point you just created to add a Bézier control handle. Then drag again at a different location to append a curved segment to the end of the straight segment.

✦ **Cusp point**: After drawing a curved segment, Option/Alt+drag from the
smooth point you just created to redirect the forward Bézier control handle,
converting the smooth point to a corner point with two independent handles,
sometimes known as a cusp point. Then drag again at a new location to
append a curved segment that proceeds in a different direction than the
previous curved segment.

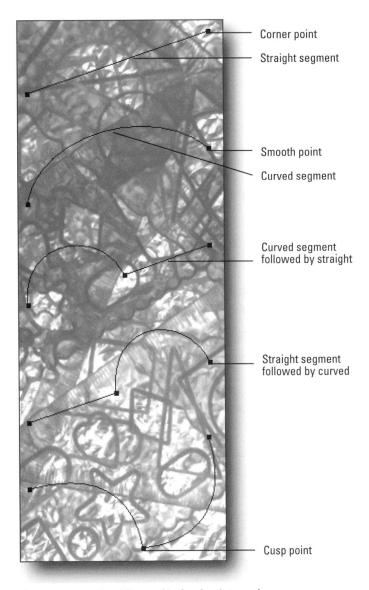

Corner point

Straight segment

Smooth point

Curved segment

Curved segment
followed by straight

Straight segment
followed by curved

Cusp point

**Figure 15-25:** The different kinds of points and
segments you can draw with the pen tool.

## Going freeform

If the pen tool is too much work, then try the freeform pen tool (two Shift+Ps over from the standard pen). As you drag with the tool, Photoshop tracks the motion of the cursor with a continuous line. After you release the mouse button, the program automatically assigns and positions the points and segments needed to create the Bézier path.

You can draw straight segments with the freeform pen by pressing Option/Alt. As you're dragging with the freeform pen, press and hold the Option/Alt key. Then click around to create points. When you're finished drawing straight segments, again drag with the freeform pen and release Option/Alt. (If you release Option/Alt when the mouse button is not pressed, Photoshop completes the path.)

Alas, automation is rarely perfect. (If it were, what need would these machines have for us?) When the program finishes its calculations, a path may appear riddled with far too many points or equipped with too few.

Fortunately, you can adjust the performance of the freeform pen to accommodate your personal drawing style using the Curve Fit option in the Freeform Pen Options palette. When the freeform pen is active, just press Return/Enter to highlight the Curve Fit value. You can enter any new value between 0.5 and 10, which Photoshop interprets in screen pixels. The default value of 2, for example, instructs the program to ignore any jags in your mouse movements that do not exceed 2 pixels in length or width. Setting the value to 0.5 makes the freeform pen extremely sensitive; setting the value to 10 smoothes the roughest of gestures.

A Curve Fit from 2 to 4 is generally adequate for most folks, but you should experiment to determine the best setting. Like the magic wand's Tolerance setting, you can't alter the Curve Fit value for a path after you've drawn it. Photoshop calculates the points for a path only once, after you release the mouse button.

## Going magnetic

The magnetic pen works like a combination of the magnetic lasso and the freeform pen. Like the magnetic lasso, you begin by clicking anywhere along the edge of the image element you want to select. (For a pertinent blast from the past, see Figure 15-4.) Then move the cursor—no need to drag—around the perimeter of the element and watch Photoshop do its work. To set an anchor point, click. When you come full circle, click on the point where you started to complete the path.

As with the freeform pen, you can Option/Alt+click to create straight segments. And you have access to a Curve Fit option (in the Magnetic Pen Options palette) that controls the smoothness of the path. Lower values trace the edges more carefully, higher values result in fewer points and smoother edges.

The remaining options in the Magnetic Pen Options palette—Lasso Width, Frequency, Edge Contrast, and Stylus—are lifted right out of the magnetic lasso playbook. Read "Modifying the magnetic lasso options" near the beginning of this chapter for complete information.

# Reshaping and transforming paths

If you take time to master the default pen tool, you'll find yourself drawing accurate paths more and more frequently. But you'll never get it right 100 percent of the time—or even 50 percent of the time. And when you rely on the freeform or magnetic pen tools, the results are never dead on. From your first timid steps until you develop into a seasoned pro, you'll rely heavily on Photoshop's ability to *reshape* paths by moving points and handles, adding and deleting points, and converting points to change the curvature of segments. So don't worry too much if your path looks like an erratic stitch on the forehead of Frankenstein's monster. The path-edit tools provide all the second chances you'll ever need.

## Using the arrow tool

The arrow tool (which you get by pressing the A key) represents the foremost path-reshaping function in Photoshop. After selecting this tool, you can perform any of the following functions:

✦ **Selecting points**: Click on a point to select it independently of other points in a path. Shift+click to select an additional point, even if the point belongs to a different path than other selected points. Option/Alt+click on a path to select all its points in one fell swoop. You can even marquee points by dragging in a rectangle around them. You cannot, however, apply commands from the Select menu, such as All or None, to the selection of paths.

✦ **Drag selected points**: To move one or more points in a path, select the points you want to move and then drag one of the selected points. All selected points move the same distance and direction. When you move a point while a neighboring point remains stationary, the segment between the two points shrinks, stretches, and bends to accommodate the change in distance. Segments located between two selected or deselected points remain unchanged during a move.

You can move selected points in 1-pixel increments by pressing arrow keys. If both a portion of the image and points in a path are selected, the arrow keys move the point only. Because paths reside on a higher layer, they take precedence in all functions that might concern them.

✦ **Drag a straight segment**: You also can reshape a path by dragging its segments. When you drag a straight segment, the two corner points on either side of the segment move, as well. As illustrated in Figure 15-26, the neighboring segments stretch, shrink, or bend to accommodate the drag.

This technique works best with straight segments drawn with the default pen tool. Segments created by Option/Alt+clicking with the freeform or magnetic pens may include trace control handles that make Photoshop think the segment is actually curved.

✦ **Drag a curved segment**: When you drag a curved segment, you stretch, shrink, or bend that segment, as demonstrated in Figure 15-27.

Tip

When you drag a curved segment, drag from the middle of the segment, approximately equidistant from both its points. This method provides the best leverage and ensures the segment doesn't go flying off in some weird direction you hadn't anticipated.

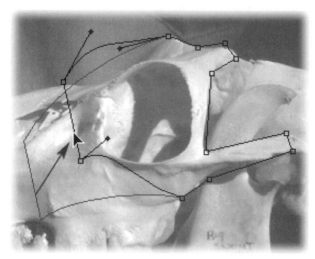

**Figure 15-26:** Drag a straight segment to move the segment and change the length, direction, and curvature of the neighboring segments.

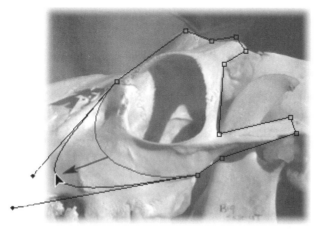

**Figure 15-27:** Drag a curved segment to change the curvature of that segment only and leave the neighboring segments unchanged.

✦ **Drag a Bézier control handle**: Select a point and drag either of its Bézier control handles to change the curvature of the corresponding segment without moving any of the points in the path. If the point is a smooth point, moving one handle moves both handles in the path. If you want to move a smooth handle independently of its partner, you must use the convert point tool, as discussed in the "Converting points" section later in this chapter.

✦ **Clone a path**: To make a duplicate of a selected path, Option/Alt+drag it to a new location in the image window. Photoshop automatically stores the new path under the same name as the original.

✦ **Deselect a path**: Click with the arrow tool outside any path to deselect all active paths. Because many options affect the selected path only, deselecting the paths before choosing a command you want to apply to all visible paths is often a good idea.

**Tip**

Press and hold the ⌘/Ctrl key to access the arrow tool temporarily when one of the pen or path-edit tools are selected. When you release the ⌘/Ctrl key, the cursor returns to the selected tool. This is a great way to edit the path while you're still drawing it.

## Adding and deleting points

The quantity of points and segments in a path is forever subject to change. Whether a path is closed or open, you can reshape it by adding and deleting points, which, in turn, forces the addition or deletion of a segment:

✦ **Appending a point to the end of an open path**: If an existing path is open, you can activate one of its endpoints by either clicking or dragging it with the pen tool, depending on the identity of the endpoint and whether you want the next segment to be straight or curved. Photoshop is then prepared to draw a segment between the endpoint and the next point you create.

✦ **Closing an open path**: You also can use the technique I just described to close an open path. Just select one endpoint, click or drag on it with the pen tool to activate it, and then click or drag on the opposite endpoint. Photoshop draws a segment between the two endpoints, closing the path and eliminating both endpoints by converting them to interior points, which simply means the points are bound on both sides by segments.

✦ **Joining two open paths**: You can join two open paths to create one longer open path. To do so, activate an endpoint of the first path, then click or drag with the pen tool on an endpoint of the second path.

✦ **Inserting a point in a segment**: Select the insert point tool (by pressing the + key) and click anywhere along an open or closed path to insert a point and divide the segment on which you click into two segments. Photoshop automatically inserts a corner or smooth point, depending on its reading of the path. If the point does not exactly meet your needs, use the convert point tool to change it.

Any of the three pen tools changes to the insert point cursor when you hover it over a segment in an existing path. Just click on the segment, and Photoshop inserts a point. You can also insert points with the remove point tool by Option/Alt+clicking.

✦ **Deleting a point and breaking the path**: The simplest way to delete a point is to select it with the arrow tool and press either the Delete or Clear key. (You also can choose Edit ⇨ Clear, though why you would want to expend so much effort is beyond me.) When you delete an interior point, you delete both segments associated with that point, resulting in a break in the path. If you delete an endpoint from an open path, you delete the single segment associated with the point.

✦ **Removing a point without breaking the path**: Select the remove point tool (by pressing the – key) and click on a point in an open or closed path to delete the point and draw a new segment between the two points that neighbor it. The remove point tool ensures no break occurs in a path.

To access the remove point tool when using one of the pen tools, hover your cursor over a selected interior point in an existing path. Click on the point and it goes away. Alternately, you can remove a point when the insert point tool is active by Option/Alt+clicking.

✦ **Deleting a segment**: You can delete a single interior segment from a path without affecting any point. To do so, first click outside the path with the arrow tool to deselect the path. Then click on the segment you want to delete and press the Delete key. When you delete an interior segment, you create a break in your path.

✦ **Deleting a whole path**: To delete an entire path, select any portion of it and press the Delete key twice. The first time you press Delete, Photoshop deletes the selected point or segment and automatically selects all other points in the path. The second time you press Delete, Photoshop eliminates everything it missed the first time around.

### Converting points

Photoshop lets you change the identity of an interior point. You can convert a corner point to a smooth point and vice versa. You perform all point conversions using the convert point tool as follows:

✦ **Smooth to corner**: Click on an existing smooth point to convert it to a corner point with no Bézier control handle.

✦ **Smooth to cusp**: Drag one of the handles of a smooth point to move it independently of the other, thus converting the smooth point to a cusp.

✦ **Corner to smooth**: Drag from a corner point to convert it to a smooth point with two symmetrical Bézier control handles.

✦ **Cusp to smooth**: Drag one of the handles of a cusp point to lock both handles back into alignment, thus converting the cusp to a smooth point.

Photoshop **5.0**

**Tip** Press the Option/Alt key to temporarily access the convert point tool when one of the three pen tools is active and positioned over a selected point. To do the same when the arrow tool is active, press ⌘/Ctrl and Option/Alt.

## Transforming paths

Photoshop 5 broadens your range of path editing options by permitting you to scale, rotate, skew, and otherwise transform paths independently of the image. First, select the arrow key (by pressing the A key) to enter path editing mode. Then do one of the following:

✦ To transform all paths in a group — such as both the eye and skull outline in the first example of Figure 15-28 — select the arrow tool and click off a path to make sure all paths are deselected. Then choose Edit ➪ Free Transform Path.

Rotate cursor        Transformation origin

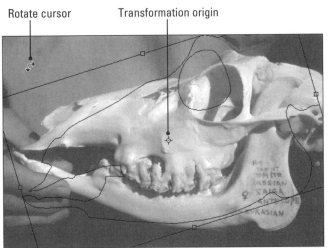

**Figure 15-28:** To transform multiple paths at once (top), deselect all paths and press ⌘/Ctrl+T. You can alternatively transform independent paths or points by selecting them with the arrow tool and pressing ⌘/Ctrl+T (bottom).

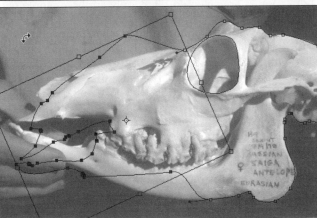

✦ To transform a single path independently of others in a group, Option/Alt+ click on it with the arrow tool. Then choose Edit ➪ Free Transform Points.

✦ Photoshop even lets you transform some points independently of others inside a single path, as demonstrated in the second example of Figure 15-28. Just select the points you want to modify and choose Edit ➪ Free Transform Points.

The keyboard shortcut for all of these operations is ⌘/Ctrl+T. If you select an independent path — or specific points inside a path — press ⌘/Ctrl+Option/Alt+T to transform a duplicate of the path and leave the original unaffected.

In an attempt to conserve tree matter — which is being wasted liberally enough in this tome — I explain the larger topic of transformation in one central location, the "Applying Transformations" section of Chapter 17. Even so, here's a brief rundown of your transformation options after you press ⌘/Ctrl+T:

✦ **Scale**: To scale a path, drag one of the eight square handles that adorn the transformation boundary. Option/Alt+drag a handle to scale with respect to the origin point. (You can move the origin by dragging it.)

✦ **Rotate**: Drag outside the boundary to rotate the paths or points, as demonstrated in Figure 15-28.

✦ **Flip**: Control right-click in the transformation mode to access a pop-up menu of transformation options. Choose Flip Horizontal or Flip Vertical to create a mirror image of the path.

✦ **Skew**: ⌘/Ctrl+drag one of the side handles to slant the paths. Press the Shift key along with ⌘/Ctrl to constrain the slant along a consistent axis.

✦ **Distort**: ⌘/Ctrl+drag one of the corner handles to distort the paths.

✦ **Perspective**: ⌘/Ctrl+Shift+Option/Alt+drag a corner handle to achieve a perspective effect.

Note that you can't take advantage of the distortion or perspective feature when individual points are selected. They only apply to whole paths.

✦ **Numerical transformations**: If you need to transform a path by a very specific amount, Control/right-click in the image window and choose the Numeric command. The Numeric Transform dialog box tracks the changes you've made so far. Modify the values as desired and press Return/Enter.

When you finish stretching and distorting your paths, press Return/Enter or double-click inside the boundary to apply the transformation. You can undo the last transformation inside the transform mode by pressing ⌘/Ctrl+Z or bag the whole thing by pressing the Escape key.

To repeat the last transformation on another path, press ⌘/Ctrl+Shift+T.

# Filling paths

After you finish drawing a path and getting it exactly the way you want it, you can convert it to a selection outline — as described in the upcoming "Converting paths to selections" section — or you can paint it. You can either paint the interior of the path by choosing the Fill Path command from the Paths palette menu, or you can paint the outline of the path by choosing Stroke Path.

The Fill Path command works much like Edit ⇨ Fill. After drawing a path, choose the Fill Path command or Option/Alt+click on the fill path icon in the lower-left corner of the palette (the one that looks like a filled circle). Photoshop displays a slight variation of the Fill dialog box discussed in Chapter 9, the only difference being the inclusion of two Rendering options. Enter a value into the Feather Radius option box to blur the edges of the fill, as if the path were a selection with a feathered outline. Select the Anti-aliased check box to soften slightly the outline of the filled area.

If one path falls inside another, Photoshop leaves the intersection of the two paths unfilled. Suppose you draw two round paths, one fully inside the other. If you deselect both paths and then choose the Fill Path command, Photoshop fills only the area between the two paths, resulting in the letter *O*.

If the Fill Path command fills only part or none of the path, the path probably falls outside the selection outline. Choose Select ⇨ Deselect (⌘/Ctrl+D) to deselect the image and then choose the Fill Path command again.

If you select one or more paths with the arrow tool, the Fill Path command changes to Fill Subpaths, enabling you to fill the selected paths only. The fill path icon also affects only the selected paths.

# Painting along a path

Unlike the Fill Path command, which bears a strong resemblance to Edit ⇨ Fill, the Stroke Path command is altogether different than Edit ⇨ Stroke. Where Edit ⇨ Stroke creates outlines and arrowheads, the Stroke Path command enables you to paint a brush stroke along the contours of a path. This may not sound like a big deal at first, but this feature enables you to combine the spontaneity of the paint and edit tools with the structure and precision of a path.

To paint a path, choose the Stroke Path command from the Paths palette menu to display the Stroke Path dialog box shown in Figure 15-29. In this dialog box, you can choose the paint or edit tool with which you want to stroke the path (which only means to paint a brush stroke along a path). Photoshop drags the chosen tool along the exact route of the path, retaining any tool or brush shape settings that were in force when you chose the tool.

You can also display the Stroke Path dialog box by Option/Alt+clicking on the stroke path icon, the second icon at the bottom of the Paths palette (labeled back in Figure 15-23). If you prefer to bypass the dialog box, select a paint or edit tool and then either click on the stroke path icon or simply press the Enter key on the numeric keypad. Instead of displaying the dialog box, Photoshop assumes you want to use the selected tool and strokes away.

**Note**

If the path is selected, the Stroke Path command becomes a Stroke Subpath command. Photoshop then only strokes the selected path, rather than all paths saved under the current name.

**Figure 15-29:** Photoshop displays this dialog box when you choose the Stroke Path command while a tool other than a paint or edit tool is selected.

**Tip**

If you're really feeling precise—I think they have a clinical term for that—you can specify the location of every single blob of paint laid down in an image. When the Spacing option in the Brush Options dialog box is deselected, Photoshop applies a single blob of paint for each point in a path. If this isn't sufficient control, I'm a monkey's uncle. (What a terrible thing to say about one's nephew!)

## Converting and saving paths

Photoshop provides two commands to switch between paths and selections, both of which are located in the Paths palette menu. The Make Selection command converts a path to a selection outline; the Make Path command converts a selection to a path. And regardless of how you create a path, you can save it with the current image, which enables you not only to reuse the path but also to hide and display it at will.

### Converting paths to selections

When you choose the Make Selection command or Option/Alt+click on the make selection icon (which looks like a dotted circle, as labeled back in Figure 15-23), Photoshop displays the dialog box shown in Figure 15-30. You can specify whether to antialias or feather the selection and to what degree. You can also instruct Photoshop to combine the prospective selection outline with any existing selection in the image. The Operation options correspond to the keyboard functions discussed in the "Manually adding and subtracting" section earlier in this chapter.

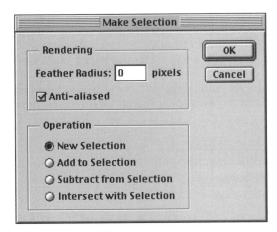

**Figure 15-30:** When you choose the Make Selection command, you have the option of combining the path with an existing selection.

Photoshop offers several alternative ways to convert a path to a selection outline, all of which are more convenient than the Make Selection command:

✦ **Press the Enter key on the numeric keypad**: As long as a path or selection tool is active, the keypad Enter key converts the path to a selection.

✦ **⌘/Ctrl+click on the path name**: If some other tool is selected, you can ⌘/Ctrl+ click on the name of a path in the Paths palette. The path needn't be active.

✦ **Shift+Enter or ⌘/Ctrl+Shift+click**: To add the path to an existing selection, press Shift with one of the above techniques. You can press Shift+Enter. (Again, use the Enter key on the keypad.) Or ⌘/Ctrl+Shift+click on a path name in the palette.

✦ **Option/Alt+Enter or ⌘/Ctrl+Option/Alt+click**: Naturally, if you can add, you can subtract. Just press the Option/Alt key with Enter or ⌘/Ctrl+clicking to subtract the path from the selection.

✦ **Shift+Option/Alt+Enter or ⌘/Ctrl+Shift+Option/Alt+click**: Now we're starting to get into some obscure stuff, but what's possible is possible. You select the intersection of a path and a selection outline by pressing a whole mess of keys.

All of these wonderful techniques have the added advantage of hiding the path when converting the path to a selection. This way, you have full, unobstructed access to your selection outline.

By contrast, the Make Selection command leaves the path on screen in front of the converted selection. If you try to copy, cut, delete, or nudge the selection, you perform the operation on the path instead.

## Converting selections to paths

When you choose the Make Paths command, Photoshop produces a single Tolerance option. Unlike the Tolerance options you've encountered so far, this one is accurate to ⅒ pixel and has nothing to do with colors or brightness values. Rather, it works like the Curve Fit option in the Freeform Pen Options palette — that is, it permits you to specify Photoshop's sensitivity to twists and turns in a selection outline. The value you enter determines how far the path can vary from the original selection. The lowest possible value, 0.5, not only ensures Photoshop retains every nuance of the selection, but it can also result in overly complicated paths with an abundance of points. If you enter the highest value, 10, Photoshop rounds out the path and uses few points. If you plan on editing the path, you probably won't want to venture any lower than 2.0, the default setting.

To bypass the Make Work Path dialog box and turn your selection into a path using the current Tolerance settings, click on the make path icon.

### Saving paths with an image

As mentioned at the beginning of the paths discussion, saving a path is an integral step in the path-creation process. You can store every path you draw and keep it handy in case you decide later to select an area again. Because Photoshop defines paths as compact mathematical equations, they take up virtually no room when you save an image to disk.

You save one or more paths by choosing the Save Path command from the Paths palette menu or by simply double-clicking on the italicized *Work Path* item in the scrolling list. After you perform the save operation, the path name appears in upright characters. A path name can include any number of separate paths. In fact, if you save a path and then set about drawing another one, Photoshop automatically adds that path in with the saved path. To start a new path under a new name, you first must hide the existing path. Or click on the new path icon — the little page at the bottom of the Paths palette — to establish an independent path.

To hide all paths, click on the empty portion of the scrolling list below the last saved path name. You can even hide unsaved paths in this way. If you hide an unsaved path and then begin drawing a new one, however, the unsaved path is deleted, never to return again.

To hide all paths when the Paths palette is all full up and there is no empty area at the bottom of the scrolling list, choose Turn Off Path from the Paths palette menu. If you typically create five or six paths in a single image, you're going to love this command.

# Swapping Paths with Illustrator

Photoshop can swap paths directly with the most recent versions of Illustrator and FreeHand. All you must do is copy a path to the Clipboard and paste it into the other program. Or, if you own Illustrator 8, you can simply drag and drop paths from Photoshop to Illustrator and vice versa. This special cross-application compatibility feature expands and simplifies a variety of path-editing functions. For example, suppose you want to scale and rotate a path:

If you own Illustrator, select the path in Photoshop with the arrow tool and copy it to the Clipboard (⌘/Ctrl+C). Then switch to Illustrator, paste the path, and edit as desired. About 95 percent of Illustrator's capabilities are devoted to the task of editing paths, so you have many more options at your disposal than in Photoshop. When you finish modifying the path, copy it again, switch to Photoshop, and paste.

When you paste an Illustrator path into Photoshop, the dialog box shown in Figure 15-31 offers you the option of rendering the path to pixels — just as you can render an Illustrator EPS document using File ⇨ Open — or keeping the path information intact. Select the Paste as Paths option to add the copied paths to the selected item in the Paths palette. (If no item is selected, Photoshop creates a new *Work Path* item.) You can then use the path to create a selection outline or whatever.

**Figure 15-31:** When pasting a path copied from Illustrator, Photoshop greets you with this dialog box.

Things can get pretty muddled in the Clipboard, especially when you're switching applications. If you copy something from Illustrator, but the Paste command is dimmed inside Photoshop, you may be able to force the issue a little. You may simply need to wake up the Clipboard. On a Mac, press the Option key inside Illustrator and choose Edit ⇨ Copy. This is intended to copy a PICT version of the path, but it sometimes has the added benefit of alerting the Clipboard to the fact that, yes indeed, there is something in here that Photoshop can use. If you're using Windows, open the Windows Clipbook Viewer (Start ⇨ Programs ⇨ Accessories ⇨ Clipbook Viewer). Don't worry if you see a message about an unsupported format, or if the image looks a complete mess. Just minimize the viewer window and try to paste again. (Computers are kind of slow sometimes. Every once in a while, you must give them a kick in the pants.)

You can copy paths from Photoshop and paste them into Illustrator or some other drawing program regardless of the setting of the Export Clipboard check box in the Preferences dialog box. That option affects pixels only. Paths are so tiny, Photoshop always exports them.

## Exporting to Illustrator

If you don't have enough memory to run both Illustrator and Photoshop at the same time, you can export Photoshop paths to disk and then open them in Illustrator. To export all paths in the current image, choose File ⇨ Export ⇨ Paths to Illustrator. Photoshop saves the paths as a fully editable Illustrator document. This scheme enables you to trace images exactly with paths in Photoshop and then combine these paths as objects with the exported EPS version of the image inside

Illustrator. Whereas tracing an image in Illustrator can prove a little tricky because of resolution differences and other previewing limitations, you can trace images in Photoshop as accurately as you like.

**Note**

Unfortunately, Illustrator provides no equivalent function to export paths for use in Photoshop; nor can Photoshop open Illustrator documents from disk and interpret them as paths. This means the Clipboard is the only way to take a path created or edited in Illustrator and use it in Photoshop.

**Cross-Reference**

Only about half of Photoshop users own Illustrator. Meanwhile, close to 90 percent of Illustrator users own Photoshop. This is why I cover the special relationship between Illustrator and Photoshop in-depth in Chapter 13 of my Illustrator book, *Real World Illustrator 8*. You'll find out more about using Photoshop with FreeHand in the *FreeHand 8 Bible* (IDG Books Worldwide, 1998).

### Retaining transparent areas in an image

When you import an image into Illustrator, FreeHand, CorelDraw, QuarkXPress, PageMaker, or some other object-oriented program, the image comes in as a rectangle with opaque pixels. Even if the image appeared partially transparent in Photoshop — on a layer, for example — the pixels are filled with white or some other color in the receiving application. These same object-oriented applications, however, do enable you to mask portions of an image you want to appear transparent by establishing a clipping path. Elements that lie inside the clipping path are opaque; elements outside the clipping path are transparent. Photoshop enables you to export an image in the EPS format with an object-oriented clipping path intact. When you import the image into the object-oriented program, it appears premasked with a perfectly smooth perimeter, as illustrated by the clipped image in Figure 15-32.

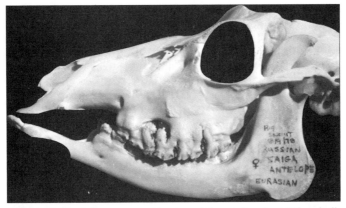

**Figure 15-32:** I drew one path around the perimeter of the skull and another around the eye socket. After defining the paths as clipping paths, I exported the image in the EPS format, imported it into Illustrator, and set it against a black background for contrast.

The following steps explain how to assign a set of saved paths as clipping paths.

## Steps: Saving an Image with Clipping Paths

1. **Draw one or more paths around the portions of the image you want to appear opaque.** Areas outside the paths will be transparent.

2. **Save the paths.** Double-click on the *Work Path* item in the Paths palette, enter a name, and press Return/Enter. (Try to use a name that will make sense three years from now when you have to revisit this document and determine what the heck you did.)

3. **Choose the Clipping Path command from the Paths palette menu.** Photoshop displays the dialog box shown in Figure 15-33, which asks you to select the saved paths you want to assign as the clipping path.

   **Note**

   If you like, enter a value into the Flatness option box. This option enables you to simplify the clipping paths by printing otherwise fluid curves as polygons. The Flatness value represents the distance—between 0.2 and 100, in printer pixels—the polygon may vary from the true mathematical curve. A higher value leads to a polygon with fewer sides. This means it looks chunkier, but it also prints more quickly. I recommend a value of 3. Many experts say you can go as high as 7 when printing to an imagesetter without seeing the straight edges. But I strongly suspect it depends on how much of a perfectionist you are. Me? I like 3.

   After you set a path to a clipping path, Photoshop identifies it in the Paths palette by displaying its name in bold type (or outline type on a Mac), as illustrated in Figure 15-33.

**Figure 15-33:** After you choose the Clipping Path command (top), Photoshop identifies the clipping path name in the Paths palette with bold type (bottom).

4. **Choose File ⇨ Save As and select Photoshop EPS from the Save As pop-up menu (or Format pop-up menu on a Mac).** Select the desired Preview and Encoding settings, and press the Return/Enter key. Photoshop saves the EPS image with masked transparencies to disk.

**Note** PageMaker is unique in that it supports clipping paths saved in the TIFF format. So if you plan on placing the image in PageMaker, you can save the image in TIFF instead of EPS in Step 4.

Figure 15-34 shows an enhanced version of the clipped skull from Figure 15-32. In addition to exporting the image with clipping paths in the EPS format, I saved the paths to disk by choosing File ⇨ Export ⇨ Paths to Illustrator. Inside Illustrator, I used the exported paths to create the outline around the clipped image. I also used them to create the shadow behind the image. The white of the eyeball is a reduced version of the eye socket, as are the iris and pupil. The background features a bunch of flipped and reduced versions of the paths. This may look like a lot of work, but the only drawing required was to create the two initial Photoshop paths.

**Figure 15-34:** It's amazing what you can accomplish by combining scans edited in a painting program with smooth lines created in a drawing program.

Be prepared for your images to grow by leaps and bounds when imported into Illustrator. The EPS illustration shown in Figure 15-34 consumes six times as much space on disk as the original Photoshop image saved in the TIFF format.

**Caution** When used in excess, clipping paths present problems for the most sophisticated printing devices. You should use a clipping path only when it's absolutely necessary and can't be avoided. If you want to place an image against a bitmapped background, for example, do it in Photoshop, not in Illustrator, QuarkXPress, or any other application. This will invariably speed printing and may mean the difference between whether or not a file prints successfully.

✦         ✦         ✦

# Creating Masks

## Selecting via Masks

Most Photoshop users don't use masks. If my personal experience is any indication, it's not only because masks seem complicated, it's because they strike most folks as being more trouble than they're worth. Like nearly everyone, when I first started using Photoshop, I couldn't even imagine a possible application for a mask. I have my lasso tool and my magic wand. If I'm really in a rut, I can pull out my pen tool. What more could I possibly want?

Quite a bit, as it turns out. Every one of the tools I just mentioned is only moderately suited to the task of selecting images. The lasso tools let you create free-form selections, but none of them — not even the magnetic lasso — can account for differences in focus levels. The magic wand selects areas of color, but it usually leaves important colors behind and the edges of its selection outlines often appear ragged and ugly. The pen tool is extremely precise, but it results in mechanical outlines that may appear incongruous with the natural imagery they contain.

Masks offer all the benefits of the other tools. With masks, you can create free-form selections, select areas of color, and generate amazingly precise selections. Masks also address all the deficiencies associated with the selection tools. They can account for different levels of focus, they give you absolute control over the look of the edges, and they create selections every bit as natural as the image itself.

In fact, a mask *is* the image itself. Masks use pixels to select pixels. Masks are your way to make Photoshop see what you see using the data inherent in the photograph. Masks enable you to devote every one of Photoshop's powerful capabilities to the task of creating a selection outline. Masks are, without a doubt, the most accurate selection mechanism available in Photoshop.

### Masking defined

For those folks who aren't clear on what a mask is, I'll tell you: A *mask* is a selection outline expressed as a grayscale image.

✦ Selected areas appear white.

✦ Deselected areas appear black.

✦ Partially selected parts of the image appear in gray. Feathered edges are also expressed in shades of gray, from light gray near the selected area to dark gray near the deselected area.

Figure 16-1 shows two selection outlines and their equivalent masks. The top-left example shows a rectangular selection that has been inverted (using Image ⇨ Adjust ⇨ Invert, ⌘/Ctrl+I). Below this example is the same selection expressed as a mask. Because the selection is hard-edged with no anti-aliasing or feathering, the mask appears hard-edged, as well. The selected area is white and is said to be *unmasked*; the deselected area is black, or *masked*.

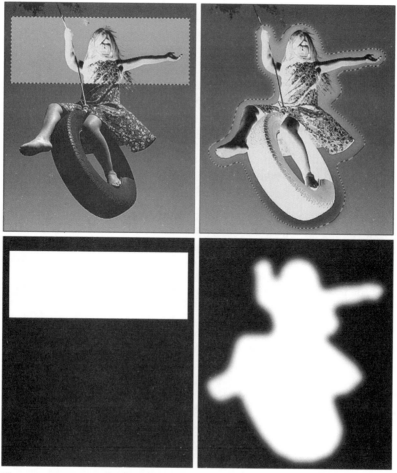

**Figure 16-1:** Two selection outlines with inverted interiors (top) and their equivalent masks (bottom).

The top-right example in Figure 16-1 shows a feathered selection outline. Again, I've inverted the selection so you can better see the extent of the selection outline. (Marching ants can't accurately express softened edges, so the inversion helps show things off more.) The bottom-right image is the equivalent mask. Here, the feathering effect is completely visible.

When you look at the masks along the bottom of Figure 16-1, you may wonder where the heck the image went. One of the wonderful things about masks is they can be viewed independently of an image, as in Figure 16-1, or with an image, as in Figure 16-2. In the second figure, the mask is expressed as a color overlay. By default, the color of the overlay is a translucent red, like a conventional rubylith. (To see the overlay in its full, natural color, see Color Plate 16-1.) Areas covered with the rubylith are masked (deselected); areas that appear normal—without any red tint—are unmasked (selected). When you return to the standard marching ants mode, any changes you make to your image will affect only the unmasked areas.

**Figure 16-2:** Here are the masks from Figure 16-1, shown as they appear when viewed along with an image.

Now that you know roughly what masks are (the definition will become progressively clearer throughout this chapter), the question remains, what good are they? Because a mask is essentially an independent grayscale image, you can edit the mask using any of the paint and edit tools discussed in Chapters 8 through 10, any of the filters discussed in Chapters 23 and 24, any of the color correction options discussed in Chapter 30, and virtually any of the functions described in the other chapters. You can even use the selection tools, as discussed in the previous chapter. With all these features at your disposal, you can't help but create a more accurate selection outline in a shorter amount of time.

# Painting and Editing Inside Selections

Before we immerse ourselves in masking techniques, let's start with a warm-up topic, *selection masking*. When you were in grade school, you might have had a teacher who nagged you to color within the lines. (I didn't. My teachers were more concerned about preventing me from writing on the walls and coloring on the other kids, or so I'm told.) If so, he would have been pleased by this incredibly straightforward feature. If you dread to paint inside an image because you're afraid you'll screw it up, selection masking is the answer. Regardless of which tool you use to create the selection—marquee, lasso, magic wand, or pen—Photoshop permits you to paint or edit only the selected area. The paint can't enter the deselected (or protected) portions of the image, so you can't help but paint inside the lines. As a result, all selection outlines act as masks, hence the term *selection masking*. (And you thought this chapter was going to be hard.)

Figures 16-3 through 16-6 show the familiar skull image subject to some pretty free-and-easy use of the paint and edit tools. (You think I ought to lay off the heavy metal or what?) The following steps describe how I created these images using a selection mask.

## Steps: Painting and Editing inside a Selection Mask

1. **I selected the slightly rotting skull of the enchanting Russian Saiga antelope.** You can see the selection outline in such golden oldies as Figures 15-19 and 15-21. If those figures are too remote, just look at the top example in Figure 16-3. For the record, I drew this selection outline using the pen tool.

2. **I reversed the selection with the Inverse command.** I wanted to edit the area surrounding the skull, so I chose Select ⇨ Inverse (⌘/Ctrl+Shift+I) to reverse which areas were selected and which were not.

3. **I pressed ⌘/Ctrl+Delete/Backspace to fill the selected area with the background color.** In this case, the background color was white—as shown in the bottom half of Figure 16-3.

4. **I painted inside the selection mask.** But before I began, I chose Select ⇨ Hide Edges (⌘/Ctrl+H). This enabled me to paint without being distracted by those infernal marching ants. (In fact, this is one of the most essential uses for the Hide Edges command.)

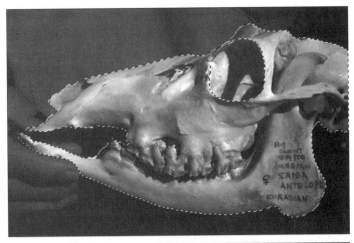

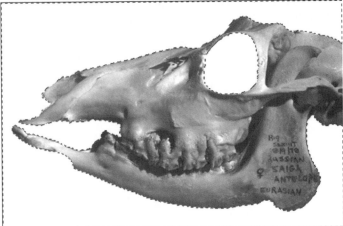

**Figure 16-3:** After drawing a selection outline around the antelope skull (top), I inversed the selection and deleted the background (bottom).

5. **I selected the paintbrush tool and expressed myself.** I selected the 21-pixel soft brush shape in the Brushes palette. With the foreground color set to black, I dragged the paintbrush around the perimeter of the skull to set it apart from its white background, as shown in Figure 16-4. No matter how sloppily I painted, the skull remained unscathed.

*(continued)*

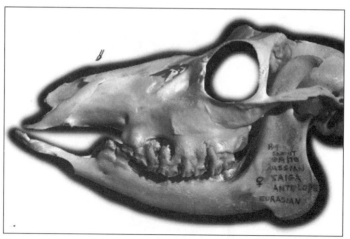

**Figure 16-4:** I painted inside the selection mask with a 21-pixel soft brush shape.

6. **I next selected and used the smudge tool.** I set the Pressure slider bar inside the Smudge Options palette to 80 percent by pressing the 8 key. I dragged from inside the skull outward 20 or so times to create a series of curlicues. I also dragged from outside the skull inward to create white gaps between the curlicues. As shown in Figure 16-5, the smudge tool can smear colors from inside the protected area, but it does not apply these colors until you go inside the selection. This is an important point to remember, because it demonstrates that although the protected area is safe from all changes, the selected area may be influenced by colors from protected pixels.

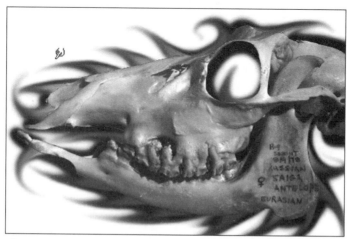

**Figure 16-5:** Dragging with the smudge tool here smeared colors from pixels outside the selection mask without changing the appearance of those pixels.

**7. I double-click on the airbrush tool icon in the toolbox to display the Airbrush Options palette.** Then I selected the Fade check box and set the Fade value to 20, leaving the Transparent option selected in the pop-up menu. I then selected a 60-pixel soft brush shape and, again, dragged outward from various points along the perimeter of the skull. As demonstrated in Figure 16-6, combining airbrush and mask is as useful in Photoshop as it is in the real world.

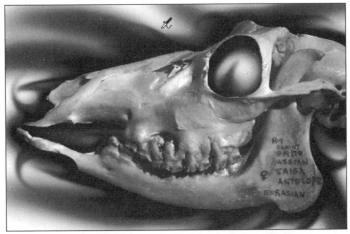

**Figure 16-6:** I dragged around the skull with the airbrush to distinguish it further from its background. Pretty cool effect, huh? Well, if this is not your cup of tea, maybe you can track down a teenager who will appreciate it.

# Working in Quick Mask Mode

Selection masks give you an idea of what masks are all about, but they only scrape the surface. The rest of the discussions in this chapter revolve around using masks to define complex selection outlines.

The most straightforward environment for creating a mask is the *quick mask mode*. In the quick mask mode, a selection is expressed as a rubylith overlay. All the deselected areas in your image appear coated with red and the selected areas appear without red coating, as shown in the middle examples of Color Plate 16-1. You can then edit the mask as desired and exit the mode to return to the standard selection outline. The quick mask mode is — as its name implies — expeditious and convenient, with none of the trappings or permanence of more conventional masks. It's kind of like a fast food restaurant — you use it when you aren't overly concerned about quality and you aim to get in and out in a hurry.

## How the quick mask mode works

Typically, you'll at least want to rough out a selection with the standard selection tools before entering the quick mask mode. Then you can concentrate on refining and modifying your selection inside the quick mask, rather than having to create the selection from scratch. (Naturally, this is only a rule of thumb. I violate the rule several times throughout this chapter, but only because the quick mask mode and I are such tight friends.)

To enter the quick mask mode, click on the quick mask mode icon, as I've done in Figure 16-7. Or press the Q key. When I pressed *Q* after wreaking my most recent havoc on the extinct antelope skull, I got the image shown in Figure 16-7. The skull receives the mask because it is not selected. (In Figure 16-7, the mask appears as a light gray coating; on your color screen, the mask appears in red.) The area outside the skull looks the same as it always did because it's selected and, therefore, not masked.

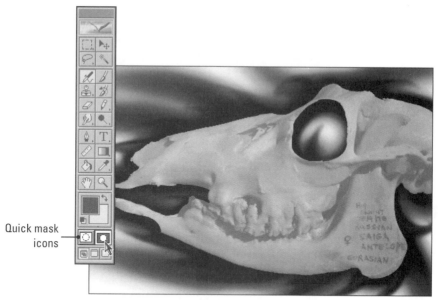

Quick mask
icons

**Figure 16-7:** Click on the quick mask mode icon (highlighted in the toolbox) to instruct Photoshop to express the selection temporarily as a grayscale image.

Notice the selection outline disappears when you enter the quick mask mode. This is because it temporarily ceases to exist. Any operations you apply affect the mask itself and leave the underlying image untouched. When you click on the marching ants mode icon (to the left of the quick mask mode icon) or again press the Q key, Photoshop converts the mask back into a selection outline and again enables you to edit the image.

**Note**

If you click on the quick mask mode icon without seeing anything change on screen, your computer isn't broken, it simply means you didn't select anything before you entered the mode. When nothing is selected, Photoshop makes the whole image open for editing; in other words, everything's selected. (Only a smattering of commands under the Edit, Layer, and Select menus require something to be selected before they work.) If everything is selected, the mask is white; therefore, the quick mask overlay is transparent and you don't see any difference on screen. This is another reason it's better to select something before you enter the quick mask mode — you get an immediate sense you're accomplishing something.

Also, Photoshop enables you to specify whether you want the red mask coating to cover selected areas or deselected areas. For information on how to change this setting, see "Changing the red coating," later in this chapter.

Once in the quick mask mode, you can edit the mask in the following ways:

✦ **Subtracting from a selection:** Paint with black to add red coating and, thus, deselect areas of the image, as demonstrated in the top half of Figure 16-8. This means you can selectively protect portions of your image by merely painting over them.

✦ **Adding to a selection:** Paint with white to remove red coating and, thus, add to the selection outline. You can use the eraser tool to whittle away at the masked area (assuming the background color is set to white). Or you can swap the foreground and background colors so you can paint in white with one of the painting tools.

✦ **Adding feathered selections:** If you paint with a shade of gray, you add feathered selections. You also can feather an outline by painting with black or white with a soft brush shape, as shown in the bottom image in Figure 16-8.

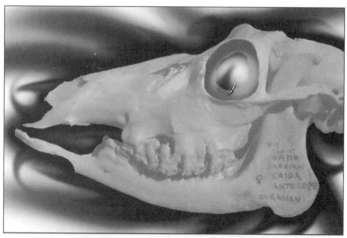

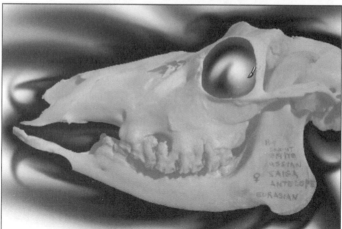

**Figure 16-8:** After subtracting some of the selected area inside the eye socket by painting in black with the paintbrush tool (top), I feathered the outline by painting with white, using a soft 45-pixel brush shape (bottom).

✦ **Clone selection outlines:** If you have a selection outline that you want to repeat in several locations throughout the image, the quick mask is your friend. Select the transparent area with one of the standard selection tools and ⌘/Ctrl+Option/Alt+drag it to a new location in the image, as shown in Figure 16-9. Although I use the lasso tool in the figure, the magic wand tool also works well for this purpose. To select an anti-aliased selection outline with the wand tool, set the tolerance to about 10 and be sure the Anti-aliased check box is active. Then click inside the selection. It's that easy.

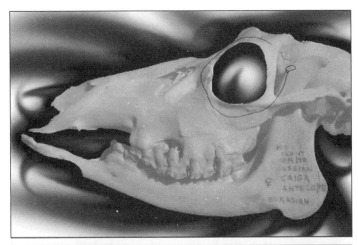

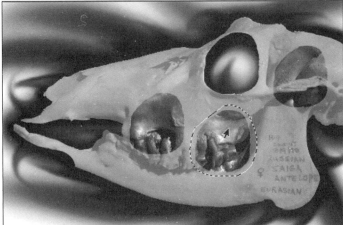

**Figure 16-9:** To clone the eye socket selection, I lassoed around it (top) and ⌘/Ctrl+Option/Alt+dragged it (bottom).

✦ **Transform selection outlines:** You can scale or rotate a selection independently of the image, just as you can with the Transform Selection command (covered in Chapter 15). Enter the quick mask mode, select the mask using one of the standard selection tools, and choose Edit ➪ Free Transform or press ⌘/Ctrl+T. (See Chapter 17 for more information on Free Transform and related commands.)

These are only a few of the unique effects you can achieve by editing a selection in the quick mask mode. Others involve tools and capabilities I haven't yet discussed, such as filters and color corrections.

When you finish editing your selection outlines, click on the marching ants mode icon (to the left of the quick mask mode icon) or press the Q key again to return to the marching ants mode. Your selection outlines again appear flanked by marching ants, and all tools and commands return to their normal image-editing functions. Figure 16-10 shows the results of switching to the marching ants mode and deleting the contents of the selection outlines created in the last examples of the previous two figures.

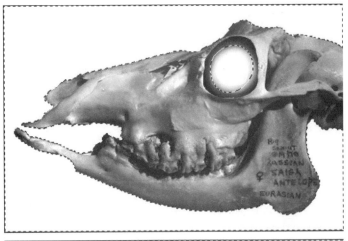

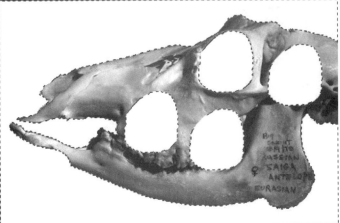

**Figure 16-10:** The results of deleting the regions selected in the final examples of Figures 16-8 (top) and 16-9 (bottom). Kind of makes me want to rent *It's the Great Pumpkin, Charlie Brown.* I mean, who wouldn't give this antelope a rock?

**Tip**

As demonstrated in the top example of Figure 16-10, the quick mask mode offers a splendid environment for feathering one selection outline, while leaving another hard-edged or anti-aliased. Granted, because most selection tools offer built-in feathering options, you can accomplish this task without resorting to the quick mask mode. But the quick mask mode enables you to change feathering selectively after drawing selection outlines, something you can't accomplish with Select ⇨ Feather. The quick mask mode also enables you to see exactly what you're doing. Kind of makes those marching ants look piddly and insignificant, huh?

## Changing the red coating

By default, the protected region of an image appears in translucent red in the quick mask mode, but if your image contains a lot of red, the mask can be difficult to see. Luckily, you can change it to any color and any degree of opacity that you like. To do so, double-click on the quick mask icon in the toolbox (or double-click on the *Quick Mask* item in the Channels palette) to display the dialog box shown in Figure 16-11.

> ✦ **Color Indicates:** Select the Selected Areas option to reverse the color coating, that is, to cover the selected areas in a translucent coat of red and view the deselected areas normally. Select the Masked Areas option (the default setting) to cover the deselected areas in color.

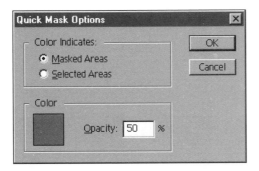

**Figure 16-11:** Double-click on the quick mask mode icon to access the Quick Mask Options dialog box. You then can change the color and opacity of the protected or selected areas when viewed in the quick mask mode.

**Tip**

You can reverse the color coating without ever entering the Quick Mask Options dialog box. Simply Option/Alt+click on the quick mask icon in the toolbox to toggle between coating the masked or selected portions of the image. The icon itself changes to reflect your choice.

> ✦ **Color:** Click on the Color icon to display the Color Picker dialog box and select a different color coating. (If you don't know how to use this dialog box, see the "Using the Color Picker" section of Chapter C on CD-ROM #2.) You can lift a color from the image with the eyedropper after the Color Picker dialog box comes up, but you probably want to use a color that isn't in the image so you can better see the mask.

> ✦ **Opacity:** Enter a value to change the opacity of the translucent color that coats the image. A value of 100 percent is absolutely opaque.

Change the color coating to achieve the most acceptable balance between being able to view and edit your selection and being able to view your image. For example, the default red coating shows up badly on my grayscale screen shots, so I changed the color coating to light blue and the Opacity value to 65 percent before shooting the screens featured in Figures 16-7 through 16-9.

## Gradations as masks

If you think the Feather command is a hot tool for creating softened selection outlines, wait until you get a load of gradations in the quick mask mode. No better way exists to create fading effects than selecting an image with one of the gradient tools.

### Fading an image

Consider the U.S. Capitol building shown in Figure 16-12. Whether you care for the folks who reside inside — personally, I'm sick of all this cynicism about the government, but I'm happy to exploit it for a few cheap laughs — you must admit, this is one beautiful building. Still, you might reckon the structure would be even more impressive if it were to fade into view out of a river of hot Hawaiian lava, like the one to the Capitol's immediate right. Well, you're in luck, because this is one of the easiest effects to pull off in Photoshop.

**Figure 16-12:** You can use the linear gradient tool in the quick mask mode to make the Capitol (left) fade out of the lava (right).

Switch to the quick mask mode by pressing the Q key. Then use the linear gradient tool to draw a gradation from black to white. (You can set the gradient style in the Linear Gradient Options palette to either Foreground to Background or Black, White.) The white portion of the gradation represents the area you want to select. I decided to select the top portion of the Capitol, so I drew the gradation from the top of the second tier to the top of the flag, as shown in the first example of Figure 16-13. Because the gradient line is a little hard to see, I've added a little arrow to show the direction of the drag. (To see the mask in full color, check out the first image in Color Plate 16-2.)

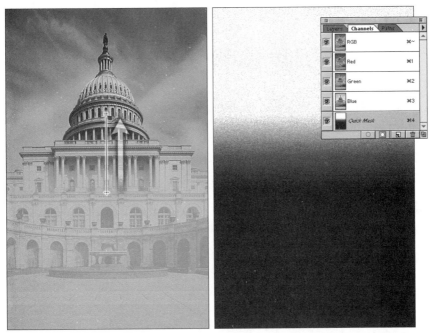

**Figure 16-13:** After drawing a linear gradation in the quick mask mode near the center of the image (left), I hid the image and applied the Add Noise filter with an Amount of 24 (right).

Banding can be a problem when you use a gradation as a mask. To eliminate the banding effect, therefore, apply the Add Noise filter at a low setting several times. To create the right example in Figure 16-13, I applied Add Noise using an Amount value of 24 and the Uniform distribution option.

**Tip**

Notice in the right example of Figure 16-13, I've hidden the image so only the mask is visible. As the figure shows, the Channels palette lists the *Quick Mask* in italics. This is because Photoshop regards the quick mask as a temporary channel. You can hide the image and view the mask in black and white by clicking on the eyeball in front of the color composite view, in this case RGB. Or just press the tilde key (~) to hide the image. Press tilde again to view mask and image together.

To apply the gradation as a selection, I returned to the marching ants mode by again pressing Q. I then ⌘/Ctrl+dragged the selected portion of the Capitol and dropped it into the lava image to achieve the effect shown in Figure 16-14. I could say something about Congress rising up from the ashes, but I have no idea what I'd mean by this. For the color version of this splendid image, see Color Plate 16-2.

**Figure 16-14:** The result of selecting the top portion of the Capitol using a gradient mask and then ⌘/Ctrl+dragging and dropping the selection into the lava image.

## Applying special effects gradually

You also can use gradations in the quick mask mode to fade the outcomes of filters and other automated special effects. For example, I wanted to apply a filter around the edges of the Lincoln colossus that appears in Figure 16-15. I began by deselecting everything in the image (⌘/Ctrl+D) and switching to the quick mask mode. Then I brought up the Linear Gradient Options palette and selected the Foreground to Transparent option from the Gradient pop-up menu.

I pressed the D key to make the foreground color black and the background color white. Then I dragged with the linear gradient tool from each of the four edges of the image inward to create a series of short gradations that trace around the boundaries of the image, as shown in Figure 16-16. (As you can see, I've hidden the image so you see the mask in black and white.) Because I've selected the Foreground to Transparent option, Photoshop adds each gradation to the last one.

**Figure 16-15:** This time around, my intention is to surround Lincoln with a gradual filtering effect.

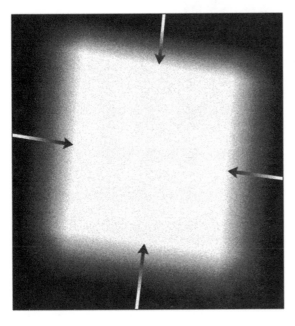

**Figure 16-16:** Inside the quick mask mode, I dragged from each of the four edges with the gradient tool (as indicated by the arrows).

To jumble the pixels in the mask, I applied Filter ➪ Noise ➪ Add Noise with an Amount value of 24. This is the effect that appears in Figure 16-16.

The only problem is I want to select the outside of the image, not the inside. So I need the edges to appear black and the inside to appear white, the opposite of what you see in Figure 16-16. No problem. All I do is press ⌘/Ctrl+I (Image ➪ Adjust ➪ Invert) to invert the image. Inverting inside the quick mask mode produces the same effect as applying Select ➪ Inverse to a selection.

Finally, I switched back to the marching ants mode by again pressing Q. Then I applied Filter ➪ Render ➪ Clouds to get the atmospheric effect you see in Figure 16-17. Yes, he's Abe the Illusionist — Lincoln as you've never seen him before! Once he gets to Vegas, he'll wipe the floor with David Copperfield.

**Figure 16-17:** After switching back to the marching ants mode, I chose Filter ➪ Render ➪ Clouds to create the foggy effect shown here.

Notice the corners in the mask in Figure 16-16? These corners are rounded, but you can achieve all kinds of corner effects with the linear gradient tool. For harsher corners, select the Foreground to Background option and set the brush mode to Lighten. For some *really* unusual corner treatments, try out the Difference and Exclusion brush modes. Wild stuff.

# Creating gradient arrows

A few sections ago, Figure 16-13 featured an upward-pointing arrow that faded into view with a dark halo around it. I could have created this arrowhead in a drawing program to get nice sharp points and smooth outlines. But I chose to create it in Photoshop, so I could take advantage of two options drawing programs don't offer: gradient lines and halos. Naturally, you can create both in the quick mask mode.

The following steps explain how to add cool fading arrows to any image, as demonstrated in Figures 16-18 and 16-19. The steps involve the quick mask mode, the gradient tool, the Fill command, and good old Delete/Backspace.

## Steps: Creating Fading Arrows with Halos

1. **Choose the New Snapshot command from the History palette menu.** Photoshop adds a new snapshot thumbnail at the top of the palette. Click in front of it to make it the source state. Now you're ready to revert to this state if need be, as called for in Step 15.

2. **Deselect everything (⌘/Ctrl+D) and switch to the quick mask mode (Q).** The image should appear absolutely normal.

3. **Select the line tool (Shift+N twice) and press Return/Enter.** Adjust the line weight and arrowhead settings in the Line Options palette to fit your needs. To create my first arrows (the ones that come inward from the corners in Figure 16-19), I set the Weight value to 20 and the Width, Length, and Concavity values in the Arrowhead Shape dialog box to 400, 600, and 20, respectively.

4. **Press D to switch to the default colors.**

5. **Draw your line, which will show up in red.** If you don't get it right the first time — as is often the case with this tool — press ⌘/Ctrl+Z and try again. The beauty of drawing a line in the quick mask mode is you can edit it after the fact without damaging the image. (You could also do the same on a separate layer, but the quick mask mode affords you a little more flexibility in this specific exercise.)

6. **Select the linear gradient tool (G) and press Return/Enter.** Make sure the Gradient pop-up menu in the Options palette is set to Foreground to Background. Also set the Opacity value to 100 percent. Then choose Lighten from the brush mode pop-up menu.

7. **Use the gradient tool to fade the base of the line.** Drag with the linear gradient tool from the point at which you want the line to begin to fade, down to the base of the line. Try to make the direction of your drag parallel to the line itself, thus ensuring a smooth fade. The first example in Figure 16-18 shows me in the progress of dragging along one of my arrows with the gradient tool. The small white arrow shows the direction of my drag. (The black line shows the actual cursor you see on screen.) The second image shows the result of the drag.

*(continued)*

**Figure 16-18:** Drag from the point at which you want the arrow to begin fading to the base of the line (left) parallel to the line itself (indicated here by the white arrow) to fade the line out (right).

**Figure 16-19:** I don't know whether this guy's in store for a cold front or what, but if you ever need to annotate an image with arrows, this gradient-arrowhead trick is certainly the way to do it.

8. **Choose Image ➪ Adjust ➪ Invert (⌘/Ctrl+I).** This inverts the quick mask, thus making the arrow the selected area.

9. **Copy the quick mask to a separate channel.** Drag the *Quick Mask* item in the Channels palette onto the little page icon at the bottom of the palette to copy the quick mask to a permanent mask channel. You'll need it again.

10. **Press Q to switch back to the marching ants mode.** Your arrow appears as a selection outline.

11. **Expand the selection to create the halo.** Choose Select ➪ Modify ➪ Expand and enter the desired value, based on the size and resolution of your image. I entered 6 to expand the selection outline 6 pixels.

12. **Choose Select ➪ Feather (⌘/Ctrl+Option/Alt+D).** Enter the same value and press Return/Enter.

13. **Fill the selection with white for a light halo, or black for a dark one.** I wanted a white halo, so I pressed the D key to restore the default foreground and background colors. Then I pressed ⌘/Ctrl+Delete/Backspace to fill the selection with white.

14. **⌘/Ctrl+click on the Quick Mask Copy item in the Channels palette.** This regains your original arrow-shaped selection outline. (I explain channel masks in detail later in this chapter, but for now, just ⌘/Ctrl+click.)

15. **Press ⌘/Ctrl+Option/Alt+Delete/Backspace.** If you set the source state properly in Step 1, this shortcut reverts the portion of the image inside the arrows to its original appearance.

16. **Copy the selection to an independent layer.** Press ⌘/Ctrl+J or choose Layer ➪ New ➪ Layer via Copy.

17. **Fill the layered arrow with a color.** Change the foreground color to anything you like and press Shift+Option/Alt+Delete/Backspace to fill the arrow (and only the arrow).

18. **Choose Multiply from the blend mode pop-up menu in the upper-left corner of the Layers palette.** This burns the colored arrow into the image. Then set the Opacity value to the desired level. I pressed the 4 key to change the Opacity to 40 percent.

---

After that, I simply kept adding more and more arrows by repeating the process. I saved occasional snapshot states so I could create arrows on top of arrows. Most notably, I made a snapshot of the image before adding the last, big arrow that shoots up from the bottom. Then I filled the arrow with the snapshot to bring back bits and pieces of a few of the other arrows. (Had I not filled back in time via the History palette, the arrow fragments behind the big arrow would have disappeared.)

# Generating Masks Automatically

Another convenient method for creating a mask is the Color Range command under the Select menu. This command enables you to generate selections based on color ranges. You use the familiar eyedropper cursor to specify colors that should be considered for selection, and other colors you want to rule out. The Color Range command is a lot like the magic wand tool, except it enables you to select colors with more precision and to change the tolerance of the selection on the fly.

## Using the Color Range command

When you choose Select ➪ Color Range, Photoshop displays the Color Range dialog box shown in Figure 16-20. Like the magic wand combined with the Similar command, Color Range selects areas of related color all across the image, whether or not the colors are immediate neighbors. You click in the image window to select and deselect colors, as you do with the wand. But rather than adjusting a Tolerance value before you use the tool, you adjust a Fuzziness option any old time you like. Photoshop dynamically updates the selection according to the new value. Think of Color Range as the magic wand on steroids.

**Note**

So why didn't the folks at Adobe merely enhance the functionality of the magic wand rather than adding this strange command? The Color Range dialog box offers a preview of the mask—something a tool can't do—which is pretty essential for gauging the accuracy of your selection. And the magic wand is convenient, if nothing else. If Adobe were to combine the two functions, you would lose functionality.

Notice, when you move your cursor outside the Color Range dialog box, it changes to an eyedropper. Click with the eyedropper to specify the color on which you want to base the selection—I call this the base color—as if you were using the magic wand. Or you can click inside the preview area, labeled in Figure 16-20. In either case, the preview area updates to show the resulting mask.

You can also do the following:

✦ **Add colors to the selection:** To add base colors to the selection, select the add color tool inside the Color Range dialog box and click inside the image window or preview area. You can also access the tool while the standard eyedropper is selected by Shift+clicking (just as you Shift+click with the magic wand to add colors to a selection). You can even Shift+drag with the eyedropper to add multiple colors in a single pass, something you can't do with the wand tool.

✦ **Remove colors from the selection:** To remove base colors from the selection, click with the remove color tool or Option/Alt+click with the eyedropper. You can also drag or Option/Alt+drag to remove many colors at a time.

**Tip**

If adding or removing a color sends your selection careening in the wrong direction, press ⌘/Ctrl+Z. Yes, the Undo command works inside the Color Range dialog box as well as out of it.

Preview

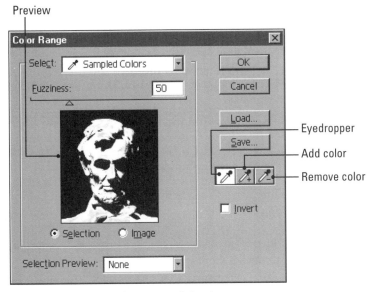

— Eyedropper

— Add color

— Remove color

**Figure 16-20:** The Color Range dialog box enables you to generate a mask by dragging with the eyedropper tool and adjusting the Fuzziness option.

✦ **Adjust the Fuzziness value:** This option resembles the Tolerance value in the Magic Wand Options palette because it determines the range of colors to be selected beyond the ones on which you click. Raise the Fuzziness value to expand the selected area; lower the value to contract the selection. A value of 0 selects the clicked color only. Unlike changes to Tolerance, however, changing the Fuzziness value adjusts the selection on the fly; no repeat clicking is required, as it is with the wand tool.

Fuzziness and Tolerance also differ in the kind of selection outlines they generate. Tolerance entirely selects all colors within the specified range and adds antialiased edges. If the selection was a mask, most of it would be white with a few gray pixels around the perimeter. By contrast, Fuzziness entirely selects only the colors on which you click and Shift+click, and partially selects the other colors in the range. That's why most of the mask is expressed in shades of gray. The light grays in the mask represent the most similar colors; the dark grays represent the least similar pixels that still fall within the Fuzziness range. The result is a tapering, gradual selection, much more likely to produce natural results.

✦ **Reverse the selection:** Select the Invert check box to reverse the selection, changing black to white and white to black. As when using the magic wand, it may be easier to isolate the area you don't want to select than the area you do want to select. When you encounter such a situation, select Invert.

✦ **Toggle the preview area:** Use the two radio buttons below the preview area to control the preview's contents. If you select the first option, Selection, you see the mask that will be generated when you press Return/Enter. If you select the Image option, the preview shows a reduced version of the image.

You can toggle between the two previews by pressing and holding the ⌘/Ctrl key. My advice is to leave the option set to Selection and press the ⌘/Ctrl key when you want to view the image.

✦ **Control the contents of the image window:** The Selection Preview pop-up menu at the bottom of the dialog box enables you to change what you see in the image window. Leave the option set to None—the default setting—to view the image normally in the image window. Select Grayscale to see the mask on its own. Select Quick Mask to see the mask and image together. Select Black Matte or White Matte to see what the selection would look like against a black or white background.

Although they may sound weird, the Matte options enable you to get an accurate picture of how the selected image will mesh with a different background. Figure 16-21 shows Lincoln's head at the top with the grayscale mask on the right. The mask calls for the shadows in Lincoln's face to be selected, with the highlights deselected. The two Matte views help you see how this particular selection looks against two backgrounds as different as night and day. Use the Fuzziness option in combination with Black Matte or White Matte to come up with a softness setting that will ensure a smooth transition.

✦ **Select by predefined colors:** Choose an option from the Select pop-up menu at the top of the dialog box to specify the means of selecting a base color. If you choose any option besides Sampled Colors, the Fuzziness option and eyedropper tools become dimmed to show they are no longer operable. Rather, Photoshop selects colors based on their relationship to a predefined color. For example, if you select Red, the program entirely selects red and partially selects other colors based on the amount of red they contain. Colors composed exclusively of blue and green are not selected.

The most useful option in this pop-up menu is Out of Gamut, which selects all the colors in an RGB or Lab image that fall outside the CMYK color space. You can use this option to select and modify the out-of-gamut colors before converting an image to CMYK.

✦ **Load and save settings:** Click on the Save button to save the current settings to disk. Click on Load to open a saved settings file.

When you define the mask to your satisfaction, click on the OK button or press Return/Enter to generate the selection outline. Although the Color Range command is more flexible than the magic wand, you can no more expect it to generate perfect selections than any other automated tool. After Photoshop draws the selection outline, therefore, you'll probably want to switch to the quick mask mode and paint and edit the mask to taste.

None                                    Grayscale

Black Matte                         White Matte

**Figure 16-21:** Selecting an option from the Selection Preview pop-up menu changes the way the Color Range command previews the selection in the image window.

If you learn nothing else about the Color Range dialog box, at least learn to use the Fuzziness option and the eyedropper tools. Basically there are two ways to approach these options. If you want to create a diffused selection with gradual edges, set the Fuzziness option to a high value — 60 or more — and click and Shift+click two or three times with the eyedropper. To create a more precise selection, enter a Fuzziness of 40 or lower and Shift+drag and Option/Alt+drag with the eyedropper until you get the exact colors you want.

Figure 16-22 shows some sample results. To create the left images, I clicked with the eyedropper tool once in Lincoln's face and set the Fuzziness to 160. To create the right images, I lowered the Fuzziness value to 20; then I clicked, Shift+clicked, and Option/Alt+clicked with the eyedropper to lift exactly the colors I wanted. The top examples show the effects of stroking the selections, first with 6-pixel white strokes, and then with 2-pixel black ones. In the two bottom examples, I copied the selections and pasted them against an identical background of — what else? — the Lincoln Memorial. In all four cases, the higher Fuzziness value yields more generalized and softer results; the lower value results in a more exact but harsher selection.

## A few helpful Color Range hints

Tip

You can limit the portion of an image that Select ➪ Color Range affects by selecting part of the image before choosing the command. When a selection exists, the Color Range command masks only those pixels that fall inside it. Even the preview area reflects your selection. Try it and see.

You can also add or subtract from an existing selection using the Color Range command. Press Shift when choosing Select ➪ Color Range to add to a selection. Press Option/Alt when choosing Color Range to subtract from a selection.

If you get hopelessly lost when creating your selection and you can't figure out what to select and what to deselect, click with the eyedropper tool to start over. This clears all the colors from the selection except the one you click. Or you can press Option/Alt to change the Cancel button to a Reset button. Option/Alt+click on the button to return the settings inside the dialog box to those in force when you first chose Select ➪ Color Range.

# Creating an Independent Mask Channel

The problem with masks generated via the quick mask mode and Color Range command is that they're here one day and gone the next. Photoshop is no more prepared to remember them than it is a lasso or wand selection.

Most of the time, that's okay. You'll only use the selection once, so there's no reason to sweat it. But what if the selection takes you a long time to create? What if, after a quarter hour of Shift+clicking here and Option/Alt+dragging there, adding a few strokes in the quick mask mode, and getting the selection outline exactly right, your boss calls a sudden meeting or the dinner bell rings? You can't just drop everything; you're in the middle of a selection. But nor can you convey your predicament to non-Photoshop users because they'll have no idea what you're talking about and no sympathy for your plight.

The simplest solution is to back up your selection, save your file, and move on to the next phase of your life. In fact, anytime that you spend 15 minutes or more on a selection, I'd save it. After all, you never know when all heck is going to break loose and 15 minutes is just too big a chunk of your life to repeat it. (The average person racks up a mere 2.5 million quarter hours, so use them wisely!) You wouldn't let 15 minutes of image-editing go by without saving, and the rules don't change just because you're working on a selection.

Fuzziness: 160    Fuzziness: 20

**Figure 16-22:** After creating two selections with the Color Range command — one with a high Fuzziness value (left) and one with a low one (right) — I alternately stroked the selections (top) and pasted them against a different background (bottom).

## Saving a selection outline to a mask channel

The following steps describe how to back up a selection to an independent mask channel, which is any channel above and beyond those required to represent a grayscale or color image. Mask channels are saved along with the image itself, making it a safe and sturdy solution.

## Steps: Transferring a Selection to an Independent Channel

1. **Convert the selection to a mask channel.** One way to do this is to choose Select ➪ Save Selection (or Control/right-click in the image window and choose Save Selection from the pop-up menu), which saves the selection as a mask. The dialog box shown in Figure 16-23 appears, asking you where you want to put the mask. In most cases, you'll want to save the mask to a separate channel inside the current image. To do so, make sure the name of the current image appears in the Document pop-up menu. Then select New from the Channel pop-up menu, enter any name for the channel that you like, and press Return/Enter.

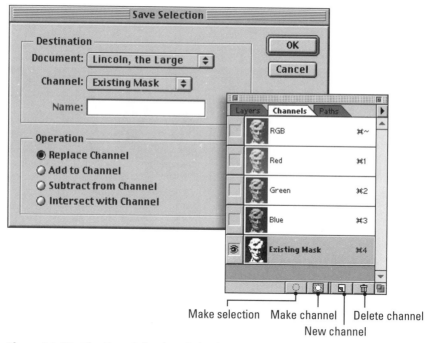

Make selection    Make channel    Delete channel
New channel

**Figure 16-23:** The Save Selection dialog box enables you to convert your selection outline to a mask and save it to a new or existing channel.

If you have an old channel you want to replace, select the channel's name from the Channel pop-up menu. The radio buttons at the bottom of the dialog box become available, permitting you to add the mask to the channel, subtract it, or intersect it. These radio buttons work like the equivalent options that appear when you make a path into a selection outline (as discussed in the previous chapter) but, instead, they blend the masks together. The result is the same as if you were adding, subtracting, or intersecting selection outlines, except it's expressed as a mask.

Or you can save the mask to a new multichannel document all its own. To do this, choose New from the Document pop-up menu and press Return/Enter.

Man, what a lot of options! If you only want to save the selection to a new channel and be done with it, you needn't bother with the Save Selection command or dialog box. Just click on the make channel icon at the bottom of the Channels palette (labeled in Figure 16-23). Photoshop automatically creates a new channel, converts the selection to a mask, and places the mask in the channel.

Regardless of which of these many methods you choose, your selection outline remains intact.

2. **View the mask in the Channels palette.** To do so, click on the appropriate channel name in the Channels palette — automatically named *Alpha 1* unless you assigned a name of your own. In Figure 16-23, I replaced the contents of a channel called Existing Mask, so this is where my mask now resides.

This step isn't the least bit mandatory. It just lets you see your mask and generally familiarize yourself with how masks look. Remember, white represents selection, black is deselected, and gray is partial selection.

If you didn't name your mask in Step 1 and you want to name it now, double-click on the Alpha 1 item in the Channels palette and enter a name in the active option box.

3. **Return to the standard image-editing mode by clicking on the first channel name in the Channels palette.** Better yet, press ⌘/Ctrl+1 if you're editing a grayscale image or ⌘/Ctrl+tilde (~) if the image is in color.

4. **Save the image to disk to store the selection permanently as part of the file.** A handful of formats — FlashPix, PICT, Pixar, PNG, TIFF, Targa, and native Photoshop — accommodate RGB images with an extra mask channel. But only the TIFF and native .psd format can handle more than four channels, both saving up to 24 channels in all. I generally use the TIFF format with LZW compression when saving images with masks — unless the image contains layers, in which case you have no choice but to save in the Photoshop format.

Both the native Photoshop format and TIFF are capable of compressing the sizes of masks so that they take up substantially less room on disk. The Photoshop format does this automatically. When saving a TIFF image, be sure to turn on the LZW Compression check box. In both cases, this run-line compression is entirely safe. It does not change a single pixel in the image; it merely writes the code in a more efficient manner.

Photoshop also permits you to save a mask with a GIF file. But if you do, all pixels in the masked area are saved as gray, indicating transparency. This means that all detail in the masked areas goes away, and you cannot access the mask independently of the image.

If you performed the steps in the "Creating gradient arrows" section earlier in this chapter, you know that you can also save a quick mask to its own channel for later use. But in case you missed those steps, or you're saving them for a special occasion, here's how it works. When you enter the quick mask mode, the Channels palette displays an item called *Quick Mask*. The italic letters show the channel is temporary and will not be saved with the image. (To clone it to a permanent channel, drag the *Quick Mask* item onto the page icon at the bottom of the Channels palette). Now save the image to the TIFF or Photoshop format and you're backed up.

## Converting a mask to a selection

To retrieve your selection later, choose Select ➪ Load Selection. A dialog box nearly identical to the one shown in Figure 16-23 appears except for the addition of an Invert check box. Select the document and channel that contain the mask you want to use. You can add it to a current selection, subtract it, or intersect it. Select the Invert option if you want to reverse the selected and deselected portions of the mask.

Want to avoid the Load Selection command? ⌘/Ctrl+click on the channel name in the Channels palette that contains the mask you want to use. For example, if I ⌘/Ctrl+clicked on the Existing Mask item in Figure 16-23, Photoshop would load the equivalent selection outline into the image window.

But wait, there's more:

✦ You can press ⌘/Ctrl+Option/Alt plus the channel number to convert the channel to a selection. For example, ⌘/Ctrl+Option/Alt+4 would convert the Existing Mask channel shown in the figure.

✦ You can also select the channel and click on the far-left mask selection icon at the bottom of the Channels palette. But for my money, this takes too much effort.

✦ To add a mask to the current selection outline, ⌘/Ctrl+Shift+click on the channel name in the Channels palette.

✦ ⌘/Ctrl+Option/Alt+click on a channel name to subtract the mask from the selection.

✦ And ⌘/Ctrl+Shift+Option/Alt+click to find the intersection.

You can convert color channels to selections as well as mask channels. For example, if you want to select the black pixels in a piece of scanned line art in grayscale mode, ⌘/Ctrl+click on the first item in the Channels palette. This selects the white pixels; press ⌘/Ctrl+Shift+I (or choose Select ⇨ Inverse) to reverse the selection to the black pixels.

## Viewing mask and image

Photoshop lets you view any mask channel along with an image, just as you can view mask and image together in the quick mask mode. To do so, click in the first column of the Channels palette to toggle the display of the eyeball icon. An eyeball in front of a channel name indicates you can see that channel. If you are currently viewing the image, for example, click in front of the mask channel name to view the mask as a translucent color coating, again as in the quick mask mode. Or, if the contents of the mask channel appear by themselves on screen, click in front of the image name to display it as well.

When the mask is active, you can likewise toggle the display of the image by pressing the tilde (~) key. Few folks know about this shortcut, but it's a good one to assign to memory. It works whether the Channels palette is open or not, and it permits you to focus on the mask without moving your mouse all over the screen.

Using a mask channel is different from using the quick mask mode in that you can edit either the image or the mask channel when viewing the two together. You can even edit two or more masks at once. To decide which channel you want to edit, click on the channel name in the palette. To edit two channels at once, click on one and Shift+click on another. All active channel names appear highlighted.

You can change the color and opacity of each mask independently of other mask channels and the quick mask mode. Double-click on the mask channel name or choose the Channel Options command from the Channels palette menu. (This command is dimmed when editing a standard color channel, such as Red, Green, Blue, Cyan, Magenta, Yellow, or Black.) A dialog box similar to the one shown back in Figure 16-11 appears, but this one contains a Name option box so you can change the name of the mask channel. You can then edit the color overlay as described in the "Changing the red coating" section earlier in this chapter.

If you ever need to edit a selection outline inside the mask channel using paint and edit tools, click on the quick mask mode icon in the toolbox. It may sound a little incestuous — like a play within a play, perhaps — but you can access the quick mask mode even when working within a mask channel. Make sure the mask channel color is different from the quick mask color so you can tell what's happening.

# Building a Mask from an Image

So far, everything I've discussed in this chapter has been pretty straightforward. Now it's time to see how the professionals do things. This final section in the chapter explains every step required to create a mask for a complex image — updated especially for this edition of the book. Here's how to select the image you never thought you could select, complete with wispy little details like hair.

Take a gander at Figure 16-24 and you'll see what I mean. I chose this subject not for her good looks or her generous supply of freckles, but for that hair. I mean, look at all that hair. Have you ever seen such a frightening image-editing subject in your life? Not only is this particular girl blessed with roughly 15 googol strands of hair, but every one of them is leaping out of her head in a different direction and at a different level of focus. Can you imagine selecting any one of them with the magnetic lasso or magic wand? No way. As demonstrated by the second example of Figure 16-24, these tools lack sufficient accuracy to do any good. Furthermore, you'd be fit for an asylum by the time you finished selecting the hairs with the pen tools, and the edges aren't definite enough for Select ➪ Color Range to latch onto.

**Figure 16-24:** Have you ever wanted to select wispy details, like the hair shown on left? You certainly aren't going to make it with the magnetic lasso (right) or other selection tools. But with masks, it's a piece of cake.

So what's the solution? Manual masking. Although masking styles vary as widely as artistic style, a few tried-and-true formulas work for everyone. First, you peruse the channels in an image to find the channel that will lend itself best to a mask. You're looking for high degrees of contrast, especially around the edges. Next, you copy the channel and boost the level of contrast using Image ➪ Adjust ➪ Levels. (Some folks prefer Image ➪ Adjust ➪ Curves, but Levels is more straightforward.) Then you paint inside the lines until you get the mask the way you want it.

The only way to get a feel for masking is to try it out for yourself. The following steps explain exactly how I masked this girl and pasted her against a different background. The final result is so realistic, you'd think she was born there.

## Steps: Selecting a Monstrously Complicated Image Using a Mask

1. **Browse the color channels.** Press ⌘/Ctrl+1 to see the red channel, ⌘/Ctrl+2 for green, and ⌘/Ctrl+3 for blue. (This assumes you're working inside an RGB image. You can also peruse CMYK and Lab images. If you're editing a grayscale image, you have only one channel from which to choose—Black.)

   Figure 16-25 shows the three channels in my RGB image. Of the three, the red channel offers the most contrast between the hair, which appears very light, and the background, which appears quite dark.

**Figure 16-25:** Of the three color channels, the red channel offers the best contrast between hair and background.

*(continued)*

2. **Copy the channel.** Drag the channel onto the little page icon at the bottom of the Channels palette. (I naturally copy the red channel.) Now you can work on the channel to your heart's content without harming the image itself.

3. **Choose Filter ⇨ Other ⇨ High Pass.** The next thing you want to do is to force Photoshop to bring out the edges in the image so you don't have to hunt for them manually. And when you think edges, you should think filters. All of Photoshop's edge-detection prowess is packed into the Filter menu. Several edge-detection filters are available to you — Unsharp Mask, Find Edges, and many others that I discuss in Chapter 23. But the best filter for finding edges inside a mask is Filter ⇨ Other ⇨ High Pass.

   High Pass selectively turns an image gray. High Pass may sound strange, but it's quite useful. The filter turns the non-edges completely gray while leaving the edges mostly intact, thus dividing edges and non-edges into different brightness camps, based on the Radius value in the High Pass dialog box. Unlike in most filters, a low Radius value produces a more pronounced effect than a high one, in effect locating more edges.

   Figure 16-26 shows the original red channel on left with the result of the High Pass filter on right. I used a Radius of 10, which is a nice, moderate value. The lower you go, the more edges you find and the more work you make for yourself. A Radius of 3 is accurate, but it'll take you an hour to fill in the mask. Granted, 10 is less accurate, but if you value your time, it's more sensible.

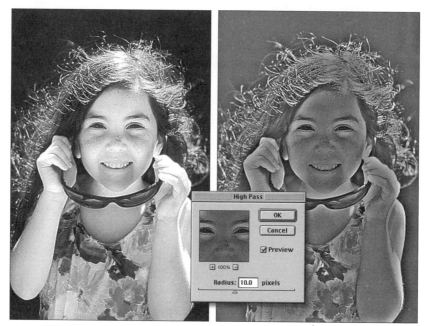

**Figure 16-26:** After copying the red channel (left), I apply the High Pass filter with a Radius value of 10 to highlight the edges in the image (right).

4. **Choose Image ⇨ Adjust ⇨ Levels (⌘/Ctrl+L).** After adding all that gray to the image, follow it up by increasing the contrast. And the best command for enhancing contrast is Levels. Although I discuss this command in-depth in Chapter 30, here's the short version: Inside the Levels dialog box, raise the first Input Levels value to make the dark colors darker, and lower the third Input Levels value to make the light colors lighter. (For now you can ignore the middle value.)

Figure 16-27 shows the result of raising the first Input Levels value to 110 and lowering the third value to 155. As you can see in the left-hand image, this gives me some excellent contrast between the white hairs and black background.

**Figure 16-27:** Here are the results of applying the Levels command to the mask after the High Pass step (left) and without High Pass (right). As you can see, High Pass has a pronounced effect on the edge detail.

To demonstrate the importance of the High Pass command in these steps, I've shown what would happen if I had skipped Step 3 in the right-hand image in Figure 16-27. Here I've applied the same Levels values as the left image, and yet the image is washed out and quite lacking in edges. Look at that wimpy hair. It simply is unacceptable.

5. **Use the lasso tool to remove the big stuff you don't need.** By way of High Pass and Levels, Photoshop has presented you with a complex coloring book. From here on, it's a matter of coloring inside the lines. To simplify things, get rid of the stuff you know you don't need. All you care

*(continued)*

about is the area where the girl meets her background — mostly hair and arms. Everything else goes to white or black.

For example, in Figure 16-28, I selected a general area inside the girl by Option/Alt+clicking with the lasso tool. Then I filled it with white by pressing ⌘/Ctrl+Delete/Backspace. I also selected around the outside of the hair and filled it with black. At all times, I was careful to stay about 10 to 20 pixels away from the hair and other edges; these I need to brush in carefully with the eraser. (Be sure to press ⌘/Ctrl+D to eliminate the selection before continuing to the next step.)

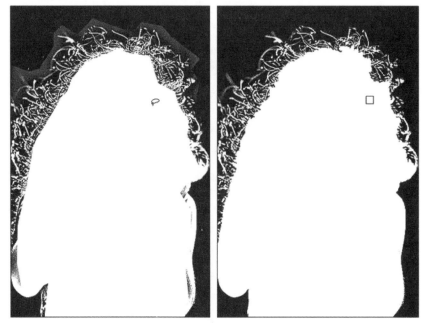

**Figure 16-28:** To tidy things up a bit, I selected the general areas inside and outside the girl with the lasso tool and filled them with white or black (left). Then I painted inside the lines with the block eraser (right).

6. **Erase inside the lines with the block eraser.** This is the most time-consuming part. You now have to paint inside the lines to make the edge pixels white (selected) or black (not). I like to use the block eraser because it's a hard-edged block. See, Photoshop has already presented me with these lovely and accurate edges. I don't want to gum things up by introducing new edges with a soft paintbrush or airbrush. The block eraser is hard, you can easily see its exact boundaries, and it automatically adjusts as you zoom in and out — affecting fewer pixels at higher levels of magnification, which is what you need. When working in a mask, the eraser always paints in the background color. So use the X key to toggle the background color between white and black.

The second example in Figure 16-28 shows the fruits of my erasing. As you can see, I make a few judgment calls and decide — sometimes arbitrarily —

where the hair gets so thick that background imagery won't show through. You may even disagree with some of my eraser strokes. But you know what? It doesn't matter. Despite whatever flaws I may have introduced, my mask is more than accurate enough to select the girl and her unruly hair, as I'll soon demonstrate.

7. **Switch to the color composite view.** Press ⌘/Ctrl+tilde (~). Or if you're working in a grayscale image, press ⌘/Ctrl+1. By the way, now is a good time to save the image if you haven't already done so.

8. **⌘/Ctrl+click on the mask channel to convert it to a selection.** This mask is ready to go prime time.

9. **⌘/Ctrl+drag the selection and drop it into a different image.** Figure 16-29 shows the result of dropping the girl into a background of rolling California hills. Thanks to my mask, she looks as natural in her new environment as she did in her previous one. In fact, an uninitiated viewer might have difficulty believing this isn't how she was originally photographed. But if you take a peek at Figure 16-24, you can confirm that Figure 16-29 is indeed an artificial composite. I lost a few strands of hair in the transition, but she can afford it.

**Figure 16-29:** Thanks to masking, our girl has found a new life in southern California. Now she's ready to finally put on those sunglasses.

The grayscale Figure 16-29 looks great but, in all honesty, your compositions may not fare quite so well in color, as illustrated by the first girl in Color Plate 16-3. Her hair is fringed with blue, an unavoidable holdover from her original blue background. The solution is to brush in the color from her new background. Using the paintbrush tool set to the Color brush mode, you can Option/Alt+click in the Background layer to lift colors from the new background and then paint them into the hair. I also took the liberty of erasing a few of the more disorderly hairs, especially the dark ones above her head. (I used a soft paintbrush-style eraser, incidentally, not the block.) After a minute or two of painting and erasing, I arrived at the second girl in the color plate. Now if that isn't compositing perfection, I don't know what is.

✦　　✦　　✦

# Layers and Transformations

## Layers, Layers Everywhere

Layers are at once Photoshop's most overrated and most underused feature. On one hand — and let's be perfectly clear about this — they add absolutely no functionality to Photoshop. Anything you can accomplish with layers, you can also accomplish without layers. Photoshop artists have been devising fantastic compositions, applying all varieties of selections, and masking and blending images since the program was first released. Very wisely, in my opinion, Adobe has yet to make any feature exclusive to layers.

What layers add is flexibility. Because each layer in a composition is altogether independent of other layers, you can change your mind on a moment's notice. Consider Figure 17-1. Here I've compiled the ingredients for a very bad day at the doctor's office. (By golly, this may explain the reason for my chronic heartburn.) Each of the bits and pieces of hardware are located on a separate layer, all of which float above the surface of the background X-ray. Even though the pixels from the hardware blend with the X-ray and with each other, I can easily reposition and modify them as the mood strikes me. Photoshop automatically reblends the pixels on the fly.

To show what I mean, I've repositioned and transformed every single layer in the second example in Figure 17-1. The MO cartridge is smaller and rotated, the mess of cords hangs up instead of down, and the lock and key are just plain skewed. I can also exchange the order of the layers, merge layers together, and adjust their translucency until I keel over from sheer alternative overload.

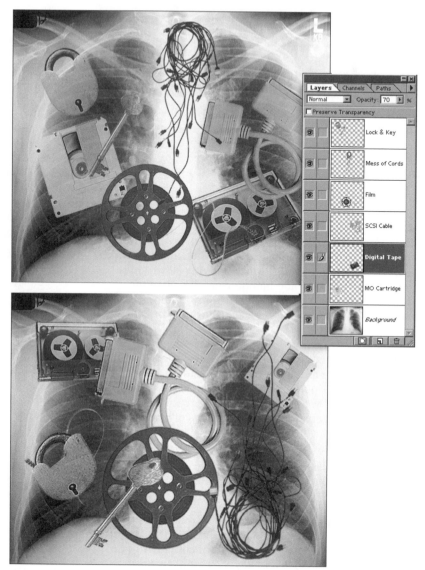

**Figure 17-1:** So that's what I did with my SCSI cable! Thanks to the flexibility of layers, you can arrange a bunch of images one way one moment (top) and quite differently the next (bottom). Layers enable you to modify a composition without sacrificing quality.

Layers are also uniquely versatile. You can apply three levels of masking to layers — all of which can be in force simultaneously, if you like. You can move and transform multiple layers at a time. You can create a special kind of layer that adjusts the colors in the layers below it (as I explain in Chapter 30), and mix layers together using predefined mathematical calculations (Chapter 31). Again, you can do it all without layers if you want, but with layers, the world becomes an infinitely editable place.

Thanks to the further demise of floating selections, Photoshop 5 forces you to use layers in many situations. Whether you like this iron-hand approach or not—I happen to think Adobe went a tad overboard—you can't argue with the logic. We should all use layers more often. Layers make it harder to make mistakes, they make it easier to make changes, and they expand your range of options. If a layer might help, there's very little reason not to add one. You may not appreciate having to use layers, but at least they're for your own good.

# Sending a Selection to a Layer

To its credit, Photoshop lets you establish a new layer in roughly a billion different ways. If you want to add a selected portion of one image to another image, the easiest method is to ⌘/Ctrl+drag the selection and drop it into its new home, as demonstrated in Figure 17-2. Photoshop makes you a new layer, lickety-split.

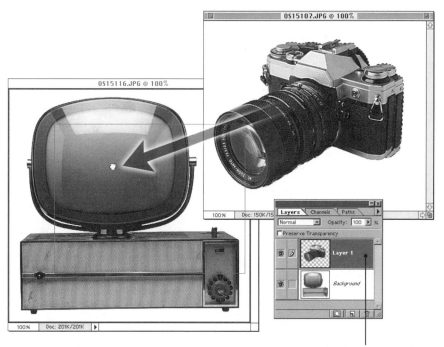

Dropped selection becomes new layer

**Figure 17-2:** ⌘/Ctrl+drag a selection and drop it into a different image window to introduce the selection as a new layer. As you can see in the Layers palette, the camera becomes a new layer in front of the television.

**Caution**

Be sure to ⌘/Ctrl+drag or use the move tool. If you merely drag the selection with the marquee, lasso, or wand, you drop an empty selection outline into the new image window.

When you drop the selection, your selection outline disappears. Not to worry, though. Now that the image resides on an independent layer, the selection outline is no longer needed. You can move the layer using the move tool — as you would move a selection. You can even paint inside what was once the selection by selecting the Preserve Transparency check box in the Layers palette. I explain both the move tool and Preserve Transparency in greater detail throughout this chapter.

If you want to clone a selection to a new layer inside the same image window — useful when performing complex filter routines and color corrections — choose Layer ⇨ New ⇨ Layer Via Copy. Or press ⌘/Ctrl+J, as in Jump.

## Other ways to make a layer

Those are only two of many different ways to create a new layer in Photoshop. Here are a few others:

✦ Copy a selection (⌘/Ctrl+C) and paste it into another image (⌘/Ctrl+V). Photoshop pastes the selection as a new layer.

✦ If you want to relegate a selection exclusively to a new layer, choose Layer ⇨ New ⇨ Layer Via Cut or press ⌘/Ctrl+Shift+J. Rather than cloning the selection, Layer Via Cut removes the selection from the background image and places it on its own layer.

✦ To convert a floating selection — one which you've moved or cloned — to a new layer, press ⌘/Ctrl+Shift+J. The Shift key is very important. If you press ⌘/Ctrl+J without Shift, Photoshop clones the selection and leaves an imprint of the image on the layer below.

✦ To create an empty layer — as when you want to paint a few brushstrokes without harming the original image — choose Layer ⇨ New ⇨ Layer or press ⌘Ctrl+Shift+N. Or click on the new layer icon at the bottom of the Layers palette (labeled in Figure 17-3).

Incidentally, you can also create a new layer by choosing New Layer from the Layers palette menu. But as you can see in the wonderfully easy-to-follow Figure 17-3 — can you imagine a more illuminating piece of info art? — nearly all the palette commands are duplicated in the Layer menu. The only unique palette command is Palette Options (circled in the figure), which lets you change the size of the thumbnails in front of the layer names.

**Tip**

When you choose the Layer Via Copy or Layer Via Cut command or click on the new layer icon, Photoshop automatically names the new layer for you. Unfortunately, the automatic names — Layer 1, Layer 2, and so on — are fairly meaningless and don't help to convey the contents of the layer. (Dammit,

Photoshop, don't you know a camera when you see one?) If you want to specify your own name, add the Option/Alt key. Press ⌘/Ctrl+Option/Alt+J to clone the selection to a layer, press ⌘/Ctrl+Shift+Option/Alt+J to cut the selection, or Option/Alt+click on the new layer icon to create a blank layer. In any case, you'll see the dialog box shown in Figure 17-4. Enter a name for the layer and press Return/Enter. (You can ignore the other options in this dialog box for now.)

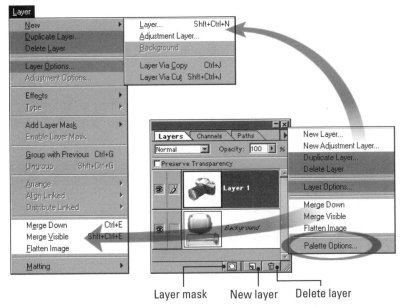

Layer mask     New layer     Delete layer

**Figure 17-3:** All but one of the commands in the Layers palette menu are duplicated in the Layer menu.

When creating a new layer from the keyboard, press ⌘/Ctrl+Shift+Option/Alt+N to bypass the dialog box. So Option/Alt works both ways, forcing the dialog box some times and suppressing it others. The only time it produces no effect is when pasting or dropping an image. Too bad—I for one would get a lot of use out of it.

Incidentally, you can also create a new layer by choosing New Layer from the Layers palette menu. But as you can see in the wonderfully easy-to-follow Figure 17-3—can you imagine a more illuminating piece of info art?—nearly all the palette commands are duplicated in the Layer menu. The only unique palette command is Palette Options (circled in the figure), which lets you change the size of the thumbnails in front of the layer names.

**Tip**

To rename a layer, double-click on its name in the Layers palette. (You can also choose Layer ➪ Layer Options, but what sane human being would go to all that effort?) Then enter a new name and whack that Return/Enter key.

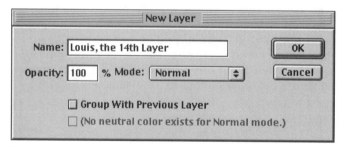

**Figure 17-4:** Press Option/Alt to force the display of the New Layer dialog box, which lets you name the new layer.

## Duplicating a layer

To clone the active layer, you can choose Layer ⇨ Duplicate Layer. But that's the sucker's way. The more convenient way is to drag the layer name you want to clone onto the new layer icon at the bottom of the Layers palette.

To specify a name for the cloned layer or to copy the layer into another image, Option/Alt+drag the layer onto the new layer icon. Always the thoughtful program, Photoshop displays the dialog box shown in Figure 17-5. You can name the cloned layer by entering something into the As option box. To jettison the layer to some other open image, choose the image name from the Document pop-up menu. Or choose New and enter the name for an entirely different image in the Name option box, as the figure shows.

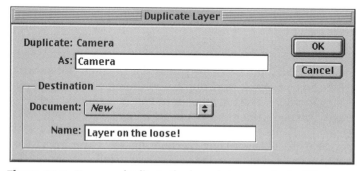

**Figure 17-5:** You can duplicate the layer into an entirely different image by Option/Alt+dragging the layer onto the new layer icon in the Layers palette.

In Photoshop 5, you can also clone a layer simply by ⌘/Ctrl+Option/Alt+dragging it. This way, you clone the layer and reposition it in one operation. Just be sure no portion of the image is selected; otherwise, you create a floating selection.

# Working with Layers

Regardless of how you create a new layer, Photoshop lists the layer along with a little thumbnail of its contents in the Layers palette. The new layer's name appears highlighted to show it's active. The little paintbrush icon in front of the layer name also indicates an active layer.

To the left of the paintbrush icon is a column of eyeballs, that invite you to hide and display layers temporarily. Click on an eyeball to hide the layer. Click where the eyeball previously was to bring it back and redisplay the layer. Whether hidden or displayed, all layers remain intact and ready for action.

To view a single layer by itself, Option/Alt+click on the eyeball icon before the layer name to hide all other layers. Option/Alt+click in front of the layer again to bring all the layers back into view.

## Switching between layers

You can select a different layer by clicking on its name in the Layers palette. This layer becomes active, enabling you to edit it. Only one layer may be active at a time in Photoshop—you can't Shift+click to select and edit multiple layers, I'm sorry to say.

If your image contains several layers—like the one back in Figure 17-1—it might prove inconvenient, or even confusing, to switch from one layer to another in the Layers palette. Luckily, Photoshop offers a better way. With any tool, containing the element. For example, ⌘/Ctrl+Option/Alt+Control/right-clicking on the SCSI cable in Figure 17-1 would take me to the SCSI Cable layer.

Why ⌘/Ctrl+Option/Alt+Control/right-clicking? Here's how it breaks down:

✦ ⌘/Ctrl gets you the move tool. (If the move tool is already selected, you don't have to press ⌘/Ctrl; Option/Alt+Control/right-clicking works just fine.)

✦ Control/right-clicking alone brings up a context-sensitive pop-up menu. When you right-click with the move tool—or ⌘/Ctrl+Control/right-click with any other tool—Photoshop displays a pop-up menu that lists the layer the image is on and any other layers in the image, as in Figure 17-6. (If a layer is completely transparent at the spot where you Control/right-click, that layer name doesn't appear in the pop-up menu.) Select the desired layer to go there.

✦ The Option/Alt key bypasses the pop-up menu and goes straight to the clicked layer.

Add them all together, and you get ⌘/Ctrl+Option/Alt+Control/right-click. It's a lot to remember, but believe me, it's a great trick once you get the hang of it.

If you'd prefer Photoshop *always* go directly to the layer on which you click and avoid all these messy keyboard tricks, then press the V key to select the move tool and press Return/Enter. Inside the Move Options dialog box, you'll find the Auto Select Layer check box. Turn it on. Now whenever you click on a layer with the move tool — or ⌘/Ctrl+click with some other tool — Photoshop goes right to that layer.

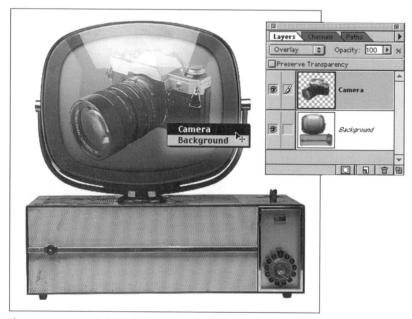

**Figure 17-6:** ⌘/Ctrl+Option/Alt+Control/right-click on an image to view a pop-up menu. The menu lists the location of the image on which you've clicked and the background layer.

## Switching layers from the keyboard

You can also ascend and descend the layer stack from the keyboard:

✦ **Option/Alt+]:** Press Option/Alt+right bracket to go to the next layer up in the stack. If you're already at the top layer, Photoshop takes you back around to the lowest one.

✦ **Option/Alt+[:** Press Option/Alt+left bracket to go down a layer. If the background layer is active, Option/Alt+[ takes you to the top layer.

✦ **Shift+Option/Alt+]:** This takes you to the top layer in the image.

✦ **Shift+Option/Alt+[:** This activates the background layer (or the lowest layer if no background exists).

## Understanding transparency

Although the selection outline disappears when you convert a selection to a layer, no information is lost. Photoshop retains every little nuance of the original selection outline—whether it's a jagged border, a little bit of anti-aliasing, or a feathered edge. Anything that wasn't selected is now transparent. The data that defines the opacity and transparency of a layer is called the *transparency mask*.

To see this transparency in action, click on the eyeball icon in front of the Background item in the Layers palette. This hides the background layer and enables you to view the new layer by itself. In Figure 17-7, I hid the background TV from Figure 17-6 to view the camera on its own. The transparent areas are covered in a checkerboard pattern. Opaque areas look like the standard image, and translucent areas—where they exist—appear as a mix of image and checkerboard.

**Figure 17-7:** When you hide the background layer, you see a checkerboard pattern that represents the transparent portions of the layer.

**Tip**    If the checkerboard pattern is hard to distinguish from the image, you can change the appearance of the pattern. Press ⌘/Ctrl+K and then ⌘/Ctrl+4 to go to the Transparency & Gamut panel of the Preferences dialog box. Then edit away.

If you apply an effect to the layer while no portion of the layer is selected, Photoshop changes the opaque and translucent portions of the image, but leaves the transparent region intact. For example, if you press ⌘/Ctrl+I (or choose Image ➪ Adjust ➪ Invert), Photoshop inverts the image but doesn't change a single pixel in the checkerboard area. If you click in the left column in front of the Background item to bring back the eyeball icon, you may notice a slight halo around the inverted image, but the edge pixels blend with the background image as well as they ever did. In fact, it's exactly as if you applied the effect to a selection, as demonstrated in Figure 17-8. The only difference is this selection is altogether independent of its background. You can do anything you want to it without running the risk of harming the underlying background.

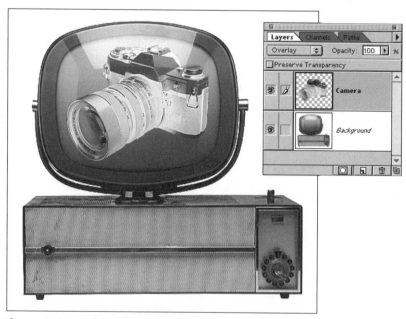

**Figure 17-8:** Applying the Invert command to the camera layer inverts only the camera without affecting any of the transparent pixels. The TV remains every bit as visible as ever.

Only a few operations affect the transparent areas of a layer, and most of these are limited to tools. You can paint on transparent pixels to make them opaque. You can clone with the rubber stamp, or smear pixels with the edit tools. But you can send pixels back to transparency using the eraser, as well. All these operations change both the contents of the layer and the composition of the transparency mask.

**Tip**

You can also fill all pixels by pressing Option/Alt+Delete/Backspace for the foreground color and ⌘/Ctrl+Delete/Backspace for the background color. To fill the pixels in a layer without altering the transparency mask, toss in the Shift key. Shift+Option/Alt+Delete/Backspace fills the opaque pixels with the foreground color, while ⌘/Ctrl+Shift+Delete/Backspace fills them with the background color. In both cases, the transparent pixels remain every bit as transparent as they ever were.

When a portion of the layer is selected, pressing plain old Delete/Backspace eliminates the selected pixels and makes them transparent, revealing the layers below.

**Note**

Transparent pixels take up next to no space in memory, but opaque and translucent pixels do. Thus, a layer containing 25 percent as many pixels as the background layer takes up roughly 25 percent as much space. I wouldn't let this influence how you work in Photoshop, but it is something to keep in mind.

## Modifying the background layer

At the bottom of the layer stack is the *background layer*, the fully opaque layer that represents the base image. The background image is as low as you go. Nothing can be slipped under the background layer and pixels in the background layer cannot be made transparent, unless you first convert the background to a "normal" layer.

To make the conversion, double-click on the background item in the Layers palette. Then enter a name for the new layer — Photoshop suggests Layer 0 — and press Return/Enter. You can now change the order of the layer or erase down to transparency.

In Figure 17-9, I converted the background television to a layer. This particular image (from the PhotoDisc Object Series) included a predrawn path that encircled the TV. I ⌘/Ctrl+clicked on the path to convert it to a selection outline, then I pressed ⌘/Ctrl+Shift+I to reverse the selection. Finally, I pressed the Delete/Backspace key to erase the pixels outside the TV, as the figure demonstrates.

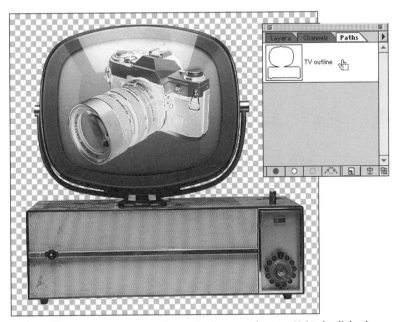

**Figure 17-9:** After converting the TV image to a layer, I ⌘/Ctrl+clicked on the path, inversed the selection, and pressed the Delete/Backspace key to reveal the transparent void below.

From this point, I can reorder the camera and television layers or add layers in back of the TV. I can also introduce a new background layer. (A program like QuarkXPress or PageMaker doesn't recognize Photoshop's transparency, so there's no point in leaving the background transparent. As I mentioned in Chapter 15, if you want to export transparency, you must use a clipping path.)

**Photoshop 5.0** To add a new background layer, choose Layer ➪ New ➪ Background. This is also a step in converting the lowest layer in the stack to the background. Choose Layer ➪ New ➪ Background, then press Option/Alt+] to select the next layer up, and press ⌘/Ctrl+E to merge it with the background.

In Figure 17-10, I added a new background layer. I used the Add Noise and Emboss filters to create a paper texture pattern (as I explained back in Chapter 10). Then I used Layer ➪ Effects ➪ Drop Shadow to add a drop shadow that matched the contours of the TV. (To learn all about the Layer ➪ Effects commands, read the "Automatic Shadows, Glows, and Bevels" section later in this chapter.)

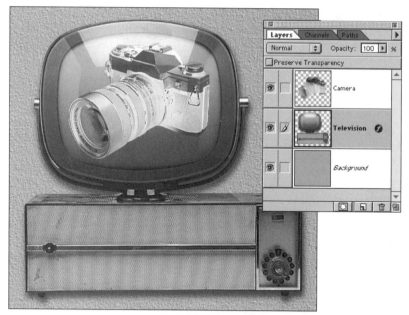

**Figure 17-10:** I added a background layer behind the television and applied a paper texture and drop shadow to give my composition a little false depth.

## Reordering layers

What good would layers be if you couldn't periodically change what's on the top and what's on the bottom? There are two ways to reorder layers. First, you can drag a layer name up or down in the scrolling list to move it forward or backward in layering order. The only trick is to make sure that the black bar appears at the point where you want to move the layer before you release the mouse button, as illustrated in Figure 17-11.

The second way to reorder layers is to choose a command from the Layer ⇨ Arrange submenu. For example, choose Layer ⇨ Arrange ⇨ Bring Forward to move the active layer up one level; choose Layer ⇨ Arrange ⇨ Send to Back to move the layer to above the background layer.

You can move faster if you remember the following keyboard shortcuts:

✦ **⌘/Ctrl+Shift+]**: Press ⌘/Ctrl+right bracket to move the active layer to the top of the stack.

✦ **⌘/Ctrl+Shift+[**: This shortcut moves the active layer to the bottom of the stack, just above the background layer.

✦ **⌘/Ctrl+]**: This nudges the layer up one level.

✦ **Ctrl+[**: This nudges the layer down.

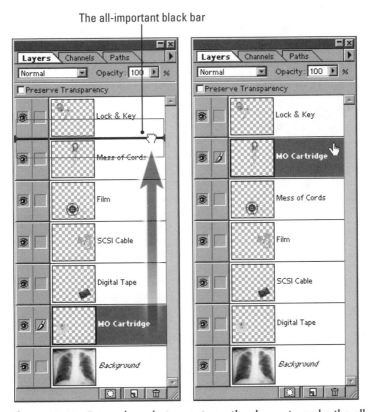

**Figure 17-11:** Drag a layer between two other layers to make the all-important black bar appear (left). Then release to change the hierarchy of the layer (right).

**Note** You can neither reorder the background layer nor move any other layer below the background until you first convert the background to a normal layer, as explained in the previous section.

## Automated matting techniques

When you convert an anti-aliased selection to a layer, you sometimes take with you a few pixels from the selection's previous background. These *fringe pixels* can result in an unrealistic outline around your layer that cries out, "This image was edited by a hack." For example, Figure 17-12 shows a magnified detail from one of my original attempts to add a drop shadow to the TV. Although the selection outline was accurate, I managed to retain a few white pixels around the edges, as you can see around the outline of the picture tube and arm that holds the tube.

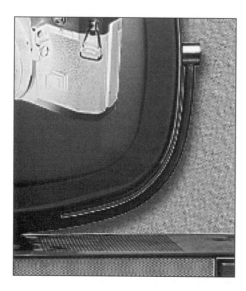

**Figure 17-12:** This enlarged detail of the TV layer against the textured background shows the fringe pixels left over from the TV's original white background.

You can instruct Photoshop to replace the fringe pixels with colors from neighboring pixels by choosing Layer ➪ Matting ➪ Defringe. Enter the thickness of the perceived fringe in the Width option box to tell Photoshop which pixels you want to replace. To create the image shown in Figure 17-13, I entered a Width value of 1. But even at this low value, the effect is pretty significant, leaving gummy edges in its wake.

Photoshop provides two additional commands under the Layer ➪ Matting submenu: Remove Black Matte and Remove White Matte. Frankly, it's unlikely you'll have much call to use them, but here's the scoop:

✦ **Remove Black Matte**: This command removes the residue around the perimeter of a layer that was lifted from a black background.

✦ **Remove White Matte**: This command removes a white ring around a layer.

**Figure 17-13:** Here I used the Defringe command set to a Width value of 1 to replace the pixels around the perimeter of the layer with colors borrowed from neighboring pixels.

Adobe tells me these commands were designed specifically for compositing a scene rendered in a 3-D drawing program against a black or white background. But for other purposes, they almost never work. For example, my television is a prime candidate for Remove White Matte — it originated from a white background — and yet it leaves behind more white pixels than the Defringe command set to its lowest setting.

Tip

If you encounter unrealistic edge pixels and the automatic matting commands don't solve your problem, you may be able to achieve better results by fixing the edges manually. First, switch to the layer that's giving you fits and ⌘/Ctrl+click on its name in the Layers palette. This creates a tight selection around the contents of the layer. Then choose Select ⇨ Modify ⇨ Contract and enter the width of the fringe in the Contract By option box. Next, choose Select ⇨ Feather (⌘/Ctrl+Shift+D) and enter this same value into the Feather Radius option box. Finally, press ⌘/Ctrl+Shift+I to inverse the selection and press Delete/Backspace to eliminate the edge pixels.

Figure 17-14 shows the results of applying this technique to my television. By setting the Contract and Feather commands to 1 pixel, I managed to remove the edges without harming the layer itself. And the effect looks better than that produced by the Defringe command (as you can compare for yourself with Figure 17-13).

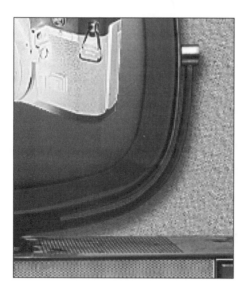

**Figure 17-14:** Here I removed the edges manually using the Contract, Feather, and Inverse commands. This looks way better than anything Photoshop can do automatically.

## Blending layers

Photoshop lets you blend layers with each other like no other program in the business. In fact, Photoshop does such a great job that it takes me an entire chapter — Chapter 31 — to explain these options in detail. I offer this section only by way of introduction, so you're at least aware of the basics. If you have bigger questions, then Chapter 31 is ready to tell all.

The Layers palette provides three basic ways to blend pixels between layers. None of these techniques changes as much as a pixel in any layer, so you can always return and reblend the layers at a later date (see Figure 17-15).

✦ **The Opacity value:** Enter a value into the Opacity option box near the top of the Layers palette to change the opacity of the active layer or floating selection. If you reduce the Opacity value to 50 percent, for example, Photoshop makes the pixels on the active layer translucent, so the colors in the active layer mix evenly with the colors in the layers below.

If any tool other than a paint or edit tool is active — including the selection and navigation tools — you can press a number key to change the Opacity value. Press 1 for 10 percent, 2 for 20 percent, up to 0 for 100 percent. Or you can enter a specific Opacity value by pressing two number keys in a row. For example, press 3 and then 7 for 37 percent.

✦ **The blend mode pop-up menu:** Choose an option from the blend mode pop-up menu — open in Figure 17-15 — to mix every pixel in the active layer with the pixels below it, according to one of several mathematical equations. For example, when you choose Multiply, Photoshop really does multiply the brightness values of the pixels and then divide the result by 255, the maximum brightness value. Blend modes use the exact same math as the brush modes covered in Chapter 8. But you can accomplish a lot more with blend modes, which is why I spend so much time examining them in Chapter 31.

In Photoshop 5, you can select a blend mode from the keyboard when a selection or navigation tool is active. Press Shift+plus to advance incrementally down the list; press Shift+minus to inch back up. You can also press Shift+Option/Alt plus a letter key to select a specific mode. For example, Shift+Option/Alt+M selects the Multiply mode. Shift+Option/Alt+N restores the mode to Normal.

✦ **Layer Options**: Choose Layer ➪ Layer Options or double-click on a layer name to display the Layer Options dialog box. This dialog box provides access to an Opacity value and a Mode pop-up menu, but it also offers a few unique functions. Using the Blend If slider bars, you can specify which colors are visible in the active layer and which colors show through from the layers behind it. You can also mix the colors using special fuzziness controls and change the slider bar settings for an individual color channel.

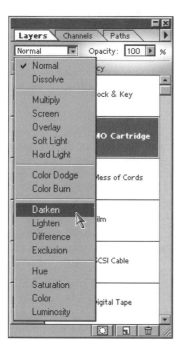

**Figure 17-15:** The blend mode pop-up menu and the Opacity option box enable you to mix layers together without making any permanent changes to the pixels.

This is enough to prepare you for anything I might throw at you between now and Chapter 31. But as I've mentioned four times now, Chapter 31 contains the whole story. (Oops, make that five.)

## Fusing several layers into one

Although layers are wonderful and marvelous creatures, they have their price. Layers expand the size of an image in RAM and ultimately lead to slower performance. And as explained in Chapter 4, you can save layered images in only one format, the native Photoshop format.

In the name of slimming down the size of your image, Photoshop provides the following methods for merging layers together:

✦ **Merge Down (⌘/Ctrl+E)**: Choose Layer ➪ Merge Down to merge a layer with the layer immediately below it. When generating screen shots, I use this command 50 or 60 times a day. I paste the screen shot into the image window, edit the layer as desired, and then press ⌘/Ctrl+E to set it down. Then I can save the screen shot in any format I like.

If the active layer is linked to other layers or part of a clipping group — two conditions I discuss later in this chapter — the Merge Down command changes to Merge Linked or Merge Group, respectively. Again, these commands use ⌘/Ctrl+E as a shortcut. Merge Down is forever changing to suit the situation.

✦ **Merge Visible (⌘/Ctrl+Shift+E)**: Choose the Merge Visible command to merge all visible layers into a single layer. If the layer is not visible — that is, if no eyeball icon appears in front of the layer name — Photoshop doesn't eliminate it; the layer simply remains independent.

To create a merged clone, press the Option/Alt key when applying either Layer ➪ Merge Down or Layer ➪ Merge Visible. Option/Alt+choosing Merge Down (or pressing ⌘/Ctrl+Option/Alt+E) clones the contents of the active layer into the layer below it. Option/Alt+choosing Merge Visible (or pressing ⌘/Ctrl+Shift+Option/Alt+E) copies the contents of all visible layers to the active layer.

To copy the merged contents of a selected area, choose Edit ➪ Copy Merged or press ⌘/Ctrl+Shift+C. You can then paste the selection into a layer or make it part of a different image.

✦ **Flatten Image**: This command, on the other hand, merges all visible layers and throws away the invisible ones. The result is a single, opaque background layer. Photoshop does not give this command a keyboard shortcut because it's so dangerous. More often than not, you'll want to flatten an image incrementally using the two Merge commands.

Note that Photoshop suggests that you flatten an image when converting from one color mode to another by choosing a command from the Image ➪ Mode submenu. You can choose not to flatten the image (by pressing the D key) but this may come at the expense of some of the brighter colors in your image.

## Dumping layers

You can also merely throw a layer away: Drag the layer name onto the trash can icon at the bottom of the Layers palette. Or click on the trash can icon to delete the active layer.

When you click on the trash can icon, Photoshop displays a message asking whether you really want to toss the layer. To give this message the slip in the future, Option/Alt+click on the trash can icon.

## Saving a flattened version of an image

Only one file format, the native Photoshop format, saves images with layers. If you want to save a flattened version of your image — that is, with all layers fused together into a single image — in some other file format, choose File ➪ Save a Copy (⌘/Ctrl+Option/Alt+S) and select the desired format from the Save As pop-up menu (or Format pop-up menu on a Mac). If you select any format other than Photoshop, the program selects and dims the Flatten Image check box in the lower-left corner of the dialog box.

The Save a Copy command neither affects the image on screen — all layers remain intact — nor changes the name of the image in the title bar. It merely creates a flattened duplicate of the image on disk.

# Selecting the Contents of Layers

A few sections back, I mentioned every layer (except the background) includes a *transparency mask*. This mask tells Photoshop which pixels are opaque, which are translucent, and which are transparent. Like any mask, Photoshop lets you convert the transparency mask for any layer — active or not — to a selection outline. In fact, you use the same keyboard techniques you use to convert paths to selections (as explained in Chapter 15) and channels to selections (Chapter 16):

✦ ⌘/Ctrl+click on an item in the Layers palette to convert the transparency mask for that layer to a selection outline.

✦ To add the transparency mask to an existing selection outline, ⌘/Ctrl+ Shift+click on the layer name. The little selection cursor includes a plus sign to show you that you're about to add.

✦ To subtract the transparency mask, ⌘/Ctrl+Option/Alt+click on the layer name.

✦ And to find the intersection of the transparency mask and the current selection outline, ⌘/Ctrl+Shift+Option/Alt+click on the layer name.

If you're uncertain you'll remember all these keyboard shortcuts, you can use Select ➪ Load Selection instead. After choosing the command, select the Transparency item from the Channel pop-up menu. (You can even load a transparency mask from another open image if the image is exactly the same size as the one in which you're working.) Then use the Operation radio buttons to merge the mask with an existing selection, as described in the "Converting a mask to a selection" section of Chapter 16.

Selection outlines exist independently of layers, so you can use the transparency mask from one layer to select part of another layer. For example, to select part of the background layer that exactly matches the contents of another layer, you press Shift+Option/Alt+[ to descend to the background layer and then ⌘/Ctrl+click on the name of the layer you want to match.

The most common reason to borrow a selection from one layer and apply it to another is to create manual shadow and lighting effects. After ⌘/Ctrl+clicking on a layer, you can use this selection to create a drop shadow that precisely matches the contours of the layer itself. No messing with the airbrush or the lasso tool — Photoshop does the tough work for you.

Now, you might think with Photoshop 5's new automated effects (found in the Layer ⇨ Effects submenu), manual drop shadows and the like would be a thing of the past. After all, you have only to choose Layer ⇨ Effects ⇨ Drop Shadow and, bang, the program adds a drop shadow. But the old, manual methods still have their advantages. You don't have to visit a dialog box to edit a manual drop shadow, you can reposition a manual shadow from the keyboard, and you can expand and contract a manual shadow with more precision than an automatic one.

On the other hand, this is not to say the old ways are always better. A shadow created with the Drop Shadow command takes up less room in memory, it moves and rotates with a layer, and you can edit the softness of the shadow long after creating it.

What we have is two equally powerful solutions, each with its own characteristic pros and cons. Therefore, the wise electronic artist will develop a working knowledge of both. This way, you're ready and able to apply the technique that makes the most sense for the job at hand.

The following sections explore the manual drop shadows, highlights, and spotlights. For everything you ever wanted to know about the Layer ⇨ Effects commands, read the section "Automatic Shadows, Glows, and Bevels" a few pages from now in this same chapter.

## Drop shadows

In these first steps, I'll take the dolphin from Figure 17-16 and insert a drop shadow behind it. This might not be the exact subject to which you'll apply drop shadows — sea critters so rarely cast such shadows onto the water's surface — but it accurately demonstrates how the effect works.

**Figure 17-16:** A dolphin in dire need of a drop shadow.

## Steps: Creating a Drop Shadow

1. **Select the subject you want to cast the shadow.** In my case, I selected the dolphin by painting the mask shown in Figure 17-17 inside a separate mask channel. These days, I add a mask to nearly every image I create to distinguish the foreground image from its background. I converted the mask to a selection outline by ⌘/Ctrl+clicking on the mask name in the Channels palette and then pressing ⌘/Ctrl+tilde (~) to switch back to the composite view.

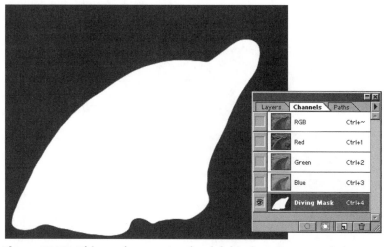

**Figure 17-17:** This mask separates the dolphin from its watery home.

*Continued*

2. **Send the image to a separate layer by pressing ⌘/Ctrl+J.** Now that the selection is elevated, you can slip in the drop shadow beneath it.

3. **Retrieve the selection outline for your new layer and apply it to the background layer.** To do this, ⌘/Ctrl+click on the new layer name (presumably Layer 1), then press Shift+Option/Alt+[ to switch to the background layer. (Because I saved the mask to a separate channel, I could have, instead, ⌘/Ctrl+clicked on the Mask item in the Channels panel to retrieve the selection. Or I could have pressed ⌘/Ctrl+Option/Alt+4.)

4. **To create a softened drop shadow – indicative of a diffused light source – choose Select ⇨ Feather (⌘/Ctrl+Option/Alt+D).** The Radius value you enter depends on the resolution of your image. I recommend dividing the resolution of your image by 20. When working on a 200 ppi image, for example, enter a Radius value of 10. My image is a mere 140 ppi, so I entered 7. Then press Return/Enter to soften the image.

5. **Press ⌘/Ctrl+J to send the feathered selection to a new layer.**

6. **Fill the feathered area with black.** If necessary, press the D key to make the foreground color black. Then press Shift+Option/Alt+Delete/Backspace to fill only the area inside the transparency mask. A slight halo of dark pixels forms around the edges of the image.

7. **Press ⌘/Ctrl with the arrow keys to nudge the shadow to the desired location.** In Figure 17-18, I nudged the shadow 12 pixels to the right. (Press ⌘/Ctrl+Shift+arrow key to nudge the shadow 10 pixels.)

**Figure 17-18:** A drop shadow nudged is 12 pixels due right from the dolphin head, which is situated on the layer above it.

8. **Lower the Opacity setting.** If the shadow is too dark – black lacks a little subtlety – change the Opacity value in the Layers palette to change the opacity of the shadow. Or press M to make sure a selection tool is active and then press a number key to change the opacity. I typically press 7 for 70 percent, but I'm probably in a rut.

Tip

If you don't like a black drop shadow, you can make a colored one with only slightly more effort. Instead of filling the shadow with black in Step 6, select a different foreground color and press Shift+Option/Alt+Delete/Backspace. For the best result, select a color that is the complimentary opposite of your background color. In Color Plate 17-1, for example, the background is blue, so I selected a reddish orange as the foreground color. Next, choose Multiply from the blend mode pop-up menu in the Layers palette (or press Shift+Option/Alt+M). This burns the colors in the shadow into those in the lower layers to create a darkened mix. Finally, press a number key to specify the opacity. (In the color plate, I again used 70 percent. I'm definitely in a rut.)

## Halos

Creating a halo is similar to creating a drop shadow. The only differences are you must expand the selection outline and fill the halo with white (or some other light color) instead of black. The following steps tell all.

### Steps: Creating a Downright Angelic Halo

1. **Follow Steps 1 through 3 of the previous instructions.** You'll end up with a version of the selected image on an independent layer and a matching selection outline applied to the background image. (See, I told you this was like creating a drop shadow.)

2. **Expand the selection outline.** Unlike a drop shadow, which is offset slightly from an image, a halo fringes the perimeter of an image pretty evenly. You need to expand the selection outline beyond the edges of the image so you can see the halo clearly. To do this, choose Select ⇨ Modify ⇨ Expand. You'll be greeted by an Expand By option box. Generally speaking, you want the expansion to match the size of your feathering, so the softening occurs outward. Therefore, I entered 7. (The maximum permissible value is 16; if you want to expand more than 16 pixels, you must apply the command twice.)

3. **Choose Select ⇨ Feather and enter the same value you entered in the Expand By option box.** Again, you decide this value by dividing the resolution of your image by 20 (or thereabouts).

4. **Send the selection to a new layer. Press ⌘/Ctrl+J.**

5. **Fill the halo with white.** Assuming the background color is white, press ⌘/Ctrl+Shift+Delete/Backspace.

That's it. Figure 17-19 shows an enlightened-looking dolphin set against a halo effect. I also drew a conventional halo above its head, added some sparklies, and even changed my finned friend's eye using the eyeball brush shape included in the Assorted Brushes document. I mean, if this aquatic mammal's not bound for glory, I don't know who is.

**Tip**

Incidentally, you needn't create a white halo any more than you must create a black drop shadow. In Step 5, set the background color to something other than white. Then select the Screen option from the blend mode pop-up menu in the Layers palette (Shift+Option/Alt+S), thus mixing the colors and lightening them at the same time. If you don't like the effect, select a different background color and press ⌘/Ctrl+Shift+Delete/Backspace again. With the halo on a separate layer, you can do just about anything to it without running a risk of harming the underlying original.

**Figure 17-19:** Few dolphins reach this level of spiritual awareness, even if you do set them off from their backgrounds using the halo effect. He kind of looks like one of the cast members from *Cocoon*, don't you think?

## Spotlights

Now, finally, for the spotlight effect. I use spotlights about a billion times in this book to highlight some special option I want you to look at in a palette or dialog box. I've received so many questions (from fellow authors mostly) on how to perform this effect, I've decided to write the information in this book and be done with it. So here goes.

### Steps: Shining a Spotlight on Something Inside an Image

1. **Draw an oval selection inside your image.** Obviously, the best tool for this purpose is the elliptical marquee tool. The selection represents the area where the spotlight will shine. If you don't like where the oval is located, but you basically like its size and shape, drag the outline to a more satisfactory location.

2. **Choose Select ⇨ Feather and enter whatever Radius value you please.** Again, you may want to follow the divide-the-resolution-by-20 rule, but use whatever value you like. (There's no such thing as a wrong Radius value.)

To create Figure 17-20, I doubled my Radius value to 14 pixels to create a soft effect.

3. **Press ⌘/Ctrl+Shift+I.** Most likely, you really want to darken the area outside the spotlight, not lighten the spotlight itself. So choose Select ⇨ Inverse (⌘/Ctrl+Shift+I) to swap what's selected and what's not.

4. **Send the selection to a new layer.** That's ⌘/Ctrl+J, of course.

5. **Fill the transparency mask with black.** With the foreground color set to black, press Shift+Option/Alt+Delete/Backspace.

6. **Lower the Opacity setting by pressing a number key.** To get the effect in Figure 17-20, I pressed 6 for 60 percent.

**Figure 17-20:** Create an elliptical selection, feather it, inverse it, layer it, fill it with black, and lower the opacity to create a spotlight effect like this one.

Actually, the image in Figure 17-20 isn't all that convincing. Although the preceding steps are fine for spotlighting flat images such as screen shots, they tend to rob photographs of some of their depth. After all, in real life, the spotlight wouldn't hit the water in the same way it hits the dolphin.

**Tip**

But there is a way around this. You can combine the oval selection outline with the mask used to select the foreground image, thereby eliminating the background from the equation entirely. First establish the selection and feather it (Steps 1 and 2). Assuming your image has a mask saved in a separate channel, ⌘/Ctrl+Shift+ Option/Alt+click on the mask name in the Channels palette. This retains just the intersection of the mask and the spotlight selection. Then perform the preceding Steps 3 through 6 — that is, inverse the selection (⌘/Ctrl+Shift+I), send it to a layer (⌘/Ctrl+J), fill the transparency mask with black (Shift+Option/Alt+Delete/

Backspace), and change the opacity. For my part, I first rotated the oval selection using Select ⇨ Transform Selection. Then I found the intersection of the mask and rotated oval to achieve the more natural spotlight shown in Figure 17-21.

**Figure 17-21:** You can mix the feathered selection with the contents of a mask channel to limit the spotlighting effect to the foreground character only.

Sometimes, the darkness of the area around the spotlight appears sufficiently dark that it starts bringing the spotlighted area down with it. To brighten the spotlight, inverse the selection (⌘/Ctrl+Shift+I) so the spotlight is selected again. Then apply the Levels command (⌘/Ctrl+L) to brighten the spotlighted area. The Levels command is explained at length in Chapter 30.

Just for fun—what other possible reason would there be?—Color Plate 17-2 shows one result of combining the spotlight effect with the halo effect. After selecting the oval area, feathering it, and rotating it with the Transform Selection command, I inversed the selection (⌘/Ctrl+Shift+I). Then I ⌘/Ctrl+Shift+Option/Alt+clicked on the dolphin mask in the Channels palette to retain the area outside the oval and inside the dolphin. (The background was therefore deselected.) I cloned this area to a separate layer, filled it with a deep blue, and applied the Multiply blend mode. Then, using my original dolphin mask, I sent the dolphin to a separate layer and created a yellowish, pinkish halo behind it. Finally, I returned to the background layer and inverted it by pressing ⌘/Ctrl+I. An interestingly lit dolphin in a radioactive bath is the result.

# Automatic Shadows, Glows, and Bevels

Photoshop 5 adds a series of so-called *layer effects* that automate the application of shadows, glows, and beveled edges. To apply a layer effect, select a foreground element in your image, press ⌘/Ctrl+J to copy it to an independent layer, and choose one of the first five commands from the Layer ⇨ Effects submenu:

✦ **Drop Shadow:** The Drop Shadow command applies a common, everyday drop shadow. You specify the color, opacity, blend mode, position, and softness of the shadow, Photoshop does the rest.

✦ **Inner Shadow:** This command applies a drop shadow inside the layer, as demonstrated by the second example in Figure 17-22. The command simulates the kind of shadow you'd get if the layer was punched out of the background — that is, the background looks like it's in front, casting a shadow onto the layer. Inner Shadow is especially effective with type, as I explain in Chapter 18.

✦ **Outer Glow:** The Outer Glow command creates a traditional halo, like the one I applied to our aquatic friend back in the "Halos" section. You specify color, opacity, blend mode, and softness.

✦ **Inner Glow:** This command applies the effect inside the layer rather than outside, as demonstrated in the second row of Figure 17-22.

To create a neon strip around the perimeter of a layer, apply both the Outer Glow and Inner glow commands. For an example of a neon edge, see the bottom right image in Figure 17-22.

✦ **Bevel and Emboss:** Layer ➪ Effects ➪ Bevel and Emboss produces four distinct edge effects, each of which appears in Figure 17-23. You can add a three-dimensional beveled edge around the outside of the layer, as in the first example in the figure. The Inner Bevel effect produces a beveled edge inside the layer. The Emboss effect combines inner and outer bevels. And the Pillow Emboss reverses the inner bevel so the image appears to sink in and then rise back up along the edge of the layer.

Layer effects are a godsend to beginners, but experienced users might be tempted to dismiss them. After all, you can create every one of these effects manually using layers, selection outlines, and blends modes. But there is much to like about the Layer ➪ Effects commands:

✦ First, they stick to the layer. Move or transform the layer and the effect tags along with it.

✦ Second, the effect is temporary. So long as you save the image in the native Photoshop format, you can edit the shadows, glows, and bevels long into the future.

✦ Third, layer effects are equally applicable to both standard layers and editable text layers. (As explained in Chapter 18, editable text resides on a special kind of layer that prohibits certain kinds of edits.)

✦ Fourth, you can combine multiple effects on a single layer. Fifth, you can copy an effect from one layer and paste it onto another. Sixth, you can temporarily disable and enable using simple keyboard tricks. Seventh — why the heck do you need a seventh advantage? Isn't six enough?

Now that you're chomping at the bit — or as the dolphins say, "bonkin' at the beach ball" — to get your flippers on these effects, the following sections tell you how, why, and what for.

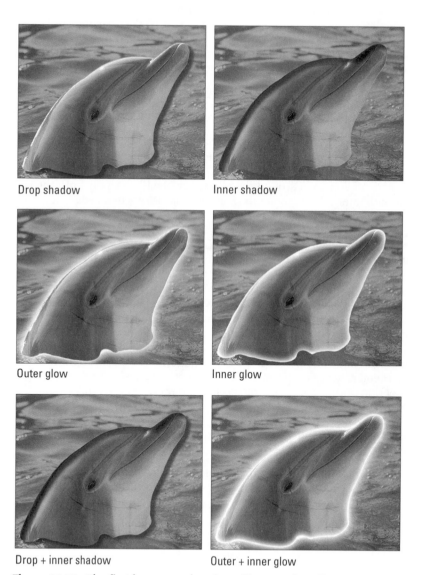

Drop shadow           Inner shadow

Outer glow           Inner glow

Drop + inner shadow        Outer + inner glow

**Figure 17-22:** The first four examples above illustrate the effects of the first four commands under the Layer ⇨ Effects submenu. You can also combine multiple effects on a single layer, as demonstrated by the two images at bottom.

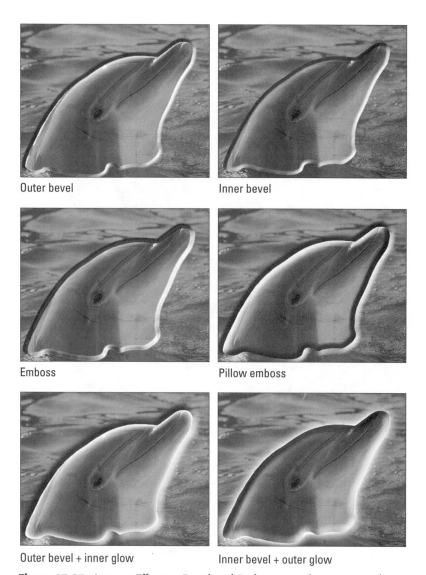

Outer bevel

Inner bevel

Emboss

Pillow emboss

Outer bevel + inner glow

Inner bevel + outer glow

**Figure 17-23:** Layer ➪ Effects ➪ Bevel and Emboss permits you to apply one of four effects, demonstrated in the first four examples above. The last row of images show what happens when you combine beveled edges with glows.

## Working inside the Effects dialog box

When you choose one of the first five commands from the Layer ➪ Effects submenu, Photoshop displays the Effects dialog box, featured in Figure 17-24. This one dialog box provides access to all five effects. Just select the desired effect from the first pop-up menu (labeled in the figure), then select the Apply check box to apply the effect, or deselect the check box to turn it off.

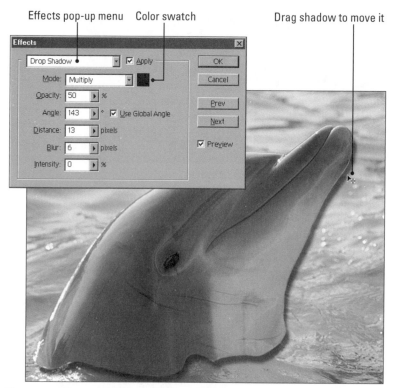

Effects pop-up menu    Color swatch    Drag shadow to move it

**Figure 17-24:** To position a shadow when the Effects dialog box is up on screen, just drag inside the image window.

Most of the options in the Effects dialog box are self-explanatory. You select a blend mode from the Mode pop-up menu. You change the opacity by entering a value in the Opacity option box. (Everybody say, "Duh!") Still, not every option is so transparent. Here's how the more unusual features work:

✦ **Switching effects:** To switch between effects from the keyboard, press ⌘/Ctrl+1 for Drop Shadow, ⌘/Ctrl+2 for Inner Shadow, and on up to ⌘/Ctrl+5 for Bevel and Emboss.

✦ **Color swatch:** To change the color of the shadow, glow, or beveled edge, click on the color swatch. (Okay, you could have figured that out, but you're smarter than most.)

✦ **Mode:** The Mode pop-up menu controls the blend mode. That much is obvious. But did you know that you can use the Mode menu to turn an effect upside-down? Select a light color and apply the Screen mode to change a drop shadow into a directional halo. Or use a dark color with Multiply to change an outer glow into a shadow that evenly traces the edge of the layer. Don't be constrained by pedestrian notions of shadows and glows. Layer effects can be anything.

✦ **Angle and Distance:** The Drop Shadow and Inner Shadow panels feature Angle and Distance values that determine the distance between the farthest edge of the effect and the corresponding edge of the layer.

Again, fairly obvious. But what you may not know is that you can avoid these numerical options and simply drag the shadow to the desired location. When the Effect dialog box is visible, move your cursor into the image window and drag away. Photoshop gives you the standard move cursor, as illustrated in Figure 17-24.

✦ **Use Global Angle:** In the real world, the sun casts all shadows in the same direction. Oh, sure, the shadows change minutely from one object to the next, but what with the sun being 90 million miles away and all, the changes are astronomically subtle. I doubt if a single-celled organism, upon admiring its shadow compared with that of its neighbor, could perceive the slightest difference. (The fact that single-celled organisms lack eyes, brains, and other perceptual organs does not in any way lessen the truth of this powerful argument.)

As I was saying, one sun means one lightness and one darkness. By turning on the Use Global Angle check box, you tell Photoshop to cast all direction-dependent effects — drop shadows, inner shadows, and the four kinds of bevels — in the same direction. If you change the angle of a drop shadow applied to Layer 1, Photoshop rotates the sun in its heaven and so changes the angle of the pillow emboss applied to Layer 9, thus proving that even a computer program may subscribe to the immutable laws of nature.

Conversely, if you turn the check box off, you tell nature to take a hike. You can change an Angle value in any which way you like and none of the other layers will care.

If you have established a consistent universe, you can edit the angle of the sun by choosing Layer ⇨ Effects ⇨ Global Angle. Enter a new angle and all shadows and bevels created with Use Global Angle turned on will move in unison. "Sun rise, sun set," as the Yiddish fiddlers say. That doesn't shed any light on the topic, of course, but when in doubt, I like to quote a great musical to class up the joint.

✦ **Blur:** This option works like the Feather command, softening the boundary of the effect.

✦ **Intensity:** By itself, the Intensity option does nothing. But combined with the Blur value, it permits you to spread the effect. Figure 17-25 shows how raising the Intensity value from 0 percent to its maximum setting, 600 percent, gradually grows the shadow outward from its layer. Raising the Blur value creates more pronounced effects.

✦ **Up, Down:** When working in the Bevel and Emboss panel, you'll notice two radio buttons named Up and Down (spotlighted in Figure 17-26). If the Angle value denotes the direction of the sun (or other light source), then Up positions the highlight along the edge near the sun and the shadow along the opposite edge. Down swaps things around, positioning the shadow near the light source. Presumably, this means the layer sinks into its background rather than protrudes out from it. But in practice, the layer typically appears merely as though it's lit differently.

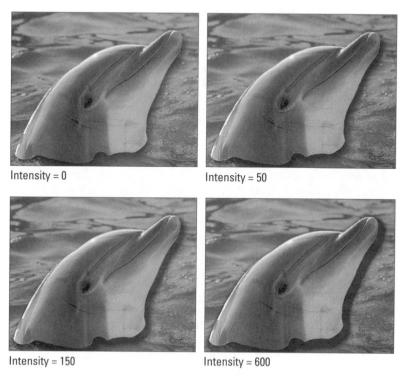

Intensity = 0                    Intensity = 50

Intensity = 150                  Intensity = 600

**Figure 17-25:** Several Intensity values combined with an Opacity value of 50 percent and a Blur of 20 pixels. As you can see, higher Intensity values spread the drop shadow out from the layer.

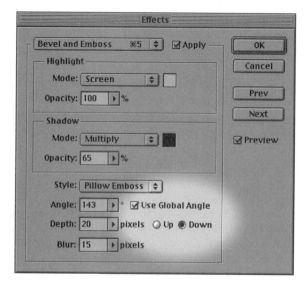

**Figure 17-26:** The Up and Down options specify whether an embossed layer swells outward from its background or sinks into it.

## Modifying and resolving effects

After you apply a layer effect, Photoshop stamps the layer with a small florin symbol (cursive *f*), as shown in Figure 17-27. From that point, you can edit the effect by double-clicking on the florin. Be sure to double-click inside the florin circle; if you double-click anywhere else on the layer, Photoshop brings up the Layer Options dialog box.

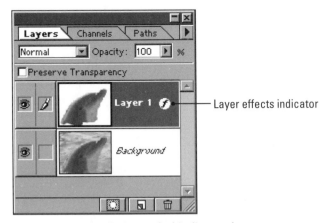

Layer effects indicator

**Figure 17-27:** The florin symbol indicates that one or more layer effects have been applied to the layer.

### Disabling effects

To temporarily disable all effects applied to a layer, choose Layer ⇨ Effects ⇨ Hide All Effects. To turn the effects back on, choose the Show All Effects command.

To permanently disable an effect, Option/Alt+double-click on the florin symbol in the Layers palette. If many effects are applied to the layer, Option/Alt+choose the specific effect you want to turn off from the Layer ⇨ Effects submenu.

### Duplicating effects

Once you apply a layer effect to any layer, the effect becomes an element that you can copy and apply to other layers. Select the layer with the effect you want to duplicate and choose Layer ⇨ Effects ⇨ Copy Effects. Then select another layer and choose Layer ⇨ Effects ⇨ Paste Effects. To repeat a copied effect onto multiple layers at a time, link then together (as explained in the upcoming "Linking layers" section) and then choose the Paste Effects to Linked command.

The Copy and Pasting Effects commands bypass the Clipboard. This means you can copy an image and then copy an effect without displacing the image.

**Tip**

If you spend a lot of time copying and pasting effects, you'll quickly tire of burrowing your way into the inconvenient Layer ➪ Effects submenu. The better way to bring up the Effects commands is to Control/right-click on the florin symbol in the Layers palette.

### Scattering effects to the four winds

When you apply an effect, Photoshop is actually doing all the manual layer work for you in the background. This means if Photoshop doesn't seem to be generating the precise effect you want, you can take over and edit the layers to your satisfaction. Choose Layer ➪ Effects ➪ Create Layers to resolve the automated effect into a series of layers and clipping groups. Then edit at will.

**Caution**

After choosing Create Layers, you're on your own. From that point on, you lose the ability to edit the effects using the Layer ➪ Effects commands (unless, of course, you decide to go back in time via the History palette).

# Moving and Aligning Layers

You can move an entire layer or the selected portion of a layer by dragging in the image window with the move tool. If you have a selection going, drag inside the marching-ants outline to move only the selection; drag outside the selection to move the entire layer.

As I mentioned in Chapter 15, you can temporarily access the move tool when some other tool is active by pressing the ⌘/Ctrl key. To nudge a layer, press ⌘/Ctrl with an arrow key. Press ⌘/Ctrl and Shift together to nudge in 10-pixel increments.

If part of the layer disappears beyond the edge of the window, no problem. As long as you don't move your cursor outside the image window, Photoshop saves even the hidden pixels in the layer, enabling you to drag it into view later. (This only works when moving all of a layer. If you move a selection beyond the edge of the image window using the move tool, Photoshop clips the selection at the window's edge the moment you deselect it.) If you move your cursor outside the image window, however, Photoshop thinks you are trying to drag-and-drop pixels from one image to another and responds accordingly.

If you ⌘/Ctrl+drag the background image — either when no portion of the image is selected or by dragging outside the selection outline — Photoshop automatically converts the background to a new layer (called Layer 0). The area revealed by the move appears as checkerboard transparency. Photoshop saves the hidden portions of the background image in case you ever decide to move the background back into its original position.

**Note**

If you regularly work on huge images or your machine is old and kind of slow, Photoshop lets you speed up the display of whole layers on the move. Press the V key to select the move tool, press Return/Enter to display the Move Options palette, and select the Pixel Doubling check box. From now on, Photoshop will show you a low-resolution proxy of the layer as you drag it (or ⌘/Ctrl+drag it) across the screen.

Pixel Doubling has no effect when you ⌘/Ctrl+drag selections. It only works when you move entire layers.

## Linking layers

Photoshop lets you move multiple layers at a time. To do so, you have to establish a *link* between the layers you want to move and the active layer. Begin by selecting the first layer in the Layers palette you want to link. Then click in the second column to the left of the other layer you want to link. A chain link icon appears in front of each linked layer, as in Figure 17-28. This icon shows the linked layers will move in unison when you ⌘/Ctrl+drag the active layer. To break the link, click on a link icon, which hides it.

**Note** Dragging inside a selection outline moves the selection independently of any linked layers. Dragging outside the selection moves all linked layers at once.

**Tip** To link many layers at a time, drag up and down the link column. To unlink the active layer from all others, Option/Alt+click on the paintbrush icon in the link column.

Link column

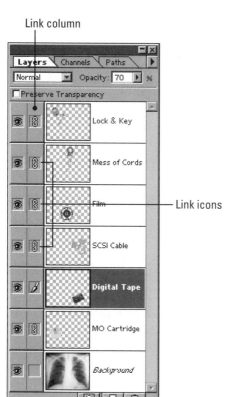

Link icons

**Figure 17-28:** Click in the second column in the Layers palette to display or hide link icons. Here I've linked all layers except the background, so I can ⌘/Ctrl+drag them in unison.

In Photoshop 5, you can also link layers via the context-sensitive pop-up menu. As you may recall from the "Switching between layers" section earlier in this chapter, you can bring up a pop-up menu listing the layers in an image by ⌘/Ctrl+Control/ right-clicking on an image element with any tool. Add Shift while selecting a layer from the pop-up menu to link or unlink the layer rather than switch to it. But that's not all. If you're plum crazy for shortcuts, you can change the link state without visiting the pop-up menu by — drum roll please — ⌘/Ctrl+Shift+Option/Alt+Control/ right-clicking on an element in the image window. Okay, I love shortcuts, but even *I* have to admit this one is gratuitous!

When you drag-and-drop linked layers into another document, all linked layers move together and the layers retain their original order. If you hold down Shift when dropping, Photoshop centers the layers in the document. If the document is exactly the same size as the one from which you dragged the layers, then Shift+dropping lands the image elements in the same position they held in the original document. And finally, if something is selected in the document, the Shift+dropped layers are centered inside that selection.

## Using guides

Photoshop grids and guides allow you to move selections and layers into alignment. Together with the move tool, grids and guides enable you to create rows and columns of image elements, and even align layers by their centers.

To create a guide, press ⌘/Ctrl+R (View ⇨ Show Rulers) to display the horizontal and vertical rulers. Then drag a guideline from the ruler. At the top of Figure 17-29, you can see me dragging a horizontal guide down from the top ruler. Then ⌘/Ctrl+drag layers and selections in alignment with the guide. In the bottom portion of the figure, I've dragged the MO disk, film reel, and tape — each on different layers — so they snap into alignment at their centers. (The reel has some film hanging from it, which Photoshop considers in calculating the center.) You'll know when the layer snaps into alignment because the move cursor becomes hollow, like the labeled cursor in Figure 17-29.

Text layers snap to guides a little differently than other kinds of layers. Rather than snapping by the top or bottom edge of the layer, Photoshop snaps a text guide by its baseline. It's just what you need when aligning type.

Guides are pretty straightforward creatures. I mean, you don't have to study them rigorously for years to understand them — a few minutes are all you need to master them. But there are a few hidden treats:

✦ You can show and hide all guides by pressing ⌘/Ctrl+semicolon (;) or by choosing the Hide (or Show) Guides command from the View menu. When the guides are hidden, layers and selections do not snap into alignment.

✦ You can turn on and off guide snappiness while the guides remain visible by pressing ⌘/Ctrl+Shift+semicolon (or choosing View ⇨ Snap to Guides).

✦ As with all image elements in Photoshop, you can move a guide with the move tool. If some other tool is active, ⌘/Ctrl+dragging also works.

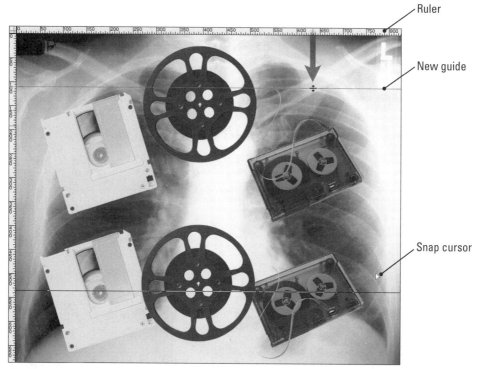

**Figure 17-29:** Drag from one of the rulers to create a guide (top), and then ⌘/Ctrl+drag each layer or selection into alignment (bottom).

✦ To lock all guides so you can't accidentally move them while you're trying to ⌘/Ctrl+drag something else, press ⌘/Ctrl+Option/Alt+semicolon or choose View➪Lock Guides. Press ⌘/Ctrl+Option/Alt+semicolon again to unlock all guides.

✦ When moving a guide, press the Shift key to snap the guide to the nearest ruler tick mark.

✦ To convert a horizontal guide to a vertical guide, or vice versa, press the Option/Alt key while moving the guide.

✦ If you rotate your document in exact multiples of 90 degrees or flip the image horizontally or vertically, your guides also rotate unless they are locked.

✦ You can position a guide outside the image if you want. To do so, make the image window larger than the image. Now you can drag a guide into the empty canvas surrounding the image. You can then snap a layer or selection into alignment with the guide.

✦ To edit the color of the guides, ⌘/Ctrl+double-click on a guide to display the Guides & Grid panel of the Preferences dialog box. You can also change the guides from solid lines to dashed. (This is for screen purposes, by the way. Guides don't print.)

✦ Like paths, Photoshop saves guides with any file format. If you export the image into another program, the guides are invisible. However, the only formats that support guides on a cross-format basis — so you can use your Photoshop guides on a Mac or a PC — are Photoshop, JPEG, TIFF, and EPS.

✦ If you don't need your guides anymore, choose View ➪ Clear Guides to delete them all in one housekeeping operation. (I wish I had a command like this built into my office — I'd choose Maid ➪ Clear Dust and be done with it.)

## Automatic alignment and distribution

Photoshop 5 also lets you align and distribute layers by choosing a command from the Layer ➪ Align Linked or Distribute Linked submenu. The commands are pretty straightforward — quite familiar if you've ever used a drawing or page-layout program — but applying them is a little unusual.

Here's how to align two or more layers:

### Steps: Aligning Layers

1. **Select the layer that will serve as the anchor.** Whenever you align layers, one layer remains still and the others align to it. The still layer is the one you select.

2. **Link the layers you want to align.** Click in front of the layers you want to align to display the link icon. (And be sure to unlink any layers you don't want to align.) You have to link at least two layers — after all, there's no point in aligning a layer to itself.

3. **Choose a command from the Layer ➪ Align Linked submenu.** If you don't like the result, press ⌘/Ctrl+Z and try a different command.

The Distribute Linked commands space linked layers apart evenly. So it doesn't matter which of the linked layers is selected — the command distributes all linked layers with respect to the two horizontal or vertical extremes. Naturally, it's meaningless to space apart one or two layers, so the Distribute Linked commands require three or more layers to be linked together.

## Setting up the grid

Photoshop also offers a grid, which is a regular series of snapping increments. You view the grid — and turn it on — by pressing ⌘/Ctrl+quote (") or choosing View ➪ Show Grid. Turn the snapping forces of the grid on and off by pressing ⌘/Ctrl+Shift+quote or choosing View ➪ Snap to Grid.

You edit the grid in the Guides & Grid panel of the Preferences dialog box (which you can get to by pressing ⌘/Ctrl+K and ⌘/Ctrl+6 or by ⌘/Ctrl+double-clicking on a guide). I explain how to use these options in the "Guides & Grid" section of Chapter

B on CD-ROM #2. But, for the record, you enter the major grid increments in the Gridline Every option box and enter the minor increments in the Subdivisions option box. For example, in Figure 17-30, I set the Gridline Every value to 50 pixels and the Subdivisions value to 5. This means a moved layer will snap in 10-pixel (50 pixels divide by 5) increments. Figure 17-30 also demonstrates each of the three Style settings.

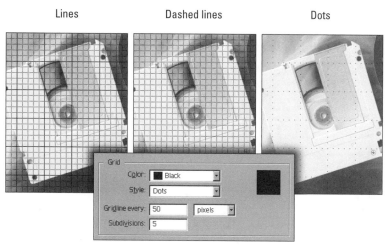

**Figure 17-30:** Here are the three styles of grid with the Grid Preferences options shown at the bottom.

## Using the measure tool

The final method for controlling movements in Photoshop 5 is the measure tool. Press the U key to select the tool. Then drag from one point to another point in the image window. Photoshop itemizes the distance and angle between the two points in the Info palette. The measure tool is even smart enough to automatically display the Info palette if it's hidden.

From that point on, any time you select the measure tool, Photoshop displays the original measurement line. This way, you can measure a distance, edit the image, and press U at any time to refer back to the measurement.

To measure the distance and angle between two other points, you can draw a new line with the measure tool. Or drag the endpoints of the existing measurement line.

Photoshop accommodates only one measurement line per document. But you can break the line in two using what Adobe calls the "protractor" feature. Option/Alt+drag on one of the endpoints to draw forth a second segment. The Info palette then measures the angle between the two segments. As demonstrated in Figure 17-31, the D1 item in the Info palette lists the length of the first segment, D2 lists the length of the second segment, and A tells the angle between the segments.

Measure cursor

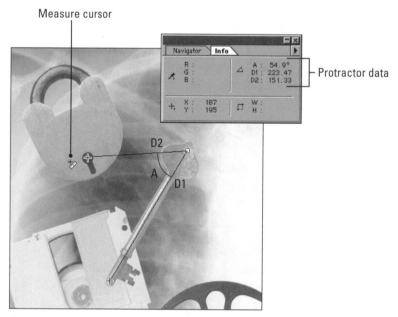

Protractor data

**Figure 17-31:** Here I measured the angle of the key, and then Option/Alt+dragged from the top endpoint to measure the angle between the key and lock.

**Tip**    The measure tool is great for straightening crooked layers. After drawing a line with the measure tool, choose Edit ➪ Transform ➪ Numeric. The Rotate value automatically conforms to the A (angle) value listed in the Info palette. If you look closely, the two values may not exactly match. That's because Photoshop intelligently translates the value to between -45 and +45 degrees, which happens to be the simplest way to express any rotation. If you're unclear what I'm talking about, just trust in Photoshop. It does the math so you don't have to.

# Applying Transformations

Photoshop and other graphics treat some kinds of edits differently than others. Edits that affect the geometry of a selection or layer are known collectively as *transformations*. These transformations include scaling, rotating, flipping, slanting, and distorting. (Technically, moving is a transformation as well.) Transformations are special because they can affect a selection, a layer, multiple layers, or an entire image at a time.

## Transforming the entire image

There are two varieties of transformations in Photoshop. Transformation commands that affect the entire image — including all layers, paths, guides, and so on — are listed in the Image menu. Those that affect layers and selected portions of layers are found in the Edit menu.

The following list explains how to apply transformations to every pixel in an image, regardless of whether the image is selected or not:

✦ **Scale:** To resize the image, use Image ⇨ Image Size. Because this command is one of the most essential low-level functions in the program, I covered it way back in Chapter 4.

✦ **Rotate:** To rotate the entire image, choose a command from the Image ⇨ Rotate Canvas submenu. To rotate an image scanned on its side, choose the 90° CW or 90° CCW command. (That's clockwise and counterclockwise, respectively.) Choose 180° to spin the image on its head. To enter some other specific value, choose Image ⇨ Rotate Canvas ⇨ Arbitrary.

To fix a slightly crooked scanned image, for example, select the measure tool by pressing the U key. Then drag along the edge of the image and note the A value in the Info palette. When you figure out the proper angle, choose Image Í Rotate Canvas Í Arbitrary and enter it into the Angle option box.

Whenever you apply the Arbitrary command, Photoshop has to expand the canvas size to avoid clipping any of your image. This results in background-colored wedges at each of the four corners of the image. You'll need to either clone with the rubber stamp tool to fill in the wedges or to clip them away with the crop tool.

✦ **Flip:** Choose Image ⇨ Rotate Canvas ⇨ Flip Horizontal to flip the image so left is right and right is left. To flip the image upside-down, choose Image ⇨ Rotate Canvas ⇨ Flip Vertical.

No command is specifically designed to slant or distort the entire image. In the unlikely event you're keen to do this, you'll have to link all layers and apply one of the commands under the Edit ⇨ Transform submenu, as explained in the next section.

## Transforming layers and selected pixels

To transform a layer or selection, you can apply one of the commands in the Edit ⇨ Transform submenu. Nearly a dozen commands are here, all of which you can explore on your own. I'm not copping out; it's unlikely you'll use any of these commands on a regular basis. (The notable exception is Numeric, which I discuss in the following section.) These commands aren't bad, but one command — Free Transform — is infinitely better.

With Free Transform, you can scale, flip, rotate, slant, distort, and move a selection or layer in one continuous operation. This one command lets you get all your transformations exactly right before pressing Return/Enter to apply the final changes.

To initiate the command, press ⌘/Ctrl+T or choose Edit ⇨ Free Transform. Photoshop surrounds the layer or selection with an eight-handle marquee. You are now in the Free Transform mode, which prevents you from doing anything except transform the image until you apply the operation or cancel it.

Here's how to work in the Free Transform mode:

✦ **Scale:** Drag one of the eight square handles to scale the image inside the marquee. To scale proportionally, Shift+drag a corner handle. To scale about the central *transformation origin* (labeled in Figure 17-32), Option/Alt+drag a corner handle.

By default, the origin is located in the center of the layer or selection. But you can move it to any place inside the image by dragging it. The origin snaps to the grid and guides, as well as the center or any corner of the layer.

✦ **Flip:** You can flip the image by dragging one handle past its opposite handle. For example, dragging the left side handle past the right handle flips the image horizontally.

If you want to perform a simple flip, it's generally easier to choose Edit ➪ Transform ➪ Flip Horizontal or Flip Vertical. Better yet, Control/right-click in the image window and choose one of the Flip commands from the pop-up menu. Quite surprisingly, you can choose either command while working in the Free Transform mode.

✦ **Rotate:** To rotate the image, drag outside the marquee, as demonstrated in the first example in Figure 17-32. Shift+drag to rotate in 15-degree increments.

✦ **Skew:** ⌘/Ctrl+drag a side handle (including the top or bottom handle) to slant the image. To constrain the slant, useful for producing perspective effects, ⌘/Ctrl+Shift+drag a side handle.

✦ **Distort:** You can distort the image by ⌘/Ctrl+dragging a corner handle. You can tug the image to stretch it in any of four directions.

To tug two opposite corner handles in symmetrical directions, ⌘/Ctrl+Option/Alt+drag either of the handles. I show this technique in the second example in Figure 17-32.

✦ **Perspective**: For a one-point perspective effect, ⌘/Ctrl+Shift+drag a corner handle. To move two points in unison, ⌘/Ctrl+Shift+Option/Alt+drag a corner handle.

✦ **Move:** Drag inside the marquee to move the image. This is useful when you're trying to align the selection or layer with a background image and you want to make sure the transformations match up properly.

✦ **Undo:** To undo the last modification without leaving the Free Transform mode altogether, press ⌘/Ctrl+Z.

✦ **Zoom:** You can change the view size by choosing one of the commands in the View menu. You can also use the keyboard zoom shortcuts (⌘/Ctrl+spacebar+click, Option/Alt+spacebar+click, ⌘/Ctrl+plus, ⌘/Ctrl+minus).

✦ **Apply:** Press Return/Enter to apply the final transformation and interpolate the new pixels. You can also double-click inside the marquee.

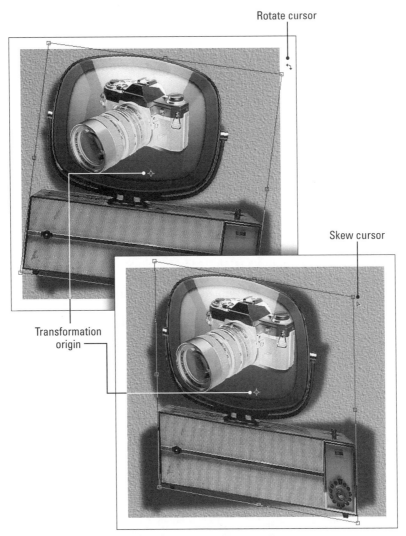

**Figure 17-32:** After pressing ⌘/Ctrl+T to initiate the Free Transform command, drag outside the marquee to rotate the layer (top). You can also ⌘/Ctrl+Option/ Alt+drag a corner handle to move the opposite corner handle symmetrically.

**Tip**

If the finished effect looks jagged, it's probably because you selected Nearest Neighbor from the Interpolation pop-up menu in the Preferences dialog box. To fix this problem, press ⌘/Ctrl+Z to undo the transformation, and then press ⌘/Ctrl+K and select the Bicubic option from the General panel of the Preferences dialog box. Then press ⌘/Ctrl+Shift+T to reapply the transformation.

✦ **Cancel:** To cancel the Free Transform operation, press the Escape key.

To transform a clone of a selected area, press Alt when choosing the Free Transform command, or press ⌘/Ctrl+Option/Alt+T. This only works with selected areas — you can't clone an entire layer any more than you can by Option/Alt+dragging with the move tool.

If no part of the image is selected, you can transform multiple layers at a time by linking them, as described in the "Linking layers" section earlier in this chapter. For example, I could have linked the TV and camera layers to transform the two in unison back in Figure 17-32.

To replay the last transformation on any layer or selection, press ⌘/Ctrl+Shift+T. This is a great technique to use if you forgot to link all the layers that you want to transform. You can even transform a path or selection outline to match a transformed layer. It's a handy feature.

## Numerical transformations

To track your transformations numerically, display the Info palette (F8) before you apply the Free Transform command. After you initiate Free Transform, you can't change the visible palettes until you complete or cancel the operation.

Alternatively, choose Edit ⇨ Transform ⇨ Numeric. You can apply this command while working in the Free Transform mode, or apply the entire transformation numerically by choosing the Numeric command at the outset. In any case, you get the dialog box shown in Figure 17-33. If you're in the middle of a Free Transform operation, the dialog box reflects the changes you've made so far (minus the distortions). Otherwise, Photoshop displays the last settings applied.

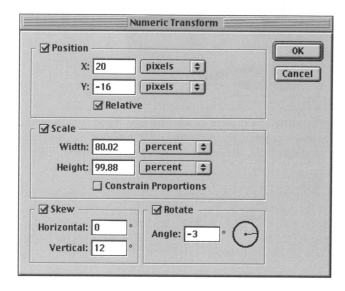

**Figure 17-33:** Press ⌘/Ctrl+Shift+T to transform a selection or layer numerically.

For the most part, this dialog box is pretty straightforward. Use the check boxes to decide which kinds of transformations you want to apply. The Relative check box controls whether a move is measured relative to the previous position of the element or with respect to the absolute 0,0 coordinate (generally in the upper-left corner of the image).

I imagine that most folks will use this dialog box strictly for scaling and rotating. You'd need the spatial awareness of a NASA navigation system to predict a numerical slant.

# Masking and Layers

Layers offer special masking options unto themselves. You can paint inside the confines of a layer as if it were a selection mask; you can add a special mask for a single layer; or you can group multiple layers together and have the bottom layer in the group serve as the mask. Quite honestly, these are the kinds of thoughtful and useful functions I've come to expect from Photoshop. Although they're fairly complicated to use — you must be on your toes once you start juggling layer masks — these functions provide new realms of opportunities.

## Preserving transparency

You may have already noticed a little check box called Preserve Transparency near the top of the Layers palette. If not, the option appears spotlighted in Figure 17-34. When checked, it prevents you from painting inside the transparent portions of the layer.

Suppose I want to paint inside the girl shown in Figure 17-34. If this were a flat, nonlayered image, I'd have to draw a selection outline carefully around her hair and arms, as I did back in Chapter 16. But there's no need to do this when using layers. Because the girl lies on a different layer than her background, a permanent selection outline tells Photoshop which pixels are transparent and which are opaque. This is the transparency mask.

The first example in Figure 17-35 shows the girl on her own with the background hidden. The transparent areas outside the mask appear in the checkerboard pattern. When the Preserve Transparency option is turned off, you can paint anywhere you want inside the layer. Selecting Preserve Transparency activates the transparency mask and places the checkerboard area off limits.

The right image in Figure 17-35 shows what happens after I select Preserve Transparency and paint around the girl with the airbrush. (The foreground color is set to white.) Notice, no matter how much paint I may apply, none of it leaks out onto the background.

**Figure 17-34:** The Preserve Transparency check box (upper right) enables you to paint inside the layer's transparency mask without harming the transparent pixels.

**Figure 17-35:** The layered girl as she appears on her own (left) and when airbrushed with the Preserve Transparency check box turned on (right).

Although this enlightening discussion pretty well covers it, I feel compelled to share a few additional words about Preserve Transparency:

**Tip**

> You can turn Preserve Transparency on and off from the keyboard by pressing the standard slash character, /, right there on the same key with the question mark.

✦ Remember, you can fill only the opaque pixels in a layer, whether Preserve Transparency is on or off. Use ⌘/Ctrl+Shift+Delete/Backspace to fill with the background color, and Shift+Option/Alt+Delete/Backspace to fill with the foreground color.

✦ The Preserve Transparency check box is dimmed when the background layer is active because this layer is entirely opaque. There's no transparency to preserve, eh? (That's my impression of a Canadian explaining layer theory. It needs a little work, but I think I'm getting close.)

And finally, here's a question for all you folks who think you may have Photoshop mastered. Which of the brush modes (explained in Chapter 8) is the exact opposite of Preserve Transparency? The answer is Behind. If you turn off Preserve Transparency and select the Behind brush mode in, say, the Paintbrush Options palette, you paint exclusively outside the transparency mask, thus protecting the opaque pixels. So it follows, when Preserve Transparency is turned on, the Behind brush mode is dimmed.

The moral? Behind is not a true brush mode and should not be grouped with the brush modes. The better solution would be a Preserve Opacity check box. Alas, Adobe's engineers have so far ignored my advice, but after they were so kind as to implement a dozen or so suggestions from the previous edition, I remain optimistic for the future.

## Creating layer-specific masks

In addition to the transparency mask that accompanies every layer (except the background), you can add a mask to a layer to make certain pixels in the layer transparent. Now, you might ask, "Won't simply erasing portions of a layer make those portions transparent?" (I just love these little chats we have.) The answer is yes, but when you erase, you delete pixels permanently. By creating a layer mask, you instead make pixels temporarily transparent. You can return several months later and bring those pixels back to life again simply by adjusting the mask. So layer masks add yet another level of flexibility to a program that's already a veritable image-editing contortionist.

To create a layer mask, select the layer you want to mask and choose Layer ⇨ Add Layer Mask ⇨ Reveal All. Or more simply, click on the layer mask icon at the bottom of the Layers palette, as labeled in Figure 17-36. A second thumbnail preview appears to the left of the layer name, also labeled in the figure. A heavy outline around the preview shows the layer mask is active.

**Tip**

If the heavy outline is hard to see, keep your eye on the icon directly to the left of the layer name. If the icon is a paintbrush, the layer and not the mask is active. If the icon is a little dotted circle, the mask is active.

To edit the mask, simply paint in the image window. Paint with black to make pixels transparent. Because black represents deselected pixels in an image, it makes these pixels transparent in a layer. Paint with white to make pixels opaque.

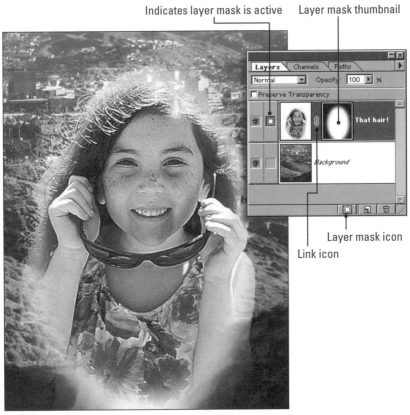

Indicates layer mask is active    Layer mask thumbnail

Layer mask icon

Link icon

**Figure 17-36:** The black area in the layer mask (which you can see in the thumbnail view, top right) translates to transparent pixels in the layer itself.

Thankfully, Photoshop is smart enough to make the default foreground color in a layer mask white and the default background color black. This ensures painting with the paintbrush or airbrush makes pixels opaque, where painting with the eraser makes them transparent, just as you would expect.

In Figure 17-36, I created a feathered oval, inversed it, and filled it with black by pressing ⌘/Ctrl+Delete/Backspace. This results in a soft vignette around the layer. If I decide I eliminated too much of the hair, not to worry. I merely paint with white to bring it back again.

Photoshop goes nuts in the layer mask department, adding lots of bells and whistles to make the function both convenient and powerful. Here's everything you need to know:

✦ **Reveal Selection:** If you select some portion of your layer, Photoshop automatically converts the selection to a layer mask when you click on the layer mask icon at the bottom of the palette. The area outside the selection becomes transparent. (The corresponding command is Layer ⇨ Add Layer Mask ⇨ Reveal Selection.)

✦ **Hide Selection:** You can also choose to reverse the prospective mask, making the area inside the selection transparent and the area outside opaque. To do this, choose Layer ⇨ Add Layer Mask ⇨ Hide Selection. Or, better yet, Option/Alt+click on the layer mask icon in the Layers palette.

✦ **Hide everything:** To begin with a black mask that hides everything, choose Layer ⇨ Add Layer Mask ⇨ Hide All. Or press ⌘/Ctrl+D to deselect everything and Option/Alt+click on the layer mask icon.

✦ **View the mask:** Photoshop regards a layer mask as a layer-specific channel. You can actually see it listed in italics in the Channels palette. To view the mask on its own — as a black-and-white image — Option/Alt+click on the layer mask thumbnail in the Layers palette. Option/Alt+click again to view the image instead.

✦ **Layer mask rubylith:** To view the mask as a red overlay, Shift+Option/Alt+ click on the layer mask icon. Or simply press the backslash key, \, above Return/Enter.

After you have both layer and mask visible at once, you can hide the mask by pressing \, or hide the layer and view only the mask by pressing the tilde key (~). So many alternatives!

✦ **Change the overlay color:** Double-click on the layer mask thumbnail to access the Layer Mask Display Options dialog box, which enables you to change the color and opacity of the rubylith.

✦ **Turn off the mask:** You can temporarily disable the mask by Shift+clicking on the mask thumbnail. A red *X* covers the thumbnail when it's disabled, and all masked pixels in the layer appear opaque. Shift+click again to put the mask in working order again.

✦ **Switch between layer and mask:** As you become more familiar with layer masks, you'll switch back and forth between layer and mask quite frequently, editing the layer one minute, editing the mask the next. You can switch between layer and mask by clicking on their respective thumbnails. As I mentioned before, look to the icon to the left of the layer name to see whether the layer or the mask is active.

You can also switch between layer and mask from the keyboard. Press ⌘/Ctrl+ tilde (~) to make the layer active. Press ⌘/Ctrl+\ to switch to the mask.

✦ **Link layer and mask:** A little link icon appears between the layer and mask thumbnails in the Layers palette. When the link icon is visible, you can move or transform the mask and layer as one. If you click on the link icon to turn it off, layer and mask move independently. (You can always move a selected region of the mask or layer independently of the other.)

✦ **Convert mask to selection:** As with all masks, you can convert a layer mask to a selection. To do so, ⌘/Ctrl+click on the layer mask icon. Throw in the Shift and Option/Alt keys if you want to add or subtract the layer mask with an existing selection outline.

When and if you finish using the mask — you can leave it in force as long as you like — you can choose Layer ➪ Remove Layer Mask. Or just drag the layer mask thumbnail to the trash can icon. Either way, an alert box asks you if you want to discard the mask or permanently apply it to the layer. Click on the button that corresponds to your innermost desires.

## Pasting inside a selection outline

One command, Edit ➪ Paste Into (⌘/Ctrl+Shift+V), creates a layer mask automatically. Choose Paste Into command to paste the contents of the Clipboard into the current selection, so the selection acts as a mask. Because Photoshop pastes to a new layer, it converts the selection into a layer mask. But here's the interesting part: By default, Photoshop turns off the link between layer and mask. This way, you can ⌘/Ctrl+drag the layer inside a fixed mask to position the pasted image.

Once upon a time in Photoshop, a command existed named Edit ➪ Paste Behind. (Or something like that. It might have been Paste in Back. My memory's a little hazy.) The command (whatever its name) pasted a copied image in back of a selection. But while the command is gone, its spirit still lives. Now you press the Alt key when choosing Edit ➪ Paste Into. Or just press ⌘/Ctrl+Shift+Option/Alt+V. Photoshop creates a new layer with an inverted layer mask, masking away the selected area.

## Masking groups of layers

About now, you may be growing fatigued with the topic of layer masking. But one more option requires your immediate attention. You can group multiple layers into something called a *clipping group*, in which the lowest layer in the group masks the others. Where the lowest layer is transparent, the other layers are hidden; where the lowest layer is opaque, the contents of the other layers are visible.

Despite the similarities in name, a clipping group bears no relation to a clipping path. That is, a clipping group doesn't allow you to prepare transparent areas for import into QuarkXPress and the like.

There are two ways to create a clipping group:

✦ Option/Alt+click on the horizontal line between any two layers to group them into a single unit. Your cursor changes to the group cursor labeled in Figure 17-37 when you press Option/Alt; the horizontal line becomes dotted after you click. To break the layers apart again, Option/Alt+click on the dotted line to make it solid.

**Figure 17-37:** Option/Alt+click on the horizontal line between two layers to group them together.

✦ Select the higher of the two layers you want to combine into a clipping group. Then choose Layer ➭ Group with Previous, or press ⌘/Ctrl+G. To make the layers independent again, choose Layer ➭ Ungroup (⌘/Ctrl+Shift+G).

Figures 17-37 and 17-38 demonstrate two steps in a piece of artwork I created for *Macworld* magazine. I had already created some text on an independent layer using the type tool (the subject of the next chapter), and I wanted to fill the text with water. So I added some photographs I shot of a swimming pool to a layer above the text, as shown in Figure 17-37. Then I combined text and pool images into a clipping group. Because the text was beneath the water, Photoshop masked the pool images according to the transparency mask assigned to the text. The result is a water pattern that exactly fills the type, as in Figure 17-38. (For a full-color version of these figures, see Color Plate 17-3.)

**Figure 17-38:** After combining pool water and type layers into a single clipping group, Photoshop applies the type layer's transparency mask to the pool layer.

**Note**

If you're familiar with Illustrator, you may recognize this clipping group metaphor as a relative to Illustrator's clipping path. One object in the illustration acts as a mask for a collection of additional objects. In Illustrator, however, the topmost object in the group is the mask, not the bottom one. So much for consistency.

✦　　✦　　✦

# Amazing Text Stuff

## The State of Type in Photoshop 5

Photoshop 5 has given us something you don't see very often — editable bitmapped type. Long after you create a line or two of text, you have the option of changing the words, typeface, size, leading, kerning, and so on, just as you can in other graphics and electronic publishing programs. You can also mix and match formatting attributes inside a single text block, something you couldn't do in Version 4 and earlier. In only one upgrade cycle, Photoshop has made a quantum leap from grim Stone Age letter wrangling to something that might actually pass for contemporary typesetting.

Now, the astute reader might discern that my tone — while generally enthusiastic — falls short of effusive. Although undeniably improved, Photoshop's type capabilities suffer two enduring flaws. First, you still have to work inside a dialog box. This means that you can't edit and format type directly in the image window. And second, as with all things in Photoshop, type is made of pixels. Each character invariably conforms to the exact same resolution as the rest of the image. So if you want to add super-smooth object-oriented type, you'll have to import the image into a program like Illustrator or QuarkXPress, just as you have in the past.

But don't let these shortcomings make you bitter and resentful. You can rest assured that Photoshop 5's brave new type tool runs circles around the old one. Even if it only does 75 percent of what you'd like it to do, that's a tremendous improvement.

## The limitation of bitmapped type

When you come right down to it, type is just another kind of graphic. A typeface is nothing more than a library of clip art that you can access from the keyboard. So it's little surprise that Photoshop treats type like any other collection of pixels.

The legibility of your type is therefore dependent upon the size and resolution of your image.

For example, Figure 18-1, shows four lines of type printed at equal sizes but different resolutions. (If these lines were printed at the same resolution, each line would be twice as large as the line that precedes it.) As you can see, the low-resolution type at top is jagged, and high-resolution type at bottom is smooth. Hence, big type printed at a high resolution yields smooth, legible output, just as a big image printed at a high resolution yields smooth, detailed output. In fact, everything that you can say about an image is true of bitmapped type.

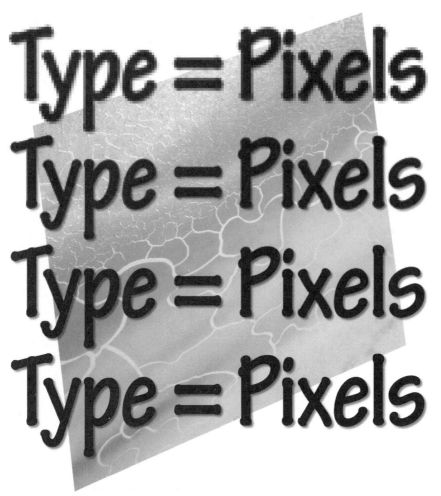

**Figure 18-1:** Four lines of type set in the PostScript font Tekton. Each line is printed at twice the resolution as the line that precedes it, starting at 37.5 ppi (top) and working up to 300 ppi (bottom).

The disadvantage of working with pixel-based type is painfully obvious. Rather than matching the resolution of your printer—a function provided by virtually every program from word processors on up—Photoshop prints type at the same resolution it prints the rest of the image. A pixel is a pixel.

## The benefits of bitmapped type

What Photoshop gives you in exchange is a whole lot of flexibility. Simply put, you can do all kinds of things with pixel-based type that you could never hope to accomplish in Illustrator, FreeHand, or a host of other programs. Here are a few examples:

✦ **Create translucent type:** Because Photoshop automatically creates type on a new layer, you can change the translucency of type as easily as adjusting the Opacity value in the Layers palette. Using this simple technique, you can merge type and images to create subtle overlay effects, as illustrated in Figure 18-2.

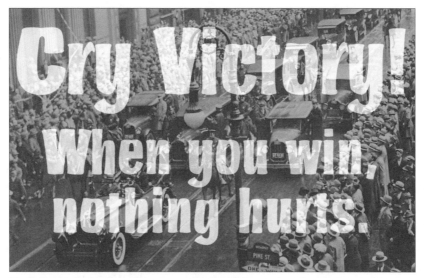

**Figure 18-2:** After creating some white type layered against a vintage photo, I lowered the opacity setting to 70 percent. Though child's play in Photoshop, this effect is virtually impossible in most drawing programs.

✦ **Use type as a selection:** Photoshop provides two type tools that create letter-shaped selection outlines. This means you can use type to select a portion of an image and then move, copy, or transform it. To create Figure 18-3, for example, I used my text to select the vintage photo. Then dragged it into a different stock photo background and applied the Multiply blend mode from the Layers palette. Naturally, you'd be hard-pressed to tell that there's a parade inside those letters, but it serves as an interesting texture.

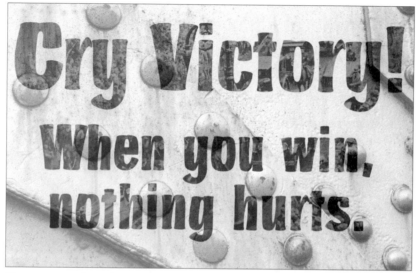

**Figure 18-3:** Photoshop is virtually unique in permitting you to select an image using type. Here I selected the image from Figure 18-2 and dragged the selection into a different background.

✦ **Apply layer effects:** Photoshop 5's new layer effects are fully applicable to type. In Figure 18-4, I replaced the industrial background from Figure 18-3 with a background texture created with the Clouds and Emboss filters (see Chapter 10). Then I applied a pillow emboss effect to the text layer using Layer ➪ Effects ➪ Bevel and Emboss.

✦ **Edit type as part of the image:** Once converted to a standard layer using the Render Layer command, you can paint type, erase it, smear it, fill it with a gradation, apply a filter or two, or do anything else that you can do to pixels. In Figure 18-5, I embossed the type, flattened it against its background, applied a few effects filters, and made it sway with the Wave filter. Don't even think about trying to accomplish this without pixels.

✦ **Trade images freely:** If you've ever shared a document created in a word processor, you know what a nightmare fonts can be. If your associate's machine isn't equipped with the fonts you used, then your document comes up all wrong. When you work with images, your font worries are over. The other guy doesn't need special screen or printer fonts to view your image exactly as you created it. He won't be able to edit the image using your font, but that's to be expected.

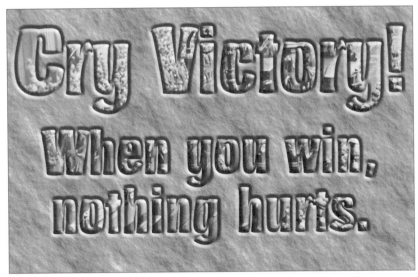

**Figure 18-4:** I used the Bevel and Emboss command to apply a pillow emboss effect. Again, an effect that takes a minute or two in Photoshop would be absolutely impossible in an object-oriented program.

**Figure 18-5:** This image is the result of going nuts for 15 minutes or so using the commands under the Filter menu. Emboss, Radial Blur, Colored Pencil, Craquelure, and Wave are all represented.

# Using the Type Tool

In a drawing or desktop publishing program, the type tool typically serves two purposes: you can create text with the tool or you can edit existing text by highlighting characters and either replacing them or applying formatting commands. In Photoshop, the primary purpose of the type tool is to create text. As a convenience, you can click on an existing text layer to edit it, but this is just a sideline. First and foremost, the type tool creates.

To create a new layer of text, select the type tool — the one that looks like a solid T — and click in the image window. (Not coincidentally, you can select the type tool from the keyboard by pressing the T key.) Instead of producing a blinking insertion marker in the window, as in other graphics programs, Photoshop displays the Type Tool dialog box shown in Figure 18-6.

The lower portion of the Type Tool dialog box is taken up by the text-entry area. This is where you enter and edit the text that you want to add to your image. As you enter the text, Photoshop gives you two simultaneous previews. You can monitor the type in black-and-white in the text-entry area and in color in the background image window. You can also zoom either preview to get a better look. To zoom the preview inside the text-entry area, use the zoom controls in the bottom left corner of the dialog box. Zoom outside the dialog box by ⌘/Ctrl+spacebar+clicking and Option/Alt+spacebar+clicking, or by pressing ⌘/Ctrl+plus and ⌘/Ctrl+minus.

But the image window isn't just for previewing. If you don't like the placement of the type inside the image, you can move the text simply by dragging it, as demonstrated in Figure 18-6. So while Photoshop 5 technically doesn't let you edit text directly in the image window, it comes awfully darn close. What we have here is a special blend of the best and worst worlds that I like to call Direct Text Editing with a Big Fat Dialog Box in Your Way.

As you enter text, it's bound to reach the right edge of the text-entry area. But instead of knocking the text to a new line, as in the old days, Photoshop scrolls your view in the dialog box. If you want to see the entire line from start to finish, drag the resize box in the lower right corner to scale the dialog box. Photoshop 5 has made significant strides in making the Type Tool dialog box present an accurate picture of your text.

Photoshop has no concept of column width, so it never breaks a line of text automatically, no matter how long it gets. You have to add a manual break by pressing the Return/Enter key. It's like using a typewriter, but without the little bell. (Dang, I miss that bell.)

Drag type to move it

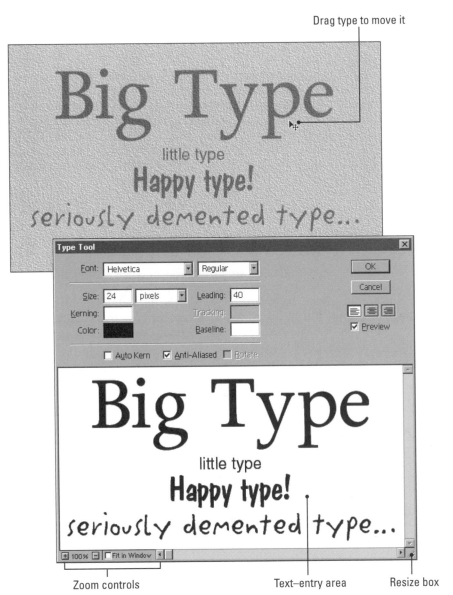

**Figure 18-6:** To create type in Photoshop, enter it into the Type Tool dialog box, which appears after you click with the type tool. You can now drag in the background window to move type, as shown at top.

## Accepting and editing

To accept the text and return to the image window, press the Enter key on the keypad. If one of the option boxes is active—Size, Leading, Kerning, Tracking, or Baseline—you can alternatively press the standard Return/Enter key. But it's a good idea to get in the habit of pressing the keypad Enter since otherwise you run the risk of inserting a line break in the text-entry area. Train yourself and avoid irritation, that's my motto. (My other motto is "Click softly and carry a big Nerf gun." But in this particular case, that advice seems counterproductive.)

Upon pressing Enter (or clicking on the OK button if you're a conventionalist), Photoshop creates your text as a new layer. But not just any layer—a special type layer. As you can see in Figure 18-7, Photoshop even adds a little T to the right of the layer name to show what a special layer it is. This T indicates two things:

✦ First, the text is fully editable. You can revisit it time and time again and make any changes you like.

✦ Second, many pixel-level edits are prohibited. You can change the color of the type, modify the blend mode or Opacity value, press ⌘/Ctrl+T to transform it, and apply as many layer effects as you like. But before you can paint on the text or apply filters, you have to convert the type to a standard layer by choosing Layer ⇨ Type ⇨ Render Layer. The tradeoff is that after that point, the type is no longer editable.

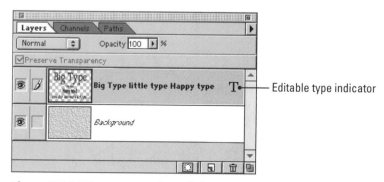

**Figure 18-7:** When you see the telltale T next to a layer, you know it's editable type.

To give you an idea, the text back in Figures 18-2 and 18-4 was 100 percent editable. (Figure 18-3 shows the effect of creating selection outlines in the shapes of letters, which is never editable.) But before going off the deep end into Figure 18-5, I had to choose the Render Layer command and forsake future editing. There is a perfectly good reason for this — pixel-level edits fundamentally change the composition of the text so it has nothing to do with its original character forms. But if that doesn't do it for you, then just remember, such is the way of Photoshop.

To revisit the Type Tool dialog box and edit a text block, you have two options:

✦ Double-click on the layer name or the T icon in the Layers palette. (Don't double-click on the thumbnail preview — that brings up the Layer Options dialog box.)

✦ When the text layer is active, use the type tool to click on a letter inside the image window. The cursor appears as a plain I-beam (no dotted outline) to show that Photoshop is ready to edit the type.

If you want to create a new text block when an editable type layer is active, Shift+click with the type tool. When a standard layer is active, just click with the type tool. Either way, the Type Tool dialog box brings up the last text you created.

By now, you may have noticed that Photoshop 5 automatically names text layers after the first 31 characters. This is a handy feature, but you can change the layer name to anything you like without affecting the editability of the text. Double-click on the thumbnail preview for the layer in the Layers palette to bring up the Layer Options dialog box, then enter a name more to your liking.

## Selecting type

Prior to Version 5, Photoshop formatted all type entered into the text-entry area identically according to a global set of specifications. The fact that Photoshop 5 lets you mix and match formatting attributes is at once helpful and confusing. The benefits are obvious — now you have more control and flexibility. But if you're used to entering a bit of text, applying some formatting settings, and hitting Enter, then prepare for some extra steps.

Before you can modify so much as a word of type, you have to select it. Fortunately, selecting has improved a bit in Photoshop 5. You can still drag over characters to highlight them, but you also have access to a wider range of keyboard tricks, as outlined in Table 18-1.

Table 18-1
### Selecting Text from the Keyboard

| Text Selection | Keystrokes |
| --- | --- |
| Select character to left or right | Shift+left or right arrow |
| Select whole word | double-click on word |
| Move left or right one word | ⌘/Ctrl+left or right arrow |
| Select word to left or right | ⌘/Ctrl+Shift+left or right arrow |
| Select one line up or down | Shift+up or down arrow |
| Select range of characters | click at one point, Shift+click at another |
| Select all text | ⌘/Ctrl+A |

After selecting type, you can replace it by entering new text from the keyboard. You can likewise cut, copy, or paste text by pressing the standard keyboard shortcuts (⌘/Ctrl+X, C, and V) or by choosing commands from the Edit menu. You can undo a text modification by pressing ⌘/Ctrl+Z or choosing Edit ➪ Undo. And if things go terribly wrong, press the Option/Alt key to change the Cancel button to Reset. Option/Alt+click on this button to reset the type to its appearance when you first opened the dialog box.

## Formatting type

Now that you know the basics of creating, selecting, and mucking about with type, it's time to cover the specific formatting attributes that do so much to make your type readable and alluring. The following sections explain the formatting options in the order they appear at the top of the Type Tool dialog box.

### Font

Select the typeface and type style you want to use from the side-by-side Font pop-up menus. Rather than offering lowest-common-denominator Bold and Italic check boxes (as was the case for Photoshop 4), Version 5 is smart enough to present a full list of designer style options. For example, while Times is limited to Bold and Italic, the Helvetica family may yield such stylistic variations as Oblique, Light, Black, Condensed, Inserat, and Ultra Compressed.

**Photoshop 5.0**

The old Underline, Outline, and Shadow check boxes are gone, and I say good riddance. Few folks want or need underlined type in Photoshop — if you do you can easily draw one. And the outline and shadow styles were truly awful. The colloquial contraction "b'ugly" comes to mind, and b'ugly is something we can all do without.

## Size

Type size is measured either in points or pixels. You can select the desired measurement from the pop-up menu to the right of the Size option box. If the resolution of your image is 72 ppi, points and pixels are equal. (There are 72 points in an inch, so 72 ppi means one pixel per point.) If the resolution is higher, however, a single point may include many pixels. The moral is to select the points option when you want to scale text according to the image resolution; select pixels when you want to map text to an exact number of pixels in an image.

**Note**

Type is measured from the top of its *ascenders*—letters like *b, d,* and *h* that rise above the level of most lowercase characters—to the bottom of its *descenders*—letters like *g, p,* and *q* that sink below the baseline. That's the way it's supposed to work, anyway. But throughout history, designers have played pretty loose and free with type size. To illustrate, Figure 18-8 shows the two standards Times and Helvetica along with a typical display font and a typical script. Each line is set to a type size of 180 pixels and then placed inside a 180-pixel box. The dotted horizontal lines indicate the baselines. As you can see, the only font that comes close to measuring the full 180 pixels is Tekton. The Brush Script sample is relatively minuscule (and Brush Script is husky compared with most scripts). So if you're looking to fill a specific space, be prepared to experiment. The only thing you can be sure of is that the type *won't* measure the precise dimensions you enter into the Size option box.

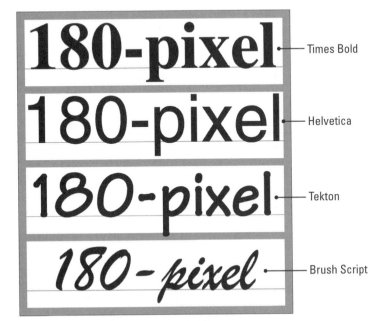

**Figure 18-8:** Four samples of 180-pixel type set inside 180-pixel boxes. As you can see, type size is an art, not a science.

In Photoshop 5, you can change every numerical formatting attribute from the keyboard. To increase the type size in 2-point (or pixel) increments, press ⌘/Ctrl+ Shift+greater than (>). To similarly decrease the size, press ⌘/Ctrl+Shift+less than (<). Add the Option/Alt key to raise or lower the type size in 10-point (or pixel) increments.

## Leading

Also called line spacing, *leading* is the vertical distance between the baseline of one line of type and the baseline of the next line of type, as illustrated in Figure 18-9. Leading is measured in the unit you selected from the Size pop-up menu. If you leave the Leading value blank, Photoshop automatically applies a leading equal to 125 percent of the type size.

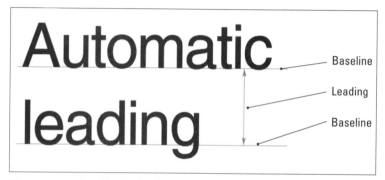

**Figure 18-9:** Leading is the distance between any two baselines in a single paragraph of text. Here, the type size is 120 pixels and the leading is 150 pixels.

The easiest way to change the distance between one line and another is like so: First, when adjusting the space between a pair of lines, select the bottom of the two. Then press Option/Alt+up arrow to decrease the leading in 2-point (pixel) increments and move the lines closer together. Press Option/Alt+down arrow to increase the leading and spread the lines apart. To work in 10-point (pixel) increments, press ⌘/Ctrl+Option/Alt+up or down arrow.

## Kerning and Auto Kern

Technically, *kern* is the predetermined amount of space that surrounds each character of type and separates it from its immediate neighbors. (Some type-heads also call it *side bearing*.) But as is so frequently the case with our molten magma of a language, kern has found new popularity in recent years as a verb. So if a friend says, "Let's kern!" don't reach for your rowing oars. Get psyched to adjust the amount of room between characters of type. (Yes, there are people who love to kern and, yes, it is sad.)

The first line of defense in the battle against ugly character spacing is the Auto Kern check box. When turned off, Photoshop applies the default amount of side bearing to each character, as prescribed by the specifications included in the individual font file on your hard drive. But some character combinations don't look right when subjected to the default bearing. The spacing that separates a *T* and an *h* doesn't look so good when you scrap the *h* and insert an *r*. Therefore, the character combination *T* and *r* is a special-needs pair, a typographic marriage that requires kern counseling.

When you turn on the Auto Kern check box, Photoshop digs farther into the font specifications and pulls out a list of special-needs letter pairs. Then it applies a prescribed amount of spacing compensation, as illustrated by the second line in Figure 18-10.

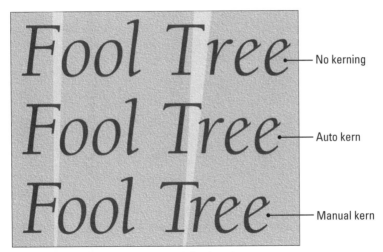

— No kerning

— Auto kern

— Manual kern

**Figure 18-10:** Three examples of the kerning options in Photoshop 5. I've added wedges to track the ever-decreasing space between the difficult pairs *Fo* and *Tr*.

In most cases, you'll want to leave Auto Kern turned on and trust in the designers' pair kerning expertise. But there may be times when the prescribed kerning isn't to your liking. In this case, Photoshop 5 lets you kern manually. Inside the Type Tool dialog box, click between two badly spaced characters of type. Then turn off the Auto Kern check box to enable the Kerning option box. Enter a negative value to shift the letters closer together. Enter a positive value to kern them farther apart. The last line in Figure 18-10 shows examples of my tighter manual kerns.

To decrease the Kerning value (and thereby tighten the spacing) in increments of 20, press Option/Alt+left arrow. To increase the Kerning value by 20, press Option/Alt+right arrow. You can also modify the kerning in increments of 100 by pressing ⌘/Ctrl+Option/Alt+left or right arrow.

Incidentally, the Kerning and Tracking values are measured in $\frac{1}{1000}$ em, where an *em* (or *em space*) is the width of the letter *m* in the current font at the current size. This may sound weird, but it's actually very helpful. Working in ems ensures that your character spacing automatically updates to accommodate changes in font and type size.

## Tracking

The Tracking value is virtually identical to Kerning. It affects character spacing, as measured in em spaces. It even reacts to the same keyboard shortcuts. The only differences are that you can apply Tracking to multiple characters at a time. And Photoshop permits you to apply a Tracking value on top of either automatic or manual kerning. (For folks experienced with Photoshop 4 and earlier, Tracking is more or less the equivalent of the old Spacing option, but measured in ems.)

## Color

Click on the Color swatch to display the Color Picker dialog box. This is the one attribute that Photoshop applies to all text in the dialog box, whether selected or not. Personally, I find it more convenient to apply color outside the Type Tool dialog box by selecting a color from the Color palette and pressing Option/Alt+ Delete/Backspace. The effect is the same.

## Baseline

The Baseline value raises or lowers the selected text with respect to the baseline, as measured in pixels or points depending on the Size pop-up menu setting. In type parlance, this is called *baseline shift*. Raising type results in a superscript. Lowering type results in a subscript. An example of each appears in Figure 18-11.

You can also raise type to create a built fraction. (To access the special fraction slash on a Mac, press Shift+Option+1.) Select the number before the slash (the *numerator*) and enter a positive value into the Baseline option box. Reduce the size of the value after the slash (the *denominator*) but leave the Baseline blank. That's all I did to get the fraction at the bottom of Figure 18-11.

Press Shift+Option/Alt+up arrow to raise the Baseline value by 2 or Shift+Option/ Alt+down arrow to lower the value by 2. To change the value in increments of 10, add in the ⌘/Ctrl key.

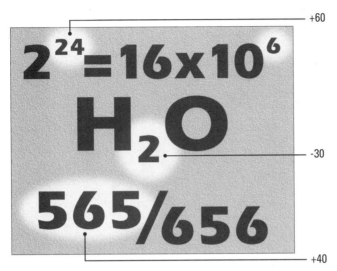

+60

$$2^{24} = 16 \times 10^6$$

$$H_2O$$ -30

565/656 +40

**Figure 18-11:** Baseline shift frequently finds its way into the worlds of math and science. The labels show the Baseline values.

## Alignment

The three nameless icons below the Cancel button control how lines of type align with each other. By default, the alignment is measured from the point at which you originally clicked with the type tool. But as I mentioned earlier, you can move this alignment point by dragging in the image window even when the Type Tool dialog box is open. Photoshop lets you align text left, center, or right. Because it has no concept of column width, there is no justification setting.

Old timers will notice the last of vertical alignment options. To create vertical text, exit the Type Tool dialog box and choose Layer ➪ Type ➪ Vertical. Or create the type from the outset with the vertical type tool, as I explain later in this chapter.

You can change the alignment using standard keyboard tricks. Press ⌘/Ctrl+Shift+L to align selected lines to the left. ⌘/Ctrl+Shift+C centers text and ⌘/Ctrl+Shift+R aligns it to the right.

## Anti-Aliased

When you select the Anti-Aliased check box, Photoshop softens characters by slightly blurring pixels around the perimeter. Unless you want to create very small type or you intend to match the resolution of your output device — printing a 300 ppi image to a 300 dpi printer, for example — you should turn this option on. Unless otherwise indicated, I created all figures in this chapter with the Anti-Aliased check box selected. In fact, the only exception I can think of is the second example in Figure 18-12.

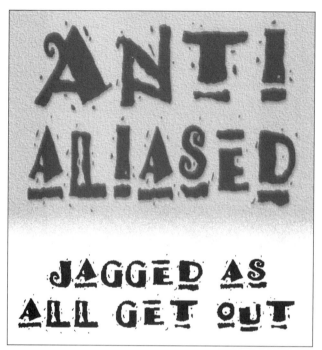

**Figure 18-12:** I created the top example with the Anti-Aliased check box turn on and the bottom with the option turned off. Unless you're looking for a harsh, exacting effect, leave Anti-Aliased on.

## Creating vertical type

For Westerners, Photoshop 5 offers a new vertical type tool for aligning type from top to bottom instead of left to right. To get to this tool, press Shift+T twice when the type tool is active. In truth, the vertical type tool is nothing more than the standard type tool lifted from the Japanese version of Photoshop. As shown in the first example of Figure 18-13, it creates vertical columns of type that read right to left, as in Japan. If you want to make columns of type that read left to right, you'll have to create each column as an independent text block.

When editing vertical type, the Type Tool dialog box presents you with a Rotate check box. Select this check box to rotate each character 90 degrees and achieve the effect illustrated by the second example of Figure 18-13.

You can convert vertical text to horizontal by choosing Layer ➪ Type ➪ Horizontal. To go the other way, choose Layer ➪ Type ➪ Vertical.

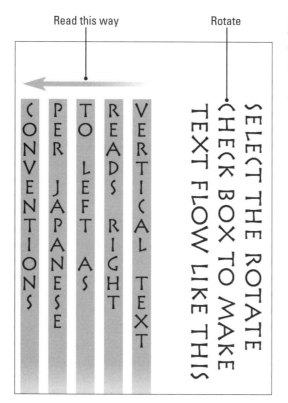

Read this way      Rotate

**Figure 18-13:** By default, vertical type reads right to left, as shown in the first example. If you select the Rotate check box in the Type Tool dialog box, Photoshop creates the effect on right.

# Character Masks and Layer Effects

Photoshop offers two more type tools. Known as the type mask tools (regular and vertical), they create character-shaped selection outlines. You can switch to the type mask tool by pressing Shift+T when the standard type tool is active. Or select the T with the dotted outline in the pop-up in the toolbox. If you want to select the vertical type mask tool (unlikely, but you never know), press Shift+T twice more.

Generally speaking, the type mask tool works like any other type tool, the one exception being that you can't edit the type in the same way as a self-contained type layer. If you misspell a word or you change your mind about the type size, press ⌘/Ctrl+D to deselect the image and click again with the type mask tool to bring up your last settings.

The type mask tools are ultimately selection tools, so they work a lot like the magic wand, lasso, and others:

    ✦ Click with a type mask tool to create a new selection outline.

    ✦ Shift+click to add the character outlines to an existing selection.

✦ Option/Alt+click to subtract from a selection.

✦ And Shift+Option/Alt+click to find the intersection.

## Type masks on the march

The most obvious use for the type mask tool is to select a portion of an image. In a matter of seconds, you get type filled with photographic imagery. While nifty in theory, finding a use for photographic type is another matter. In the following steps, I use the type mask tool to select a portion of an image, send it to a new layer, and then modify brightness values to distinguish the text from its background. Though very easy, it yields some interesting results.

### Steps: Selecting Part of an Image Using Character Outlines

1. **Assemble the image you want to mask.** In my case, I start with the classic eel erupting from a clock pictured in Figure 18-14. I know, you're thinking, "Deke, how do you come up with such attractive stuff?" It's a knack, I guess. Try not to be jealous.

**Figure 18-14:** I created this image by selecting an eel, layering it against a clock, and using a layer mask to blend the two images. Then I flattened the image and saved it.

2. **Create your text.** Select the type mask tool and click in the image window. Enter the text you want to use into the Type Tool dialog box, format it as desired, and press the Enter key on the keypad to display the type outlines in the image window. Bear in mind, Photoshop does not preview type masks in the image window, so you'll have to rely on the preview inside the Type Tool dialog box.

3. **Modify the selection outlines an needed.** I chose Select ⇨ Transform Selection and then ⌘/Ctrl+dragged the corner handles to distort my character outlines, as in Figure 18-15. (The character outlines are hard to see, so I've added a translucent white fill to make the text more legible. The fill is there merely for the purpose of the screen shot.)

**Figure 18-15:** The Transform Selection command enabled me to apply a perspective effect to my character outlines before using them to select the image.

4. **Send the selected text to a separate layer by pressing ⌘/Ctrl+J.** The selection outlines disappear, so the image looks like it did before you started. But rest assured, you have characters filled with imagery on a separate layer.

*(continued)*

5. **Return to the background layer and create a new layer by clicking on the page icon at the bottom of the Layers palette.** The easiest way to distinguish text from background image is to darken the background image and lighten the text (or vice versa). This new layer is just the ticket.

6. **Fill the layer with a dark color.** Then choose the Multiply mode (Shift+Option/Alt+M) and lower the Opacity value. For my part, I added a black-to-white gradation starting from the lower left and ending in the upper right portion of the image. Thanks to the Multiply mode, just the area behind the text was darkened, as shown in Figure 18-16. I also lowered the Opacity to 40 percent.

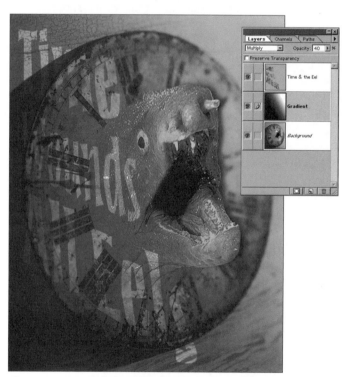

**Figure 18-16:** To darken the area behind the type, I added a black-to-white gradation on a new layer and set the layer to the Multiply mode.

7. **Switch to the type layer.** Now to make the type a lighter color.

8. **Create a new layer and fill it with a light color.** Set the blend mode to Screen (Shift+Option/Alt+S) and adjust the Opacity value as desired. I filled my layer with white and set the Opacity to 80 percent.

9. **Press ⌘/Ctrl+G.** This groups the light layer with the type below it, as demonstrated in Figure 18-17. The light area outside the type goes away. Now the type stands out clearly from its background, even though you can see the image both inside and outside the letters.

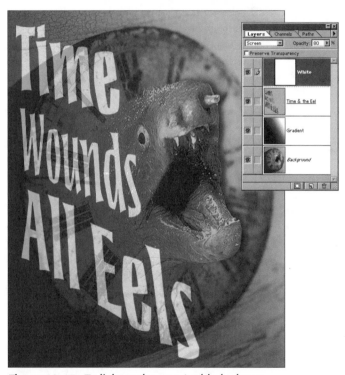

**Figure 18-17:** To lighten the text, I added a layer filled entirely with white and grouped it with the type layer.

*(continued)*

10. **Apply whatever additional effects strike your fancy.** I returned to the type layer and chose Layer ⇨ Effects ⇨ Bevel and Emboss. Then I selected the Outer Bevel setting to create the letters shown in Figure 18-18. I also applied the Drop Shadow effect to the text in the upper right corner and the Pillow Emboss effect to the Jelly-Vision logo.

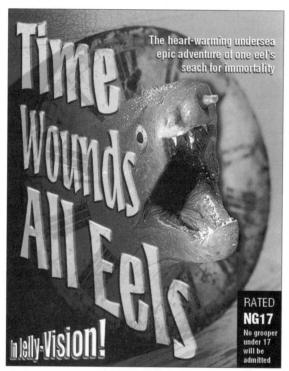

**Figure 18-18:** I managed to transform a strange, drab composition into this mighty attractive poster art using nothing but text.

As the enlarged view of the Jelly-Vision logo in Figure 18-19 shows, Photoshop's layer effects can work super-fast miracles on type. In a matter of seconds, I was able to transform the top example in the figure into the bottom one. (Note that in order to distort the type to achieve the perspective effect, I had to first convert it to a standard layer using Layer ⇨ Type ⇨ Render Layer.)

**Figure 18-19:** Creating the Jelly-Vision logo was as simple as distorting the text and applying a Pillow Emboss layer effect.

## Layer effects bonanza

You'll have a blast experimenting with layer effects and type. Layer effects are fast, flexible, easy to use, and they were designed largely with editable type in mind. I have no doubt that they'll get *waaaay* overused. But as with any cool feature, you can stay ahead of the curve by applying your effects creatively.

Figure 18-20 shows three very simple but unusual implementations of layer effects. All three effects rely on character masks, but I created these selection outlines using the standard type tool. I clicked with the type tool; entered the words *Shake*, *Murder*, and *Imprint*; formatted them; and hit the keypad Enter to create a new type layer. Then I ⌘/Ctrl+clicked on the layer to draw out the selection outlines as I needed them.

Why use the standard type tool to create selection outlines instead of the type mask tool? Two reasons. First, the type tool shows you what it's up to in the image window, which is invaluable when formatting type to fit in a confined space. Second, I can always go back and edit my type when it's on an independent layer. (These edits won't affect my existing character masks, but I can ⌘/Ctrl+click to generate new masks any time I like.) The wonderful thing about the standard type tool is that it permits you to create both editable text and type masks. This one tool does everything you need, which is why I for one never change type tools; I always work with the upright black T.

**Figure 18-20:** Three examples of childishly simple layer effects applied creatively to character masks.

That's really the key to creating cool effects. The rest is just "scribbling and bibbling" as a dramatized Mozart once said. But because the scribbles and bibbles may prove of minor interest to you, here's how I made each effect:

✦ **Shake:** First, the boring stuff. I extracted the layer mask for the word Shake by ⌘/Ctrl+clicking on my type layer and Shift+Option/Alt+dragging around the word Shake with the rectangular marquee tool to deselect Murder and Imprint.

Then I switched to the background layer and pressed ⌘/Ctrl+J to send Shake to an independent layer. Finally I pressed the / key to turn on Preserve Transparency, so I could edit the type and only the type.

Now for the fun stuff. I created a pattern from the embossed texture back in Figure 18-5 using Edit ➪ Define Pattern. Then I used Edit ➪ Fill to fill Shake with the pattern. Last, I brought up the Effects dialog box and applied a drop shadow set to black and Multiply, and an Inner Shadow set to white and Screen. The upshot is that the drop shadow darkens the background and the inner shadow lightens the characters. Figure 18-21 shows my settings.

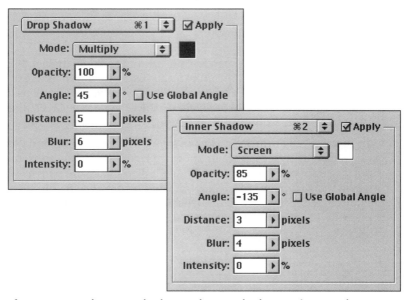

**Figure 18-21:** The Drop Shadow and Inner Shadow settings used to create the word Shake in Figure 18-20.

✦ **Murder:** I filled the background layer behind the word Murder with black. Then I did all the boring stuff that I mentioned two paragraphs ago — ⌘/Ctrl+clicked the type layer, intersected Murder with the marquee tool, pressed ⌘/Ctrl+J to send Murder to its own layer, and selected Preserve Transparency.

I set the foreground color to white and brushed across the Murder layer with the paintbrush set to 40 percent opacity. Because Preserve Transparency was on, I painted inside the letters only. Finally, I chose Layer ➪ Effects ➪ Drop Shadow and applied a white halo set to Screen according to the settings in Figure 18-22. The result is a directional glow.

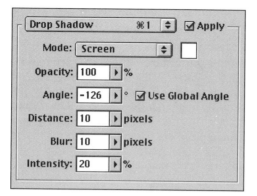

**Figure 18-22:** I used the Drop Shadow effect to add a halo behind the word Murder.

✦ **Imprint:** I filled the area behind imprint with the same pattern I defined for Shake, then I mushed the pattern together using the filters Noise ➪ Median and Blur ➪ Gaussian Blur (both explained in Chapter 23). Then, as usual, I did the boring stuff — ⌘/Ctrl+clicked on the original type layer, intersected Imprint with the marquee tool, and pressed ⌘/Ctrl+J and the / key.

With Imprint on its own layer, I chose Layer ➪ Effects ➪ Bevel and Emboss, and applied the fairly typical settings shown in Figure 18-23. The subsequent effect was a bit disappointing. Muted and dark, it didn't have the punch I wanted. To brighten it up, I duplicated the Imprint layer by dragging it onto the page icon at the bottom of the Layers palette. Then I pressed Shift+Option/Alt+S to apply the Screen mode. The final result is the much sharper effect you see in Figure 18-20.

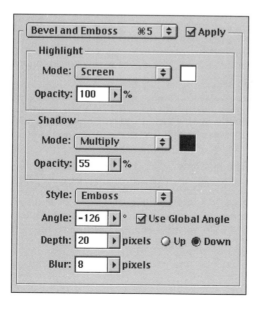

**Figure 18-23:** After applying these settings to the word Imprint, I duplicated the layer and selected the Screen blend mode.

# Other Type Options

While Version 5's type capabilities have changed pretty radically, Photoshop still has its limitations. Take type on a curve, for example. While you can rest assured Adobe intends to add type on a curve to a future version of Photoshop, the feature isn't available yet.

One option is to align your type to a curve in a drawing program such as Illustrator or FreeHand, and then drag and drop it into Photoshop. If you don't own a drawing program—or if you're looking for an integrated solution that doesn't require you to leave Photoshop—then you might want to purchase a good third-party plug-in. The one that looks most promising is PhotoText, part of the PhotoDraw suite which should be available in Fall of 1998 from Extensis (*www.extensis.com*). As the screen shot from Figure 18-24 shows, PhotoText will let you bind text to primitive shapes like ellipses and regular polygons, as well as free-form Bézier paths. PhotoText will also support justified paragraphs, tabs, and custom styles, all advantages over Photoshop 5.

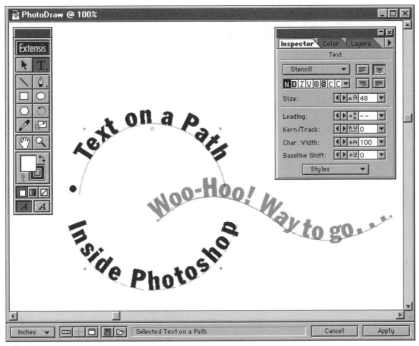

**Figure 18-24:** PhotoText from Extensis serves as a fully functioning text-editing environment, complete with type on a curve. Bear in mind, this is an early alpha screen shot sneaked to me months before PhotoText is to ship. The final interface may look different.

If you want to create three-dimensional type effects inside Photoshop, you have two third-party plug-ins to choose from. The first is the $200 TypeCaster from Xaos Tools (*www.xaostools.com*). To use the plug-in, you simply open a dialog box, enter some text, select a font, and modify the type in 3D space. You can rotate, scale, and adjust the depth of the extrusion. You can also apply and modify surface textures to the face, bevel, and extruded sides of the type, as demonstrated in Figure 18-25. Finally, you can assign and position light sources inside a separate dialog box. TypeCaster isn't perfect — live previews, manual kerning, and letter warping would all go a long way — but it's an excellent addition to Photoshop.

**Figure 18-25:** TypeCaster lets you create 3-D type inside Photoshop. But because it doesn't permit you to hand-kern letters, you'll probably need to adjust the type manually on a separate layer.

The second 3-D type product is HotText from Vertigo (*www.vertigo3d.com*). Priced $50 cheaper than TypeCaster, HotText shares TypeCaster's inability to kern and lacks the option to create beveled edges. But in exchange, HotText lets you align your text to a free-form path so that the characters dip, pivot, and spin in 3-D space. It's just the thing for making type that rushes toward the viewer. Naturally, all of the products mentioned here — PhotoGraphics, TypeCaster, and HotText — are available for the Mac, Windows 95, and Windows NT.

✦    ✦    ✦

# PART VI
## THINGS ONLY PHOTOSHOP CAN DO

**The Tao of Layering**
**Enhancing Vector Artwork**
**Special Type Effects**
**Setting Up Clipping Paths**

# CHAPTER 19
# THE TAO OF LAYERING

G reg Vander Houwen is easily one of the most cerebral Photoshop artists I know. To his credit, the guy spends as much time analyzing and reflecting on what he does as he spends doing it. In the eight years he's worked with Photoshop, he's discovered three broad and unifying principles of computer imaging:

"First — and I think everyone has discovered this — computers don't like us for the way we use them, and they pay us back by stealing our time. Probably one out of every ten times I walk up to my machine, there's some new problem that I have to mess with. It's no use fighting; the computer always has the upper hand. It literally owns your data." You have to coax the machine to share its data through attentiveness and patient problem solving.

"Second, Photoshop is a great program, but it's by no means perfect. It's not even intelligent in any conventional sense. So it's up to you to recognize its shortcomings and anticipate them. Photoshop is like a force of nature that you do well to understand and embrace.

"Third, simplicity is key to the way I work. I'm not keen on complex sequences. The bottom line is, even though I'm technically capable, I can't remember long procedures. The best techniques are the simple ones that I can mix and match like jazz licks. If I can quickly recall and 'play' the operation, only then does it become practical."

The net result is an artistic philosophy based on anticipating mistakes and working with as little fanfare as possible. Vander Houwen's primary ally in this quest is the common layer. "Layers have made my life

*Photoshop is like a force of nature that you do well to understand and embrace.*

**GREG VANDER HOUWEN**

substantially better. I have clients who perpetually come back to me and say, 'Gee, Greg, that's great, but you know, what we were thinking was *this*.' It always translates to me having to change something. But so long as I stick with virtual compositing — relying on blend modes, layer options, layer masks, and adjustment layers — then I can always go back and retrieve the original data." With layers, Vander Houwen makes it easy and keeps it safe.

## BASE CAMPS AND SERIOUS ALTERATIONS

"There are two concepts that are central to the way I think — 'base camps' and 'serious alterations.' A base camp is just a saved version of a file at a certain stage in its development. Back in Photoshop 2.5, before layers came along, I was constantly saving versions so that I could revert back to previous stages of the artwork. Now that I have layers, I still use base camps as an added precaution. I tend to save a base camp whenever my gut says, 'You know, if you lost this, it could be very bad.'

"A serious alteration is a modification that you apply directly to a pixel. For example, applying the Levels command directly to an image is a serious alteration; using an adjustment layer is not. . . . I try not to commit a serious alteration when an alternative is available. But many serious alterations are unavoidable. The trick is, before I commit a serious alteration, I make sure to create a base camp. Then, I'm covered."

Vander Houwen even goes so far as to archive many base camps to CD-ROM on the off-chance he might need it in the future. "On CD, I can go back years and extract bits and pieces from files because I've been working this way. It doesn't happen very often, but I've had situations where the client calls up and says, 'Now, we know this is a big change and we know it was six months ago, but the thing is, we got this deadline. We realize you'll have to work through the night, and this is going to cost us a huge sum of money.' I'm tempted to say, 'Yeah, it is. That's going to hurt a lot. Boy, are you right.' But instead, I pop in the CD, grab the right base camp, and surprise the client with a miracle turnaround."

The figures (19.1, 19.2, 19.3) demonstrate the lengths Vander Houwen goes to in his virtual compositing. "Don't get hung up on the numbers. These are just demonstration composites, but they should give you a good idea of how I work."

**19.1 (26 LAYERS, 2 BASE CAMPS)**

## ROUGHING OUT A COMPOSITION

"I always start off by blocking out the basic composite. I throw things onto their own layers, so as not to damage them. Then, I add layer masks using gradients and brushes. I might play with the Opacity setting, too. The bottom line is, I'm trying to build the roughest, fastest composite I can, so I can make decisions and figure out if there are any problems with the composite. You might have a nice sketch put together, but until you get the images nested, you can't see exactly where things work and where they might go wrong."

**ARTIST:**
Greg Vander Houwen

**ORGANIZATION:**
Interact
P.O. Box 498
Issaquah, Washington 98027
(206) 999-2584
gregvh@netcandy.com

**SYSTEM:**
Power Mac 8100/110
6GB storage

**RAM:**
110MB total
90MB assigned to Photoshop

**MONITOR:**
Apple 17-inch

**EXTRAS:**
Wacom 12 × 12 electrostatic tablet

**VERSION USED:**
Photoshop 5.0

**OTHER APPLICATIONS:**
Adobe Illustrator, Fractal Design Painter, ElectricImage Broadcast

19.2 (16 LAYERS, 3 BASE CAMPS)

19.3 (21 LAYERS, 3 BASE CAMPS)

**WORK HISTORY:**

<u>1977</u> — Sold photographs for $200 to farming magazine at 14 years old.

<u>1983</u> — Searched around in vain for job in Los Angeles video industry, retreated to home-town computer store and began to pursue computer graphics.

<u>1989</u> — Acquired alpha version of Photoshop, created first published image for *Verbum* magazine.

<u>1991</u> — Started his own design firm, which now includes Apple, Adobe, and Microsoft as clients.

<u>1992</u> — Learned compositing and retouching techniques at Ivey Seright imaging lab.

<u>1997</u> — Helped Microsoft develop new graphical interface.

**FAVORITE CARTOON CHARACTER:**

The Tick ("Aside from Buddha, he's the most enlightened intellect I've ever encountered.")

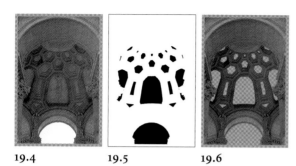

19.4          19.5          19.6

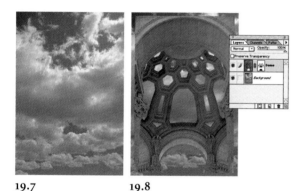

19.7          19.8

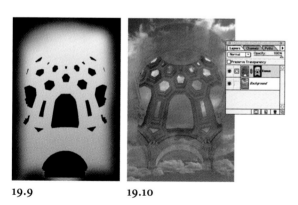

19.9          19.10

## CHAIN SAWING A LAYER MASK

As an example, Vander Houwen had an idea to create a dome with transparent windows looking up into a cloudy sky. Up front, there was one obvious problem: the dome didn't have any windows (19.4). But it did have indented panels that could be removed to serve as windows. Rather than deleting these panels, Vander Houwen converted the dome to a floating layer and added a layer mask (19.5).

"I clicked around with the polygon lasso tool until I selected the panels. It's like chain sawing — I just hacked through it in rough slashes. After I got a halfway decent selection, I Option-clicked the layer mask icon at the bottom of the Layers palette to mask away the selected areas. Then, with the layer mask on, I took out my brushes and tweaked it. I used the Shift key and clicked from point to point along the straight edges." The result is a windowed dome, without so much as a pixel in the original image harmed (19.6).

## DROPPING THE DOME

Compositing the dome against the sky (19.7) was a simple matter of dragging the dome with the move tool (or ⌘/Ctrl-dragging with some other tool) and dropping it into the sky. By pressing the Shift key during the drop, Vander Houwen center-registered the dome inside the sky (19.8).

The layered image wasn't quite the same size as the sky, so the dome had a harsh rectangular edge around it. Rather than resizing the dome or cropping the sky, Vander Houwen decided to simply brush around the layer mask some more. He applied a black fringe with the paintbrush tool (19.9), starting with a big fuzzy brush and working down to smaller ones. "Begin big and general, then work toward precision," Vander Houwen advises. Although the fringe took just a minute or two to create, it rendered a very serviceable fade (19.10).

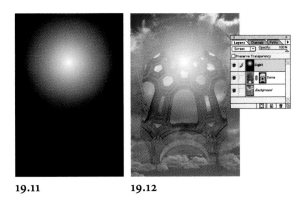

**19.11**          **19.12**

## THE LIGHT FROM ON HIGH

Finally, the dome needed a bright, glorious light streaming in from the sky. Vander Houwen created a new layer and filled it with a very simple white-to-black radial gradation (19.11). Then, he applied the Screen blend mode from the Layers palette to drop out the black and highlight the layers below (19.12). "I always tell people, Screen and Multiply are 90 percent of what they need to know about blend modes. Screen stacks lightness; Multiply stacks darkness. So I use Screen to keep light stuff like glows, and Multiply to keep dark stuff like shadows."

No special filter, a very simple approach, and not a single serious alteration — it's the ideal composition. "My first goal is always to assemble the rough elements together so I can quickly adapt if needed, or call the art director and say, 'Mayday! This is never going to work!' A rough composite gives you a basis for negotiation and compromise."

**19.13** (TOP), **19.14** (BOTTOM)

## USING LAYER OPTIONS

"For another composition, I was asked to layer some lightning (19.13) against some clouds (19.14). Obviously, I wanted to keep the light stuff and make the dark stuff go away. Blend modes and layer options are great for that. You don't need to use the magic wand tool and get those jagged halos around the edges, and you don't need to resort to a complex mask. Let Photoshop do the work for you."

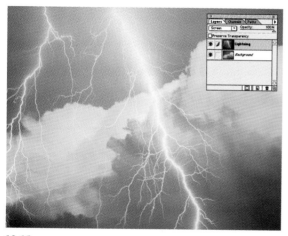

**19.15**

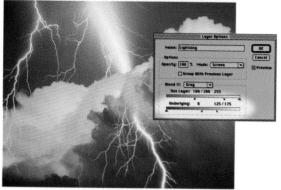

**19.16** (TOP), **19.17** (BOTTOM)

Vander Houwen started by layering the lightning in front of the clouds and applying the Screen blend mode from the Layers palette (19.15). But this resulted in a universal lightening effect that washed out the clouds below. The trick is to keep only the lightest pixels in the lightning layer and make the others invisible. Sounds like a job for layer options.

### DROPPING OUT AND FORCING THROUGH

Vander Houwen double-clicked the Lightning layer in the Layers palette to bring up the Layer Options dialog box. Then, he adjusted the black triangle in the slider bar labeled This Layer. This dropped out the original background for the layer. To soften the transition between visible and invisible pixels, he Option/Alt-dragged the triangle to break it in half. The result is lightning that looks like it was photographed with the original image (19.16).

But that wasn't enough. Vander Houwen also wanted to force the lightest colors in the clouds in front of the lightning. So he dragged and then Option/Alt-dragged the white triangle in the Underlying slider bar. This created the effect of the lightning going through the clouds (19.17).

### NEVER TRY TO MASK LIGHTNING

"I had a client who said, 'We know how hard it is to knock out lightning because it's got all those fingers. Maybe you could use an alpha channel or something.' And I thought, if I had to create a mask for lightning, it would take me a week and it probably wouldn't look right. The layer options effect takes a few seconds to pull off, it doesn't harm the original image, and it looks better than anything I could accomplish with a mask," as the magnified detail shows (19.18). "And it's not just lightning. It's stars, it's city lights, it's anything light. Or anything dark — for example, layer options are great for compositing scanned logos against different backgrounds. I just move the white slider, and the paper goes away.

"Along with blend modes, layer options are basically your way to control the overlay of light and dark stuff. If you can get your head around that, then you can even control how individual color channels land by editing red, green, and blue separately. For example, blue skies can be made to go away rather easily by tweaking the sliders in the blue component."

## TONAL ADJUSTMENTS IN LAYER MASKS

"One of my favorite little techniques to show people that they should care about layer masks is just to put a couple of images together and run gradients across them. If you don't like the way the effect works, you don't need to undo. Just run gradient after gradient after gradient. Each new gradient will obliterate the last one. Or you can run a simple black-to-white gradient. And then use a tonal control like Levels or Curves to manipulate the mask transitions."

### GRADIENT LAYER MASKS

For this example, Vander Houwen took a photograph of a woman's face (19.19) and layered it against a sunset (19.20) so the woman's right eye aligned exactly on top of the sun. "I just dragged on the eye and dropped onto the sun. If you know a little about your composition ahead of time, alignment is easy."

Vander Houwen added a layer mask by clicking the left-hand icon at the bottom of the Layers palette. He selected the gradient tool and chose Foreground to Background in the Gradient Tool Options palette (with the foreground and background colors set to their defaults of black and white). Then, he dragged from the lower-right to the upper-left corner in the mask (19.21). The lower-right corner became transparent and faded into opacity (19.22), again without upsetting a pixel in the original images.

Using the Curves command, Vander Houwen created a spiky color map that resulted in an alternating series of blacks and whites inside the layer mask (19.23). "A simple black-to-white gradation can yield all kinds of effects with Curves." The upshot is a strobe effect that flashes the face on and off over the course of the image (19.24).

19.18

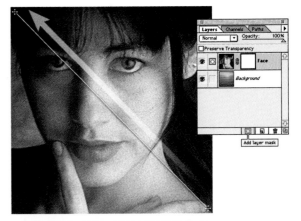

**19.21** (TOP), **19.22** (BOTTOM)

**19.19** (TOP), **19.20** (BOTTOM)

## TONAL EDGE ADJUSTMENTS

"I also use this technique to refine selections. I make a hasty selection around an image element that's just roughly in the shape of the thing. Then, I convert the selection to a layer mask (19.25), blur the heck out of it (19.26), and go into Levels or Curves and manipulate the edge (19.27). This way, I can draw the layer into the background or draw it away from the background, without a lot of work. In most cases, I have to go back and edit the mask further (19.28), but this simple spreading and choking technique eliminates about 70 percent of the job."

The lasso isn't the only selection tool that can benefit from this technique. "One of the key things I've

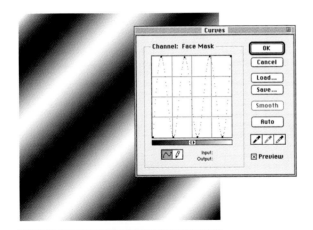

**19.23 (TOP), 19.24 (BOTTOM)**

**19.25 (TOP), 19.26 (BOTTOM)**

learned about Photoshop is that if I had to rely exclusively on the magic wand to make a selection, I'd be a sad puppy. So I use the magic wand to get me half the way, and then play with layer masking from there. Suddenly, it's a cool tool that quickly eliminates a large part of my work."

## QUICK EFFECT MASKS

"A lot of special effects can be achieved with the help of layer masks. For example, Photoshop doesn't offer a unidirectional motion trail filter. That's okay, because you can easily whip one together yourself."

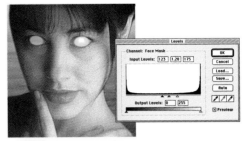

**19.27 (TOP), 19.28 (BOTTOM)**

The jet fighter (19.29) is an image that's just begging for a motion trail. Vander Houwen duplicated the image to a new layer and applied a hefty dose of Motion Blur filter. "I matched the Angle value to the angle of the jet, and I changed the Distance to 300 pixels." That's a pretty huge value considering the modest resolution of this image. In fact, the jet is pretty well blown to bits (19.30).

Vander Houwen then added a layer mask and painted in the forward part of the blurred plane to reveal the original underneath. "I start painting with huge brushes — the bigger the brush, the better to start with. I just knock it out at first, then I refine with smaller brushes. I hit the number and bracket keys like a madman to adjust the brush settings on the fly. I never touch the palettes if I can help it — it takes too long and interrupts the flow."

He Shift-clicked along the sides of the wings — with the grain of the motion blur — to get rid of any blurring Photoshop may have applied to the sky. And he filled in a few spots inside the jet with light grays to bring back some of the detail. The finished mask appears in grayscale (19.31) with the resulting motion trail effect shown below it (19.32).

"Sometimes the simplicity of these effects is a little painful. This one in particular makes me flinch a little because, in the past, I did it so badly. I would hand-draw the motion trail with the smudge tool or something equally difficult. But that's the way it is, right? The price of today's success is often yesterday's pain."

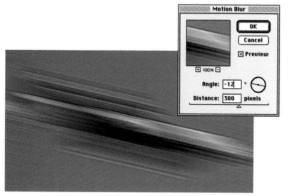

19.29

19.30

19.31 (TOP), 19.32 (BOTTOM)

## WALKING THE VIRTUAL MILE

"This last file includes a bunch of good examples of how you can easily layer image elements using the techniques I explained before, all working together in concert. I started by dragging and dropping all my elements into a single composition. I have to say that I've really embraced drag-and-drop lately because I finally figured out its advantage. Everyone tells you that drag and drop doesn't take up any Clipboard memory. But you know what that means? You aren't leaving the picture of the 5MB duck or whatever up in the Clipboard for two hours while you wait for it to cause an out-of-memory error. Besides, it's easier — you just grab the thing and haul it over."

## BUILDING THE LAYERS

Vander Houwen started this particular image by filling a layer with black and adding stars to it (19.33). To make the stars, he applied the Add Noise filter and turned on both the Gaussian and Monochrome options. Then, he applied Gaussian Blur with a Radius of 1.0 and used the Levels command to exaggerate the brightness of the blurred dots.

He next dragged in a sky photo and set the blend mode to Screen so the stars would remain visible (19.34). Then, he introduced two more elements — the Golden Gate Bridge and a statue in harsh light (19.35). Both elements consume relatively small chunks of the image window and require blending. Vander Houwen dropped away the sky pixels in the bridge layer using the Layer Options dialog box. He set the Blend If pop-up menu to Blue and adjusted the white This Layer triangle. (Try this on any bright sky image, and you'll quickly see how well it works.) Then, he added gradient layer masks to both layers to create even fades (19.36).

The last image to be tossed on the stack was the rolling fog (19.37). This image completely covered the stuff behind it, so Vander Houwen again relied on his friends, the layer options. By adjusting the black triangle in the This Layer slider bar, he was able to drop the black sky away and melt the fog gracefully into its background (19.38).

19.33 (TOP), 19.34 (BOTTOM)

## STRIKING BASE CAMP

"I often modify the position of the elements with the arrow keys and Shift-arrow. It's fast and accurate — whether you have a dirty mouse or what, the arrow keys let you get the layer exactly where you want it. Also, up here in Seattle, my caffeine intake makes it impossible to nudge stuff by any other method.

"When I get it all together and everything's basically in place, I save my base camp. This is a separate file — dot 2 or whatever — so that the previous file remains fixed in time. Of course, I save the base camp in the Photoshop native format; and I can't think of any reason for using another format until my image is 100 percent finished. And even then, I always keep a Photoshop file as backup."

**19.35 (TOP), 19.36 (BOTTOM)**

**19.37 (TOP), 19.38 (BOTTOM)**

## THE FINISHING TOUCHES

The text is Helvetica Compressed, further squished and skewed using the Free Transform command, and then filtered with Motion Blur. Vander Houwen also added a gradient layer mask to fade the text in the corners (19.39). Finally, he added a layer mask to the second-to-bottom sky layer. Then, he airbrushed in black with the airbrush to uncover an area of starry night behind the text (19.40).

"When I was doing 9-to-5 production work, I learned the hard way that you don't worry about the details until the end. You concentrate on the biggest problems — the major composite parts — and work your way down to increasing levels of refinement. Otherwise, you end up blowing away that detail work you did earlier, and you waste a lot of time."

## FOLLOWING THE PATH THAT IS ALWAYS IN MOTION

"Ideally, the goal for me is to play Photoshop like an instrument. Playing jazz Photoshop is where I'd like to be someday. But I figure I need about ten more years — if they'd just quit changing the program. Imagine if you were playing the sax, and they kept moving the buttons on you every couple of years. Not that I don't like the changes — sometimes they're great. But becoming a musician with an instrument that's in constant flux is a challenge."

"Even if the program stood still, I might never master it. Every week it seems like I figure out a better way to do something and realize how hard it was to do it the old way. In fact, I kind of hope I never get it down completely. I hope I always cringe at the way I used to do things because that means I'll be getting better."

Once again, we have an example of a composition in which no scanned image was directly modified. "I messed with the text, but I can redo that in a few seconds. After I get the image finessed to the point I'm more or less happy with it, I save another base camp. Then, I merge some layers or flatten the image and move on. It gives me piece of mind and sheer naked freedom to continue on to the next job without any worries of losing my work."

19.39 (TOP), 19.40 (BOTTOM)

## GREG KEEPS THE SKETCH HANDY

**V**ander Houwen likes to scan his original sketch (19.41) and stick it in a mask channel. This way, he can refer to the sketch at any time by clicking the eyeball in front of the mask name in the Channels palette. The sketch channel appears as a color overlay (19.42) without affecting his ability to edit the image file. "This lets me position, rotate, scale, and distort elements with extreme accuracy. But it can also help when explaining images to art directors. When there's an approved sketch, it's hard to argue. The sketch is like a visual contract."

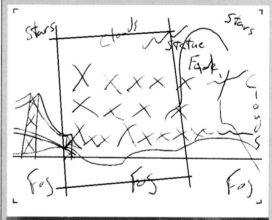

19.41 (TOP), 19.42 (BOTTOM)

# CHAPTER 20
# ENHANCING VECTOR ARTWORK

I f there's one program that every computer artist uses, it has to be Photoshop. Some folks are primarily vector artists; others are famous for their 3-D work, and still others do videos and animation. But they all spend some amount of time in Photoshop — sketching roughs, rasterizing artwork, editing renderings, and performing hundreds of other chores. It's the closest thing there is to an industry-standard graphics application.

So call me sick, but I thought it'd be a lot of fun to find a prominent computer artist who *didn't* use Photoshop. Had never touched it. Simply didn't have any call to play with it. There must be — oh, gosh — two or three such examples in the country, but the best one I know is Ron Chan. Chan is a San Francisco–based freelance artist who is best known for his Illustrator work. My job — invite Chan to join the Photoshop-using majority and turn him into a pixel kind of guy. Resistance is futile; Chan will be assimilated.

## PORTRAIT OF A VECTOR GUY

Just to give you a sense of who Ron Chan is, I've taken the liberty of including a few examples of his artwork over the years. These pages feature an early cover from *Macworld* magazine (20.1), the ubiquitous announcer guy who long adorned Macromedia Director boxes (20.2), and the eye-catching mandrill roll-out for Illustrator 5 (20.3). If you're more interested in type tricks, check out the cover of the *TV Guide* big fall preview issue (20.4) or the more interesting version that was deemed too chaotic for the publication's audience (20.5). Sadly, the artwork

*As I see it, Illustrator is the creation tool and Photoshop is the editing tool. My goal is to take the strengths of both and marry them into a single überprogram.*

RON CHAN

20.1

didn't quite measure up to Chan's expectations. "I thought the *TV Guide* cover would be a great job because my mom would see it," the artist confides. "But she forgot to buy it that week."

20.2

20.3

Whether Mother Chan is aware of it or not, everything her son creates is pure PostScript vector art. Sharp outlines, stylized forms, vivid colors — this stuff wouldn't know a pixel from a pancake.

**ARTIST:**
Ron Chan

**STUDIO:**
24 Nelson Avenue
Mill Valley, CA 94941
415/389-6549
*http://www.ronchan.com*
ron@ronchan.com

**SYSTEM:**
PowerWave 604/150 (Power Computing)
6GB storage

**RAM:**
160MB total
80MB assigned to Photoshop

**MONITOR:**
ViewSonic PT810

**VERSION USED:**
Photoshop 5.0

**OTHER APPLICATIONS:**
Adobe Illustrator, Fractal Design Painter, Macromedia Director

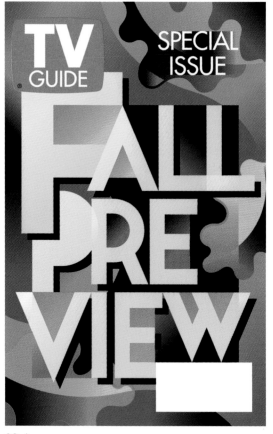

20.4

20.5

**WORK HISTORY:**

1979 — Instead of going to art school, started working at Hallmark Cards ("so I never really did learn how to draw").

1984 — Hired as part-time staff artist at the *San Francisco Chronicle*.

1986 — Tested illustration program from Adobe code-named Picasso (later named Illustrator).

1989 — Created cover for first all-digitally produced issue of *Macworld* magazine.

1995 — Cover for "Fall Preview" issue of *TV Guide*.

1997 — Participated in this book, forever changing the way he works!

**FAVORITE CHILDHOOD TOY:**

Major Matt Mason ("When you bend the arms too much, the wires pop out and poke you.")

## FEAR OF PHOTOSHOP

Chan is obviously both talented and technically proficient. He was one of the first artists to ever touch Illustrator, a year before Adobe released it publicly. So why this avoidance of Photoshop? It can't be ease of use, because it's more difficult to manipulate a Bézier curve in Illustrator than change the color of a pixel in Photoshop. And it can't be that he doesn't own a copy of the program, because he's had it on his hard disk for years. Just what is the story?

"For one thing, I'm used to manageable file sizes. A really complicated magazine cover might take up 700K to 800K in Illustrator. To have an equivalent resolution in Photoshop, it'd have to be at least 20MB. To me, that seems like an enormous file. I can't quickly e-mail it to a client." And for Chan, JPEG compression isn't an option because it would gum up his high-contrast edges. "Then there's the problem of archiving. Right now, I can put two or three years of work on a Zip cartridge. If I used Photoshop, that would hold maybe two or three jobs.

Photoshop also makes you worry about resolution all the time, where Illustrator doesn't. But, I suppose it ultimately boils down to the fact that I'm making a steady living using Illustrator and I haven't really been forced to use Photoshop."

Chan considers and then adds, "Well, not until you started bugging me."

## THE ATTRACTION OF PIXELS

But surely Photoshop offers some advantages over Illustrator. "Blends in Illustrator are a real chore. You have to set up a beginning and ending shape, and you have to enter the right number of steps to avoid banding. In Photoshop, adding a blend is as easy as filling a feathered selection or painting with a soft brush. Glows and shadows are especially easy to throw together. And you can get a more natural, less sterile effect.

"Another thing I'd like to do with Photoshop is add textures. I've been looking at some WPA silk-screens from the 1940s that combine gritty textures with high-contrast poster art. I suppose I could try to get this effect with Illustrator's Ink Pen filter, but it would be so much trouble that I doubt it'd be worth it. Photoshop seems like a much better program for this purpose."

I suggested to Chan another way Photoshop could be used to enhance his artwork. By relegating elements to different layers and discreetly applying the Gaussian Blur filter, he could create a depth-of-field effect. This would impose a sense of visual hierarchy, literally focusing attention on the foreground elements and downplaying the background, as in the revised take on Chan's Sarazen World Open Championship poster (20.6). Chan ventured that he wasn't terribly keen on the idea. "Gee, I don't think I own any 3-D glasses." But he generously gave me permission to take a whack at it myself, as I do later in this chapter.

20.6

## ADDING TEXTURES TO AN ILLUSTRATION

The first project Chan decided to texturize in Photoshop was a poster he created for a concert featuring young soloists with disabilities (20.7). The piece is clean and precise, composed mostly of simple shapes with flat fills. Chan stripped out the handful of blends that used to serve as highlights and color transitions. In place of these, he resolved to substitute textural fades inside Photoshop.

20.8

20.7

### MAKING THE TEXTURE

To safeguard the visual harmony of his artwork, Chan decided to start with a single texture pattern and repeat it over and over throughout the image. He created his texture (20.8) by making a transparent image and painting in the empty layer with the airbrush tool set to Dissolve in the Airbrush Options palette. All of the pixels were either black or transparent. Because it's a small trick to later fill the black pixels with color while leaving the transparent pixels intact, this small file is ideally suited to Chan's needs.

### BRINGING IN PATHS FROM ILLUSTRATOR

The next step was to rasterize the Illustrator artwork in Photoshop and then transfer Illustrator's paths to use as masks for the textures. "When opening the artwork in Photoshop, I modified the resolution; but I never changed the inch measurements of the image. This way, I could drag individual paths over from Illustrator and have them align exactly.

"I used Illustrator's Trim filter to simplify the illustration so none of the paths overlapped. Mostly, that worked out fine. When it didn't quite work, I used Unite or another Pathfinder filter to get the shapes I wanted. Then I copied the paths I needed, pasted them into Photoshop, and positioned them with the direct selection tool (the white arrow in the same slot as the pen). Actually, I was surprised how well it worked. I didn't have much problem at all lining up the paths exactly the way I wanted them."

20.9

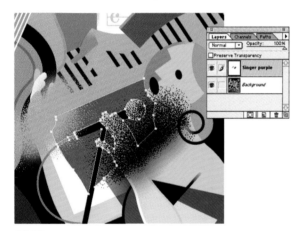

20.10

20.11

## FILLING PATHS WITH TEXTURES

The best way to see how Chan used the paths to mask his textures is to focus in on a detail in the image. The purple area around the singer's hand and microphone includes a total of four paths. After Chan imported and aligned these paths (20.9), he named them in the Paths palette to ensure that Photoshop didn't automatically delete them when he imported more paths later.

Chan imported his texture (20.8) onto a new layer. He positioned the texture in the area below the microphone and left it painted black. Next, he cloned the texture, rotated it 180 degrees, and positioned the clone to the right of the singer's raised hand. He sampled the lavender color from the piano with the eyedropper. Then with the cloned texture still selected, he filled it with lavender by pressing Shift-Option/Alt+Delete. Chan also used the airbrush (set to Normal) to fill in the texture with a little additional color (20.10).

As you can see, Chan made no attempt to keep his textures inside the lines. This is the purpose of the paths. He converted the paths to selection outlines by pressing Enter. Then he converted the selection to a layer mask by clicking the layer mask icon at the bottom of the Layers palette. The result was a perfect stencil to contain the textures (20.11).

## REPEAT, REPEAT, REPEAT

Chan repeated this process over and over again to add texture to the other elements in the image (20.12). The completed image contained 14 layers with as many named paths. "Sometimes I had to edit the layer masks a little to get the textures aligned properly. And once or twice, I played around with the blend mode. When the texture overlapped the black piano keys, for example, I set the layer to Darken so the texture covered only the lavender area."

The final effect is splendid (20.13), but importing all those paths must have gotten a little tedious after a while. "Oh, I don't know; it wasn't too bad. If I did it again, I'd probably use fewer layers. I might also dab on the texture directly using the airbrush set to Dissolve. I guess it took me longer than setting up blends in Illustrator, but I like the effect better, too. And I bet I'll get a lot more efficient with time."

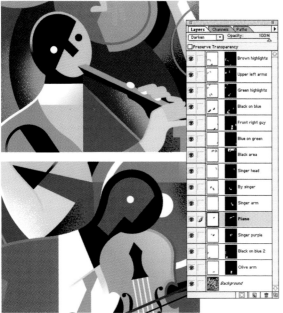

**20.12**

**20.13**

20.14

20.15

20.16 (TOP), 20.17 (BOTTOM)

## THE BIG OIL TEXTURE

At my urging, Chan experimented with adding textures to a couple of other images at low resolutions. In the case of a client's annual report illustration (20.14), Chan decided to apply a more complex texture over a few large areas of color. He started by creating a grayscale oil paint texture inside Fractal Design Painter (20.15). "I really like the natural media tools in Painter, but I don't like its layering controls. It's just too confusing to mask images." So he rasterized the illustration inside Photoshop, imported the paths he needed for layer masks from Illustrator, and opened the Painter texture.

This time, Chan was able to get by with far fewer layers — six to be exact. "I'd just roughly position and rotate the texture against one of the elements in my illustration. If the texture didn't quite cover an element, I either stretch it or repeat it (20.16)." The texture wasn't designed to repeat, so Chan sometimes had to cover up the seam. "In the red clouds, I had to align the seam above the box — where the clouds are thinnest — to make the seam as unobtrusive as possible (20.17)."

As before, Chan used paths to make layer masks. But how did he color the texture? "Filling the texture with a flat color would have ruined it. I could have colorized the texture with Hue/Saturation, but then I couldn't exactly match the colors I had set up in Illustrator. I tried rendering each texture layer as a duotone, but that was way too much work.

"Finally, I discovered a *reeeally* easy solution. I left the texture layer grayscale and applied the Screen mode with the Opacity set to about 30 percent. This worked great because it made the texture follow the blends from the original illustration. Once I figured that out, it took me like a half hour to finish the whole thing (20.18)."

**20.18**

## THE CUSTOMIZED FADE TEXTURE

According to Chan, his final experiment was the most successful. "I wouldn't have any hesitation about sending this to a client." Chan started by rasterizing the office supply illustration (20.19). Then he created a rough brush texture in Painter (20.20). The problem was, the texture was painted onto a white background, making it nearly impossible to colorize and overlay onto different backgrounds. The challenge: Turn this flat brush into a flexible layer with an accurate transparency mask.

Selecting the brush with the magic wand or Color Range command wouldn't have caught all the delicate edges in the texture. The correct solution was a bit more obscure, so naturally it fell to me, keeper of obscure facts, to do the honors. I switched to the Channels palette and ⌘/Ctrl-clicked on the top channel item to convert the tonal range to a selection. This selected the white pixels, so I chose Select ➤ Inverse to select the black ones. Then I copied the selection to a new layer (⌘/Ctrl+J). And now for the weirdest step: I pressed Shift+Option/Alt+Delete to fill the texture with solid black. Then I deleted the Background layer, leaving the layered black texture (20.21). It was an exact match to Chan's original.

**20.19**

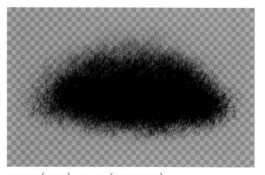

**20.20 (TOP), 20.21 (BOTTOM)**

Chan then used the texture to create highlights and color transitions, just as he had back in the Young Soloists poster. But this time, instead of using a black-and-white MacPaint-style pattern, Chan's texture supplied a full range of gray values. He was able to colorize it by pressing Shift+Option/Alt+Delete, just as before, because the layer's transparency mask was the only factor controlling the softness of the edges. The result is an elegant rendering that any professional would be proud to see on his or her ink blotter (20.22).

**20.22**

## LAYERS IN FOCUS

The next few paragraphs explain how to add depth to a two-dimensional piece of vector art. But I should warn you up front that this technique is mine. Don't blame Chan; it's not his fault. Although the subject of the technique is Chan's Young Soloists poster, I am the cheeky monkey responsible for its execution.

No doubt, some of you may think it's presumptuous for me to modify another artist's work, even if said artist gave me permission. After all, Chan deliberately violates the rules of depth and perspective in favor of geometric form and a stylized convergence of elements. Isn't it possible that the technique I'm about to suggest may have a trivializing effect on Chan's artwork? I guess it is, particularly with a half-wit like me at the helm. But my philosophy is this: If Leonardo Da Vinci sees fit to give Quasimodo a stab at the *Mona Lisa*, who are we to judge?

The idea is simple: Isolate elements on different planes according to the distance from the viewer, assign each plane to a separate layer, and blur the layers that lie in front or in back of the viewer's plane of focus. You can use different blur filters to get different effects, but for this demonstration, I'll stick with Gaussian Blur.

I assume you recall the unmodified Young Soloists illustration (20.7). Inside Illustrator, I established four planes, each on a separate layer. I placed the clarinet and violin players on the front layer, the singer on the next one back, the guitarist and pianist on the third layer, and the background at the rear (20.23).

Using Illustrator 8, I exported the layered illustration as a layered Photoshop 5 file. This ensured that Photoshop automatically respected each of the four layers created in Illustrator, from background up to clarinet and violin players.

To focus the viewer's attention on the singer, I needed to apply varying amounts of blur to all the other layers. (No sense in sharpening the singer; she's already as sharp as rasterized vector art gets.) Using the Gaussian Blur filter, I applied Radius values of 4.0 to the front layer, 2.0 to the guitarist and pianist, and 10.0 to the background. I also used the Levels command to reduce the contrast of the two rear layers and darken the front layer (20.24).

The effect was too subtle for a Philistine like me. I added some gradations in between layers to serve as simple lighting effects. I started by adding a layer to the front of the stack and drawing a black-to-transparent gradation from the base of the image to the base of the clarinet. I inserted a similar white-to-transparent gradient layer in front of the singer. I also added a circular drop shadow behind her head.

**20.23**

20.24

The finished composition imposes a kind of View Master sensibility on Chan's artwork (20.25). What does the artist think? "Mm hmm. And the advantage of this is what?" Not quite the ringing endorsement I was hoping for, but he's not threatening a lawsuit either. All things considered, I'd call that a success.

## CHAN'S IMAGING REFLECTIONS

A year after this chapter was first written, Chan now regularly creates his flat vector art in Illustrator (20.26) and adds textures and depth in Photoshop (20.27). As of late, Chan has become more adventurous with his textures, introducing organic elements such as photographic surfaces and airbrushed clouds (20.28).

20.25

20.26

20.27

"At first, I had this fear of large files. But I went ahead and upgraded my computer to 160MB of RAM and a 6GB hard drive. Now I can work with large, layered images in Photoshop pretty quickly. Some things are slower than they are in Illustrator, but it's usually worth the wait . . . and the wait and the wait. Gives me time to read the newspaper."

Any complaints? "Photoshop's a great program and everything, but there are a few things that irritate me about both Versions 4 and 5. In particular, I wish I could paste multiple elements into a single layer instead of constantly creating new layers. Then I could set up a single layer mask and paste several images into it. It really should be a toggle — paste as a new layer or paste as a floater. Let me decide."

Would Chan ever create artwork directly in Photoshop? "I don't see what I would gain by doing that. Illustrator's drawing tools give me the precision I expect from the computer. If I want to sketch or paint, I'll turn to traditional tools before Photoshop. As I see it, Illustrator is the creation tool and Photoshop is the editing tool. My goal is to take the strengths of both and marry them into a single überprogram."

20.28

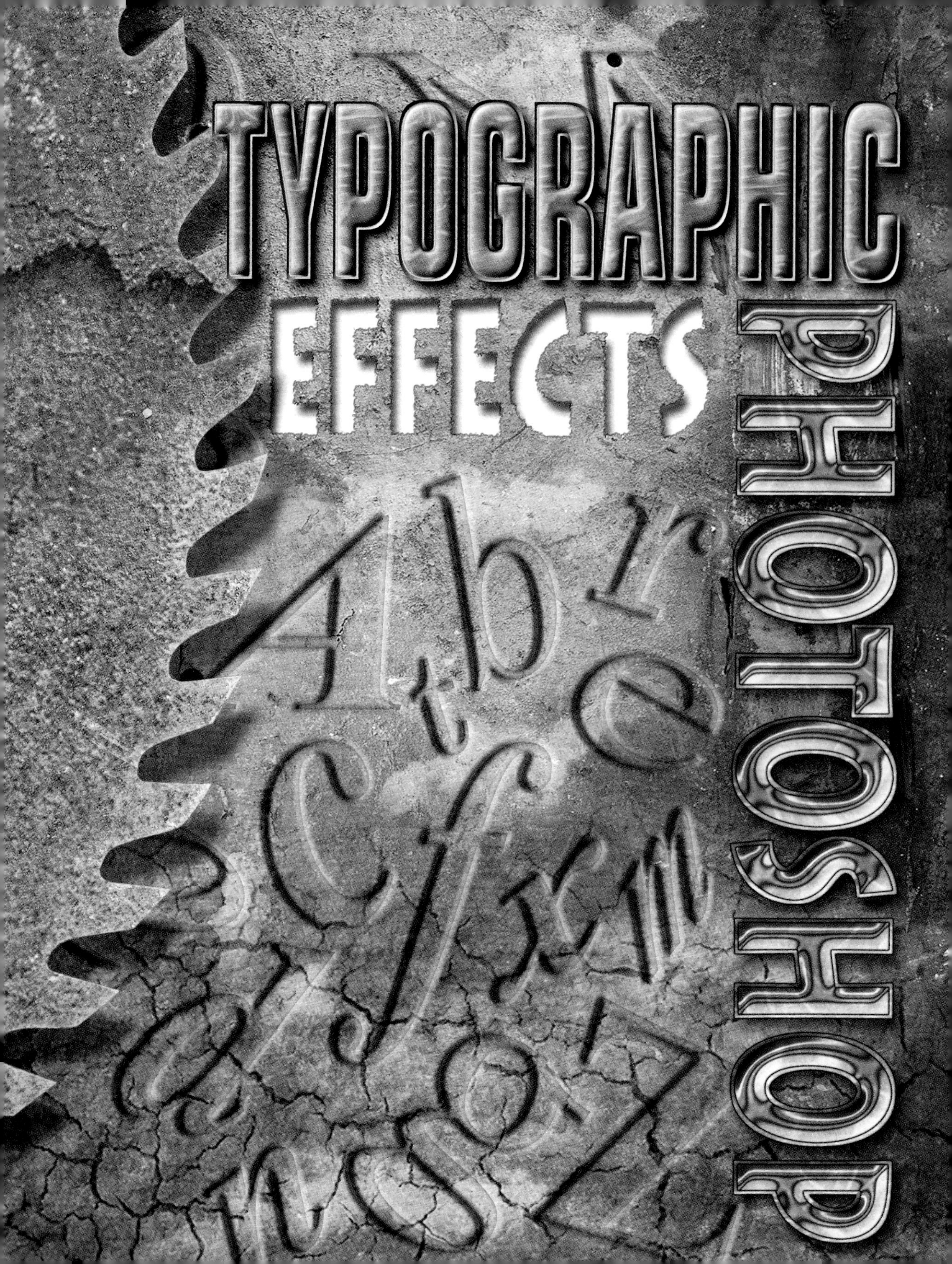
TYPOGRAPHIC
EFFECTS
PHOTOSHOP

## CHAPTER 21
# SPECIAL TYPE EFFECTS

W hether a picture is really worth a thousand words is a subject for debate. Take a masterwork by Eugène Delacroix and display it within sight of countryman and contemporary Victor Hugo, and you can count on 1,000 words minimum. But flash an Easter card in front of the character Lenny in *Of Mice and Men*, and about the best you can expect is, "Duh, dat's a pretty bunny, George!"

Even so, there's clearly some magic that occurs when you combine pictures and words into a single element. In his cover art for *Sports Illustrated*'s baseball and football calendars (21.1), Brooklyn-based artist Eric Reinfeld proves that text can both tell and show its message. "Photoshop's not the kind of program where you set some type, kern it a little, and say 'gee, nice headline.' I mean, you *can* do that, but if you do, you're not bringing any creativity to bear; you're just plopping words together. Photoshop gives you an opportunity to distort type, add dimension, and hopefully infuse it with a little of your own aesthetic energy."

Reinfeld should know. The artist derives a significant part of his income from turning type into full-fledged artistic elements with genuine form and substance. From the raised lettering of the *Sports Illustrated* cover art (21.1) to the waxy edges of the Marét logo (21.2), Reinfeld gives us the sense that his type is actually made of something. Even the corporate-cool letters in Time-Warner's empire ads (21.3) convey a subtle presence of depth.

In this chapter, Reinfeld shows you how to mold matter into abstraction. After all, when working in

> **Photoshop gives you an opportunity to distort type, add dimension, and hopefully infuse it with a little of your own aesthetic energy.**
>
> ERIC REINFELD

Photoshop, your goal is not so much to create real-world type as it is to build letters from the essence of life. You know the photograph is an image. We can plainly see that the artwork is an image. But lest we forget, the type is every bit an image as well.

### THE BASIC APPROACH

Reinfeld uses two programs to make his text. "Photoshop is a heck of a program for stylizing type, but I think everyone agrees that it's not the best program for creating the letters in the first place. There's a plug-in from Extensis called PhotoTools that improves Photoshop's type capabilities. I use it when I'm making quick comps, just to get ideas across and see how they look. But when I start on the final artwork, I create the type in Illustrator and then bring it into Photoshop. The antialiasing is much better that way."

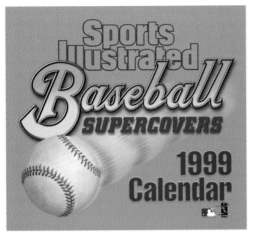

21.2

21.3

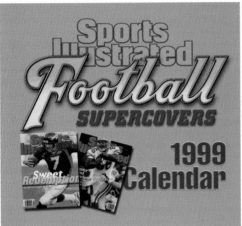

21.1

*Artwork by Eric Reinfeld*

**ARTIST:**
Eric Reinfeld

**STUDIO:**
87 Seventh Avenue
Brooklyn, New York 11217
718/783-2313
reinfeld1@aol.com
macsushi@earthlink.net

**SYSTEM:**
SuperMac S900 604e/225 (Umax)
18GB storage (including Quantum Atlas
and Micronet HotSwapable arrays)

**RAM:**
300MB total
275MB assigned to Photoshop

**MONITORS:**
Apple 17- and 20-inchers

**EXTRAS:**
Targa 2000 Pro video-capture board

**VERSION USED:**
Photoshop 5.0

Reinfeld saves his type in the native Illustrator (ai) format, and then he opens it up in Photoshop. "Note that I don't Place the file (with File ➤ Place), I open it. That way, I can enter the resolution I want to use, specify RGB or CMYK, and so on. Then, I increase the canvas size by an inch or so all the way around to give myself room to work."

At this point, Reinfeld might import a background. "Because I opened the type from an EPS illustration, the background is transparent. Just as an example, I took in a generic stock image of some clouds and dragged it in as a new layer behind the text (21.4)."

"Now, what I'm about to show you is the simplest kind of type treatment you can do in Photoshop — type filled with an image surrounded by a shiny halo. Of course, it could just as easily be a drop shadow or a color fringe or whatever. Try it a couple of times and you'll see that this basic approach works for a dozen different effects. A clipping group here, some expanding and blurring there, and you're done."

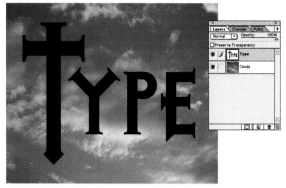

**21.4**

**OTHER APPLICATIONS:**
Adobe Illustrator, Adobe After Effects, QuarkXPress, ElectricImage Broadcast, Form·Z

**WORK HISTORY:**
1985 — Opened up independent branch of father's dry cleaning business.
1987 — Purchased color Mac II system, learned to use PixelPaint and Illustrator.
1990 — Designed belts in Photoshop for New York fashion company.
1992 — Converted *The American Kennel Club Gazette* from traditional to electronic publishing.

1993 — Left job as Senior Desktop Color Technician at high-end service bureau to freelance for Time, Sony, Paramount, and others.
1997 — Authored *Real World After Effects* (Peachpit Press).

**FAVORITE COLLECTIBLE:**
Antique advertising signs ("If you have old signs in the house, contact me immediately.")

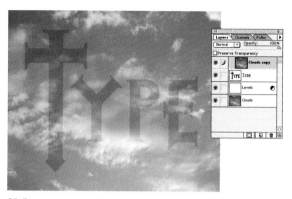

**21.5**

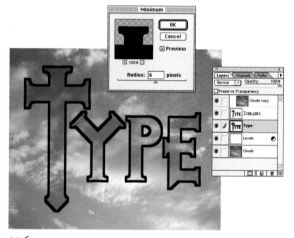

**21.6**

**21.7**

### CLIPPING IMAGE AGAINST IMAGE

"The clouds were a little muddy, so I went ahead and added a Levels adjustment layer on top of the cloud layer to brighten it up a bit. I didn't apply the Levels command directly, I used an adjustment layer because I still wanted to have access to the original dark clouds. My feeling is, always use adjustment layers when you can. No sense in applying the effect for good until you get everything exactly the way you want it."

Reinfeld's next step was to fill the type with the darker clouds. "I made a copy of the clouds by dragging the layer onto the little page icon. (By the way, I have to say, I hate the way the page and trash icons are right next to each other at the bottom of the Layers palette. I'm constantly throwing away a layer when I mean to copy it.)

"Anyway, I dragged the cloned clouds to the top of the layer stack. Then, I combined the cloud layer with the type below it to make a clipping group." You can do this by pressing ⌘/Ctrl+G. The result is a darker patch of clouds masked by the text (21.5).

### EXPANDING THE TYPE FOR THE HALO

"Even though I've got this clipping group, my text is unharmed, same as it ever was. The great thing about this technique is that I can get to my original text any time I need it. Like now."

To make the halo, Reinfeld started by duplicating the text layer. "The weird thing here is that Photoshop makes the duplicated layer part of the clipping group and releases the original. It doesn't matter, of course — it just affects how the layers are named — but I've seen it confuse people."

To make the cloned type thicker, Reinfeld applies Filter ➤ Other ➤ Minimum. "When working with a layer like this, the Minimum filter shrinks the transparency mask and expands the letters. It's a little counterintuitive — seems like Maximum would do the expanding. If you can't keep Minimum and Maximum straight, just try one. If it's wrong, undo and try the other. You've got a 50/50 chance.

"I entered a Radius of 6. But you can do less or more — whatever you want. It just tells Photoshop how far to blow up the text (21.6)." Incidentally, if you create your text directly in Photoshop instead of importing it from Illustrator, make sure you turn off the Preserve Transparency check box before choosing Minimum. Otherwise, the letters are immutable.

### BLURRING AND DODGING

"Next, I applied a nice Gaussian Blur so the type spreads out. Some folks like to match the Gaussian Blur radius to the Minimum radius. I usually take it a few notches higher. You just want to get a gradual separation between type and background." At this point, Reinfeld ended up with a drop shadow. To turn it into a halo, he filled the layer with white by pressing ⌘/Ctrl+Shift+Delete (21.7).

"From here, there are a million different things you can do. Apply blend modes, change the Opacity, modify the other layers. Knock yourself out." To demonstrate, Reinfeld selected Color Dodge from the blend mode pop-up menu in the Layers palette and reduced the Opacity setting to 70 percent. This resulted in a more dramatic halo with hot, glowing edges. Then, he selected the text layer inside the clipping group and applied the Motion Blur filter at a 90 degree angle and a Distance value of 30 pixels. This blurred the halo into the tops and bottoms of the characters without harming the cloud pattern (21.8).

21.8

## THE BENEFITS OF LAYERED TYPE

**B**y keeping your effects and text variations on separate layers, you ensure absolute flexibility. "Here's where things become interesting. Try linking the two type layers with that chain icon in the Layers palette. Then, you can move the type mask and halo together. I can even apply Free Transform and flip or distort the two text layers without affecting the cloud patterns at all (21.9). I might also link the top cloud texture with the type to get yet another look."

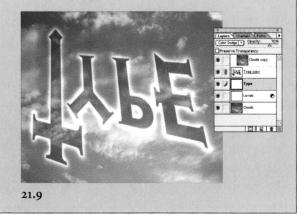

21.9

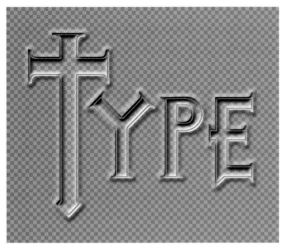

**21.10**

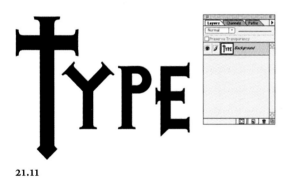

**21.11**

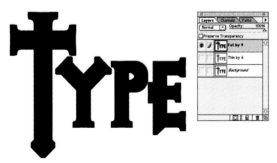

**21.12**

## CREATING SOURCE VARIATIONS

"Okay, that was easy. If you want more sophisticated effects (21.10), you have to do a little more work." Reinfeld marries the old-school approach of building depth via channel operations with some of Photoshop's newer layering functions. "Whenever I create serious type effects, I work in two files. One file is a source file, the other is the target. The source contains the original type and a few layers of simple variations; the target's where I build the actual composition. Then, I use the Apply Image and Calculations commands to bounce back and forth between these two files.

"I start off the source file by opening type I've created in Illustrator and flattening the image so I have one background layer — black type against a white background (21.11). This layer is sacred. I will never, ever, ever touch it, except to duplicate it. Every text effect I create stems from this one background layer."

### CHANGING THE WEIGHT

Reinfeld then duplicated the layer twice and created two weight variations using the Minimum and Maximum filters. "Because this is black type against a white background — no transparency — you use Minimum to expand the weight of the type and Maximum to contract it." Reinfeld created a thinner variation with Filter ➢ Other ➢ Maximum set to a radius of 6 pixels, and a fatter version using Minimum and a radius of 9 pixels (21.12). As you'll soon see, these will define the inner and outer edges of his embossed text effects.

## MAKING OUTLINES

Next, Reinfeld duplicated his existing base layers — Background, Thin by 6, and Fat by 9 — and applied a trio of effects to each. "First, I apply outline effects. You think, 'Oh, the Find Edges filter,' right? No way, not enough control. I use a layering trick that involves Gaussian Blur and the Difference mode. It's really easy.

"Say I want to start with the original type. I duplicate the background layer and apply the Gaussian Blur set to 1.5 pixels. This gives me a subtle soft edge that will determine the thickness of the outline. Then, I duplicate this new layer, invert it (⌘/Ctrl+I), and apply the Difference blend mode. Then, I do a ⌘/Ctrl+E to merge the two outline layers into one." The result is a soft outline about 3 pixels thick (21.13). Reinfeld repeated this operation on the Thin by 6 and Fat by 9 layers as well.

## SOFT EMBOSS EFFECTS

"I use the Emboss filter to give the text depth. But before I can do that, I have to blur the type. Emboss doesn't like hard edges." Reinfeld duplicated the three original type layers — our friends Background, Thin by 6, and Fat by 9 — and applied the Gaussian Blur filter to each with a Radius value of 6. Then, he duplicated each of the blurred layers and applied the Emboss filter. "The settings you use are totally up to you. But you'll probably want to be consistent." For this example, Reinfeld used an Angle value of -60 degrees, a Height of 6 pixels, and an Amount value of 150 percent (21.14).

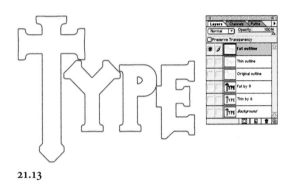

21.13

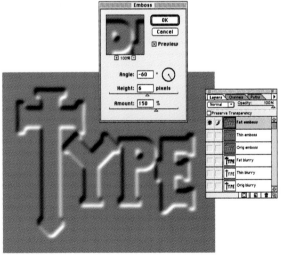

21.14

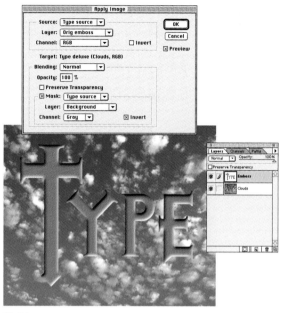

21.15

## THE SOLID BLACK LAYER

"Last and certainly least, I create a new layer at the top of the stack and fill it with black. It's nearly always a good idea to have a black layer handy when using channel operations. Many of the layers I've created I'll use as masks, and I'll need to fill the masked areas with black or white. So long as I've got this black layer sitting around, I can make black, white, or any shade of gray."

## ASSEMBLING THE ACTUAL COMPOSITION

"When creating your target image, you need to make sure it's the same size as the source." After you choose the New command, select the name of the source file from the Window menu. This ensures a pixel-for-pixel match. "Then, import the image that you want to use as a background for your type. You can use the Place command, or just drag and drop an image from an open file." For this example, Reinfeld used another cloud image.

## THE FIRST EMBOSS EFFECT

After dropping in the cloud background, Reinfeld created a new layer for his first emboss effect. "As I mentioned earlier, the Emboss filter works best with blurry edges. But that doesn't mean you want your type to be blurry. The solution is to mask the emboss effect."

Reinfeld chose Image ➢ Apply Image to display the Apply Image dialog box. He selected his source image from the Source pop-up menu, and then selected the standard-weight emboss layer from the Layer pop-up menu. The Blending options were set to Normal and 100 percent. "Be sure to turn the Preview check box on when you're inside this dialog box so you can see what you're doing."

To define the edges of the emboss effect, Reinfeld turned on the Mask check box and again selected the source image from the pop-up menu. This time, however, he selected Background from the Layer pop-up, and turned on the Invert check box. The result is embossed text inside a precise text mask (21.15).

Some may wonder why Reinfeld didn't convert the type to a selection outline and use that to drag and drop the emboss effect. "Hey, try it. It works, but it isn't any easier. You have to hide everything but the background layer and then go to the Channels palette and retrieve the selection. Then, you have to switch to the emboss layer — it's a lot of busy work. I prefer to just send everything through masks, like I did here. The Apply Image dialog box may look tough at first, but once you become familiar with it, it's quite easy to navigate."

After creating the new emboss layer, Reinfeld applied Hard Light from the blend mode pop-up menu in the Layers palette. This etched the type into the cloudy background (21.16). "See, now that alone is a pretty good type effect. Thank you folks, and have a nice day." But Reinfeld has no intention of stopping there.

21.16

### THE RED INNER EMBOSS

Reinfeld then set about creating another level of emboss inside the first. Like before, he created a new layer and chose Image ➢ Apply Image. The dialog box came up with the same settings he applied before. All he changed were the two Layers settings. He selected the layer that contains the thin emboss effect from the top Layer pop-up menu. Then, he set the lower Layer pop-up to Thin by 6. This masked the thin emboss effect with the thin type (21.17).

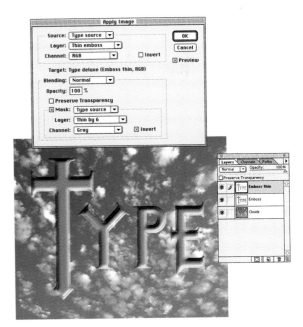

21.17

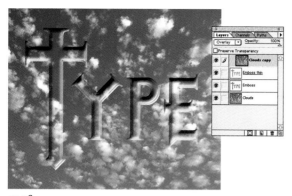

**21.18**

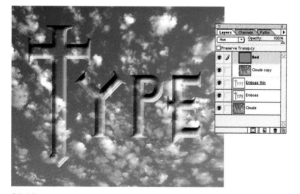

**21.19**

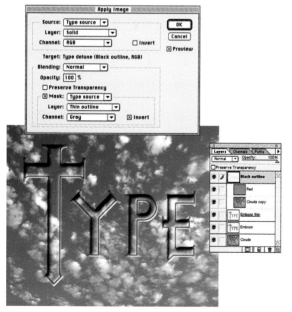

**21.20**

Reinfeld could have applied the Hard Light mode to this layer as well, but he didn't. "My intention is to give the new emboss layer some additional definition by adding outline effects behind it. This means the new layer has to be opaque." To blend the clouds into this opaque layer, Reinfeld duplicated the cloud layer, dragged it to the top of the Layers palette, and grouped it with the thin emboss effect by pressing ⌘/Ctrl+G. Then, he applied the Overlay mode, which is the exact inverse of Hard Light. As a result, the thin emboss layer appeared to blend in with the clouds exactly like the original emboss effect (21.18).

Just for the heck of it, Reinfeld added a layer to colorize the thin emboss effect with red. After adding yet another new layer, he filled the whole thing with 100 percent red and added it to the clipping group below by pressing ⌘/Ctrl+G. Then, he applied the Hue blend mode. This made the clouds inside the thin embossed type red while leaving both the luminosity and saturation values of the underlying pixels intact (21.19).

"When you have embossed text that's on its own layer and you're using it as the parent of a clipping group, you're ready for anything. If you work much with art directors, you know they like to see stuff really quick. If the art director wants me to try out a new color, I just go to the red layer and press Option/Alt+Delete. Bang, there it is: no work, new color. Everyone can visualize what's going on really easily."

### INNER EMBOSS HIGHLIGHTS

Reinfeld's next step was to trace around the red emboss effect using the outline layers from the source file that he had created earlier. Again, he added a new layer, and again he chose the Apply Image command. This time, he switched the top Layer option to the solid black layer, and then he set the bottom Layer option to the thin outline layer. This instructed Photoshop to use the thin outline as a mask and fill it with black (21.20).

Reinfeld moved the new black outline layer to behind the inner emboss clipping group. Then, he pressed ⌘/Ctrl+down arrow and ⌘/Ctrl+right arrow to nudge the outline one pixel down and to the right. He set the Opacity of this layer to 70 percent. This made a subtle black outline underneath the red text.

Naturally, Reinfeld needed a white outline to compliment the black one. So he duplicated the outline layer, inverted it to white by pressing ⌘/Ctrl+I, and nudged the layer two pixels each up and to the left. I've zoomed in on this effect so you can see it in detail (21.21).

### THE BIG BACKGROUND EMBOSS

Finally, Reinfeld set about denting the letters into the background sky, as if the type was resting on cloud-patterned fabric. As is his habit, he made a new layer and chose Image ➢ Apply Image. But this time, he did things a little differently. He selected the emboss effect applied to the fat letters from the first Layer pop-up menu. Then, he selected the accompanying Invert check box. The idea here was to switch the highlights and shadows in the emboss effect to better set off the existing emboss layers. For the mask layer, he selected the fat blurry layer from the source image, giving the type soft edges (21.22).

As the *coup de resistance*, Reinfeld dragged the new layer to the bottom of the stack, just above the clouds. He applied the Hard Light blend mode and set the Opacity to 80 percent. The end product is a sight to behold (21.23).

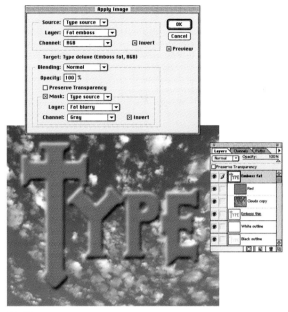

**21.22**

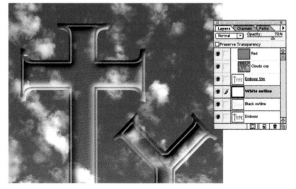

**21.21**

**21.23**

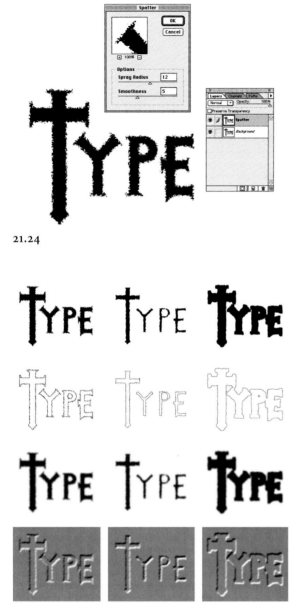

21.24

21.25

"What you've got here is an infinitely flexible composition, with a full set of source layers to go along with it. You'll notice, I didn't use all the source layers — hey, that's my prerogative. But later, maybe I will. The point is, I can go back and change my mind any time I want. This leaves me free to learn new effects and explore fresh territory."

### ROUGHING IT

"By now, you're probably starting to get an idea of what I do. The specific steps aren't all that important. It's the approach that really matters. Put together a source file full of outline, Gaussian Blur, and Emboss variations, and you can experiment for days."

If you harbor any doubts about this, Reinfeld's next demonstration puts them to rest. Starting with a copy of the same gothic text that he's used in previous examples, Reinfeld applied Filter ➢ Brush Strokes ➢ Spatter. "I don't care for most of the Gallery Effects filters that were added to Photoshop 4, but this one's very handy." The filter roughs up the edges of the type, giving the letters a frayed appearance (21.24).

"That one simple modification makes a tremendous difference. From here on out, it's just a matter of repeating the thin, fat, outline, blur, and emboss stuff that I did earlier (21.25). Then, when you go into your composition file, you can have a field day." Reinfeld isn't exaggerating. The berry images feature three different adaptations of Reinfeld's technique, one of which he created (21.26) and two of which I designed (21.27 and 21.28). Every nuance is the result of retrieving outlined, blurred, and embossed layers from a source file and sending them through thin, fat, outlined, and blurred masks. Speaking from personal experience, it's a lot of fun.

## ERIC'S CLOSING PEARLS OF WISDOM

"Before you go, I have to pass along a few parting shots here. First, if you decide to work in RGB, that's fine. Just be careful to pick the colors for your type properly. And by that, I mean set your color picker to CMYK. Even in the RGB color space, this ensures that while you may get an ugly color, you won't get a color that won't print.

"Second, the beauty of this whole approach is that you can take a composition you've applied to one background and substitute in a whole different background. For example, in a matter of seconds, I could replace the clouds or the berries with a new image and completely change the look of my type.

"Third, a lot of folks have asked me my impression of Photoshop 5's layer effects. For the most part, I just use them for comping. They help me to add quick lighting effects, toss together some glows and shadows, things like that. But I've also experienced some banding issues. When you use layer effects on their own, you can run into artifacts and weird blends. So when I finish roughing out a layer effect, I'll choose Layer ➤ Effects ➤ Create Layer to break up the effects onto their own layers. Then I'll rebuild the effect by hand, or modify it with an adjustment layer, whatever. The point is, don't just accept the first thing Photoshop spits out. You can edit the effect to get exactly what you want.

"And last, if nothing else, this little exercise proves that text in Photoshop can look awesome. Zoom in on your type and check out how sharp your edges are. Some people say that you can't get sharp type out of Photoshop, but they're wrong. At 300 pixels per inch or better, you can count on your text looking great. Take my word for it — this stuff works."

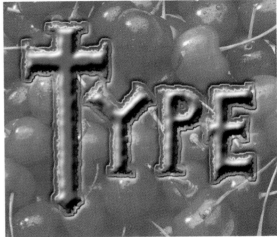

**21.26 (TOP), 21.27 (MIDDLE), 21.28 (BOTTOM)**

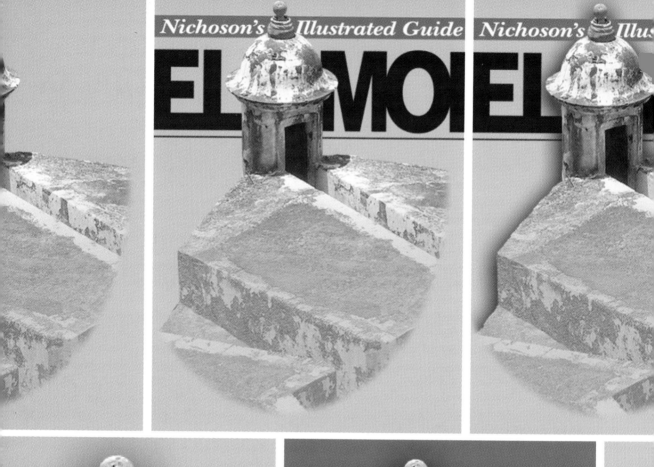

EL MOIEL

on's Illust

son's

| Layers | Channels | Paths | ▶ |
|---|---|---|---|

Normal ▾ Opacity: 100 ▶ %

☐ Preserve Transparency

👁 | 🖼 | **Fort wall** | 𝑓
👁 | ✏ | **Bar red** |
👁 | | *Background* |

# CHAPTER 22
# SETTING UP CLIPPING PATHS

T he clipping path is a wonderful invention. Without one, every image brought into Illustrator, QuarkXPress, or any other object-oriented program would import as an opaque rectangle. But use Photoshop or another image editor to draw a clipping path around an image, and suddenly the rectangular wall comes tumbling down. Everything inside the clipping path is opaque, and everything outside is transparent. The image becomes another free-form element of your page design that you can mix and match with type and other vector objects.

Unfortunately, all is not happiness in the world of clipping paths. They're a pain in the neck to draw, they increase the complexity of a document, and they prolong print time. But the biggest problem with clipping paths is that they're mercilessly uncompromising. Like any PostScript object, a clipping path is always sharp and discrete. You can't feather it, blur it, or blend it with another object, as you can with pixels.

Does this eliminate any potential for adding soft drop shadows and gradual fades to your printed pages? Certainly not. The trick is to know where to use clipping paths and where to use plain rectangular images. Suppose you want an image element to rise up out of an object-oriented headline, but you also want that image to cast a soft drop shadow onto the type and background (22.1). Just place the clipped image in front of the type and the opaque shadow image behind. It's a simple trick, but the results appear to violate all laws of PostScript. And in design, breaking the rules is a very good thing.

Creating a clipping path effect is a two-part process. First you have to prepare the image in Photoshop, and then you have to combine the image with type and other objects in a drawing or page layout program. I use Illustrator 8.0 as the sample layout program in this chapter, but rest assured that the technique is equally applicable to QuarkXPress, PageMaker, FreeHand, and CorelDraw.

22.1

22.2

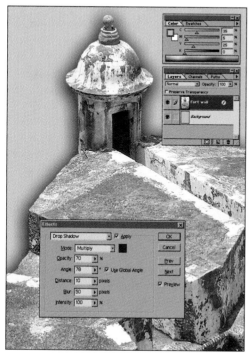

22.3

## PREPARING THE IMAGE IN PHOTOSHOP

One of the keys to getting great image and object compositions is to prepare your artwork as meticulously as possible in Photoshop. If you want an image to appear against a green background in Illustrator or QuarkXPress, for example, set it against a green background in Photoshop. This eliminates the possibility of matting problems — a fringe of incongruously colored pixels around the edges of the clipped image — when you import the image into the layout program.

Start by selecting the exact portion of the image you want to clip and sending it to a new layer. In Photoshop 5, the best way to select an image is to create a mask. However, you can use the Color Range command (22.2), quick mask mode, lasso tool, or whatever method you feel most comfortable with, so long as it delivers satisfactory results. Press ⌘/Ctrl+J to float the selected image to a new layer.

Now, switch to the background layer in the Layers palette and fill it with the background color that you intend to use in your layout program. To guarantee an accurate match, you should convert the image to the CMYK mode (if you haven't done so already) and specify the background color using CMYK values. Assuming the layout program doesn't attempt to make any automatic color conversions when importing the image, the CMYK color you specify in Photoshop will jibe with the one you specify in the layout program, ensuring a seamless transition between image and objects.

If you want to add a drop shadow or other effect to the image, this is a good time to do it. In Photoshop 5, Control/right-click the layer name of the masked image in the Layers palette to gain access to the Effects menu (22.3). Next, choose Drop Shadow, Outer Glow, or whatever effect you want to apply. Don't worry about the fact that you can't clip the shadow — you'll work around that pesky problem in your layout program.

Draw the clipping path. The skilled artist will want to trace around the edge of the masked image layer using the pen tool. If drawing a path is too much work, you can take the lazy person's approach and generate a path automatically: ⌘/Ctrl-click the masked image item in the Layers palette to retrieve the selection outline, and then convert the selection to a path using the Make Work Path command in the Paths palette menu. But bear in mind, the resulting path is likely to be pretty rough. Automatic paths simply aren't as precise as the old-fashioned hand-drawn variety. When you finish drawing the path, give it a name by double-clicking it; identify it as a clipping path by selecting Clipping Path in the Paths palette menu (22.4).

Want to introduce more feathering and fading effects (22.5)? Go for it. So long as you make the image blend with the particular CMYK background color you specified earlier, you can't go wrong. As with the drop shadow, you'll deal with the results of your blending madness later.

Save the layered image in the Photoshop (PSD) format. Flatten it and choose Save As to save it in a format recognized by your layout program. Recent versions of QuarkXPress and PageMaker recognize clipping paths inside TIFF images. But if you have any doubt, save the image in the EPS format.

When you finish, go back to the Paths palette and delete the clipping path. Use the Save As command to save the unclipped image as a separate file. You'll need both the clipped and unclipped version of the file to make the effect work in the layout program.

## LAYERING THE OBJECTS IN ILLUSTRATOR 8

So much for the hard stuff. Now on to the easier steps in the layout program—in this case, Illustrator 8. Illustrator has never been the most with-it program on the planet, so it's little surprise that Version 8 still doesn't recognize clipping paths in TIFF files. The clipped image has to be saved in the EPS format.

First create the border and background for your document. Draw a rectangle (or whatever shape you prefer) and fill it with the CMYK background color you specified in Photoshop.

Choose Place from the File menu to import the EPS file that you saved with the clipping path. Position the clipped image as desired (22.6). Onscreen, the clipped image won't appear nearly as smooth as it will when printed. And if the clipped image includes areas colored with the background color, those areas won't match the background color you specified in

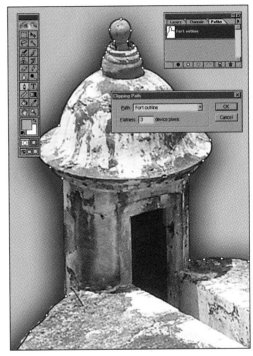

22.4

22.5

Illustrator. These are inevitable results of the limitations of the EPS preview and differing calibration settings between Photoshop and your layout program. When you print the page, it should look fine.

With the clipped image in place, create your headline text and stack it behind the image (22.7). The portion of the image inside the clipping path will overlap the text, but the pixels outside the clipping path are transparent, permitting you to see through the image to the text behind it.

Lastly, choose Place again to import the unclipped version of the image. Use the options in the Align palette to align the newly imported image to the clipped image, so they exactly overlap. Stack the clipped image in back of the text but in front of the background rectangle. The drop shadows and fading effects blend into the background rectangle, creating a seamless transition of images and objects (22.8).

22.6          22.7          22.8

## HEIGHTENING THE EFFECT

This technique works best when the color of your headline text is a saturated CMYK black (that is, 100 percent black with 50 to 60 percent each of cyan, magenta, and yellow). Because saturated black is as dark as is gets, the shadow from the unclipped image appears to blend in with the text. But if the text is colored with something other than black, it looks like it's in front of the shadow (which indeed it is), lessening the impact of the effect, as shown by the white text and red bar in this example (22.9).

Fortunately, if you're familiar with masking, it's easy to solve this problem. Return to your original layered image in Photoshop and fill the background layer with the color of your text or, in this case, the bar (22.10). Flatten the image and crop it so it's just slightly bigger than the text. (A smaller image will take less time to print.) Be sure to leave at least one original corner of the image intact so you have a point of reference from which to align in your layout program. Delete the clipping path and choose Save As to save a separate version of the image.

Inside Illustrator, import the new image and align it to the others. Copy the colored text and paste it in front of the new image (⌘/Ctrl+F). Shift+click the new image to add it to the selection and press ⌘/Ctrl+7 to mask the image with the type. Stack the mask behind the clipped image, and you're good to go (22.11).

22.9          22.10          22.11

## OF MASKS AND CLIPPING PATHS

The perceptive reader will notice that masking in Illustrator (and other object-oriented programs) is analogous to creating a clipping path in Photoshop. Both operations let you sculpt the shape of the image into something other than rectangular. In fact, the two operations are mathematically identical. This means, if you prefer, you can import an image without a clipping path and mask it in the layout program (assuming the program provides sufficiently capable drawing tools). Despite the limitations of the PostScript printing language, it seems pixels and objects can coexist after all.

# Filters and Special Effects

# Corrective Filtering

## Filter Basics

In Photoshop, *filters* enable you to apply automated effects to an image. Although named after photographer's filters, which typically correct lighting and perspective fluctuations, Photoshop's filters can accomplish a great deal more. You can slightly increase the focus of an image, introduce random pixels, add depth to an image, or completely rip it apart and reassemble it into a hurky pile of goo. Any number of special effects are made available via filters.

At this point, a little bell should be ringing in your head, telling you to beware of standardized special effects. Why? Because everyone has access to the same filters that you do. If you rely on filters to edit your images for you, your audience will quickly recognize your work as poor or at least unremarkable art.

Imagine this scenario: You're wasting away in front of your TV, flipping aimlessly through the channels. Just as your brain is about to shrivel and implode, you stumble across the classic "Sledgehammer" video. Outrageous effects, right? Peter Gabriel rides an imaginary roller coaster, bumper cars crash playfully into his face, fish leap over his head. You couldn't be more amused or impressed.

As the video fades, you're so busy basking in the glow that you neglect for a split second to whack the channel-changer. Before you know it, you're midway through an advertisement for a monster truck rally. Like the video, the ad is riddled with special effects — spinning letters, a reverberating voice-over slowed down to an octave below the narrator's normal pitch, and lots of big machines filled with little men filled with single brain cells working overtime.

In and of themselves, these special effects aren't bad. There was probably even a time when you thought that spinning letters and reverberating voice-overs were hot stuff. But sometime after you passed beyond preadolescence, you managed to grow tired of these particular effects. You've come to associate them with raunchy, local car-oriented commercials. Certainly, these effects are devoid of substance, but more importantly, they're devoid of creativity.

This chapter and the one that follows, therefore, are about the creative application of special effects. Rather than trying to show an image subject to every single filter — a service already performed quite adequately by the manual included with your software — these chapters explain exactly how the most important filters work and offer some concrete ways to use them.

You'll also learn how to apply several filters in tandem and how to use filters to edit images and selection outlines. My goal is not so much to teach you what filters are available — you can find that out by tugging on the Filter menu — but how and when to use filters.

## A first look at filters

You access Photoshop's special effects filters by choosing commands from the Filter menu. These commands fall into two general camps — *corrective* and *destructive*.

### Corrective filters

Corrective filters are workaday tools used to modify scanned images and prepare an image for printing or screen display. In many cases, the effects are subtle enough that the viewer won't even notice that you applied a corrective filter. As demonstrated in Figure 23-1 and Color Plate 23-1, these filters change the focus of an image, enhance color transitions, and average the colors of neighboring pixels, among other effects. You'll find these filters in the Filter ⇨ Blur, Noise, Sharpen, and Other submenus.

Many corrective filters have direct opposites. Blur is the opposite of Sharpen, Add Noise is the opposite of Median, and so forth. This is not to say that one filter entirely removes the effect of the other; only reversion functions such as the History palette provide that capability. Instead, two opposite filters produce contrasting effects.

Corrective filters are the subject of this chapter. Although they number fewer than their destructive counterparts, I spend more time on them because they represent the functions you're most likely to use on a day-to-day basis.

Unsharp Mask

Gaussian Blur

Median

High Pass

**Figure 23-1:** The gigantic head of 4th-century Roman emperor Constantine subject to four corrective filters, including one each from the Sharpen, Blur, Other, and Noise submenus (reading clockwise from upper left).

## Destructive filters

The destructive filters produce effects so dramatic that they can, if used improperly, completely overwhelm your artwork, making the filter more important than the image itself. For the most part, destructive filters reside in the Filter ➪ Distort, Pixelate, Render, and Stylize submenus. A few examples of overwhelmed images appear in Figure 23-2 and Color Plate 23-2.

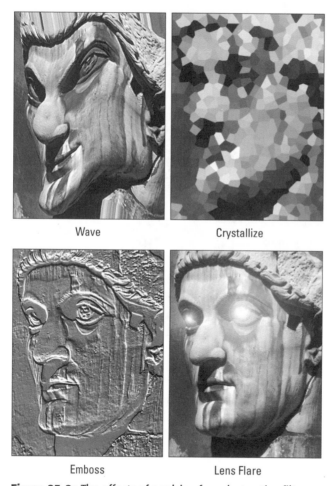

Wave                Crystallize

Emboss                Lens Flare

**Figure 23-2:** The effects of applying four destructive filters, one each from the Distort, Pixelate, Render, and Stylize submenus (clockwise from upper left). Note that Lens Flare is applicable to color images only, so I had to convert Constantine to the RGB mode before applying the filter.

Destructive filters produce way-cool effects, and many people gravitate toward them when first experimenting with Photoshop. But the filters invariably destroy the original clarity and composition of the image. Granted, every Photoshop function is destructive to a certain extent, but destructive filters change your image so extensively that you can't easily disguise the changes later by applying other filters or editing techniques.

Destructive filters are the subject of Chapter 24. Rather than explaining every one of these filters in detail, I try to provide a general overview.

## Effects filters

Photoshop also provides a subset of destructive filters called the "effects" filters. These 47 filters originally sire from the Gallery Effects collection developed by Silicon Beach, which got gobbled up by Aldus (of PageMaker fame) and finally acquired by Adobe Systems. Not knowing what exactly to do with this grab bag of plug-ins, Adobe integrated them into Photoshop.

Little about these filters has changed since Gallery Effects 1.5 came out in 1993. A couple of filters have been renamed — the old GE Ripple filter is now Ocean Ripple to avoid confusion with Photoshop's own Ripple filter. One filter, GE Emboss, is gone, presumably because it detracted from the popular Filter ➪ Stylize ➪ Emboss. But Adobe hasn't bothered with any meaningful retooling. You can't raise or lower a GE dialog box value using the arrow keys, you can't preview the effect in the image window, on a Mac you can't switch applications when an effects dialog box is visible, and a few are dreadfully slow.

As a result, I devote only passing attention to the effects filters, explaining those few that fulfill a real need. Of course, I encourage you to experiment and derive your own conclusions. After all, as Figure 23-3 illustrates, these filters do produce intriguing special effects. I mean, that Plaster effect is just plain cool. For the record, most of the effects filters reside in the Filter ➪ Artistic, Brush Strokes, Sketch, and Texture submenus. A few have trickled out into other submenus, including Filter ➪ Distort ➪ Diffuse Glow, Glass, and Ocean Ripple; and Filter ➪ Stylize ➪ Glowing Edges.

**Tip**

If your experimentation leads you to my conclusion — you can live through most days without the effects filters — you can turn them off to save a whole lot of space in RAM better devoted to storing pixels. All the effects filters are stored in the Effects folder inside the Plug-Ins folder on your hard drive. Move the Effects folder out of the Plug-Ins folder and all 47 filters will be turned off.

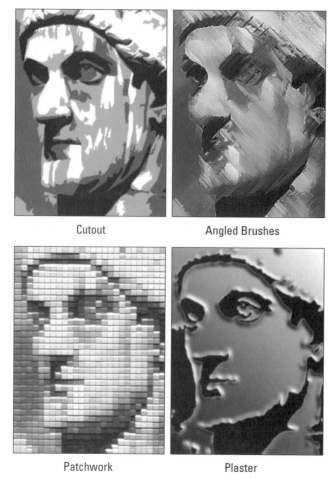

Cutout

Angled Brushes

Patchwork

Plaster

**Figure 23-3:** The "effects" filters come from Gallery Effects, a little toy surprise that Adobe accidentally acquired when it purchased Aldus Corporation. Here we see the impact of one filter each from the Filter ⇨ Artistic, Brush Strokes, Sketch, and Texture submenus (clockwise from upper left).

# How filters work

When you choose a command from the Filter menu, Photoshop applies the filter to the selected portion of the image. If no portion of the image is selected, Photoshop applies the filter to the entire image. Therefore, if you want to filter every nook and cranny of an image, press ⌘/Ctrl+D and then choose the desired command.

## External plug-ins

Some filters are built into the Photoshop application. Others are external modules that reside in the Plug-Ins folder. This enables you to add functionality to Photoshop by purchasing additional filters from third-party collections. Gallery Effects used to be such a collection. Others include PhotoTools from Extensis, Eye Candy from Alien Skin, the Series collections from Andromeda, Paint Alchemy from Xaos Tools, and Kai's Power Tools from MetaCreations.

If you open the Plug-Ins folder inside the Photoshop folder, you'll see that it contains several subfolders. By default, Photoshop places the filters in the Filters and Effects subfolders, but you can place additional filters anywhere inside the Plug-Ins folder. Even if you create a new folder inside the Plug-Ins folder and call it *No Filters Here,* create another folder inside that called *Honest, Fresh Out of Filters,* toss in one more folder called *Carpet Beetles Only,* and put every plug-in you own inside this latest folder, Photoshop sees through your clever ruse and displays the exact same filters you always see under their same submenus in the Filter menu. The only purpose of the subfolders is to keep things tidy, so that you don't have to look through a list of 6,000 files.

## Previewing filters

For years, the biggest problem with Photoshop's filters was that they did not offer previews to help you predict the outcome of an effect. You just had to tweak your 23,000 meaningless settings and hope for the best. But today, life is much better. Photoshop 3 introduced previews, Version 4 made them commonly available to all but the most gnarly filters, and Version 5 had the good sense to leave well enough alone.

Photoshop offers two previewing capabilities:

✦ **Dialog box previews:** Labeled in Figure 23-4, the $100 \times 100$-pixel preview box is now a common feature to all filter dialog boxes. Drag inside the preview box to scroll the portion of the image you want to preview. Move the cursor outside the dialog box to get the square preview cursor (labeled in the figure). Click with the cursor to center the contents of the preview box at the clicked position in the image.

Click on the zoom buttons (+ and –) to reduce the image inside the preview box. You can even take advantage of the standard zoom tool by pressing ⌘/Ctrl+spacebar or Option/Alt+spacebar, depending on whether you want to zoom in or out.

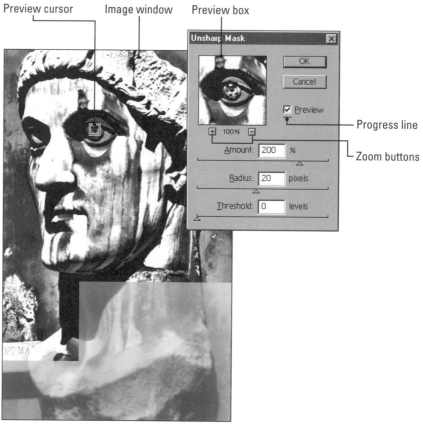

**Figure 23-4:** Most filter dialog boxes let you preview the effects of the filter both inside the dialog box and in the image window.

✦ **Image window previews:** Most corrective filters — as well as a couple of destructives like Mosaic and Emboss — also preview effects in the full image window. Just select the Preview check box to activate this function. While the effect is previewing, a blinking progress line appears under the check box. In Figure 23-4, for example, you can see that the bottom of the image still hasn't finished previewing, so the progress line strobes away. If you're working on a relatively poky computer, you'll probably want to turn this check box off to speed up the pace at which the filter functions.

Incidentally, the Preview check box has no affect on the contents of the preview box. The latter continually monitors the effects of your settings, whether you like it or not.

Use the Preview check box to compare the before and after effects of a corrective filter in the image window. Turn it on to see the effect; turn it off to see the original image. You can also compare the image in the preview box by clicking in the box. Mouse down to see the old image; release to see the filtered image. It's like an electronic, high-priced, adult version of peek-a-boo. But not nearly as likely to induce giggles.

Even though a dialog box is on-screen and active, you can zoom and scroll the contents of the image window. ⌘/Ctrl+spacebar+click to zoom in, Option/Alt+ spacebar+click to zoom out, and spacebar+drag to scroll. You can also choose commands from the View and Window menus. Feel free to switch applications.

One more tip: When you press the Option/Alt key, the Cancel button changes to a Reset button. Option/Alt+click on this button to restore the settings that appeared when you first opened the dialog box. (These are not necessarily the factory default settings; they are the settings you last applied to an image.)

Most destructive filters make no attempt to preview effects in the image window. Seven filters continue to offer no previews whatsoever: Radial Blur, Displace, Color Halftone, Extrude, Tiles, De-Interlace, and Offset. Of course, single-shot filters — the ones that don't bring up dialog boxes — don't need previews because there aren't any settings to adjust.

### Reapplying the last filter

To reapply the last filter used in the current Photoshop session, choose the first command from the Filter menu or simply press ⌘/Ctrl+F. If you want to reapply the filter subject to different settings, Option/Alt+choose the first Filter command or press ⌘/Ctrl+Option/Alt+F to redisplay that filter's dialog box.

Both techniques work even if you undo the last application of a filter. If you cancel a filter while in progress, however, pressing ⌘/Ctrl+F or ⌘/Ctrl+Option/Alt+F applies the last uncanceled filter.

### Nudging numerical values

In addition to entering specific numerical values inside filter dialog boxes, you can nudge the values using the up and down arrow keys. When working with percentage values, press an arrow key to raise or lower the value by 1. Press Shift+up or down arrow to change the value in increments of 10.

If the value accommodates decimal values, it's probably more sensitive to the arrow key. Press an arrow for a 0.1 change; press Shift+arrow for 1.0.

As I mentioned earlier, these tricks don't work in some of the destructive filters dialog boxes, most notably those associated with old Gallery Effects filters.

## Fading a filter

In many cases, you apply filters to a selection or image at full intensity — meaning that you marquee an area using a selection tool, choose a filter command, enter whatever settings you deem appropriate if a dialog box appears, and sit back and watch the fireworks.

What's so "full intensity" about that? Sounds normal, right? Well, the fact is, you can reduce the intensity of the last filter applied by choosing the Filter ➪ Fade command or pressing ⌘/Ctrl+Shift+F. This command permits you to mix the filtered image with the original, unfiltered one.

As shown in Figure 23-5, the Fade dialog box provides you with the basic tools of image mixing — an Opacity value and a blend mode pop-up menu. To demonstrate the wonders of Filter ➪ Fade, I've applied two particularly destructive Gallery Effects filters to the colossal marble head — Filter ➪ Stylize ➪ Glowing Edges and Filter ➪ Sketch ➪ Note Paper. In the second column of heads, I pressed ⌘/Ctrl+Shift+F and lowered the Opacity of the two effects to 30 percent. The right-hand images show the effects of two blend modes, Lighten and Overlay, with the Opacity value restored to 100 percent.

Despite its placement in the Filter menu, the Fade command also affects the opacity of floating selections, as explained in Chapter 15. You can likewise choose Filter ➪ Fade to change the intensity of the last color correction command, as explained in Chapter 30.

Caution

### Creating layered effects

The drawback of the Fade command is that it's only available immediately after you apply a filter (or color correction). If you so much as modify a selection outline after applying the filter, the Fade command dims, only to return when you apply the next filter.

Therefore, you may find it more helpful to copy a selection to a separate layer (⌘/Ctrl+J) before applying a filter. This way, you can perform other operations, and even apply many filters in a row, before mixing the filtered image with the underlying original.

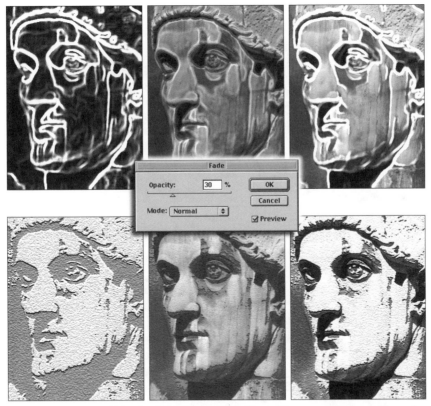

**Figure 23-5:** Press ⌘/Ctrl+Shift+F to mix the filtered image with the unfiltered original. Now, is it me, or is Constantine on Note Paper the spitting image of Rambo? That's got to be keeping some art historian awake at night.

## Filtering inside a border

Here's another reason to layer before you filter: If your image has a border around it — like the ones shown in Figure 23-6 — you don't want Photoshop to factor the border into the filtering operation. To avoid this, select the image inside the border and press ⌘/Ctrl+J to layer it prior to applying the filter. The reason is that most filters take neighboring pixels into consideration even if they are not selected. By contrast, when a selection floats, it has no neighboring pixels, and therefore the filter affects the selected pixels only.

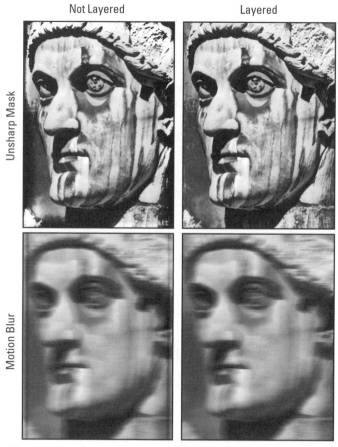

**Figure 23-6:** The results of applying two sample filters to images surrounded by borders. In each case, only the image was selected; the border was not. Layering the right examples prevented the borders from affecting the performance of the filters.

Figure 23-6 shows the results of applying two filters discussed in this chapter — Unsharp Mask and Motion Blur — when the image is anchored in place and when it's layered. In all cases, the 2-pixel border was not selected. In the left examples, the Unsharp Mask filter leaves a high-contrast residue around the edge of the image, while Motion Blur duplicates the left and right edges of the border. Both problems vanish when the filters are applied to layered images, as seen on the right.

Even if the area outside the selection is not a border per se — perhaps it's just a comparatively dark or light area that serves as a visual frame — layering comes in handy. You should always layer the selection unless you specifically want edge pixels to be calculated by the filter.

### Undoing a sequence of filters

Okay, here's one last reason to layer before you filter. Copying an image to a layer protects the underlying image. If you just want to experiment a little, pressing ⌘/Ctrl+J is often more convenient than restoring a state in the History palette. After applying four or five effects to a floating image, you can undo all that automated abuse by Option/Alt+clicking on the trash icon at the bottom of the Layers palette. The underlying original remains unharmed.

# Heightening Focus and Contrast

If you've experimented at all with Photoshop, you've no doubt had your way with many of the commands in the Filter ⇨ Sharpen submenu. By increasing the contrast between neighboring pixels, the sharpening filters enable you to compensate for image elements that were photographed or scanned slightly out of focus.

The Sharpen, Sharpen More, and Sharpen Edges commands are easy to use and immediate in their effect. You can achieve better results and widen your range of sharpening options, however, if you learn how to use the Unsharp Mask and High Pass commands, which I discuss at length in the following pages.

## Using the Unsharp Mask filter

The first thing you need to know about the Unsharp Mask filter is that it has a weird name. The filter has nothing to do with "unsharpening" — whatever that is — nor is it tied into Photoshop's masking capabilities. Unsharp Mask is named after a traditional film compositing technique (which is also oddly named) that highlights the edges in an image by combining a blurred film negative with the original film positive.

That's all very well and good, but most Photoshop artists have never touched a stat camera (an expensive piece of machinery, roughly twice the size of a washing machine, used by image editors of the late Jurassic, pre-Photoshop epoch). Even folks like me who used to operate stat cameras professionally never had the time to delve into the world of unsharp masking. In addition — and much to the filter's credit — Unsharp Mask goes beyond traditional camera techniques.

To understand Unsharp Mask — or Photoshop's other sharpening filters, for that matter — you first need to understand some basic terminology. When you apply one of the sharpening filters, Photoshop increases the contrast between neighboring pixels. The effect is similar to what you see when you adjust a camera to bring a scene into sharper focus.

Two of Photoshop's sharpening filters, Sharpen and Sharpen More, affect whatever area of your image is selected. The Sharpen Edges filter, however, performs its sharpening operations only on the *edges* in the image — those areas that feature the highest amount of contrast.

Unsharp Mask gives you both sharpening options. It can sharpen only the edges in an image or it can sharpen any portion of an image according to your exact specifications, whether it finds an edge or not. It fulfills the exact same purposes as the Sharpen, Sharpen Edges, and Sharpen More commands, but it's much more versatile. Simply put, the Unsharp Mask tool is the only sharpening filter you'll ever need.

When you choose Filter ⇨ Sharpen ⇨ Unsharp Mask, Photoshop displays the Unsharp Mask dialog box, shown in Figure 23-7, which offers the following options:

✦ **Amount:** Enter a value between 1 and 500 percent to specify the degree to which you want to sharpen the selected image. Higher values produce more pronounced effects.

✦ **Radius:** This option determines the thickness of the sharpened edge. Low values produce crisp edges. High values produce thicker edges with more contrast throughout the image.

✦ **Threshold:** Enter a value between 0 and 255 to control how Photoshop recognizes edges in an image. The value indicates the numerical difference between the brightness values of two neighboring pixels that must occur if Photoshop is to sharpen those pixels. A low value sharpens lots of pixels; a high value excludes most pixels from the running.

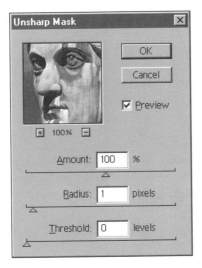

**Figure 23-7:** Despite any conclusions you may glean from its bizarre name, the Unsharp Mask filter sharpens images according to your specifications in this dialog box.

The preview options offered by the Unsharp Mask dialog box are absolutely essential visual aids that you're likely to find tremendously useful throughout your Photoshop career. Just the same, you'll be better prepared to experiment with the Amount, Radius, and Threshold options and less surprised by the results if you read the following sections, which explain and demonstrate the effects of these options in detail.

## Specifying the amount of sharpening

If Amount were the only Unsharp Mask option, no one would have any problems understanding this filter. If you want to sharpen an image ever so slightly, enter a low percentage value. Values between 25 and 50 percent are ideal for producing subtle effects. If you want to sharpen an image beyond the point of good taste, enter a value somewhere in the 300 to 500 percent range. And if you're looking for moderate sharpening, try out some value between 50 and 300 percent. Figure 23-8 shows the results of applying different Amount values while leaving the Radius and Threshold values at their default settings of 1.0 and 0, respectively.

**Figure 23-8:** The results of sharpening an image with the Unsharp Mask filter using eight different Amount values. The Radius and Threshold values used for all images were 1.0 and 0, respectively (the default settings).

If you're not sure how much you want to sharpen an image, try out a small value, in the 25 to 50 percent range. Then reapply that setting repeatedly by pressing ⌘/ Ctrl+F. As you can see in Figure 23-9, repeatedly applying the filter at a low setting produces a nearly identical result to applying the filter once at a higher setting. For example, you can achieve the effect shown in the middle image in the figure by applying the Unsharp Mask filter three times at 50 percent or once at 250 percent. I created the top-row results in Figure 23-9 using a constant Radius value of 1.0. In the second row, I lowered the Radius progressively from 1.0 (left) to 0.8 (middle) to 0.6 (right).

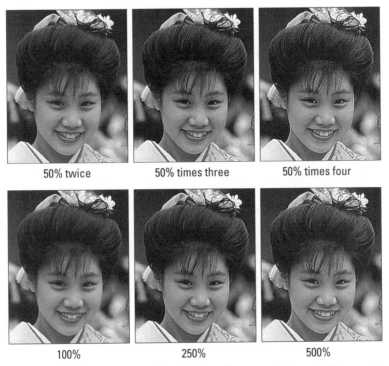

**Figure 23-9:** Repeatedly applying the Unsharp Mask filter at 50 percent (top row) is nearly equivalent on a pixel-by-pixel basis to applying the filter once at higher settings (bottom row).

The benefit of using small values is that they enable you to experiment with sharpening incrementally. As the figure demonstrates, you can add sharpening bit by bit to increase the focus of an image. You can't, however, reduce sharpening incrementally if you apply too high a value; you must press ⌘/Ctrl+Z and start again.

Just for fun, Color Plate 23-3 shows the results of applying the Unsharp Mask filter to each of the color channels in an RGB image independently. In each case, I maxed out the Amount value to 500 percent and set the Radius and Threshold to 4.0 and 0 respectively. The top row shows the results of applying the filter to a single channel; in the second row, I applied the filter to two of the three channels (leaving only one channel unfiltered). You can see how the filter creates a crisp halo of color around the chess pieces. Sharpening the red channel creates a red halo, sharpening the red and green channels together creates a yellow halo, and so forth. Applying the filter to the red and green channels produced the most noticeable effects because these channels contain the lion's share of the image detail. The blue channel contained the least detail — as is typical — so sharpening this channel produced the least dramatic results.

If you're a little foggy on how to access individual color channels, read Chapter 3. Incidentally, you can achieve similar effects by sharpening the individual channels in a Lab or CMYK image.

As I mentioned in Chapter 3, Photoshop is ultimately a grayscale editor, so when you apply the Unsharp Mask command to a full-color image, Photoshop actually applies the command in a separate pass to each of the color channels. Therefore, the command always results in the color halos shown in Color Plate 23-3 — it's just that the halos get mixed together, minimizing the effect. To avoid any haloing whatsoever, convert the image to the Lab mode (Image ➪ Mode ➪ Lab Color) and apply Unsharp Mask to only the Lightness channel in the Channels palette. (Do not filter the *a* and *b* channels.) This sharpens the brightness values in the image and leaves the colors 100 percent untouched.

## Setting the thickness of the edges

The Unsharp Mask filter works by identifying edges and increasing the contrast around those edges. The Radius value tells Photoshop how thick you want your edges. Large values produce thicker edges than small values.

The ideal Radius value depends on the resolution of your image and the quality of its edges:

✦ When creating screen images — such as Web graphics — use a very low Radius value such as 0.5. This results in terrific hair-line edges that look so crisp, you'll think you washed your bifocals.

✦ If a low Radius value brings out weird little imperfections — such as grain, scan lines, or JPEG compression artifacts — raise the value to 1.0 or higher. If that doesn't help, don't fret. I include two different sure-fire image fixing techniques later in this chapter, one designed to sharpen grainy old photos, and another that accommodates compressed images.

✦ When printing an image at a moderate resolution — anywhere from 120 to 180 ppi — use a Radius value of 1.0. The edges will look a little thick on-screen, but they'll print fine.

✦ For high-resolution images — around 300 ppi — try a Radius of 2.0. Because Photoshop prints more pixels per inch, the edges have to be thicker to remain nice and visible.

If you're looking for a simple formula, I'd recommend 0.1 of Radius for every 23 ppi of final image resolution. That means 75 ppi warrants a Radius of 0.5, 120 ppi warrants 0.8, 180 ppi warrants 1.2, and so on. If you have a calculator, just divide the intended resolution by 150 to get the ideal Radius value.

You can of course enter higher Radius values — as high as 250, in fact. Higher values produce heightened contrast effects, almost as if the image had been photocopied too many times, which are generally useful for producing special effects.

But don't take my word for it; you be the judge. Figure 23-10 demonstrates the results of specific Radius values. In each case, the Amount and Threshold values remain constant at 100 percent and 0, respectively.

**Figure 23-10:** The results of applying eight different Radius values, ranging from precise edges to very gooey.

Figure 23-11 shows the results of combining different Amount and Radius values. You can see that a large Amount value helps to offset the softening of a high Radius value. For example, when the Amount is set to 200 percent, as in the first row, the Radius value appears to mainly enhance contrast when raised from 0.5 to 2.0. When the Amount value is lowered to 50 percent, however, the higher Radius value does more to distribute the effect than boost contrast.

**Figure 23-11:** The effects of combining different Amount and Radius settings. The Threshold value for each image was set to 0, the default setting.

For those few folks who are thinking, "By gum, I wonder what would happen if you applied an unusually high Radius value to each color channel independently," you have only to consult Color Plate 23-4. In this figure, I again applied the Unsharp Mask filter to each channel and each pair of channels in the RGB chess image independently. But I changed the Amount value to 250 percent, raised the Radius value to a whopping 20.0 pixels, and left the Threshold at 0. To make the splash more apparent, I applied the filter twice to each image. The colors now bound out from the king, queen, and knight, bleeding into the gray background by as much as 20 pixels, the Radius value. Notice how the color fades away from the pieces, almost as if I had selected and feathered them? A high Radius value spreads the sharpening effect and, in doing so, allows colors to bleed. Because you normally apply the filter to all channels simultaneously, the colors bleed uniformly to create thick edges and high-contrast effects.

## Recognizing edges

By default, the Unsharp Mask filter sharpens every pixel in a selection. You can instruct the filter to sharpen only the edges in an image by raising the Threshold value from zero to some other number, however. The Threshold value represents the difference between two neighboring pixels — as measured in brightness levels — that must occur for Photoshop to recognize them as an edge.

Suppose that the brightness values of neighboring pixels are 10 and 20. If you set the Threshold value to 5, Photoshop reads both pixels, notes that the difference between their brightness values is more than 5, and treats them as an edge. If you set the Threshold value to 20, however, Photoshop passes them by. A low Threshold value, therefore, causes the Unsharp Mask Filter to affect a high number of pixels, and vice versa.

In the top row of images in Figure 23-12, the high Threshold values result in tiny slivers of sharpness that outline only the most substantial edges in the woman's face. As I lower the Threshold value incrementally in the second and third rows, the sharpening effect takes over more and more of the face, ultimately sharpening all details uniformly in the lower right example.

**Figure 23-12:** The results of applying nine different Threshold values. To best show off the differences between each image, I set the Amount and Radius values to 500 percent and 2.0, respectively.

## Using the preset sharpening filters

So how do the Sharpen, Sharpen Edges, and Sharpen More commands compare with the Unsharp Mask filter? First of all, none of the preset commands permit you to vary the thickness of your edges, a function provided by Unsharp Mask's Radius option. Secondly, only the Sharpen Edges command can recognize high-contrast areas in an image. Finally, all three commands are set in stone — you can't adjust their effects in any way. Figure 23-13 shows the effect of each preset command and the nearly equivalent effect created with the Unsharp Mask filter.

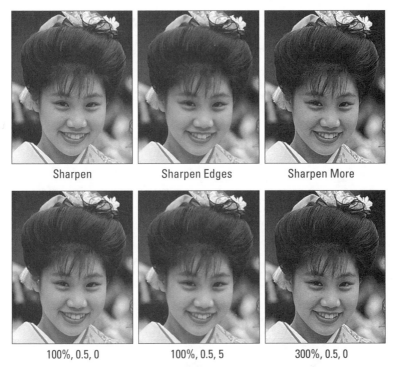

Sharpen    Sharpen Edges    Sharpen More

100%, 0.5, 0    100%, 0.5, 5    300%, 0.5, 0

**Figure 23-13:** The effects of the three preset sharpening filters (top row) compared with the Unsharp Mask equivalents (bottom row). Unsharp Mask values are listed in the following order: Amount, Radius, Threshold.

## Sharpening grainy photographs

Having completed my neutral discussion of Unsharp Mask, king of the Sharpen filters, I hasten to interject a little bit of commentary, along with a helpful solution to a common sharpening problem.

First, the commentary: While Amount and Radius are the kinds of superior options that will serve you well throughout the foreseeable future, I urge young and old to observe Threshold with the utmost scorn and rancor. The idea is fine — we can all agree that you need some way to draw a dividing line between those pixels that you want to sharpen and those that you want to leave unchanged. But the Threshold setting is nothing more than a glorified on/off switch that results in harsh transitions between sharpened and unsharpened pixels.

Consider the picture of pre-presidential Eisenhower in Figure 23-14. Like so many vintage photographs, this particular image of Ike is a little softer than we're used to seeing these days. But if I apply a heaping helping of Unsharp Mask — as in the second example in the figure — I bring out as much film grain as image detail. The official Photoshop solution is to raise the Threshold value, but the option's intrinsic harshness results in a pock-marked effect, as shown on the right. Photoshop has simply replaced one kind of grain with another.

Soft

Sharpened, Threshold: 0

Sharpened, Threshold: 20

**Figure 23-14:** The original Ike is a bit soft (left), a condition I can remedy with Unsharp Mask. Leaving the Threshold value set to 0 brings out the film grain (middle), but raising the value results in equally unattractive artifacts (right).

These abrupt transitions are quite out of keeping with Photoshop's normal approach. Paintbrushes have anti-aliased edges, selections can be feathered, the Color Range command offers Fuzziness — in short, everything mimics the softness found in real life. Yet right here, inside what is indisputably Photoshop's most essential filter, we find no mechanism for softness whatsoever.

While we wait for Photoshop to give us a better Threshold — one with a Fuzziness slider or similar control — you can create a better Threshold using a simple masking technique. Using a few filters that I explore at greater length throughout this chapter and the next, you can devise a selection outline that traces the essential edges in the image — complete with fuzzy transitions — and leaves the non-edges unmolested. So get out your favorite old vintage photograph and follow along with these steps.

## Steps: Creating and Using an Edge Mask

1. **Duplicate one of the color channels.** Bring up the Channels palette and drag one of the color channels onto the little page icon. Ike is a grayscale image, so I duplicate the one and only channel.

2. **Choose Filter ⇨ Stylize ⇨ Find Edges.** As I explain in Chapter 24, the Find Edges filter automatically traces the edges of your image with thick, gooey outlines that are ideal for creating edge masks.

3. **Press ⌘/Ctrl+I or choose Image ⇨ Adjust ⇨ Invert.** Find Edges produces black lines against a white background, but to select your edges, you need white lines against a black background. The Invert command reverses the lights and darks in the mask, as in the first example in Figure 23-15.

4. **Choose Filter ⇨ Noise ⇨ Median.** You need fat, gooey edges, and the current ones are a bit tenuous. To firm up the edges, choose the Median filter, enter a value of 2 (or thereabouts), and press Return/Enter.

5. **Choose Filter ⇨ Other ⇨ Maximum.** The next step is to thicken up the edges. The Maximum filter expands the white areas in the image, serving much the same function in a mask as Select ⇨ Modify ⇨ Expand serves when editing a selection outline. Enter 4 for the Radius value and press Return/Enter.

6. **Choose Filter ⇨ Blur ⇨ Gaussian Blur.** Unfortunately, the Maximum filter results in a bunch of little squares that don't do much for our cause. You can merge the squares into a seamless line by choosing the Gaussian Blur command and entering 4, the same radius you entered for Maximum. Then press Return/Enter.

The completed mask is pictured in the second example of Figure 23-15. Although hardly an impressive sight to the uninitiated eye, you're looking at the perfect edge mask — soft, natural, and extremely accurate.

*(continued)*

Find Edges, Invert

Sharpened edges

Find edge mask

**Figure 23-15:** I copy a channel, find the edges, and invert (left). I then apply a string of filters to expand and soften the edges (middle). After converting the mask to a selection outline, I reapply Unsharp Mask with winning results (right).

7. **Return to the standard composite view.** Press ⌘/Ctrl+tilde (~) in a color image. Because I'm working in a grayscale image, I press ⌘/Ctrl+1.

8. **Convert the mask to a selection outline.** Ctrl+click on the mask name in the Channels palette. Photoshop selects the most essential edges in the image without selecting the grain.

9. **Choose Filter ➪ Sharpen ➪ Unsharp Mask.** In the last example in Figure 23-15, I applied the highest permitted Amount value, 500 percent, and a Radius of 2.0.

10. **Whatever values you use, make sure the Threshold is set to 0.** Always leave it at 0 from this day forward.

In case Figures 23-14 and 23-15 are a little too subtle, I include enlarged views of the great general's eyes in Figure 23-16. The top eyes show the result of using the Threshold value, the bottom eyes were created using the edge mask. Which ones appear sharper and less grainy to you?

**Figure 23-16:** Enlarged views of the last examples from Figures 23-14 (top) and 23-15 (bottom). A good edge mask beats the Threshold value every time.

## Using the High Pass filter

The High Pass filter falls more or less in the same camp as the sharpening filters but is not located under the Filter ➪ Sharpen submenu. This frequently overlooked gem enables you to isolate high-contrast image areas from their low-contrast counterparts.

When you choose Filter ➪ Other ➪ High Pass, Photoshop offers a single option: the familiar Radius value, which can vary from 0.1 to 250.0. As demonstrated in Figure 23-17, high Radius values distinguish areas of high and low contrast only slightly. Low values change all high-contrast areas to dark gray and low-contrast areas to a slightly lighter gray. A value of 0.1 (not shown) changes all pixels in an image to a single gray value and is therefore useless.

### Applying High Pass to individual color channels

In my continuing series of color plates devoted to adding a bit of digital color to the ages-old chess pieces, Color Plate 23-5 shows the results of applying the High Pass filter set to a Radius value of 5.0 to the various color channels. This application is actually a pretty interesting use for this filter. When applied to all channels at once, High Pass has an irritating habit of robbing the image of color in the low-contrast areas, just where the color is needed most. But when applied to a single channel, there's no color to steal. In fact, the filter adds color. For example, because there is almost no contrast in the dark shadows, High Pass elevates the black to gray in each of the affected color channels. The gray in the red channel appears red, the gray in the red channel mixed with the gray in the green channel appears yellow, and so forth. As a result, the filter imbues each image with a chalky glow.

**Note**

I enhanced the High Pass effect slightly in Color Plate 23-5 by increasing the contrast of each affected color channel using the Levels command. Using the three Input option boxes at the top of the Levels dialog box, I changed the first value to 65 and the third value to 190, thereby compressing the color space equally on both the black and white sides. Had I not done this, the images would appear a little more washed out. (Not a lot, but I figure that you deserve the best color I can deliver.) For detailed information on the Levels command, read Chapter 30.

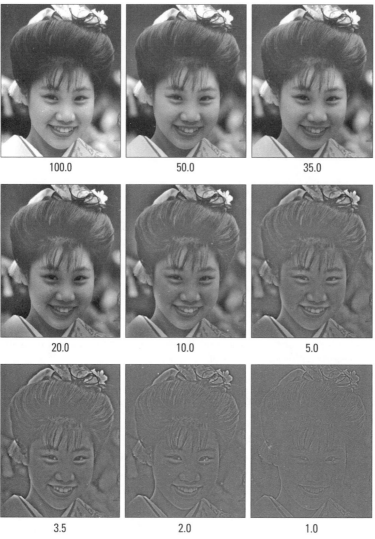

**Figure 23-17:** The results of separating high- and low-contrast areas in an image with the High Pass filter set at eight different Radius values.

## Converting an image into a line drawing

The High Pass filter is especially useful as a precursor to Image ➪ Adjust ➪ Threshold, which converts all pixels in an image to black and white (again, covered in Chapter 30). As illustrated in Figure 23-18, the Threshold command produces entirely different effects on images before and after you alter them with the High Pass filter. In fact, applying the High Pass filter with a low Radius value and then issuing the Threshold command converts your image into a line drawing.

In the second row of examples in the figure, I followed Threshold with Filter ➪ Blur ➪ Gaussian Blur (the subject of the next section). I set the Gaussian Blur Radius value to 1.0. Like the Threshold option in the Unsharp Mask dialog box, the Threshold command results in harsh transitions; Gaussian Blur softens them to produce a more natural effect.

Why change your image to a bunch of slightly different gray values and then apply a command such as Threshold? One reason is to create a mask, as discussed at length in the "Building a Mask from an Image" section of Chapter 16. (In Chapter 16, I used Levels instead of Threshold, but both are variations on the same theme.)

You might also want to bolster the edges in an image. For example, to achieve the last row of examples in Figure 23-18, I layered the images prior to applying High Pass, Threshold, and Gaussian Blur. Then I monkeyed around with the Opacity setting and the blend mode to achieve an edge-tracing effect.

**Note**

I should mention that Photoshop provides several automated edge-tracing filters — including Find Edges, Trace Contour, and the Gallery Effects acquisition, Glowing Edges. But High Pass affords more control than any of these commands and permits you to explore a wider range of alternatives. Also worth noting, several Gallery Effects filters — most obviously Filter ➪ Sketch ➪ Photocopy — lift much of their code directly from High Pass. Although it may seem at first glance a strange effect, High Pass is one of the seminal filters in Photoshop.

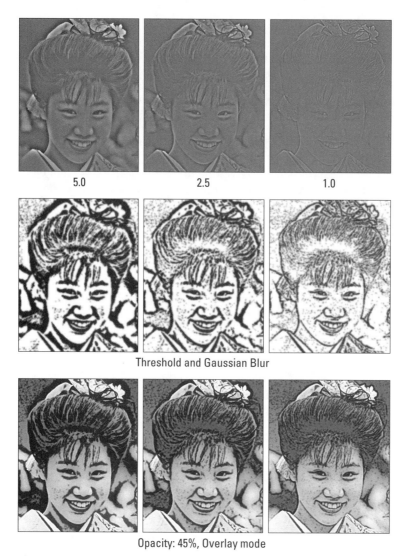

5.0                    2.5                    1.0

Threshold and Gaussian Blur

Opacity: 45%, Overlay mode

**Figure 23-18:** Several applications of the High Pass filter with low Radius values (top row), followed by the same images subject to Image ➪ Adjust ➪ Threshold and Filter ➪ Blur ➪ Gaussian Blur (middle). I then layered the second row onto the first and modified the Opacity and blend mode settings.

# Blurring an Image

The commands under the Filter ⇨ Blur submenu produce the opposite effects of their counterparts under the Filter ⇨ Sharpen submenu. Rather than enhancing the amount of contrast between neighboring pixels, the Blur filters diminish contrast to create softening effects.

## Applying the Gaussian Blur filter

The preeminent Blur filter, Gaussian Blur, blends a specified number of pixels incrementally, following the bell-shaped Gaussian distribution curve I touched on earlier. When you choose Filter ⇨ Blur ⇨ Gaussian Blur, Photoshop produces a single Radius option box, in which you can enter any value from 0.1 to 250.0. (Beginning to sound familiar?) As demonstrated in Figure 23-19, Radius values of 1.0 and smaller blur an image slightly; moderate values, between 1.0 and 5.0, turn an image into a rude approximation of life without my glasses on; and higher values blur the image beyond recognition.

Moderate to high Radius values can be especially useful for creating that hugely amusing *Star Trek* Iridescent Female effect. This is the old *Star Trek,* of course. Captain Kirk meets some bewitching ambassador or scientist who has just beamed on board. He takes her hand in sincere welcome as he gives out with a lecherous grin and explains how truly honored he is to have such a renowned guest in his transporter room, and so charming to boot. Then we see it — the close-up of the fetching actress shrouded in a kind of gleaming halo that prevents us from discerning if her lips are chapped or perhaps she's hiding an old acne scar, because some cockeyed cinematographer smeared Vaseline all over the camera lens. I mean, what *wouldn't* you give to be able to re-create this effect in Photoshop?

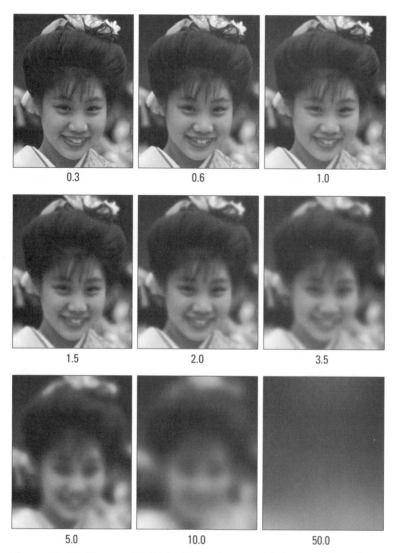

**Figure 23-19:** The results of blurring an image with the Gaussian Blur filter using eight different Radius values, ranging from slightly out of focus to Bad Day at the Ophthalmologist's Office.

Unfortunately, I don't have any images of actresses adorned in futuristic go-go boots, so Constantine cum Rambo will have to do in a pinch. The following steps explain how to make the colossal head glow as demonstrated in Figure 23-20.

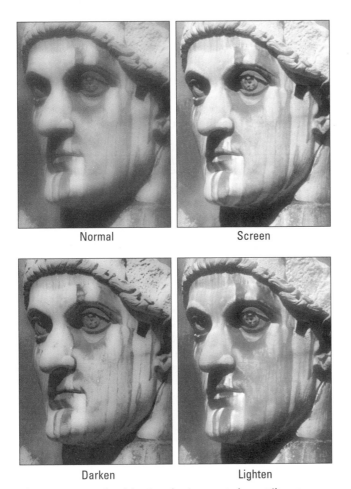

Normal        Screen

Darken        Lighten

**Figure 23-20:** After blurring the image, I chose Filter ⇨ Fade Gaussian Blur and changed the Opacity value to 70 percent. Then I applied the labeled blend modes to alter the image further.

## Steps: The Captain Kirk Myopia Effect

1. **Press ⌘/Ctrl+A to select the entire image.** If you only want to apply the effect to a portion of the image, be sure to feather the selection with a radius in the neighborhood of 5 to 8 pixels.

2. **Choose Filter ⇨ Blur ⇨ Gaussian Blur.** Enter some unusually large value into the Radius option box — say, 8.0 — and press Return/Enter.

3. **Press ⌘/Ctrl+Shift+F to bring up the Fade dialog box.** To achieve the effects shown in Figure 23-20, I reduced the Opacity value to 70 percent, making the blurred image slightly translucent. This way, you can see the hard edges of the original image through the filtered one.

4. **You can achieve additional effects by selecting options from the Mode pop-up menu.** For example, I created the upper right example in the figure by selecting the Screen option, which uses the colors in the filtered image to lighten the original. I created the two bottom examples in the figure by applying the Darken and Lighten options.

Color Plate 23-6 shows an image that's more likely to interest Captain Kirk. It shows a young agrarian woman subject to most of the same settings I applied earlier to Constantine. Again, I applied the Gaussian Blur filter with a Radius of 8.0. Then I used Filter ⇨ Fade Gaussian Blur to adjust the Opacity value and blend mode. The upper left image shows the Normal mode, but the upper right image shows the Luminosity mode. In this case, the Screen mode resulted in a washed-out effect, whereas Luminosity yielded an image with crisp color detail and fuzzy brightness values. As a result, there are some interesting places where the colors leap off her checkered dress. As in Figure 23-20, the bottom two images show the effects of the Darken and Lighten modes.

You know, though, as I look at this woman, I'm beginning to have my doubts about her and Captain Kirk. I mean, she has Scotty written all over her.

## The preset blurring filters

Neither of the two preset commands in the Filter ⇨ Blur submenu, Blur and Blur More, can distribute its blurring effect over a bell-shaped Gaussian curve. For that reason, these two commands are less functional than the Gaussian Blur filter. Just so you know where they stand in the grand Photoshop focusing scheme, Figure 23-21 shows the effect of each preset command and the nearly equivalent effect created with the Gaussian Blur filter.

Blur                    Blur More

0.3                    0.7

**Figure 23-21:** The effects of the two preset blurring filters (top row) compared with their Gaussian Blur equivalents (bottom row), which are labeled according to Radius values.

## Anti-aliasing an image

If you have a particularly jagged image, such as a 256-color GIF file, there's a better way to soften the rough edges than applying the Gaussian Blur filter. The best solution is to antialias the image. How? After all, Photoshop doesn't offer an Anti-alias filter. Well, think about it. Back in the "Softening selection outlines" section of Chapter 15, I described how Photoshop anti-aliases a brushstroke or selection outline at twice its normal size and then reduces it by 50 percent and applies bicubic interpolation. You can do the same thing with an image.

Choose Image ➪ Image Size and enlarge the image to 200 percent of its present size. Make sure that the Resample Image check box is turned on and set to Bicubic. (You can also experiment with Bilinear for a slightly different effect, but don't use Nearest Neighbor.) Next, turn right around and choose Image ➪ Image Size again, but this time shrink the image by 50 percent.

The top left example in Figure 23-22 shows a jagged image subject to this effect. I used Image ⇨ Adjust ⇨ Posterize to reduce Moses to four colors. It's ugly, but it's not unlike the kind of images you may encounter, particularly if you have access to an aging image library. To the right is the same image subject to Gaussian Blur with a very low Radius value of 0.5. Rather than appearing softened, the result is just plain fuzzy.

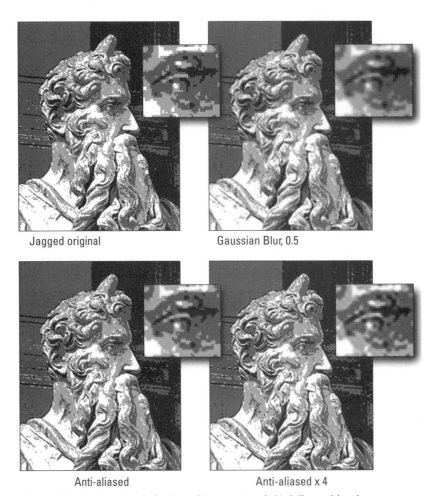

Jagged original                    Gaussian Blur, 0.5

Anti-aliased                       Anti-aliased x 4

**Figure 23-22:** A particularly jagged image (top left) followed by the image blurred using a filter (top right). By enlarging and reducing the image one or more times (bottom left and right), I soften the pixels without making them appear blurry. The enlarged details show each operation's effect on the individual pixels.

If I instead enlarge and reduce the image with the Image Size command, however, I achieve a true softening effect, as shown in the lower left example in the figure, commensurate with Photoshop's anti-aliasing options. Even after enlarging and reducing the image four times in a row — as in the bottom right example — I don't make the image blurry, I simply make it softer.

## Directional blurring

In addition to its everyday blurring functions, Photoshop provides two *directional blurring* filters, Motion Blur and Radial Blur. Instead of blurring pixels in feathered clusters like the Gaussian Blur filter, the Motion Blur filter blurs pixels in straight lines over a specified distance. The Radial Blur filter blurs pixels in varying degrees depending on their distance from the center of the blur. The following pages explain both of these filters in detail.

### Motion blurring

The Motion Blur filter makes an image appear as if either the image or camera was moving when you shot the photo. When you choose Filter ➪ Blur ➪ Motion Blur, Photoshop displays the dialog box shown in Figure 23-23. You enter the angle of movement into the Angle option box. Alternatively, you can indicate the angle by dragging the straight line inside the circle on the right side of the dialog box, as shown in the figure. (You'll notice that the arrow cursor actually appears outside the circle. Once you begin dragging on the line, you can move the cursor anywhere you want and still affect the angle.)

**Figure 23-23:** Drag the line inside the circle to change the angle of the blur.

You then enter the distance of the movement in the Distance option box. Photoshop permits any value between 1 and 999 pixels. The filter distributes the effect of the blur over the course of the Distance value, as illustrated by the examples in Figure 23-24.

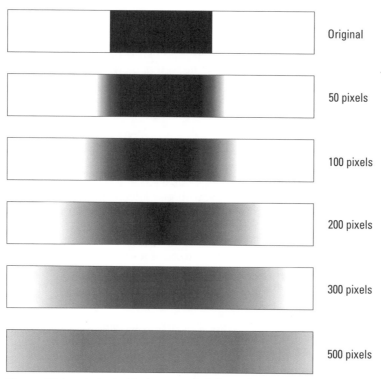

Original

50 pixels

100 pixels

200 pixels

300 pixels

500 pixels

**Figure 23-24:** A single black rectangle followed by five different applications of the Motion Blur filter. Only the Distance value varied, as labeled. A 0-degree Angle value was used in all five examples.

**Note**

Mathematically speaking, Motion Blur is one of Photoshop's simpler filters. Rather than distributing the effect over a Gaussian curve—which one might argue would produce a more believable effect—Photoshop creates a simple linear distribution, peaking in the center and fading at either end. It's as if the program took the value you specified in the Distance option, created that many clones of the image, offset half the clones in one direction and half the clones in the other — all spaced 1 pixel apart — and then varied the opacity of each.

## Using the Wind filter

The problem with the Motion Blur filter is that it blurs pixels in two directions. If you want to distribute pixels in one absolute direction or the other, try out the Wind filter, which you can use either on its own or in tandem with Motion Blur.

When you choose Filter ➪ Stylize ➪ Wind, Photoshop displays the Wind dialog box shown in Figure 23-25. You can select from three methods and two directions to distribute the selected pixels. Figure 23-26 compares the effect of the Motion Blur filter to each of the three methods offered by the Wind filter. Notice that the Wind filter does not blur pixels. Rather, it evaluates a selection in 1-pixel-tall horizontal strips and offsets the strips randomly inside the image.

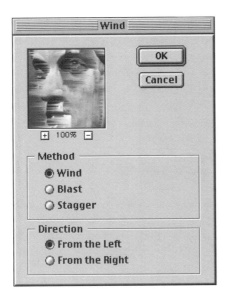

**Figure 23-25:** Use the Wind filter to randomly distribute a selection in 1-pixel horizontal strips in one of two directions.

Motion Blur

Wind

Blast

Stagger

**Figure 23-26:** Here is the difference between the effects of the Motion Blur filter (upper left) and the Wind filter (other three). In each case, I selected From the Right from the Direction radio buttons.

To get the best results, try combining the Motion Blur and Wind filters with a translucent selection. For example, to create Figure 23-27, I cloned the entire image to a new layer and applied the Wind command twice, first selecting the Stagger option and then selecting Blast. Next, I applied the Motion Blur command with a 0-degree angle and a Distance value of 30. I then set the Opacity option in the Layers palette to 80 percent and selected Lighten from the blend mode pop-up menu.

The result is a perfect blend between two worlds. The motion effect in Figure 23-27 doesn't obliterate the image detail, as the Wind filter does in Figure 23-26. The motion also appears to run in a single direction — to the right — something you can't accomplish using Motion Blur on its own.

**Figure 23-27:** Here is the result of combining the Wind and Motion Blur filters with a translucent selection.

## Radial blurring

Choosing Filter ➪ Blur ➪ Radial Blur displays the Radial Blur dialog box shown in Figure 23-28. The dialog box offers two Blur Method options: Spin and Zoom.

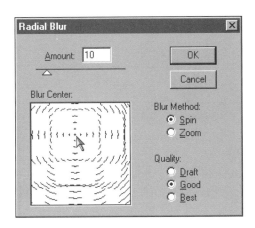

**Figure 23-28:** Drag inside the Blur Center grid to change the point about which the Radial Blur filter spins or zooms the image.

If you select Spin, the image appears to be rotating about a central point. You specify that point by dragging in the grid inside the Blur Center box (as demonstrated in the figure). If you select Zoom, the image appears to rush away from you, as if you were zooming the camera while shooting the photograph. Again, you specify the central point of the Zoom by dragging in the Blur Center box. Figure 23-29 features examples of both settings.

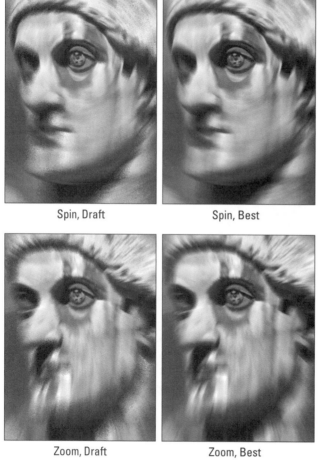

Spin, Draft                    Spin, Best

Zoom, Draft                    Zoom, Best

**Figure 23-29:** Four examples of the Radial Blur filter set to both Spin and Zoom, subject to different Quality settings (left and right). I specified Amount values of 10 pixels for the Spin examples and 30 for the Zooms. Each effect is centered about the right eye (your right, that is).

After selecting a Blur Method option, you can enter any value between 1 and 100 in the Amount option box to specify the maximum distance over which the filter blurs pixels. (You can enter a value of 0, but doing so merely causes the filter to waste time without producing an effect.) Pixels farthest away from the center point move the most; pixels close to the center point barely move at all. Keep in mind that large values take more time to apply than small values. The Radial Blur filter, incidentally, qualifies as one of Photoshop's most time-consuming operations.

Select a Quality option to specify your favorite time/quality compromise. The Good and Best Quality options ensure smooth results by respectively applying bilinear and bicubic interpolation (as explained in the "General preferences" section of Chapter B on CD-ROM #2). They also prolong the amount of time the filter spends calculating pixels in your image, however.

The Draft option *diffuses* an image, which leaves a trail of loose and randomized pixels but takes less time to complete. I used the Draft setting to create the left-hand images in Figure 23-29; I selected the Best option to create the images on the right.

## Blurring with a threshold

The purpose of the new Filter ➪ Blur ➪ Smart Blur is to blur the low-contrast portions of an image while retaining the edges. This way, you can downplay photo grain, blemishes, and artifacts without harming the real edges in the image. (If you're familiar with Filter ➪ Pixelate ➪ Facet, then it may help to know Smart Blur is essentially a customizable version of that filter.)

The two key options inside the Smart Blur dialog box (see Figure 23-30) are the Radius and Threshold slider bars. As with all Radius options, this one expands the number of pixels calculated at a time as you increase the value. Meanwhile, the Threshold value works just like the one in the Unsharp Mask dialog box, specifying how different two neighboring pixels must be to be considered an edge.

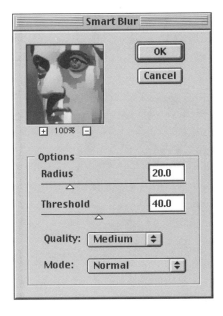

**Figure 23-30:** The Smart Blur filter lets you blur the low-contrast areas of an image without harming the edges.

But the Threshold value has a peculiar and unexpected effect on the Radius. The Radius value actually produces more subtle effects if you raise the value beyond the Threshold. For example, take a look at Figure 23-31. Here we have a grid of images subject to different Radius and Threshold values. (The first value below each image is the radius.) In the top row of the figure, the 5.0 radius actually produces a more pronounced effect than its 20.0 and 60.0 cousins. This is because 5.0 is less than the 10.0 threshold, while 20.0 and 60.0 are more.

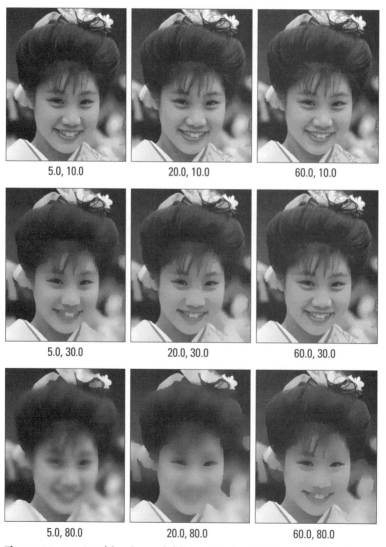

**Figure 23-31:** Combinations of different Radius (first number) and Threshold (second) values. Notice that the most dramatic effects occur when the radius is equal to about half the threshold.

The Quality settings control the smoothness of the edges. The High setting takes more time than Medium and Low, but it looks smoother as well. (All of the effects in Figure 23-31 were set to High.) The two additional Mode options enable you to trace the edges defined by the Threshold value with white lines. Overlay Edges shows image and lines, while Edges Only shows just the traced lines. About the only practical purpose for these options is to monitor the precise effect of the Threshold setting in the preview box. Otherwise, the Edges options are clearly relegated to special effects.

Frankly, I'm not convinced that Smart Blur is quite ready for prime time. You already know what I think of the Threshold option, and it hasn't gotten any better here. Without control over the transitions between focused and unfocused areas, things are going to look pretty strange.

**Tip**

The better way to blur low-contrast areas is to create an edge mask, as I explained back in the "Sharpening grainy photographs" section. Just reverse the selection by choosing Select ⇨ Inverse and apply the Gaussian Blur filter.

Figure 23-32 shows how the masking technique compares with Smart Blur. In the first image, I applied Unsharp Mask with a Threshold of 20. Then I turned around and applied Smart Blur with a Radius of 2.0 and a Threshold of 20.0, matching the Unsharp Mask value. The result makes Ike look like he has dandruff coming out of every pore in his face.

**Figure 23-32:** The difference between relying on Photoshop's automated Threshold capabilities (left) and sharpening and blurring with the aid of an edge mask (right). Despite the advent of computers, a little manual labor still wins out over automation.

In the second image, I created an edge mask — as explained in the "Creating and Using an Edge Mask" steps — and applied Unsharp Mask with a Threshold of 0. Then I pressed ⌘/Ctrl+Shift+I to reverse the selection and applied Gaussian Blur with a Radius of 2.0. The result is a smooth image with sharp edges that any president would be proud to hang in the Oval Office.

## Softening a selection outline

Gaussian Blur and other Blur filters are equally as useful when editing masks as they are when editing image pixels. As I mentioned earlier, applying Gaussian Blur to a mask has the same effect as applying Select ➪ Feather to a selection outline. But Gaussian Blur affords more control. Where the Feather command affects all portions of a selection outline uniformly, you can apply Gaussian Blur selectively to a mask, permitting you to mix soft and hard edges within a single selection outline easily.

Another advantage to blurring a mask is that you can see the results of your adjustments on-screen, instead of relying on the seldom-helpful marching ants. For example, suppose that you want to establish a buffer zone between a foreground image and its background. You've managed to select the foreground image accurately — how do you now feather the selection exclusively outward, so that no portion of the foreground image becomes selected? Although you can pull off this feat using selection commands like Expand and Feather, it's much easier to apply filters such as Maximum and Gaussian Blur inside a mask. But before I go any farther, I need to back up and explain how Maximum and its pal Minimum work.

### Maximum and Minimum

Filter ➪ Other ➪ Maximum expands the light portions of an image, spreading them outward into other pixels. Its opposite, Filter ➪ Other ➪ Minimum, expands the dark portions of an image. In traditional stat photography, these techniques are known as *spreading* and *choking*.

When you are working in the quick mask mode or an independent mask channel, applying the Maximum filter has the effect of incrementally expanding the selected area, adding pixels uniformly around the edges of the selection outline. The Maximum dialog box presents you with a single Radius value, which tells Photoshop how many edge pixels to expand. Just the opposite, the Minimum filter incrementally decreases the size of white areas, which subtracts pixels uniformly around the edges of a selection.

### Feathering outward from a selection outline

The following steps describe how to use the Maximum and Gaussian Blur filters to feather an existing selection outline outward so that it doesn't encroach on the foreground image.

## Steps: Adding a Soft Edge in the Quick Mask Mode

1. **Select the foreground image.** As shown in Figure 23-33, my foreground image is the layered television that figured so heavily into Chapter 17. I convert the layer's transparency mask to a selection outline by ⌘/Ctrl+clicking on the layer's name in the Layers palette.

2. **If you're working on a layer, switch to the background image.** The quickest route is Shift+Option/Alt+[.

3. **Press Q to enter the quick mask mode.** You can create a new mask channel if you prefer, but the quick mask mode is more convenient.

4. **Choose Filter ➪ Other ➪ Maximum.** Enter a Radius value to expand the transparent area into the rubylith. In Figure 23-33, I've entered the highest Radius value permitted, 10 pixels. After pressing Return/Enter, I decided this wasn't enough, so I pressed ⌘/Ctrl+Option/Alt+F to bring up the filter again, and further expanded the selection by 4 pixels.

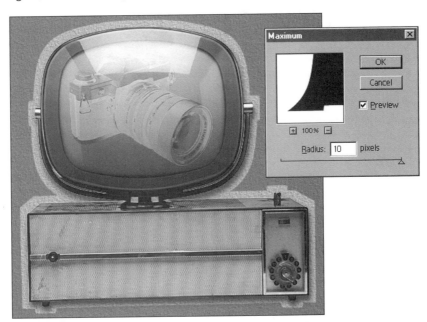

**Figure 23-33:** The Maximum filter increases the size of the transparent area inside the quick mask mode, thereby expanding the selection outline.

*(continued)*

5. **Choose Filter ⇨ Blur ⇨ Gaussian Blur.** To ensure that you don't blur into the foreground image, enter a Radius value that's no more than half the value you entered into the Maximum dialog box. Altogether, I expanded the selection by 14 pixels, so I entered 7 into the Gaussian Blur dialog box. Photoshop blurs the transparent area, as shown in Figure 23-34.

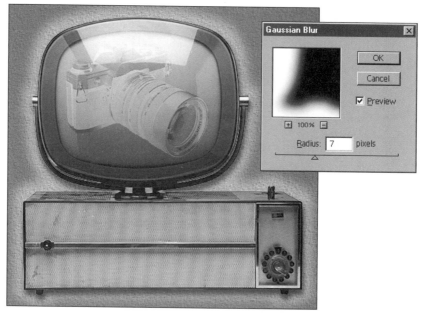

**Figure 23-34:** Use the Gaussian Blur filter to soften the transparent area, thus feathering the selection outline.

6. **Invert the mask by pressing ⌘/Ctrl+I.** So far, I've managed to select the TV, but I really want to edit the background. So I press ⌘/Ctrl+I to invert the mask and inverse the prospective selection.

7. **Press Q to exit the quick mask mode.** Ah, back in the workaday world of marching ants.

8. **Apply the desired effect.** I copied a zebra-skin pattern from another image. Then I chose Edit ⇨ Paste Into (⌘/Ctrl+Shift+V) to paste the pattern inside the selection. Photoshop created a new layer with layer mask. After ⌘/Ctrl+dragging the pattern into position, I applied the Overlay blend mode to achieve the effect shown in Figure 23-35.

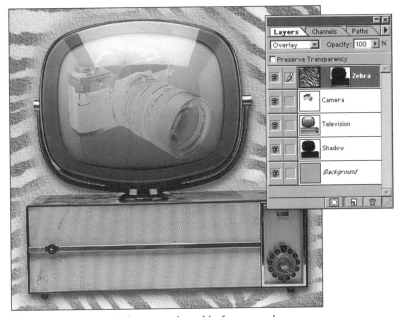

**Figure 23-35:** I copied some zebra skin from one image window and pressed ⌘/Ctrl+Shift+V to paste it into my new selection.

Thanks to my expanded and softened selection outline, the stripes fade toward the television without ever quite touching it. As I said, you can achieve this effect using Select ➪ Modify ➪ Expand and Feather, but unless you have a special aversion to the quick mask mode, it's easier to be sure of your results when you can see exactly what you're doing.

# Noise Factors

Photoshop offers four loosely associated filters in its Filter ➪ Noise submenu. One filter adds random pixels — known as *noise* — to an image. The other three, Despeckle, Dust & Scratches, and Median, average the colors of neighboring pixels in ways that theoretically remove noise from poorly scanned images. But in fact, they function nearly as well at removing essential detail as they do at removing extraneous noise. In the following sections, I show you how the Noise filters work, demonstrate a few of my favorite applications, and leave you to draw your own conclusions.

## Adding noise

Noise adds grit and texture to an image. Noise makes an image look like you shot it in New York on the Lower East Side and were lucky to get the photo at all because someone was throwing sand in your face as you sped away in your chauffeur-driven, jet-black Maserati Bora, hammering away at the shutter release. In reality, of course, a guy over at Sears shot the photo while you toodled around in your minivan trying to find a store that sold day-old bread. But that's the beauty of Noise. It makes you look cool, even when you aren't.

You add noise by choosing Filter ➪ Noise ➪ Add Noise. Shown in Figure 23-36, the Add Noise dialog box features the following options:

✦ **Amount:** Enter any value between 1 and 999 to specify the amount that pixels in the image can stray from their current colors. The value itself represents a color range rather than a brightness range. For example, if you enter a value of 10, Photoshop can apply any color that is 10 shades more or less green, more or less blue, *and* more or less red than the current color. Any value over 255 allows Photoshop to select random colors from the entire 16-million color spectrum. The higher you go above 255, the more likely Photoshop is to pick colors at opposite ends of the spectrum — that is, white and black.

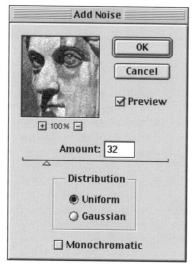

**Figure 23-36:** The Add Noise dialog box asks you to specify the amount and variety of noise you want to add to the selection.

✦ **Uniform:** Select this option to apply colors absolutely randomly within the specified range. Photoshop is no more likely to apply one color within the range than another, thus resulting in an even color distribution.

✦ **Gaussian:** When you select this option, you instruct Photoshop to prioritize colors along the Gaussian distribution curve. The effect is that most colors added by the filter either closely resemble the original colors or push the boundaries of the specified range. In other words, this option results in more light and dark pixels, thus producing a more pronounced effect.

✦ **Monochromatic:** When working on a full-color image, the Add Noise filter distributes pixels randomly throughout the different color channels. When you select the Monochrome check box, however, Photoshop distributes the noise in the same manner in all channels. The result is grayscale noise. (This option does not affect grayscale images; the noise can't get any more grayscale than it already is.)

Figure 23-37 compares three applications of Gaussian noise to identical amounts of Uniform noise. Figure 23-38 features magnified views of the noise so that you can compare the colors of individual pixels.

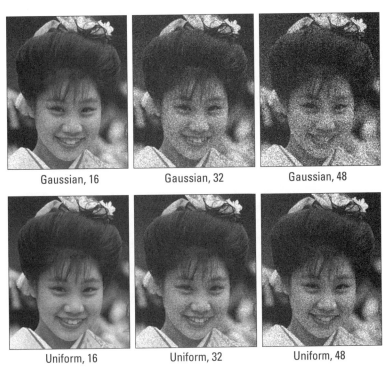

Gaussian, 16     Gaussian, 32     Gaussian, 48

Uniform, 16     Uniform, 32     Uniform, 48

**Figure 23-37:** The Gaussian option produces more pronounced effects than the Uniform option at identical Amount values.

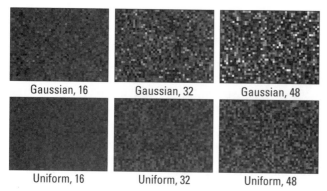

Gaussian, 16        Gaussian, 32        Gaussian, 48

Uniform, 16        Uniform, 32        Uniform, 48

**Figure 23-38:** The upper left corners of the examples from
Figure 23-37 enlarged to four times their original size.

## Noise variations

Normally, the Add Noise filter adds both lighter and darker pixels to an image.
If you prefer, however, you can limit the effect of the filter to strictly lighter or
darker pixels. To do so, apply the Add Noise filter, then choose Filter ➪ Fade
Add Noise and select the Lighten or Darken blend mode. You can also copy
the image to a new layer, apply the filter, and merge the filtered image with the
underlying original.

Figure 23-39 shows sample applications of lighter and darker noise. After
copying the image to a separate layer, I applied the Add Noise filter with an
Amount value of 100, and selected Gaussian. To create the upper left example
in the figure, I selected Lighten from the blend mode pop-up menu. To create
the right example, I selected the Darken mode. In each case, I added a layer of
strictly lighter or darker noise while at the same time retaining the clarity of
the original image.

To achieve the streaked noise effects in the bottom example of Figure 23-39, I
applied Motion Blur and Unsharp Mask to the layered images. Inside the Motion
Blur dialog box, I set the Angle value to –30 degrees and the Distance to 30 pixels.
Then I applied Unsharp Mask with an Amount value of 200 percent and a Radius
of 1. Naturally, the Threshold value was 0.

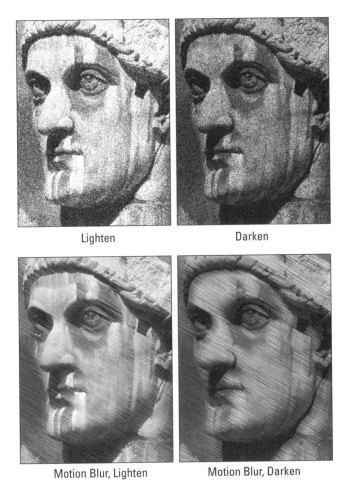

Lighten            Darken

Motion Blur, Lighten            Motion Blur, Darken

**Figure 23-39:** You can limit the Add Noise filter to strictly lighter (left) or darker (right) noise by applying the filter to a layered clone. To create the rainy and scraped effects (bottom examples), I applied Motion Blur and Unsharp Mask to the noise layers.

## Chunky noise

My biggest frustration with the Add Noise filter is that you can't specify the size of individual specks of noise. No matter how you cut it, noise only comes in 1-pixel squares. It may occur to you that you can enlarge the noise dots in a layer by applying the Maximum or Minimum filter. But in practice, doing so simply fills in the image, because there isn't sufficient space between the noise pixels to accommodate the larger dot sizes.

Luckily, Photoshop provides several alternatives. One is the Pointillize filter, which adds variable-sized dots and then colors those dots in keeping with the original colors in the image. Although Pointillize lacks the random quality of the Add Noise filter, you can use it to add texture to an image.

To create the top left image in Figure 23-40, I chose Filter ⇨ Pixelate ⇨ Pointillize and entered 5 into the Cell Size option box. After pressing Return/Enter to apply the filter, I pressed ⌘/Ctrl+Shift+F and changed the Opacity value to 50 percent. The effect is rather like applying chunky bits of noise.

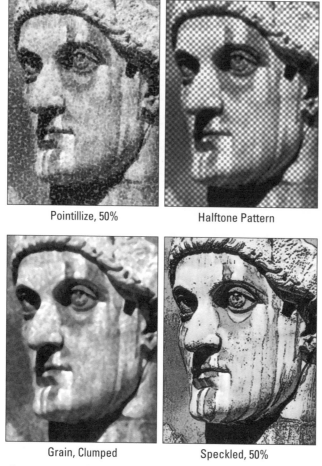

Pointillize, 50%               Halftone Pattern

Grain, Clumped               Speckled, 50%

**Figure 23-40:** The results of applying several different Add Noise-like filters, including Pointillize, Halftone Pattern, and Grain. A percentage value indicates that I modified the Opacity setting in the Fade dialog box.

The Gallery Effects filters provide a few noise alternatives. Filter ➭ Sketch ➭ Halftone Pattern adds your choice of dot patterns, as shown in the upper right example in Figure 23-40. But like all filters in the Sketch submenu, it replaces the colors in your image with the foreground and background colors. Filter ➭ Texture ➭ Grain is a regular noise smorgasbord, permitting you to select from 10 different Grain Type options, each of which produces a different kind of noise. The bottom examples in Figure 23-40 show off two of the Grain options, Clumped and Speckled. I used Filter ➭ Fade Grain to reduce the Opacity value for the Speckled effect to 50 percent.

## Removing noise with Despeckle

Now for the noise removal filters. Strictly speaking, the Despeckle command probably belongs in the Filter ➭ Blur submenu. It blurs a selection while at the same time preserving its edges — the idea being that unwanted noise is most noticeable in the continuous regions of an image. In practice, this filter is nearly the exact opposite of the Sharpen Edges filter.

The Despeckle command searches an image for edges using the equivalent of an Unsharp Mask Threshold value of 5. It then ignores the edges in the image and blurs everything else with the force of the Blur More filter, as shown in the upper left image in Figure 23-41.

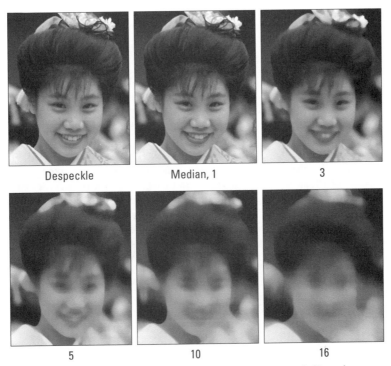

**Figure 23-41:** The effects of the Despeckle filter (upper left) and Median filter. The numbers indicate Median filter Radius values.

## Averaging pixels with Median

Another command in the Filter ➪ Noise submenu, Median removes noise by averaging the colors in an image, one pixel at a time. When you choose Filter ➪ Noise ➪ Median, Photoshop produces a Radius option box, into which you can enter any value between 1 and 16. For every pixel in a selection, the filter averages the colors of the neighboring pixels that fall inside the specified radius — ignoring any pixels that are so different that they might skew the average — and applies the average color to the central pixel. As verified by Figure 23-41, large values produce the most destructive effects.

As with Gaussian Blur, you can achieve some very interesting and useful effects by backing off the Median filter with the Fade command. But rather than creating a *Star Trek* glow, Median clumps up details, giving an image a plastic, molded quality, as demonstrated by the examples in Figure 23-42. To create every one of these images, I applied the Median Filter with a Radius of 5 pixels. Then I pressed ⌘/Ctrl+Shift+F to display the Fade dialog box and lowered the Opacity value to 70 percent. The only difference between one image and the next is the blend mode.

Another difference between Gaussian Blur and Median is that Gaussian Blur destroys edges and Median invents new ones. This means you can follow up the Median filter with Unsharp Mask to achieve even more pronounced sculptural effects. I sharpened every one of the examples in Figure 23-42 using an Amount value of 150 percent and a Radius of 1.5

## Sharpening a compressed image

Digital cameras are the hottest thing in electronic imaging. You can take as many images as you like, download them to your computer immediately, and place them into a printed document literally minutes after snapping the picture. In the next five years, I have little doubt that you — yes, *you* — will purchase a digital camera (if you haven't already).

Unfortunately, the technology is still very young. Many brands take exceptional pictures, but most of these high-end devices cost $10,000 or more. Even midrange "mega-pixel" cameras like the Kodak DC210 and Olympus D-600L cost $1,000 or more. If you're hoping for a camera under $500, you'll have to make due with a consumer model like the Fuji DX-9 or the Minolta Dimage V. Even if you pick up this book two years after I write it, and every one of these models has been discontinued, you can expect to pay $200 to $500 for a low-end model.

Normal

Screen

Darken

Lighten

**Figure 23-42:** After applying the Median filter, I reversed the effect slightly using Filter ⇨ Fade Median. Although I varied the blend mode — as labeled beneath the images — the Opacity value remained a constant 70 percent.

If you've ever used one of these cameras — it's only a matter of time, I assure you — you know how difficult it is to sharpen the photographs. Thanks to the stingy supply of pixels and the heavy-handed compression schemes (all based on JPEG), even the daintiest application of the Unsharp Mask filter can reveal a world of ragged edges and unsightly artifacts.

**Note**

The solution is to firm up the detail and smooth out the color transitions by applying a combination of filters — Median, Gaussian Blur, and Unsharp Mask — to a layered version of the image. The following steps tell all.

If you own a digital camera, I encourage you to record these steps with the Actions palette, as explained in Chapter E of CD-ROM #2. This way, you can set Photoshop to open squads of images, batch process them, and save them in a separate folder, leaving you free to do something fun, like read more of this book.

## Steps: Adjusting the Focus of Digital Photos

1. **Select the entire image and copy it to a new layer.** That's ⌘/Ctrl+A, ⌘/Ctrl+J. Figure 23-43 shows the image that I intend to sharpen, a picture of a friend's child that I snapped with a DC40 (the predecessor to the earlier-mentioned DC50). His name, in case you're interested, is Cooper.

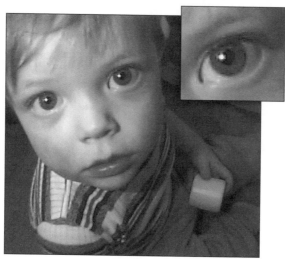

**Figure 23-43:** I captured this youthful fellow with a low-end digital camera equipped with a removable fish-eye lens. How innocent and happy he looks — obviously not a computer user.

2. **Choose Filter ⇨ Noise ⇨ Median.** After processing several thousand of these images, I've found that a Radius value of 2 is almost always the optimal choice. But if the image is particularly bad, 3 may be warranted.

3. **Choose Filter ⇨ Blur ⇨ Gaussian Blur.** Now that you've gummed up the detail a bit and rubbed out most of the compression, use the Gaussian

Blur filter with a Radius of 1.0 to blur the gummy detail slightly. This softens the edges that the Median filter creates. (You don't want any fake edges, after all.)

4. **Choose Filter ⇨ Sharpen ⇨ Unsharp Mask.** All this blurring demands some intense sharpening. So apply Unsharp Mask with a maximum Amount value of 500 percent and a Radius of 1.0 (to match the Gaussian Blur radius). This restores most of the definition to the edges, as shown in Figure 23-44.

**Figure 23-44:** Thanks to Median, Gaussian Blur, and Unsharp Mask, Cooper is a much smoother customer. In fact, he's beyond smooth — he's a gummy kid.

5. **Lower the layer's Opacity value.** By itself, the filtered layer is a bit too smooth. So mix the filtered floater with the underlying original with an Opacity value between 30 and 50 percent. I found that I could go pretty high — 45 percent — with Cooper. Kids have clearly defined details that survive filtering quite nicely.

6. **Merge the image.** Press ⌘/Ctrl+E to send the layer down.

7. **Continue to correct the image as you normally would.** The examples in Figure 23-45 show the difference between applying the Unsharp Mask filter to the original image (top) and the filtered mixture (bottom). In both cases, I applied an Amount value of 200 percent and a Radius of 1.0. The top photo displays an unfortunate wealth of artifacts — particularly visible in the magnified eye — while the bottom one appears smooth and crisp.

*(continued)*

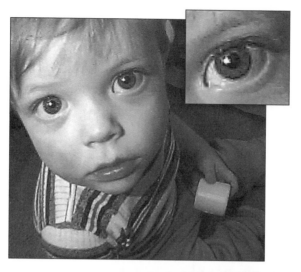

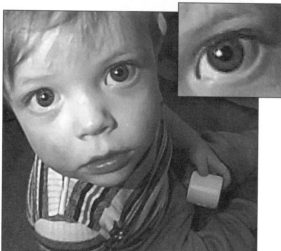

**Figure 23-45:** Here you can see the difference between sharpening a digital photograph right off the bat (top) and waiting to sharpen until after you've prepared the image with Median, Gaussian Blur, and Unsharp Mask (bottom).

These steps work well for sharpening other kinds of compressed imagery, including old photographs that you over-compressed without creating backups, and images that you've downloaded from the Internet. If applying the Unsharp Mask filter brings out the goobers, try these steps instead.

## Cleaning up scanned halftones

Photoshop offers one additional filter in the Filter ➪ Noise submenu called Dust & Scratches. The purpose of this filter is to remove dust particles, hairs, scratches, and other imperfections that may accompany a scan. The filter offers two options, Radius and Threshold. As long as the offending imperfection is smaller or thinner than the Radius value and different enough from its neighbors to satisfy the Threshold value, the filter deletes the spot or line and interpolates between the pixels around the perimeter.

But like so many automated tools, this one works only when conditions are favorable. I'm not saying that you shouldn't ever use it — in fact, you may always want to give this filter the first crack at a dusty image. But if it doesn't work (as it probably won't), don't get your nose out of joint. Just hunker down and eliminate the imperfections manually using the rubber stamp tool, as explained in the "Touching up blemishes" section of Chapter 10.

Now, as I say, Dust & Scratches was designed to get rid of gunk on a dirty scanner. But another problem that the filter may be able to eliminate is moiré patterns. These patterns appear when scanning halftoned images from books and magazines. See, any time you scan a printed image, you're actually scanning a collection of halftone dots rather than a continuous-tone photograph. In most cases, the halftone pattern clashes with the resolution of the scanned image to produce rhythmic and distracting moirés.

**Caution**

When scanning published photographs or artwork, take a moment to find out if what you're doing is legal. It's up to you to make sure that the image you scan is no longer protected by copyright — most, but not all, works over 75 years old are considered free game — or that your noncommercial application of the image falls under the fair-use umbrella of commentary or criticism.

The Dust & Scratches filter can be pretty useful for eliminating moirés, particularly if you reduce the Threshold value below 40. But this also goes a long way toward eliminating the actual image detail, as shown in Color Plate 23-7. This figure features an image scanned from a previous issue of *Macworld* magazine. (Because I created the original image, *Macworld* probably won't sue me, but you shouldn't try it.)

The left half of Color Plate 23-7 shows the individual color channels in the image; the right half shows the full-color image. I've blown up a detail in each image so that you can better see the pixels in the moiré pattern.

The top example in the color plate shows the original scanned image with its awful moirés. (Actually, I've slightly exaggerated the moirés to account for any printing anomalies; but believe me, with or without enhancement, the image is a mess on-screen.) The middle example shows the same image subject to the Dust & Scratches filter with a Radius of 2 and a Threshold value of 20. The moirés are gone, but the edges have all but disappeared as well. I'm tempted to describe this artwork using adjectives like "soft" and "doughy," and them are fightin' words in the world of image-editing.

But what about that bottom example? How did I manage to eliminate the moirés *and* preserve the detail that is shown here? Why, by applying the Gaussian Blur, Median, and Unsharp Mask filters to individual color channels.

The first step is to examine the channels independently (by pressing ⌘/Ctrl+1, ⌘/Ctrl+2, and ⌘/Ctrl+3). You'll likely find that each one is affected by the moiré pattern to a different extent. In the case of this scan, all three channels need work, but the blue channel—the usual culprit—is the worst. The trick, therefore, is to eliminate the patterns in the blue channel and draw detail from the red and green channels.

To fix the blue channel, I applied both the Gaussian Blur and Median commands in fairly hefty doses. I chose Filter ➪ Blur ➪ Gaussian Blur and specified a Radius value of 1.5 pixels, rather high considering that the image measures only about 300 pixels tall. Then I chose Filter ➪ Noise ➪ Median and specified a Radius of 2.

The result was a thickly modeled image with no moirés but little detail. To firm things up a bit, I chose Filter ➪ Sharpen ➪ Unsharp Mask and entered 200 percent for the Amount option and 1.5 for the Radius. I opted for this Radius value because it matches the Radius that I used to blur the image. When correcting moirés, a Threshold value of 0 is almost always the best choice. A higher Threshold value not only prevents the sharpening of moiré pattern edges but also ignores real edges, which are already fragile enough as it is.

The green and red channels required incrementally less attention. After switching to the green channel, I applied the Gaussian Blur filter with a Radius of 1.0. Then I sharpened the image with the Unsharp Mask filter set to 200 percent and a Radius value of 0.5. In the red channel (⌘/Ctrl+1), I applied Gaussian Blur with a Radius value of 0.5. The gradual effect wasn't enough to warrant sharpening.

When you're finished, switch back to the RGB view (⌘/Ctrl+0) to see the combined result of your labors. (Or keep an RGB view of the image up on-screen by choosing

Window ⇨ New Window.) The focus of the image will undoubtedly be softer than it was when you started. You can cure this to a limited extent by applying very discreet passes of the Unsharp Mask filter, say, with an Amount value of 100 percent and a low Radius value. Keep in mind that oversharpening may bring the patterns back to life or even uncover new ones.

**Tip**

One last tip: Always scan halftoned images at the highest resolution available to your scanner. Then resample the scan down to the desired resolution using Image ⇨ Image Size, as covered in Chapter 2. This step by itself goes a long way toward eliminating moirés.

✦　　✦　　✦

# Full-Court Filtering

## Destructive Filters

Corrective filters allow you to both eliminate flaws in an image and apply special effects. Destructive filters, on the other hand, are devoted solely to special effects. That's why this chapter is actually shorter than its predecessor, even though Photoshop offers nearly twice as many destructive filters as corrective counterparts. Quite simply, destructive filters are less frequently used and ultimately less useful.

Don't get me wrong — these filters are a superb bunch. But because of their more limited appeal, I don't explain each and every one of them. Rather, I concentrate on the ones that I think you'll use most often, breeze over a handful of others, and let you discover on your own the ones that I ignore.

### A million wacky effects

Oh heck, I guess I can't just go and ignore half of the commands under the Filter menu — they're not completely useless, after all. It's just that you aren't likely to use them more than once every lunar eclipse. So here are the briefest of all possible descriptions of these filters:

✦ **Color Halftone:** Located under the Filter ⇨ Pixelate submenu, this command turns an image into a piece of Roy Lichtenstein artwork, with big, comic-book halftone dots. While scads of fun, the filter is ultimately a novelty that takes about a year and a half to apply.

✦ **Fragment:** Ooh, it's an earthquake! This lame filter repeats an image four times in a square formation and lowers the opacity of each to create a sort of jiggly effect. You don't even have any options to control it. It's quite possible I'm somehow missing the genius behind Filter ⇨ Pixelate ⇨ Fragment. Then again, maybe it just sucks.

◆ **Lens Flare:** Found in the Render submenu, this filter adds sparkles and halos to an image to suggest light bouncing off the camera lens. Even though photographers work their behinds off trying to make sure that these sorts of reflections don't occur, you can go and add them after the fact. You can select from one of three Lens Type options, adjust the Brightness slider between 10 and 300 percent (though somewhere around 100 is bound to deliver the best results), and move the center of the reflection by dragging a point around inside the Flare Center box. On a Mac you can also Option-click inside the preview to position the center point numerically.

If you want to add a flare to a grayscale image, first convert it to the RGB mode. Then apply the filter and convert back to grayscale (like I did back in Figure 23-2). The Lens Flare filter is applicable to RGB images only.

Here's another great tip for using Lens Flare. Prior to choosing the filter, create a new layer, fill it with black, and apply the Screen blend mode (Shift+Option/Alt+S). Now apply Lens Flare. You get the same effect as you would otherwise, but the effect floats above the background image, protecting your original image from harm. You can even move the lens flare around and vary the Opacity value, giving you more control over the final effect.

◆ **Diffuse:** Located in the Stylize submenu — as are the three filters that follow — Diffuse dithers the edges of color, much like the Dissolve brush mode dithers the edges of a soft brush. Diffuse is moderately useful, but not likely to gain a place among your treasured few.

◆ **Solarize:** This single-shot command is easily Photoshop's worst filter. It's really just a color-correction effect that changes all medium grays in the image to 50 percent gray, all blacks and whites to black, and remaps the other colors to shades in between. (If you're familiar with the Curves command, the map for Solarize looks like a pyramid.) It really belongs in the Image ⇨ Adjust submenu, or better yet, on the cutting room floor.

◆ **Tiles:** This filter breaks an image up into a bunch of regularly sized but randomly spaced rectangular tiles. You specify how many tiles fit across the width and height of the image — a value of 10, for example, creates 100 tiles — and the maximum distance each tile can shift. You can fill the gaps between tiles with foreground color, background color, or an inverted or normal version of the original image. A highly intrusive and not particularly stimulating effect.

◆ **Extrude:** The more capable cousin of the Tiles filter, Extrude breaks an image into tiles and forces them toward the viewer in three-dimensional space. The

Pyramid option is a lot of fun, devolving an image into a collection of spikes. When using the Blocks option, you can select a Solid Front Faces option that renders the image as a true 3-D mosaic. The Mask Incomplete Blocks option simply leaves the image untouched around the perimeter of the selection where the filter can't draw complete tiles.

Actually, I kind of like Extrude. For the sheer heck of it, Color Plate 24-1 shows an example of Extrude applied to what was once a red rose. I set the Type to Blocks, the Size to 10, the Depth to 30 and Random, with both the Solid Front Faces and Mask Incomplete Blocks radio buttons selected. Pretty great, huh? I only wish that the filter would generate a selection outline around the masked areas of the image so that I could get rid of anything that hadn't been extruded. It's a wonderful effect, but it's not one that lends itself to many occasions.

✦ **Diffuse Glow:** The first of the Gallery Effects that I mostly ignore, Filter ➪ Distort ➪ Diffuse Glow sprays a coat of dithered, background-colored pixels onto your image. Yowsa, let me at it.

✦ **The Artistic filters:** As a rule, the effects under the Filter ➪ Artistic submenu add a painterly quality to your image. Colored Pencil, Rough Pastels, and Watercolor are examples of filters that successfully emulate traditional mediums. Other filters — Fresco, Smudge Stick, and Palette Knife — couldn't pass for their intended mediums in a dim room filled with dry ice.

✦ **The Brush Strokes filters:** I could argue that the Brush Strokes submenu contains filters that create strokes of color. This is true of some of the filters — including Angled Strokes, Crosshatch, and Sprayed Stroke. Others — Dark Strokes and Ink Outlines — generally smear colors, while still others — Accented Edges and Sumi-e — belong in the Artistic submenu. Whatever.

✦ **The Sketch filters:** In Gallery Effects parlance, Sketch means color sucker. Beware, every one of these filters replaces the colors in your image with the current foreground and background colors. If the foreground and background colors are black and white, the Sketch filter results in a grayscale image. Charcoal and Conté Crayon create artistic effects, Bas Relief and Note Paper add texture, and Photocopy and Stamp are stupid effects you could produce better and with more flexibility using High Pass.

To retrieve some of the original colors from your image after applying a Sketch filter, press ⌘/Ctrl+Shift+F to bring up the Fade dialog box and try out a few different Mode settings. Overlay and Luminosity are particularly good choices. In Color Plate 24-2, I applied the Charcoal filter with the foreground and background colors set to light blue and dark green. Then I used the Fade command to select the Overlay mode.

✦ **The Texture filters:** As a group, the commands in the Filter ➪ Texture submenu
are my favorite effects filters. Craquelure, Mosaic Tiles, and Patchwork apply
interesting depth textures to the image. And Texturizer provides access to
several scaleable textures and permits you to load your own (so long as the
pattern is saved in the Photoshop format), as demonstrated in Figure 24-1. The
one dud is Stained Glass, which creates polygon tiles like Photoshop's own
Crystallize filter, only with black lines around the tiles.

Burlap

Canvas

Sandstone

Random Strokes

**Figure 24-1:** Filter ➪ Texture ➪ Texturizer lets you select from four
built-in patterns — including the first three shown here — and load
your own. In the last example, I loaded the Random Strokes pattern
included with Photoshop.

Certainly, there is room for disagreement about which filters are good and which are awful. After I wrote a two-star *Macworld* review about the first Gallery Effects collection back in 1992 — I must admit, I've never been a big fan — a gentleman showed me page after page of excellent artwork he had created with them. Recently, a woman showed me her collection of amazing Lens Flare imagery. I mean, here's a filter that just creates a bunch of bright spots, and yet this talented person was able to go absolutely nuts with it.

The moral is that just because I consider a filter or other piece of software to be a squalid pile of unspeakably bad code doesn't mean that a creative artist can't come along and put it to remarkable use. But that's because *you* are good, not the filter. So if you're feeling particularly creative today, give the above filters a try. Otherwise, skip them with a clear conscience.

## What about the others?

Some filters don't really belong in either the corrective or destructive camp. Take Filter ➪ Video ➪ NTSC Colors and Filter ➪ Other ➪ Offset, for example. Both are examples of commands that have no business being under the filter menu, and both could have been handled much better than they are.

The NTSC Colors filter modifies the colors in your RGB or Lab image for transfer to videotape. Vivid reds and blues that might otherwise prove very unstable and bleed into their neighbors are curtailed. The problem with this function is that it's not an independent color space; it's a single-shot filter that changes your colors and is done with it. If you edit the colors after choosing the command, you may very well reintroduce colors that are incompatible with NTSC devices and therefore warrant a second application of the filter. Conversion to NTSC — another light-based system — isn't as fraught with potential disaster as conversion to CMYK pigments, but it still deserves better treatment than this.

The Offset command moves an image a specified number of pixels. Why didn't I cover it in Chapter 15 with the other movement options? Because the command actually moves the image inside the selection outline while keeping the selection outline itself stationary. It's as if you had pasted the entire image into the selection outline and were now moving it around. The command is a favorite among fans of channel operations, a topic I cover in Chapter 31. You can duplicate an image, offset the entire thing a few pixels, and then mix the duplicate and original to create highlight or shadow effects. But I much prefer the more interactive control of layering and nudging with the arrow keys. I imagine the Offset filter might find favor with folks who want to automate movements from the Actions palette, but now that Photoshop 5 records movements made with the move tool, I'm not even sure about that. Okay, I admit it; the Offset command is a primitive feature with no purpose in our high-tech modern world.

Among the filters I've omitted from this chapter is Filter ➪ Stylize ➪ Wind, which is technically a destructive filter but is covered along with the blur and noise filters in Chapter 23. I discussed Filter ➪ Render ➪ Texture Fill in Chapter 10. And finally, for complete information on the Custom, Displace, and Filter Factory filters, stay tuned for Chapter D on CD-ROM #2.

As for the other filters in the Filter ➪ Distort, Pixelate, Render, and Stylize submenus, stay tuned to this chapter to discover all the latest and greatest details.

## Third-party filters

In addition to the filters provided by Photoshop, you can purchase all sorts of plug-in filters from other companies. In fact, Photoshop supports its own flourishing cottage industry of third-party solutions from wonderful companies like Extensis, Alien Skin, Andromeda, and others.

CD #1 at the back of this book includes sample versions of some of my favorite filters. For complete information on the specific filters and the companies that provide them, read the appendix. Many of the filters are demo versions of the shipping products, which means that you can see what they do but you can't actually apply the effects or they only work for a limited period of time. I know, it's a drag, but these folks claim that they like to make money every once in a while, and I can't say that I blame them.

## One final note about RAM

Memory — that is, real RAM — is a precious commodity when applying destructive filters. The scratch disk space typically allows you to edit larger images than your computer's RAM might permit. But all the filters in the Distort submenu and most of the commands in the Render submenu operate exclusively in memory. If they run out of physical RAM, they choke.

Fortunately, there is one potential workaround: When editing a color image, try applying the filter to each of the color channels independently. One color channel requires just a third to a fourth as much RAM as the full-color composite. Sadly, this technique does not help either Lighting Effects or Lens Flare. These delicate flowers of the filter world are compatible only with full-color images; when editing a single channel, they appear dimmed.

# The Pixelate Filters

The new Filter ➪ Pixelate submenu features a handful of commands that rearrange your image into clumps of solid color:

✦ **Crystallize:** This filter organizes an image into irregularly shaped nuggets. You specify the size of the nuggets by entering a value from 3 to 300 pixels in the Cell Size option.

✦ **Facet:** Facet fuses areas of similarly colored pixels to create a sort of hand-painted effect.

✦ **Mosaic:** The Mosaic filter blends pixels together into larger squares. You specify the height and width of the squares by entering a value into the Cell Size option box.

✦ **Pointillize:** This filter is similar to Crystallize, except that it separates an image into disconnected nuggets set against the background color. As usual, you specify the size of the nuggets by changing the Cell Size value.

## The Crystal Halo effect

By applying one of these filters to a feathered selection, you can create what I call a Crystal Halo effect, named after the Crystallize filter, which tends to deliver the most successful results. (For a preview of these effects, sneak a peek at Figure 24-2.) The following steps explain how to create a Crystal Halo, using the images in Figures 24-2 and 24-3 as an example.

### Steps: Creating the Crystal Halo Effect

1. **Select the foreground element around which you want to create the halo.** Then choose Select ➪ Inverse to deselect the foreground element and select the background.

2. **Press Q to switch to the quick mask mode.**

3. **Choose Filter ➪ Other ➪ Minimum.** As I explained in Chapter 23, this filter allows you to increase the size of the deselected area around the foreground element. The size of the Radius value depends on the size of the halo you want to create. For my part, I wanted a 15-pixel halo. Unfortunately, the Radius option box in the Minimum dialog box can't accommodate a value larger than 10. So I entered 10 the first time. When Photoshop finished applying the filter, I pressed ⌘/Ctrl+Option/Alt+F to bring up the Minimum dialog box again and entered 5.

*(continued)*

4. **Choose Filter ⇨ Blur ⇨ Gaussian Blur.** Then enter a Radius value 0.1 less than the amount by which you increased the size of the deselected area. In my case, I entered 14.9. This will cut into the image slightly, but hardly enough to be visible, as you can see in the left image in Figure 24-2.

**Figure 24-2:** Create a heavily feathered selection outline (left) and then apply the Crystallize filter to refract the feathered edges (right).

5. **Choose Filter ⇨ Pixelate ⇨ Crystallize.** Enter a moderate value into the Cell Size option box. I opted for the value 12, just slightly larger than the default value. After pressing Return/Enter, you get something along the lines of the selection outline shown in the right image in Figure 24-2. The filter refracts the softened edges, as if you were viewing them through textured glass.

6. **Switch back to the marching ants mode.** Then use the selection as desired. I merely pressed ⌘/Ctrl+Delete/Backspace to fill the selection with white, as shown in the top left image in Figure 24-3.

You may find this technique particularly useful for combining images. You can copy the selection and paste it against a different background or copy a background from a different image and choose Edit ⇨ Paste Into to paste it inside the crystal halo's selection outline.

Figure 24-3 shows several variations on the Crystal Halo effect. To create the upper right image, I substituted Filter ⇨ Pixelate ⇨ Facet for Filter ⇨ Pixelate ⇨ Crystallize in Step 5. I also sharpened the result to increase the effect of the filter (which nevertheless remains subtle). To create the lower right image, I applied the Mosaic filter in place of Crystallize, using a Cell Size value of 8. Finally, to create the lower left image, I applied the Pointillize filter. Because Pointillize creates gaps in a selection, I had to paint inside Moses to fill in the gaps and isolate the halo effect to the background before returning to the marching ants mode.

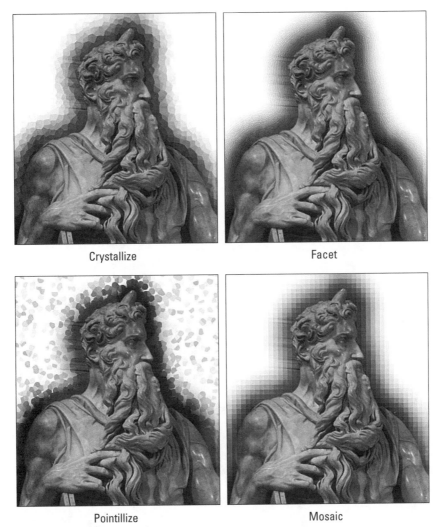

Crystallize                Facet

Pointillize                Mosaic

**Figure 24-3:** Which aura will Moses don today? The images illustrate the effects of applying each of four filters to a heavily feathered selection in the quick mask mode and pressing ⌘/Ctrl+Delete/Backspace.

## Creating a mezzotint

A *mezzotint* is a special halftone pattern that replaces dots with a random pattern of swirling lines and worm holes. Photoshop's Mezzotint filter is an attempt to emulate this effect. Although not entirely successful — true mezzotinting options can only be properly implemented as PostScript printing functions, not as filtering functions — they do lend themselves to some pretty interesting interpretations.

The filter itself is straightforward. Choose Filter ➪ Pixelate ➪ Mezzotint, select an effect from the Type submenu, and press Enter. A preview box shows each of the ten Type options. Figure 24-4 shows four of the effects at 230 ppi.

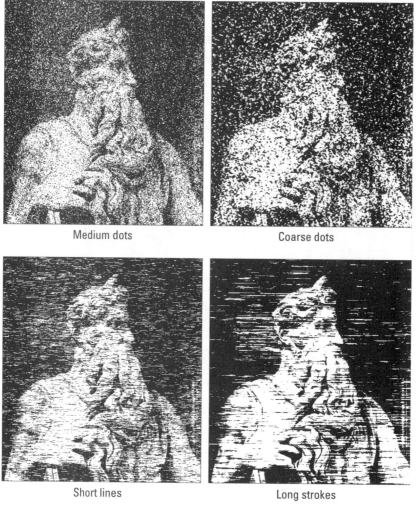

Medium dots

Coarse dots

Short lines

Long strokes

**Figure 24-4:** The results of applying the Mezzotint filter set to each of four representative effects. These line patterns are on par with the halftoning options offered when you select Mode ➪ Bitmap.

To create Figure 24-5, I applied the Mezzotint filter set to the Long Lines effect. Then I used the Filter ⇨ Fade Mezzotint command to mix filtered and original images. I selected Overlay from the Mode pop-up menu and set the Opacity value to 40 percent. The result is a scraped image. (I've decreased the resolution of the image to 180 ppi so that you can see the effect a little more clearly.)

**Figure 24-5:** To get this effect, I chose Filter ⇨ Fade after applying the Mezzotint filter. Then I selected the Overlay mode and set the Opacity value to 40 percent.

When applied to grayscale artwork, the Mezzotint filter always results in a black-and-white image. When applied to a color image, the filter automatically applies the selected effect independently to each of the color channels. Though all pixels in each channel are changed to either black or white, you can see a total of eight colors — black, red, green, blue, yellow, cyan, magenta, and white — in the RGB composite view. The upper left example of Color Plate 24-3 shows an image subject to the Mezzotint filter in the RGB mode.

If the Mezzotint filter affects each channel independently, then it follows that the color mode in which you work directly, and dramatically, affects the performance of the filter. For example, if you apply Mezzotint in the Lab mode, you again whittle the colors down to eight, but a very different eight — black, cyan, magenta, green, red, two muddy blues and a muddy rose — as shown in the top middle example of Color Plate 24-3. If you're looking for bright happy colors, don't apply Mezzotint in the Lab mode.

In CMYK, the filter produces roughly the same eight colors that you get in RGB — white, cyan, magenta, yellow, violet-blue, red, deep green, and black. However, as shown in the top right example of the color plate, the distribution of the colors is much different. The image appears much lighter and more colorful than its RGB counterpart. This happens because the filter has a lot of black to work with in the RGB mode but very little — just that in the black channel — in the CMYK mode.

The bottom row of Color Plate 24-3 shows the effects of the Mezzotint filter after using the Fade command to mix it with the original image. As in Figure 24-4, I chose Overlay from the Mode pop-up menu and set the Opacity value to 40 percent. These three very different images were all created using the same filter set to the same effect. Absolutely the only difference is color mode.

# Edge-Enhancement Filters

The Filter ➪ Stylize submenu offers access to a triad of filters that enhance the edges in an image. The most popular of these is undoubtedly Emboss, which adds dimension to an image by making it look as if it were carved in relief. The other two, Find Edges and Trace Contour, are less commonly applied, but every bit as capable and deserving of your attention.

## Embossing an image

The Emboss filter works by searching for high-contrast edges (just like the Sharpen Edge and High Pass filters), highlighting the edges with black or white pixels, and then coloring the low-contrast portions with medium gray. When you choose Filter ➪ Stylize ➪ Emboss, Photoshop displays the Emboss dialog box shown in Figure 24-6. The dialog box offers three options:

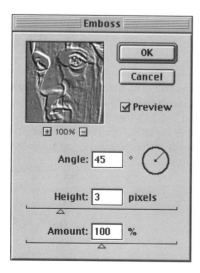

**Figure 24-6:** The Emboss dialog box lets you control the depth of the filtered image and the angle from which it is lit.

✦ **Angle:** The value in this option box determines the angle at which Photoshop lights the image in relief. For example, if you enter a value of 90 degrees, you light the relief from the bottom straight upward. The white pixels therefore appear on the bottom sides of the edges, and the black pixels appear on the top sides. Figure 24-7 shows eight reliefs lit from different angles. I positioned the images so that they appear lit from a single source.

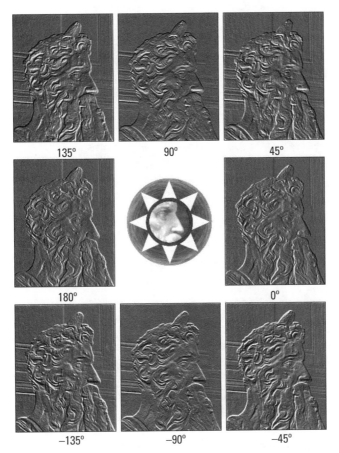

**Figure 24-7:** Reliefs lighted from eight different angles, in 45-degree increments. In all cases, the central sun image indicates the location of the light source. Height and Amount values of 1 pixel and 250 percent were used for all images.

✦ **Height:** The Emboss filter accomplishes its highlighting effect by displacing one copy of an image relative to another. You specify the distance between the copies using the Height option, which can vary from 1 to 10 pixels. Lower values produce crisp effects, as demonstrated in Figure 24-8. Values above 3 goop up things pretty good unless you also enter a high Amount value. Together, the Height and Amount values determine the depth of the image in relief.

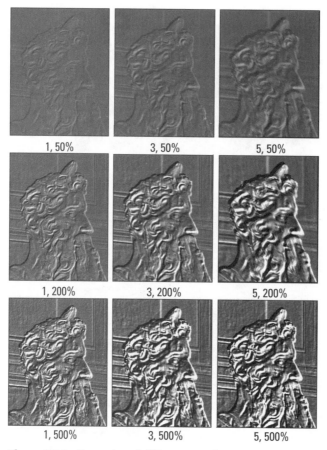

**Figure 24-8:** Examples of different Height settings (first value) and Amount settings (second value). The Angle value used for each image was 135 degrees.

**Tip**

The Height value is analogous to the Radius value in the Unsharp Mask dialog box. You should therefore set the value according to the resolution of your image—1 for 150 ppi, 2 for 300 ppi, and so on.

✦ **Amount:** Enter a value between 1 and 500 percent to determine the amount of black and white assigned to pixels along the edges. Values of 50 percent and lower produce almost entirely gray images, as you can see in the top row of Figure 24-8. Higher values produce sharper edges, as if the relief were carved more deeply.

As a stand-alone effect, Emboss is only okey-dokey. It's one of those filters that makes you gasp with delight the first time you see it but never quite lends itself to any practical application after you become acquainted with Photoshop. But if you think of Emboss as an extension of the High Pass filter, it takes on new meaning. You can use it to edit selection outlines in the quick mask mode, just as you might use the High Pass filter. You also can use it to draw out detail in an image.

Figure 24-9 shows the result of using the Fade command immediately after applying the Emboss filter. First, I applied the Emboss filter at an Angle of 135 degrees, a Height of 2 pixels, and an Amount of 250 percent. Then I pressed ⌘/Ctrl+Shift+F to display the Fade dialog box. To create the left example, I selected Darken from the Mode pop-up menu. This added shadows to the edges of the image, thus boosting the texture without unduly upsetting the original brightness values. I selected the Lighten blend mode to create the right example. In both cases, I set the Opacity value to 70 percent.

**Figure 24-9:** After applying the Emboss filter, I used my old friend the Fade command to darken (left) and lighten (right) the image.

**Tip**

To create a color relief effect, apply the Emboss filter and then select the Luminosity option in the Fade dialog box. This retains the colors from the original image while applying the lightness and darkness of the pixels from the filtered selection. The effect looks something like an inked lithographic plate, with steel grays and vivid colors mixing together. An example of this effect at 80 percent Opacity appears in the first example of Color Plate 24-4.

The second example in that same color plate shows a more impressive — if less practical — technique. Rather than applying Luminosity, I chose the Difference mode inside the Fade dialog box. With its hard edges and vivid colors, this image looks like some impossible frame from an educational film on genetic engineering. I can just hear the narrator commenting, "Prom dates have changed dramatically since scientists discovered how to splice the red rose with the poppy."

## Tracing around edges

Photoshop provides three filters that trace around pixels in your image and accentuate the edges, all located in the Filter ⇨ Stylize submenu:

✦ **Find Edges:** This filter detects edges similarly to High Pass. Low-contrast areas become white, medium-contrast edges become gray, and high-contrast edges become black, as in the labeled image in Figure 24-10. Hard edges become thin lines; soft edges become fat ones. The result is a thick, organic outline that you can overlay onto an image to give it a waxy appearance. To achieve the bottom left effect in the figure, I chose the Fade ⇨ Find Edges command and applied the Overlay mode and an 80 percent Opacity setting. She'll never get her hand off that canning jar as long as she lives.

✦ **Glowing Edges:** This Gallery Effects filter is a variation on Find Edges with two important differences: Glowing Edges produces an inverted effect, changing low-contrast areas to black and edges to white, as in the labeled image in Figure 24-10. It also displays a dialog box that lets you adjust the width, brightness, and smoothness of the traced edges. Glowing Edges is a great backup command. If you aren't satisfied with the effect produced by the Find Edges filter, choose the Glowing Edges command instead and adjust the options as desired. If you want black lines against a white background, press ⌘/Ctrl+I to invert the effect.

✦ **Trace Contour:** Illustrated on the right side of Figure 24-10, Trace Contour is a little more involved than the others and slightly less interesting. The filter traces a series of single-pixel lines along the border between light and dark pixels. Choosing the filter displays a dialog box containing three options: Level, Upper, and Lower. The Level value indicates the lightness value above which pixels are considered to be light and below which they are dark. For example, if you enter 128 — medium gray, as by default — Trace Contour draws a line at every spot where an area of color lighter than medium gray meets an area of color darker than medium gray. The Upper and Lower options tell the filter where to position the line — inside the lighter color's territory (Upper) or inside the space occupied by the darker color (Lower).

| Find Edges | Glowing Edges | Trace Contour |
| --- | --- | --- |

| Overlay, 80% | Overlay, 60% | Multiply, 100% |
| --- | --- | --- |

**Figure 24-10:** The top row of images demonstrates the effect of the three edge-tracing commands available from the Filter ➪ Stylize submenu. After applying each command, I used the Fade command to apply the blend modes and Opacity values demonstrated in the bottom row.

Like Mezzotint, Trace Contour applies itself to each color channel independently and renders each channel as a 1-bit image. A collection of black lines surrounds the areas of color in each channel; the RGB, Lab, or CMYK composite view shows these lines in the colors associated with the channels. When you work in RGB, a cyan line indicates a black line in the red channel (no red plus full intensity green and blue becomes cyan). A yellow line indicates a black line in the blue channel, and so on. You get a single black line when working in the grayscale mode.

# Creating a metallic coating

The edge-tracing filters are especially fun to use in combination with Filter ➪ Fade. I first got interested in playing with these filters after trying out the Chrome filter included with the first Gallery Effects collection. Now included with Photoshop as Filter ➪ Sketch ➪ Chrome, this filter turns an image into a melted pile of metallic goo. No matter how you apply Chrome, it completely wipes out your image and leaves a ton of jagged color transitions in its wake. It's really only useful with color images, and then only if you follow up with the Fade command and the Luminosity mode. Even then, I've never been particularly satisfied with the results.

But it got me thinking: How can you create a metallic coating, with gleaming highlights and crisp shadows, without resorting to Chrome? Find Edges offers a way. First, copy your image to a separate layer (⌘/Ctrl+J). Then apply the Gaussian Blur filter. A Radius value between 1.0 and 4.0 produces the best results, depending on how gooey you want the edges to be. Next, apply the Find Edges filter. Because the edges are blurry, the resulting image is light; so I recommend you darken it using Image ➪ Adjust ➪ Levels (raise the first Input Levels value to 100 or so, as explained in Chapter 30). The blurry edges appear in the top left example in Figure 24-11.

To produce the bottom left image, I mixed the layer with the underlying original using the Overlay blend mode (Shift+Option/Alt+O) and an Opacity of 80 percent. The result is a shiny effect that produces a metallic finish without altogether destroying the detail in the image.

If you decide you like this effect, there's more where that came from. The second and third columns of Figure 24-11 show the results of applying Filter ➪ Sketch ➪ Bas Relief and Filter ➪ Artistic ➪ Plastic Wrap. After applying each filter, I choose Filter ➪ Fade, selected the Overlay mode, and set the Opacity value to 80 percent, repeating the effect I applied to the Gaussian Blur and Find Edges layer.

Color Plate 24-5 shows the same effects in color. Starting with an unedited construction worker, I went through the usual calisthenics of selecting and layering the image. Next, I applied Gaussian Blur (3.0 Radius) and Find Edges. The effect was too light, so I chose Image ➪ Adjust ➪ Levels and entered 128 into the first option box. Everything darker than medium gray went to black, uniformly strengthening the effect. The result is the full-color metallic coating shown in the second example in the top row of the color plate. To get the top right image, I merely selected Overlay from the pop-up menu in the Layers palette (Shift+Option/Alt+O) and changed the Opacity value to 80 percent.

In the bottom row of Color Plate 24-5, I really went nuts. In each case, I applied one of three effects filters — Bas Relief, Plastic Wrap, and the infamous Filter ➪ Sketch ➪ Chrome. And each time, I chose Filter ➪ Fade, selected the Luminosity mode, and reduced the Opacity value to 80 percent.

Blur & Find Edges        Bas Relief        Plastic Wrap

Overlay, 80%

**Figure 24-11:** After applying Gaussian Blur and Find Edges to a layered version of the image (top left), I composited the filtered image with the original using the Overlay mode (bottom left). The second and third columns show similar effects achieved using the effects filters Bas Relief and Plastic Wrap.

Okay, okay, so Chrome still looks more metallic than the other effects, but it also plays havoc with the detail. I'm willing to settle for a more subtle effect if it means I can still recognize my subject when I'm finished.

# Distortion Filters

For the most part, commands in the Distort submenu are related by the fact that they move colors in an image to achieve unusual stretching, swirling, and vibrating effects. They're rather like the transformation commands from the Layer menu in that they perform their magic by relocating and interpolating colors rather than by altering brightness and color values.

The distinction, of course, is that while the transformation commands let you scale and distort images by manipulating four control points, the Distort filters provide the equivalent of hundreds of control points, all of which you can use to affect different portions of an image. In some cases, you're projecting an image into a fun-house mirror; other times, it's a reflective pool. You can fan images, wiggle them, and change them in ways that have no correlation to real life, as illustrated in Figure 24-12.

**Figure 24-12:** This is your image (left); this is your image on distortion filters (right). Three filters, in fact: Spherize, Ripple, and Polar Coordinates.

Distortion filters are very powerful tools. Although they are easy to apply, they are extremely difficult to use well. Here are some rules to keep in mind:

✦ **Practice makes practical:** Distortion filters are like complex vocabulary words. You don't want to use them without practicing a little first. Experiment with a distortion filter several times before trying to use it in a real project. You may even want to write down the steps you take so that you can remember how you created an effect.

✦ **Use caution during tight deadlines:** Distortion filters are enormous time-wasters. Unless you know exactly how you want to proceed, you may want to avoid using them when time is short. The last thing you need when you're working under the gun is to get trapped trying to pull off a weird effect.

✦ **Apply selectively:** The effects of distortion filters are too severe to inflict all at once. You can achieve marvelous, subtle effects by distorting feathered and layered selections. Although I wouldn't call the image in Figure 24-12 subtle, no single effect was applied to the entire image. I applied the Spherize filter to a feathered elliptical marquee that included most of the image. I then reapplied Spherize to the eye. I selected the hair and beard and applied the

Ripple filter twice. Finally, after establishing two heavily feathered vertical columns on either side of the image in the quick mask mode, I applied the Polar Coordinates filter, which reflected the front and back of the head. Turn the book upside down and you'll see a second face.

✦ **Combine creatively:** Don't expect a single distortion to achieve the desired effect. If one application isn't enough, apply the filter again. Experiment with combining different distortions.

Distortion filters interpolate between pixels to create their fantastic effects. This means that the quality of your filtered images is dependent on the setting of the Interpolation option in the General Preferences dialog box. If a filter produces jagged effects, the Nearest Neighbor option is probably selected. Try selecting the Bicubic or Bilinear option instead.

## Reflecting an image in a spoon

Most folks take their first ventures into distortion filters by using Pinch and Spherize. Pinch maps an image onto the inside of a sphere or similarly curved surface; Spherize maps it onto the outside of a sphere. It's sort of like looking at your reflection on the inside or outside of a spoon.

You can apply Pinch to a scanned face to squish the features toward the center or apply Spherize to accentuate the girth of the nose. Figure 24-13 illustrates both effects. It's a laugh, and you pretty much feel as though you're onto something that no one else ever thought of before. (At least that's how I felt — but I'm easily amazed.)

**Figure 24-13:** Constantine does the popular throbbing facial dance — well, it was popular back in 300 AD — thanks to the Pinch (left) and Spherize (right) filters.

You can pinch or spherize an image using either the Pinch or Spherize command. As shown in Figure 24-14, a positive value in the Pinch dialog box produces a similar effect to a negative value in the Spherize dialog box. There is a slight difference between the spatial curvature of the 3-D calculations: Pinch pokes the image inward or outward using a rounded cone — we're talking bell-shaped, much like a Gaussian model. Spherize wraps the image on the outside or inside of a true sphere. As a result, the two filters yield subtly different results. Pinch produces a soft transition around the perimeter of a selection; Spherize produces an abrupt transition. If this doesn't quite make sense to you, just play with one, try out the same effect with the other, and see which you like better.

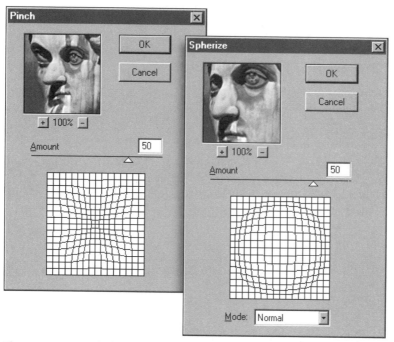

**Figure 24-14:** Both the Pinch and Spherize dialog boxes let you pinch and spherize images. Pinch wraps an image on a rounded cone; Spherize wraps onto a sphere.

Another difference between the two filters is that Spherize provides the additional options of allowing you to wrap an image onto the inside or outside of a horizontal or vertical cylinder. To try out these effects, select the Horizontal Only or Vertical Only options from the Mode pop-up menu at the bottom of the Spherize dialog box.

Tip

Both the Pinch and Spherize filters are applicable only to elliptical regions of an image. If a selection outline is not elliptical in shape, Photoshop applies the filter to the largest ellipse that fits inside the selection. As a result, the filter may leave behind a noticeable elliptical boundary between the affected and unaffected portions of the selection. To avoid this effect, select the region you want to edit with the elliptical marquee tool and then feather the selection before filtering it. This softens the effect of the filter and provides a more gradual transition (even more so than Pinch already affords).

One of the more remarkable properties of the Pinch filter is that it lets you turn any image into a conical gradation. Figure 24-15 illustrates how the process works. First, blur the image to eliminate any harsh edges between color transitions. Then apply the Pinch filter at full strength (100 percent). Reapply the filter several more times. Each time you press ⌘/Ctrl+F, the center portion of the image recedes farther and farther into the distance, as shown in Figure 24-15. After 10 repetitions, the face in the example all but disappeared.

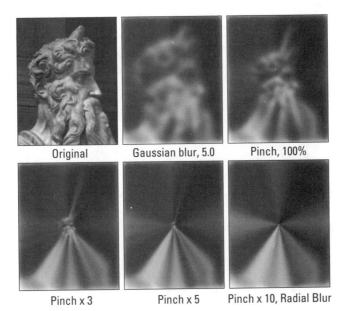

**Figure 24-15:** After applying the Gaussian Blur filter, I pinched the image 10 times and applied the Radial Blur filter to create a conical gradation.

Next, apply the Radial Blur filter set to Spin 10 pixels or so to mix the color boundaries a bit. The result is a type of gradation that you can't create using Photoshop's gradient tool.

## Twirling spirals

The Twirl filter rotates the center of a selection while leaving the sides fixed in place. The result is a spiral of colors that looks for all the world as if you poured the image into a blender set to a very slow speed.

When you choose Filter ⇨ Distort ⇨ Twirl, Photoshop displays the Twirl dialog box, shown in Figure 24-16. Enter a positive value from 1 to 999 degrees to spiral the image in a clockwise direction. Enter a negative value to spiral the image in a counterclockwise direction. As you are probably already aware, 360 degrees make a full circle, so the maximum 999-degree value equates to a spiral that circles around approximately three times, as shown in the bottom right example in Figure 24-17.

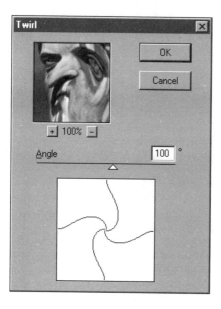

**Figure 24-16:** The Twirl dialog box lets you create spiraling images.

**Tip**    The Twirl filter produces smoother effects when you use lower Angle values. Therefore, you're better off applying a 100-degree spiral 10 times rather than applying a 999-degree spiral once, as verified by Figure 24-17.

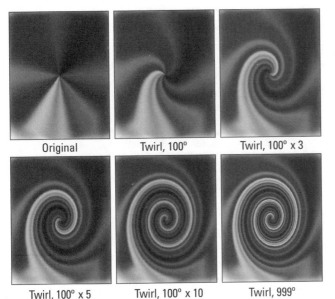

Original  Twirl, 100°  Twirl, 100° x 3

Twirl, 100° x 5  Twirl, 100° x 10  Twirl, 999°

**Figure 24-17:** The effects of applying the Twirl filter. Repeatedly applying the Twirl filter at a moderate value (bottom middle) produces a smoother effect than applying the filter once at a high value (bottom right).

In addition to creating ice-cream swirls like those shown in Figure 24-17, you can use the Twirl filter to create organic images virtually from scratch, as witnessed by Figures 24-18 and 24-19.

To create the images shown in Figure 24-18, I used the Spherize filter to flex the conical gradation vertically by entering 100 percent in the Amount option box and selecting Vertical Only from the Mode pop-up menu. After repeating this filter several times, I eventually achieved a stalactite-stalagmite effect, as shown in the center example of the figure. I then repeatedly applied the Twirl filter to curl the flexed gradations like two symmetrical hairs. The result merges the simplicity of pure math with the beauty of bitmapped imagery.

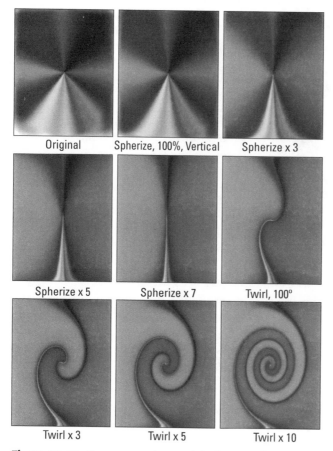

Original     Spherize, 100%, Vertical     Spherize x 3

Spherize x 5     Spherize x 7     Twirl, 100°

Twirl x 3     Twirl x 5     Twirl x 10

**Figure 24-18:** You can create surprisingly naturalistic effects using distortion filters exclusively.

Figure 24-19 illustrates a droplet technique designed by Mark Collen. I took the liberty of breaking down the technique into the following steps.

## Steps: Creating a Thick-Liquid Droplet

1. **Press the D key.** As it has so many times in the past, the D key again restores the default foreground and background colors.

2. **Select a square portion of an image.** Drag with the rectangular marquee tool while pressing the Shift key.

3. **Drag inside the selection outline with the linear gradient tool.** Drag a short distance near the center of the selection from upper left to lower right, creating the gradation shown in the top left box in Figure 24-19.

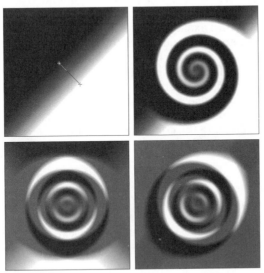

**Figure 24-19:** Though they appear as if they might be the result of the ZigZag filter, these images were created entirely by using the gradient tool, the Twirl filter, and a couple of transformations.

4. **Choose the Twirl filter and apply it at -360 degrees so that the spiral moves counterclockwise.** To create the top right image in the figure, I applied the Twirl filter three times. Each repetition of the filter adds another ring of ripples.

5. **Press ⌘/Ctrl+J to copy the selection to a layer.**

6. **Choose Edit ⇨ Transform ⇨ Flip Horizontal.**

7. **Lower the Opacity value to 50 percent.** Select the rectangular marquee tool, then press the 5 key. The result appears in the lower left example in Figure 24-19.

8. **Choose Edit ⇨ Transform ⇨ Rotate 90° CW.** This rotates the layer a quarter turn, thus creating the last image in the figure. You can achieve other interesting effects by choosing Lighten, Darken, and others from the brush modes pop-up menu.

Now, if a few twirls and transformations can produce an effect this entertaining in black and white, just imagine what you can do in color. On second thought, don't imagine; check out Color Plate 24-6 instead. The first row in this eight-part color plate is nothing more than a color version of Figure 24-19, intended merely to set the scene. As you can see, I've created a gradation using two complementary colors, blue and yellow. In the fifth example (lower left), I apply the Difference blend mode to the layer (Shift+Option/Alt+E) and return the Opacity setting to 100 percent. Next, I clone that layer and rotate it another 90 degrees clockwise to produce the sixth example. The Difference blend mode remains in effect for this cloned layer as well. Not satisfied, I clone that layer, rotate it another 90 degrees, and flip it horizontally. The result, also subject to Difference, is the seventh example. Then for the *coup de grâce*, I randomly apply the Twirl, Spherize, and ZigZag filters to the layers to mutate the concentric rings into something a little more interesting.

If that went a little fast for you, not to worry. More important than the specific effect is this general category of "distortion drawings." A filter such as Pinch or Twirl enables you to create wild imagery without ever drawing a brushstroke or scanning a photograph. If you can do this much with a simple two-color gradation, just think of what you can do if you throw in a few more colors. Pixels are little more than fodder for these very powerful functions.

## Creating concentric pond ripples

I don't know about you, but when I think of zigzags, I think of cartoon lightning bolts, wriggling snakes, scribbles — anything that alternately changes directions along an axis, like the letter *Z*. The ZigZag filter does arrange colors into zigzag patterns, but it does so in a radial fashion, meaning that the zigzags emanate from the center of the image like spokes in a wheel. The result is a series of concentric ripples. If you want parallel zigzags, check out the Ripple and Wave filters, described in the next section. (The ZigZag filter creates ripples and the Ripple filter creates zigzags. Go figure.)

When you choose Filter ➪ Distort ➪ ZigZag, Photoshop displays the ZigZag dialog box shown in Figure 24-20. The dialog box offers the following options:

✦ **Amount:** Enter an amount between negative and positive 100 in whole-number increments to specify the depth of the ripples. If you enter a negative value, the ripples descend below the surface. If you enter a positive value, the ripples protrude upward. Examples of three representative Amount values appear in Figure 24-21.

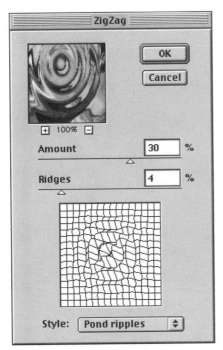

**Figure 24-20:** The ZigZag dialog box lets you add concentric ripples to an image, as if the image were reflected in a pond into which you dropped a pebble.

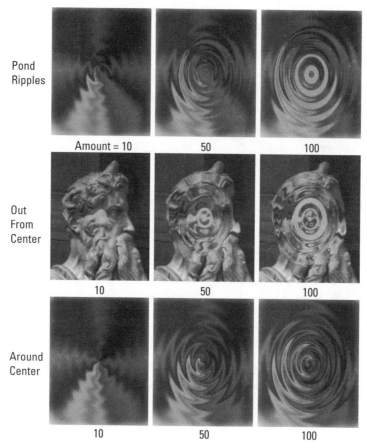

**Figure 24-21:** The effects of the ZigZag filter subject to three Amount values and the Pond Ripples, Out From Center, and Around Center settings. In all cases, the Ridges value was 5.

✦ **Ridges:** This option box controls the number of ripples in the selected area and accepts any value from 1 to 20. Figure 24-22 demonstrates the effect of three Ridges values.

✦ **Pond Ripples:** This option is really a cross between the two that follow. It moves pixels outward and rotates them around the center of the selection to create circular patterns. As demonstrated in the top rows of Figures 24-21 and 24-22, this option truly results in a pond ripple effect.

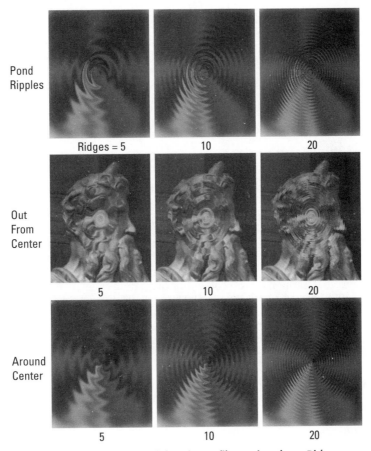

**Figure 24-22:** The effects of the ZigZag filter using three Ridges values and each of the three Style pop-up menu settings. In all cases, the Amount value was 20.

✦ **Out From Center:** When you select this option, Photoshop moves pixels outward in rhythmic bursts according to the value in the Ridges option box. Because the gradation image I created in Figure 24-14 was already arranged in a radial pattern, I brought in Moses to demonstrate the effect of the Out From Center option, as shown in the second rows of Figures 24-21 and 24-22.

✦ **Around Center:** Select this option to rotate pixels in alternating directions around the circle without moving them outward. This is the only option that produces what I would term a zigzag effect. The last rows of Figures 24-21 and 24-22 show the effects of the Around Center option.

## Creating parallel ripples and waves

Photoshop provides four means to distort an image in parallel waves, as if the image were lying on the bottom of a shimmering or undulating pool. Of the four, the ripple filters — which include Ripple, Ocean Ripple, and Glass — are only moderately sophisticated, but they're also relatively easy to apply. The fourth filter, Wave, affords you greater control, but its options are among the most complex Photoshop has to offer.

### The Ripple filter

To use the Ripple filter, choose Filter ➪ Distort ➪ Ripple. Photoshop displays the Ripple dialog box shown in Figure 24-23. You have the following options:

✦ **Amount:** Enter an amount between negative and positive 999 in whole-number increments to specify the width of the ripples from side to side. Negative and positive values change the direction of the ripples, but visually speaking, they produce identical effects. The ripples are measured as a ratio of the Size value and the dimensions of the selection — all of which translates to "Experiment and see what happens." You can count on getting ragged effects from any value over 300, as illustrated in Figure 24-24.

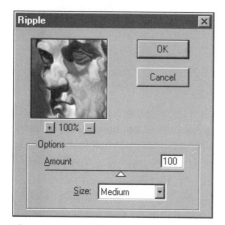

**Figure 24-23:** The Ripple filter makes an image appear as if it were refracted through flowing water.

✦ **Size:** Select one of the three options in the Size drop-down menu to change the length of the ripples. The Small option results in the shortest ripples and therefore the most ripples. As shown in the upper right corner of Figure 24-24,

**Tip**

you can create a textured glass effect by combining the Small option with a high Amount value. The Large option results in the longest and fewest ripples.

You can create a blistered effect by overlaying a negative ripple onto a positive ripple. Try this: First, copy the selection. Then apply the Ripple filter with a positive Amount value—say, 300. Next, paste the copied selection and apply the Ripple filter at the exact opposite Amount value, in this case, -300. Press 5 to change the Opacity value to 50 percent. The result is a series of diametrically opposed ripples that cross each other to create teardrop blisters.

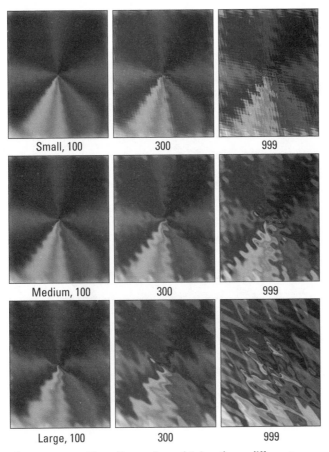

| Small, 100 | 300 | 999 |
| Medium, 100 | 300 | 999 |
| Large, 100 | 300 | 999 |

**Figure 24-24:** The effects of combining three different Ripple filter Amount values with three different Size settings.

## Ocean Ripple and Glass

The Ocean Ripple and Glass filters are gifts from Gallery Effects. Both filters emulate the effect of looking at an image through textured glass. These two distorters so closely resemble each other that they would be better merged into one. But where the effects filters are concerned, interface design is as fickle and transitory as the face on the cover of *Tiger Beat* magazine.

The Ocean Ripple and Glass dialog boxes appear joined at the hip in Figure 24-25. While the names and effects of the specific slider bars vary, the only real difference between the two filters is that Ocean Blur subscribes to a fixed ripple texture, and Glass lets you switch out the texture by selecting from a pop-up menu.

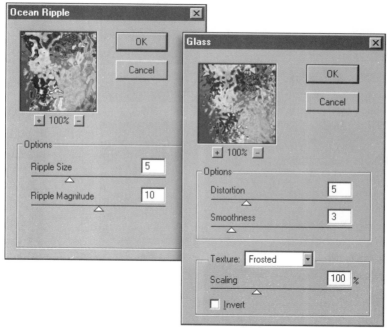

**Figure 24-25:** The Ocean Ripple and Glass effects filters are two birds of a feather, ultimately born from the same yolk.

To guide you in your experimentations, Figure 24-26 shows the Pinch gradation subject to several Ocean Blur settings. The first number represents the Ripple Size value (listed first in the dialog box); the second number in the figure represents the Ripple Magnitude value. As you can see, you can vary the Size value with impunity. But raise the Magnitude value, and you're looking through sculpted glass.

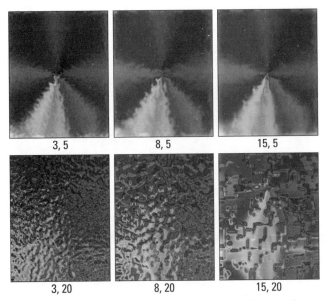

3, 5    8, 5    15, 5

3, 20    8, 20    15, 20

**Figure 24-26:** Raising the Ripple Size value (first number in each pair) spreads out the effect, while raising the Ripple Magnitude (second number) adds more depth and contrast to the ripples.

### The Wave filter

Now that you've met the ripple family, it's time to ride the Wave. I've come to love this filter — I use it all the time — but it's complex enough to warrant its own book. It wouldn't be a very big book and nobody would buy it, but you never know what a freelancer like me will do next. Keep an eye out for the *Wave Filter Bible* at your local bookstore.

In the meantime, choose Filter ➪ Distort ➪ Wave (that's the easy part) to display the Wave dialog box shown in Figure 24-27. Photoshop presents you with the following options, which make applying a distortion every bit as easy as operating an oscilloscope:

✦ **Number of Generators:** Right off the bat, the Wave dialog box boggles the brain. A friend of mine likened this option to the number of rocks you throw in the water to start it rippling. One generator means that you throw in one rock to create one set of waves, as demonstrated in Figure 24-28. You can throw in two rocks to create two sets of waves (see Figure 24-29), three rocks to create three sets of waves, and all the way up to a quarryfull of 999 rocks to create, well, you get the idea. If you enter a high value, however, be prepared to wait a few years for the preview to update. If you can't wait, press the Escape key, which turns off the preview until the next time you enter the dialog box.

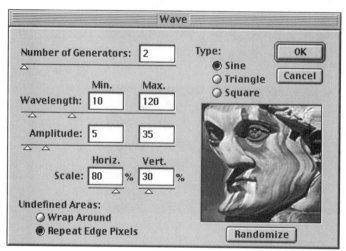

**Figure 24-27:** The Wave dialog box lets you wreak scientific havoc on an image. Put on your pocket protector, take out your slide rule, and give it a whirl.

✦ **Wavelength and Amplitude:** Beginning to feel like you're playing with a HAM radio? The Wave filter produces random results by varying the number and length of waves (Wavelength) as well as the height of the waves (Amplitude) between minimum and maximum values, which can range anywhere from 1 to 999. (The Wavelength and Amplitude options, therefore, correspond in theory to the Size and Amount options in the Ripple dialog box.) Figures 24-28 and 24-29 show examples of representative Wavelength and Amplitude values.

✦ **Scale:** You can scale the effects of the Wave filter between 1 and 100 percent horizontally and vertically. All the effects featured in Figures 24-28 and 24-29 were created by setting both Scale options to 15 percent.

✦ **Undefined Areas:** The Wave filter distorts a selection to the extent that gaps may appear around the edges. You can either fill those gaps by repeating pixels along the edge of the selection, as in the figures, or by wrapping pixels from the left side of the selection onto the right side and pixels from the top edge of the selection onto the bottom.

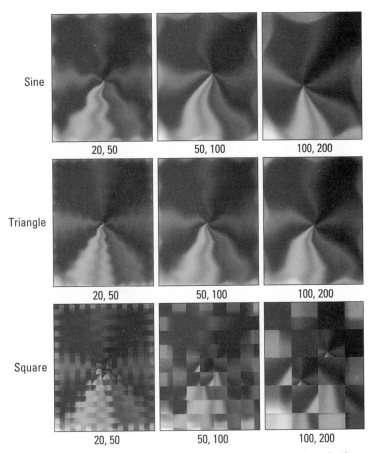

**Figure 24-28:** The effect of three sets of Maximum Wavelength (first value) and Amplitude (second value) settings when combined with each of the three Type settings. The Number of Generators value was 1 in all cases.

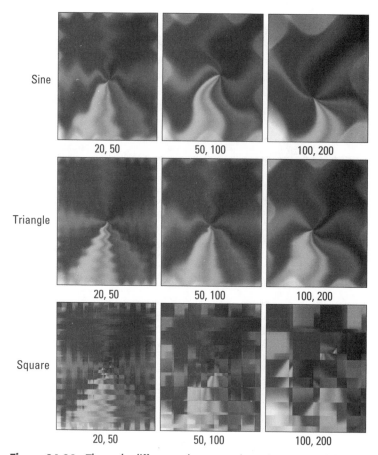

**Figure 24-29:** The only difference between these images and their counterparts in Figure 24-28 is that the Number of Generators value used for all images was 2.

✦ **Type:** You can select from three kinds of waves. The Sine option produces standard sine waves that rise and fall smoothly in bell-shaped curves, just like real waves. The Triangle option creates zigzags that rise and fall in straight lines, like the edge of a piece of fabric cut with pinking shears. The Square option has nothing to do with waves at all, but rather organizes an image into a series of rectangular groupings, reminiscent of Cubism. You might think of this option as an extension of the Mosaic filter. Figures 24-28 and 24-29 demonstrate all three options.

✦ **Randomize:** The Wave filter is random by nature. If you don't like the effect you see in the preview box, click on the Randomize button to stir things up a bit. You can keep clicking on the button until you get an effect you like.

# Distorting an image along a curve

The Distort command, which isn't discussed elsewhere in this book, creates four corner handles around an image. You drag each corner handle to distort the selected image in that direction. Unfortunately, you can't add other points around the edges to create additional distortions, which can be very frustrating if you're trying to achieve a specific effect. If you can't achieve a certain kind of distortion using Edit ⇨ Free Transform, the Shear filter may be your answer.

Shear distorts an image along a path. When you choose Filter ⇨ Distort ⇨ Shear, you get the dialog box shown in Figure 24-30. Initially, a single line that has two points at either end appears in the grid at the top of the box. When you drag the points, you slant the image in the preview. This, plus the fact that the filter is named Shear — Adobe's strange term for skewing (it appears in Illustrator as well) — leads many users to dismiss the filter as nothing more than a slanting tool. But in truth, it's more versatile than that.

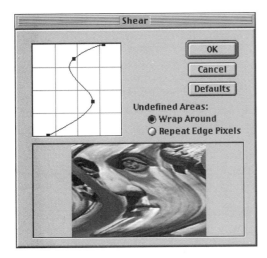

**Figure 24-30:** Click on the grid line in the left corner of the Shear dialog box to add points to the line. Drag these points to distort the image along the curve.

You can add points to the grid line simply by clicking on it. A point springs up every time you click on an empty space in the line. Drag the point to change the curvature of the line and distort the image along the new curve. To delete a point, drag it off the left or right side of the grid. To delete all points and return the line to its original vertical orientation, click on the Defaults button.

The Undefined Areas options work just as they do in the Wave dialog box (described in the preceding section). You can either fill the gaps on one side of the image with pixels shoved off the opposite side by selecting Wrap Around or you can repeat pixels along the edge of the selection by selecting Repeat Edge Pixels.

## Changing to polar coordinates

The Polar Coordinates filter is another one of those gems that a lot of folks shy away from because it doesn't make much sense at first glance. When you choose Filter ⇨ Distort ⇨ Polar Coordinates, Photoshop presents two radio buttons, as shown in Figure 24-31. You can either map an image from rectangular to polar coordinates or from polar to rectangular coordinates.

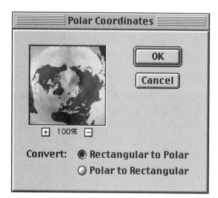

**Figure 24-31:** In effect, the Polar Coordinates dialog box lets you map an image onto a globe and view the globe from above.

All right, time for some global theory. The first image in Figure 24-32 shows a stretched detail of the world map from the Digital Stock library. This map falls under the heading of a *Mercator projection*, meaning that Greenland is all stretched out of proportion, looking as big as the United States and Mexico combined.

The reason for this has to do with the way different mapping systems handle longitude and latitude lines. On a spherical globe, lines of latitude converge at the poles. On a Mercator map, they run absolutely parallel. Because the Mercator map exaggerates the distance between longitude lines as you progress away from the equator, it likewise exaggerates the distance between lines of latitude. The result is a map that becomes infinitely enormous at each of the poles.

When you convert the map to polar coordinates (by selecting the Rectangular to Polar radio button in the Polar Coordinates dialog box), you look down on it from the extreme north or south pole. This means that the entire length of the top edge of the Mercator map becomes a single dot in the exact center of the polar projection. The length of the bottom edge of the map wraps around the entire perimeter of the circle. The second example in Figure 24-32 shows the result. As you can see, the Rectangular to Polar option is just the thing for wrapping text around a circle.

**Figure 24-32:** The world from the equator up expressed in rectangular (top) and polar (bottom) coordinates.

If you select the Polar to Rectangular option, the Polar Coordinates filter produces the opposite effect. Imagine for a moment that the conical gradation shown in the upper left corner of Figure 24-33 is a fan spread out into a full circle. Now imagine closing the fan, breaking the hinge at the top, and spreading out the rectangular fabric of the fan. The center of the fan unfolds to form the top edge of the fabric, and what was once the perimeter of the circle is now the bottom edge of the fabric.

Figure 24-33 shows two examples of what happens when you convert circular images from polar to rectangular coordinates.

The Polar Coordinates filter is a great way to edit gradations. After drawing a linear gradation with the gradient tool (as discussed in Chapter 9), try applying Filter ➪ Distort ➪ Polar Coordinates with the Polar to Rectangular option selected. (Rectangular to Polar just turns it into a radial gradation, sometimes with pretty undesirable results.) You get a redrawn gradation with highlights at the bottom of the selection. Press ⌘/Ctrl+F to reapply the filter to achieve another effect. You can keep repeating this technique until jagged edges start to appear. Then press ⌘/Ctrl+Z to go back to the last smooth effect.

**Figure 24-33:** Two familiar circular images (left) converted from polar to rectangular coordinates (right). The top example is simple enough that you can probably predict the results of the conversion in your head. The lower example looks cool, but you'd need a brain extension to predict the outcome.

## Distorting an image inside out

The following exercise describes how to achieve a sizzling Parting-of-the-Red-Sea effect. Though it incorporates several distortion filters, the star of the effect is the Polar Coordinates filter, which is used to turn the image inside out and then convert it back to polar coordinates after flipping it upside down. No scanned image or artistic talent is required. Rumor has it that Moses puts in a guest appearance in the final image.

This effect is the brainchild of Mark Collen, easily the most imaginative distortion expert I've had the pleasure of knowing. I already mentioned his name in this chapter, in connection with the "Creating a Thick-Liquid Droplet" steps. To be perfectly honest, I probably should have mentioned him more than that, because many of the ideas conveyed in this chapter were based on long, expensive telephone conversations with the guy.

At any rate, Figures 24-34 through 24-39 show the progression of the image through the following steps, starting with a simplistic throwback to Dada (the art movement, not the family member) and continuing to the fabled sea rising in billowing streams. Color Plate 24-7 shows one of Mark's most vivid images, which was created in part using many of the techniques from the steps below. Obviously, Mark used a couple of other filtering and nonfiltering techniques to create his image, but gee whiz folks, you can't expect the guy to share everything he knows in one fell swoop. He has to make a living, after all.

## Steps: The Parting-of-the-Red-Sea Effect

1. **Draw some random shapes in whatever colors you like.** My shapes appear against a black background in Figure 24-34, but you can use any shapes and colors you like. To create each shape, I used the lasso tool to draw the outline of the shape and pressed Option/Alt+Delete/Backspace to fill the lassoed selection with the foreground color. The effect works best if there's a lot of contrast between your colors.

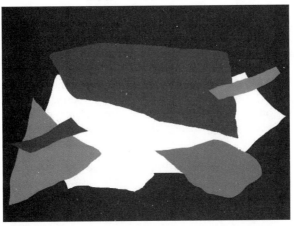

**Figure 24-34:** Draw several meaningless shapes with the lasso tool and fill each with a different color.

*(continued)*

2. **Choose Image ⇨ Rotate Canvas ⇨ 90° CCW.** In Step 3, you apply the Wind Filter to add streaks to the shapes you just created, as shown in Figure 24-35. Because the Wind filter creates horizontal streaks only, and your goal is to add vertical streaks, you must temporarily reorient your image before applying the filter.

3. **Choose Filter ⇨ Stylize ⇨ Wind.** Select Blast and From the Left and press Return. To randomize the image in both directions, choose the Wind filter again and select Blast and From the Right.

4. **Choose Image ⇨ Rotate ⇨ 90° CW.** This returns the image to its original orientation.

5. **Choose Filter ⇨ Blur ⇨ Motion Blur.** Enter 90 degrees into the Angle option and use 20 pixels for the Distance option. This blurs the image vertically to soften the blast lines, as in Figure 24-35.

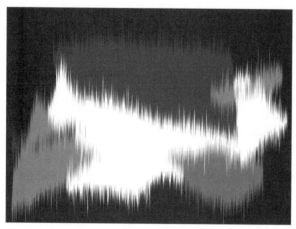

**Figure 24-35:** The result of rotating the image a quarter turn, blasting it in both directions with the Wind filter, rotating it back into place, and applying the Motion Blur filter vertically.

6. **Choose Filter ⇨ Distort ⇨ Wave.** Then enter the values shown in Figure 24-36 into the Wave option box. Most of these values are approximate. You can experiment with other settings if you like. The only essential value is 0 percent in the Vert. option box, which ensures that the filter waves the image in a horizontal direction only.

7. **Choose Filter ⇨ Distort ⇨ Ocean Ripple.** I entered 15 for the Ripple Size and 5 for the Ripple Magnitude to get the effect shown in Figure 24-37.

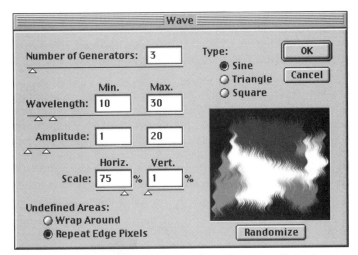

**Figure 24-36:** Apply these settings from the Wave dialog box to wave the image in a vertical direction only.

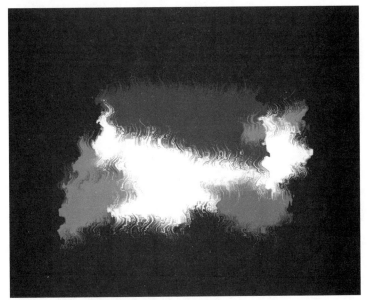

**Figure 24-37:** After applying the Ripple filter, use the Canvas Size command to add a generous amount of empty space around the image.

*(continued)*

8. **Expand the canvas size.** To perform Step 9, the Polar Coordinates filter needs lots of empty room in which to maneuver. If you filled up your canvas like I did, choose Image ⇨ Canvas Size and add 200 pixels both vertically and horizontally. The new canvas size, with generous borders, appears in Figure 24-37.

9. **Choose Filter ⇨ Distort ⇨ Polar Coordinates.** So far, you've probably been a little disappointed by your image. I mean, it's just this disgusting little hairy thing that looks like a bad rug or something. Well, now's your chance to turn it into something special. Choose Filter ⇨ Distort ⇨ Polar Coordinates and select the Polar to Rectangular radio button. Photoshop in effect turns the image inside out, sending all the hairy edges to the bottom of the screen. Finally, an image worth waiting for.

10. **Choose Image ⇨ Rotate Canvas ⇨ Flip Vertical.** This turns the image upside down. As I believe Hemingway said, the hair also rises, as shown in Figure 24-38. This step prepares the image for the next major polar conversion, due in the year 2096.

**Figure 24-38:** Convert the image from polar to rectangular coordinates to turn it inside out. Then flip it vertically to prepare it for the next polar conversion.

11. **Use the rectangular marquee tool to select the central portion of the image.** Leave about 50 pixels along the top and bottom of the image deselected, as well as 100 pixels along both sides. Then feather the selection with a 15-pixel radius.

12. **Press ⌘/Ctrl+F to reapply the Polar Coordinates filter using the same settings as before.** Okay, so it happened before 2096. How could I have known? The pixels inside the selection now billow into a fountain.

13. **Add Moses to taste.** The finished image appears in Figure 24-39.

**Figure 24-39:** Marquee the central portion of the image with a heavily feathered selection outline, convert the selection from rectangular to polar coordinates, and put Moses into the scene. My, doesn't he look natural in his new environment?

# Wrapping an Image onto a 3-D Shape

I've long maintained that three-dimensional drawing programs would catch on better if they were sold as plug-ins utilities for Photoshop. Imagine being able to import DXF objects, add a line or two of text, move the objects around in 3-D space, apply surface textures, and then render the piece directly to independent Photoshop layers. After that, you could change the stacking order of the layers, edit the pixels right there on the spot, maybe even double-click on a layer to edit it in 3-D space. Virtually every digital artist working in 3-D visits Photoshop somewhere during the process, so why not do the whole thing in Photoshop and save everyone a few steps? Experienced artists would love it and novices would take to 3-D in droves.

Frankly, my little fantasy isn't likely to take form any time in the near future. Photoshop would have to modify its plug-in specifications, and some brave programming team would have to spend a lot of time and money producing an aggressive suite of plug-ins. Even so, Adobe seems to share my dream. Filter ➪ Render ➪ 3D Transform lets you wrap an image around a three-dimensional shape. Although the drawing tools are rudimentary, the spatial controls are barely adequate, and the filter lacks any kind of lighting controls, 3D Transform is a first tentative step in the right direction.

Figure 24-40 shows exactly what 3D Transform can do. In each case, I started with the brick image shown in the upper left corner of the figure. Then I wrapped the image around the three basic kinds of *primitives* permitted by the 3D Transform filter — a cube, a sphere, and a cylinder. 3D Transform lets you add points to the side of a cylinder, as I did to get the hourglass shape. You can also mix and match primitives, as the final example in Figure 24-40 illustrates.

Notice that in each case, 3D Transform merely distorts the image. It has no affect on the brightness values of the pixels, nor does it make any attempt to light the shapes (which is why I'd prefer to see it under the Distort submenu as opposed to Render). I added the shadows using Layer ➪ Effects ➪ Drop Shadow.

**Note**    To be perfectly fair, 3D Transform is not the first three-dimensional plug-in for Photoshop. That honor went out years ago to the Series 2: 3-D Filter from Andromeda (*www.andromeda.com*). Even now, Series 2 offers features that Photoshop's 3D Transform plug-in lacks, including a wider range of numerical controls and lighting functions. But 3D Transform is easier to use.

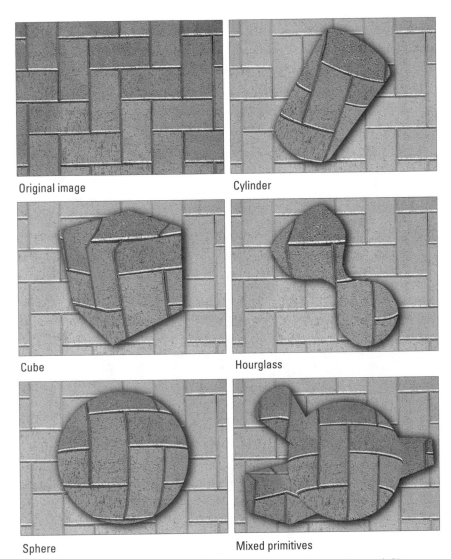

Original image

Cylinder

Cube

Hourglass

Sphere

Mixed primitives

**Figure 24-40:** The 3D Transform filter lets you wrap an image (upper left) around each of three basic primitives (cube, sphere, and cylinder), a modified cylinder (hourglass), or several shapes mixed together.

# Using the 3D Transform filter

Choose Filter ⇨ Render ⇨ 3D Transform to bring up the window shown in Figure 24-41. Less a dialog box than a separate editing environment, the 3D Transform window contains a wealth of tools and a preview area in which you can draw and evaluate your effect. There are a dozen tools in all, but they make a bit more sense if you regard them as members of five basic categories, itemized in the following sections. Like Photoshop's standard tools, you can select the 3D Transform tools from the keyboard (assuming that you have any head room left to memorize the shortcuts). Shortcut keys are listed in parentheses.

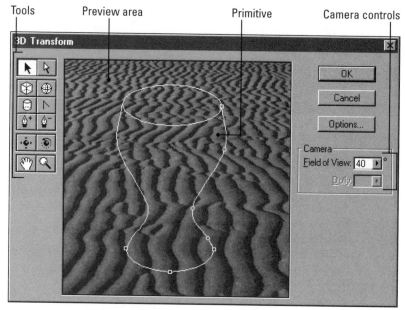

**Figure 24-41:** The 3D Transform dialog box contains a dozen tools that permit you to draw and edit three-dimensional shapes.

## Primitive shape tools

Use one of the primitive shape tools to draw a basic 3-D shape in the preview area. This is the shape around which 3D Transform will wrap the selected image.

> **Cube (M):** Use this tool to draw a six-sided box. Adobe selected M as the shortcut to match Illustrator which uses M for its rectangle tool. And that M is based in turn on Photoshop's marquee tool.

**Sphere (N):** This tool creates a perfect sphere. Again, the shortcut comes from Illustrator, this time from the ellipse tool. Just remember, N follows M. (Ironically, S goes unused. Ain't cross-application consistency a pain in the neck?)

**Cylinder (C):** This cylinder tool draws your basic, everyday, dowel-like cylinders. But you can edit them to make lots of other shapes, as I explain in the upcoming "Cylinder editors." Thankfully, Illustrator offers no equivalent for the cylinder tool, so we get a sensible shortcut, C.

## Basic edit tools

The two arrow tools — the black select tool and the white direct select — let you change a shape by dragging it around or moving the points. Both tools work just like their counterparts in Illustrator.

**Select (V):** Drag a shape with the black arrow tool to move the whole shape. If you know Illustrator, then you already know about the weird V-key shortcut. If not, think of Photoshop's own move tool.

**Direct select (A):** Use the white arrow to move individual points. Dragging a point in a sphere resizes it. Dragging a point in a cube or cylinder stretches or rotates the shape. Experiment and you'll quickly see how it works. (Unlike paths, there are no control handles. All you have to work with are anchor points.)

**Tip** You can switch between the black and white arrow tools by pressing ⌘/Ctrl+Tab. But really, there's no point. The white arrow does everything the black arrow does — just drag on a segment to move the entire shape. In fact, there's just one keyboard trick you need to remember: press ⌘/Ctrl to temporarily get the white arrow tool when any other tool is active. If you know that, the other keys are redundant.

## Cylinder editors

The three path-edit tools are applicable exclusively to cylinders. Why? Because cylinders can be modified to create a whole family of tubular shapes. Throw the cylinder on the lathe and you can make an hourglass, a goblet, a cone — in short, any shape with radial symmetry and a flat top or bottom. To make these shapes, you use the following tools:

**Insert point (+):** Click on the right side of the cylinder — unless you turn it upside-down, then click on the left side — to add a point. Then drag the point with the white arrow tool to move both sides symmetrically. It's a virtual potter's wheel.

**Remove point (–):** Click on a point you've added with the insert point tool to remove it. Don't click on any of the square points that Photoshop put in there or the program will whine at you.

**Convert point:** The insert point tool adds circular smooth points which create continuous arcs in the side of the cylinder. To change the point to a sharp corner, click on it with the convert point tool. Click again to change it back to a smooth point.

## Moving in 3-D space

The next two tools are the most powerful and the hardest to use. They permit you to move the object in 3-D space. When you switch to one of these tools, Photoshop renders the preview so you can see the image wrapped on the shape, as in Figure 24-42.

**Pan camera (E):** Drag the image to move it up, down, left, or right. How is this different than moving the primitive with the arrow tool? This time, you're moving the image in 3-D space across your field of vision. (To be more precise, you're moving the camera — which is your window into the image — while the object remains still.) As you move the image to the left, you see more of its right side. Move it up, and you see its bottom.

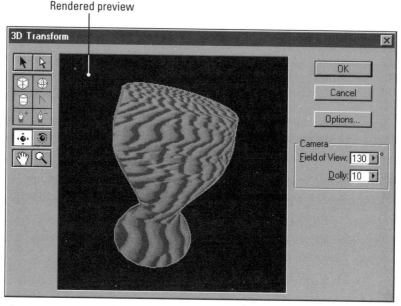

Rendered preview

**Figure 24-42:** When you select either the pan camera or trackball tool, Photoshop renders the image inside the preview area.

**Trackball (R):** The trackball rotates the image in 3-D space. Meanwhile, it's ultimately a 2-D control — you can't move your cursor in or out of the screen; just up, down, and side to side — making it difficult to predict the outcome of a drag.

**Tip**

Inevitably, you'll end up exposing the back, empty side of a shape. When this happens, spin the shape by dragging against the grain. To spin the shape head over heels, for example, drag directly up or down. To spin the shape sideways, drag horizontally. Don't fret too much about moving through the 3-D world, just watch how the program behaves when you move your mouse from one location to another. In time, you'll see some very simple patterns that you can exploit to your advantage.

In case you're wondering "What is with the shortcuts for these tools?" permit me to explain. The R key selects the rotate tool in Illustrator; because the trackball rotates, it was likewise assigned R. As for the pan camera tool, it had no equivalent in Illustrator 7, so it got one of the few keys that was never assigned in Illustrator 7: E. Crawl inside the mind of an Adobe engineer and it all makes perfect sense.

## The camera controls

When you select the pan camera or trackball tool, Photoshop offers two Camera options on the right side of the dialog box. At first, the two options seem to do the same thing. A low value moves you in; a high value takes you out. But in truth they produce subtly different effects. Think of the Field of View option as a wide-angle lens and the Dolly option as a zoom lens both operating at the same time. A low Field of View with a high Dolly results in shallow shapes. A high Field of View with a low Dolly shrinks you down to the size of a bug so that the depth is really coming at you.

## Basic navigation

The last two tools in the 3D Transform dialog box are the standard hand and magnifying glass. They work just like their counterparts outside the 3D Transform dialog box, which is to say:

**Hand (H):** Drag the image to move it around inside the preview area. You can press either the H key or the spacebar to get this tool.

**Zoom (Z):** Click with this tool to zoom in, Option/Alt+click to zoom out. ⌘/Ctrl+spacebar and Option/Alt+spacebar work as well.

# Layer before you apply

When you press Return/Enter, Photoshop merges your new 3-D shape with the original image. Because the 3D Transform filter provides no lighting controls, the shape may be virtually indistinguishable from its background, as Figure 24-43 makes abundantly clear. And that, dear friends, is a giant drag.

Luckily, you can force Photoshop to deliver the 3-D shape on a separate layer. Here's what you do. First copy the image to a separate layer by dragging it onto the page icon at the bottom of the Layers palette. Then choose Filter ➪ Render ➪ 3D Transform and click on the Options button inside the dialog box. Turn off the Display Background check box, spotlighted in Figure 24-44, and press Return/Enter.

**Figure 24-43:** By default, the 3D Transform filter merges the 3-D image into the original image, making for an extraordinarily subtle effect.

**Figure 24-44:** Copy the image to a separate layer and turn off the Display Background check box to make the area outside the 3-D shape transparent.

Not only will the 3D Transform filter restrict its efforts to the active layer, it will also make the area outside the 3-D shape transparent, as in the first example of Figure 24-45. Then you can apply layer effects or other lighting techniques to distinguish the 3-D shape from its background, as in the second example.

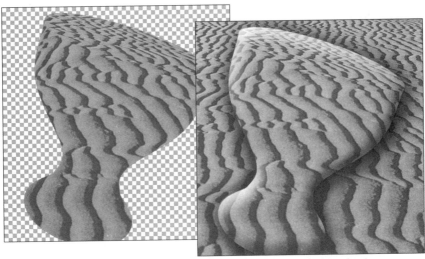

**Figure 24-45:** After applying the 3-D shape to a separate layer (shown by itself at left), I used the Drop Shadow and Inner Bevel effects to add some fake volumetric lighting to my goblet (right).

Color Plates 24-8 and 24-9 demonstrate some of the fun you can have with 3D Transform. In Color Plate 24-8, I relied entirely on the Drop Shadow and Inner Bevel layer effects to light the layered 3-D goblet. I also added a bit of red to the goblet using Image ➪ Adjust ➪ Hue/Saturation to distinguish the layer from its sandy background.

Color Plate 24-9 illustrates the merits of manual lighting techniques. After setting the goblet against a different background, I applied the drop shadow and haloing techniques that I discussed back in the "Selecting the Contents of Layers" section of Chapter 17. I also applied the airbrush tool set alternatively to the Multiply and Screen brush modes to hand-brush some natural tinting. Finally, I darkened the top of the goblet with the help of the elliptical marquee tool. After drawing my initial marquee, I chose Select ➪ Transform to rotate and scale it into position, pressed ⌘/Ctrl+J to send the selection to a separate layer, and applied the Multiply blend mode set to a low opacity. Admittedly, the finished effect involved a lot of effort, but it looks significantly more realistic than anything Photoshop can approximate automatically.

**Cross-Reference** See Chapter 27 for more details on creating special 3-D effects.

# Adding Clouds and Spotlights

The remaining five filters in the Render submenu produce lighting effects. You can use Clouds and Difference Clouds to create a layer of haze over an image. Lens Flare creates light flashes and reflections (as I mentioned earlier). Lighting Effects lights an image as if it were hanging on a gallery wall. You can even use the unremarkable Texture Fill command to add an embossed texture to a piece embellished with the Lighting Effects filter.

## Creating clouds

The Clouds filter creates an abstract and random haze between the foreground and background colors. Difference Clouds works exactly like layering the image, applying the Clouds filter, and selecting the Difference blend mode in the Layers palette.

Why on earth should Difference Clouds make special provisions for a single blend mode? Because you can create cumulative effects. Try this: Select blue as the foreground color and then choose Filter ⇨ Render ⇨ Clouds. Ah, just like a real sky, huh? Now choose Filter ⇨ Render ⇨ Difference Clouds. It's like some kind of weird Halloween motif, all blacks and oranges. Press ⌘/Ctrl+F to repeat the filter. Back to the blue sky. Keep pressing ⌘/Ctrl+F over and over and notice the results. A pink cancer starts invading the blue sky; a green cancer invades the orange one. Multiple applications of the Difference Clouds filter generate organic oil-on-water effects.

**Tip**    To strengthen the colors created by the Clouds filter, press Shift when choosing the command. This same technique works when using the Difference Clouds filter as well. In fact, I don't know of any reason *not* to Shift+choose these commands, unless you have some specific need for washed-out effects.

Color Plate 24-10 shows some pretty entertaining applications of the Clouds filters. With the foreground and background colors set to blue and orange respectively, I applied the Clouds filter to a layered copy of the rose image. For maximum effect, I Shift+chose the filter to create the top left image in the color plate. I then Shift+chose the Difference Clouds filter to create the purple montage in the figure, and pressed ⌘/Ctrl+F ten times to achieve the top right image. Looks to me like I definitely have something growing in my Petri dish.

Yeah, so really groovy stuff, right? Shades of "Purple Haze" and all that. But now that I've created this murky mess, what the heck do I do with it? Composite it, of course. The bottom row of Color Plate 24-10 shows examples of mixing each of the images from the top row with the original rose. In the left example, I chose the Overlay option from the Layers palette (Shift+Option/Alt+O). In the middle example, I chose the Screen mode(Shift+Option/Alt+S). And in the last example, I chose Hue (Shift+Option/Alt+U). This last one is particularly exciting, completely transforming the colors in the rose while leaving the gray (and therefore unsaturated) background untouched. Without a mask, without anything but a rectangular marquee, I've managed to precisely color the interior of the rose.

## Lighting an image

Photoshop ventures further into 3-D drawing territory with the Lighting Effects filter. This very complex function allows you to shine lights on an image, color the lights, position them, focus them, specify the reflectivity of the surface, and even create a surface map. In many ways, it's a direct lift from MetaCreations' Painter. But, whereas Painter provides predefined paper textures and light refraction effects that bolster the capabilities of its excellent tool, Photoshop offers better controls and more lighting options.

**Caution**

The Lighting Effects filter is applicable exclusively to RGB images. Also, don't expect to be able to apply 3-D lighting to shapes created with the 3D Transform filter. Sadly, the two filters share no common elements that would permit them to work directly with each other.

When you choose Filter ⇨ Render ⇨ Lighting Effects, Photoshop displays what is easily its most complex dialog box, as shown in Figure 24-46. The dialog box has two halves: One in which you actually position light with respect to a thumbnail of the selected image, and one that contains about a billion intimidating options. Between you and me, I think Adobe could have done a better job, but the dialog box is functional.

No bones about it, this dialog box is a bear. The easiest way to apply the filter is to choose one of the predefined lighting effects from the Style pop-up menu at the top of the right side of the dialog box, see how it looks in the preview area, and — if you like it — press Return/Enter to apply the effect.

But if you want to create your own effects, you'll have to work a little harder. Here are the basic steps involved in creating a custom effect.

Preview area (stage)

Footprint Hotspot    Focus spot                          Color swatches

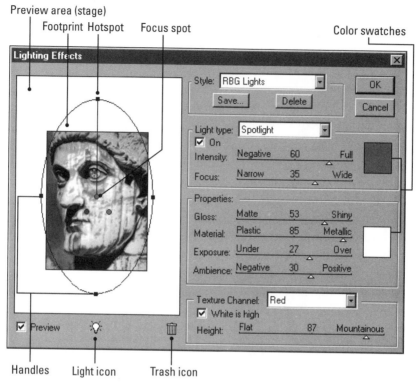

Handles    Light icon    Trash icon

**Figure 24-46:** The Lighting Effects dialog box enables you to light an image as if it were hanging in a gallery, or lying on a floor, or perhaps resting too near a hot flame.

## Steps: Lighting an Image

1. **Drag from the light icon at the bottom of the dialog box into the preview area to create a new light source.** I call this area the *stage* because it's as if the image is painted on the floor of a stage and the lights are hanging above it.

2. **Select the kind of light you want from the Light Type pop-up menu.** It's just below the Style pop-up menu. You can select from Directional, Omni, and Spotlight:

   • Directional works like the sun, being a general, unfocused light that hits a target from an angle.

- Omni is a bare light bulb hanging in the middle of the room, shining in all directions from a center point.

- And Spotlight is a focused beam that is brightest at the source and tapers off gradually.

3. **Specify the color of the light by clicking on the top color swatch.** You also can muck about with the Intensity slider bar to control the brightness of the light. If Spotlight is selected, the Focus slider becomes available. Drag the slider toward Narrow to create a bright laser of light; drag toward Wide to diffuse the light and spread it over a larger area.

4. **Move the light source by dragging at the *focus point* (the colored circle in the stage).** When Directional or Spotlight is selected, the focus point represents the spot at which the light is pointing. When Omni is active, the focus point is the actual bulb. (Don't burn yourself.)

5. **If Directional or Spotlight is active, you can change the angle of the light by dragging the *hot spot*.** The hot spot represents the location in the image that's liable to receive the most light. When you use a Directional light, the hot spot appears as a black square at the end of a line joined to the focus point. The same holds true when you edit a Spotlight; the confusing thing is that there are four black squares altogether. The light source is joined to the focus point by a line, the three *handles* are not.

**Tip**

To make the light brighter, drag the hot spot closer to the focus point. Dragging the hot spot away from the focus point dims the light by increasing the distance that it has to travel. It's like putting a flashlight in the living room when you're in the garage — the light gets dimmer as you move farther away from it.

6. **With Omni or Spotlight in force, you can edit the elliptical footprint of the light.** When Omni is in force, a circle surrounds the focus point. When editing a Spotlight, you see an ellipse. Either way, this shape represents the *footprint* of the light, which is the approximate area of the image affected by the light. You can change the size of the light by dragging the handles around the footprint. Enlarging the shape is like raising the light source. When the footprint is small, the light is close to the image, so it's concentrated and very bright. When the footprint is large, the light is high above the image, so it's more generalized.

**Tip**

When editing the footprint of a Spotlight, Shift+drag a handle to adjust the width or height of the ellipse without affecting the angle. To change the angle without affecting the size, ⌘/Ctrl+drag a handle.

*(continued)*

Tip

7. Introduce more lights as you see fit.

There are a bunch of different techniques you can use to add and subtract lights on the stage. Press the Tab key to switch from one light to the next. You can duplicate a light in the stage by Option/Alt+dragging its focus point. To delete the active light, just press the Delete key. Or if you prefer, you can drag the focus point onto the trash can icon at the bottom of the dialog box.

8. **Change the Properties and Texture Channel options as you see fit.** I explain these in detail after the steps.

9. **If you want to save your settings for future use, click on the Save button.** Photoshop invites you to name the setup, which then appears as an option in the Style pop-up menu. If you want to get rid of one of the presets, select it from the pop-up menu and click on the Delete button.

10. **Press Return/Enter to apply your settings to the image.**

That's almost everything. The only parts I left out are the Properties and Texture Channel options. The Properties slider bars control how light reflects off the surface of your image:

✦ **Gloss:** Is the surface dull or shiny? Drag the slider toward Matte to make the surface flat and nonreflective, like dull enamel paint. Drag the slider toward Shiny to make it glossy, as if you had slapped on a coat of lacquer.

✦ **Material:** This option determines the color of the light that reflects back off the image. According to the logic employed by this option, Plastic reflects back the color of the light; Metallic reflects the color of the object itself. If only I had a bright, shiny plastic thing and a bright, shiny metal thing, I could check to see if this logic holds true in real life (like maybe that matters).

✦ **Exposure:** I'd like this option better if you could vary it between Sun Block 65 and Melanoma. Unfortunately, the more prosaic titles are Under and Over — exposed, that is. This option controls the brightness of all lights like a big dimmer switch. You can control a single selected light using the Intensity slider, but the Exposure slider offers the added control of changing all lights in the stage area and the ambient light (described next) together.

✦ **Ambience:** The last slider allows you to add *ambient light,* which is a general, diffused light that hits all surfaces evenly. First, select the color of the light by clicking on the color swatch to the right. Then drag the slider to cast a subtle hue over the stage. Drag toward Positive to tint the image with the color in the swatch; drag toward Negative to tint the stage with the swatch's opposite. Keep the slider set to 0 — dead in the center — to cast no hue.

The Texture Channel options let you treat one channel in the image as a *texture map,* which is a grayscale surface in which white indicates peaks and black indicates valleys. (As long as White is High is selected, that is. If you deselect that option, everything flips, and black becomes the peak.) It's as if one channel has a surface to it. By selecting a channel from the pop-up menu, you create an emboss effect, much like that created with the Emboss filter, except much better because you can light the surface from many angles at once, and it's in color to boot.

Choose a channel to serve as the embossed surface from the pop-up menu. Then change the Height slider to indicate more or less Flat terrain or huge Mountainous cliffs of surface texture.

Color Plate 24-11 shows an image lit with a total of five spotlights, two from above and three from below. In the first example, I left the Texture Channel option set to None. In the second example, I selected the green channel as the surface map. And in the third example, I filled a separate mask channel with a bunch of white and black dollops using Filter ➪ Pixelate ➪ Pointillize, then I selected the mask from the Texture Channel pop-up menu in the Lighting Effects dialog box. The result is a wonderfully rough paper texture.

✦     ✦     ✦

# PART VIII
## SPECIAL EFFECTS
## MADE PRACTICAL

**The Face-Melting Power of
  Distortions**
**Popping Type Off the Page**
**Wrapping Images Around
  3-D Shapes**
**Photographing for Photoshop**
**Inventing Photo-Realistic Worlds**

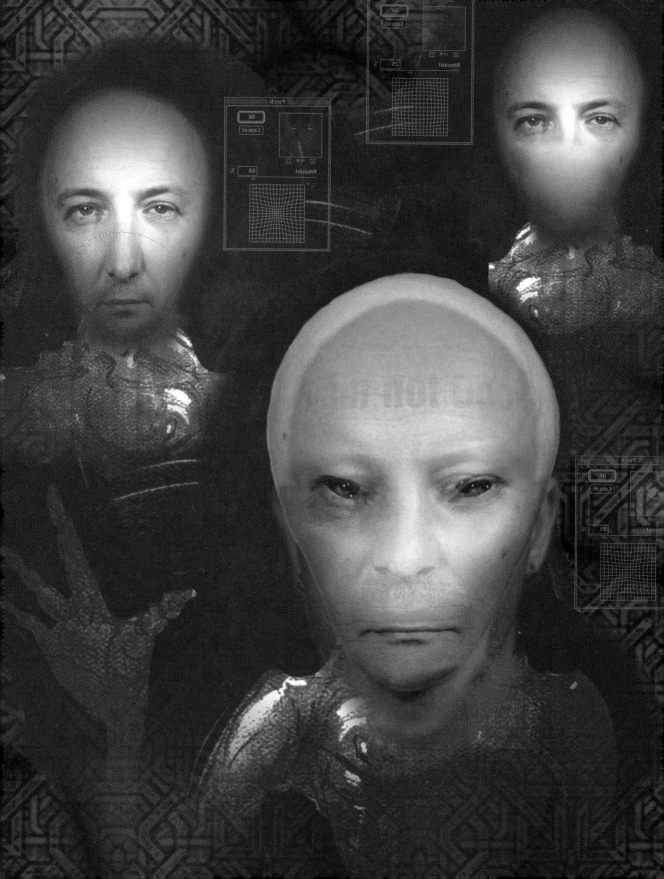

# CHAPTER 25
# THE FACE-MELTING POWER OF DISTORTIONS

The commands in the Filter ➢ Distort submenu leave most artists covering their gaping mouths with one hand and scratching their heads with the other. Oh sure, Spherize (25.1), Pinch (25.2), and fellow pixel mutilators are a lot of fun, but what do you do with them? The chance of a client asking you to contort the holy heck out of some poor guy's face seems awfully remote.

To find out how someone might apply these strange commands in a professional capacity, I went to the original stomping ground for the Distort filters, George Lucas' Industrial Light & Magic (ILM). All but a couple of the commands were written by John Knoll, an effects supervisor at ILM. Knoll wrote the filters not only to amuse himself, but also to generate the occasional special effect.

Fellow ILM artist (and subject of this chapter) Mark Moore claims distortions were the feature that first drew him to Photoshop. He recalls his reaction to an early prerelease demonstration of the program just a few months after he joined ILM: "We all knew John was working on an image editor, so we had a rough idea of what to expect. But when he opened up a picture of his wife and applied a few distortions, that's when my jaw fell on the floor. I thought, 'This is going to change how all artwork is done.' And sure enough, it has."

## THE VISUAL EFFECTS ART DIRECTOR AT WORK

In order to understand how and why Moore uses distortions, it's helpful to see how his job fits into the special effects puzzle. "When we first start a project,

*This is going to change how all artwork is done.*

MARK MOORE

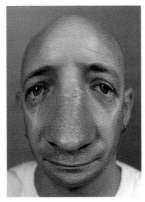

25.1     25.2

the effects supervisor breaks down the script and decides which shots are going to be visual effects. Then I step in and oversee the creation of the storyboards, which are comic book–like panels that illustrate the effects sequences. After that, I'll pick out key panels and flesh them out into full-fledged concept art. I create detailed pencil sketches to block out the composition and show what the basic scene should look like. Then I'll take the sketches I like and work them into photo-realistic renderings in Photoshop. That way, the director can look at them and get a pretty exact idea of what he can expect."

In 1993, Moore worked as art director on an alien-abduction movie called *Fire in the Sky*. Very briefly, *Fire in the Sky* is the belabored story of Travis Walton, a freelance tree chopper who gets kidnapped by a pack of fiendish extraterrestrials. He spends half the movie missing in action and the other half freaked out by his strange ordeal. The ordeal is revealed near the end of the film in a creepy scene that takes place inside the alien spaceship. Devoid of any dialog — which in this movie is a very, very good thing — it features lead character Travis waking up inside a slimy pod, fighting his way out of a huge cocoon of equally slimy pods, discovering some sleeping aliens, and unwisely electing to pause and scrutinize them. Suddenly, a couple of tiny but feisty aliens seize young Travis, fling him onto an operating table, and prepare him for the most appalling medical examination this side of *Marathon Man*. Et tu, space friend?

According to Moore, this one scene was the beginning and end of ILM's involvement in the movie. "We built the entire alien set — including the cocoon and the interior of the spaceship — on our main stage. There was just one actor, D. B. Sweeny, and the rest was puppeteers."

## DISSECTING THE ALIEN

Moore was put in charge of designing the main alien, a critter nicknamed Doc. "The director thought that Doc should look like a burn victim. He was basically humanoid, but something was very wrong with him. I also had to make him seem tough but vulnerable. The aliens wore these skintight space suits that looked like the classic large-headed, big-eyed E.T.s to protect them from our environment (25.3). The idea was that the space suits were organic and actually grew onto their bodies. But inside the ship, it was like being in a big womb, so they could walk around naked. This was also the rationale for why Doc is operating on Travis. The aliens believe we have superior bodies, and they might be able to use them for their own purposes." Ah ha, that explains Ross Perot.

"So I started by putting together some pencil sketches of the operating room and Doc (25.4). The problem was, I couldn't come up with anything that was specific enough. The director wanted to see polished renderings, not sketches. Photoshop was perfect for this, because I could scan some faces,

**ARTIST:**
Mark Moore

**ORGANIZATION:**
Industrial Light & Magic
San Rafael, California
mtwo@kerner.com

**SYSTEM:**
Power Mac 7500/100
2GB storage

**RAM:**
80MB total
50MB assigned to Photoshop

**MONITOR:**
Radius 20-inch

**VERSION USED:**
Photoshop 3.0.5

**OTHER APPLICATIONS:**
Macromedia FreeHand, Adobe Texture-Maker

**WORK HISTORY:**
1976 — Turned 20, saw *Star Wars*, understood for the first time what he wanted to do for a living.

rearrange them, and come up with a look that spelled it out very accurately. There was no room for misinterpretation."

Normally at this point, I would include content from the actual movie, just as I do for *The Empire Strikes Back* and *Dynotopia* in Chapter 29. But Paramount — the studio that owns *Fire in the Sky* — wanted to charge us more than we could afford to reprint the images. (I guess that's one way to recoup costs.) So Moore agreed to show us the steps he used to arrive at Doc as applied to a different original image. The result will be a wholly unique character whom I will christen Bones, in deference to a different Paramount-owned character.

For Moore's technique to work, he has to start with a person with a shaved head. Hence, Moore has selected as raw material a fellow ILM employee whose scalp is appropriately bereft of hair (25.5). Known as Sir Guy of Hudson in the credits to *Fire in the Sky*, this mysterious individual served as lead alien puppeteer. It is therefore ironic that in this chapter, he serves as puppet.

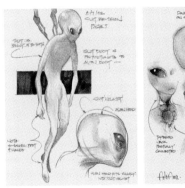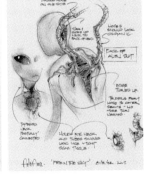

25.3

25.4

## TRANSFORMING SIR GUY INTO BONES

"Before I started work on the sketches, I got some books on alien abductions. A couple of them said that the bad aliens are called Grays. They're the ones you look out for. So we decided to make the aliens a sort of gray-brown. Meanwhile, I was working on a

1982 — Received degrees in Graphic and Industrial Design from the University of Washington in Seattle.

1989 — Landed job as concept artist for LucasArts Attractions, worked on theme park rides including "Star Tours."

1990 — First movie credit, Mechanical Model Design for flying train in *Back to the Future III*.

1993 — Met stop-motion innovator Ray Harryhausen at *Jurassic Park* opening in Los Angeles.

1997 — Visual effects art director for *Star Wars: Special Edition*.

**FAVORITE GUILTY PLEASURE:**

Godzilla movies ("The only person I've ever talked to who likes Godzilla more than me is Tim Burton.")

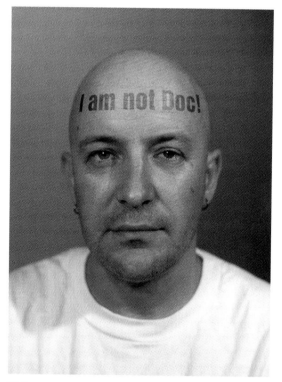

25.5

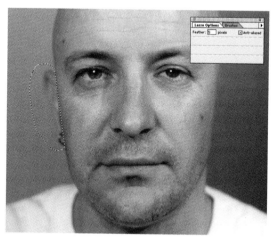

25.6

Mac IIfx at the time (equivalent to a 386 PC), and it was taking forever. So I decided, hey, if they're gray, why not work in grayscale?" For the purposes of this book, I've colorized the screen shots to get a duotone effect. Having finally gotten my publisher to spring for color, I'm dang well going to use it.

### THE IMMUTABLE LAW OF ALIEN LIGHT BULBS

When you're crafting an alien, the ears are the first thing you have to change. According to the grand tradition of Movie Logic, alien beings either have big ears or no ears at all. Bones falls into the latter camp. "The helmet design was based on the classic Whitley Strieber *Communion* alien, with a tapering face, giant eyes, and a gentle mouth (25.3). The heads needed to be able to fit inside these light bulb-shaped helmets. So I was trying to streamline the head as much as possible."

Moore used the lasso tool with the Feather value set to 5 to select each ear (25.6). Then he used that selection to grab an empty portion of the background and drag it on top of the ear. To taper Guy's head like a light bulb, Moore selected the bottom half of the face and applied Filter ➤ Distort ➤ Pinch set to an Amount value of 60 percent (25.7).

### MASKING FEATURES WITH FOREHEAD

Another feature that aliens frequently lack is the nose. So Moore set about eliminating the nose by cloning the forehead on top of it. He started by setting the Feather value in the Lasso Options palette to 11. Then he selected the area around the nose and mouth (25.8). He moved the selection outline straight up to the forehead, then he ⌘/Ctrl+Option/Alt-dragged to clone the forehead onto the lower half of the face (25.9). Finally, he used the Levels command to darken the chunk of forehead and lessen the contrast (25.10). Then he touched up the edges with the dodge and burn tools.

"Thanks to the fact that Guy is bald, I had a nice big patch of skin I could use to cover up the bottom of the face. If you look carefully, you can see that I have a bit of eyebrow down at the bottom of the chin, but I could easily clone that away if I wanted to. The point is, by cloning bits and pieces of the face, I can match the tone and texture of his skin. You get a halfway realistic effect with little work."

### MAKING THE FIERCE LITTLE EYES

"The classic alien has gigantic eyes that make it look cute. We wanted tiny beady fierce eyes so that you'd think, 'Yikes, this guy is scary.' We wanted him to look smart like a human, but cold like a predator.

"I started by going in and painting the whites of his eyes (25.11). For the most part, I just painted in the whites with black using the airbrush. I also highlighted the irises just a bit with the dodge tool and rubber stamped a couple of reflections. I figured the black eyes went a long way toward erasing his humanity.

"The model I used for the movie didn't have eyebrows. I don't know if he had shaved them off or they were super light, but I didn't have to worry about them. Unfortunately, I couldn't ask Guy to shave his eyebrows, so I had to eliminate them by cloning some more of the forehead." As before, Moore selected the area he wanted to replace with the lasso tool, moved the selection outline over a piece of the forehead, and ⌘/Ctrl+Option/Alt-dragged the selection to clone the forehead back onto the eyebrow (25.12). Then he used the dodge and burn tools to touch up the edges.

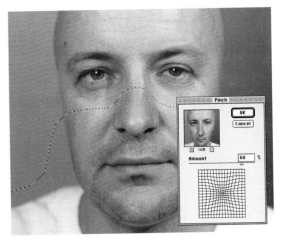

25.7

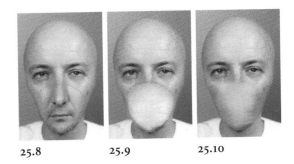

25.8          25.9          25.10

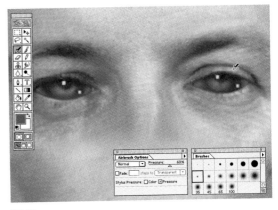

25.11

"Next, I tilted the eyes to give them a kind of cat quality." In each case, Moore selected the eye and pressed ⌘/Ctrl+Option/Alt+T. This simultaneously clones the selection and enters the Free Transform mode. Then he rotated the eye about 20 degrees (25.13). "I purposely rotated the eyes to slightly different angles. Many artists have a habit of maintaining absolute symmetry in Photoshop, and it just doesn't look natural. A little bit of asymmetry really sends the effect home."

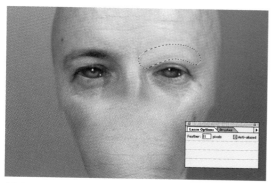

**25.12**

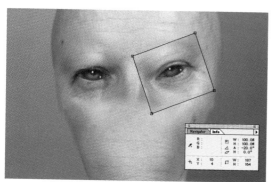

**25.13**

"To reduce the size of the eyes, I pinched them each 35 percent (25.14). This had the effect of not only shrinking the eyes, but also stretching the bags and wrinkles around the eyes. It helped to age the creature and make it more believable." The finished eyes appear savage and malevolent (25.15), just what you want in a doctor from outer space.

**EXPANDING THE CRANIUM**

"Guy has such a strong bridge to his nose that I had to touch it up with some more forehead. Again, I just selected the area, moved the selection over the forehead, and cloned the forehead into position (25.16). Then I did the usual Levels adjustment and touch-up."

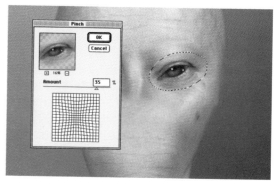

**25.14**

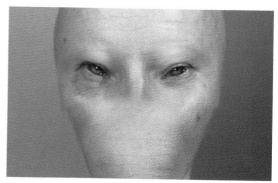

**25.15**

Moore next selected the top portion of the image and applied Filter ➤ Distort ➤ Spherize (25.17). He set the Amount value to 25 percent to swell the skull ever so slightly (25.18). "After all the work on the eyes, he was starting to look pretty beastly. The brain expansion helped him to look more intelligent."

## CLEANING UP DISTORTION BLURS

When you distort feathered selections, you tend to get blurred edges and stretch marks. In the spherized version of Bones (25.18), the stretching is evident under the bridge of the nose, around the eyes, and below the cheekbones. "These motion blur trails are a real telltale sign of digital manipulation. To get rid of them, I'll usually go in and lay down some noise with the Add Noise command set to Monochromatic. That helps to simulate the film grain. Then I'll apply a very low Gaussian Blur radius, maybe 0.3. After that, I'll do spot work with the rubber stamp tool.

"Of course, cleanup takes time, and around here time is a scarce commodity. So we typically toss it together as quickly as we can. Then when the show's released and it's successful, we go back and do it over again like we did with *Star Wars*."

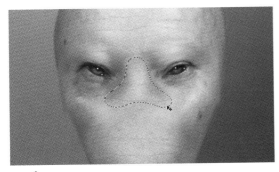

**25.16**

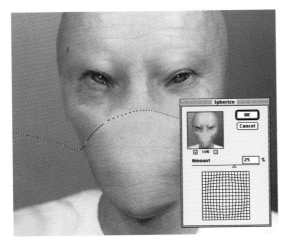

**25.17**

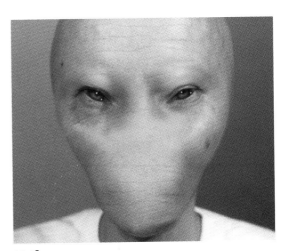

**25.18**

## RESTORING THE NUTRIENT INPUT ORIFICE

"I still wanted my alien to have a mouth, so I went back to the original image and selected the mouth using a feathered lasso. Then I copied the mouth and pasted it into the Bones image. Then I scaled the mouth to make the lips super thin (25.19). It was really fun to have this free-floating mouth because I could nudge it around to get different expressions. I could make him look like a real dummy by positioning the mouth high. If I put the mouth too low, he just looked ridiculous. I even put it on his forehead just for laughs."

## ALIEN INTERVENTION

Moore eventually arrived at three variations on the Doc theme, including Bones (25.20) and two additional operating room characters, Intern (25.21) and Nurse (25.22). "You notice I kept Guy's mole in all three images. It's a little detail you don't expect to see in visitors from another planet. But I imagine they have skin blemishes and other defects just like we do."

Moore should know. Legend has it that he was inspired by beings beyond our solar system. "Before the movie came out, there was an article in a local psychic publication. The writer claimed she was notified by aliens that they were controlling the production of the movie. They were paying special attention to the person who was designing the aliens. And I thought, cool, that should speed up the approval process."

I guess it just goes to show you: Even hyper-intelligent aliens have their limitations. They may have built the great pyramids and they're clearly the people to call if you need a nice crop circle, but their movie directing skills are a bit hit and miss. *A* for special effects; *D* for drama.

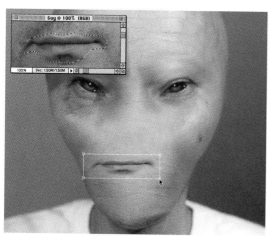

25.19

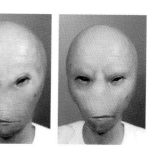

25.20             25.21             25.22

## FROM PHOTOSHOP TO CREATURE SHOP

"After the director approved my design for Doc, I sent the Photoshop sketch off to our creature shop and they used it to sculpt the clay model for the puppet. I worked with the creature shop to figure out the depth and decide how the puppet should move. In the end, less turned out to be more. We ended up inserting cables to move his eyes and eyelids. Then we added pulsating areas around his temples. That was all there was to the face. Then the arms and body were puppeted. Somehow he was scarier if he was largely immobile."

## KIDS, DON'T TRY THIS AT HOME

Moore is one of the few artists who gets to play with his stuff after he makes it. As visual effects director, he was on hand when the operation scene was filmed, so he had a chance to experience some of the props up close and personal.

In the movie, a big sheet of plastic sucks the actor down onto the operating table. It covers his whole body, including his face. The plastic sinks into the actor's open mouth and it looks to all the world like he's suffocating. "That's actually true. I took a turn as a stand-in and you can't breath at all. There's this huge compressor that sucks the sheet onto you. It was loud as heck. The director's wife, the actress Marilu Henner, was standing there and all I could hear over the motor was her screams. It scared her so bad she ran and hid behind a cabinet. I finally had to break the suction by lifting my leg. After I got my breath back, I asked, 'How was it?' And they said, 'Yeah, it looked great. Real scary.'

"Our big limitation in scripting the operating scene was that none of the people who claim they've been abducted have any marks. So we figured, what kind of operating can you do without leaving scars? We decided to concentrate on the orifices — the eye, the ear, the mouth. We even fooled around with going a little lower. In the final cut, the aliens put a pipe down Travis' mouth. But we were going to have another pipe come in from the other end. At some point, we'd see the pipes right under the skin as the one from above met up with the one from below. But the director was like, 'Er, no. That's just too disgusting.' He might have been right.

"Right after the pipes, the aliens pour some fluid into Travis' eye. Originally, the fluid was going to be really dark, but it didn't read very well on camera. So we decided to try something light. Unfortunately, we were all set up and ready to go. So one of the guys from the model shop ran off and came back with some white stuff. The director asked him, 'What is it?', but the model shop guy just said, 'Believe me, it's safe. I tested it on my own eye.' So we poured it into the actor's eye, and it looked great. You know what it was? Mocha mix." Wow, it's both a stimulant and an eye whitener.

# CHAPTER 26
# POPPING TYPE OFF THE PAGE

Where text is concerned, few publishing programs are as inept at applying basic formatting attributes as Photoshop. For example, Photoshop 5 remains incapable of the simple act of combining two type styles inside a single text block. Once you get the letters on-screen, however, Photoshop lets you edit them with unparalleled flexibility. Whatever its formatting failings, the program permits you to experiment with special-effect treatments that other image editors can't touch.

Embossing is a case in point. Photoshop lets you create raised letters that look like they were rendered in a three-dimensional drawing program. Using a simple mask and a handful of filters, you can instruct Photoshop to not only calculate highlights and shadows, but actually bend a background image around the surfaces of the letters as well. This is no half-baked Emboss filter effect; it's picture-perfect embossing that you'll be proud to submit to the most finicky clients.

## MAKING THE TYPE MASK

Photoshop provides two filters that work together to produce photo-realistic embossing: Lighting Effects and Displace. But before you can apply either of them, you have to create your text in a separate mask channel. The type mask acts as an essential surface texture for the filters.

First, open the image that you want to use as the background for your embossed type (26.1). (A low-contrast pattern with repeating elements works best.)

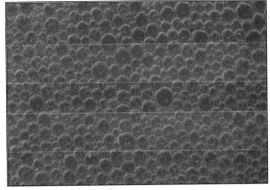

26.1

Then go to the Channels palette and click the Create a New Channel icon at the bottom. Photoshop creates a new channel filled entirely with black.

Get the type tool and create the text that you want to emboss. The type will automatically appear in white against the black background of the channel (26.2). This is precisely the effect you want. Position the text as desired.

For the text to convey depth, it has to have blurred edges. With the text still selected, choose Filter ➤ Blur ➤ Gaussian Blur and enter the desired Radius value. Higher values result in more depth: I recommend somewhere in the neighborhood of 3 pixels of Radius for every 100 pixels of type size. For example, if the letters are 400 pixels tall, set the Radius to 12.0.

Then deselect the text by pressing ⌘/Ctrl+D and reapply the Gaussian Blur filter with a Radius in the neighborhood of 2.0 (26.3). This helps smooth out the type so that the Light Effects filter doesn't cause ragged edges.

That's it for the Lighting Effects mask. But because no two Photoshop filters work quite the same, you need to duplicate the text mask to a separate file to satisfy the Displace filter. Choose the Duplicate Channel command from the Channels palette menu, then select New from the Document pop-up menu. Next, press ⌘/Ctrl+L to bring up the Levels dialog box and change the first Output Levels value to 128. This lightens the image so the darkest color is medium gray (26.4), the neutral value for the Displace filter. Finally, save the image in the native Photoshop format (.PSD) — the only format that Displace supports — and close the file. In Photoshop parlance, this file is known as the "displacement map."

## EMBOSSING WITH LIGHTING EFFECTS

Return to the RGB view, and then create a new layer and fill it with 50 percent gray. This provides a neutral layer for the Light Effects filter. Technically, you *can* apply Lighting Effects directly to the image, but the separate layer gives you more room to experiment and the flexibility to change your mind.

With the gray layer active, choose Filter ➤ Render ➤ Lighting Effects. (If you encounter an out-of-memory error, try closing all files except the image you're working on and purging the Clipboard and Snapshot buffers with the Edit ➤ Purge commands.) Select the type channel — probably #4 — from the Texture Channel pop-up menu in the lower-right corner of the sprawling Lighting Effects dialog box. Now set the angle and intensity of the light as desired in the preview area on the left (26.5). The light appears to ripple across the text channel, producing a true 3-D emboss (26.6).

26.2

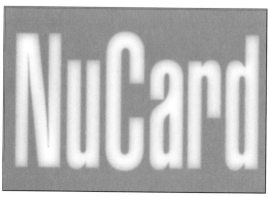

26.4

26.3

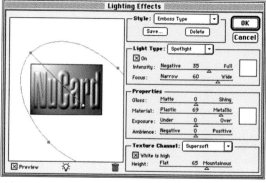

26.5

After you apply the filter, select the Overlay blend mode from the pop-up menu in the Layers palette. This burns the emboss layer into the background image (26.7). If selecting Overlay doesn't produce a significant enough effect, try duplicating the gray layer and adjusting the Opacity setting. You may also find it helpful to lower the contrast of the background image using the Levels command.

### MOLDING THE TEXT WITH DISPLACE

The only thing left to do is mold the background image onto the type. Select the Background layer and choose Filter ➤ Distort ➤ Displace. The Horizontal and Vertical Scale values determine the degree to which Photoshop shifts the pixels in the image. Larger values result in a deeper emboss effect. Feel free to experiment, but I recommend that you set the Vertical Scale to the same amount you used for the first Gaussian Blur radius—e.g., 12 for 400-pixel type—and the Horizontal Scale value to about half that. This way, the text will appear to bow upward and slightly to the left.

Select the Tile radio button from the Displacement Map options; the Undefined Areas setting is irrelevant. After you click OK, Photoshop will ask you what file you want to use as the displacement map. Select the separate PSD file you saved earlier. Photoshop shifts the pixels according to the lightness of the pixels in the displacement map, with white shifting the most and gray shifting the least. The result is a gradual bending of the background pattern across the blurred pixels (26.8).

### A WORLD OF VARIATIONS

If you spend some time experimenting with this technique, you'll quickly discover dozens of permutations. The truth is, you can combine the Lighting Effects and Displace filters to produce all kinds of 3-D effects, from raised letters to engraved type to embossed icons. Try different Gaussian Blur values when creating the text mask to get different emboss edges. And experiment with the direction of the light source in the Lighting Effects dialog box to make the text appear raised or sunken. These are some of Photoshop's most obscure filters, but once you learn how to use them, they can become some of your most powerful allies. Isn't that always how it is with the complicated stuff?

**26.6**

**26.7**

**26.8**

# CHAPTER 27
# WRAPPING IMAGES AROUND 3-D SHAPES

I f you're one of the tenacious few who've managed to successfully tackle three-dimensional drawing programs, congratulations. If not, you probably look at 3-D art with a combination of envy and trepidation. As a general rule, 3-D drawing applications demand effort, patience, spatial-reasoning skills, and a whole lot of hardware.

But you don't necessarily need a full-blown 3-D program to create 3-D art. Photoshop serves as a splendid backdoor into the third dimension. After all, the final output of virtually all 3-D applications is the rendered image file. Why not eliminate the middle man and create the image file directly in the image editor?

There are plenty of excellent 3-D plug-ins for Photoshop, including Zaxwerks 3D Invigorator; Andromeda Series 2, 3D; and Vertigo QuickSpace. But if you just want to get your feet wet, Photoshop 5 includes its own attempt at 3-D modeling called 3D Transform. Designed to test out packaging concepts,

the 3D Transform filter allows you to wrap an image around a 3-D primitive such as a cube, sphere, or cylinder. 3D Transform lacks lighting options and its controls are quite limited, but with a little effort and some help from Photoshop 5's layer effects, you can produce simple 3-D artwork (27.1) directly inside Photoshop without learning a new program.

27.1

## SCULPTING AN HOURGLASS WITH 3D TRANSFORM

The first step in wrapping an image around a 3-D shape is to select the grayscale or RGB image that you want to wrap. You do this by copying the image to its own independent layer. Although you *can* apply 3D Transform directly to the Background layer, it's not a good idea because Photoshop fuses the 3-D shape to the background, preventing you from moving it. By starting with a separate layer, you give yourself the freedom to modify the 3-D shape long after you create it.

Choose Filter ➤ Render ➤ 3D Transform. Photoshop brings up a dialog box of 3-D drawing tools. To draw an hourglass, select the cylinder tool (by pressing the C key) and drag inside the central image area of the dialog box. The cylinder is the only kind of shape to which you can add and subtract points—perfect for making cones, goblets, and hourglasses. Press the + key to select the add-point tool and click in the middle of the right side of the cylinder. This inserts a new smooth point. Then click twice more on the right side—once midway above the middle point and again midway below the point. You should now have three evenly spaced points along the right side of the cylinder.

Now to edit the shape. Using the hollow arrow tool (which you get by pressing the A key), drag the middle point inward. This narrows the waist of the cylinder symmetrically, producing an hourglass (27.2). Drag the points along the top and bottom of the shape to scale and rotate it into the desired position. Drag other points to finesse the curves. The best way to get a sense of what moving a point does is to just jump in and test it. If you don't like the result, just drag the point back where it was. (Strangely, the Undo command doesn't work inside the 3D Transform dialog box.) Press ⌘/Ctrl+spacebar and click to zoom in and get a closer look.

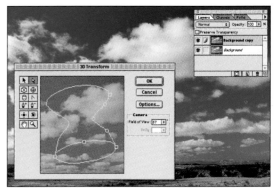

27.2

Once you get the basic wireframe shape exactly the way you want it, select the pan camera tool (by pressing the E key). This previews the shape in 3-D space. To hide the pixels outside the shape, click the Options button, turn off the Display Background check box (27.3), and click OK to return to the 3D Transform dialog box.

If you're feeling brave, you can move and rotate the hourglass in 3-D space using the pan camera and trackball tools. But if you're new to 3-D drawing, I don't recommend it. The trackball tool in particular is very difficult to anticipate: It has a habit of revealing gray areas toward the back of the 3-D shape (especially when you're working with cylinders), and without an undo, you can really mess things up fast.

Press Return/Enter to tell Photoshop to render the shape. The process can take a minute or more — especially when you're working with high-resolution images — but if you switch applications, Photoshop will keep rendering in the background. Once the rendering is complete, it's up to you. For my part, I duplicated the 3-D shape to create a series of increasingly smaller hourglasses rounding the horizon (27.4).

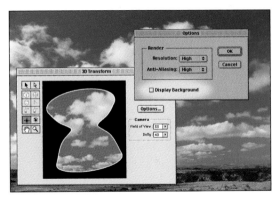

**27.3**

**27.4**

## LIGHTING WITH LAYER EFFECTS

The 3D Transform filter wraps the image around the hourglass, but it makes no attempt to light the shape, so you get no sense of dimension or depth. Sadly, Photoshop provides no easy means to apply true volumetric lighting. (You can use the Lighting Effects filter to create a plane-of-glass effect, but this makes the hourglass look flatter than ever.) The easiest way to fake 3-D lighting is with Photoshop 5's layer effects.

Control/right-click on the hourglass layer in the Layers palette to display a pop-up menu of commands. Choose the Effects command to bring up the five-paneled Effects dialog box, which enables you to apply shadows, glows, and bevels. The Effects command automatically applies a drop shadow by default. Edit the shadow's color, opacity, distance, and blur to get the effect you want. If you aren't interested in a drop shadow, turn off the Apply check box.

**27.5**

To apply a glow or bevel, select the desired option from the pop-up menu at the top of the Effects dialog box, and then click the Apply check box to enable the effect. Beveling the edges usually produces the best results. After selecting Bevel and Emboss from the top menu and turning on the Apply check box, choose Inner Bevel from the Style pop-up menu in the lower half of the dialog box (27.5). Raise the Depth and Blur values to their maximums of 20 and 50 pixels, respectively, to achieve the most gradual lighting possible. Edit the colors and other settings to your liking.

Once you've established the basic layer effects, you can modify the lighting in several ways. For example, suppose you want to create a row of hourglasses, as I did back in the introductory artwork (27.1). After creating the first hourglass layer, I duplicated the layer twice. Then I scaled and rotated the duplicates so they appeared to drift toward the horizon. I now had three unlit layers. Photoshop enables me to apply a new layer effect to just one layer at a time, so I tested out a few drop shadow and bevel effects on the first hourglass layer. When I got the effect I wanted, I copied the effect by Control/right-clicking on the cursive *f* symbol in the Layers palette and choosing the Copy Effects command. I then linked the two unlit hourglass layers together, Control/right-clicked on one of them, and chose Paste Effects To Linked (27.6). This subjected all three hourglasses to exactly the same effect. The benefit of having established a consistent point of reference is that at any time in the future I can choose the Global Angle command (27.7), which enables me to change the direction and distance of all highlights and shadows simultaneously.

## BOLSTERING THE BEVEL

The Inner Bevel effect is, of course, pure fakery, and it may or may not produce the volumetric lighting you're hoping to achieve. The most likely culprit for a bad bevel is Photoshop's maximum Depth setting of 20 pixels, which is insufficient to produce soft lighting in high-resolution artwork. Luckily, you can enhance the bevel by heaping one effect on top of another. First, resolve the layer effects onto layers of their own. Control/right-click on a beveled hourglass in the Layers palette and choose the Create Layers command. This separates the beveled edges onto two

grouped layers, labeled Inner Bevel Shadows and Inner Bevel Highlights, respectively. To enhance the Shadows layer, apply drop shadow and inner shadow effects to it. To enhance the Highlights layer, apply an outer glow effect. With little effort, you can create fake lighting to accommodate any resolution. You won't mistake 3D Transform for a true 3-D drawing environment, but it's a heck of a lot easier to use than the real thing.

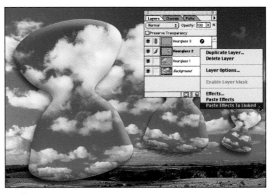

27.6

27.7

# CHAPTER 28
# PHOTOGRAPHING
# FOR PHOTOSHOP

Prior to the advent of computer imaging, photographers' choices were relatively limited. Compositing was by no means impossible, but the costs were high and the results were frequently crude. More often than not, the ideal solution was to set up a shot as commissioned and steer clear of special effects.

For example, if a client asked you to come up with a picture of a pig wearing a baseball cap and tennis shoes, your most efficient approach may have involved calling a few local animal trainers and asking if by chance they handle porkers who enjoy playing dress-up. If such a ham could be hired, the real fun would begin. The fact that clothes are generally designed to fit humans presents a few costuming challenges. How do you keep tapering hooves inside shoes? How do you attach a hat to an animal whose neck is higher than its forehead? And if by chance the beast is not as enthusiastic about fashion as advertised, how much time is wasted as the trainer pulls the battling bacon off the photographer's flattened form?

Chicago-based photographer Jeff Schewe has little doubt that the new ways for creating such images are an improvement over the old ways. Having graduated from the prestigious Rochester Institute of Technology more than a decade before anyone had even heard of Photoshop, Schewe is steeped in the traditional studio experience. He continues to use traditional tools, and his conventional training is every bit as applicable now as it was 20 years ago. The difference is that these days, he sets up his shots with an eye toward editing them in Photoshop.

So, if the need arises for Schewe to put clothes on a pig — as indeed it did — he photographs animal and clothing separately and combines them digitally.

*Each time I start a job, I establish one strategy that encompasses both the photography and the imaging. I can shoot exactly what I need and put it together exactly the way I want.*

JEFF SCHEWE

Schewe explains: "Each time I start a job, I establish one strategy that encompasses both the photography and the imaging. I can shoot exactly what I need and put it together exactly the way I want." Together, camera and computer give you absolute control over the creative process.

### HOW EXACTLY DO YOU DRESS UP A PIG?

"The Chicago Board of Trade commissioned me to do a piece that promoted trading in pork bellies. The headline was, 'Hogs are hipper than you think.' So we got this hog in the studio. He was someone's 4-H pet — his name was Pork Chop — and he came in a large dog carrier. I shot him on a white background (28.1). At first, it freaked him out because he couldn't see anything to stand on. Then, shortly after we got that problem resolved, he got this really relaxed look on his face; then he peed."

721

28.1

28.2

"Any time you photograph animals, you have to operate inside the framework of what they'll do. The art director wanted the pig's head up, but pigs are made to keep their noses in the dirt. We went through half a dozen types of food to see which one would get him to lift his head. The one he liked best was whole wheat bread. After a lot of messing around, we got fifty or so shots off. And out of those fifty, the art director and I got it down to three or four where he looked like he was smiling.

"After we selected the pig picture we wanted, I bought two pairs of kid's sneakers and positioned them very carefully to match the location and angle of the pig's feet. Then, I flew in a scrim to cast a pig-like shadow (28.2). And I put the hat up on a balloon."

I've gone ahead and composited the pig against his clothes to show how well they line up (28.3). The alignment isn't exact, but it's close enough to make the lighting consistent and keep the compositing time in Photoshop to an absolute minimum. How does Schewe line up his shots? "Back in the early days, I used to do complicated tracings. Now, I just hold up the transparency and eyeball it."

The final composition (28.4) involved more than nudging the shoes and hats into place and slapping them onto the pig. "It's very unusual to find an old pig with a curly tail. Their tails are typically docked,

**ARTIST:**
Jeff Schewe

**ORGANIZATION:**
Schewe Photography
624 West Willow
Chicago, Illinois 60614
312/951-6334
schewe@aol.com

**SYSTEM:**
Genesis 720 (DayStar, four 180MHz 604e CPUs)
16GB storage (two 8GB Seagate arrays with JackHammers SCSI accelerators)

**RAM:**
1GB total
925MB assigned to Photoshop

**MONITOR:**
Radius 17- and 21-inch PrecisionViews

**EXTRAS:**
Wacom 12 × 12 tablet, Light Source Colortron color sampler, Leaf 45 slider scanner, Shinko ColorStream II

**VERSION USED:**
Photoshop 5.0.

and this guy was no exception. So I had to curl the tail by cloning it inside Photoshop. I used the Spherize filter to distort his body and give him an extra 50 pounds. I think pigs look a little happier when they're fattened up." Then, there's that bizarre concern that never fails to pop up in commercial mammal photography. "The art director wasn't terribly comfortable with the exact state of the genitalia, so I more or less unisexed him."

## MATCHING BACKGROUNDS

When photographing his raw images, Schewe is always careful to match the position of his elements and the lighting conditions. But he's equally careful to match backgrounds. "According to the old wisdom — prior to computer imaging — you used a white background whenever you wanted to composite something, so the printer could make a knockout litho. In this day and age, unless you want white as your final background, it's the worst color to shoot against. Your edges become overly hot, making compositing very difficult.

"So, I try to make sure that I photograph all elements against a background that matches or is at least appropriate to the final background. For example, the Fruit of the Loom ad shows a bull's head

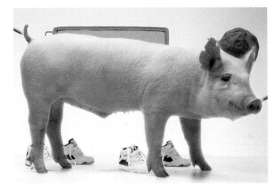

28.3

28.4

**OTHER APPLICATIONS:**
Adobe Illustrator, QuarkXPress, Valis MetaFlow, Live Picture, Fractal Design Painter, Specular Collage

**WORK HISTORY:**
1978 — Received B.S. in Commercial Photography from Rochester Institute of Technology, graduated with highest honors.
1981 — Opened commercial advertising studio, specializing in large negative compositing and multiple-exposure work.

1984 — Bought first Mac out of back of semi, created first computer imaging job on proprietary system.
1991 — Created first job in Photoshop, structured Photoshop course at Center for Creative Imaging.
1993 — Bought into early adopter program for Live Picture, later brought in as alpha tester for the likes of xRes and Photoshop.

**FAVORITE MOTORCYCLE:**
BMW R1100GS ("After sitting in a darkened room for hours on end, I like to sit outside for a few hours on end.")

28.5

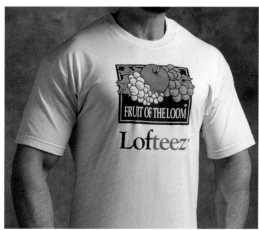

28.6

coming out of a muscular guy's body (28.5). I shot the live human element first (28.6) because the live element requires the most care. The art director and I had to figure out the pose, adjust the appearance of the lighting on the T-shirt, play with the body language, and make all the little decisions that come into play when setting up a shot.

"After we picked out a shot we were both happy with, I photographed the bull's head under the same light and against the same background (28.7). I positioned it so that the angle of the head and neck pretty much matched the body." With several days between the shots, Schewe must occasionally strike and repitch his backdrops. Doesn't that make it difficult to get everything exactly right? "I don't spend any time trying to register the background for one element to the background of another. I care about the density and the hue, so that the darkness is similar and the colors are approximately the same.

"Finally, I almost always shoot the background by itself. This gives me the option of working with the background as a separate element. So in this case, I masked the body, masked the head, put the head and the body together, and then put them both against the empty background. Because the backgrounds are consistent, I don't have any problems with haloing or weird edge artifacts. I have a little bit of latitude with my masks, and yet my edges appear completely nat-

28.7

ural, as if I had shot everything exactly as you see it."

Just out of curiosity, where in the world did Schewe come across such a photogenic bull's head? "One of the advantages of working in a big city is that there's no end to the weird stuff a photo-stylist can find. You wouldn't believe the junk you can find if you search long enough. As I recall, we rented two bull's heads for this job, one black and one brown. I think it cost me around $100." Decapitated bulls at $50 a head — there's an offer you can't refuse.

## MIXING MULTIPLE LIVE ELEMENTS

When Schewe combines living and inanimate elements, he always starts off by shooting the less predictable living item. Then, he sets up the more obedient inanimate objects based on the position and lighting of the live ones. By starting with the most chaotic element in a composition, he can achieve higher levels of control and order as he works through the job.

But how does it work when he has to shoot two or more live elements? "One job I did called for a centaur — in this case, half woman, half Shetland pony (28.8). Even in Chicago, you can't rent one of those, so I had to merge a woman and a pony together. Any time I work with two live elements, I start with the less intelligent and less versatile of the two. So I had to shoot the pony first and work within the limitations of what he could do.

"After taking a lot of shots, we managed to get an attentive pose with the head high up (28.9). I'm imagining the woman taking the place of the pony's head, so I need the neck nice and vertical. Once I got the transparency back from the lab, I was able to position the woman so she stood at the same three-quarter angle as the animal's head (28.10). We also outfitted her in a wig that was more or less the same color as the pony's mane."

28.8

28.9

28.10

28.11        28.12            28.13

28.14

## METICULOUS PATHS FOR INTRICATE EDGES

Obviously, Schewe's compositions involve some complex masking. But he works a little bit differently from other artists. "I use paths to create about 80 percent of my selections (28.11). I usually draw the paths at 200 percent view size so that I can clearly see the line of demarcation between the subject and the background (28.12). I can literally decide while I'm creating the path exactly where I'm going to clip something. If I see a piece of material that looks goofy, no problem; I just clip it away."

Schewe acknowledges that paths can be exasperating and time consuming, particularly when taken to these extremes. "But I've found that if you spend the time up front making a really excellent selection, you spend far less time fixing problems in your final composition."

After Schewe completes his paths, he converts them to a selection, saves the selection as a mask, and adds soft edges where needed using filters such as Median and Gaussian Blur (28.13). "One of my strategies is to mimic the photographic resolution of an image as accurately as possible. If something is critically sharp in the photograph, I'll make sure it's critically sharp in the selection. If it's slightly soft in the photo, it'll be slightly soft in the selection. Again, it takes a while to get it just right, but it's worth it in the end."

## ALL AGAINST A GRADIENT BACKGROUND

Here again, Schewe layered his elements against an empty version of the background. "But this time I lit the background more dramatically, so that it was dark at the top and lighter at the bottom. Then, I played with the gradation and lighting inside Photoshop to get the final effect I was looking for (28.14)."

Merging the elements together was mostly a matter of blending the horse's neck into the woman's torso. "I selected the horse from the neck down and the woman from the waist up, then I layered them against my empty background with the woman in front (28.15). I added a layer mask to the front layer to fade out the woman's torso (28.16). I also had to distort the pony's mane to send it flowing into her hair, and I lightened her hair to match the mane. There's always a lot of back and forth work in an image like this, even when the original elements are so painstakingly matched."

28.15                         28.16

## PLAYING WITH SCALE

If a shot involves strictly inanimate objects, you might expect Schewe to set up the scene exactly as he wants it and steer clear of Photoshop. But that's rarely the case. "There are all kinds of reasons to shoot inanimate elements in groups and composite them in Photoshop." A good example is the spud family portrait that Schewe created for a potato fungicide ad (28.17), which toys with the notion of relative scale. "I've got three different levels of scale going on here. A potato isn't really big enough to wear a hat or jewelry. And both the potatoes and their accessories would have been dwarfed by the TV if they were really seated as close as they're pictured in the ad. So I had to shoot each of the three groups of items separately.

"The main background shot is the TV against a plain wall with this kind of skylight lighting (28.18). That's relatively a straight shot — I may have gone in there and experimented a little bit with the gradations. Then, I propped the potatoes against a little model of a sofa (28.19). The pattern on the sofa is even miniaturized so that the flowers look the same relative size as they would on a real sofa.

28.17

**28.18**

**28.19**

"I had to play with the light so that the potatoes cast the same shadows as the TV, despite their smaller size. This was largely a matter of bringing the lights in closer and adjusting the intensity. I also included a little blue light down in front so it looked like a glow was coming from the TV. You can see that the blue glow doesn't exactly match the blue from the TV screen — it's a little more purple — but I was able to correct that when I composited the images in Photoshop (28.20). The light was really just a color cue so I could see how a cool glow would reflect off the potato bodies.

"Then, I needed the beanie for the baby spud, the pearls for Mom, and the glasses and pipe for Dad (28.21). I shot two pipes because the art director couldn't decide which one he wanted to use. There was also a discussion about whether we should add earrings to the side of Mom, so the mannequin actually has a couple of earrings stuck to her head. As usual, I had to adjust the lighting, including bringing the blue glow in from the left side. That sheet next to the mannequin is there to reflect the glow onto the beanie. Then, I shot it all to a single piece of film to keep the scanning to a minimum.

"The one element that's strictly digital is the smoke coming off the pipe (28.22). I added the smoke inside Photoshop by airbrushing with a small brush and light Exposure settings. I believe I split the pipe and glasses onto separate layers and then added the smoke on another layer in between the two. That way, I could erase the smoke and adjust the Opacity without harming any of my original elements.

"My one big conceptual contribution was to put a bowl of potato chips on top of the TV (28.23). The art director loved that. But then, somebody actually wrote the company to complain about the suggestion of cannibalism." Either it's a tuber-based homage to *Soylent Green*, or these are some very sick taters.

28.20

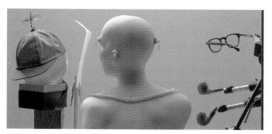

28.21

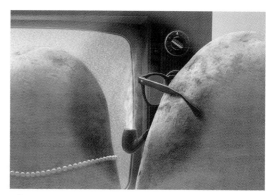

28.22

28.23

28.24

28.25                          28.26

## REFLECTIONS AND REFRACTIONS

According to Schewe, glass and water are some of the hardest substances to photograph. "Because of the way they reflect and refract the elements around them, you have to be very careful with your lighting." Things become even more complicated in the compositing phase. Any time you position an element near glass or water, you duplicate and distort the element to account for reflecting and refracting.

Schewe's snowglobe artwork is an example of just how difficult the process can get. "The concept was to take a snowglobe filled with a little snowy golf scene and then composite it against a stock photo of a golf course (28.24). Again, we have an issue of scale — an enlarged globe against a reduced background — but the more complex task is the globe itself. I guess I could have built a little golf scene inside the globe, kind of like a ship in a bottle. But I doubt that would have given me enough control over the lighting and refraction. For me, it was easier to photograph the pieces and glue them together inside Photoshop."

## WITH AND WITHOUT FLAKES

"I started by shooting a snowglobe on a stand, under what appeared to be hard outdoor light (28.25). I set the globe against a green background with a blue overhead to simulate the general appearance of grass and sky. The globe had a rubber stopper at the bottom of it so I could empty the water and fill it up again. After shooting it empty, I took several shots of the globe with the snow floating around inside it (28.26). Interestingly enough, to get the amount of snow I wanted, I had to break open three small Jesus snowglobes and steal the snowflakes from them."

Schewe modeled the contents of the globe from scratch (28.27). "I contoured the base out of foam and coated it with fake snow. The miniature trees came from a model train set. I painted a long thin dowel to make the flagpole, then I added a piece of red tape for the flag."

## INNER AND OUTER REFRACTIONS

Having photographed his raw materials, Schewe began to assemble them in a layered Photoshop file. "I started by masking away the background behind my snowy golf scene. Then, I used Filter ➢ Distort ➢ Spherize to warp the scene around the globe (28.28)." Schewe spent some time examining the way a globe refracts light to get his layers just right. "A glass ball is a curious thing. It bulges elements inside it, but it flips and pinches the stuff behind it. If you look at the original globe shot (28.25), you'll notice a layer of blue along the bottom of the glass. That blue is actually hovering a few feet above the frame." Peering through two surfaces of curved glass — one concave, the other convex — turns the world upside-down.

"To get this effect, I selected a portion of the stock photo background, rotated it 180 degrees, and then applied Filter ➢ Distort ➢ Pinch two or three times in a row (28.29). I think I also used Spherize with a negative setting a couple of times to give it some roundness. After that, I added my spherized golf scene (28.30). Since it's just behind one layer of glass, it appears rightside up."

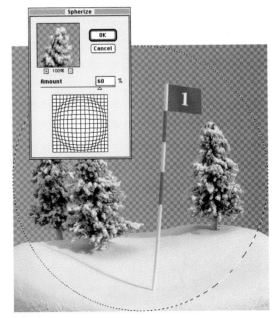

**28.28**

**28.29**

**28.30**

**28.27**

## REINSTATING THE REFLECTIONS

By this point, Schewe had covered up the reflections from the original globe, which diminished much of the realism of the image. To restore the reflections, he selected some of the highlights from the base globe layer and duplicated them onto a new layer.

"The best selection tool for this purpose is Select ➤ Color Range. The Color Range command has a great inclusion/exclusion capability, but it's global — that is, it selects colors from all over the image that fall inside the range. So, when I use Color Range, I make three passes. With the same colors selected, I'll run high, medium, and low Fuzziness values. I'll save each selection to a separate channel. Then, I'll combine elements from each of those channels to create the final mask."

After arriving at a satisfactory mask, Schewe selected the highlights — which I've set against black to make them easier to see (28.31) — and copied them to a new layer, which he dragged to the top of the stack. Then, he selected Lighten from the blend mode pop-up menu in the Layers palette, which instructed Photoshop to hide any pixels in the reflection layer that were darker than the pixels below. The result was a universally lightening effect (28.32).

## SPRINKLING THE SNOWFLAKES

The last step was to add the floating snowflakes. "The snowflakes needed to be in front of the trees and pinched background, so I had to select them from the snowflake shot and composite them on top." Again, Schewe selected the flakes with the Color Range command (28.33). Then, he pasted the flakes on top of the composition (28.34). "The interesting thing here is that the flakes already had reflections built into them, because I photographed them inside the globe. So it didn't matter if I stacked them on top of the reflection layer or underneath; either way, it looked the same."

## MERGING PASSION AND PROFIT

In the periodic skirmishes between photographers and digital artists, Schewe manages to occupy both fronts. It's a lucky thing, too, because his photography gives him a clear advantage over artists who depend on stock images. "One of the things I try to emphasize is that you just can't take disparate images, jam them together in Photoshop, and expect them to be convincing. You can be really skilled and create an interesting montage, but you'll never achieve realism. It's the difference between a photographic marriage and a digital relationship."

Schewe manages to marry image capture and image manipulation so seamlessly (28.35, 28.36) that you'd swear there was never any doubt in his mind that he wanted to be a digital artist. But in truth, his transition to computers had as much to do with maintaining his livelihood as following his creative passions. At the risk of sounding crass, Photoshop is where the money is.

"Right about the time Photoshop came out, I had a couple of jobs where the computer imaging paid twice as much as I made for the photography. It was immediately clear to me that these computer people were taking a big chunk of the overall production pie."

Schewe did what any enterprising photographer would do. After quickly assessing that there was no beating 'em, he joined 'em. "I rented a Macintosh IIci (roughly equivalent to a 386 PC) and spent the weekend doing a job and learning Photoshop at the same time. I picked up the computer Friday night, and I

28.31

28.32

28.33

28.34

had the job done Monday morning. My wife came in and found me asleep at the keyboard.

"The final piece was output to 4 × 5 film, and the client was tickled to death. At that time, I charged just about what it cost me to rent the computer for the imaging. It was definitely a valuable way to start out." Schewe has been evolving his craft on the job ever since.

28.35

28.36

# CHAPTER 29
# INVENTING PHOTO-REALISTIC WORLDS

Eric Chauvin has a dream job. From his home on the coast of northern Washington, about 45 minutes south of the Canadian border, he creates digital matte paintings for major studio movies and television shows. "I've created the mattes for every episode of *Babylon 5* that has a matte shot in it, with the exception of the original pilot." How did Chauvin land such a cushy client? "While I was working at Industrial Light & Magic (ILM), I was hired to do a single painting for the first regular episode of the show. I created this little 1MB painting entirely in Photoshop on my home computer and then e-mailed it down to the production in Los Angeles. Two weeks later a check arrived in the mail. It couldn't have gone any easier."

While at ILM, Chauvin worked on several feature film projects including *The Mask, Forrest Gump, Jumangi,* and *The American President.* After three years at ILM, he left to pursue his burgeoning freelance career. "By the end of the first season, I was averaging one painting for every episode. By the end of the second season, I was up to three or four shots per episode. It exponentially increased as the seasons progressed. They've also given me a great deal of creative latitude; very rarely will I turn something in and have them send it back and ask me to make some changes. As far as clients go, they're wonderful people to work with."

For the studio, hiring a talented artist with low overhead has its rewards as well. "Warner Brothers owns and distributes *Babylon 5,* but a team of independent producers really runs the show. They took over a warehouse in Sun Valley, retrofitted it to shoot sound,

> *I use Photoshop to paint in elements, add shadows and haze, adjust the lighting, and fill in textures. I can take an entirely fabricated 3-D rendering and turn it into something that looks like a real set.*
>
> ERIC CHAUVIN

and built their own sets. Because of that, they can do an episode — including all these effects shots — for under a million bucks. For an hour-long sci-fi show, that's a bargain."

From his house, Chauvin has also worked on all three recent *Star Trek* television series, as well as such films as *Sleepers* and the 20th anniversary *Star Wars: Special Edition* trilogy. When I first spoke with Chauvin he was working on the Robert Zemeckis film *Contact,* less than a month away from its scheduled debut. Having already seen three or four previews myself, I figured *Contact* would already be in the can. "Oh no, they'll be working on it until the absolute last minute. The shot that's going to kill me is due in seven days.

"I'm really fortunate. I knew at some point I'd be able to break away and work freelance. But I had no idea I'd be able to do it this soon. Almost all my peers have been doing matte painting longer than I have, and they're all very talented. My advantage is really

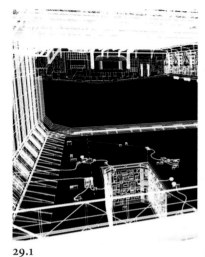

29.1                              29.2                                        29.3

the computer. Programs like Photoshop have permitted me to be competitively priced, turn out a good product, and do it much quicker than I could if I were using older techniques and materials."

## THE BASIC MATTE PROCESS

Up until five years ago, a matte painting was a still background image painted onto glass. But with the help of digital technology, modern mattes are actually short animated sequences that feature tiny people milling about, birds flying through the air, and water cascading over falls. Chauvin creates his digital scenes by constructing a three-dimensional wireframe model in Form·Z (29.1), rendering and sometimes animating elements from ElectricImage (29.2), editing and compositing the still portion of the backdrop in Photoshop (29.3), and putting the whole thing together in After Effects.

"I spend most of my time in Form·Z simply because the modeling is such an intricate process. The rest of my time is pretty evenly split between ElectricImage,

**ARTIST:**
Eric Chauvin

**ORGANIZATION:**
BlackPool Studios
P O Box 175
Bow, Washington 98232
360/766-6140
*http://www.blackpoolstudios.com*
echauvin@sos.net

**SYSTEM:**
PowerTower Pro 225 (Power Computing)
15GB storage

**RAM:**
500MB total
125MB assigned to Photoshop

**MONITOR:**
ViewSonic Pro Series 21-inch PT810 and 15-inch 15ES

**EXTRAS:**
Radius VideoVision, Exabyte 8mm tape drive, Polaroid SprintScan, Wacom 9 × 12 inch ArtZ

Photoshop, and After Effects. The Photoshop work is probably the most subtle, but it's also some of the most important. Without Photoshop, the 3-D images would have a synthetic appearance that would immediately brand them as fake. I use Photoshop to paint in elements, add shadows and haze, adjust the lighting, and fill in textures. I can take an entirely fabricated 3-D rendering and turn it into something that looks like a real set."

## CAN'T AFFORD THE HIGH-END?

Together, the full versions of Form•Z and ElectricImage cost somewhere in the neighborhood of $6,500, as much as a highly sophisticated computer system. Chauvin saved a little money by splitting the cost of ElectricImage with the producers of *Babylon 5*, but what's a mere mortal with limited means to do?

You could do the same thing Chauvin did when he was first starting out. Not so long ago, Chauvin did all his 3-D work in Specular International's Infini-D, an all-in-one 3-D program for the Mac that runs about $450. "A lot of the early episodes of *Babylon 5* feature mattes that I created in Infini-D. I haven't used Infini-D in about three years now, but I still look back on it fondly. It served my needs at the time, and it gave me the rudimentary knowledge I needed to create images using 3-D tools."

## LITTLE IMAGES FOR BIG MOVIES

When you see a spectacular other-worldly landscape projected onto a massive two-story screen, you naturally assume that the resolution of the image must be fantastic. If a magazine cover equates to a 20MB file, a film image must be 10 or 20 times that large. But in fact, Chauvin's images are relatively modest in size. "Different studios have different pixel dimensions that they want you to work in, and they're all very secretive about it. But in general, we're talking in the neighborhood of 2,000 pixels wide × 1,000 pixels or less tall, depending on the aspect ratio of the movie." And because it's film, Chauvin spends all his time in RGB. This means the largest digital frame for a major film such as *Star Wars* weighs in at less than 10MB.

"That doesn't sound like many pixels when you think how big the image appears on screen. But the best you can do is to resolve at the resolution of the film. Even 70mm film stock is relatively small — each frame is less than three inches wide. The resolution we use makes the digital images look every bit as smooth as the live-action stuff." Sometimes too smooth. Occasionally, Chauvin has to add a little bit of noise so that his matte painting matches the graininess of the film.

### VERSION USED:
Photoshop 5.0

### OTHER APPLICATIONS:
Adobe After Effects, ElectricImage Animation System, Autodessys Form•Z

### WORK HISTORY:
1987 — Hired at mortgage company — got so bored he spent most time writing golf statistic program in Lotus 1-2-3.
1989 — Entered graduate school, introduced to ILM matte painter who critiqued his paintings.

1991 — Got job as "glorified brush cleaner" for Steven Spielberg movie *Hook*; painted mattes for *Star Trek V* and *Memoirs of an Invisible Man*.
1993 — Landed full-time job at ILM; used Photoshop for the first time to paint digital mattes for *Young Indiana Jones*; won Emmy for visual effects.
1995 — After moonlighting as matte artist for *Babylon 5*, eventually left ILM to freelance full time.

### FAVORITE RIDING MOWER:
Craftsman 19.5HP ("With 2.5 acres of lawn, I really need it.")

**29.4**

## THE EMPIRE SHUTTLE BAY

A good example of the very least that Chauvin does in Photoshop is the shuttle bay matte he created for the rerelease of *The Empire Strikes Back* (29.4). "This shot is supposed to take place inside one of the big star destroyers. In the original movie, there was no shuttle bay shot of any kind, but George Lucas decided it was necessary to show Darth Vader moving from one scene to another. So they lifted a sequence of Vader walking down a gangplank that was originally shot for *Return of the Jedi*. They had me create this establishing scene to edit in front of it."

If the scene is new, why does it look so familiar? "The art director reasoned that the Empire liked to use a generic docking bay plan, so I modeled this scene after the old Death Star bays in *Star Wars* and *Return of the Jedi*. But they gave me total freedom to enhance the design and set the camera angle. I created the ceiling and gantry from scratch. I also added some cables and other elements to give the painting some depth. But the walls and floors are almost identical to the sets they built back in the '70s and '80s."

Although Chauvin modeled every cable, box, and crevice in Form·Z and rendered the surface textures from ElectricImage, he assembled the bits and pieces into a complex layered file in Photoshop (29.5). Why render groups of elements in a 3-D program and composite them in Photoshop when you can simply render the whole scene out of ElectricImage in one fell swoop? "It takes a little effort to break up the scene into pieces, but it doesn't take any more time for ElectricImage to do the rendering. Another plus is that Photoshop gives me a lot more flexibility by allowing me to isolate elements and apply different lighting effects. For example, in the case of the shuttle bay, I was able to quickly use the Levels command to make the walls a little lighter than the floor. I can also filter individual elements and make other minor tweaks that would involve a lot of work in ElectricImage."

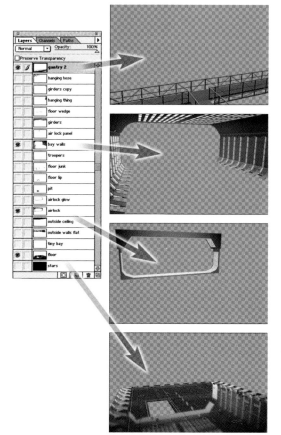

**29.5**

**PAINTING THE VOID OF SPACE**

One of the few elements that Chauvin created entirely in Photoshop was the layer of stars at the bottom of the stack. While his basic approach is similar to the one used by Greg Vander Houwen (Chapter 19), Chauvin's medium compels him to employ more subtlety. Chauvin's stars are projected onto huge movie screens, where a single pixel may grow to a half inch tall. If the stars are too numerous or too bright, the effect looks garish and fake. By contrast, Vander Houwen has to exaggerate his stars slightly so they survive dot gain and other darkening factors unique to the printing process.

That said, here's how Chauvin made his stars: He started by filling his background layer with black. Then he duplicated that layer and applied the Add Noise filter with a value of 68 set to Uniform. After pressing ⌘/Ctrl+F to reapply the filter and disperse the noise more evenly, he applied Image ➢ Adjust ➢ Threshold set to about 100 (29.6). He applied the Screen blend mode to the layer and set the Opacity to 50 percent to complete the dim background stars.

Next, he returned to the background layer and applied the Add Noise filter twice more with two whacks at ⌘/Ctrl+F. He again chose the Threshold command, but this time he set the value to 115 to create the effect of fewer bright stars. With Screen applied to the layer above, the work of combining bright and dim stars was already done (29.7), so he merged the two layers into one.

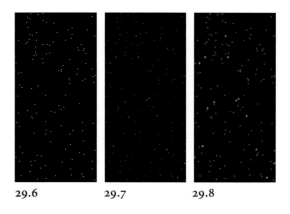

29.6                    29.7                    29.8

"If I were to send this directly to TV or film, these white and gray pixels would pop out like pinholes in the film. To fix this, I applied a little Gaussian Blur." Chauvin used a Radius value of 0.5. Then he chose the Levels command (⌘/Ctrl+L) and lowered the third Input Levels value to 70. This restored the brightness of the blurred stars (29.8).

Chauvin cautions that not all the starfields in *Star Wars* were created in this way. But in every star scene created by Chauvin, these are the stars you see. Who would have guessed that Luke Skywalker battles the Dark Force in a tumult of Add Noise?

29.9

29.10

## PLAYING WITH THE LIGHT

Chauvin spends a good half of his time in Photoshop adjusting lights and shadows. "It's very rare that I can set up my lights in ElectricImage exactly the way I want them. Also, ElectricImage doesn't do ray tracing, so it can't accurately match the way reflections look in real life. Sometimes I'll render an image with several different lighting variations and combine them inside Photoshop. I'll put the two renderings on different layers and just erase through one to reveal the other. I also spend a lot of time with the dodge and burn tools, which are great for creating highlights and shadows based on the original colors in the image. There's just no sense knocking yourself out over lighting in ElectricImage when you can create more realistic effects inside Photoshop."

The floor of the bay is an example of an area that required lots of image-editing attention (29.9). "First, I rendered the reflected light and floor onto separate layers. Then I created a separate file with noise in it. I used Layer ➤ Transform ➤ Perspective to splay the noise so it was larger at the bottom and smaller at the top. Then I applied it to the light layer as a displacement map (using Filter ➤ Distort ➤ Displace) to give the light a modeled look (29.10). I also created a gradient mask that went from white at the bottom to black at the top and then blurred the light within that mask. This way, the light grows less focused, and it moves farther away from the floor's surface."

Chauvin tells ElectricImage to automatically generate an alpha channel along with each rendered image. These alpha channels prove useful not only for compositing the rendered elements in Photoshop, but also for adding lighting effects. "The lights around the air lock and bay walls looked a little flat right after I rendered them (29.11). So I generated alpha channels for the lights from ElectricImage.

"In Photoshop, I blurred the alpha channels to soften them a little (29.12). Then I loaded the side lights from the alpha channel as a selection and lightened these areas with the Levels command. This created the reflections along the wall (29.13). To get that blue glow around the air lock, I created a new layer and loaded the middle lights as a new selection. Then I filled the selection with light blue and applied the Screen mode."

## THE TINY BAY ACROSS THE WAY

If you look closely at the final painting (29.14), you may spy a tiny bay on the far side of the shuttle entrance (highlighted orange in 29.14). "That's really just a distant shot of this same bay. In ElectricImage, I moved my camera so it was really far away from the model and looking in the opposite direction. Then I rendered it independently and added it to the Photoshop composition."

## THE ARCHITECTURE OF CLOUD CITY

Chauvin also provided a couple of new matte paintings for the Cloud City sequence, home of Lando Calrissian and demise of Han Solo. "The Cloud City sequence features these humongous cylindrical buildings set against an orange sunset sky. Rather than trying to render the sky, I just went out and shot a few rolls of film with a 35mm camera (29.15)."

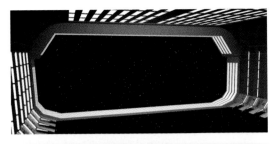

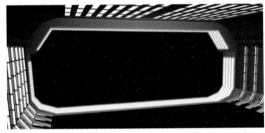

29.11 (TOP), 29.12 (MIDDLE), 29.13 (BOTTOM)

29.14

29.15

## ELIMINATING FILM GRAIN

Film grain on a still image is death at the box office. Normally, film grain is in constant motion because it changes from one frame to the next. But grain on a matte image just sits there. Even a hint of grain can make a still painting look like a cheesy backdrop. To kill the grain in his Cloud City sky, Chauvin took several pictures in a row and averaged them. He mounted a 35mm camera on a tripod and shot a dozen or more pictures to standard print film. Then he scanned them and layered the 10 best copies inside a single Photoshop document.

After aligning the images as best he could — "the registration wasn't exact, I just eyeballed them" — he adjusted the Opacity of each layer according to a secret formula hitherto known only at ILM. "The background layer is always opaque. You set the Opacity of the next layer up to 50 percent, then the layer above that to 33 percent, then 25, 20, 17, 14, 12, 11, and finally 10. In each case, you're taking the layer's number and dividing it into 100. So Layer 2 into 100 is 50 percent; Layer 3 into 100 is 33. You keep going until you get to Layer 10, which goes into 100 10 times."

Are 35mm pictures common elements in big-budget Hollywood movies? "Normally, I like to work from better source material than a handful of marginally registered snapshots. But clouds are pretty amorphous objects so a little softness didn't hurt them."

**29.16**

**29.17**

**29.18**

**29.19**

## ADDING BUILDINGS IN THE SKY

Chauvin designed the models for his Cloud City (29.16) from concept art provided by Lucasfilm. As with the shuttle bay art, Chauvin rendered his buildings in groups and assembled the pieces in Photoshop, starting with the background buildings (29.17) and working forward (29.18). "This gave me the freedom to change the relative locations of the foreground and background buildings. In the final version of the painting (29.19), you'll notice that I've moved the background buildings around and I have a lot more of them. In some cases, I copied and pasted parts of buildings to make the town look more crowded. I worked very carefully, of course; I don't think there are any two buildings that are absolutely identical. I may have spent close to an hour cloning elements in Photoshop, but it was a heck of a lot easier than rerendering the scene in ElectricImage."

## TURNING DOWN THE LIGHTS

The issue of light raises its head in this painting just as it did in the shuttle bay scene. Most of the buildings had rings of office lights ringing their perimeters. Chauvin rendered the lights out of ElectricImage, but later decided he had gone a little overboard. "The original windows were too bright (29.20). It was like every office was filled to capacity with fluorescent bulbs. In print, the effect probably looks kind of cool. But you have to remember, the scale of these buildings on screen was gigantic. Sizzling windows would have really distracted from the foreground activity."

Naturally, Chauvin turned down the lights in Photoshop. "In ElectricImage, I turned off all my light sources and made the windows totally luminous. This made the windows white and everything else black. Then I rendered that view (29.21), brought it into Photoshop as an alpha channel, and loaded it as a selection."

The next step was to stroke black around the outline of the selection. Chauvin could have used Edit ➤ Stroke or he could have gone with Select ➤ Modify ➤ Border. But he had something slightly more elaborate in mind. "In my experience, Border does a terrible job of making an even antialiased edge. I used Select ➤ Modify ➤ Contract to make the selection slightly smaller, I think I feathered it to soften the edges, then I saved it to a separate channel." In the Channels palette, Chauvin ⌘/Ctrl-clicked the first channel to load it and ⌘/Ctrl+ Option/Alt-clicked the second channel to subtract it from the first. Then he made a new layer and filled the selection with black (29.22). When composited at full opacity against the buildings, these window outlines had the magical effect of dimming the lights (29.23).

### THE TEAMING MASSES

Every thriving metropolis swarms with activity, and Cloud City is no exception. "If you look closely at the

29.20     29.21     29.22     29.23

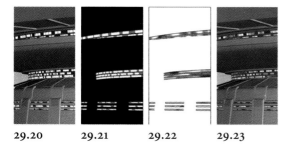

29.24 (TOP), 29.25 (BOTTOM)

finished painting, you'll notice that the floor of the balcony (lower right corner, 29.19) isn't very polished. That's because in the movie, this area is totally filled with people. This particular iteration of the scene appeared at the end of *Return of the Jedi*, where people across the galaxy are celebrating the Empire's defeat. You can't even see the railing through the crowds."

A hundred or so extras on the balcony wasn't deemed sufficient, so Chauvin was instructed to paint tiny crowds into the background. "Originally, I had painted a handful of tiny people in the lower courtyard off in the distance (29.24). But someone decided it didn't make sense for the background to be so sparse, so I added a ton of little specks to indicate the cheering crowds (29.25). I just scaled some noise and then painted on top of it."

If you compare Chauvin's early rendered models (29.18) to the finished city (29.19), you'll see that he's also added tiny spotlights, shadows, rust drools, spindly roof paraphernalia, and literally hundreds of other subtle elements, all inside Photoshop. "I keep massaging the image until it looks real. Most of the time, *real* means uneven and scuffed up. I guess I could return to ElectricImage and render this kind of stuff, but it's almost always easier to add the finishing touches in Photoshop."

### THE DINOSAUR MOVIE THAT NEVER GOT MADE

Not being acquainted with every one of Chauvin's matte paintings, it's terribly presumptuous of me to say this. But from what I've seen, Chauvin's masterpiece never made it to the big screen. "I created this painting (29.26) a couple of years ago for a movie version of *Dinotopia*, based on the children's book series by Jim Gurney. He's a very talented artist, so the illustrations in his book worked great as concept art. Unfortunately, the studio abandoned the project pretty early on so it was never finished. This is the first time I've ever displayed these images outside my demo tapes."

**29.26**

**29.27**

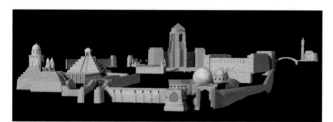

**29.28**

**29.29**

## MODELING DINOTOPIA

"When I model something in Form·Z, I almost always work in the wireframe mode. After using the program more or less every day of my life, I'm pretty familiar with what I'm doing, so the pieces usually come out the way I expect them to. But this model was an exception. The Dinotopia city had become sufficiently complex that I found it helpful to take the model into ElectricImage and do a quick render while I was modeling. I even assigned a few parts different colors — like green and blue — so I could discern them from the purple walls and buildings around them (29.27).

"After importing the model into ElectricImage, I applied the basic texture maps (29.28). The nice thing about having assigned garish colors up front is that I can see right off the bat where I've applied textures and where I haven't. After adding 20 or so textures, it's very easy to get mixed up and accidentally leave something unmapped. This way, if I see something that's electric purple, I can say, 'Oh, there's something I forgot to map.' It makes for fewer surprises when I start playing with the image in Photoshop."

## INTEGRATING THE NATURAL WORLD

"That's about as far as I took this in Form·Z and ElectricImage. I generally make my textures fairly generic, just enough to approximate the effect that I want. Then I go into Photoshop and age the walls, add the stains, paint the little statues, and generally add the realism. In this case, I also surrounded the city with a bunch of photographic elements like buildings, mountains, rocks, trees, and lots and lots of water. I suppose I could have tried to model this stuff, but it takes less time and ends up looking better if I do it in Photoshop.

"The first thing I did in Photoshop was fill in the central area of the city (29.29). I actually lifted these little buildings out of a book, which raises an interesting point. I prefer to use my own photo reference or work from royalty-free CDs. But it's sometimes necessary to reference copyrighted material.

"When I was at ILM, the company attorney spoke with us on the topic of sampling photographs. He explained that it was a gray area, but that it was kind of like sampling music, which he said is legal as long as the sample isn't too long and the song isn't dependent on the sample for its success. So on the rare occasions that I scan copyrighted material, I make sure I work the images until you can't find any specific similarities between the original photo and my edited version. In this case, I've cloned the buildings into different locations, scaled the buildings independently, combined two half buildings from different photos, painted in extra details, changed the lighting, and made absolutely every other modification I could think of." In effect, the original photograph serves as a template; Chauvin's finished piece is something altogether different.

"If the foothills in back of the city (29.30) look suspiciously like the Headlands in Marin County, California, it's because that's exactly what they are. This was back in the ILM days, so I just went out with my camera and took pictures of nearby hills that looked like they might go with the *Dinotopia* illustrations. The distant mountains are stock photos of the Swiss Alps."

29.30

29.31

## THE CASCADING FALLS

"I spent a lot of time looking at the waterfalls in Gurney's paintings to try and determine which falls I needed to shoot and from which angles. I finally came to the conclusion that if I was going to get the right kind of water, I would have to go to Niagara Falls. So I called a cameraman friend of mine, and we were on a plane for Buffalo, New York, three days later. We scouted the whole thing out that afternoon, spent the night at the Holiday Inn near the Falls, shot the water elements I needed the next day, and were back on a plane that night. I had the film transferred to videotape so I could see which sections I wanted to digitize. Then I had to go back and scale them, paint on them, and make the masks so they all fit into place (29.31). The payoff is that it's all real water so it moves exactly like you'd expect it to."

Naturally, Chauvin can't add full-motion video inside Photoshop. "The water you see here is just for reference. I replaced it with the moving footage inside After Effects. Since After Effects retains Photoshop's layering scheme, I can just sandwich the various falls in between the layers of building and rock." To see the completed scene in motion, play the QuickTime movie included on CD #2 at the back of this book.

### ERIC'S INTERMITTENT FLASHES OF FAME

You might envy Chauvin for the visibility of his work. After all, how many of us can name a piece we've done and hold out even a remote hope that someone has actually seen it? Yet here's a guy who can site a few examples and be relatively sure that no one in earshot has missed his paintings.

But Chauvin's work doesn't necessarily have the bang for the buck you might think. "If I had to create a complex matte painting from beginning to end without doing anything else, it would probably take me three weeks. Full time." And what are we talking about? Maybe a minute of film time? "No way. My work is usually measured in under 10 seconds. I've worked on shots that have been on screen for 2 seconds."

So just because we've all seen Chauvin's paintings doesn't mean we saw them for long. Good thing Mother Technology in Her infinite wisdom has equipped us with the Pause button.

# Corrections, Composites, and the Web

# Mapping and Correcting Colors

## What Is Color Mapping?

*Color mapping* is just a fancy name for shuffling colors around. For example, to map Color A to Color B simply means to take all the A-colored pixels and convert them to B-colored pixels. Photoshop provides several commands that enable you to map entire ranges of colors based on their hues, saturation levels, and, most frequently, brightness values.

### Color effects and corrections

Why would you want to change colors around? For one reason, to achieve special effects. You know those psychedelic horror movies that show some guy's hair turning blue while his face turns purple and the palms of his hands glow a sort of cornflower yellow? A grayscale version of this very effect appears in the second example of Figure 30-1. Although not the most attractive effect by modern standards — you may be able to harvest more tasteful results if you put your shoulder to the color wheel — psychedelic qualifies as color mapping for the simple reason that each color shifts incrementally to a new color.

But the more common reason to map colors is to enhance the appearance of a scanned image or digital photograph, as demonstrated in the third example in Figure 30-1. In this case, you're not creating special effects — you're just making straightforward color adjustments, known in the biz as *color corrections*. Scans are never perfect, no matter how much money you spend on a scanning device or a service bureau. They can always benefit from tweaking and subtle adjustments, if not outright overhauls, in the color department.

**Figure 30-1:** Nobody's perfect, and neither is the best of scanned photos (left). You can modify colors in an image to achieve special effects (middle) or simply fix the image with a few well-targeted color corrections (right). Too bad Photoshop hasn't delivered on its promised Remove Excessive Jewelry filter.

Keep in mind, however, that Photoshop can't make something from nothing. In creating the illusion of more and better colors, most of the color-adjustment operations that you perform actually take some small amount of color away from the image. Somewhere in your image, two pixels that were two different colors before you started the correction change to the same color. The image may look 10 times better, but it will in fact be less colorful than when you started.

It's important to keep this principle in mind because it demonstrates that color mapping is a balancing act. The first nine operations you perform may make an image look progressively better, but the tenth may send it into decline. There's no magic formula; the amount of color mapping you need to apply varies from image to image. But if you follow my usual recommendations — use the commands in moderation, know when to stop, and save your image to disk before doing anything drastic — you should be fine.

## The good, the bad, and the wacky

Photoshop stores all of its color mapping commands under the Image ⇨ Adjust submenu. These commands fall into three basic categories:

✦ **Color mappers**: Commands such as Invert and Threshold are quick-and-dirty color mappers. They don't fix images, but they can be useful for creating special effects and adjusting masks.

✦ **Easy color correctors**: Brightness/Contrast and Color Balance are true color correction commands, but they sacrifice functionality for ease of use. If I had my way, these commands would be removed from the Image ⇨ Adjust submenu and thrown in the dust heap.

✦ **Expert color correctors**: The third, more complicated variety of color correction commands provide better control, but they take a fair amount of effort to learn. Levels, Curves, and Hue/Saturation are examples of color correcting at its best and most complicated.

This chapter contains little information about the second category of commands for the simple reason that some of them are inadequate and ultimately a big waste of time. There are exceptions of course — Auto Levels is a decent quick fixer, and Variations offers deceptively straightforward sophistication — but Brightness/Contrast and Color Balance sacrifice accuracy in their attempt to be straightforward. They are as liable to damage your image as fix it, making them quite dangerous in a dull, pedestrian sort of way. I know because I spent my first year with Photoshop relying exclusively on Brightness/Contrast and Color Balance, all the while wondering why I couldn't achieve the effects I wanted. Then, one happy day, I spent about a half an hour learning Levels and Curves, and the quality of my images skyrocketed. So wouldn't you just rather learn it right in the first place? I hope so, because the die is cast.

# Quick Color Effects

Before we get into all the high-end gunk, however, I'll take a moment to explain the first category of commands, all of which happen to occupy one of the lower sections in the Image ⇨ Adjust submenu. These commands — Invert, Equalize, Threshold, and Posterize — produce immediate effects that are either difficult to duplicate or not worth attempting with the more full-featured commands.

## Invert

When you choose Image ⇨ Adjust ⇨ Invert (⌘/Ctrl+I), Photoshop converts every color in your image to its exact opposite, as in a photographic negative. As demonstrated in Figure 30-2, black becomes white, white becomes black, fire becomes water, good becomes evil, dogs romance cats, and the brightness value of every primary color component changes to 255 minus the original brightness value.

By itself, the Invert command is not sufficient to convert a scanned color photographic negative to a positive. Negative film produces an orange cast that the Invert command does not address. After inverting, you can use the Variations command to remove the color cast. Or avoid Invert altogether and use the Levels command to invert the image. Both Variations and Levels are explained later in this chapter.

Image ⇨ Adjust ⇨ Invert is just about the only color mapping command that retains every single drop of color in an image. (The Hue/Saturation command also retains colors under specific conditions.) If you apply the Invert command twice in a row, you arrive at your original image.

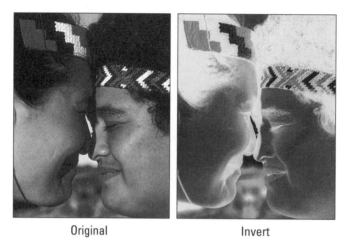

Original                    Invert

**Figure 30-2:** An image before the advent of the Invert command
(left) and after (right).

When you're working on a full-color image, the Invert command simply inverts the contents of each color channel. This means that the command produces very different results when applied to RGB, Lab, and especially CMYK images. Color Plate 30-1 shows the results of inverting a single image in each of these modes. The RGB and Lab images share some similarities, but you'll find all kinds of subtle differences if you study the backgrounds and the basic colors of the faces.

Inverting in CMYK is much different. Typically, the Invert command changes much of a CMYK image to black. Except in rare instances — such as in night scenes — the black channel contains lots of light shades and few dark shades. So when you invert the channel, it becomes extremely dark. To reverse this effect, I inverted only the cyan, magenta, and yellow channels in the right example of Color Plate 30-1. (I did this by inverting the entire image and then going to the black channel — ⌘/Ctrl+4 — and pressing ⌘/Ctrl+I again.) Though this approach is preferable to inverting the black channel, it prevents the blacks in the hair and shadows from turning white (which would be the only portions even remotely light had I inverted the black channel as well).

**Note**

Just so you know, when I refer to applying color corrections in the CMYK mode, I mean applying them after choosing Mode ⇨ CMYK Color. Applying corrections in the RGB mode when View ⇨ Preview ⇨ CMYK is active produces the same effect as when CMYK Preview is not selected; the only difference is that the on-screen colors are curtailed slightly to fit inside the CMYK color space. You're still editing inside the same old red, green, and blue color channels, so the effects are the same.

**Cross-Reference**

As I mentioned back in Chapter 16, inverting the contents of the mask channel is the same as applying Select ⇨ Inverse to a selection outline in the marching ants mode. In fact, this is one of the most useful applications of the filter. If you're considering inverting a color image, however, I strongly urge you to try out the SuperInvert filter contained in the Tormentia folder on CD-ROM #1 at the back of this book. It permits you to invert each channel independently and incrementally. Any setting under 128 lessens the contrast of the channel; 128 makes it completely gray; and any value over 128 inverts it to some degree.

## Equalize

Equalize is the smartest and at the same time least useful of the Image ➪ Adjust pack. When you invoke this command, Photoshop searches for the lightest and darkest color values in a selection. Then it maps the lightest color in all the color channels to white, maps the darkest color in the channels to black, and distributes the remaining colors to other brightness levels in an effort to evenly distribute pixels over the entire brightness spectrum. This doesn't mean that any one pixel will actually appear white or black after you apply Equalize; rather, that one pixel in at least one channel will be white and another pixel in at least one channel will be black. In an RGB image, for example, the red, green, or blue component of one pixel would be white, but the other two components of that same pixel might be black. The result is a higher contrast image with white and black pixels scattered throughout the color channels.

If no portion of the image is selected when you choose Image ➪ Adjust ➪ Equalize, Photoshop automatically maps out the entire image across the brightness spectrum, as shown in the upper right example of Figure 30-3. However, if you select a portion of the image before choosing the Equalize command, Photoshop displays a dialog box containing the following two radio buttons:

✦ **Selected Area Only**: Select this option to apply the Equalize command strictly within the confines of the selection. The lightest pixel in the selection becomes white, the darkest pixel becomes black, and so on.

✦ **Entire Image Based on Area**: If you select the second radio button, which is the default setting, Photoshop applies the Equalize command to the entire image based on the lightest and darkest colors in the selection. All colors in the image that are lighter than the lightest color in the selection become white, and all colors darker than the darkest color in the selection become black.

The bottom two examples in Figure 30-3 show the effects of selecting different parts of the image when the Entire Image Based on Area option is in force. In the left example, I selected a dark portion of the image, which resulted in over-lightening of the entire image. In the right example, I selected an area with both light and dark values, which boosted the amount of contrast between highlights and shadows in the image.

The problem with the Equalize command is that it relies too heavily on some pretty bizarre automation to be of much use as a color correction tool. Certainly, you can create some interesting special effects. But if you'd prefer to automatically adjust the colors in an image from black to white regardless of the color mode and composition of the individual channels, choose Image ➪ Adjust ➪ Auto Levels (⌘/Ctrl+Shift+L). If you want to adjust the tonal balance manually and therefore with a higher degree of accuracy, the Levels and Curves commands are tops. I explain all of these commands at length later in this chapter.

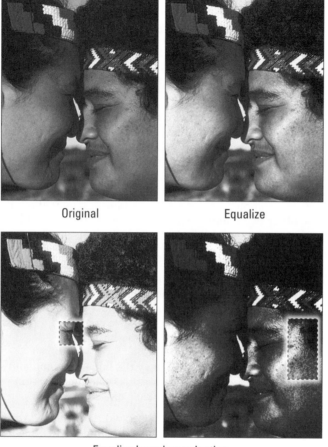

Original

Equalize

**Figure 30-3:** An image before (top left) and after (top right) applying the Equalize command when no portion of the image is selected. You can also use the brightness values in a selected region as the basis for equalizing an entire image (bottom left and right).

Equalize based on selection

## Threshold

I touched on the Threshold command a couple of times in previous chapters. As you may recall, Threshold converts all colors to either black or white based on their brightness values. When you choose Image ➪ Adjust ➪ Threshold, Photoshop displays the Threshold dialog box shown in Figure 30-4. The dialog box offers a single option box and a slider bar, either of which you can use to specify the medium brightness value in the image. Photoshop changes any color lighter than the value in the Threshold option box to white, and changes any color darker than the value to black.

Histogram

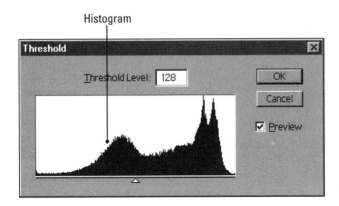

**Figure 30-4:** The histogram in the Threshold dialog box shows the distribution of brightness values in the selection.

The dialog box also includes a graph of all the colors in the image—even if only a portion of the image is selected. This graph is called a *histogram*. The width of the histogram represents all 256 possible brightness values, starting at black on the left and progressing through white on the right. The height of each vertical line in the graph demonstrates the number of pixels currently associated with that brightness value. Therefore, you can use the histogram to gauge the distribution of lights and darks in your image. It may seem weird at first, but with enough experience, the histogram becomes an invaluable tool, permitting you to corroborate the colors that you see on-screen.

**Tip**

Generally speaking, you achieve the best effects if you change an equal number of pixels to black as you change to white (and vice versa). So rather than moving the slider bar to 128, which is the medium brightness value, move it to the point at which the area of the vertical lines to the left of the slider triangle looks roughly equivalent to the area of the vertical lines to the right of the slider triangle.

The upper left example in Figure 30-5 shows the result of applying the Threshold command with a Threshold Level value of 120 (as in Figure 30-4). Although this value more or less evenly distributes black and white pixels, I lost a lot of detail in the dark areas.

As you may recall from my "Using the High Pass filter" discussion in Chapter 23, you can use Filter ⇨ Other ⇨ High Pass in advance of the Threshold command to retain areas of contrast. In the upper left image in Figure 30-5, I applied the High Pass filter with a radius of 1.0 pixel, followed by the Threshold command with a value of 125. In the two bottom images, I first chose an effects filter—Filter ⇨ Artistic ⇨ Watercolor on the left and Filter ⇨ Sketch ⇨ Bas Relief on the right—then I applied High Pass with a radius of 1.0 pixel followed by the Threshold command.

If the Threshold effects in Figure 30-5 are a bit austere, first clone the image to a layer and then mix the layer with the underlying original. Figure 30-6 shows all the effects from Figure 30-5 applied to layers subject to the Overlay blend mode and 50 percent Opacity. In each example, the translucent selection helps to add contrast and reinforce details in the original image.

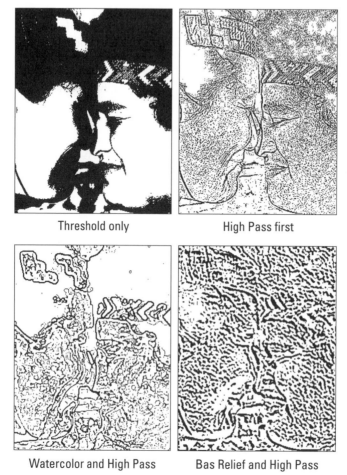

Threshold only

High Pass first

Watercolor and High Pass

Bas Relief and High Pass

**Figure 30-5:** By itself, the Threshold command tends to deliver flat results (top left). To better articulate the detail, apply High Pass and other filters prior to choosing Threshold.

Note

On a Mac, you can compare the before and after effects of any color correction command that includes a Preview check box in its dialog box by turning the check box off and then mousing down on the title bar. If the Video LUT Animation option in the Display & Cursors panel of the Preferences dialog box is active (as by default), turning the Preview check box off causes Photoshop to apply the Threshold settings to the entire screen. Unfortunately, Photoshop applies the effect separately to each color channel, creating a series of brightly colored areas that bear little resemblance to the actual black-and-white effect. To get a realistic picture of your image, leave the Preview check box turned on.

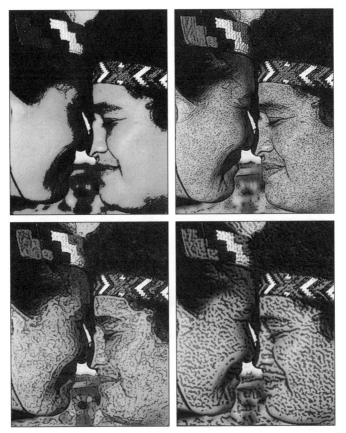

**Figure 30-6:** The Threshold operations from Figure 30-5 applied to separate layers, blended with the Overlay mode and an Opacity value of 50 percent.

If you want to achieve a colorful Threshold effect (like the one that appears when using Video LUT Animation on a Mac), try applying the Threshold command independently to each color channel. In an RGB image, for example, press ⌘/Ctrl+1 and then apply Image ⇨ Adjust ⇨ Threshold. Then press ⌘/Ctrl+2 and repeat the command, and press ⌘/Ctrl+3 and do it again. Color Plate 30-2 shows examples of what happens when I apply High Pass (with a Radius value of 3.0) and Threshold to independent color channels in the RGB, Lab, and CMYK modes. To soften the transitions and avoid trapping problems, I resampled each image up and down a couple of times, as described back in the "Antialiasing an image" section of Chapter 23.

# Posterize

The Posterize command is Threshold's rich cousin. Whereas Threshold boils down an image into two colors only, Posterize can retain as many colors as you like. However, you can't control how colors are mapped, as you can when you use Threshold. The Posterize dialog box does not provide a histogram or slider bar. Instead, Posterize automatically divides the full range of 256 brightness values into a specified number of equal increments.

To use this command, choose Image ➪ Adjust ➪ Posterize and enter a value into the Levels option box. The Levels value represents the number of brightness values that the Posterize command retains. Higher values result in subtle color adjustments; lower values produce more dramatic effects. The first example in Figure 30-7 shows an image subject to a Levels value of 8.

 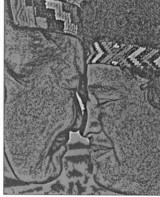

Posterize                    High Pass first

**Figure 30-7:** An image subject to the Posterize command with a Levels value of 8 (left). You can retain more detail in an image by applying the High Pass filter before using Posterize (right).

By now, you may be thinking, "By golly, if Posterize is so similar to Threshold, I wonder how it works when applied after the High Pass filter?" Well, you're in luck, because this is exactly the purpose of the second example in Figure 30-7. Here I chose the High Pass filter and entered 3.0 for the Radius. Then I applied the Posterize command with the same Levels value as before (8).

Now, just in case you've tried this same effect on your full-color image and thought, "Yech, this looks terrible—half the color just disappeared," the key is to apply High Pass and Posterize to a layered version of the image and then mix the effect with the underlying original. Color Plate 30-3 shows the results of applying the High Pass filter with a Radius of 3.0 and the Posterize command with a setting of 8 to the layered clone and then compositing layer and underlying original using each of three overlay modes from the Layers palette. The Luminosity option applies only the lights and darks in the layered image, allowing the colors in the underlying image to show through; Hard Light strengthens the light and dark shades; and Hue applies the colors from the layer with the saturation and brightness values from the original.

After flattening each image, I increase the saturation of the colors using Image ➪ Adjust ➪ Hue/Saturation (⌘/Ctrl+U), which I discuss in an upcoming section.

# Quick Corrections

Photoshop offers two quick-correctors under the Image ➪ Adjust submenu that I want to discuss before entering into the larger world of advanced color correction. Both are single-shot commands that alter your image without any dialog boxes or special options. The first, Desaturate, sucks the saturation out of a selection and leaves it looking like a grayscale image. The second, Auto Levels, automatically increases the contrast of an image according to what Photoshop deems to be the ideal brightness values.

## Sucking saturation

There's little reason to apply the Desaturate command to an entire image; you can just as easily choose Image ➪ Mode ➪ Grayscale to accomplish the same thing and dispose of the extra channels that would otherwise consume room in memory and on disk. I know of only two reasons to sacrifice all colors in the RGB mode:

✦ You want to retain the option of applying RGB-only filters, such as Lens Flare, Lighting Effects, and anything created with the Filter Factory.

✦ You intend to downsize the colors using Image ➪ Mode ➪ Indexed Colors and save the final image in the GIF format for use on the World Wide Web (as I discuss in Chapter 32).

But mostly, you'll use Desaturate to rob color from discrete selections or independent layers, neither of which the Grayscale mode can accommodate. For example, in Color Plate 30-4, I used Select ➪ Color Range to select all of the pumpkin except the eyes and mouth and a few speckly bits here and there. (I could have used the quick mask mode to tweak the selection and get it just right, but it didn't strike me as particularly important in this case.) I then applied Image ➪ Adjust ➪ Desaturate (⌘/Ctrl+Shift+U) to achieve the first example. To create the top right pumpkin, I chose Filter ➪ Fade Desaturate and changed the Opacity value to 50 percent, bringing back some of the original colors from the full-color original and achieving an only slightly desaturated pumpkin.

**Tip**

In case you missed that last paragraph, you can use Filter ➪ Fade (⌘/Ctrl+Shift+F) to back off the effects of any command under the Image ➪ Adjust submenu. As always, the Fade command is available immediately after you apply the color correction; if you so much as alter a selection outline, Fade goes dim.

Desaturate isn't the only way to suck colors out of an image. You can also invert the colors and mix them with their original counterparts to achieve a slightly different effect. The bottom row of Color Plate 30-4 shows what I mean. In the lower left example, I applied Invert (⌘/Ctrl+I) to my same Color Range selection. Then I pressed ⌘/Ctrl+Shift+F, changed the Opacity setting to 50 percent, and — here's the important part — selected Color from the Mode pop-up menu.

Note that the inverted and mixed colors are slightly different than the desaturated tones in the pumpkin above. When set to the Color blend mode, the colors in the inverted image should theoretically cancel out the colors in the underlying original. However, the Invert command doesn't change the saturation of the pixels, so the saturation of the inverted and original pixels are the same. As a result, some colors from the underlying image are allowed to show through, as the bottom left image shows.

The bottom right example shows what happened when I changed the Opacity to 70 percent, thus favoring the inverted colors. Why'd I do that? Maybe I just like blue pumpkins. Or more likely, I had a fourth spot to fill in the figure, and a blue pumpkin seemed like the guy to fill it.

By the way, you might be wondering why Adobe selected ⌘/Ctrl+Shift+U as the keyboard shortcut for Desaturate. Well, Desaturate is actually a renegade element from the Hue/Saturation command, which lets you raise and lower saturation levels to any degree you like. The shortcut for Hue/Saturation is ⌘/Ctrl+U — for hUUUe, don't you know — so Desaturate is ⌘/Ctrl+Shift+U.

## Auto contrast correction

Image ➪ Adjust ➪ Auto Levels (⌘/Ctrl+Shift+L) goes through each color channel and changes the lightest pixel to white, changes the darkest pixel to black, and stretches out all the shades of gray to fill out the spectrum. In Figure 30-8, I started with a drab and murky image. But when I applied Auto Levels, Photoshop pumped up the lights and darks, bolstering the contrast. Although I would argue that the corrected image is too dark, it's not half bad for an automated, no-brainer command that you just choose and let rip.

Unlike the Equalize command, which considers all color channels as a whole, Auto Levels looks at each channel independently. So as with the Invert command, the active color mode has a profound effect on Auto Levels. Color Plate 30-5 shows our friendly jack o' lantern prior to color corrections, followed by the same image corrected with Auto Levels in the RGB, Lab, and CMYK modes. Quite frankly, the RGB image is the only one that's acceptable. The Lab image is far too orange, and the CMYK image is too dark, thanks to the exaggeration of the black channel. Auto Levels has also darkened the cyan channel, turning the pumpkin a bright red that one rarely sees in today's sincere pumpkin patches.

Like Invert, Equalize, and other automatic color mappers, Auto Levels is designed specifically for use in the RGB mode. If you use it in CMYK, you're more likely to achieve special effects than color correction.

The Auto Levels command serves the same purpose and produces the same effect as the Auto button in the Levels dialog box. You shouldn't really rely on either. What you should do is read the rest of this chapter and learn about the bigger and better color correction commands.

**Figure 30-8:** A grayscale image before (left) and after (right) applying the Auto Levels command.

# Hue Shifting and Colorizing

The following sections cover commands that are specifically designed to change the distribution of colors in an image. You can rotate the hues around the color spectrum, change the saturation of colors, adjust highlights and shadows, and even tint an image. Two of these commands — Hue/Saturation and Selective Color — are applicable exclusively to color images. The other two — Replace Color and Variations — can be applied to grayscale images, but are not the best solutions. Although both permit you to select specific ranges of brightness values that you want to edit, they apply their corrections with less finesse than either the Levels or Curves commands (discussed toward the end of the chapter).

**Tip**

Before I go any further, I should mention one awesome little bit of advice. Remember that ⌘/Ctrl+Option/Alt+F redisplays the last filter dialog box so that you can tweak the effect? Well, a similar shortcut is available when you're applying color corrections. Press the Option/Alt key when choosing any of the commands described throughout the rest of this chapter to display that command's dialog box with the settings last applied to the image. If the command has a keyboard equivalent, just add Option/Alt to restore the last settings. ⌘/Ctrl+Option/Alt+U, for example, brings up the Hue/Saturation dialog box with the settings you last used.

## Using the Hue/Saturation command

The Hue/Saturation command provides two functions. First, it enables you to adjust colors in an image according to their hues and saturation levels. You can apply the changes to specific ranges of colors or modify all colors equally across the spectrum. And second, the command lets you colorize images by applying new hue and saturation values while retaining the core brightness information from the original image.

This command is perfect for colorizing grayscale images. I know, I know, Woody Allen wouldn't approve, but with some effort, you can make Ted Turner green with envy. Just scan him and change the Hue value to 140 degrees.

When you choose Image ⇨ Adjust ⇨ Hue/Saturation (⌘/Ctrl+U), Photoshop displays the Hue/Saturation dialog box, shown in Figure 30-9. Before I explain how to use this dialog box to produce specific effects, let me briefly introduce the options, starting with the three option boxes and then moving to the other options:

✦ **Hue**: The Hue slider bar measures colors on the 360-degree color circle. You can adjust the Hue value from negative to positive 180 degrees. As you do, Photoshop rotates the colors around the Hue wheel. Consider the example of flesh tones. A Hue value of +30 moves the flesh into the orange range; a value of +100 makes it green. Going the other direction, a Hue of –30 makes the flesh red and –100 makes it purple.

When the Colorize check box is selected, Hue becomes an absolute value measured from 0 to 360 degrees. A Hue value of 0 is red, 30 is orange, and so on.

✦ **Saturation**: The Saturation value changes the intensity of the colors. Normally, the Saturation value varies from –100 for gray to +100 for incredibly vivid hues. The only exception occurs when the Colorize check box is active, in which case saturation becomes an absolute value, measured from 0 for gray to 100 for maximum saturation.

✦ **Lightness**: You can darken or lighten an image by varying the Lightness value from negative to positive 100.

Because this value invariably changes *all* brightness levels in an image to an equal extent — whether or not Colorize is selected — it permanently dulls highlights and shadows. I advise that you avoid this option like the plague and rely instead on the Levels or Curves command to edit brightness and contrast.

**Edit**: The Edit pop-up menu controls which colors in the active selection or layer are affected by the Hue/Saturation command. If you select the Master option, as by default, Hue/Saturation adjusts all colors equally. If you prefer to adjust some colors in the layer differently than others, choose one of the other Edit options or press the keyboard equivalent — ⌘/Ctrl+1 for Reds, ⌘/Ctrl+2 for Yellows, and so on.

Each of the Edit options isolates a predefined range of colors inside the image. For example, the Reds option selects the range measured from 345 to 15 degrees on the Hue wheel. Naturally, if you were to modify just the red pixels and left all non-red pixels unchanged, you'd end up with some jagged transitions in your image. So Photoshop softens the edges with 30 degrees of fuzziness at either end of the red spectrum (the same kind of fuzziness described in the "Using the Color Range command" section of Chapter 16).

You can apply different Hue, Saturation, and Lightness settings for every one of the color ranges. For example, to change all reds in an image to green and all cyans to gray, do like so: Choose the Reds option and change the Hue value to +50, then choose Cyans and change the Saturation value to –100.

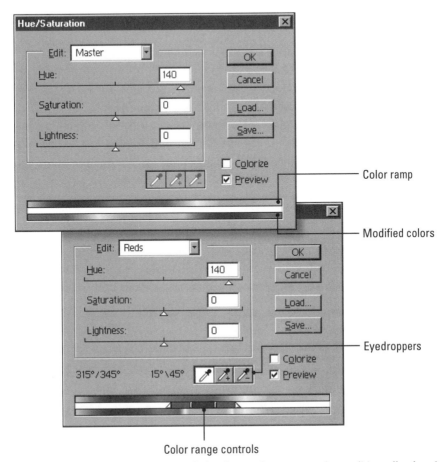

**Figure 30-9:** The Hue/Saturation dialog box as it appears when editing all colors in a layer (top) or just a specific range of colors (bottom).

✦ **Color ramps**: There are two ways to track changes made to colors in the Hue/Saturation dialog box. One way is to select the Preview check box and keep an eye on the changes in the image window. The second way is to observe the color ramps at the bottom of the dialog box. The first ramp shows the 360-degree color spectrum; the second ramp shows what the color ramp looks like after your edits.

✦ **Range controls**: You can also use the color ramps to broaden or narrow the range of colors affected by Hue/Saturation. When you choose any option other than Master from the Edit pop-up menu, a collection of color range controls appears between the color ramps. The range bar identifies the selected colors, but it also permits you to edit them.

Figure 30-10 shows the color range controls up close and personal. Here's how they work:

- Drag the central range bar to move the entire color range.

- To broaden or narrow the color range without affecting the fuzziness, drag one of the two lighter-colored fuzziness bars.

- Drag the vertical range control (labeled in Figure 30-10) to change the range while leaving the fuzziness points fixed in place. This means expanding the range and condensing the fuzziness, or vice versa.

- Drag the triangular fuzziness control to lengthen or contract the fuzziness independently of the color range.

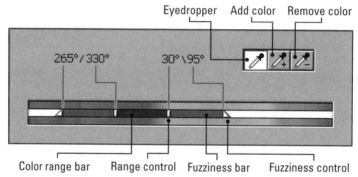

**Figure 30-10:** After defining a basic range using the Edit pop-up menu, use the color range controls to modify the range or the fuzziness.

By default, red is the central color in the color ramps with blue at either side. This is great when the range is red or some other warm color. But if you're working with a blue range, the controls get split between the two ends. To move a different color to the central position, ⌘/Ctrl+drag in the color ramp. The spectrum revolves around the ramp as you drag.

✦ **Eyedroppers:** To lift a color range from the image window, click inside the image window with the eyedropper cursor. (The cursor automatically changes to an eyedropper when you move it outside the Hue/Saturation dialog box.) Photoshop centers the range on the exact color on which you click.

To expand the range to include more colors, Shift+click or drag in the image window. To remove colors from the range, Option/Alt+click or drag in the image. You can also use the alternative plus and minus eyedropper tools, but why bother. Shift and Option/Alt do the job just fine.

✦ **Load/Save:** As in all the best color correction dialog boxes, you can load and save settings to disk in case you want to reapply the options to other images. These options are especially useful if you find a magic combination of color-correction settings that account for most of the color mistakes produced by your scanner.

✦ **Colorize**: Select this check box to apply a single hue and a single saturation level to the entire selection or layer, regardless of how it was previously colored. (Notice that Photoshop 5 sets the Saturation to 25 percent by default, a much more satisfactory setting than the previous overblown default of 100 percent.) All brightness levels remain intact, although you can adjust them incrementally using the Lightness slider bar (a practice that I strongly advise against, as I mentioned earlier).

Color ranges are not permitted when colorizing. The moment you select the Colorize check box, Photoshop dims the Edit pop-up menu and sets it to Master.

✦ **Restore**: You can restore the options in the Hue/Saturation, Levels, and Curves dialog boxes to their original settings by Option/Alt+clicking on the Reset button (the Cancel button changes to Reset when you press the Option/Alt key). Or, on a Mac, you can simply press Option+Escape.

**Tip**

To track the behavior of specific colors when using Hue/Saturation or any of Photoshop's other powerful color adjustment commands, display the Info palette (F8) before choosing the Hue/Saturation command. Then move the cursor inside the image window. As shown in Figure 30-11, the Info palette tracks the individual RGB and CMYK values of the pixel beneath the cursor. The number before the slash is the value before the color adjustment; the number after the slash is the value after the adjustment.

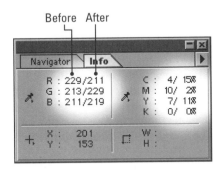

Before  After

**Figure 30-11:** When you move the eyedropper outside a color adjustment dialog box and into the image window, the Info palette lists the color values of the pixel beneath the cursor before and after adjustment.

**Photoshop 5.0**

In Photoshop 5, you don't have to settle for just one color readout. Shift+click in the image window to add up to four fixed color samples (like those created with the color sample tool, described in Chapter C on CD-ROM #2). To move a color sample once you've set it in place, Shift+drag it.

In the case of the Hue/Saturation dialog box, you can set color sample points only when the Edit pop-up menu is set to Master. After you set the samples, then select some other options from the pop-up menu to modify a specific range.

# Adjusting hue and saturation

All right, now that you know how the copious Hue/Saturation options work, it's time to give them a whirl. One caveat before I launch into things: Grayscale figures won't help you one whit in understanding the Hue/Saturation options, so I'll be referring you to three color plates. You may want to take a moment to slap a Post-it note on the page that contains Color Plates 30-6, 30-7, and 30-8 before you begin reading so that you can easily flip back and forth between text and figures.

## Changing hues

When the Colorize check box is inactive, the Hue slider bar shifts colors in an image around the color wheel. It's as if the pixels were playing a colorful game of musical chairs, except that none of the chairs disappear. If you select the Master option and enter a value of +60 degrees, for example, all pixels stand up, march one sixth of the way around the color wheel, and sit down, assuming the colors of their new chairs. A pixel that was red becomes yellow, a pixel that was yellow becomes green, and so on. The top row of Color Plate 30-6 shows the result of applying various Hue values to a single image. Note that in each case, all colors in the image change to an equal degree.

As long as you select only the Master option and edit only the Hue value, Photoshop retains all colors in an image. In other words, after shifting the hues in an image +60 degrees, you can later choose Hue/Saturation and shift the hues –60 degrees to restore the original colors.

If you select any Edit option other than Master, the musical chairs metaphor breaks down a little. All pixels that correspond to the selected color range move while pixels outside the color range remain seated. The pixels that move must sit on the non-moving pixels' laps, meaning that you sacrifice colors in the image.

For example, I edited the images in the second row of Color Plate 30-6 by applying Hue values exclusively while the Cyan option was selected. (In other words, I didn't apply Hue changes in combination with any other color range.) All pixels that fell inside the cyan range shifted to new hues; all non-cyan pixels remained unchanged. Despite the fact that the Hue values in each column of the color plate are identical, the colors in the horse changed less dramatically when Cyan was selected than when I used the Master option. Even the pixels in the primarily cyan areas contain trace amounts of blue and green, which are excluded from the Cyan range.

## Changing saturation levels

When I was a little kid, I loved watching my grandmother's television, because she kept the Color knob cranked at all times. The images leapt off the screen, like they were radioactive or something. Way cool. Well, the Saturation option works just like that Color knob. I don't recommend that you follow my grandmother's example and send the saturation for every image through the roof, but it can prove helpful for enhancing or downplaying the colors in an image. If the image looks washed out, try adding saturation; if colors leap off the screen so that everybody in the image looks like they're wearing neon makeup, subtract saturation.

**Note**

Just as the Saturation option works like the Color knob on a TV set, the Hue value serves the same purpose as the Tint knob, and the Lightness value works like the Brightness knob. So you see, your mother was quite mistaken when she told you that sitting on your butt and staring at the TV wasn't going to teach you anything. Little did she know, you were getting a head start on electronic art

The top row of Color Plate 30-7 shows the results of applying Saturation values when the Master option is selected. As you can see, all colors in the image fade or fortify equally. However, by applying the Saturation values to specific color ranges only, you can selectively fade and fortify colors, as demonstrated in the second row of the color plate. The lower left image in the color plate shows the result of selecting every color range except Cyan and Blue and lowering the Saturation to –100, which translates to no saturation whatsoever. The result is that all colors outside the cyan and blue ranges turn gray. In the lower right image, I lowered the Saturation for the Cyan and Blue options to –100 and raised the saturation of all other color ranges to +50, thus eliminating the image's most prominent colors and enhancing the remaining weaker ones.

The Saturation option is especially useful for toning down images captured with low-end scanners and digital cameras, which have a tendency to exaggerate certain colors. Back in the early years, I used to work with an Epson ES-300C. Although a good device for its time, it would digitize flesh tones in varieties of vivid oranges and red. I couldn't for the life of me figure out how to peel the colors off the ceiling until I tried the Saturation option in the Hue/Saturation dialog box. By selecting the Red color range and dragging the slider down to about –50, I was usually able to eliminate the problem. You can, too.

### Correcting out-of-gamut colors

Another common use for the Saturation option is to prepare RGB images for process-color printing. Many colors in the RGB spectrum are considered "out of gamut," meaning that they fall outside the smaller CMYK color space. Photoshop now provides a means for recognizing such colors while remaining inside the RGB color space. Choose View ➪ Gamut Warning (⌘/Ctrl+Shift+Y) to color all out-of-gamut colors with gray (or some other color that you specify using the Preferences command). The pixels don't actually change to gray; they just appear gray on-screen as long as the command is active. To turn View ➪ Gamut Warning off, choose the command again.

How do you eliminate such problem colors? Well, you have three options:

✦ Let Photoshop take care of the problem automatically when you convert the image by choosing Image ➪ Mode ➪ CMYK Color. This tactic is risky, because Photoshop simply cuts off colors that are outside the gamut and converts them to their nearest CMYK equivalents. What was once an abundant range of differently saturated hues becomes abruptly flattened, like some kind of cruel buzz haircut. Choosing View ➪ Preview ➪ CMYK (⌘/Ctrl+Y) while working in the RGB color space gives you an idea of how dramatic the buzz can be. Sometimes the effect is hardly noticeable, in which case no additional attention may be warranted. Other times, the results can be disastrous.

✦ Another method is to scrub away with the sponge tool. In Chapter 8, I discussed how much I dislike this alternative, and despite the passage of ten chapters, I haven't changed my mind. Although it theoretically offers selective control — you just scrub at areas that need attention until the gray pixels created by the Gamut Warning command disappear — the process leaves too much to chance and frequently does more damage than simply choosing Image ➪ Mode ➪ CMYK Color.

✦ The third and best solution involves the Saturation option inside the Hue/Saturation dialog box.

No doubt that last item comes as a huge surprise, given that I decided to broach the whole out-of-gamut topic in the middle of examining the Saturation option. But try to scoop your jaw up off the floor long enough to peruse the following steps, which outline the proper procedure for bringing out-of-gamut colors back into the CMYK color space.

## Steps: Eliminating Out-of-Gamut Colors

1. **Create a duplicate of your image to serve as a CMYK preview.** Choose Image ➪ Duplicate to create a copy of your image. Then choose View ➪ Preview ➪ CMYK or press ⌘/Ctrl+Y. This image represents what Photoshop will do with your image if you don't make any corrections whatsoever. It's good to have around for comparative purposes.

2. **Return to your original image and choose Select ➪ Color Range.** Then select the Out Of Gamut option from the Select pop-up menu and press Return/Enter. You have now selected all the nonconformist anti-gamut pixels throughout your image. These radicals must be expunged.

3. **To monitor your progress, choose View ➪ Gamut Warning to display the gray pixels.** Oh, and don't forget to press ⌘/Ctrl+H to get rid of those pesky ants.

4. **Press ⌘/Ctrl+U to display the Hue/Saturation dialog box.**

5. **Lower the saturation of individual color ranges.** Don't change any settings while Master is selected; it's not exacting enough. Rather, experiment with specifying your own color ranges and lowering the Saturation value. Every time you see one of the pixels change from gray to color, it means that another happy pixel has joined the CMYK collective. You may want to shout, "It's pointless to resist the invasion of the gamut snatchers!" and laugh mockingly just to make your work more entertaining.

6. **When only a few hundred sporadic gray spots remain on screen, click on the OK button to return to the image window.** Bellow imperiously, "You may think you have won, you little gray pixels, but I have a secret weapon!" Then choose Image ➪ Mode ➪ CMYK Color and watch as Photoshop forcibly thrusts them into the gamut.

Mind you, the differences between your duplicate image and the one you manually turned away from the evils of RGB excess will be subtle, but they may prove enough to produce a better looking image with a more dynamic range of colors.

### Avoiding gamut-correction edges

The one problem with the previous steps is that the Color Range command selects only the out-of-gamut pixels without even partially selecting their neighbors. As a result, you desaturate out-of-gamut colors while leaving similar colors fully saturated, an effect that may result in jagged and unnatural edges.

**Tip**

One solution is to insert a step between Steps 2 and 3 in which you do the following: Change the Tolerance value in the Magic Wand Options palette to, say, 12. Next, choose Select ⇨ Similar, which expands the selected area to incorporate all pixels that fall within the Tolerance range. Finally, choose Select ⇨ Feather and enter a Feather Radius value that's about half the Tolerance — in this case, 6.

This solution isn't perfect — ideally, the Color Range option box wouldn't dim the Fuzziness slider when you choose Out Of Gamut — but it does succeed in partially selecting a few neighboring pixels without sacrificing too many of the out-of-gamut bunch.

## Colorizing images

When you select the Colorize check box in the Hue/Saturation dialog box, the options perform differently. Returning to that wonderful musical chairs analogy, the pixels no longer walk around a circle of chairs; they all get up and go sit in the same chair. Every pixel in the selection receives the same hue and the same level of saturation. Only the brightness values remain intact to ensure that the image remains recognizable.

The top row of Color Plate 30-8 shows the results of shifting the hues in an image in two different directions around the color wheel. In each case, the Colorize option is turned off. The second row shows similar colors applied separately to the blue and non-blue portions of the image using the Colorize option. (Because you can't specify color ranges in the Hue/Saturation dialog box when Colorize is on, I selected the blue regions using the Color Range command prior to choosing the Hue/Saturation command.) The colors look similar within each column in the color plate. However, the Hue values are different in the shifted images than those in the colorized images because the shifted colors are based on relative adjustments while the colorized changes are absolute.

In most cases, you'll only want to colorize grayscale images or bad color scans. After all, colorizing ruins the original color composition of an image. For the best results, you'll want to set the Saturation values to somewhere in the neighborhood of 25 to 75. All the colors in the second-row images in Color Plate 30-8 err on the high side, with Saturation values of 80.

**Tip**    To touch up the edges of a colorized selection, change the foreground color to match the Hue and Saturation values that you used in the Hue/Saturation dialog box. You can do this by choosing the HSB Sliders command from the Color palette menu, and entering the values into the H and S option boxes. Set the B (Brightness) value to 100 percent. Next, select the paintbrush tool and change the brush mode to Color (Shift+Option/Alt+C). Then paint away.

## Shifting selected colors

The Replace Color command allows you to select an area of related colors and adjust the hue and saturation of that area. When you select Image ⇨ Adjust ⇨ Replace Color, you get a dialog box much like the Color Range dialog box. Shown in Figure 30-12, the Replace Color dialog box varies in only a few respects: It's missing the Select and Selection Preview pop-up menus and it offers three slider bars, taken right out of the Hue/Saturation dialog box.

**Figure 30-12:** The Replace Color dialog box works like the Color Range dialog box described back in Chapter 16, with a few Hue/Saturation options thrown in.

In fact, this dialog box works exactly as if you were to select a portion of an image using Select ⇨ Color Range and edit it with the Hue/Saturation command. You don't have as many options to work with, but the outcome is the same. The Replace Color and Color Range dialog boxes even share the same default settings. If you change the Fuzziness value in one, the default Fuzziness value of the other changes as well. It's like they're identical twins or something.

So why does the Replace Color command even exist? Because it allows you to change the selection outline and apply different colors without affecting the image in any way. Just select the Preview check box to see the results of your changes on screen, and you're in business.

The top row of Color Plate 30-9 shows two effects created by selecting an area and changing the Hue value to +148 and the Saturation value to –12 (as in Figure 30-12). In the first example, I selected the pumpkin face by setting the Fuzziness value to 40 and clicking and Shift+clicking a few times with the eyedropper tool. In the right example, I clicked just once in the area behind the pumpkin and changed the Fuzziness to 200, the maximum setting. I was able to experiment freely without once leaving the dialog box or redrawing the selection outline.

If you're not clear on how to use all the options in the Replace Color dialog box, read the "Using the Color Range command" section in Chapter 16. It tells you all about the eyedropper tools and the Fuzziness option.

## Shifting predefined colors

The Selective Color command permits you to adjust the colors in CMYK images. You can use the command when working on RGB or Lab images, but because it permits you to adjust the levels of cyan, magenta, yellow, and black inks, Selective Color makes more sense in the CMYK color space.

Frankly, I'm not very keen on this command. For general image editing, the Variations command provides better control and more intuitive options. Adobe created the Selective Color command to accommodate traditional press managers who prefer to have direct control over ink levels rather than monkeying around with hue, saturation, and other observational color controls. If Selective Color works for you, great. But don't get hung up on it if it never quite gels. You can accomplish all this and more with the Variations command, described in the next section.

Choosing Image ➪ Adjust ➪ Selective Color brings up the dialog box shown in Figure 30-13. To use the dialog box, choose the predefined color that you want to edit from the Colors pop-up menu and then adjust the four process-color slider bars to change the predefined color. When the Relative radio button is selected, you add or subtract color, much as if you were moving the color around the musical chairs using the Hue slider bar. When you select Absolute, you change the predefined color to the exact value entered into the Cyan, Magenta, Yellow, and Black option boxes. The Absolute option is therefore very much like the Colorize check box in the Hue/Saturation dialog box.

If you examine it closely, you'll notice that the Selective Color dialog box is very much like the Hue/Saturation dialog box. You have access to predefined colors in the form of a pop-up menu instead of radio buttons, and you can adjust slider bars to alter the color. The key differences are that the pop-up menu lets you adjust whites, medium grays (Neutrals), and blacks — options missing from Hue/Saturation — and the slider bars are always measured in CMYK color space.

The bottom row of Color Plate 30-9 includes two examples that show how this dialog box works. To create the first, I chose Red from the Colors pop-up menu and dragged the Cyan slider bar all the way up to +100 percent and the Yellow slider all the way down to –100 percent. I also selected the Relative radio button, which retains a lot of pink in the pumpkin's face. To create the second example, I reapplied the same colors but selected the Absolute radio button, making the entire pumpkin purple. I also chose Black from the Colors pop-up menu and dragged the Black slider to –100 percent.

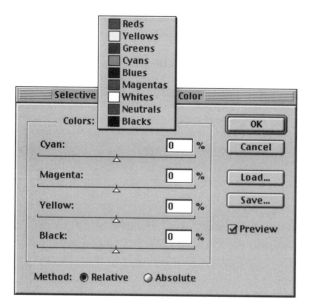

**Figure 30-13:** Select a predefined color from the Colors pop-up menu and adjust the slider bars to change that color.

As I mentioned at the outset, the Selective Color command produces the most predictable results when you're working on a CMYK image. When you drag the Cyan slider triangle to the right, for example, you're actually transferring brightness values to the cyan channel. However, you have to keep an eye out for a few anomalies, particularly when editing Black. In the CMYK mode, areas of your image that appear black include not only black, but also shades of cyan, magenta, and yellow, resulting in what printers call a rich black (or saturated black). Therefore, to change black to white, as I did in the lower right example of Color Plate 30-9, you have to set the Black slider to –100 percent and also set the Cyan, Magenta, and Yellow sliders to the same value.

## Using the Variations command

The Variations command is at once Photoshop's most essential color correction function and its funkiest:

✦ On one hand, you can adjust hues and luminosity levels based on the brightness values of the pixels. This gives you a selective degree of control unmatched by Hue/Saturation. You can also see what you're doing by clicking on little thumbnail previews (see Figure 30-14), which takes much of the guesswork out of the correction process.

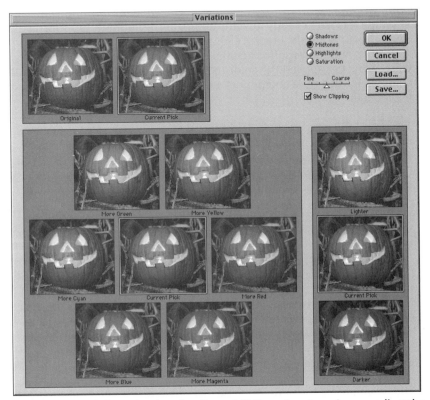

**Figure 30-14:** Click on the thumbnails to shift the colors in an image; adjust the slider bar in the upper right corner to change the sensitivity of the thumbnails; and use the radio buttons to determine which part of an image is selected.

✦ On the other hand, the Variations dialog box takes over your screen and prevents you from previewing corrections in the image window. Furthermore, you can't see the area outside of a selection, which proves disconcerting when making relative color adjustments.

Variations is therefore best suited to correcting an image in its entirety. Here's how it works: To infuse color into the image, click on one of the thumbnails in the central portion of the dialog box. The thumbnail labeled More Cyan, for example, shifts the colors toward cyan. The thumbnail even shows how the additional cyan will look when added to the image. In case you're interested in seeing how these thumbnails actually affect a final printed image in the CMYK color space, check out Color Plate 30-10.

Now notice that each thumbnail is positioned directly opposite its complementary color. More Cyan is across from More Red, More Blue is across from More Yellow, and so on. In fact, clicking on a thumbnail not only shifts colors toward the named color but away from the opposite color. For example, if you click on More Cyan and then click on its opposite, More Red, you arrive at the original image.

Although this isn't exactly how the colors in the additive and subtractive worlds work — cyan is not the empirical opposite of red — the colors are theoretical opposites, and the Variations command makes the theory a practicality. After all, you haven't yet applied the color to the image, so the dialog box can calculate its adjustments in a pure and perfect world. Cyan and red ought to be opposites, so for the moment, they are.

To control the amount of color shifting that occurs when you click on a thumbnail, move the slider triangle in the upper right corner of the dialog box. Fine produces very minute changes; Coarse creates massive changes. Just to give you an idea of the difference between the two, you have to click on a thumbnail about 40 times when the slider is set to Fine to equal one click when it's set to Coarse.

The radio buttons at the top control which colors in the image are affected. Select Shadows to change the darkest colors, Highlights to change the lightest colors, and Midtones to change everything in between.

In fact, if you're familiar with the Levels dialog box — as you will be when you read "The Levels command" section later in this chapter — the first three radio buttons have direct counterparts in the slider triangles in the Levels dialog box. For example, when you click on the Lighter thumbnail when the Highlights option is selected in the Variations dialog box, you perform the same action as moving the white triangle in the Levels dialog box to the left — that is, you make the lightest colors in the image even lighter.

The Saturation radio button lets you increase or decrease the saturation of colors in an image. Only one thumbnail appears on either side of the Current Pick image — one that decreases the saturation, and another that increases it. The Variations command modifies saturation differently than Hue/Saturation — where Hue/Saturation will push the saturation of a color as far as it will go, Variations attempts to modify the saturation without changing overall brightness values. As a result, an image saturated with Hue/Saturation will look lighter than one saturated with Variations.

As you click on the options — particularly when modifying saturation — you may notice that weird colors spring up inside the thumbnails. These brightly colored pixels are gamut warnings, highlighting colors that exceed the boundaries of the current color space. For example, if you're working in the RGB mode, these colors extend beyond the RGB gamut. Although the colors won't actually appear inverted as they do in the dialog box, it's not a good idea to exceed the color space because it results in areas of flat color, just as when you convert between the RGB and CMYK spaces. To view the thumbnails without the weirdly colored pixels, turn off the Show Clipping check box. (Incidentally, this use of the word *clipping* — Photoshop's third, in case you're counting — has nothing to do with paths or masks.)

# Enhancing colors in a compressed image

Now that you know every possible way to adjust hues and saturation levels in Photoshop, it's time to discuss some of the possible stumbling blocks. The danger of rotating colors or increasing the saturation of an image is that you can bring out some very unstable colors. Adjusting the hues can switch ratty pixels from colors that your eyes aren't very sensitive to—particularly blue—into colors that you're eye sees very well—reds and greens. Drab color can also hide poor detail, which becomes painfully obvious when you make the colors bright and vivid.

Consider the digital photograph featured in Color Plate 30-11. Snapped in Boston's Copley Square with a Kodak DC50 digital camera, the original image at the top of the color plate is drab and lifeless. If I used the Hue/Saturation command to pump up the saturation levels, a world of ugly detail rises out of the muck, as shown in the second example. (Obviously, I've taken the saturation a little too high, but only to demonstrate a point.) The detail would have faired no better if I had used the Variations command to boost the saturation.

Unstable colors may be the result of JPEG compression, as in the case of the digital photo. Or you may have bad scanning or poor lighting to thank. In any case, you can fix the problem using our friends the Median and Gaussian Blur commands, as I explain in the following steps.

If you find yourself working with heavily compressed images on a regular basis, you may want to record these steps with the Actions palette, as explained in Chapter E on CD-ROM #2. Unlike the "Adjusting the Focus of Digital Photos" steps back in Chapter 23, you won't want to apply these steps to every digital photograph you take—or even most of them—but they come in handy more often than you might think.

## Steps: Boosting the Saturation of Digital Photos

1. **Select the entire image and copy it to a new layer.** It seems like half of all Photoshop techniques begin with ⌘/Ctrl+A and ⌘/Ctrl+J.

2. **Press ⌘/Ctrl+U to display the Hue/Saturation dialog box.** Then raise the Saturation value to whatever setting you desire. Don't worry if your image starts to fall apart—that's the whole point of these steps. Pay attention to the color and don't worry about the rest. In the second example in Color Plate 30-11, I raised the Saturation to +80.

3. **Choose Filter ➪ Noise ➪ Median.** As you may recall from the last module, Median is the preeminent JPEG image fixer. A Radius value of 4 or 5 pixels works well for most images. You can take it even higher when working with resolutions of 200 ppi or more. I used 5. This destroys the detail, but that's not important. The color is all that matters.

*Continued*

4. **Choose Filter ⇨ Blur ⇨ Gaussian Blur.** As always, the Median filter introduces its own edges. And this is one case where you don't want to add any edges whatsoever. So blur the heck out of the layer. I used a Radius of 4.0, just 1 pixel less than my Median Radius value.

5. **Select Color from the blend mode pop-up menu in the Layers palette.** Photoshop mixes the gummy, blurry color with the crisp detail underneath. I also lowered the Opacity to 70 percent to produce the third example in Color Plate 30-11.

My image was still a little soft, so I applied the digital-photo sharpening steps from Chapter 23. After flattening the image, I pressed ⌘/Ctrl+A and ⌘/Ctrl+J again to copy it to yet another new layer. Then I applied the Median, Gaussian Blur, and Unsharp Mask filters, flattened the image one last time, and sharpened the image to taste. The finished result appears at the bottom of Color Plate 30-11. Although a tad bit too colorful — Boston's a lovely city, but it's not quite this resplendent — the edges look every bit as good as they did in the original photograph, and in many ways better.

# Making Custom Brightness Adjustments

The Lighter and Darker options in the Variations dialog box are preferable to the Lightness slider bar inside the Hue/Saturation dialog box because you can specify whether to edit the darkest, lightest, or medium colors in an image. But neither command is adequate for making precise adjustments to the brightness and contrast of an image. Photoshop provides two expert-level commands for adjusting the brightness levels in both grayscale and color images:

✦ The Levels command is great for most color corrections. It lets adjust the darkest values, lightest values, and midrange colors with a minimum of fuss and a generous amount of control.

✦ The Curves command is great for creating special effects and correcting images that are beyond the help of the Levels command. Using the Curves command, you can map every brightness value in every color channel to an entirely different brightness value.

**Note**

There seems to be a controversy brewing in the back rooms of some print houses and art shops over which command is better, Levels or Curves. Based on a few letters I've received over the years, it seems that some folks consider Curves to be the command for real men and Levels suitable only for color-correcting wimps.

Naturally, this is a big wad of hooey. Levels provides a histogram, which is absolutely essential for gauging the proper setting for black and white points. Meanwhile, Curves lets you map out a virtually infinite number of significant points on a graph. The point is, both commands have their advantages, and both offer practical benefits for intermediate and advanced users alike.

There's no substitute for a good histogram, so I prefer to use Levels for my day-to-day color correcting. If you can't quite get the effect you want with Levels, or you know that you need to map specific brightness values in an image to other values, then use Curves. The Curves command is the more powerful function, but it is likewise more cumbersome.

## The Levels command

When you choose Image ⇨ Adjust ⇨ Levels (⌘/Ctrl+L), Photoshop displays the Levels dialog box shown in Figure 30-15. The dialog box offers a histogram, as explained in the "Threshold" section earlier in this chapter, as well as two sets of slider bars with corresponding option boxes and a few automated eyedropper options in the lower right corner. You can compress and expand the range of brightness values in an image by manipulating the Input Levels options and then mapping those brightness values to new brightness values by adjusting the Output Levels options.

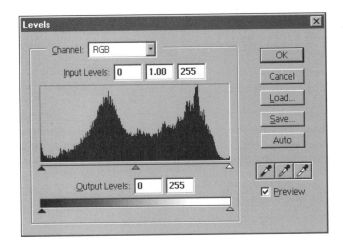

**Figure 30-15:** Use the Levels dialog box to map brightness values in the image (Input Levels) to new brightness values (Output Levels).

The options in the Levels dialog box work as follows:

✦ **Channel**: Select the color channel that you want to edit from this pop-up menu. You can apply different Input Levels and Output Levels values to each color channel. However, the options along the right side of the dialog box affect all colors in the selected portion of an image regardless of which Channel option is active.

✦ **Input Levels**: Use these options to modify the contrast of the image by darkening the darkest colors and lightening the lightest ones. The Input Levels option boxes correspond to the slider bar immediately below the histogram. You map pixels to black (or the darkest Output Levels value) by entering a number from 0 to 255 into the first option box or by dragging the black slider triangle. For example, if you raise the value to 55, all colors with brightness values of 55 or less in the original image become black, darkening the image as shown in the first example of Figure 30-16.

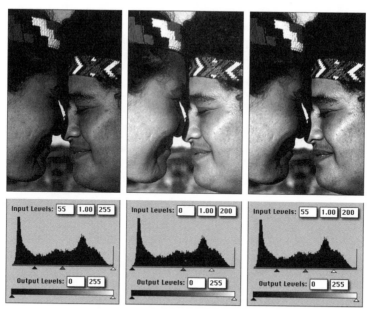

**Figure 30-16:** The results of raising the first Input Levels value to 55 (left), lowering the last value to 200 (middle), and combining the two (right).

You can map pixels at the opposite end of the brightness scale to white (or the lightest Output Levels value) by entering a number from 0 to 255 into the last option box or by dragging the white slider triangle. If you lower the value to 200, all colors with brightness values of 200 or greater become white, lightening the image as shown in the second example of Figure 30-16. In the last example of the figure, I raised the first value and lowered the last value, thereby increasing the amount of contrast in the image.

**Tip**    One of my favorite ways to edit the Input Levels values is to press the up and down arrow keys. Each press of an arrow key raises or lowers the value by 1. Press Shift with an arrow key to change the value in increments of 10.

✦ **Gamma**: The middle Input Levels option box and the corresponding gray triangle in the slider bar (shown highlighted in Figure 30-17) represent the gamma value, which is the brightness level of the medium gray value in the image. The gamma value can range from 0.10 to 9.99, with 1.00 being dead-on medium gray. Any change to the gamma value has the effect of decreasing the amount of contrast in the image by lightening or darkening grays without changing shadows and highlights. Increase the gamma value or drag the gray slider triangle to the left to lighten the medium grays (also called *midtones*), as in the first and second examples of Figure 30-18. Lower the gamma value or drag the gray triangle to the right to darken the medium grays, as in the last example in the figure.

You can also edit the gamma value by pressing the up and down arrow keys. Pressing an arrow key changes the value by 0.01, while pressing Shift+arrow changes the value by 0.10. I can't stress enough how useful this technique is. I rarely do anything except press arrow keys inside the Levels dialog box anymore.

✦ **Output Levels**: Use these options to curtail the range of brightness levels in an image by lightening the darkest pixels and darkening the lightest pixels. You adjust the brightness of the darkest pixels — those that correspond to the black Input Levels slider triangle — by entering a number from 0 to 255 into the first option box or by dragging the black slider triangle. For example, if you raise the value to 55, no color can be darker than that brightness level (roughly 80 percent black), which lightens the image as shown in the first example of Figure 30-19. You adjust the brightness of the lightest pixels — those that correspond to the white Input Levels slider triangle — by entering a number from 0 to 255 into the second option box or by dragging the white slider triangle. If you lower the value to 200, no color can be lighter than that brightness level (roughly 20 percent black), darkening the image as shown in the second example of Figure 30-19. In the last example of the figure, I raised the first value and lowered the second value, thereby dramatically decreasing the amount of contrast in the image.

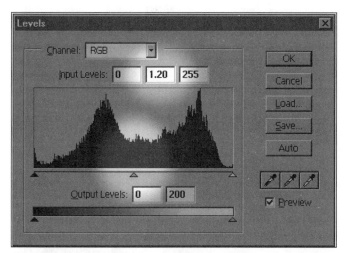

**Figure 30-17:** To create the spotlighting effects you see here, I selected the circular areas, inversed the selection, and applied the values shown in this very dialog box.

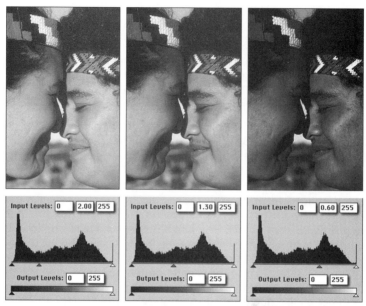

**Figure 30-18:** The results of raising (left and middle) and lowering (right) the gamma value to lighten and darken the midtones in an image.

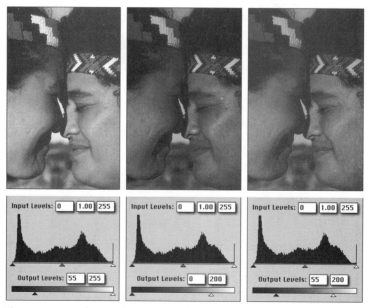

**Figure 30-19:** The result of raising the first Output Levels value to 55 (left), lowering the second value to 200 (middle), and combining the two (right).

You can fully or partially invert an image using the Output Levels slider triangles. Just drag the black triangle to the right and drag the white triangle to the left past the black triangle. The colors flip, whites mapping to dark colors and blacks mapping to light colors.

✦ **Load/Save**: You can load and save settings to disk using these buttons.

✦ **Auto**: Click on the Auto button to automatically map the darkest pixel in your selection to black and the lightest pixel to white, as if you had chosen Image ⇨ Adjust ⇨ Auto Levels. Photoshop actually darkens and lightens the image by an extra half a percent just in case the darkest and lightest pixels are statistically inconsistent with the rest of the image.

To enter a percentage of your own, Option/Alt+click on the Auto button (the button name changes to Options). This displays two additional options, Black Clip and White Clip. Enter higher values to increase the number of pixels mapped to black and white; decrease the values to lessen the effect. Figure 30-20 compares the effect of the default 0.50 percent values to higher values of 2.50 and 9.99 percent. As you can see, raising the Clip value produces higher contrast effects.

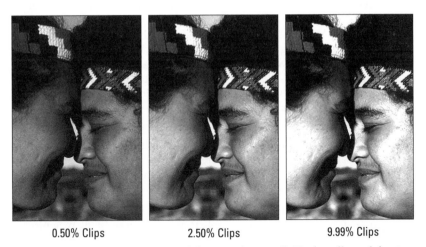

0.50% Clips          2.50% Clips          9.99% Clips

**Figure 30-20:** The default effect of the Auto button (left), the effect of the Auto button after raising the Clip values (middle), and the effect of the Equalize filter (right).

**Note**

Any changes made inside the Auto Range Options dialog box also affect the performance of the Auto Levels command. At all times, the effects of the Auto button and Auto Levels command are absolutely identical.

✦ **Eyedroppers**: Select one of the eyedropper tools in the Levels dialog box and click on a pixel in the image window to automatically adjust the color of that pixel. If you click on a pixel with the black eyedropper tool (the first of the three), Photoshop maps the color of the pixel and all darker colors to black. If you click on a pixel with the white eyedropper tool (last of the three), Photoshop maps it and all lighter colors to white. Use the gray eyedropper tool (middle) to change the exact color on which you click to medium gray and adjust all other colors in accordance. For example, if you click on a white pixel, all white pixels change to medium gray and all other pixels change to even darker colors.

One way to use the eyedropper tools is to color-correct scans without a lot of messing around. Include a neutral swatch of gray with the photograph you want to scan. (If you own a Pantone swatch book, Cool Gray 5 or 6 is your best bet.) After opening the scan in Photoshop, choose the Levels command, select the gray eyedropper tool, and click on the neutral gray swatch in the image window. This technique won't perform miracles, but it will help you to distribute lights and darks in the image more evenly. You then can fine-tune the image using the Input Levels and Output Levels options.

✦ **Preview (Mac only):** Select this option to preview the effects of your settings in the image window. The effect of turning Preview off depends on the setting of the Video LUT Animation check box in the Display & Cursors panel of the Preferences dialog box (⌘+K, ⌘+3). When Video LUT Animation is inactive, turning off Preview simply displays the image prior to choosing the Levels command. When Video LUT Animation is active, turning off Preview applies the Levels settings to the entire screen. Click and hold on the title bar to see the original image prior to the correction, release to again apply the settings to the entire screen.

I discuss why I hate Video LUT Animation in Chapter B on CD-ROM #2 — it applies adjustments to both selected and deselected areas in an image alike, and the preview is inaccurate in the Lab and CMYK modes. But there is one good thing about Video LUT Animation:

With Video LUT Animation turned on and the Preview check box turned off, you can preview the exact pixels that will turn to black or white in the image window. Just Option+drag the black or white triangle in the Input Levels slider bar. When Option+dragging the black handle, all pixels that appear some color other than white will change to black. When Option+dragging the white handle, look for the pixels that are not black to change to white.

To give you a sense of how the Levels command works, the following steps describe how to improve the appearance of an overly dark, low-contrast image such as the first example in Color Plate 30-12. Thanks to natural lighting and the dark color of the stone, this statue of Thomas Jefferson is hardly recognizable. Luckily, you can bring out the highlights using Levels.

## Steps: Correcting Brightness and Contrast with the Levels Command

1. **Press ⌘/Ctrl+L to display the Levels dialog box.** The histogram for the Jefferson image appears superimposed in white in front of the great man's chest. As you can see, most of the colors are clustered together on the left side of the graph, showing that there are far more dark colors than light.

2. **Press ⌘/Ctrl+1 to examine the red channel.** Assuming that you're editing an RGB image, ⌘/Ctrl+1 displays a histogram for the red channel. The channel-specific histograms appear below Jefferson, colorized for your viewing pleasure.

3. **Edit the black Input Levels value as needed.** Drag the black slider triangle to below the point at which the histogram begins. In the case of Jefferson, you can see a spike in the histogram about a half pica in from the left side of the graph. I dragged the black triangle directly underneath that spike, changing the first Input Levels value to 14, as you can see in the red histogram on the right side of Color Plate 30-12.

4. **Edit the white Input Levels value.** Drag the white slider triangle to below the point at which the histogram ends. In the color plate, the histogram features a tall spike on the far right side. This means a whole lot of pixels are already white. I don't want to create a flat hot spot, so I leave the white triangle alone.

5. **Edit the gamma value.** Drag the gray triangle to the gravitational center of the histogram. Imagine that the histogram is a big mass, and you're trying to balance the mass evenly on top of the gray triangle. Because my histogram is weighted too heavily to the left, I had to drag the gray triangle far to the left, until the middle Input Levels value changed to 2.40, which represents a radical shift.

6. **Repeat Steps 2 through 5 for the green and blue channels.** Your image probably has a significant preponderance of red about it. To fix this, you need to edit the green and blue channels in kind. The graphs on the right side of Color Plate 30-12 show how I edited my histograms. Feel free to switch back and forth between channels as much as you like to get everything just right.

7. **Press ⌘/Ctrl+tilde (~) to return to the composite RGB histogram.** Once you get the color balance right, you can switch back to the composite mode and further edit the Input Levels. I typically bump up the gamma a few notches—to 1.2 or so—to account for dot gain.

   You may notice that your RGB histogram has changed. Although the histograms in the individual color channels remain fixed, the composite histogram updates to reflect the red, green, and blue modifications. I've superimposed the updated histogram in white on the corrected Jefferson on the right side of Color Plate 30-12. As you can see, the colors are now better distributed across the brightness range.

*Continued*

**8. Press Return/Enter to apply your changes.** Just for fun, press ⌘/Ctrl+Z a few times to see the before and after shots. Quite the transformation, eh?

If you decide after looking at the before and after views that you could do a better job, undo the color correction and press ⌘/Ctrl+Option/Alt+L to bring up the Levels dialog box with the previous settings intact. Now you can take up where you left off.

## The Curves command

If you want to be able to map any brightness value in an image to absolutely any other brightness value — no holds barred, as they say at the drive-in movies — you want the Curves command. When you choose Image ➪ Adjust ➪ Curves (⌘/Ctrl+M), Photoshop displays the Curves dialog box, shown in Figure 30-21, which offers access to the most complex and powerful color correction options on the planet.

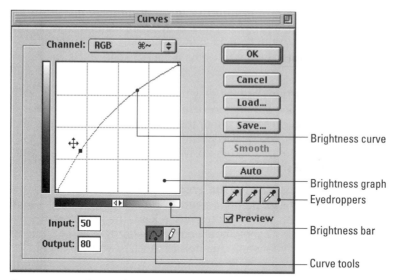

**Figure 30-21:** The Curves dialog box lets you distribute brightness values by drawing curves on a graph.

Quickly, here's how the options work:

✦ **Channel**: Surely you know how this option works by now. You select the color channel that you want to edit from this pop-up menu. You can apply different mapping functions to different channels by drawing in the graph below the pop-up menu. But, as is always the case, the options along the right side of the dialog box affect all colors in the selected portion of an image regardless of which Channel option is active.

✦ **Brightness graph**: The brightness graph is where you map brightness values in the original image to new brightness values. The horizontal axis of the graph represents input levels; the vertical axis represents output levels. The *brightness curve* charts the relationship between input and output levels. The lower left corner is the origin of the graph (the point at which both input and output values are 0). Move right in the graph for higher input values, up for higher output values. Because the brightness graph is the core of this dialog box, upcoming sections explain it in more detail.

By default, a trio of horizontal and vertical dotted lines crisscross the brightness graph, subdividing it into quarters. For added precision, you can divide the graph into horizontal and vertical tenths. Just Option/Alt+click inside the graph to toggle between tenths and quarters.

✦ **Brightness bar**: The horizontal brightness bar shows the direction of light and dark values in the graph. When the dark end of the brightness bar appears on the left — as by default when editing an RGB image — colors are measured in terms of brightness values. The colors in the graph proceed from black on the left to white on the right, as demonstrated in the left example of Figure 30-22. Therefore, higher values produce lighter colors. This is my preferred setting, because it measures colors in the same direction as the Levels dialog box.

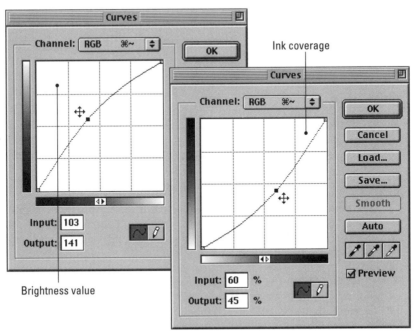

**Figure 30-22:** Click on the brightness bar to change the way in which the graph measures color: by brightness values (left) or by ink coverage (right).

If you click on the brightness bar, white and black switch places, as shown in the second example of the figure. The result is that Photoshop measures the colors in terms of ink coverage, from 0 percent of the primary color to 100 percent of the primary color. Higher values now produce darker colors. This is the default setting for grayscale and CMYK images.

✦ **Curve tools**: Use the curve tools to draw the curve inside the brightness graph. The point tool (labeled in Figure 30-23) is selected by default. Click in the graph with this tool to add a point to the curve. Drag a point to move it. To delete a point, ⌘/Ctrl+click on it.

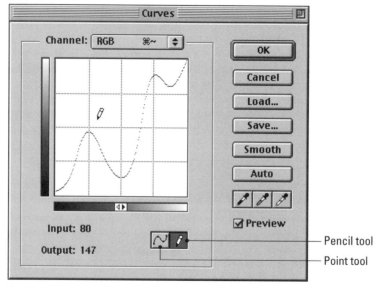

**Figure 30-23:** Use the pencil tool to draw free-form lines in the brightness graph. If the lines appear rough, you can soften them by clicking on the Smooth button.

The pencil tool lets you draw free-form curves simply by dragging inside the graph, as illustrated in Figure 30-23. This pencil works much like Photoshop's standard pencil tool. This means you can draw straight lines by clicking at one location in the graph and Shift+clicking at a different point.

✦ **Input and Output values**: The Input and Output values monitor the location of your cursor in the graph according to brightness values or ink coverage, depending on the setting of the brightness bar. In Photoshop 5, you can modify the Input or Output value when working with the point tool. Just click on the point on the graph you want to adjust, then enter new values. The Input number represents the brightness or ink value of the point before you entered the Curves dialog box; the Output number represents the new brightness or ink value.

Photoshop 5 also lets you change the Output value from the keyboard. Click on the point you want to modify. Then press the up or down arrow key to raise or lower the Output value by 1. Press Shift+up or down arrow to change the Output value in increments of 10. Note that these techniques — and ones that follow — work only when the point tool is active. (You can't change points with the pencil tool.)

Naturally, when editing multiple graph points from the keyboard, it's helpful to be able to activate the points from the keyboard as well. To advance from one point to the next, press ⌘/Ctrl+Tab. To select the previous point, press ⌘/Ctrl+Shift+Tab. To deselect all points, press ⌘/Ctrl+D.

✦ **Load/Save**: Use these buttons to load and save settings to disk.

Okay, here's *the* weirdest tip in all of Photoshop. It's not very practical, but it's about as wild as you can get. You can use a gradation as a Curves map. First, click on the Edit button in the Gradient Tool Options palette, select one of the more garish gradients, like Spectrum. Then ⌘/Ctrl+click on the Save button to save the gradient as a map settings (.amp) file. Next, bring up the Curves dialog box (⌘/Ctrl+M), click on the Load button, select Map Settings from the Files of Type pop-up menu (Windows only), open the saved gradation, and stand back and watch the fireworks.

In the psychedelic Color Plate 30-13, I cloned Constantine to a new layer and applied a heavy dose of Gaussian Blur. Then I used the Curves command to apply one of three gradient maps. In the bottom row, I mixed each of the fantastic images with its underlying original using the Color blend mode.

✦ **Smooth**: Click on the Smooth button to smooth out curves drawn with the pencil tool. Doing so leads to smoother color transitions in the image window. This button is dimmed except when you use the pencil tool.

✦ **Auto**: Click on this button to automatically map the darkest pixel in your selection to black and the lightest pixel to white. Photoshop throws in some additional darkening and lightening according to the Clip percentages, which you can edit by Option/Alt+clicking on the button.

✦ **Eyedroppers**: If you move the cursor out of the dialog box into the image window, you get the standard eyedropper cursor. Click on a pixel in the image to locate the brightness value of that pixel in the graph. A circle appears in the graph, and the input and output numbers list the value for as long as you hold down the mouse button, as shown in the first example in Figure 30-24.

The other eyedroppers work as they do in the Levels dialog box, mapping pixels to black, medium gray, or white. For example, the second image in Figure 30-24 shows the white eyedropper tool clicking on a light pixel, thereby mapping that value to white, as shown in the highlighted portion of the graph below the image. (Photoshop maps the value to each color channel independently. So when editing a full-color image inside the Curves dialog box, you'll have to switch channels to see the results of clicking with the eyedropper.) You can further adjust the brightness value of that pixel by dragging the corresponding point in the graph, as demonstrated in the last example of the figure.

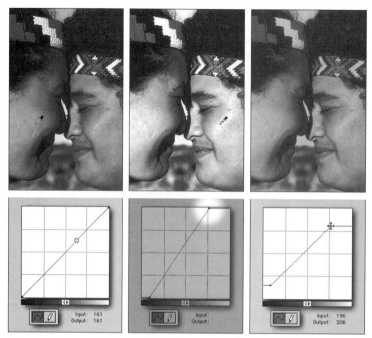

**Figure 30-24:** Use the standard eye-dropper cursor to locate a color in the brightness graph (left). Click with one of the eyedropper tools from the Curves dialog box to map the color of that pixel in the graph (middle). You then can edit the location of the point in the graph by dragging it (right).

The eyedropper tools aren't the only way to add points to a curve from the image window. Photoshop 5 adds two keyboard tricks that greatly simplify the process of pinpointing and adjusting colors inside the Curves dialog box. Bear in mind, both of these techniques work only when the point tool is active.

✦ To add a color as a point along the Curves graph, ⌘/Ctrl+click on a pixel in the image window. Photoshop adds the point to the channel displayed in the dialog box. So if the RGB composite channel is visible, the point is added to the RGB composite curve. If the Red channel is visible, Photoshop adds the point to the red graph and leaves the green and blue graphs unchanged.

✦ To add a color to all graphs, regardless of which channel is visible in the Curves dialog box, ⌘/Ctrl+Shift+click on a pixel in the image window. In the case of an RGB image, Photoshop maps the red, green, and blue brightness values for that pixel to each of the red, green, and blue graphs in the Curves dialog box. The RGB composite graph will show no change — switch to the individual channels to see the new point.

## Continuous curves

All discussions in the few remaining pages of this section assume that the brightness bar is set to edit brightness values (in which case the gradation in the bar lightens from left to right). If you set the bar to edit ink coverage (the bar darkens from left to right), you can still achieve the effects I describe, but you must drag in the opposite direction. For example, if I tell you to lighten colors by dragging upward, then you would drag downward. In a world backward live the people ink coverage.

When you first enter the Curves dialog box, the brightness curve appears as a straight line strung between two points, as shown in the first example of Figure 30-25, mapping every input level from black (the lower left point) to white (the upper right point) to an identical output level. If you want to perform seamless color corrections, the point tool is your best bet because it enables you to edit the levels in the brightness graph while maintaining a continuous curve.

To lighten the colors, click near the middle of the curve with the point tool to create a new point and then drag the point upward, as demonstrated in the second example of Figure 30-25. To darken the image, drag the point downward, as in the third example.

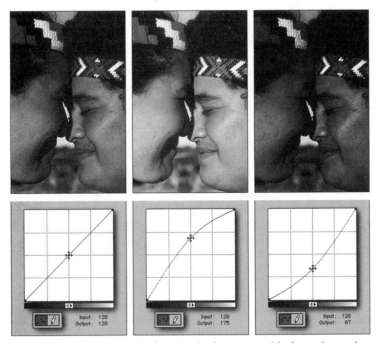

**Figure 30-25:** Create a single point in the curve with the point tool (left) and then drag it upward (middle) or downward (right) to lighten or darken the image evenly.

Create two points in the curve to boost or lessen the contrast between colors in the image. In the first example of Figure 30-26, I created one point very near the white point in the curve and another point very close to the black point. I then dragged down on the left point and up on the right point to make the dark pixels darker and the light pixels lighter, which translates to higher contrast.

In the second example of the figure, I did just the opposite, dragging up on the left point to lighten the dark pixels and down on the right point to darken the light pixels. As you can see in the second image, this lessens the contrast between colors, making the image more gray.

In the last example in Figure 30-26, I bolstered the contrast with a vengeance by dragging the right point down and to the left. This has the effect of springing the right half of the curve farther upward, thus increasing the brightness of the light pixels in the image.

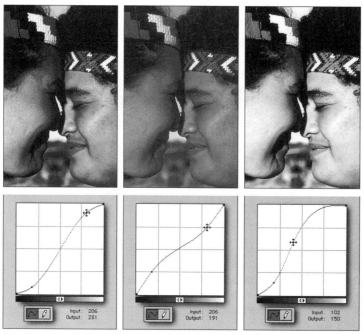

**Figure 30-26:** Create two points in the curve to change the appearance of contrast in an image, whether by increasing it mildly (left), decreasing it (middle), or boosting it dramatically (right).

## Arbitrary curves

You can create some mind-numbing color variations by adjusting the brightness curve arbitrarily, mapping light pixels to dark, dark pixels to light, and in-between pixels all over the place. In the first example of Figure 30-27, I used the point tool to achieve an arbitrary curve. By dragging the left point severely upward and the right point severely downward, I caused dark and light pixels alike to soar across the spectrum.

If you're interested in something a little more subtle, try applying an arbitrary curve to a single channel in a color image. Color Plate 30-14, for example, shows an image subject to relatively basic color manipulations in the red and green channels, followed by an arbitrary adjustment to the blue channel.

Although you can certainly achieve arbitrary effects using the point tool, the pencil tool is more versatile and less inhibiting. As shown in the second example of Figure 30-27, I created an effect that would alarm Carlos Castaneda just by zigzagging my way across the graph and clicking on the Smooth button.

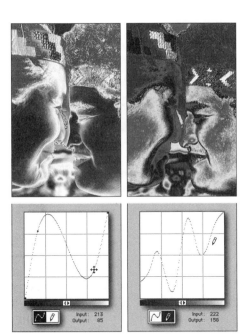

**Figure 30-27:** These arbitrary brightness curves were created using the point tool (left) and the pencil tool (right).

In fact, the Smooth button is an integral part of using the pencil tool. Try this little experiment: Draw a bunch of completely random lines and squiggles with the pencil tool in the brightness graph. As shown in the first example of Figure 30-28, your efforts will most likely yield an unspeakably hideous and utterly unrecognizable effect.

Next, click on the Smooth button. Photoshop automatically connects all portions of the curve, miraculously smoothing out the color-mapping effect and rescuing some semblance of your image, as shown in the second example of the figure. If the effect is still too radical, you can continue to smooth it out by clicking additional times on the Smooth button. I clicked on the button twice more to create the right image in Figure 30-28. Eventually, the Smooth button restores the curve to a straight line.

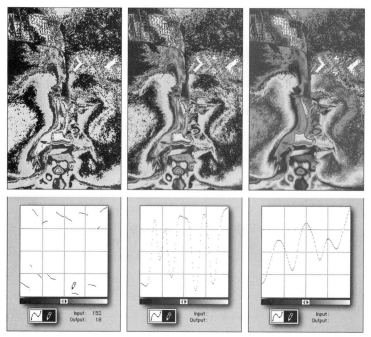

**Figure 30-28:** After drawing a series of completely random lines with the pencil tool (left), I clicked on the Smooth button once to connect the lines into a frenetic curve (middle) and then twice more to even out the curve, thus preserving more of the original image (right).

# Adjustment Layers

Every one of the commands I've discussed in this chapter is applicable to a single layer at a time. If you want to correct the colors in multiple layers, you have to create a special kind of layer called an *adjustment layer*. Adjustment layers are layers that contain mathematical color correction information. The layer applies its corrections to all layers below it, without affecting any layers above.

You can create an adjustment layer in one of two ways:

✦ Choose Layer ➪ New ➪ Adjustment Layer.

✦ ⌘/Ctrl+click on the page icon at the bottom of the Layers palette.

Either way, Photoshop displays the New Adjustment Layer dialog box shown in Figure 30-29. This dialog box contains the standard Name, Opacity, and Mode options that accompany any kind of layer. But you also get a Type pop-up menu, which offers some of Photoshop's most important color correction commands. Select the kind of color correction that you want to apply from the menu, and press Return/Enter.

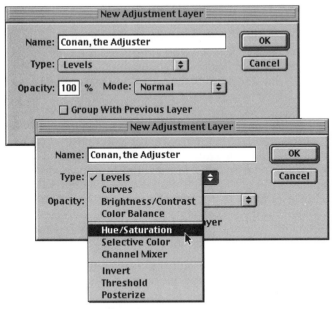

**Figure 30-29:** The New Adjustment Layer dialog box, as it appears normally (top) and with Type pop-up menu unfurled (bottom).

Photoshop then displays the dialog box for the selected correction (unless you choose Invert, which does not offer a dialog box). Change the settings as desired and press Return/Enter as you normally would. The completed color correction appears as a new layer in the Layers palette. In Figure 30-30, for example, I've added a total of three adjustment layers. Photoshop marks adjustment layers with half-black circles so that you can readily tell them apart from image layers.

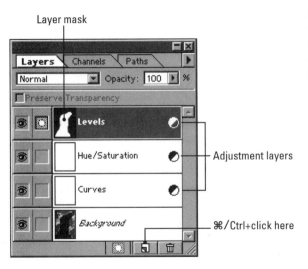

Layer mask

Adjustment layers

⌘/Ctrl+click here

**Figure 30-30:** Here I've created three layers of color correction in front of a single background image.

# The advantages of layer-based corrections

Now at this point, you might think, "Big whoop. You can apply corrections to multiple layers. That doesn't seem like such a great feature." Not only would that be an unkind assessment of adjustment layers — hey, computer code has feelings too — but an inaccurate assessment as well. Here are a few reasons adjustment layers are so great:

✦ **Forever editable**: So long as the adjustment layer remains intact — stored in the native Photoshop format, of course — you can edit the color correction over and over again without damaging the underlying pixels. Unlike standard color corrections, which alter selected pixels directly, adjustment layers have no permanent affect on the pixels whatsoever. On the slightest whim, you can double-click on the layer name in the palette to bring up the color correction dialog box, complete with the settings that are currently in force. Tweak the settings as the mood hits you and press Return/Enter to make changes on the fly. You can't get any more flexible than this.

✦ **Versatile layer masking**: You can also adjust the affected area to your heart's content. An adjustment layer covers the entire image like an adjustable wall-to-wall carpet. You modify the affected area by painting inside the layer. The layer doesn't contain any pixels of its own, so painting in an adjustment layer changes its layer mask. Paint with black to remove the correction from an area, use white to paint the correction back in.

Tip

In fact, if a selection is active when you create a new adjustment layer, Photoshop automatically creates a layer mask according to the selection outline. For example, in Color Plate 30-15, I selected the topiary dinosaur before creating the Levels layer. Photoshop thoughtfully converted my selection into a mask, as labeled in Figure 30-30. And like any layer mask, I can edit it well into the future without any adverse side effects.

✦ **Reorder your corrections**: As with any layers, you can shuffle adjustment layers up and down in stacking order. For example, if you decide you don't want the correction to affect a specific layer, just drag the adjustment layer to a level in the Layers palette below the layer you want to exclude. If you're juggling multiple adjustment layers, as in Figure 30-30 and Color Plate 30-15, you can shuffle the adjustment layers to change the order in which they're applied. This includes the standard reordering keyboard shortcuts, ⌘/Ctrl+[ and ⌘/Ctrl+].

✦ **Fade corrections**: You can fade a standard color correction right after you apply it using Filter ⇨ Fade. But you can fade a correction applied with an adjustment layer any old time. Just change the Opacity and blend mode settings in the Layers palette.

✦ **Correct with blend modes**: Some folks prefer to correct overly light or dark images using blend modes. Take an image, copy it to a new layer, and apply the Multiply mode to darken the layer or Screen to lighten it. The problem with this trick is that it increases the size of the image in memory. Duplicating the image to a new layer requires Photoshop to double the size of the image in RAM.

Adjustment layers permit you to apply this same technique without adding pixels to RAM. Create a new adjustment layer with the Levels option selected. After the Levels dialog box comes up, press Return/Enter to ignore it. Now select Multiply or Screen from the blend mode pop-up menu in the Layers palette. The adjustment layer serves as a surrogate duplicate of the layers below it, mocking every merged pixel. And it doesn't add so much as a K to the file size. It's an image-editing miracle — layers without the pain.

## Correcting a flat image using layers

Although many artists will use this new feature to edit multilayer compositions, adjustment layers are equally applicable to flat photos. Originally printed in the February, 1996 issue of *Macworld* magazine, Color Plate 30-15 shows how I corrected an image shot with a Polaroid PDC-2000 using a total of three color corrections, layered one on top of the other. (Much of this text also comes from that same article.) At first glance, the original photo on the left side of the color plate is a textbook example of what happens if you ignore backlighting. But as you have probably figured out by now, an image that appears black may actually contain several thousands of colors just itching to get out. Adjustment layers make it easier than ever to free these colors and make them fully visible to the world.

Because my image was in such rotten shape, I decided to start with the expert Curves command. I ⌘/Ctrl+clicked on the new layer icon and selected Curves from the  Type pop-up menu. Then I used the pencil tool in the Curves dialog box to draw a radical upswing on the left side of the graph, dramatically lightening the blacks right out of the gate. I clicked on the Smooth button a few times to even out the color transitions, as demonstrated in the second example in Color Plate 30-15.

All this lightening resulted in some very washed-out colors (a typical side effect), so I created a second adjustment layer using the Hue/Saturation command. By raising the Saturation value, I quickly breathed a little enthusiasm into these tired old hues — a sufficient amount, in fact, to make it clear how soft the focus was. So I went back to the original image layer and applied the Unsharp Mask filter. Had it not been for the advent of adjustment layers, I would have either had to sharpen the image before color correcting it, making it impossible to accurately gauge the results, or sharpen the image after correcting, which might bring out compression artifacts and other undesirable anomalies. With adjustment layers, however, I can sharpen and correct at the same time, giving no operation precedent over the other.

The hedge monster remained a little dark, so I selected it with the Color Range command and then created a third adjustment layer for the Levels command. Using Levels, I quickly enhanced the brightness and contrast of the green beast, bringing him out into the full light of day. As I mentioned earlier, Photoshop automatically generated a layer mask for my selection, which appears as a tiny white silhouette in the Layers palette.

To be fair, I should mention that adjustment layers are not an original invention for Photoshop. Just as Painter/X2 offered bitmapped layers more than a year before Photoshop, Live Picture introduced correction layers two years prior to the arrival of Photoshop. Live Picture's layers also permit you to temporarily sharpen, blur, and distort underlying pixels, three operations that are currently beyond Photoshop's reach. Although Adobe made no changes to adjustment layers in Version 5, my guess is that Photoshop will continue to grow in this direction in the future. The day you can apply filters with adjustment layers is the day the feature will be complete. (Photoshop 6 perhaps? We can only hope.)

✦    ✦    ✦

# The Wonders of Blend Modes

## Mixing Images Together

There must be 50 ways to combine and compare differently
colored pixels in Photoshop. So far, we've seen how you can
smear and blur pixels into each other, select pixels using other
pixels, layer pixels in front of pixels, compare a pixel to
its neighbors using automated filters, and map the colors
of pixels to other colors. Any time that you edit, mask,
composite, filter, or color correct an image, you're actually
breeding the image with itself or with other images to create
a new and unique offspring.

This chapter explores the final and ultimate experiment in
Photoshop's great genetics laboratory. *Blend modes*, also
called *calculations*, permit you to mix the color of a pixel
with that of every pixel in a straight line beneath it. A single
blend mode is as powerful as a mask, a filter, and a color
map combined, and best of all, it's temporary. So long as one
image remains layered in front of another, you can replace one
calculation with another as easily as you change a letter of
text in a word processor.

To appreciate the most rudimentary power of blend modes,
consider Figure 31-1. The first image shows a terrestrial thrill
seeker composited in front of the Apollo crew's old stomping
grounds. Both layers are as opaque as if you had cut them out
with scissors and glued them together. (Granted, you'd have
to be very skilled with scissors.) The anti-aliased edges of the
parachute mix slightly with the moon pixels below them. But
beyond that, every pixel is a digital hermit, steadfastly
avoiding interaction.

The second image in Figure 31-1 paints a different picture.
Here I've created several clones of the parachute and moon
and mixed them together using Photoshop's considerable

array of calculation capabilities. Although I used just two images, I composited them onto ten layers, only one of which — the background layer — was fully opaque. I don't know if it's moon men invading earth or the other way around, but whatever it is, it wouldn't have been possible without blend modes and their ilk.

**Figure 31-1:** Layers permit you to combine images from different sources (left), but blend modes permit you to mix images together to create intriguing if sometimes unexpected interactions (right).

Photoshop gives you three ways to mix images:

✦ **The Layers palette:** You can combine the active layer with underlying pixels using the Opacity value and blend mode pop-up menu, both members of the Layers palette. Figure 31-2 shows these two illustrious items in the context of the layers list for Figure 31-1. To learn everything there is to know about the Opacity value and blend mode pop-up menu, read the next section.

Blend mode pop-up menu

Opacity slider

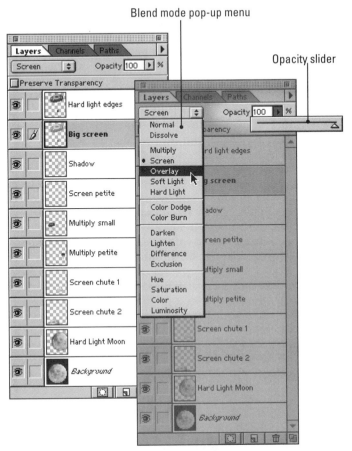

**Figure 31-2:** The list of layers in the Invasion Moon composition, with the blend mode pop-up menu proudly displayed on the right.

✦ **The Blend If sliders:** You can double-click on a layer name in the Layers palette to display the Layers Options dialog box. Many of the options in this dialog box are found elsewhere, but the two slider bars are unique. They allow you to drop colors out of the active layer and force colors to show through from layers below. This is one of Photoshop's oldest, finest, and least used features, as I discuss later in the "Dropping Out and Forcing Through" section.

✦ **Channel operations:** The so-called channel operations permit you to combine two open images of identical size, or one image with itself. Photoshop offers two commands for this purpose, Image ⇨ Apply Image and Image ⇨ Calculations. Unusually complex and completely lacking in sizing and placement functions, these commands provide access to two unique blend modes named Add and Subtract. Simply put, unless a technique involves the Add or Subtract mode, or you want to clone two images into a third image window, you can mix images with greater ease, flexibility, and feedback using the Layers palette. For more on this lively topic, see the "Using Channel Operation Commands" section later in this chapter.

Blend modes are not Photoshop's most straightforward feature. There may even come a time when you utter the words, "Blend modes are stupid." They demand a generous supply of experimentation, and even then they'll fool you. I was a math major in college (with a double-major in art, for what it's worth), so I well understand the elementary arithmetic behind Photoshop's calculations. And yet, despite roughly a decade of experience with blend modes in Photoshop and other programs, I am frequently surprised by their outcome.

The key, therefore, is to combine a basic understanding of how blend modes and other compositing features work with your natural willingness to experiment. And now that Photoshop 5 permits you to switch blend modes from the keyboard, you can experiment more easily than ever. Sometime when you don't have a deadline looming over your head, take some multilayered composition you have lying around and hit it with a few calculations. Even if the end result is a disaster that you wouldn't share with your mother, let alone a client, you can consider it time well spent.

# Using Opacity and Blend Modes

This is not the first time in this book that I've touched on the Opacity value or the blend mode pop-up menu. And given that the Layer palette's blend modes mimic the brush modes (both in name and in function) as I discussed in "The 18 paint tool modes" section near the end of Chapter 8, we're covering some familiar territory. But you'll soon find that there's a significant difference between laying down a single color with a brush, and merging the hundred or so thousand colors that inhabit a typical layer. This difference is the stuff of the following pages.

Incidentally, both the Opacity and blend mode options are dimmed when working on the background layer or in a single-layer image. There's nothing underneath, so there's nothing to mix. Naturally, this goes double when editing black and white and indexed images or when editing masks, since neither of these circumstances supports layers.

## The Opacity setting

The Opacity value is the easiest of the layer mixers to understand. It permits you to mix the active layer with the layers below in prescribed portions. It's sort of like mixing a drink. Suppose you pour one part vermouth and four parts gin into a martini glass. (Any martini enthusiast knows that's too much vermouth, but bear with me on this one.) The resulting beverage is ⅕ vermouth and ⅘ gin. If the vermouth were a layer, you could achieve the same effect by setting the Opacity to 20 percent. This implies that 20 percent of what you see is vermouth and the remaining 80 percent is underlying gin.

When any selection or navigation tool is active, you can change the Opacity setting for a layer from the keyboard. Press a single number key to change the Opacity in 10-percent increments. That's 1 for 10 percent, 2 for 20 percent, up to 0 for 100 percent — in order along the top of your keyboard. If you have the urge to be more precise, press two keys in a row to specify an exact two-digit Opacity value.

Yes, I know, I already mentioned the previous tip in Chapter 17, but it bears repeating. Besides, here's something I didn't mention. In Photoshop 5, the old Opacity slider bar has gone into hiding. Click on the arrowhead to the right of the Opacity value to display the slider bar. Then drag the triangle to change the value. Or press the up and down arrows to nudge the triangle along. Press Shift with the arrow key to nudge in 10-percent increments. Press Return/Enter to confirm the slider setting. Press Escape to cancel and restore the previous setting.

## The blend modes

Photoshop 5 offers a total of 17 blend modes. That's actually two down from Version 4. Thanks to the diminished role of floating selections, Behind and Clear are now officially ex-modes. Once upon a time — circa Photoshop 3 and earlier — Behind and Clear were quite useful for slipping floaters behind layers and cutting movable holes. But they became significantly more cumbersome in Version 4. Let us take a moment of silence to mourn their passing.

While the Behind and Clear modes are no longer available for layers, they are still available for use with the Line and Paintbucket tools and the Edit ⇨ Fill and Edit ⇨ Stroke commands.

Okay, enough of that. The remaining 17 modes — Normal through Luminosity — are still alive and well, so I suppose we should count our blessings. As you read through my upcoming discussions, you can check out examples of the blend modes both in the accompanying grayscale figures and in Color Plate 31-1. The grayscale figures show the results of compositing the two images shown in Figure 31-3. The thinker is on top, the sunset is on bottom. The color plate features a series of Saturns layered against the stormy gaseous planet of Jupiter. Although the planets aren't to scale — I understand that both bodies are several times larger than this book, for example — they do a fair job of showing the effects of Photoshop's modes.

**Figure 31-3:** To demonstrate the effects of Photoshop's blend modes, I composited the thinker (top) against a sunset background (bottom). In each case, the blend mode is applied to the thinker.

In Photoshop 5, you can access every one of the blend modes from the keyboard by pressing Shift+Option/Alt plus a letter. Some letters make perfect sense — Shift+Option/Alt+N for Normal, for example — others are a bit of a stretch — Shift+Option/Alt+I for Dissolve. Whether predictable or not, I list the letter in parentheses with each blend mode description.

One more note: Every so often, I allude to a little something called a *composite pixel*. By this I mean the pixel color that results from all the mixing that's going on in back of the active layer. For example, your document may contain hoards of layers with all sorts of blend modes in effect, but as long as you work on, say, Layer 23, Photoshop treats the image formed by Layers 1 through 22 as if it were one flattened image filled with a bunch of static composite pixels.

Cool? Keen. So without any further notes and clarifications, here they are, the 17 blend modes, in order of appearance:

✦ **Normal (N):** In combination with an Opacity setting of 100 percent, this option displays every pixel in the active layer normally regardless of the colors of the underlying image. When you use an Opacity of less than 100 percent, the color of each pixel in the active layer is averaged with the composite pixel in the layers behind it according to the Opacity value.

✦ **Dissolve (I):** This option specifically affects feathered or softened edges. If the active layer is entirely opaque with hard edges, this option has no effect. But when the edges of the layer are feathered, the Dissolve option randomizes the pixels along the edges. The first two images in Figure 31-4 compare a feathered layer subjected to the Normal and Dissolve modes. Dissolve also randomizes pixels when the Opacity value is set below 100 percent, as demonstrated in the final example in the figure.

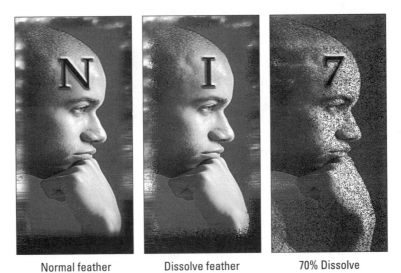

Normal feather        Dissolve feather        70% Dissolve

**Figure 31-4:** Here I applied Normal (left) and Dissolve (middle) to a layer with heavily feathered edges. The final example shows the effect of Dissolve when I reduce the Opacity value to 70 percent. (The superimposed characters indicate the keyboard shortcuts Shift+Option/Alt+N for Normal, Shift+Option/Alt+I for Dissolve, and 7 for 70 percent opacity.)

✦ **Multiply (M):** To understand the Multiply and Screen modes, you have to use a little imagination. So here goes: Imagine that the active layer and the underlying image are both photos on transparent slides. The Multiply mode produces the same effect as holding those slides up to the light, one slide in front of the other. Because the light has to travel through two slides, the outcome is invariably a darker image that contains elements from both images. An example of the Multiply blend mode appears in Figure 31-5.

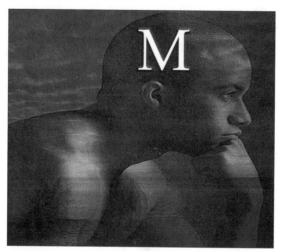

**Figure 31-5:** The Multiply blend mode produces the same effect as holding two overlapping transparencies up to the light. It always results in a darker image.

✦ **Screen (S):** Still have those transparent slides from the Multiply analogy? Well, place them both in separate projectors and point them at the same screen and you'll get the same effect as Screen. Rather than creating a darker image, as you do with Multiply, you create a lighter image, as demonstrated in Figure 31-6 and Color Plate 31-1.

You can use the Screen blend mode to emulate film that has been exposed multiple times. Ever seen Thomas Eakin's pioneering *Jumping Figure,* which shows rapid-fire exposures of a naked man jumping from one location to another? Each shot is effectively screened onto the other, lightening the film with each and every exposure. The photographer was smart enough to limit the exposure time so as not to overexpose the film; likewise, you should only apply Screen when working with images that are sufficiently dark so that you avoid overlightening.

**Figure 31-6:** The Screen mode produces the same effect as shining two projectors at the same screen. It always results in a lighter image.

✦ **Overlay (O), Soft Light (F), and Hard Light (H):** You just can't separate these guys. All three multiply the dark colors in the active layer and screen the light colors into the composite pixels in the layers below. But they apply their effects to different degrees. Overlay favors the composite pixels while Hard Light favors the layered pixels. (In fact, the two are direct opposites.) Soft Light is a washed out version of Hard Light that results in a low-contrast effect.

The left-hand examples in Figure 31-7 show each Overlay, Soft Light, and Hard Light applied to the thinking fellow. I then duplicated the thinker layer with the blend mode still in force to get the effects on the right. As these examples demonstrate, the modes effectively tattoo one image onto the image behind it. Even after multiple applications of the thinker layer, the sunset image still shows through as if the thinker were appliquéd on.

I recommend starting with the Overlay mode any time you want to mix both the active layer and the layers behind it to create a reciprocal blend. By this, I mean a blend that mixes the colors evenly without eliminating any of the detail in either layer. After you apply Overlay, vary the Opacity to favor the composite pixels. I've said it before and I'll say it again, Overlay is Photoshop's most practical blend mode, the one you should always try first.

If you can't quite get the effect you want at lower Opacity settings, switch to the Soft Light mode and give that a try. On the other hand, if the Overlay mode at 100 percent seems too subtle, switch to Hard Light. You can even clone the layer to darn well emblazon the layer onto its background, as in the bottom right image in Figure 31-7.

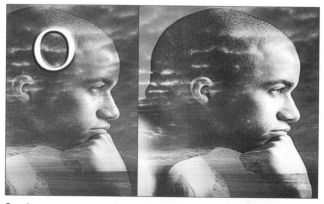

Overlay                     x 2

Soft Light                  x 2

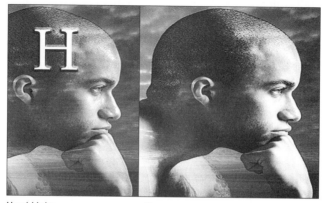

Hard Light                  x 2

**Figure 31-7:** The results of the Overlay, Soft Light, and Hard Light blend modes as they appear when applied to a single version of the thinker layer (left) and a second thinker layer (right).

✦ **Color Dodge (D):** When you apply the Color Dodge mode, each color in the layer becomes a brightness value multiplier. Light colors like white produce the greatest effect and black produces no effect. As a result, Color Dodge is Photoshop's most dramatic whitening agent, the equivalent of applying bleach to colored fabric. When applied to the thinker in Figure 31-8, Color Dodge exaggerates the sunset, resulting in a rougher effect than either Screen or the upcoming Lighten.

✦ **Color Burn (B):** If Color Dodge is bleach, then Color Burn is the charred surface of burnt toast. It uses the colors in the active layer to reduce brightness values, resulting in a radical darkening effect. Like Color Dodge, the Color Burn mode results in a radical, high-contrast effect, as shown in Figure 31-9. You may also want to sneak a peek at Color Plate 31-1, which illustrates how both Color Dodge and Color Burn sap the colors out of the active layer more surely than any other blend mode except Luminosity. If you want high-contrast stamping effects, these are the blend modes to use.

✦ **Darken (K):** When you select this option, Photoshop applies colors in the active layer only if they are darker than the corresponding pixels below. Keep in mind that Photoshop compares the brightness levels of pixels in a full-color image on a channel-by-channel basis. So although the red component of a pixel in the active layer may be darker than the red component of the underlying composite pixel, the green and blue components may be lighter. In this case, Photoshop would assign the red component but not the green or blue, thereby subtracting some red and making the pixel slightly more turquoise. Compare the predictable grayscale example in Figure 31-10 to its more challenging color counterpart in Color Plate 31-1.

**Figure 31-8:** Color Dodge uses the active layer to bleach the pixels in the layer below. There is nothing subtle about this effect.

**Figure 31-9:** Color Burn sears an image charcoal black. No other darkening mode is this severe.

**Figure 31-10:** The same active layer subject to the Darken blend mode. Only those pixels in the thinker layer that are darker than the pixels in the underlying sunset remain visible.

✦ **Lighten (G):** If you select this option, Photoshop applies colors in the active layer only if they are lighter than the corresponding pixels in the underlying image. Again, Photoshop compares the brightness levels in all channels of a full-color image. Examples of the Lighten blend mode appear in Figure 31-11 and Color Plate 31-1.

**Figure 31-11:** Our friend the thinker subject to the Lighten blend mode. Only those pixels in the selection that are lighter than the pixels in the underlying sunset remain visible.

✦ **Difference (E) and Exclusion (X):** Difference inverts lower layers according to the brightness values in the active layer. White inverts the composite pixels absolutely, black inverts them not at all, and the other brightness values invert it to some degree in between. In the first example of Figure 31-12, the light sunset shows through the black pixels at the back of the thinker's head, while the light areas along the front of the man's face invert the sky and clouds.

Exclusion works just like Difference, except for one, er, difference. Shown in the second example of Figure 31-12, Exclusion sends medium colored pixels to gray, creating a lower contrast effect, much as Soft Light is a low-contrast version of Hard Light.

**Cross-Reference**

One of my favorite uses for the Difference and Exclusion modes is to create a "Difference sandwich," in which you slide a filtered version of an image on a layer between two originals. I explain this technique and others in the upcoming section "Sandwiching a filtered image."

✦ **Hue (U):** The Hue mode and the following three blend modes make use of the HSL color model to mix colors between active layer and underlying composite. When you select Hue, Photoshop retains the hue values from the active layer and mixes them with the saturation and luminosity values from the underlying image. An example of this mode appears in the right column of Color Plate 31-1.

**Note**

I don't include grayscale figures for the Hue, Saturation, Color, and Luminosity blend modes for the simple reason that these modes affect color images only. In fact, all four options are dimmed when editing a grayscale document.

Difference

Exclusion

**Figure 31-12:** When you apply the Difference mode (top), white pixels invert the pixels beneath them, while black pixels leave the background untouched. The Exclusion mode (bottom) performs a similar effect, but instead of inverting medium colors, it changes them to gray.

✦ **Saturation (T):** When you select this option, Photoshop retains the saturation values from the active layer and mixes them with the hue and luminosity values from the underlying image. This mode rarely results in anything but very subtle effects, as demonstrated by the bright orange Saturn in Color Plate 31-1. You'll usually want to apply it in combination with some other blend mode. For example, after applying a random blend mode to a layer, you might duplicate the layer and then apply the Saturation mode to either boost or downplay the colors, much like printing a gloss or matte coating over the image.

✦ **Color (C):** This option combines hue and saturation. Photoshop retains both the hue and saturation values from the active layer and mixes them with the luminosity values from the underlying image. Because the saturation portion of the Color mode has such a slight effect, Color frequently produces an almost identical effect to Hue. For example, the Hue and Color versions of Saturn in Color Plate 31-1 are very similar, with the former appearing only slightly less bright than the latter.

✦ **Luminosity (Y):** The Luminosity blend mode retains the lightness values from the active layer and mixes them with the hue and saturation values from the underlying image. An example of this mode appears in the lower right corner in Color Plate 31-1. Here Saturn appears every bit as clearly defined as the Normal example in the upper left corner, but it assumes the orange color of its Jupiterian background. So just as the Color mode uses the layer to colorize its background, the Luminosity mode uses the background to colorize the layer.

The best way to get a feel for blend modes is to give them a whirl. Just start whacking the Shift+Option/Alt+key combos and see what you come up with. A handful of keys won't produce any effect. The beginning of the alphabet contains the motherload of shortcuts. Of the first 15 letters (up through and including O), only A, J, and L go unused. That's BO – JL. The other good ones are S, T, U, X, and Y, which just happens to spell "Stuxy." Summing up, the magic formula is:

> *BO – JL + Stuxy*

Remember that and you're golden.

## Blend mode madness

Remember that scene in *Amadeus* where Mozart is telling the king about some obscure opera that he's writing — "Marriage of Franz Joseph Haydn" or something like that — and he's bragging about how many folks he has singing on stage at the same time? Remember that scene? Oh, you're not even trying. Anyway, you can do that same thing with Photoshop. Not with melody or recitative or anything like that, but with imagery. Just as Mozart might juggle several different melodies and harmonies at once, you can juggle layers upon layers of images, each filtered differently and mixed differently with the images below it.

Predicting the outcome of these monumental compositions takes a brain the magnitude of Mozart's. But screwing around with different settings takes no intelligence at all, which is where I come in.

## The hierarchy of blend modes

The most direct method for juggling multiple images is "sandwiching." By this I mean placing a heavily filtered version of an image between two originals. This technique is based on the principal that most blend modes — all but Multiply, Screen, Difference, and Exclusion — change depending on which of two images is on top.

For example, Figure 31-13 shows two layers, A and B, and what happens when I blend them with the Overlay mode. When the leaf is on top, as in the third example, the Overlay mode favors the woman; but when the woman appears on the top layer, the Overlay mode favors the leaf.

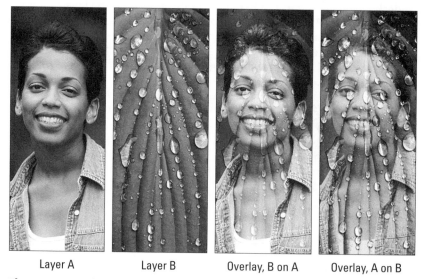

Layer A          Layer B          Overlay, B on A          Overlay, A on B

**Figure 31-13:** After establishing two layers, woman and leaf, I placed the leaf on top and applied Overlay to get the third image. Then I switched the order of the layers and applied the Overlay mode to the woman to get the last image.

As I mentioned earlier, the Overlay mode always favors the lower layer. Its opposite, Hard Light, favors the active layer. Therefore, I could have achieved the exact effect shown in the third example of Figure 31-13 by placing the leaf underneath and setting the woman layer to Hard Light. Flip-flop the layers and apply Hard Light to the leaf to get the last example.

Other blend modes have opposites as well. Take the Normal mode, for example. When you apply Normal, whichever image is on top is the one that you see.

However, if you change the Opacity, you reveal the underlying image. At 50 percent Opacity, it doesn't matter which image is on top. The color of every pair of pixels in both images is merely averaged. So an inverse relationship exists. If the filtered image is on top, an Opacity setting of 25 percent produces the same effect as if you reversed the order of the images and changed the Opacity to 75 percent.

The other obvious opposites are Color and Luminosity. If I were to position the green leaf in front of the woman and apply Color, the woman would turn green. The very same thing would happen if I placed the woman in front and applied Luminosity.

The moral of this minutia is that the order in which you stack your layers is as important as the blend modes you apply. Even filters that have no stacking opposites — Soft Light, Color Dodge, Hue, and others — will produce different effects depending on which layer is on top. Just for your general edification, Figure 31-14 and possibly more enlightening Color Plate 31-2 show a few examples.

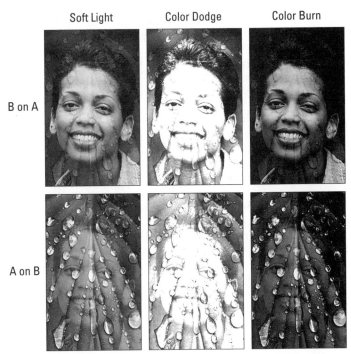

**Figure 31-14:** Examples of a few additional blend modes with the leaf on the front layer (top row) and the woman in front (bottom row).

## Sandwiching a filtered image

When you sandwich a filtered image between two originals — which, as you may recall, is what all this is leading up to — you can lessen the effect of the filter and achieve different effects than those I discussed in Chapter 23. Layers and blend modes give you the flexibility to experiment as much as you want and for as long as you please.

In Color Plate 31-3, I copied the woman's face to a new layer, then I applied Filter ⇨ Sketch ⇨ Charcoal with the foreground color set to dark purple and the background color set to green. The top row of images in the color plate show what happened when I used three different blend modes — Hard Light, Color, and Difference — to mix the Charcoal image with the underlying original.

I next cloned the background layer and moved it above the Charcoal layer, so that the filtered image resided between two originals, creating a sandwich. The originals are the bread of the sandwich, and the Charcoal layer is the meat (or the eggplant, for you vegetarians). The bottom row demonstrates the effects of applying each of three blend modes to the top slice of bread, which interacts with the blend mode applied to the Charcoal meat shown above. For example, in the second column, I applied the Hard Light mode to the filtered image to achieve the top effect. Then I created the top layer and applied the Soft Light mode to get the bottom effect.

## Creating a Difference sandwich

Ask your local deli guy, and he'll tell you that everyone has a favorite sandwich. Where blend modes are concerned, my favorite is the Difference sandwich. By applying Difference to both the filtered layer and the cloned original on top, you effectively invert the filter into the original image, and then reinvert the image to create a more subtle and utterly unique effect.

Figure 31-15 and Color Plate 31-4 show a small sampling of the several thousand possible variations on the Difference sandwich theme. In the top rows of both figures, I've vigorously applied a series of standard filters — so vigorously, in fact, that I've pretty well ruined the image. But no fear. By stacking it on top of the original, cloning the original on top of it, and applying the Difference mode to both layers, you can restore much of the original image detail, as shown in the bottom examples of the two figures. (I corrected the colors of the images by adding an adjustment layer on top of the sandwich, but otherwise you see the effects in their raw form.)

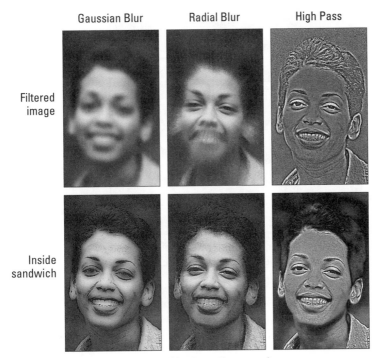

Gaussian Blur    Radial Blur    High Pass

Filtered image

Inside sandwich

**Figure 31-15:** Three different filtering effects as they appear on their own (top row) and when inserted into a Difference sandwich (bottom row).

**Note**

A few notes about the Difference sandwich. First of all, the effect doesn't work nearly so well if you start reducing the Opacity values. Second, try using the Exclusion mode instead of Difference if you want to lower the contrast. And finally, Difference is one of those few blend modes that produces the same effect regardless of how you order the layers. This means you can filter either the middle layer or the bottom layer in the sandwich and get the exact same effect. But the top layer must be the original image.

# Dropping Out and Forcing Through

When you double-click on a layer name in the Layers palette, Photoshop displays the Layer Options dialog box shown in Figure 31-16. In addition to permitting you to name a layer, change the Opacity value, and select a blend mode, you can drop out pixels in the active layer and force through pixels from lower layers according to their brightness values.

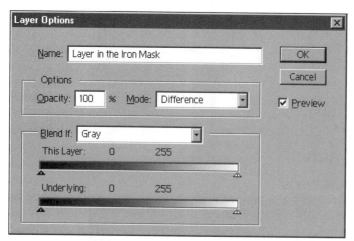

**Figure 31-16:** When editing a layer, you can access a dialog box of options to selectively mix the colors in the active layer with the colors in the image below.

For the record, the Layer Options dialog box offers the following seven options:

✦ **Name:** Use this option box to change the layer name that appears in the Layers palette.

✦ **Opacity:** Enter a value to change the translucency of the active layer. This option works identically to the Opacity value in the Layers palette.

✦ **Mode:** Here's where you select one of the 17 blend modes you could already access in the Layers palette pop-up menu.

✦ **Blend If:** Select a color channel from the Blend If pop-up menu to apply the effects of the slider bars beneath the menu to one color channel independently of the others. When the Gray option is active, as it is by default, your changes affect all color channels equally. (To my knowledge, this is the only instance where Gray means all color channels; elsewhere, Gray means a gray composite, just like Gray ought to mean.) Just for the record, the Opacity value and Mode option affect all channels regardless of the color channel you select from Blend If.

✦ **This Layer:** This slider bar lets you exclude ranges of colors according to brightness values in the active layer. When you exclude colors by dragging the black triangle to the right or the white triangle to the left, the colors disappear from view.

✦ **Underlying:** This slider forces colors from the underlying layers to poke through the active layer. Any colors not included in the range set by the black and white triangles cannot be covered and are therefore visible regardless of the colors in the active layer.

✦ **Preview:** Select the Preview check box to continually update the image window every time you adjust a setting.

The slider bars are far too complicated to explain in a bulleted list. To find out more about these options as well as the Blend If pop-up menu, read the following sections.

## Color exclusion sliders

The first slider bar, This Layer, hides pixels in the active layer according to their brightness values. You can abandon dark pixels by dragging the left slider triangle or light pixels by dragging the right slider triangle. Figure 31-17 shows examples of each.

Screen, This Layer: 170, 255

**Figure 31-17:** Two examples of modifying the blend mode and This Layer settings inside the Layer Options dialog box.

Multiply, This Layer: 0, 120

✦ To create the first example, I first set the blend mode to Screen. Then I dragged the left slider bar until the value immediately to the right of the *This Layer* label read 170, thereby hiding all pixels whose brightness values were 170 or lower.

✦ To create the second example, I changed the blend mode to Multiply. I reset the left slider triangle to 0 and dragged the right slider triangle to 120, which hid those pixels with brightness values of 120 or higher.

Drag the triangles along the Underlying slider bar to force pixels in the underlying layers to show through, again according to their brightness values. To force dark pixels in the underlying image to show through, drag the left slider triangle; to force light pixels to show through, drag the right slider triangle.

Here's how I achieved the effects in Figure 31-18:

✦ To achieve the effect in the top example in Figure 31-18, I started off by applying the Hard Light mode. (Those blend modes, they're keepers.) Then I dragged the left slider triangle until the first Underlying value read 140. This forced the pixels in the sunset that had brightness values of 140 or lower to show through.

✦ In the second example, I changed the blend mode to Overlay. Then I dragged the right Underlying slider triangle to 150, uncovering pixels at the bright end of the spectrum.

Bear in mind, every single adjustment made inside the Layer Options dialog box is temporary. The slider bars hide pixels, they don't delete them. So long as the layer remains intact, you can revisit Layer Options and restore hidden pixels or hide new ones.

## Fuzziness

The problem with hiding and forcing colors with the slider bars is that you achieve some pretty harsh color transitions. Both Figures 31-17 and 31-18 bear witness to this fact. Talk about your jagged edges! Luckily, you can soften the color transitions by abandoning and forcing pixels gradually over a fuzziness range, which works much like the Fuzziness value in the Color range dialog box, leaving some pixels opaque and tapering others off into transparency.

Hard Light, Underlying: 140, 255

Overlay, Underlying: 0, 150

**Figure 31-18:** Here I changed the Underlying slider bar settings to force through the darkest (top) and lightest (bottom) pixels in the sunset.

To taper off the opacity of pixels in either the active layers or the underlying image, Option/Alt+drag one of the triangles in the appropriate slider bar. The triangle splits into two halves, and the corresponding value above the slider bar splits into two values separated by a slash, as demonstrated in Figure 31-19.

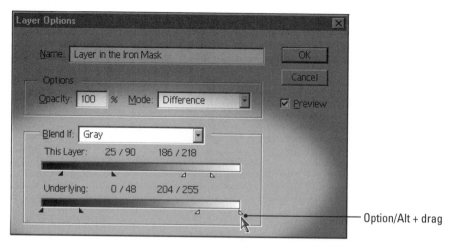

**Figure 31-19:** Option/Alt+drag a slider triangle to split it in half. You can then specify a fuzziness range across which brightness values will gradually fade into transparency.

The left triangle half represents the beginning of the fuzziness range—that is, the brightness values at which the pixels begin to fade into or away from view. The right half represents the end of the range—that is, the point at which the pixels are fully visible or invisible.

Figure 31-20 shows some fuzziness applied to the This Layer slider. Here are the specifics:

✦ In the top example of Figure 31-20, I set the blend mode to Multiply. I left the first This Layer triangle set to 0. I Option/Alt+dragged the second triangle to split it. And I moved the left half of the split triangle to 55 and the right half to 128. The result is a gradual drop off. All pixels with brightness values of 0 to 55 are opaque, the pixels become gradually more translucent from 56 to 127, and pixels brighter than 128 are transparent.

✦ Next, I duplicated my layer and switched the blend mode to Screen. After splitting the first slider triangle with an Option/Alt+drag, I set one half of the triangle to 128 and the other to 220. I dragged both halves of the second This Layer triangle back to 255. The darkest pixels are transparent, they fade into view from 129 to 219, and become opaque from 220 on up. As shown in the second example in Figure 31-20, the result is a perfect blending of Multiply and Screen, with the sunset showing through in the gray areas.

**Figure 31-20:** By Option/Alt+ dragging a This Layer slider triangle, you can create gradual transitions between the opaque and transparent portions of a layer.

Multiply, This Layer: 0, 55/128

Duplicate layer, Screen, This Layer: 128/220, 255

Using the Underlying slider is a bit trickier. It typically works best when you're trying to force through very bright or dark details, like the highlights in the sunset sky and the shadows in the water. It also helps to work with a foreground layer that has lots of flat areas of color for the background to show through. Here's what I did to create Figure 31-21:

✦ For starters, I applied Filter ➪ Other ➪ High Pass to my thinker layer, as in the first example of Figure 31-21. This created lots of gray areas for the underlying pixels to shine through.

✦ I applied the radical Color Dodge mode to this layer. I left the first Underlying triangle at 0. Then I split the second one and moved the left half to 80 and the right half to 200. This forced through the darkest pixels, fading out as they got lighter.

✦ Next, I duplicated the layer, applied the Color Burn mode, and fiddled with the Underlying triangles until the values read 100/150 and 180/255. The result is a vibrant composition that nicely sets off the thinker's tattoos.

High Pass filter

Color Dodge, Underlying: 0, 80/200

Duplicate layer, Color Burn, Underlying: 100/150, 180/255

**Figure 31-21:** After combining a High Pass effect with the radical Color Dodge and Color Burn blend modes, I used the Underlying slider bar to force through pixels from the background so the sunset and ocean didn't get lost.

## Color channel options

The options in the Blend If pop-up menu are applicable exclusively to the settings you apply using the This Layer and Underlying slider bars. When you work with a grayscale image, the Blend If pop-up menu offers one option only — Black — meaning that the Blend If option has no effect on grayscale editing. However, when you work in the RGB, CMYK, or Lab mode, you can hide and force ranges of pixels based on the brightness values of a single color channel.

To do so, select a color channel from the Blend If pop-up menu and then set the slider triangles as desired. Each time you select a different Blend If option, the slider triangles change to the positions at which you last set them for that color channel.

# Using Channel Operation Commands

Image ⇨ Apply Image and Image ⇨ Calculations provide access to Photoshop's *channel operations,* which composite one or more channels with others according to predefined mathematical calculations. Although once hailed as Photoshop's most powerful capabilities, channel operations have been eclipsed by the standard and more accessible functions available from the Layers and Channels palettes. One day, I suspect Adobe will scrap Apply Image and Calculations altogether. But until that day, I will dutifully document them both.

The Apply Image and Calculations commands allow you to merge one or two identically sized images using 12 of the 17 blend modes discussed earlier plus two additional modes, Add and Subtract. In a nutshell, the commands duplicate the process of dragging and dropping one image onto another (or cloning an image onto a new layer), and using the blend mode and Opacity settings in the Layers palette to mix the two images together.

Although Apply Image and Calculations are more similar than different, each command fulfills a specific — if not entirely unique — function:

✦ **Apply Image:** This command takes an open image and merges it with the foreground image (or takes the foreground image and composites it onto itself). You can apply the command to either the full-color image or one or more of the individual channels.

✦ **Calculations:** The Calculations command works on individual channels only. It takes a channel from one image, mixes it with a channel from another (or the same) image, and puts the result inside an open image or in a new image window.

The primary advantage of these commands over other, more straightforward compositing methods is that they allow you to access and composite the contents of individual color channels without a lot of selecting, copying and pasting, cloning, floating, and layering. You also get two extra blend modes, Add and Subtract, which may prove useful on a rainy day.

The Apply Image and Calculations commands provide previewing options, so that you can see how an effect will look in the image window. But thanks to the sheer quantity of unfriendly options offered by the two commands, I suggest that you use them on a very occasional basis. The Calculations command can be a handy way to combine masks and layer transparencies to create precise selection outlines. And Apply Image is good for compositing images in different color models, such as RGB and Lab (as I explain in the "Mixing images in different color modes" section later in this chapter).

But if your time is limited and you want to concentrate your efforts on learning Photoshop's most essential features, then feel free to skip Apply Image and Calculations. I assure you, you won't be missing much.

## The Apply Image command

Channel operations work by taking one or more channels from an image, called the *source,* and duplicating them to another image, called the *target.* When you use the Apply Image command, the foreground image is always the target, and you can select only one source image. Photoshop then takes the source and target, mixes them together, and puts the result in the target image. Therefore, the target image is the only image that the command actually changes. The source image remains unaffected.

When you choose Image ⇨ Apply Image, Photoshop displays the dialog box shown in Figure 31-22. Notice that you can select from a pop-up menu of images to specify the Source, but the Target item — listed just above the Blending box — is fixed. This is the active layer in the foreground image.

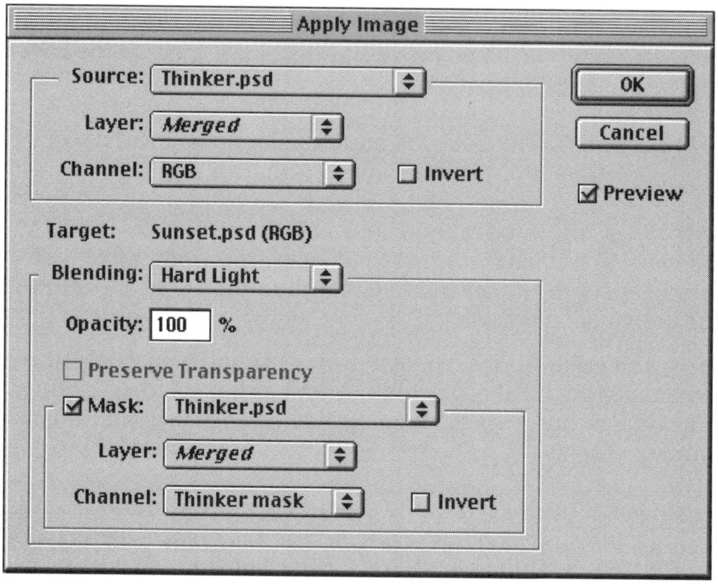

**Figure 31-22:** The Apply Image command lets you mix one source image with a target image and make the result the new target.

If this sounds a little dense, just think of it this way: The source image is the floating selection and the target is the underlying original. Meanwhile, the Blending options are the blend modes pop-up menu and Opacity value in the Layers palette.

Using the Apply Image command is a five-step process. You can always simply choose the command and hope for the best, but you'll get the most use out of it if you do the following:

## Steps: Applying the Apply Image Command

1. **Open the two images that you want to mix.** If you want to mix the image with itself to create some effect, just open the one image.

2. **Make sure that the two images are exactly the same size, down to the last pixel.** Use the crop tool and Image Size command as necessary. (You don't have to worry about this step when mixing an image with itself.)

3. **Inside the target image, switch to the channel and layer that you want to edit.** If you want to edit all channels, press ⌘/Ctrl+tilde (~) to remain in the composite view.

   When you're editing a single channel, I strongly advise you to display all channels on-screen. For example, after pressing ⌘/Ctrl+1 to switch to the red channel, click in front of the RGB item in the Channels palette to display the eyeball icon and show all channels. Only one channel is active, but all are visible. This way, you can see how your edits inside the Apply Image dialog box will affect the entire image, not just the one channel.

4. **Select the portion of the target image that you want to edit.** If you want to affect the entire image, don't select anything.

5. **Choose Image ⇨ Apply Image and have a go at it.**

Obviously, that last step is a little more difficult than it sounds. That's why I've put together the following list to explain how all those options in the Apply Image dialog box work:

✦ **Source:** The Source pop-up menu contains the name of the foreground image as well as any other images that are both open and exactly the same size as the foreground image. If the image you want to merge is not available, you must not have been paying much attention to Step 2. Press Escape to cancel, then resize and crop as needed, choose Image ⇨ Apply Image, and try again.

✦ **Layer:** This pop-up menu lists all layers in the selected source image. If the image doesn't have any layers, Background is your only option. Otherwise, select the layer that contains the prospective source image. Select Merged to mix all visible layers in the source image with the target image.

✦ **Channel:** Select the channels that you want to mix from this pop-up menu. Both composite views and individual color and mask channels are included. Keep in mind that you'll be mixing these channels with the channels that you made available in the target image before choosing the command.

For example, if the target image is an RGB image shown in the full-color composite view, and you choose RGB from the Channel pop-up menu in the Apply Image dialog box, Photoshop mixes the red, green, and blue channels in the source mage with the corresponding red, green, and blue channels in the target image. However, if you switched to the red channel before choosing Apply Image and then selected the RGB option, the program mixes a composite grayscale version of the RGB source image with the red channel in the target and leaves the other target channels unaffected.

✦ **Selection, Transparency, and Layer Mask:** If a portion of the source image is selected, the pop-up menu offers a Selection option, which lets you apply the selection outline as if it were a grayscale image, just like a selection viewed in the quick mask mode. If you selected a specific layer from the Layer pop-up menu, you'll find a Transparency option that represents the transparency mask. If the layer includes its own layer mask, a Layer Mask option also appears.

None of the three options is particularly useful when you work in the composite view of the target image; you'll usually want to apply the Selection, Transparency, or Layer Mask option only to a single channel, as described in "The Calculations command" section toward the end of this chapter. (For an exception, see the upcoming tip.)

✦ **Invert:** Select this check box to invert the contents of the source image before compositing it with the target image. This option permits you to experiment with different effects. The last example in Color Plate 31-5, for example, shows one use for the Invert check box. I inverted the *b* channel before compositing it with the RGB image to create an early dawn effect.

✦ **Target:** You can't change this item. It merely shows which image, which channels, and which layers are being affected by the command.

✦ **Blending:** This pop-up menu offers access to 12 of the blend modes I discussed in "The remaining 17 blend modes" section earlier in this chapter. The Dissolve, Hue, Saturation, Color, and Luminosity options are missing. Two additional options, Add and Subtract, are discussed in the "Add and Subtract" section later in this chapter.

✦ **Opacity:** By now, I gather you're well aware of how this one works.

✦ **Preserve Transparency:** When you're editing a layer in the target image—that is, you activated a specific layer before choosing Image ➪ Apply Image—the Preserve Transparency check box becomes available. Select it to protect transparent portions of the layer from any compositing, much as if the transparent portions were not selected and are therefore masked.

✦ **Mask:** Select this option to mask off a portion of the source image. I already mentioned that you can specify the exact portion of the target image you want to edit by selecting that portion before choosing the Apply Image command. But you also can control which portion of the source image is composited on top of the target through the use of a mask. When you select the Mask check box, three new pop-up menus and an Invert check box appear at the bottom of the Apply Image dialog box. For complete information on these options, see the upcoming "Compositing with a mask" section.

### Mixing images in different color modes

Throughout my laborious explanations of all those options in the Apply Image dialog box, I've been eagerly waiting to share with you the command's one truly unique capability. Image ➪ Apply Image is the only way to composite images in different color modes without setting the modes to match. For example, you could mix the lightness channel from a Lab image with each of the channels from an RGB image, or mix the green channel from an RGB image with each of the channels in a CMYK image. By contrast, if you were to simply drag and drop a Lab image into an RGB image, Photoshop would automatically convert the image to the RGB color space, which would result in a very different effect.

To help make things a little more clear, Color Plate 31-5 shows four examples of an image composited onto itself using the Hard Light blend mode. The first example shows the result of selecting the RGB image as both source and target. As always, this exaggerates the colors in the image and enhances contrast, but retains the same basic color composition as before.

The other examples in the color plate show what happened when I duplicated the image by choosing Image ➪ Duplicate, converted the duplicate to the Lab mode (Mode ➪ Lab Color), and then composited the Lab and RGB images together. To do this, I switched to the RGB image, chose Image ➪ Apply Image, and selected the Lab image from the Source pop-up menu. In the top right example, I chose Lightness from the Channel pop-up menu, which mixed the lightness channel with all three RGB channels. And in the bottom left image, I chose *b* from the Channel pop-up menu and selected the Invert check box, which inverted the *b* channel before applying it. For the final, moderately psychedelic effect in Color Plate 31-5, I used the Lab image as the destination. I switched to the Lab image, chose the Apply Image command, selected the RGB image as the Source, and selected Blue from the Channel pop-up menu.

### Compositing with a mask

The Mask option in the Apply Image dialog box provides a method for you to import only a selected portion of the source image into the target image. Select the Mask check box and choose the image that contains the mask from the pop-up menu on the immediate right. As with the Source pop-up menu, the Mask menu lists only those images that are open and happen to be the exact same size as the target image. If necessary, select the layer on which the mask appears from the Layer pop-up menu. Then select the specific mask channel from the final pop-up menu. This doesn't have to be a mask channel; you can use any color channel as a mask.

After you select all the necessary options, the mask works like so: Where the mask is white, the source image shows through and mixes in with the target image, just as if it were a selected portion of the floating image. Where the mask is black, the source image is absent. Gray values in the mask mix the source and target with progressive emphasis on the target as the grays darken.

If you prefer to swap the masked and unmasked areas of the source image, select the Invert check box at the bottom of the dialog box. Now, where the mask is black, you see the source image; where the mask is white, you don't.

The first example in Color Plate 31-6 shows a mask viewed as a rubylith overlay with the image. To make the mask, I selected the background with the Color Range command, inversed the selection, and saved the result as a separate channel. In the other examples in the color plate, I again composited the RGB and Lab versions of the image — as in the previous section — using Photoshop's most outrageous blend modes. No matter how dramatically the Apply Image command affected the thinker, his background remained unscathed, thanks to the mask. If the Mask option had not been turned on, the background would have changed with the mode, turning light blue for Color Dodge, black for Color Burn, and deep red for Difference.

**Tip**

You can even use a selection outline or layer as a mask. If you select some portion of the source image before switching to the target image and choosing Image ➪ Apply Image, you can access the selection by choosing Selection from the Channel pop-up menu at the very bottom of the dialog box. Those pixels from the source image that fall inside the selection remain visible; those that do not are transparent. Use the Invert check box to inverse the selection outline. To use the boundaries of a layer selected from the Layer pop-up menu as a mask, choose the Transparency option from the Channel menu. Where the layer is opaque, the source image is opaque (assuming that the Opacity option is set to 100 percent, of course); where the layer is transparent, so too is the source image.

## Add and Subtract

The Add and Subtract blend modes found in the Apply Image dialog box (and also in the Calculations dialog box) work a bit like the Custom filter that I discuss in Chapter D on CD-ROM #2 at the back of the book. However, instead of multiplying brightness values by matrix numbers and calculating a sum, as the Custom filter does, these modes add and subtract the brightness values of pixels in different channels.

The Add option adds the brightness value of each pixel in the source image to that of its corresponding pixel in the target image. The Subtract option takes the brightness value of each pixel in the target image and subtracts the brightness value of its corresponding pixel in the source image. When you select either Add or Subtract, the Apply Image dialog box offers two additional option boxes, Scale and Offset. Photoshop divides the sum or difference of the Add or Subtract mode by the Scale value (from 1.000 to 2.000) and then adds the Offset value (from negative to positive 255).

If equations will help, here's the equation for the Add blend mode:

*Resulting brightness value = (Target + Source) ÷ Scale + Offset*

And here's the equation for the Subtract mode:

*Resulting brightness value = (Target − Source) ÷ Scale + Offset*

If equations only confuse you, just remember this: The Add option results in a destination image that is lighter than either source; the Subtract option results in a destination image that is darker than either source. If you want to darken the image further, raise the Scale value. To darken each pixel in the target image by a constant amount, which is useful when applying the Add option, enter a negative Offset value. If you want to lighten each pixel, as when applying the Subtract option, enter a positive Offset value.

## Applying the Add command

The best way to demonstrate how these commands work is to offer an example. To create the effects shown in Figures 31-23 and 31-24, I began with the thinker and sunset shown way back in Figure 31-3.

After switching to the Sunset image and choosing Image ⇨ Apply Image, I selected the Thinker image from the Source pop-up menu. (I happened to be working with flat, grayscale images, so I didn't have to worry about the Layer and Channel options.) I selected the Add option from the Blending pop-up menu and accepted the default Scale and Offset values of 1 and 0, respectively, to achieve the first example in Figure 31-23. The thinker went blindingly white, much lighter than he would under any other blend mode, even Color Dodge. To improve the quality and detail of the image, I changed the Scale value to 1.2 to slightly downplay the brightness values and entered an Offset value of −60 to darken the colors uniformly. The result of this operation is the more satisfactory image shown in the second example of the figure.

Add, Scale: 1, Offset: 0

Add, Scale: 1.2, Offset: -60

**Figure 31-23:** Two applications of the Add blend mode from the Apply Image command, each subject to different Scale and Offset values.

## Applying the Subtract command

To create the first example in Figure 31-24, I selected the Subtract option from the Blending pop-up menu, once again accepting the default Scale and Offset values of 1 and 0, respectively. This time, the thinker turned pitch black because I subtracted the light values of his face from the light values in the sky, leaving no brightness value at all. Meanwhile, the thinker's hair had virtually no effect on the sunset because the hair pixels were very dark and in some cases black. Subtracting black from a color is like subtracting 0 from a number — it leaves the value unchanged.

The result struck me as too dark, so I lightened it by raising the Scale and Offset values. To create the second image in Figure 31-24, I upped the Scale value to 1.2, just as in the second Add example, which actually darkened the image slightly. Then I raised the Offset value to 180, thus adding 180 points of brightness value to each pixel. This second image is more likely to survive reproduction with all detail intact.

Subtract, Scale: 1, Offset: 0

Subtract, Scale: 1.2, Offset: 180

**Figure 31-24:** Two applications of the Subtract command on the images from Figure 31-23, one subject to Scale and Offset values of 1 and 0 (top) and the other subject to values of 1.2 and 180 (bottom).

## The Calculations command

Though its options are nearly identical, the Calculations command performs a slightly different function than Apply Image. Rather than compositing a source image on top of the current target image, Image ➪ Calculations combines two source channels and puts the result in a target channel. You can use a single image for both sources, a source and the target, or all three. The target doesn't have to be the foreground image (although Photoshop previews the effect in the foreground image window). And the target can even be a new image. But the biggest difference is that instead of affecting entire full-color images, the Calculations command affects individual color channels only. Only one channel changes as a result of this command.

Choosing Image ➪ Calculations displays the dialog box shown in Figure 31-25. Rather than explaining this dialog box option by option — I'd just end up wasting 35 pages and repeating myself every other sentence — I'll attack the topic in a less structured but more expedient fashion.

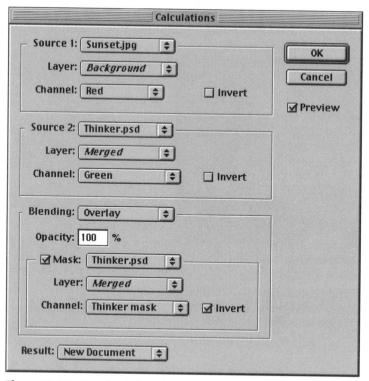

**Figure 31-25:** Use the Calculations command to mix two source channels and place them inside a new or existing target channel.

When you arrive inside the dialog box, you select your source images from the Source 1 and Source 2 pop-up menus. As with Apply Image, the images have to be exactly the same size. You can composite individual layers using the Layer menus. Select the channels you want to mix together from the Channel options. In place of the full-color options — RGB, Lab, CMYK — each Channel menu offers a Gray option, which represents the grayscale composite of all channels in an image.

The Blending pop-up menu offers the same 14 blend modes — including Add and Subtract — that are found in the Apply Image dialog box. But it's important to keep in mind how the Calculations dialog box organizes the source images when working with blend modes. The Source 1 image is equivalent to the source when using the Apply Image command (or the floating selection when compositing conventionally); the Source 2 image is equivalent to the target (or the underlying original). Therefore, choosing the Normal blend mode displays the Source 1 image. The Subtract command subtracts the Source 1 image from the Source 2 image.

Half of the blend modes perform identically regardless of which of the two images is Source 1 and which is Source 2. The other half — including Normal, Overlay, Soft Light, and Hard Light — produce different results based on the image you assign to each spot. But as long as you keep in mind that Source 1 is the floater — hey, it's at the top of the dialog box, right? — you should be okay.

**Tip**

The only one that throws me off is Subtract, because I see Source 1 at the top of the dialog box and naturally assume that Photoshop will subtract Source 2, which is underneath it. Unfortunately, this is exactly opposite to the way it really works. If you find yourself similarly confused and set up the equation backwards, you can reverse it by selecting both Invert options. Source 2 minus Source 1 results in the exact same effect as an inverted Source 1 minus an inverted Source 2. (After all, the equation (255 – Source 1) – (255 – Source 2), which represents an inverted Source 1 minus an inverted Source 2, simplifies down to *Source 2 – Source 1*. If math isn't your strong point, don't worry. I was just showing my work.)

As you can in the Apply Image dialog box, you can specify a mask using the Mask options in the Calculations dialog box. The difference here is that the mask applies to the first source image and protects the second one. So where the mask is white, the two sources mix together normally. Where the mask is black, you see the second source image only.

The Result option determines the target for the composited channels. If you select New Document from the Result pop-up menu, as in Figure 31-25, Photoshop creates a new grayscale image. Alternatively, you can stick the result of the composited channels in any channel inside any image that is the same size as the source images.

# Combining masks

As described for the Apply Image command, Selection, Transparency, and Layer Mask may be available as options from any of the Channel pop-up menus. But here they have more purpose. You can composite layer masks to form selection outlines, selection outlines to form masks, and all sorts of other pragmatic combinations.

Figure 31-26 shows how the Calculations command sees selected areas. Whether you're working with masks, selection outlines, transparency masks, or layer masks, the Calculations command sees the area as a grayscale image. So in Figure 31-28, the white areas are selected or opaque, and the black areas are deselected or transparent.

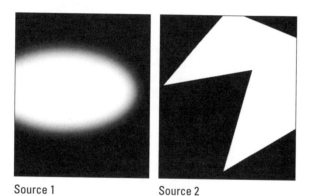

Source 1                Source 2

**Figure 31-26:** Two selections expressed as grayscale images (a.k.a. masks). The left image is the first source, and the right image is the second.

Assuming that I've chosen Image ⇨ Calculations and selected the images using the Source 1 and Source 2 options, the only remaining step is to select the proper blend mode from the Blending pop-up menu. Screen, Multiply, and Difference are the best solutions. The top row in Figure 31-27 shows the common methods for combining selection outlines. In the first example, I added the two together using the Screen mode, just as in the previous steps. In fact, Screening masks and adding selection outlines are exact equivalents. To subtract the Source 1 selection from Source 2, I inverted the former (by selecting the Invert check box in the Source 1 area) and applied the Multiply blend mode. To find the intersection of the two masks, I simply applied Multiply without inverting.

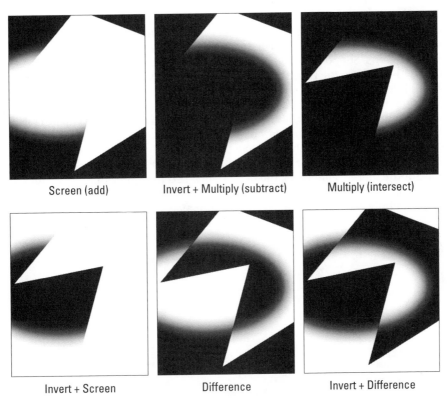

| Screen (add) | Invert + Multiply (subtract) | Multiply (intersect) |

| Invert + Screen | Difference | Invert + Difference |

**Figure 31-27:** Starting with the masks shown in Figure 31-28, I combined them in traditional (top row) and nontraditional (bottom row) ways using the Calculations command.

But the Calculations command doesn't stop at the standard three — add, subtract, and intersect. The bottom row of Figure 31-27 shows three methods of combining selection outlines that are not possible using keyboard shortcuts. For example, if I invert the Source 1 mask and combine it with the Screen mode, I add the inverse of the elliptical selection and add it to the polygonal one. The Difference mode adds the portion of the elliptical selection that doesn't intersect the polygonal one and subtracts the intersection. And inverting Source 1 and then applying Difference retains the intersection, subtracts the portion of the polygonal selection that is not intersected, and inverts the elliptical selection where it does not intersect. These may not be options you use every day, but they are extremely powerful if you can manage to wrap your brain around them.

Depending on how well you've been keeping up with this discussion, you may be asking yourself, "Why not apply Lighten or Add in place of Screen, or Darken or Subtract in place of Multiply?" The reason becomes evident when you combine two soft selections. Suppose that I blurred the Source 2 mask to give it a feathered edge. Figure 31-28 shows the results of combining the newly blurred polygonal mask with the elliptical mask using a series of blend modes. In the top row, I added the two selection outlines together using the Lighten, Add, and Screen modes. Lighten results in harsh corner transitions, while Add cuts off the interior edges. Only Screen does it just right. The bottom row of the figure shows the results of subtracting the elliptical mask from the polygonal one by occasionally inverting the elliptical mask and applying Darken, Subtract, and Multiply. Again, Darken results in sharp corners. The Subtract mode eliminates the need to invert the elliptical marquee, but it brings the black area too far into the blurred edges, resulting in an overly abrupt interior cusp. Multiply ensures that all transitions remain smooth as silk.

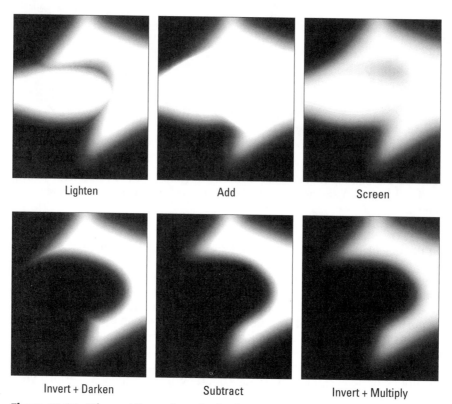

Lighten                 Add                 Screen

Invert + Darken         Subtract            Invert + Multiply

**Figure 31-28:** When adding softened selections (top row) and subtracting them (bottom row), the Screen and Multiply modes provide the most even and continuous transitions.

The reason for the success of the Screen and Multiply modes is that they mix colors together. Lighten and Darken simply settle on the color of one source image or the other — no mixing occurs — hence the harsh transitions. Add and Subtract rely on overly simplistic arithmetic equations — as I explained earlier, they really just add and subtract brightness values — which result in steep fall-off and build-up rates; in other words, there are cliffs of color transition where there ought to be rolling hills. Both Screen and Multiply soften the transitions using variations on color averaging that makes colors incrementally lighter or darker.

✦    ✦    ✦

# Web Graphics Primer

## The World of Web Imagery

The Internet may well be the most chaotic, anarchic force ever unleashed on the planet. It has no boundaries, it has no unifying purpose, it is controlled by no one, and it is owned by everyone. It's also incomprehensibly enormous, larger than any single government or business entity on the planet. If the ten richest men in the world pooled their resources, they still couldn't purchase all the computers and cables that keep the Internet alive. In terms of pure size and volume, the Web makes the great thoroughfares of the Roman empire look like a paper boy's route.

As a result, it's impossible to get a bead on the World Wide Web. With several million hands in the pie, and several million more hands groping for a slice, the Web is as subject to casual comprehension as are the depths of the oceans, the infinity of the cosmos, or the meaning of life. And the Web mutates faster than any of those forces. Something just changed while you were reading the last sentence. An important new Web technology hit the market during the sentence you're reading now. It's enough to drive any sane human bonkers.

Fortunately, I'm not altogether sane, so I find the Web quite intriguing. Even so, whatever I write today will very likely change by the time you read this. We may all have the Internet cabled into our homes, animation and video images may rule the day, and the Web as I presently know it may be stone cold dead. All of this will happen gradually, of course — even lightning-fast changes take some time to occur. And were a new technology to come along that combined the power of Java, the versatility of HTML, and the ease of use of a bar of soap, every one of the untold millions of Web content providers would continue to create their millions of different pages in millions of different ways. The most brilliant of technologies is forever mitigated by the willingness of humans to adapt to it.

I include the preceding by way of a disclaimer for the general thesis of this chapter, which is simply this: Bitmapped graphics rule the Web. Sure, text-based content, file libraries, and hyperlinks are the main stock and trade of the Internet, but the graphics are what make the Web intelligible and invite us to come back for more. Graphics have brought the masses to the Web, images account for 90 percent of all Web graphics, and Photoshop is the world's number one image editor. As a result, Photoshop has become as inextricably linked to the Web as Netscape Navigator, Adobe PageMill, RealAudio, and a hundred other programs. It's just another happy accident in Photoshop's runaway success.

## The smaller, the speedier

If you have any experience with the Web, then you know that small images are speedy images. By "small," I don't mean small in physical size (although that often helps). I mean small in terms of disk space. A 20K image that fills your screen takes less time to download and display than a 50K file no larger than a sticky note. It's the act of getting the data through the cables and phone lines that takes the time; by comparison, the time it takes your browser software to interpret the data is insignificant.

Therefore, the main focus of this chapter is file size. How can you squish the finest graphics you're capable of creating into the smallest amount of disk space with the least amount of sacrifice? This is the single most important challenge facing Web artists today. And while the Web-wide world is certain to change by the time you read this, I have a sneaking suspicion that small and speedy will remain the watchwords for some time to come.

## Preparing screen images

Many Web artists come from a background in print media, and while much of what you've learned while preparing printed photographs is equally applicable to online artwork, there are differences. Foremost among them, you never need worry about converting images to the CMYK color space. All Web graphics are RGB (or a subset of indexed colors or gray values). This is extremely good news, because it means that for once in the history of electronic publishing, what you see on-screen is really, truly what you're going to get.

Well, almost. Ignoring the differences in the ways people perceive colors and the variances in ambient light from one office or study to the next, there are measurable differences between monitors. Some monitors produce highly accurate colors, others — especially older screens — are entirely unreliable. But more importantly, some screens display images more brightly than others.

For example, the typical Macintosh user with an Apple-brand monitor is cursed with a very bright screen. Apple monitors — and many non-Apple brands developed for the Mac — are calibrated to a gamma of 1.8. Meanwhile, most PC monitors are calibrated to 2.2, which is roughly equivalent to a standard television.

Higher gamma values translate to darker displays because they indicate degrees of compensation. That is, an image has to be lightened only to 1.8 on the Mac to look as light as an image corrected to 2.2 on the PC.

Figures 32-1 and 32-2 show a test image subjected to various brightness settings. The upper left example in Figure 32-1 shows how the image looks when corrected for a typical Macintosh screen. The upper right example shows that very same image displayed on a typical PC monitor. The upper left example in Figure 32-2 shows how the image looks when corrected for a typical PC screen, and the upper right example shows the image displayed on a typical Macintosh monitor. While it's safe to assume that most folks who visit your Web page own PCs, the graphics community is still very large and active on the Mac side. So it pays to keep both Mac and PC users in mind when preparing your artwork.

**Figure 32-1:** Although most Web images are prepared on the Mac, they are more often viewed on PCs. Therefore, Mac users have to be aware that PC screens are typically darker.

Corrected on Mac          Very dark on PC

Slightly light for Mac          Slightly light for PC

The solution is to strike a compromise. Choose Image ➪ Adjust ➪ Levels (⌘/Ctrl+L). If you're using a Mac, raise the gamma (the middle Input Levels value) to between 1.2 and 1.25. If you're using a PC, lower the gamma to between 0.8 and 0.75. This strikes a nice balance between PC darkness and Mac brightness. The bottom two examples in Figure 32-1 show what happens when I raise the gamma to 1.25 on my Mac and display the image on a Mac screen (left) and a PC screen (right). The bottom two examples in Figure 32-2 show what happens when I lower the gamma to 0.75 on my PC and display the image on a PC screen (left) and a Mac screen (right). A little light on one, a little dark on the other, but ultimately an equitable compromise.

Photoshop 5.0

You can use File ➪ Color Settings ➪ RGB Setup to preview how your image will look on a foreign monitor. Assuming your monitor is properly calibrated using Gamma or a similar calibration tool (as explained in Chapter 3), here's what you do: Choose the RGB Setup command. Make sure the two check boxes — Preview and Display Using Monitor Compensation — are turned on. Then select an option from the RGB pop-up menu. Select the Apple RGB option to check out the view on a typical Mac screen, choose sRGB to preview the image on a typical PC. Photoshop updates the image in the background. When you finish appraising the situations, press Escape to return to your previous screen settings.

Corrected on PC

Washed out on Mac

**Figure 32-2:**
An image corrected for a PC screen will lighten up dramatically when viewed on a typical Macintosh monitor.

Slightly dark for PC

Slightly light for Mac

## More rules of Web imagery

Here are a few more items to remember when creating Web graphics:

✦ **Resolution doesn't matter**: Regardless of the Resolution value you enter into the Image Size dialog box, the Web browser displays one image pixel for every screen pixel (unless you specify an alternative image size in your HTML file). All that counts, therefore, is the pixel measurements — the number of pixels wide by the number of pixels tall.

✦ **GIF, JPEG, and PNG**: GIF and JPEG are the file formats of choice for Web graphics. GIF supports just 256 colors, so it's better for high-contrast artwork and text. JPEG applies lossy compression, so it's better for photographs and other continuous-tone images. The upstart format is PNG, which is essentially a 24-bit version of GIF designed for small full-color images that you don't want to compress.

✦ **Indexing colors**: Before you can save an image in the GIF format, you have to reduce the number of colors to 256 or fewer. Photoshop uses a technique called indexing, which reassigns colors according to a fixed index, which serves much the same purpose as the index in the back of this book.

Tip

**Use the Save a Copy command**: To keep your file sizes as small as possible, choose File ⇨ Save a Copy (⌘/Ctrl+Option/Alt+S) and select the Exclude Non-Image Data check box. This dumps the previews, color settings, file info, and all other data that isn't absolutely necessary to display the image on screen. This one operation can shave as much as 10K off a typical image, and that's a big savings on the Internet.

By recognizing which formats to use when, and how best to reduce colors, you can better ensure that visitors to your Web site will spend less time sitting on their hands and more time enjoying your site. I explain the fine points of the file formats and color indexing in the following sections.

# Saving JPEG Images

When it comes to saving photographic images, no format results in smaller file sizes than JPEG. As explained in gory detail in Chapter 2, the JPEG format decreases the file size by applying a lossy compression scheme that actually redraws details in the image. Inside the JPEG Options dialog box, select lower Quality settings to put the screws to the image and squish it as low as it will go. But in doing so, you also sacrifice image detail. (Revisit the first color plate in this book, Color Plate 2-1, to see an example of JPEG compression at work.)

Just to show you how well the JPEG format works, Figure 32-3 shows a series of images saved in the JPEG and GIF formats, along with their file sizes. The original file consumed 62K in memory. Yet by lowering the Quality setting to Medium, I was able to get the file size down to 28K on disk. To accomplish similar savings using the GIF format, I had to reduce the color palette to 3 bits, or a mere 8 colors. (For the record, this same file saved in the PNG format consumed 63K on disk.) As you can plainly see in the enlarged details, applying JPEG compression has a less destructive effect on the appearance of the image than reducing the color palette.

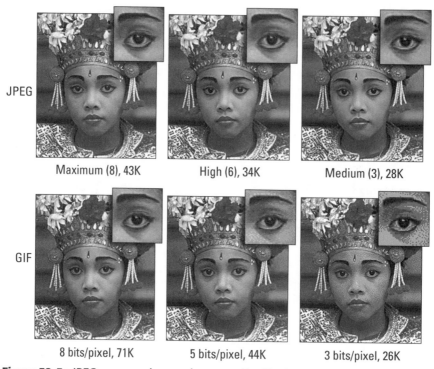

JPEG

Maximum (8), 43K    High (6), 34K    Medium (3), 28K

GIF

8 bits/pixel, 71K    5 bits/pixel, 44K    3 bits/pixel, 26K

**Figure 32-3:** JPEG compression produces smaller file sizes with less impact than reducing the color palette and saving in GIF. The number in parentheses indicates the Quality value entered into the JPEG Options dialog box.

Tip

When judging small differences in file size, be sure to right-click on the file at the desktop level and choose the Properties command. Or, on a Mac, select the file at the Finder desktop and choose File ➪ Get Info (⌘+I). Then check the Size item listed in bytes. For example, the Size item in Figure 32-4 reads *16KB (16,551 bytes), 32,768 bytes used*. The value in parentheses is the true reading, accurate to the byte. The second value — in this case, 32,768 bytes — is measured in drive blocks, which are the smallest parcels of disk that the system can write to. This makes for a misleading measurement that is invariably larger than the actual file size, and that grows in proportion to the capacity of the hard drive (or drive partition). On a Mac, the value listed in the Size column inside a directory window, and the value Photoshop shows in the Open dialog box, are likewise measured in drive blocks. Whatever you do, don't believe the size listed in the preview box in the bottom left corner of the image window on a Mac and at the far left end of the status bar on a PC. This is the size of the image in memory, but where Web graphics are concerned, all that counts is the size of the file on disk.

**Figure 32-4:**
To gauge the
true size of a
file — accurate
to the byte —
observe the
value in
parentheses.

When you save a JPEG image, Photoshop displays the JPEG Options dialog box shown in Figure 32-5. Here's how the options contained inside affect Web images:

✦ **Image Options**: Use the Quality option to specify the amount of compression applied to your image. Lower values mean smaller file sizes and more JPEG compression gook. Many experts say Medium (3) is the best setting for Web graphics, but I think it looks pretty awful, especially on-screen. I prefer a Quality value of 5 or better.

✦ **Format Options**: Most Web browsers support two variations on the JPEG format. The so-called *baseline* (or *sequentially displayed*) format displays images in line-by-line passes on-screen. The *progressive* JPEG format displays an image on-screen in multiple passes, permitting visitors to your page to get an idea of how an image looks right off the bat, without waiting for the entire image to arrive.

To save a baseline image for use on the Web, select Baseline Optimized. This format includes better Huffman encoding that makes the file even smaller than Baseline ("Standard"). You can generally reduce the file size by 5 to 10 percent using this option. Select the Progressive option to save an image that gradually appears on-screen in passes.

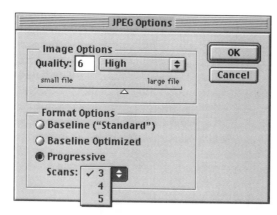

**Figure 32-5:** Select the Baseline Optimized or Progressive radio button when saving a JPEG image for use on the Web.

✦ **Scans**: If you select the Progressive radio button, you can pick a number of passes from the Scans pop-up menu. A higher value results in a faster display of the initial image on your page, but it also takes longer to display completely on screen because of all the incremental refreshing (although some browsers are smart enough not to redisplay individual JPEG scans if they already have received data for subsequent ones). A medium value of 4 is probably best, but it doesn't particularly matter.

There's a fair amount of debate over whether you should use progressive JPEG (and other incremental display options such as GIF interlacing). Certainly, some older Web browsers don't support progressive JPEG files, but that's not much of a problem these days. More controversial, some artists believe that progressive JPEGs are somehow tacky, because they have a rough appearance in the first few passes.

If that bothers you, and you don't want the viewer to see your image until it's in its final form, then select Baseline Optimized. But if you want my opinion, that would be doing your visitors a disservice. By providing an immediate, unfinished pass at your image, you're giving the viewer an early right of refusal. And that's what the Web's all about — providing the viewer with the tools of page customization and navigation. I mean, heck, guests can turn your graphics completely off if they want to. If you get too hung up on making your visitors see things your way, you'll go bonkers. Too many things are out of your control.

# Preparing and Saving GIF Images

So much for JPEG, now on to GIF. The GIF format came into being during a time when only the super savvy owned 1200-bps modems. It supports a maximum of 8 bits per pixel (256 colors), and it uses LZW compression, just like TIFF. GIF comes in two varieties, known by the snappy monikers 87a and 89a, with the latter supporting transparent pixels.

Frankly, GIF is getting a little long in the tooth. Most online pundits figure PNG will replace GIF in the next few years. But for the time being, GIF is an extremely popular and widely supported format. And despite its obvious limitations, it has its uses. GIF is a much better format than JPEG for saving high-contrast line art or text. Figure 32-6 shows two versions of the same image; the top image was saved in the JPEG format, and the bottom one was saved in GIF. As you can see, the JPEG compression utterly ruins the image. And I had to reduce the Quality setting to 0 — the absolute minimum — to get the file size down to 16K. Meanwhile, saving the image in the GIF format sacrificed no detail whatsoever and resulted in a file size of 18K. GIF's LZW compression is well suited to high-resolution artwork with large areas of flat color.

**Figure 32-6:** The JPEG format creates weird patterns in high-contrast images (top) and saves relatively little space on disk. Meanwhile, GIF keeps the sharp edges very much intact (bottom).

But before you can save a color image in the GIF format, you have to reduce the number of colors using Image ➪ Mode ➪ Indexed Color. The following section explains how this command works.

## Using the Indexed Color command

Choose Image ➪ Mode ➪ Indexed Color to display the dialog box shown in Figure 32-7. This command permits you to strip an image of all but its most essential colors. Photoshop then generates a color look-up table (or LUT) which describes the few remaining colors in the image. The LUT serves as an index, which is why the process is called *indexing*.

Photoshop 5 has greatly improved upon its indexing capabilities. The program not only generates better colors, it also permits you to preview effects before you apply them. So turn that Preview check box on and keep an eye on the image window.

Photoshop **5.0**

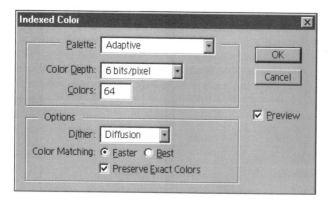

**Figure 32-7:** Use the Palette options to select the kinds of colors that remain in the image. Use the Color Depth option to specify how many colors remain.

For some reason, Photoshop doesn't let you index grayscale, Lab, or CMYK images. If the Indexed Color command is dimmed, choose Image ➪ Mode ➪ RGB to convert the image to the RGB mode and then choose Image ➪ Mode ➪ Indexed Color.

Caution

Don't expect to be able to edit your image after indexing it. Most of Photoshop's functions — including the gradient tool, all the edit tools, and the filters — refuse to work. Others, like feathering and the paintbrush and airbrush tools, produce undesirable effects. If you plan on editing an 8-bit image much in Photoshop, convert it to the RGB mode, edit it as desired, and then switch back to the indexed color mode when you finish.

Now that I've gotten all the warnings and special advice out of the way, the following sections explain how to use the options inside the Indexed Color dialog box. Enjoy.

## Specifying the palette

The first pop-up menu — Palette — tells Photoshop how to compute the colors in the look-up table. Most of the time, you'll want to select the Adaptive option, as in Figure 32-7. But just so you're prepared to be all you can be, the following list explains how each of the options works:

✦ **Exact**: If the image already contains fewer than 256 colors, the Exact option appears by default. This only occurs if you've created an extremely high-contrast image — such as a screen shot — or you're working from an image that originally started out as grayscale. If Exact is selected, just press Return/Enter and let the command do its stuff. No sense messing with a good thing.

✦ **System**: Photoshop offers two System options, which are used by the Macintosh and Windows operating systems. The only reason to select either of these options is if you want to add a bit of imagery to the system. For example, it's a good idea to select the System (Windows) or System (Macintosh) option when creating a background pattern, a custom file icon, a wallpaper image, or some other item that appears at the desktop level. Color Plate 32-1 shows examples of a 24-bit image downsized to the Mac and Windows system palettes.

✦ **Web**: Just to make things as confusing as possible, Web browsers subscribe to their own variety of color palette. According to folklore, this 216-color LUT is an intersection of colors found in the Mac and Windows system palettes. But in fact, the Web palette includes those 216 colors whose R, G, and B values are divisible by 51. That means each primary color can be set to 0, 51, 102, 153, 204, or 255. Calculate all possible combinations, and you get 216 colors.

When displaying an image on an 8-bit screen, the browser invariably changes all colors to those in the Web palette. Therefore, converting your colors to the Web palette ensures that what you see on your screen is what your guests see as well. But for most folks, I still argue in favor of Adaptive. An image with an adaptive palette will look far better on 16-bit and better monitors, and these days, high-color screens are in the majority. (The notable exceptions are portables, which often max out at 8-bit screens. But these LCD screens hardly do your color graphics justice, so it seems silly to let such lowest-common-denominator concerns dictate your work.)

✦ **Uniform**: This is the dumbest option of them all. It merely retains a uniform sampling of colors from the spectrum. I've never heard of anyone finding a use for it — but as always, I welcome your suggestions.

✦ **Adaptive**: This option selects the most frequently used colors in your image, which typically delivers the best possible results. Because it ignores all system and Web palettes, images downsized with Adaptive look best on high-color monitors, as I mentioned above. To demonstrate just how much better they look, the bottom row of Color Plate 32-1 shows three images subject to the Adaptive palette at various Color Depth settings. Even with a mere 64 and 16 colors, the middle and right images look as good or better than the 256-color system-palette images above them.

You can influence the performance of the Adaptive option by selecting an area of your image before choosing the Indexed Color command. Photoshop will then favor the selected area when creating the palette. For example, before indexing the image in Color Plate 32-1 down to the 8-color palette (bottom right), I selected the fellow's face to avoid losing all the flesh tones.

✦ **Custom**: Select this option to load a look-up table from disk. This is useful when creating multimedia content, but rarely serves any purpose for Web graphics. You can save a custom palette using Image ⇨ Mode ⇨ Color Table, as I explain in this chapter.

✦ **Previous**: This option uses the last look-up table created by the Indexed Color command. If you're trying to create a series of high-contrast graphics that you want to look as homogenous as possible, then this is the option to use. The Previous option is dimmed unless you have used the Indexed Color command at least once during the current session.

## Color depth

Select a value from the Color Depth pop-up menu to specify the number of colors you want to retain in your image. Fewer colors results in smaller GIF files. I generally start with 6 bits/pixel, which results in 64 colors. With the Preview check box turned on, I can see the effect of this palette in the image window. If the image looks okay, I try 5 bits/pixel; if not, I try 7 bits/pixel. It's all a matter of getting the colors as low as they can go without becoming ugly. The bottom row in Color Plate 32-1 shows examples of the same image with 256, 64, and 16 colors.

**Note**

Like all computer programs, Photoshop measures color in terms of *bit depth*. As I've mentioned elsewhere in this book, an 8-bit image translates to 256 colors. Photoshop computes this figure by taking the number 2 and multiplying it by itself the number of times specified by the bit depth. 24-bit means 2 to the 24th power, which is 16 million; 4-bit means 2 to the 4th power, which is 16. You don't need to know this to select an option from a pop-up menu — Photoshop constantly keeps you apprised of the number of colors in the Colors option box — but sometimes it's nice to know what the program's up to.

## Dither

Use the Dither pop-up menu to specify how Photoshop distributes the indexed colors throughout the image:

✦ **None**: If you select None, Photoshop maps each color in the image to its closest equivalent in the look-up table, pixel for pixel. This results in the harshest color transitions. But as I'll explain in a moment, it is frequently the preferable option.

✦ **Pattern**: This option is available only if you select System (Macintosh) from the Palette options. And even then you should avoid the Pattern option like the plague. It dithers colors in a geometric pattern, which is altogether ugly. Look to the lower left example of Figure 32-8 and the middle image in Color Plate 32-2 for examples.

✦ **Diffusion**: The Diffusion option dithers colors randomly to create a naturalistic effect, as shown in the lower right example of Figure 32-8 and the last image in Color Plate 32-2.

After looking at Figure 32-8 and Color Plate 32-2, you might be inclined to think that Diffusion is the option of choice. Not necessarily. In most cases, None is the better option. First of all, None results in smaller GIF files (as Color Plate 32-2 shows). Because LZW is better suited to compressing uninterrupted expanses of color, harsh transitions mean speedier images. Second, if a guest views your page on an 8-bit monitor, the system will dither the image automatically (assuming you selected Adaptive from the Palette pop-up menu). System dithering on top of Diffusion dithering gets incredibly messy; system dithering on its own, however, is acceptable.

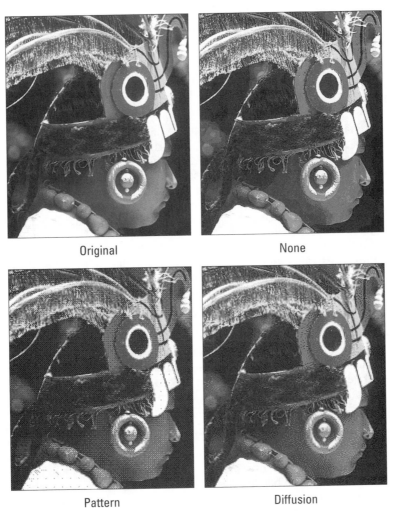

Original                          None

Pattern                          Diffusion

**Figure 32-8:** The results of converting an image (upper left) to the System palette using each of the three Dither options, None, Pattern, and Diffusion.

## Color Matching

Photoshop
**5.0**

In the past, Photoshop has done an average to poor job of maintaining decent colors in an indexed image, which was one of the reasons third-party GIF plug-ins were so popular. But Photoshop 5 fairs much better. Even if you never mess with the new Color Matching controls, you'll see your GIF images improve in quality.

Then again, I see no reason to avoid the Color Matching options. They're ridiculously easy to use. The Faster and Better check boxes permit you to adjust the quality of the color reduction. Faster is supposedly faster, and Better is typically better at maintaining colors in gradations and smooth color transitions. But I would give them both a try. When editing small images, neither option takes more than a couple of seconds to preview. So try out both and go with the one that looks best.

The Preserve Exact Colors check box is available only when the Diffusion option is selected from the Dither pop-up menu. When turned on, this option turns off dithering inside areas of flat color that exactly match a color in the active palette. Say that you've created some text in a Web-safe color. The text is antialiased, but the letters themselves are flat color. By selecting Web from the palette pop-up menu and selecting the Preserve Exact Colors check box, you tell Photoshop to dither around the edges of the letters, but leave the interiors undithered.

As I mentioned before, I recommend you avoid dithering whenever possible, in which case Preserve Exact Colors is dimmed. But if you decide to dither, it's a good idea to turn Preserve Exact Colors on. Even if you can't see a difference on your screen, it may show up on another.

## Editing indexed colors

As I said earlier, Adaptive is generally the best choice when creating Web graphics, because it scans each image for its most essential colors. But even the Adaptive option doesn't get things 100 percent right. On occasion, Photoshop selects some colors that look wildly off base.

To replace all occurrences of one color in an indexed image with a different color, choose Image ⇨ Mode ⇨ Color Table. The ensuing Color Table dialog box, shown in Figure 32-9, enables you to selectively edit the contents of the LUT. To edit any color, click on it to display the Color Picker dialog box. Then select a different color and press Return/Enter to go back to the Color Table dialog box. Then press Return/Enter again to close the Color Table dialog box and change every pixel colored in the old color to the new color.

The Color Table dialog box also enables you to open and save palettes and select predefined palettes from the Table pop-up menu. What the Color Table dialog box doesn't let you do is identify a color from the image. For example, if you're trying to fix a color in your image, you can't display the Color Table dialog box, click on the color in the image, and have the dialog box show you the corresponding color in the look-up table. The only way to be sure you're editing the correct color — and be forewarned, this is a royal pain in the behind — is to slog through the following steps, which begin before you choose Image ⇨ Mode ⇨ Color Table.

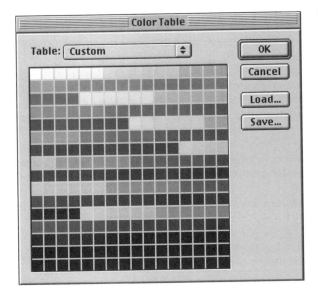

**Figure 32-9:** Use the Color Table dialog box to modify the colors in an indexed image.

## Steps: Editing a Specific CLUT Color

1. **Use the eyedropper tool to click on the offending color in the image.** This makes it the foreground color.

2. **Click on the foreground color icon to display the specs for the color in the Color Picker dialog box.** Write down the RGB values on a handy piece of paper, the palm of your hand, or a bald friend's scalp. (Don't edit the color inside the Color Picker dialog box at this time. If you do, you just change the color without changing any pixel in the image associated with that color.) Press Escape to leave the dialog box.

3. **Choose Image ⇨ Mode ⇨ Color Table.**

4. **Click on a color that looks like it might be the right one.** After the Color Picker appears, compare the color's RGB numbers to those you wrote down. If they match, boy, did you ever luck out. Go ahead and edit the color as desired. If the RGB values don't match, press the Escape key to return to the Color Table dialog box and try again. And again. And again.

Tip

To create a *color ramp* — that is, a gradual color progression — drag rather than click on the colors in the palette to select multiple colors at a time. Photoshop then displays the Color Picker dialog box, enabling you to edit the first color in the ramp. After you select the desired color and press Return/Enter, the Color Picker reappears, this time asking you to edit the last color in the ramp. After you specify this color, Photoshop automatically creates the colors between the first and last colors in the ramp in even RGB increments.

## Saving the completed GIF image

When it comes time to save your GIF image, you can save it in either the GIF87a or 89a format. To save a GIF87a image — where all pixels are opaque — choose File ➪ Save As and select the CompuServe GIF option from the Format pop-up menu. After you press Return/Enter, Photoshop presents you with two options, Normal and Interlaced. If you want the Web browser to display the image in incremental passes — similar to a progressive JPEG image — select the latter. Otherwise, select Normal.

But it's generally a better idea to save the indexed image as a GIF89a file. GIF89a is a more efficient format with better compression, which means it results in smaller files. GIF89a also supports transparent pixels, thereby permitting you to see through portions of the image to the Web page background pattern, or to other images in a Dynamic HTML file.

Choose File ➪ Export ➪ GIF89a Export to display the similarly named dialog box shown in Figure 32-10. Here you'll find an Interlace check box, which you can turn on or off as desired. There's also a Caption check box which lets you save a caption created with File ➪ File Info. The only purpose for this is to let image cataloging programs search for the file by keywords. The caption does not appear in the HTML file.

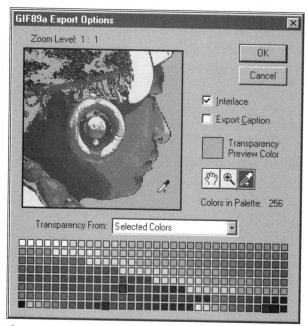

**Figure 32-10:** Click with the eyedropper cursor to make colors in the image transparent, as I have with the pixels outside the man's face.

All this is very well and good, but the real purpose of the GIF89a Export dialog box is to make pixels transparent:

✦ Click on a pixel in the image preview, or on one of the swatches in the color palette below, to make that color transparent. Keep clicking to add more transparent colors. Photoshop surrounds the transparent color swatches with heavy outlines.

✦ ⌘/Ctrl+click on a color to bring it back from transparency and return it to opacity again.

✦ You can scroll the preview by pressing the spacebar and dragging inside it. Zoom by ⌘/Ctrl+spacebar+clicking, and Option/Alt+spacebar+clicking.

✦ By default, Photoshop changes the transparent pixels to gray. But if gray is a popular color in your image, this may make it difficult to edit the image later. Because Photoshop has no method for expressing GIF transparency — the checkerboard method only works for native Photoshop files — the transparent pixels appear gray in color when you open and edit the image. So I recommend that you take the extra precaution of changing the transparent pixels to some way-out color, like bright yellow or green. To do this, click on the swatch labeled Transparency Preview Color (or Transparency Index Color on a Mac) and select a new color in the Color Picker.

**Tip**

If your image contains a mask channel, you can use the mask to define the transparent areas in the image. Just select the mask name from the Transparency From pop-up menu in the GIF89a Export dialog box. The black areas of the mask translate to transparency; the white areas are opaque. Keep in mind that GIF can handle just two levels of opacity — on and off, with no room for translucency. So if the mask includes gray pixels, the dark gray pixels become transparent and the light gray pixels become opaque.

**Cross-Reference**

For examples of transparent pixels, you might want to check out my site at *http://www.dekemc.com*. Every single graphic includes some transparent pixels, permitting the drop shadows and other gradual elements to blend in with the background.

# Third-Party JPEG and GIF Alternatives

Photoshop's own GIF and JPEG export modules are pretty good, but third-party replacements from Digital Frontiers (*www.digfrontiers.com*) and Box Top Software (*www.boxtopsoft.com*) suggest that there's ample room for improvement. The CD at the back of the book includes demonstrations of these filters so you can arrive at your own conclusions, but here's the skinny:

Digital Frontier's $150 HVS WebFocus includes separate modules for exporting JPEG and GIF images, both featured in Figure 32-11. The HVS JPEG module includes a live preview that updates when you change settings. (The preview isn't entirely accurate — you can't know the exact effects of JPEG compression until the final compression is applied—but it's a heck of a lot better than no preview at all.) HVS JPEG also estimates the size of the saved image, a terrific help when deciding how much compression to apply.

But if HVS JPEG is helpful, HVS ColorGIF is essential. First, ColorGIF gives you precise control over dithering. Instead of simply turning dithering on or off, as Photoshop lets you do, you can adjust the dithering incrementally, thereby permitting you to soften edges without speckling flat areas of color, whether the flat colors are found in the palette or not. ColorGIF also lets you adjust threshold and gamma settings to prepare images for display on foreign monitors. You can establish settings and preview the results inside a single dialog box. And like HVS JPEG, ColorGIF estimates the size of the saved file. Frankly, ColorGIF is a must for anyone who's serious about Web graphics.

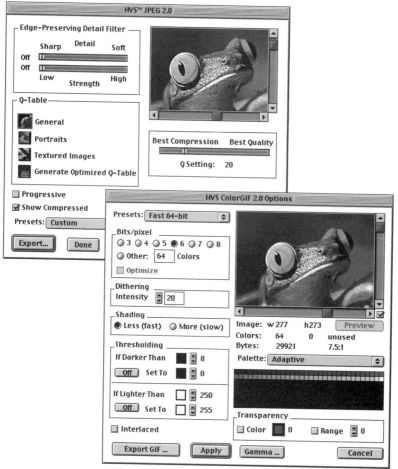

**Figure 32-11:** The HVS JPEG and ColorGIF plug-ins permit you to apply and preview effects inside a single dialog box, as well as predict file size before saving.

A less expensive solution for folks using Macs is the $70 ProJPEG and PhotoGIF bundle from BoxTop. ProJPEG does most of what HVS JPEG does, and with a simpler interface. PhotoGIF filter shares ColorGIF's ability to gradually dither an image, but it lacks the screen calibration options and you have to preview your settings in a separate dialog box. Still, at half the price of WebFocus, you may be able to live with those limitations.

Oh, and in case you were considering worrying about compatibility, don't. The JPEG and GIF formats are sufficiently standardized that your on-line guests will never know where your images came from. An image saved with HVS JPEG or ColorGIF can be opened on another machine by Photoshop without HVS. The same holds true for the BoxTop plug-ins as well.

# Saving PNG Images

As I write this, the newest Web image format is the *Portable Network Graphics* format, or PNG (pronounced *ping*). Developed by a panel of independent graphics experts, PNG was designed specifically to outperform and ultimately replace GIF. It supports 24-bit and 48-bit images, it permits you to include mask channels for gradual transparency control, and—perhaps most importantly—PNG is not patented. Starting in 1995, Unisys, the developer of GIF, began to charge royalties to Web software developers. PNG, meanwhile, is free for all, which is why some folks claim PNG unofficially stands for "PNG, Not GIF."

PNG files are typically larger than comparable JPEG or GIF images because a PNG file does not include JPEG's lossy compression, and it can contain more colors than a GIF image. (The exception is when you save a grayscale or indexed PNG file, which is frequently smaller than the same file saved in GIF.) So PNG is generally best suited to small images—buttons and thumbnails—with fine details that you don't want mangled by JPEG compression.

Photoshop supports any RGB, grayscale, or indexed image in the PNG format. PNG doesn't support layers (of course), but it does permit you to include a single mask channel. Assuming the browser supports extra PNG channels, the mask defines the opacity and transparency of the image on the page. PNG graphics can even be translucent (as defined by gray areas in the mask channel), a terrific advantage over GIF and JPEG.

When you save a PNG image, Photoshop displays the dialog box shown in Figure 32-12. Here you can select the kind of interlacing and compression that you want to apply:

> ◆ **Interlace**: The PNG format offers the strangely named "Adam7" interlacing. Adam7 draws your image on screen in seven passes, drawing the image in blocks and filling in the pixels between blocks. If you want interlacing, select Adam7. If you don't, turn it off.

✦ **Filter:** These options permit you to specify the way in which Photoshop applies PNG's special zlib compression scheme. This particular scheme compresses data in blocks, and the Filter options let you specify the way in which the blocks are calculated. Even when armed with this knowledge, only one option, None, makes any sense. It turns off the compression. The other options permit you to tweak the compression for the minimum possible file size.

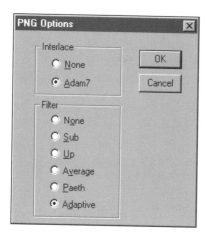

**Figure 32-12:** When saving a PNG file, Photoshop offers you some very peculiar options found nowhere else in the program.

See, GIF's LZW compression can actually lead to an increase in file size in some cases. To avoid this, PNG gives you a sufficient number of compression options to ensure smaller files. You can certainly experiment with the options to see which one gives you the smallest results. But unless you're absolutely obsessed by small file size — we're talking about saving a few hundred bytes at most — just select Adaptive and let the compression do its magic without your help.

Before you rush out to save an image to the PNG format, however, bear in mind that support is thus far spotty. As I write this, neither Netscape Navigator nor Internet Explorer directly support PNG. If you want to include a PNG image on your page, your guests will have to install a third-party plug-in, such as Siegel and Gale's PNG Live. I live in hope that this will change. I imagine that PNG support might become fairly universal by, say, the year 2001. But in the meantime, the format is more interesting than practical.

✦　　✦　　✦

# PART X
# NEW FRONTIERS

## CHAPTER 33

# THE QUICK GUIDE TO DIGITAL CAMERAS

Whether you're a photographer, a commercial artist, or a weekend Photoshop enthusiast, you've probably heard the siren call of direct-to-disk photography. The very idea that you snap an RGB photograph and download it to a hard disk in less time than it takes to drive to your local film developer and ask, "Are my prints ready?" has a certain universal appeal.

In fact, according to electronic photographer and consultant Katrin Eismann, those photographers who haven't yet gone digital can look forward to a complete transformation of their craft. "In the next five years, 80 percent of professional photographers will be involved in some form of digital imaging. That's up from about 30 percent now. Conventional photography as we know it will be a thing of the past very, very soon."

But while the long-term forecast for digital cameras is sunny, the current state of technology is a bit rough and tumble. As with any new and emerging technology, digital cameras are expensive and every device ships with its own laundry list of rewards and penalties. It's no easy matter to decide whether you should bite the bullet and buy now, or wait for things to settle down and hope that you can make a successful transition when the moment is right.

In this chapter, Eismann walks us through the three prevalent issues of digital photography: when to buy, what to look for, and how to edit images in Photoshop once you start snapping pictures. Much as we'd like to think that if you've seen one Photoshop image you've seen them all, digital photography presents its own share of special concerns.

*My advice is always: Get the image right in front of the lens and fix as little as possible in Photoshop.*

KATRIN EISMANN

### IS A DIGITAL CAMERA RIGHT FOR YOU?

Naturally, no photographer wants to trade in a tried-and-true film camera for something that isn't capable of producing at least the same level of quality. So it's important that the new technology measure up to the old. Eismann insists that it does. "If you just want a quick yes or no, then rest assured — the quality is there. Professional-level digital cameras are every bit as good as film, in some cases better."

Eismann photographed this cat (33.1) with a $10,000 Kodak DCS420, one of the least expensive of the professional models. In the magnified view (33.2), you can clearly see individual hairs around the eye and capillaries in the iris. You can even make out a reflection of a house with a silhouette of Eismann shooting the picture.

**33.1 (TOP), 33.2 (BOTTOM)**

The salt shaker (33.3) is the work of a $30,000 Leaf Digital Camera Back II affixed to a Hasselblad ELX camera body. Even when printed at 300 pixels per inch, the image manages to fill the page — and this is just a detail from the full 12MB file. "If I take a 12MB drum scan off a professional piece of film and compare it to a 12MB image shot with the Leaf DCB II, I'll be able to blow up the Leaf image more because there's no grain to get in the way (33.4)."

But while the quality is dreamy, the costs are enough to shock you wide awake. "Granted, you no longer have to pay for film or developing. But a digital camera costs anywhere from a few hundred bucks for a consumer model to $55,000 at the very high end. And that's not including the $10,000 or more for a desktop system required to process these 5MB to 150MB files. I mean, you're not borrowing your kid's IIci. We're talking about enough money to make a down payment on a very nice home."

So the real question is not whether digital measures up to film, but whether it warrants your personal investment. "For every kind of photography, you're going to get a different answer. First you have to determine what photographic niche you fit in, and then you can decide if a digital camera will work for you."

Eismann has identified three major niche criteria — time, quality, and budget. The amount of emphasis you place on each criterion determines what kind of digital camera — if any — will best satisfy your needs.

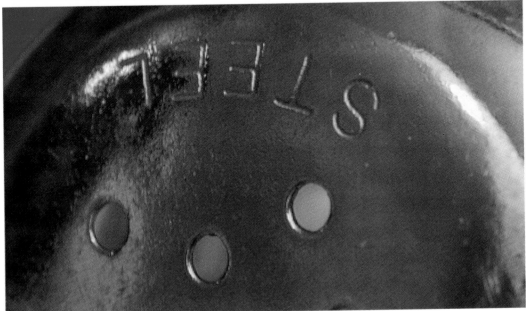

**33.3 (TOP), 33.4 (BOTTOM)**

## TIME WAITS FOR NO ONE

"As soon as time is an important factor, digital cameras win hands down," Eismann explains. This includes folks who work in news, medicine, government, or any other arena where pictures need to travel quickly. "At the major news services and USA Today, the typical picture deadline for digital files is an hour and a half later than for the guy who's shooting to film. And in the news business, an hour and a half is a major chunk of time."

Just out of curiosity, how do these roving digital journalists transfer their images? "If you're lucky, you have a land line and you use a modem. But most of these guys work with cell phones, which allow them to transmit from buses and even airplanes, as high as 6,000 feet. And in really remote situations, you might find a guy schlepping around a 40-pound satellite dish. But the payoff is that you can transfer 500K in about six to eight minutes."

## A MATTER OF QUALITY

A few digital cameras in the $20,000 range can capture more information than film, upward of 35 million pixels. But for the moment, these are scanning cameras which require long exposures — 30 seconds to 12 minutes — and continuous light. "So if you're doing high-quality, display-format photography with live models, you're not going to be working with a scanning camera. In the cosmetic industry, for example, forget it — the model would have to be dead." The exception may be the $55,000 Dicomed BigShot, which quickly captures millions of pixels with an area array. But Eismann isn't prepared to endorse this model. "I'm still hearing very mixed reviews."

But for less demanding product shots — where you can stick inanimate objects under hot lights without anyone complaining — digital cameras can't be beat. "Digital cameras are really taking over the catalog business. Sharper Image, LL Bean, Bon Marché — they're all digital. Ninety percent of catalog images are printed smaller than 8 × 10 inches. So with something like the $22,000 Kodak DCS460 (33.5), you've got it made. The catalogs are produced electronically anyway, so there's just no reason to shoot film."

**ARTIST:**
Katrin Eismann

**COMPANY:**
PRAXIS. Digital Solutions
450 7th Street, 4B
Hoboken, NJ 07030
201/659-7378
praxis1@earthlink.net

**SYSTEM:**
Power Mac 9500/180MP
8GB storage

**RAM:**
348MB total
300MB assigned to Photoshop

**MONITOR:**
Mitsubishi Diamond Pro 17TX

**OTHER STUFF:**
Ergonomic MacTable ("You have to consider your working environment. I've seen people with $15,000 systems using tables from Wal-Mart.")
6 × 9 inch Wacom tablet, and Kodak 8600 Thermal Dye-Sublimation printer

33·5

**VERSION USED:**

Photoshop 5.0

**OTHER APPLICATIONS:**

Live Picture, QuarkXPress

**WORK HISTORY:**

1987 — Following 10-year break after high school, studied fine-art photography at Rochester Institute of Technology.

1991 — First intern at Kodak Center for Creative Imaging in Camden, Maine.

1993 — One of 16 invited artists to participate in international digital imaging show, Montage '93.

1995 — Sponsored by Kodak for eight-country photoimaging tour of Asia.

1999 — Coauthored *Real World Digital Photography*, Peachpit Press.

**FAVORITE ROLE MODEL:**

Amanda from *Melrose Place* ("She's true to herself . . . well, only herself.")

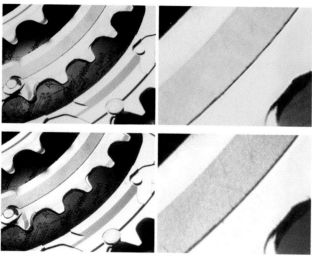

**33.6 (TOP), 33.7 (BOTTOM)**

Another quality-related issue to keep in mind is the difference between competing three-shot and one-shot technologies. Both permit you to shoot flash pictures (something the scanning backs don't permit). But where a three-shot camera back captures an image using multiple exposures with red, green, and blue filters, the one-shot camera embeds the filters onto the individual CCD cells. (Incidentally, a CCD is basically the electronic equivalent of film in a digital camera. A huge array of CCD cells — one for each pixel — makes up the imaging surface.) As a result, three-shots are studio cameras ill-suited to moving objects, while the more prevalent one-shots are portable and work like conventional 35mm devices.

But one-shots are not without their failings. "Because you have the RGB filter right on the CCD, you'll often encounter little rainbow patterns in reflective areas and in finely patterned areas such as cloth or hair (33.6). One filtered cell is seeing something that its immediate neighbor does not. With a three-shot, you don't get the rainbows because you're taking full advantage of the resolution of the monochrome array (33.7)." Eismann tells us how to eliminate the one-shot rainbows in Photoshop in the section "Fixing Rainbows" later in this chapter.

If quality isn't important, then you can get by for considerably less money. "For folks who work in documentation, real estate, or insurance (33.8), color and clarity aren't big concerns. If you intend to print the photo on inexpensive paper or post it on the Web, then why even bother with the quality film can offer you?" For these folks, the midrange "megapixel" cameras are ideal. Virtually every major imaging company — Kodak, Olympus, Nikon, Fuji — sells a digital camera that takes pictures with 1024 × 768 pixels or more for less than $1,000.

## THE COST OF DOING BUSINESS

Assessing your financial niche helps you decide if a digital camera fits in your budget. "At the professional level, this is a major business decision. You have to ask yourself, 'What am I saving by investing in this camera?' The obvious answers are film, Polaroid, processing. But more importantly, you're creating a more efficient environment. You're eliminating that delay between shooting the picture and confirming that the job is done so you can move on to another shoot."

So a digital camera may help you squeeze a few additional shoots into your schedule, or it may prevent another business from encroaching on your territory. "You know who's buying the $10,000 cameras right now? The service bureaus, the prepress houses, the professional color labs. They're offering digital photography as an added value." Therefore, the ambitious photographer will need to pay to play. "You ultimately want to get into the digital workflow and start offering retouching and compositing services. The longer you can stay with your image — shoot it, retouch it, composite it, and submit the final image file in CMYK — the longer you will literally be in business."

## FILM STILL HAS ITS MERITS

But surely, even a photographer who fits perfectly into a digital niche is going to experience some separation pangs from film. "Oh, there's no doubt. Give me a conventional camera — be it a Nikon or a Hasselblad — and 10 rolls of film, and I can shoot landscapes, portraits, still life, underwater photography — I've got the whole breadth. No digital camera can beat the versatility of conventional film. That's why finding your niche is so important. If you can identify a narrow range of requirements, you're more likely to find a digital camera that suits your needs."

33.8

**33.9** (TOP), **33.10** (BOTTOM)

## SELECTING THE BEST CAMERA

Digital cameras are in a rapid state of flux. There are several examples of a vendor introducing and discontinuing a specific model within the same year. So there's no way to create a buyer's guide within the context of this chapter. Computer magazines such as *Macworld, Publish,* and *Digital PhotoWorld* routinely print camera roundups and are better suited to releasing timely recommendations.

That said, Eismann can offer a few general guidelines for evaluating cameras on your own. "Whenever people look at digital cameras, they always ask, 'How big is the file?' The problem is, that's just one of the issues. The other issues — what does the image look like and how does the camera handle — are ultimately more important. If you have to spend too much time editing the images and you don't like working with a camera, then I don't care how big the images are, you're not going to use it. Your investment is just going to sit around and molder on a shelf."

So how do you make sure you'll enjoy using a camera? "When buying a point-and-shoot device, you want to look at the viewfinder." Eismann shot some pictures comparing one of the least expensive cameras ever produced, the $200 Kodak DC20 (33.9), with one of the most expensive rangefinder models, the $3,000 Polaroid PDC-2000 (33.10). She framed both pictures identically, and yet the DC20 shot is mostly hay. "Its viewfinder is just a hole — it's not accurate at all. Here's an example of a camera that's cheap, but what good is it if you can't frame a picture? This is parallax at its worst."

Most rangefinder devices are now adopting color LCD screens (33.11), which can serve as excellent framing aids. But refresh rates vary anywhere from a few frames per second (terrible) to 30 fps (TV quality) or better. And if you're going to use an LCD for live preview, you need lots of juice. "The batteries have to be rechargeable. Some people think this is nit-picking, but wait till you go out in the field and run out of power after half an hour. It can be devastating."

Another consideration is reaction speed. "If you're working with children or animals, having a delay — even one or two seconds — just isn't acceptable." The Polaroid PDC-2000 is an offender here. The camera spends so much time charging its flash that the shutter release may be temporarily inoperable.

"Removable storage is a definite must. This one fellow told me that his camera got digitally constipated. I was like, 'Excuse me, have we met?' But he was right. You have to be able to switch out media when the memory gets full."

For those of you in the market for a professional level camera, there's no substitute for a hands-on inspection. "Before you sink $5,000 or more into a device, make sure to give it the full digital test drive. Most reputable resellers will be happy to visit you in your studio so you can see how the camera performs on your home turf."

33.11

## SHOOTING AND EDITING YOUR PHOTOS

Much as Eismann appreciates Photoshop, she doesn't recommend it as a panacea for framing and compositional errors. "What I've seen happen when some people get digital cameras is that they'll get lazy. I was out shooting with this one guy and he takes a picture of a model so she looks like she has a telephone pole coming out of her head. He told me, 'Oh, I'll fix that with the rubber stamp.' I was like, 'Wouldn't it be easier to just move over three feet?' My advice is always: Get the image right in front of the lens and fix as little as possible in Photoshop.

33.12 (TOP), 33.13 (BOTTOM)

"Another thing: When using the low-end cameras, you should make an effort to shoot really graphic subjects. And get in close — no, I mean closer, no I mean *really* close." The chickens bear out Eismann's advice. I shot the top group of hens (33.12) with an Olympus D200L, a very good low-end camera in its time. But I made a total mess of the subject by standing five miles away. The two close-up hens (33.13) are much more successful, even though I used a Casio QV-10A, possibly the worst digital camera ever made in terms of picture quality.

## KATRIN'S LOW-END TIPS

Low-end cameras suffer from pixel shortages, and they spoil what few pixels they have with an excessive dose of compression. So you have to make the best of what little you have to work with when taking the picture. Eismann recommends:

- Get in close so your subject fills the frame.
- Beware of parallax when shooting closer than 3 feet. (If you anticipate doing a lot of close-up work, get a camera with an LCD preview.)
- Avoid fine detail, like leaves, cloth patterns, and so on.
- Avoid high-contrast light. "Don't shoot someone at noon, or he'll have dark shadows on his face like a raccoon."
- If the sunlight does create shadows on your subject, there's an easy way to fix it. "Just turn on the flash. A daylight flash is called a 'fill flash' because it opens up the dark shadows."

## ADJUSTING LIGHTING IRREGULARITIES

But even with the best of precautions, pictures will go awry. Eismann shot her fountain boys (33.14) at dusk with a Polaroid PDC-2000 — which despite its shutter release problem, produces excellent midrange images. The subject is close, the detail is smooth, and the lighting is soft. But when Eismann opened the image in Photoshop, she was surprised to see a curious vertical shaft of light running down the middle of the image.

She added a Levels adjustment layer (by ⌘/Ctrl-clicking the page icon at the bottom of the Layers palette). But in lightening the fountain boys, she managed to overlighten the bright shaft. Luckily, every adjustment layer permits a layer mask which you can use to paint away portions of the color correction. Eismann used the gradient tool to create a mask in which the black area mimicked the shaft of light in the photograph (33.15). This involved two strokes of the gradient tool — first white to black and then white to transparent in the opposite direction. (Incidentally, you don't normally see the layer mask; to make the figure, I Option/Alt-clicked the layer mask thumbnail in the Layers palette.)

Finally, Eismann set the blend mode to Screen and set the Opacity to 70 percent (33.16). The effect isn't perfect because the shaft of light is not precisely vertical. But it comes awfully close, especially given how fast you can reproduce these steps. And if you were feeling particular, you could perfect the layer mask by painting in highlights with the airbrush tool.

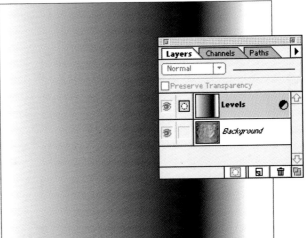

**33.14 (TOP), 33.15 (MIDDLE), 33.16 (BOTTOM)**

**33.17 (TOP), 33.18 (BOTTOM)**

## FIXING RAINBOWS

Earlier, I explained how one-shot cameras can capture unwanted rainbows along the edge of reflective surfaces. The rainbows appear in full bloom in the chrome Marina logo (33.17), which Eismann shot with a Kodak DCS420. Luckily, you can remedy this problem with little effort inside Photoshop.

The rainbow is caused by disparity between neighboring pixels. So the solution is to blur the colors slightly and then sharpen the detail, both of which you can accomplish in the Lab mode.

First choose Image ➤ Mode ➤ Lab Color to convert the RGB image to Lab. Then go to the Channels palette and click on the *a* channel. (If you want to preview the effect in color, click in the eyeball column in front of the Lab composite.) Apply the Gaussian Blur filter with a Radius of about 1 pixel for every 1MB of image data. In the case of the 4.5MB Marina logo, Eismann applied a Radius of 3. Then switch to the *b* channel and press ⌘/Ctrl+F to reapply the filter.

So far, all you've affected is the color; the detail is still saved in the luminosity (L) channel. Press ⌘/Ctrl+1 to go to the L channel and choose the Unsharp Mask filter. "I tend to raise the Amount value to 175 percent. And I play with my Radius. Usually it's between 0.75 and 1.5.

"The blurring gets rid of the color artifacting; the sharpening brings out the detail (33.18). Nowadays, I apply this technique to just about every picture I shoot; often there's artifacting that's much more subtle than the rainbows but equally harmful to the appearance of the image. And you can even script this operation from the Actions palette to apply it with a single keystroke in the future."

## SIMPLE BUT SPECIAL EFFECTS

"Every photographer occasionally wants to darken edges or burn down corners, where the edges fade in from black, to help frame the image. To do this, I go into the Layers palette and make an empty layer. I select the gradient tool and set it to Foreground to Transparent. The foreground color is black. Then I drag from a corner about a fifth of the way into the image and let go (33.19). I do that in all four corners. Now, it looks like the image has just gotten ruined. But if I set the blend mode in the Layers palette to Soft Light, I can really control how much I want to burn down those edges. Then I experiment with the Opacity until I get the effect I want (33.20).

"Another way to focus the viewer's attention on the foreground image is to blur the background. In the case of the forks (33.21), the background is a light box with gumdrops on it. I used the pen tool to select the forks and the big gumdrops, then I inversed the selection and applied the Motion Blur filter — not much, maybe 7 or 8 pixels — to give the background a little more dynamic appeal. This also enhances the depth of field, forcing the forks more into the foreground."

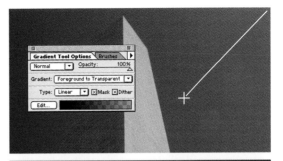

**33.19 (TOP), 33.20 (BOTTOM)**

33.21

## KEEPING YOUR PHOTOS SAFE

Eismann offers one last word of advice to photographers making the transition from film. "Archiving may be the most important issue of all for digital photographers. Once again, look at film — it's your capture device, and it's your storage device." There's a good chance that film lasts longer than magnetic media, too. The only electronic media that come close are CDs and MOs (magneto opticals), both of which may endure several decades of use. "I even archive my film shots to Photo CD, because that way, I know I'll use them." What about SyQuest, Zip, or Jaz? "I just use that stuff to transfer files."

What exactly should you save? "Media is too cheap to cut corners. So save everything. For example, a lot of the high-end cameras will automatically shoot into an archived format, with compressed files arranged neatly in folders. You then acquire the images for editing in Photoshop one picture at a time. I always save back the entire archive. As Leaf, Kodak, and other manufacturers improve their software, I can go back and reacquire the images. It's like reprocessing the images with fresh chemicals."

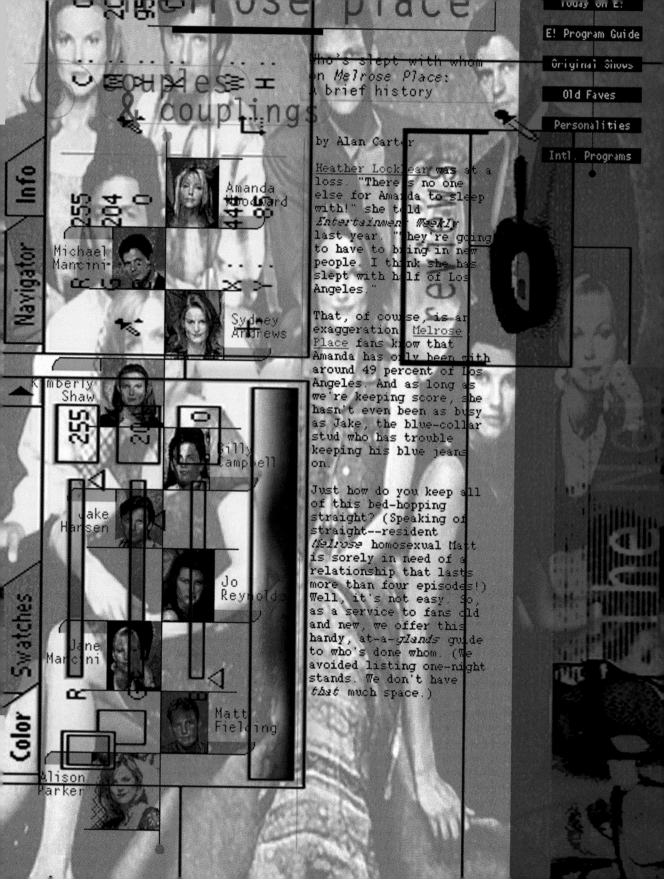

# melrose place

## couples & couplings

Today on E!

E! Program Guide

Original Shows

Old Faves

Personalities

Intl. Programs

**Info**

**Navigator**

**Swatches**

**Color**

Amanda Woodward

Michael Mancini

Sydney Andrews

Kimberly Shaw

Billy Campbell

Jake Hansen

Jo Reynolds

Jane Mancini

Matt Fielding

Alison Parker

### Who's slept with whom on *Melrose Place*: A brief history

by Alan Carter

Heather Locklear was at a loss. "There's no one else for Amanda to sleep with!" she told *Entertainment Weekly* last year. "They're going to have to bring in new people. I think she has slept with half of Los Angeles."

That, of course, is an exaggeration. *Melrose Place* fans know that Amanda has only been with around 49 percent of Los Angeles. And as long as we're keeping score, she hasn't even been as busy as Jake, the blue-collar stud who has trouble keeping his blue jeans on.

Just how do you keep all of this bed-hopping straight? (Speaking of straight—resident *Melrose* homosexual Matt is sorely in need of a relationship that lasts more than four episodes!) Well, it's not easy. So, as a service to fans old and new, we offer this handy, at-a-*glands* guide to who's done whom. (We avoided listing one-night stands. We don't have *that* much space.)

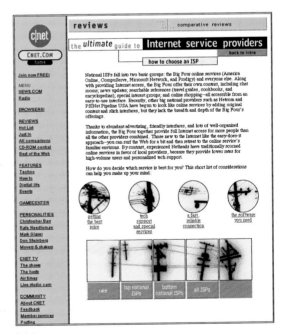

# CHAPTER 34
# CREATING IMAGES FOR THE WEB

T he World Wide Web is a truly wonderful, truly horrible medium. Its primary wonder is its ceaseless bounty. The Web is already so vast as to defy comprehension, and yet it continues to grow at an incomprehensible rate. The Web also rates high marks for anarchy. Just plain folks can post sites for little money, and there are none of the space limitations inherent in, say, print media.

The horror is the speed. It doesn't matter what kind of modem or direct wiring you use, this is one agonizingly slow delivery vehicle. Consider this comparison: When you pick up a traditional magazine, you can take in the entire full-color, high-resolution, uncompressed cover in the time it takes your brain to interpret reflected light. I'm no physicist, but I'm guessing that we're talking about a few nanoseconds, max. Now, imagine viewing that same full-color, high-resolution, uncompressed image posted on someone's Web site. I'm no telecommunications expert, but if there was a race between that image and a snail crawling from Bangor to Tijuana, I'd put my money on the snail.

## BEN WOULD KILL FOR A KILOBYTE

Having served on the launch teams for such prominent online magazines as *CNET* (34.1) and *E! Online* (34.2), full-time Web artist Ben Benjamin is all too familiar with the benefits and handicaps of packaging content for the Internet. On one hand, you can post pages until you're blue in the face and make them as long as you like. On the other hand, Benjamin wages a perpetual battle to make his images small.

"File size is absolutely the biggest constraint that I

*Compress till it hurts.*

BEN BENJAMIN

**34.1**

*Reprinted with permission from CNET, Inc., ©1995–97*

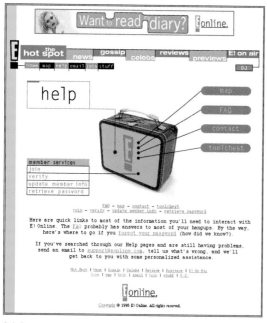

**34.2**
*©1996 E! Online*

work under," Benjamin says. "I use Photoshop and Equilibrium's DeBabelizer to automate some of the chores — like deciding the optimal bit depth of a GIF palette or the amount of compression to apply to a JPEG file. But I often revisit the image inside Photoshop and do some tedious cleanup work. With GIF files in particular, I might zoom in to the image and examine which colors I can eliminate on a pixel-by-pixel basis. Like, say a block of pixels is mostly one shade of green with a red pixel in the middle. I'll probably use the pencil tool to change the red pixel to green, as well. That not only gets rid of a color, but it makes GIF's run-length-encoding compression more efficient."

Pixel-level editing is a pretty extreme measure. Why go to that effort to shave a few bytes off the file size? "Commercial sites enforce per-page maximums — file sizes that you can't go over. It varies from site to site, usually between 20K and 50K." When you consider that each character of text and HTML code takes up a byte, and a single icon-sized button weighs in at 1K, these maximums are rather prohibitive. In print, four 50K images could fit inside one square inch.

So, how do you make the cut? "Small size is generally considered more important than appearance. So you keep the pixel dimensions of the graphics as small as possible. And you compress till it hurts. You

**ARTIST:**
Ben Benjamin

**ORGANIZATION:**
Mr. Pants — A Design Firm
60 Thirteenth Street
San Francisco, CA 94107
415/863-9666
ben@superbad.com

**SYSTEM:**
PowerTower Pro 225 (Power Computing)
2GB storage

**RAM:**
128MB total
60MB assigned to Photoshop

**MONITOR:**
Apple 21-inch

**EXTRAS:**
Global Village 28K modem

**VERSION USED:**
Photoshop 4.0

keep nudging the bit depth or compression until the image looks awful. Then, you nudge it back one and leave it there." Good enough and speedy is better than beautiful and slow.

## THE MELROSE MYSTERY

Not only have I never seen *Melrose Place*, I don't even know what channel it's on. And yet this televised testament to promiscuity has somehow managed to rear its lascivious head twice in this book (the first reference having occurred in the otherwise principled Chapter 33). Is it possible that I've uncovered a secret link between Photoshop users and Heather Locklear?

Benjamin couldn't say. "I know everybody says this, but I've really never watched the show either." I'm certain the same goes for you, O chaste reader, but we'll all have to do our best to feign interest.

### A TAWDRY LITTLE CYBERPLACE

"The *Melrose Place* story went up when we launched *E! Online* (34.3). Basically, it chronicles who slept with whom (34.4). It's a few years old now, so they've had to update the story to include new characters." I imagine the list of extramarital encounters has expanded as well.

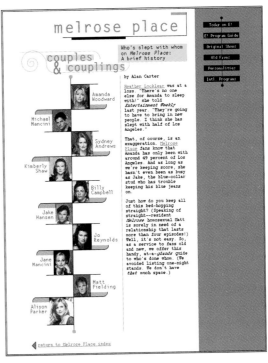

**34.3**
©*1996 E! Online*

**OTHER APPLICATIONS:**
Adobe Illustrator, Equilibrium DeBabelizer, Netscape Navigator, Bare Bones Software BBEdit, GifBuilder (shareware)

**WORK HISTORY:**
1990 — Hand-painted T-shirts and sold them to students at Indiana University.
1992 — Accepted one-day temp job shoveling dog food; created comic strip "Clod" for student newspaper.
1994 — Landed a job at Yo! Design; worked on Peachpit Press Web site back in the days of Netscape 1.0.

1995 — Joined CNET: The Computer Network as part of original launch team.
1996 — Hired as art director for *E! Online*, the Internet Entertainment magazine.

**FAVORITE AMERICAN FOLKLORE HERO:**
John Henry ("You have to admire the man's hatred of machines.")

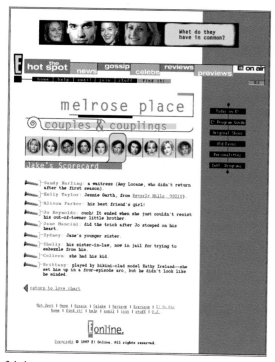

**34.4**

**34.5**

"This page went up before we had a photo editor or anything like that. So, all I had to work with was a badly digitized cast photo (34.5). It's pretty high-res, but it's a blurry, grainy, messed-up scan. But because we were posting the images online, it didn't really matter. I made it work by downsampling the heck out of it. Then, I indexed the image to the 216-color Web palette, without dithering (34.6)."

## DESIGNING PAGES IN ILLUSTRATOR

Benjamin composed his basic page design in Illustrator (34.7). "I selected each of the faces in Photoshop and then dragged and dropped them over into the Illustrator document. Then, I added the body copy and designed the headlines and other text treatments."

Why use Illustrator for this purpose? Why not use PageMill or one of the other HTML editors? "I'm not in charge of generating the HTML files. I'm just making a design that the coders will work from. I export the design as a big GIF file and post it for the editorial folks to look at in L.A. After it's approved, I save all the graphics and send them down the assembly line."

In that case, why not use a page layout program such as QuarkXPress? "Illustrator handles single-

**34.6**

page designs really well, but it also permits me to add graphic elements and create special headline treatments. When I get the effect I want, I can export the graphics as GIF files, or drag and drop elements over to Photoshop. It's way more flexible than using a page layout program."

## EXPORTING THE GIF IMAGE MAP

Benjamin exported a modified version of the "cast toolbar"—the column of characters' faces and names—as a GIF89a file (34.8). This toolbar was then tagged as an image map by the coding department. Each face became a button which would take you to a listing of the character's sexual exploits. (For the record, Illustrator 7 and 8 let you assign URLs to objects and save client-side image maps, but Benjamin was using Version 6 at the time.)

After exporting a GIF file from Illustrator, it's always a good idea to open it in Photoshop and make sure you like the results. "I usually export a few different versions of the graphic from Illustrator — one with antialiasing turned on, another with it turned off, one with dithering on, et cetera. Then, I combine the pieces I like into the final image inside Photoshop."

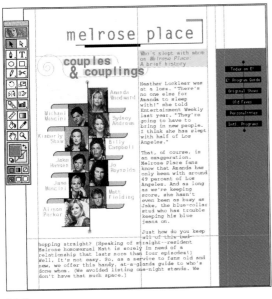

34·7

34.8

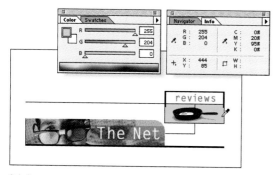

34.9

## ANTICIPATING 256-COLOR MONITORS

As a Photoshop artist, you probably own a 16-bit or 24-bit monitor. But about half the people who visit your site will be looking at 8-bit monitors. When your image is viewed on an 8-bit screen, the browser redraws the image using the Mac or Windows system palette. The two palettes share 216 common colors, which make up the so-called Web palette.

"Any color in the graphic that falls inside the Web palette looks fine; any color that isn't in the palette appears dithered. Sometimes dithering is okay. With soft edges and continuous-tone photographs, dithering doesn't usually matter. But dithering looks crummy inside flat-colored areas, like the green shapes and the text in the cast toolbar."

The solution is to fill the flat areas with a Web-safe color. Illustrator 8 offers a built-in Web palette. And Photoshop lets you downsample to the Web palette using Image ➤ Mode ➤ Indexed Color. But the best trick is to memorize the RGB recipe for Web-safe colors, as explained in the sidebar "How Ben Anticipates 256-Color Monitors."

### HOW BEN ANTICIPATES 256-COLOR MONITORS

**B**enjamin explains, "If each of the RGB values for a color is divisible by 51, then it's safe." That's a total of 6 permutations — 0, 51, 102, 153, 204, and 255 — in each of three channels. As it just so happens, $6 \times 6 \times 6 = 216$.

"When I reduce the bit depth of the image using Photoshop's Indexed Color command, I usually apply the Adaptive palette. Then, I go back and check the flat areas with the eyedropper to make sure they haven't changed (34.9). If a flat color has changed, I return to the RGB mode and use the paint bucket set to a Tolerance of 0 to make it Web-safe again."

## EXPLOITING BROWSER CACHING

As I've said, my experience with *Melrose Place* is nil, but it seems quite clear that the ambition of the show's cast is to put every known form of contraception through the most grueling test possible. To wit, each of the 10 characters had his or her own scorecard. I've grouped the headers for these pages into one big figure (34.10). As you can see, each header features a row of the characters' faces, along with elements highlighting the face and name of the character at hand.

If Benjamin had created each header as a separate graphic, the browser would have had to load a new image for each page, thereby slowing the user's enjoyment of the site. Luckily, Benjamin would have none of that. "The one common element in each header is the row of heads inside the little washing machine windows. So, I made that element a separate GIF graphic. That way, the browser downloads the image once, caches it, and doesn't have to load it again until the next session.

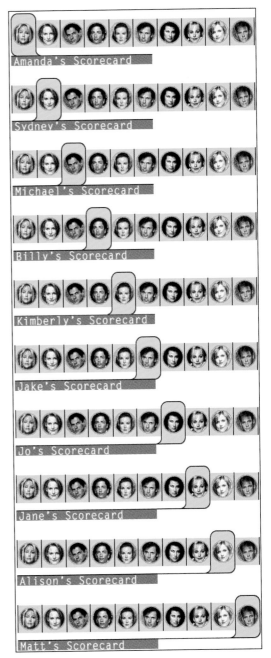

34.10

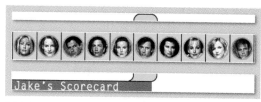

**34.11**

"The parts that change are the yellow cap above the washing machine heads and the yellow bit with the text below the heads (34.11). The cap is incredibly tiny. It's just three colors — yellow, black, and white — so that's a 2-bit GIF file with lots of flat areas for compression. Naturally, that's a Web-safe yellow. The bottom part is a little bigger, but I managed to get it down to a 4-bit palette.

"These elements have to line up perfectly, so I put together a layered file in Photoshop with the washing machine heads, all the caps, and all the bottoms. Then, I exported each layer to a separate GIF file. Because I cropped each element tight vertically, with no extra pixels hanging off above or below, they appear to merge into a single graphic inside the browser."

## ANIMATED BANNER ADS

Banner ads are the current craze for advertising on the Web. They burst and sizzle at the top of your screen in an attempt to entice you to click on them. Some folks hate banner ads because they're intrusive, they prolong the overall download time, and they generally make a mockery of the original, civic-minded intentions of the Web. But I don't have any problem with them. Advertising is the fuel for just about every prevailing medium that's come down the pike. Without advertising, some excellent professional sites would have to fold up their tents. Even with advertising, some of these outfits are running on shoestring, loss-leader budgets. What we need is *more* advertising, not less!

## HYPING TALK SOUP

Whatever your feelings are on this fascinating topic, you have Benjamin to thank for some of the banner ads you've seen. Included on CD #2 at the back of this book is an ad Benjamin created for the television show *Talk Soup*. In case you're not familiar with it, the show compiles sensational highlights from the current glut of fatuous daytime talk shows. It's like a *Reader's Digest* condensed guide to the daily sleaze. (Though I've never watched *Melrose Place*, I am guilty of having sat through entire episodes of *Talk Soup* with mouth agape like a motorist passing a train wreck.)

"E! wanted a simple animated banner for a contest they were running. It had to feature a little person rising from the *Talk Soup* bowl. That little person was you, if you won the contest.

"Like usual, I made a comp for the animation inside Illustrator (34.12)." To prepare the illustration, Benjamin set up the individual frames for the face, the soup bowl, and the shaking E! logo inside Photoshop. To keep things tidy, he painted each frame on a separate layer. Then, he dragged and dropped the layers into Illustrator. "I created this particular comp for myself so I could remember the order for the animation. I sent a more simplified version to E! for approval."

## COMPILING THE FRAMES IN GIFBUILDER

After getting the idea accepted — "no one seemed to like how I made John Henson's eyes wiggle, but everything else was okay" — Benjamin set about compiling the frames in Yves Piguet's popular shareware utility, GifBuilder. "GifBuilder does a pretty good job of dithering and reducing file sizes. And in GifBuilder 0.5, you can drag and drop whole layers directly from Photoshop. That way, I don't have to worry about adjusting the Indexed Color settings or saving GIF files out of Photoshop."

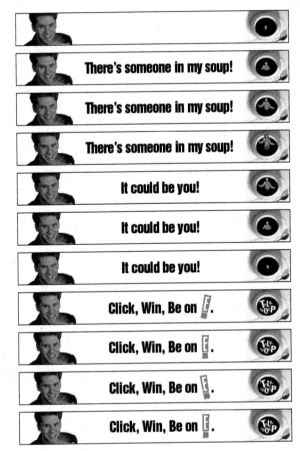

34.12
©1996 E! ONLINE

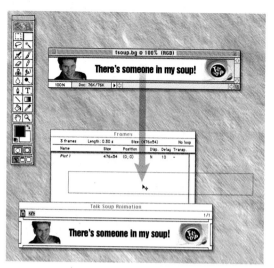

**34.13**

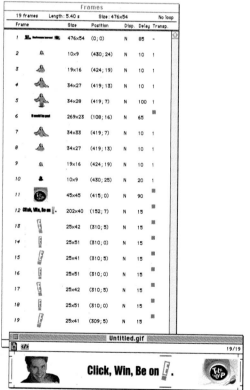

**34.14**

Benjamin started by dropping in the first frame of the animation, which included host John Henson's face on the far left side of the banner and the soup bowl on the far right (34.13). This frame served as a background for the remaining frames. Rather than drop in completed frames that measured the whole width of the banner, Benjamin dragged over different elements as separate pieces. One set of frames included different views of the bowl, another included alternate text, and the last was a thin set of frames that featured the red E! exclamation point.

GifBuilder's basic organization is a lot like Photoshop's Layers palette. The individual frames appear in a list with or without thumbnails (34.14). You can change the order of frames by dragging them up or down in the list. The program lets you specify the duration and coordinate positions of frames. You can even toggle the animation to loop repeatedly after it finishes playing the first time.

## FILE SIZE, DIMENSIONS, AND DURATION

Of course, file size is as much of a concern when working with animated GIF files as it is when creating still images. "GifBuilder provides a command called *frame optimization* that dumps any pixel that's repeated from one frame to the next. If the file is still too big after that, I look at which frames I might be able to delete. The goal is to get the entire animation under 12K or so, which is sometimes a challenge."

File size isn't the only size limitation for banner ads. There's also the issue of pixel dimensions. "Up until very recently, banner ads were a total nightmare. Every single advertising venue had different banner specifications. This ad ran on *E! Online* and *CNET* at 476 × 54 pixels. Yahoo! needed 468 × 60. So, I'd have to do four or five different versions of the same ad. Nowadays, most sites have standardized at 468 × 60 pixels.

"But there are still weird parameters that you have to watch out for. At Yahoo!, a banner ad can't be more than 8K, and the animation can't last for more than four seconds." While that makes life difficult for the ad creators, it's wonderful news for Web content consumers. The ad loads in four seconds, plays for four seconds, and the pain is over. Personally, I'm happy to give eight seconds of my time if it means keeping a site free.

### LOOPING WITH A LOW SOURCE

If you write your own HTML code, you're probably aware of the `<LOWSRC>` tag, which instructs the browser to download a preliminary version of an image. For example, the TomGirl figure (34.15) illustrates the tag `<IMG SRC="zellweg.jpg" LOWSRC="zellmono.gif">`. This tag tells the browser to load the smaller monotone image first and then gradually display the larger JPEG file in its place. The mono file serves as a proxy until the real image loads.

Benjamin suggests that you can also use this tag with animated GIF files. "I saw this used really well with an animated bee. The `<LOWSRC>` tag loaded a file that showed the bee flying toward you. Then, the GIF switched out and it became looping animation with the bee flying in space. There's really no other way to pull that off without resorting to javascript or some sort of plug-in."

34.15

# CHAPTER 35
# MASTERING TRANSPARENT GIFS

Any designer who's spent some time trying to retrofit his or her talents to the World Wide Web has quickly learned to adapt to limitations. In many ways, it's like going back in time ten years, to the rough-and-tumble pioneering days of desktop publishing. HTML offers about as many text-formatting options as an early DOS version of WordPerfect. (What new and wonderful designs can you create with one stinkin' font today?) And the graphics capabilities aren't much better. You must settle on 24-bit, rectangular, lossy JPEG images; or get really primitive with 256-color GIF graphics. (A relatively new format, PNG, merges the best of both worlds. But thanks to narrow support, the chances of your visitors being able to view PNG images are extremely slim.)

I have long been a proponent of giving GIF a proper burial alongside stone-cold formats such as MacPaint and CGM. And yet in the last year, I've taken to GIF with the enthusiasm of a strict vegetarian rediscovering ice cream. That's because GIF offers one thing JPEG lacks: transparency. Using a variation on GIF known as 89a, you can make specific pixels in your image utterly invisible, permitting you to merge the image with the background pattern assigned to your Web page. It's like attaching a clipping path, except without all the hassle.

The downside is that you have just two levels of opacity — on (opaque) and off (transparent). This means that your typical GIF89a image has a serrated edge, every bit as jagged as artwork printed from an ancient ImageWriter. Compared with the gradual transitions and sophisticated blend modes afforded by Photoshop, compositing on an HTML page is a cruel joke.

But as they say, rudimentary technology is the mother of invention. By merging portions of your background pattern into the GIF graphic, you can create images that blend seamlessly into their surroundings, regardless of how the graphic and background pattern are aligned. This technique accommodates anything from feathered drop shadows to tapering brushstrokes and translucent overlays. Just one caveat: These steps work best with continuous-tone textural backgrounds. If the background features high-contrast, readily identifiable tiles — like the repeating mouse ears that once adorned *www.disney.com* — the GIF image is unlikely to register properly. But because most sites have abandoned such distracting tiles (Disney doesn't use the ears anymore), this is a minor drawback.

**35.1**

**35.2**

## SETTING UP THE LAYERS

The first step is to create your image exactly as you want it to appear in your Web site, complete with background pattern. In Photoshop, open the image that serves as the pattern tile for your page. Select the entire image and choose the Define Pattern command from the Edit menu to save the image to memory. Next, create a new RGB document big enough to house your graphic and use the Fill command (Shift+ Delete/Backspace) to fill it with the repeating pattern. This will serve as your background (35.1).

Now build up your image layer by layer as you would normally (35.2 and 35.3). Just be careful not to modify the Background layer in any way. Feel free to monkey around with the Opacity settings and blend modes of your layers until you get the exact effect that you want (35.4). Don't worry that GIF can't accommodate the range of compositing tricks that Photoshop offers: You'll address that problem when you've finished your artwork. For now, the sky's the limit.

**35.3**

## CREATING A MASK

The key to creating a successful GIF89a file is to define a mask that precisely traces around the edges of your image and integrates portions of the background pattern. To create a mask, you first need to select the contents of every layer except Background (35.5). ⌘/Ctrl-click on the first item in the Layers palette above Background. Then Shift+⌘/Ctrl-click on each of the other layer names in ascending order. (Technically, you don't have to select the layers in any specific order, but doing so helps you remember which layers you've selected.)

Now convert the selection to a mask. Go to the Channels palette and click the Save Selection as Channel button along the bottom of the palette (35.6). Then click on the channel to make it active, and press ⌘/Ctrl+D to deselect the image. If your layers include soft edges, so will your mask. But because GIF89a accommodates just two levels of opacity, you need to change all the pixels in the mask to either black (for transparent) or white (for opaque). I generally apply the Maximum filter (in the Other submenu) with a Radius of 1 to spread the edges of the mask a little; this ensures that the soft edges don't get cut short. Then apply Image ➤ Adjust ➤ Threshold with a low value such as 40 (35.7), which changes all the pixels to black or white and further spreads the mask.

35.4

35.5

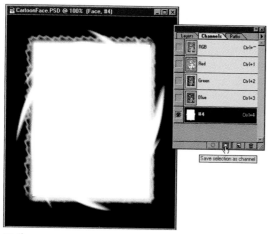

35.6

With the mask complete, switch back to the RGB view. (This is a good place to save your layered image with mask to the native Photoshop format.) Use Image ➤ Mode ➤ Indexed Color to downsample the image to 256 or fewer colors (35.8). Select the Adaptive palette; to best accommodate GIF's run-line compression, set the Dither option to None. This flattens the image, but the mask channel remains intact. To save the image to GIF, choose File ➤ Export ➤ GIF89a Export. Select the mask channel from the Transparency From pop-up menu (35.9), and press Return/Enter.

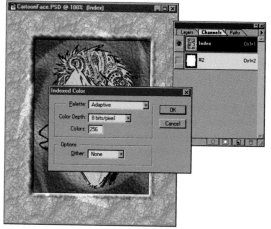

35.8

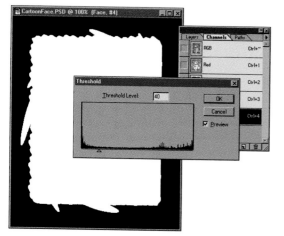

35.7

One warning: Note that the GIF89a Export command is like Save a Copy—it doesn't rename the image on-screen. So be careful not to save the image when you close it. Doing so would overwrite the layered original.

## TEST-DRIVING YOUR NEW GIF

After you save your GIF file from Photoshop, you can test it out by centering the image inside an HTML page that includes your background pattern. If you use a WYSIWYG editor like Adobe PageMill, you can preview the image right away. Otherwise, open the page in a browser like Netscape Navigator. Either way, you'll want to play around with the width of the page to align the image to different positions along the background pattern. If you notice any rough edges, you can open the GIF file in Photoshop and edit the offending pixels. More likely, however, you won't be able to detect any edges at all.

I got so hooked on this technique that I settled on GIF89a for every one of the images on my site. To see a hundred or so GIFs in action, visit *http://www. dekemc.com.*

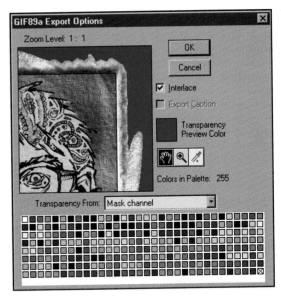

35.9

# CHAPTER 36
# BUTTONS, BUTTONS, BUTTONS

Computers have a way of completely transforming how we work in a small amount of time. Just as an example, perhaps you've seen the made-for-TV version of *The Shining* — you know, the Stephen King novel about the folks who spend the winter in a really scary hotel. The movie was inspired by and filmed at a hotel called the Stanley in Estes Park, Colorado. The story's theme is a bit gruesome — what with all the bleeding walls and killer topiary animals — but it's worth a few chuckles. It was especially comical when the mom and dad start freaking out about the snowmobile being wrecked and their being helplessly trapped, because in real life the Stanley is about a block away from a supermarket that's open all year. And supposedly, the hotel is poised at the edge of a blizzardy mountain pass that's closed over a span of about 200 miles, when clearly there isn't such a place even in Saskatchewan, much less Colorado.

But the least believable part comes right at the beginning. The lead character, Dad, is writing a play using a typewriter. King wrote the story in the 1970s, when typewriters were still common. But here it is more than 20 years later, and we're supposed to

*The best buttons are little pieces of art, as elegant and informative as characters in a typeface.*

MICHAEL NINNESS

believe that an ex-college professor in his mid-thirties hasn't managed to pick up a laptop somewhere along the way? How did he ever manage to wean himself off slide rules, rotary-dial phones, and 8-track tapes?

This is all a roundabout way of leading up to the topic of buttons. The point is, if I had shown you a collection of brightly colored buttons (36.1) three or four years ago, I would have fully expected you to utter a "Hm" or other bored commentary. Buttons are about as applicable to print-media designers as pressure-sensitive styluses are to stenographers. But

**Study Agriculture**

**Learn a New Language**

**You Can Be Mechanical**

**Learn to Love Symbols**

36.1

nowadays, I'd be surprised if you didn't examine these buttons with at least a glimmer of curiosity. The latest computing rage — the World Wide Web — has turned armies of us into interface designers. Like it or not, buttons and onscreen iconography are fast becoming a part of our everyday lives.

In celebration of this phenomenon, I contacted a fellow whose only experience with typewriters was a tenth grade typing class. Young enough to have taken up desktop publishing in high school, Myke Ninness sees buttons as miniature artwork with a purpose. "Their real function is to guide visitors through your site, multimedia presentation, or whatever. The best you can hope is that the buttons are so intuitive that no one pays much attention to them. Or maybe someone thinks, 'Wow, this is a great site,' but they don't spend a lot of time pondering over each and every button. They just click and go.

"But if you take the time to look closely, the best buttons are little pieces of art, as elegant and informative as characters in a typeface. In fact, in many ways, electronic buttons are to the '90s what Post-Script fonts were to the '80s — except you have a lot more options when creating them and they're a heck of a lot easier to make."

## THE BASIC BEVELED SQUARE

"I'd like to stress up front that none of the button effects I use rely on third-party filters. You don't need Kai's Power Tools or any of those. All the 3-D stuff is done with two filters that are built into Photoshop — Emboss and Lighting Effects. And otherwise, it's all layers and channels."

Probably the easiest kind of button to create is a beveled rectangle or square. Ninness starts off by opening a texture file and sizing it to the desired shape. When creating a square button, he usually crops the texture to about 400 × 400 pixels. For best results, the image should have a low degree of contrast. "Because Lighting Effects exaggerates the amount of contrast in an image, you may want to mute the colors a few notches using Image ➢ Adjust ➢ Levels."

To define the beveled edge of the button, Ninness selects the entire image (⌘/Ctrl+A) and chooses Select ➢ Modify ➢ Border. "Enter a Width value of 40 pixels, or about one-tenth the width of the file. This expands the selection around the edges of the window. Then switch to the channels palette and click on the save selection icon (36.2) to convert the selection to a mask." Ninness names his channel Edge Mask.

**ARTIST:**
Michael Ninness

**ORGANIZATION:**
Extensis Corporation
1800 SW First Avenue, Suite 500
Portland, OR 97201
503/274-2020
mninness@extensis.com

**SYSTEM:**
Power Mac 7250/120
2GB storage

**RAM:**
32MB total (with RAM Doubler)
24MB assigned to Photoshop

**MONITOR:**
Sony 15-inch multisync

**VERSION USED:**
Photoshop 5.0

**OTHER APPLICATIONS:**
Macromedia FreeHand, Adobe Page-
Maker, NetObjects Fusion, Bare Bones
BBEdit

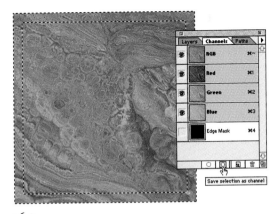

36.2

**WORK HISTORY:**

<u>1986</u> — Designed high school yearbook using Mac 512Ke and PageMaker 1.0.

<u>1990</u> — Paid way through design school training professionals to use Macs.

<u>1994</u> — Graduated from University of Washington with BFA in Graphic Design.

<u>1996</u> — Director of Computer Graphics Training Division at professional photo lab Ivey Seright.

**FAVORITE FISH:**

Clown fish ("They freakin' rock!")

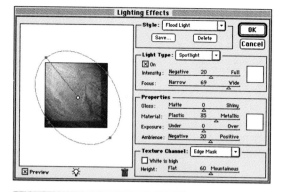

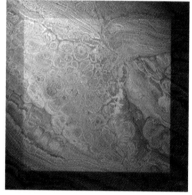

36.3 (TOP), 36.4 (BOTTOM)

"At this point, you can deselect the image (⌘/Ctrl+D) or not. If you leave the selection intact, you'll get a flat button face. If you deselect the image, you get more depth, but it can be a little more difficult to control."

For purposes of this example, Ninness deselects the image and chooses Filter ➤ Render ➤ Lighting Effects. "Keep in mind, Lighting Effects is notorious for generating out-of-memory errors. To work on a 500K button, you'll need about 20MB of RAM assigned to Photoshop." He selects the Edge Mask channel from the Texture Channel pop-up menu at the bottom of the dialog box. Then, he turns off the White is High check box. "From there, it's just a matter of tweaking the spotlight and slider bars until you get the effect you want (36.3). When you press Return, Photoshop generates your beveled button automatically (36.4)."

## MAKING BUTTONS WITH CLIPPING GROUPS

"Photoshop's clipping group function is a big help when creating buttons. You can place texture inside buttons and apply highlights and shadows, all with a simple Option-click." To demonstrate, Ninness starts with a simple collection of characters on a transparent layer (36.5). "If you're working with text, be sure to turn the Preserve Transparency check box off." He then creates a vibrant texture on a separate layer in front of the characters (36.6).

"The texture is a stock Noise and Motion Blur technique that's been around for ages. Just take a layer and fill it with whatever color you want — in this case, a reddish orange. Choose the Add Noise filter. Crank the noise as high as you want — higher values result in more streaks. Then, apply the Motion Blur filter at 45 degrees with a distance of 45 pixels. If you want, reapply the filter with the same angle but change the distance two or three times. This brings out the pattern a little bit more. Then, if you don't like the color, you can go into Hue/Saturation and modify the overall Hue. You have endless opportunities to change the overall look of this."

When you get the texture you want (and keep in mind, it doesn't have to be streaks — any texture will do), Option/Alt-click on the horizontal line between the two layers in the Layers palette to combine them into a clipping group (36.7). Alternatively, you can press ⌘/Ctrl+G in Photoshop 5. Then, Ninness recommends that you merge the two layers together (⌘/Ctrl+E).

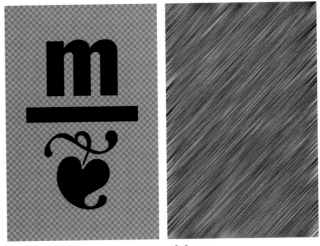

36.5            36.6

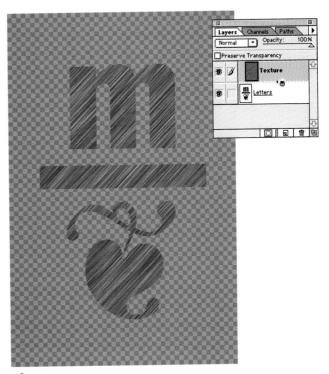

36.7

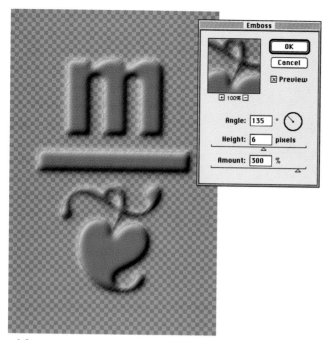

36.8

Next, Ninness duplicates the layer and fills the opaque portions with black (Shift+Option/Alt+ Delete). This layer will serve as the highlights and shadows for the button. The Emboss filter will give the button depth, while Gaussian Blur will lend some softness to the effect. "By blurring the layer, you give the Emboss filter some soft edges to work with. Trust me, Emboss can do some ugly things to hard edges." Ninness applies a Radius value of about 6.0 for a 400 × 600 pixel image.

Next, Ninness chooses Filter ➤ Stylize ➤ Emboss. He sets the Angle value to 135 degrees. "I don't know why, but I like my light to come in from the upper left corner. Then, you match the Height value to the Radius you assigned for Gaussian Blur — in this case, 6. And the Amount is 300 percent (36.8).

"After you apply the Emboss filter, you end up with this crappy gray effect. But we don't care about the gray; all we want are the highlights and shadows. So change the blend mode in the Layers palette to Hard Light. That nukes all the gray stuff and leaves the highlights and shadows intact (36.9)."

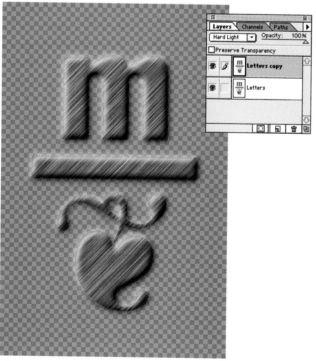

36.9

There's one final step. "Because you applied Gaussian Blur, you end up with this residue that drifts outside the original letters. If you don't like the shadow effect — sometimes it can be effective, other times not — then group the shadow with the layer below it, again by Option/Alt-clicking on the horizontal line or pressing ⌘/Ctrl+G." This will clean up the edge of the button. Then, add a drop shadow to taste.

"And here's a tip: If the highlights and shadows are too washed out, just duplicate the top layer and adjust the Opacity (36.10). Each copy of the layer remains inside the clipping group. With very little effort, you can have that button popping off the page."

## ETCHING TYPE INTO THE BEVELED SQUARE

"This clipping group technique is also a snazzy way to etch text into a button. For example, take the beveled square. A square by itself — that's not a button. But add some text and you've really got something."

Ninness sets the foreground color to 50 percent gray. Then, he uses Photoshop's type tool to add the words "Click Me" to a new layer. After he centers the text on the button, he turns off the Preserve Transparency check box (which permits blurring later). He also sets the blend mode in the Layers palette to Hard Light to make the gray text invisible.

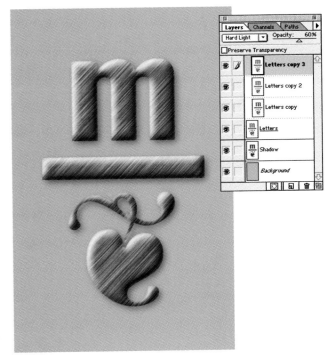

36.10

**36.11 (TOP), 36.12 (BOTTOM)**

Next, he duplicates the Click Me layer and fills it with black (by setting the foreground color to black and pressing Shift+Option/Alt+Delete). Ninness then applies the Gaussian Blur filter with a Radius value of 3.0. "The higher the radius, the deeper the etching."

After blurring, he chooses Emboss and sets the Height to 3 (matching the blur radius) and the Amount to 300 percent. "Unlike before, I'm digging the text into the button, so I rotate the Angle value to -45 degrees." The result is a soft-edged effect that looks like the type has melted into the button (36.11). To make the text nice and crisp, group the emboss layer with the text below it by pressing ⌘/Ctrl+G (36.12).

## MASS BUTTON PRODUCTION

"From a production standpoint, this technique can be a huge time saver. If you have a series of buttons on your Web site, and they're all going to be the same except for what they say, then you have one source file to go back and edit. Here, I just have to change the two text layers — which takes maybe five minutes — and export the modified button in the GIF89a format. That's because the GIF89a Export module saves just the visible layers.

"It also works in the other direction. If you change your mind about the color of the button, and you still have the original Photoshop file with the various text layers intact, you only have one layer to go back and edit — the Background layer. The text etches into the new background automatically."

## CREATING A STAMPED BUTTON

"Clipping groups are a great way to add depth to complex shapes. But they aren't the only way to go. In fact, my favorite button technique doesn't involve clipping groups at all. Using layers and channels, you can stamp an icon so it looks like someone has branded it into a button shape." The buttons at the beginning of the chapter (36.1) are cases in point.

Ninness suggests two techniques for creating stamped buttons: one that involves the Emboss filter, and a more complicated but equally more realistic method that involves Lighting Effects.

### THE SIMPLE EMBOSS APPROACH

Whether he decides to enhance his button with Emboss or Lighting Effects, Ninness starts off the same way. First, he creates a new image with the Contents set to Transparent. Then, he creates an icon for the button — shown here as a black cog (36.13) — on the default layer provided with the document. It's very important that the icon be black; even if you want to make it a different color later, use black for now.

Next, Ninness creates a new layer below the first and blocks out the shape of the button in white (36.14). "I just painted a few random strokes using the paintbrush tool with a soft brush. I figure, if the technique works with fuzzy brushstrokes, it'll work with anything." Again, it's very important that you use white for the button. You can always modify the color later.

If you're following along and creating your own button, this is a good point to save your work. In the next section, you'll start from this point when using the Lighting Effects filter. You may even want to duplicate the image so you don't harm the original.

Just so we're all on the same page, Ninness has two layers — one called Cog (black) in front of another called Button (white). With the Button layer active, he presses Option/Alt while choosing Layer ➤ Merge Visible. (On the Mac, you can alternatively press ⌘+Shift+Option+E.) This merges the contents of both layers onto the Button layer.

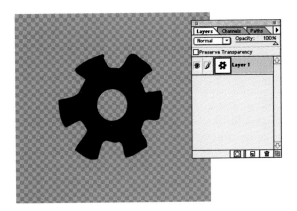

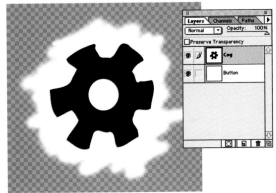

**36.13 (TOP), 36.14 (BOTTOM)**

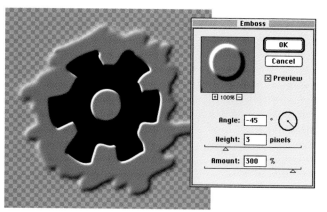

**36.15**

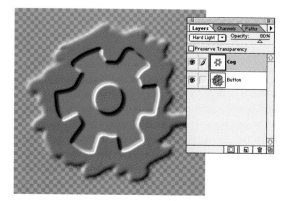

At this point, you could launch right into the Emboss filter. But again, Ninness suggests you start off with a little Gaussian Blur. "In this case, I'd go with something subtle, like a Radius of about 2.0."

Then, he chooses the Emboss filter. Because he's working with a layer of white pixels, Ninness sets the Angle value to -45 degrees to create the effect of light coming in from the upper left. "Then, I just experiment with the other settings. A Height of 3 and an Amount of 300 looks pretty good (36.15).

"That's it, really. From here, it's just a matter of assigning your button the proper colors." If you want to color the icon separately of the button, you can fill the icon with color by pressing Shift+Option/Alt+Delete. Try setting the blend mode in the Layers palette to Hard Light. Then, adjust the Opacity setting as desired. As a general rule of thumb, cool colors tend to require higher Opacity settings than warm ones (36.16).

If you prefer to color the icon and button together, Ninness recommends that you leave the icon black and reduce the Opacity to about 50 percent. You can add an adjustment layer (by ⌘/Ctrl-clicking on the new layer icon along the bottom of the Layers palette) and set the layer to Hue/Saturation. Then, inside the Hue/Saturation dialog box, select the Colorize check box and adjust the Hue and Saturation values as desired.

"This is a great way to colorize the button (36.17) because you can always go back and modify your colors later. With your button layers set to neutral grays, your coloring options are virtually unlimited."

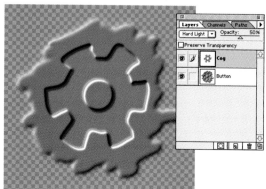

**36.16**

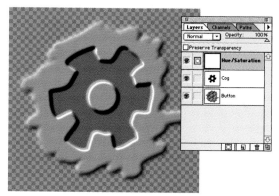

**36.17**

## THE SLIGHTLY MORE ELABORATE
## LIGHTING EFFECTS METHOD

To light your button with the Lighting Effects filter, you start with the same two-layer file — black icon in the foreground and white button in the background. You'll apply Lighting Effects to the white button layer, but first, you need to create a mask to give the button some depth. "Lighting Effects creates the best results when you have a texture channel to work with. That's where the mask comes in."

In Photoshop, Ninness ⌘/Ctrl-clicks on the Button layer in the Layers palette to select the button outline. Then, he presses both ⌘ and Option, or Ctrl and Alt under Windows, and clicks on the Cog layer. This subtracts the cog outline from the selection. Finally, Ninness switches to the Channels palette and clicks the save selection icon to convert the selection to a channel.

To keep things tidy, Ninness names his mask "Lighting FX Mask." Then, he switches to the mask channel (⌘/Ctrl+4), deselects everything (⌘/Ctrl+D), and applies the Gaussian Blur filter, again with a Radius of 2.0.

Ninness switches back to the RGB composite view (⌘/Ctrl+tilde). With the Button layer active, he chooses Filter ➤ Render ➤ Lighting Effects. Then, he selects his Lighting FX Mask channel from the Texture Channel pop-up menu (36.18), and he leaves the White is High check box turned on. "Switch the angle of the light to wherever you want it. Again, I like it coming from the upper left, but it's up to you.

"If you plan on making a series of buttons using the same basic lighting and texture settings, you might want to take a moment and save your settings. Then, once you get an effect you like, go ahead and apply the filter by pressing Return or Enter." Although Lighting Effects is a more challenging filter to use than Emboss, it also delivers a more credible rendition of depth (36.19). The figure shows the Button layer on its own, with Cog temporarily hidden.

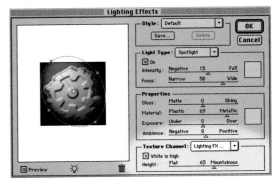

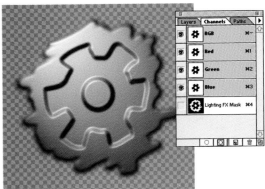

**36.18 (TOP), 36.19 (BOTTOM)**

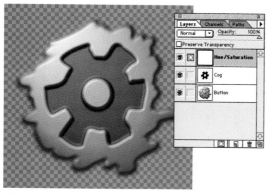

36.20

"To color the button, do the same thing you did with the Emboss effect. Set the Opacity of the icon layer to 50 percent and apply Hue/Saturation on an adjustment layer (36.20).

"You can use the buttons as is, against a white HTML page. Or use the mask channel to clean up the edges of your buttons and then add drop shadows (36.21). This effect takes some effort the first few times you run through it. But with a little practice, you'll be cranking out buttons in no time."

 **When Good Steer Go Bad**

 **Cowhands of the Orient**

 **I Was a Gear-Head Cowpoke**

 **@Home.OnThe/Range.html**

36.21

# As Extreme As You Want To Be!

## MacFriendly Graphics Machines for NT

Go to extremes on **Intergraph's ExtremeZ™ GL ViZual Workstations** — the industry's hottest Windows NT® and Intel® processor-based machines for **new media and graphic design**. From the market's only MacFriendly® NT workstation, you'll get:

- **Superior graphics & blazing performance** — especially for working with large files in networked environments
- Full peer-to-peer **Mac/NT connectivity** through AppleTalk
- Power to **read/write Mac-formatted media** on an NT box
- Great **out-of-box experience** with bundled apps and other options
- Lots of **room to expand** as your needs grow
- **Platform for leading apps** — Photoshop® QuarkXPress™, Painter, FreeHand — and enjoy the same look and feel regardless of OS
- **Service/support** from a dedicated publishing team

### For more info or a reseller's name:
## 1•800•763•0242

www.intergraph.com/publishing

## INTERGRAPH
### COMPUTER SYSTEMS

**Color Plate 2-1**
This little warlock shows off the differences between the four different JPEG compression settings, from maximum quality, minimum compression (upper left) to minimum quality, maximum compression (lower right). Inspect the enlarged eye and sharpened staff for subtle erosions in detail.

Maximum                116K    High                    66K

Medium                  50K    Low                     46K

**Color Plate 2-2**
My personal 256-color, 1024 × 768 pixel wallpaper image saved as a BMP file and applied to the desktop using the Display control panel.

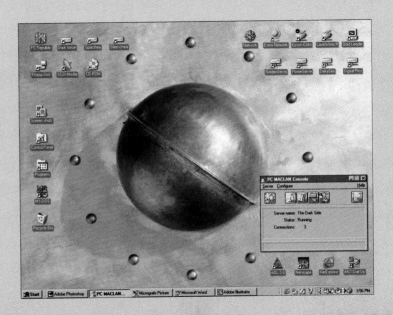

**Color Plate 2-3**
An example of a custom
1024×768-pixel startup
screen saved as a PICT
resource file.

**Color Plate 3-1**
An image created
on the Mac in the
SMPTE-240M space
(left) and then
opened on the PC
and converted to
sRGB (right). If you
look closely in the
medium blue areas,
you'll see a slight
shift toward green
on the right. Even
so, Photoshop has
done a terrific job
of converting the
colors.

**Color Plate 3-2**
This colorful image is the basis for an awful lot of channel discussions in Chapter 3. Right about now, I'm wishing I was in that inner tube instead of editing it.

**Color Plate 3-3**
One of the wonderful things about the Lab mode is that it allows you to edit the colors in an image independently of the brightness values. Here I've inverted and boosted the contrast of the *a* and *b* color channels to produce some startling effects, all without harming a smidgen of detail.

Invert a                    Auto Levels b                    Invert and Auto Levels a and b

Replace red with blue

Replace green with red

Replace blue with red

**Color Plate 3-4**
You can wreak some pretty interesting havoc on the colors in an image by replacing one color channel with another or by swapping the contents of two color channels using the Channel Mixer command.

Swap red and blue

Swap red and green

Swap green and blue

**Color Plate 4-1**
I converted this grayscale piece by Seattle-based artist Mark Collen to a quadtone using the colors navy blue, rose, teal, and dull orange. All colors were defined and printed using CMYK pigments.

**Color Plate 4-2**
After converting Mark's quadtone to a multichannel image, I experimented with hiding different channels. In the top row, I hid one spot color and left the other three visible. In the bottom row, I hid two channels per image.

Navy, Orange, Teal    Orange, Teal, Rose    Navy, Orange, Rose

Navy, Orange    Teal, Rose    Orange, Rose

**Color Plate 8-1**
Starting with an image of typical saturation (upper left), I applied the sponge tool set to Desaturate to the inside of the pepper and the corn in the background (upper right). I then repeated the effect twice more to make the areas almost gray (lower right). Returning to the original image, I then selected the Saturate icon and again scrubbed inside the pepper and in the corn to boost the colors (lower left).

Behind

Dissolve

Normal

**Color Plate 8-2**

Here I've gone and desecrated a pivotal work of European iconography by scribbling the name of America's patron saint of graffiti. Reading up from the bottom, the Normal brush mode applies paint normally. The Dissolve mode scattered pixels along the fuzzy edge of the brushstroke. And the Behind mode paints behind the current layer, in this case, a layer containing the Madonna's head.

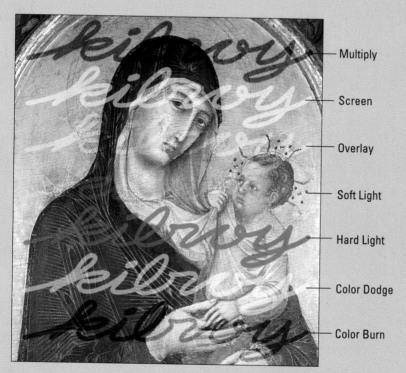

Multiply

Screen

Overlay

Soft Light

Hard Light

Color Dodge

Color Burn

**Color Plate 8-3**

Here I've painted green lines using the seven brush modes in the middle of the Options palette pop-up menu. Multiply darkens uniformly and Screen lightens uniformly. (In fact, Multiply and Screen are direct opposites.) Overlay, Soft Light, and Hard Light all multiply the darkest pixels and screen the lightest ones to produce different contrast-enhancing effects. Color Dodge and Color Burn work like dodge and burn tools that also add color to an image.

**Color Plate 8-4**

Here are the effects of the final eight entries in Photoshop 5's enormous arsenal of brush modes. Darken and Lighten are opposites, Difference and Exclusion are very closely related, and the last four apply different bits and pieces of the HSL color model. Because many of these modes produce slight effects—particularly the Saturation and Luminosity modes—I have added dark halos around the brushstrokes to offset them slightly from the background. Naturally, the halos feel right at home.

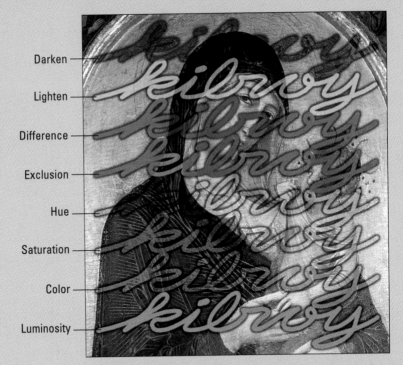

Darken

Lighten

Difference

Exclusion

Hue

Saturation

Color

Luminosity

**Color Plate 9-1**

Here I've used the paint bucket to colorize two oranges (top) with bright blue. First, I set the Tolerance value in the Paint Bucket Options palette to 120 and changed the brush mode to Color. Then I clicked at each of the four points marked with blue arrows (middle). Then, I changed the foreground color to green and clicked just once in the lower right corner of the image (marked with the green arrow). Unfortunately, the paint bucket isn't very precise, so I had to touch up the dimples and edges with the paintbrush, also set to the Color mode. Finally, I used the airbrush—set to the Color Burn mode—to deepen some of the blue shadows inside the fruit.

**Color Plate 9-2**
I started by designing a three-color gradient that fades twice into transparency, as demonstrated by the checkerboard background (left). Such a gradation is meant to be blended with an image, such as the piano keys (middle). So I selected the Overlay brush mode from the Gradient Tool Options palette and tickled my gradation across the ivories (right).

**Color Plate 10-1**
To see how I scanned this 90-year-old photograph (left) and cloned away its considerable supply of tears, creases, stains, and flaking (right), read the "Restoring an old photograph" section of Chapter 10.

## Color Plate 15-1

If you attempt to select this whimsical sign with the magic wand tool, you end up selecting odd little fragments of the yellow areas one at a time. However, by switching to the blue channel—in which both sign and Sasquatch appear black against a relatively light background—you can easily select both portions of the sign in two easy clicks. I then inverted the sign (right) by pressing ⌘/Ctrl+I. The effect isn't perfect, but it's as good as it gets with the magic wand.

## Color Plate 16-1

At top, we see two selection outlines (both from Figure 16-1) expressed as masks. The masks appear as transparent red overlays, permitting you to see mask and image at the same time. Red-tinted areas are masked, representing deselected areas in the image; untinted areas are unmasked, and represent selected areas. In the bottom examples, I inverted the selected areas to demonstrate the full extent of the selection outlines.

**Color Plate 16-2**
In the left example, I drew a black to white gradation in the quick mask mode, extending from the base of the top row of pillars to the top of the flagpole. Then I applied the Add Noise filter to jumble up the pixels a little. Finally, I exited the quick mask mode to convert the mask to a selection, and ⌘/Ctrl+dragged the Capitol into the lava image (right).

**Color Plate 16-3**
Which twin has the Toni? With the help of a very precise mask, I dragged this girl in from her old environment into this new one. But despite the mask's accuracy, I managed to bring in some blue from her prior background (left). To fix this problem, I brushed in some color from the new background, and erased a few of the overly dark hairs (right).

**Color Plate 17-1**

Photoshop lets you copy layer effects from one layer and paste them onto another. After applying the Outer Glow command to some bananas and Pillow Emboss to a pineapple (left), I decided the pillow emboss is all wrong. So I copied the pillow emboss effect from the pineapple and applied it to the new thought-balloon layer. Then I copied the outer glow from the bananas and pasted it onto the pineapple (right).

**Color Plate 17-2**

Here I've used a clipping group to fill some characters of type with a water pattern. I started by adding a couple of pool images that I shot with a digital camera to a layer above my text—which is itself on an independent layer—as demonstrated on the left. Then I just Option/Alt+clicked on the horizontal line between the two layers in the Layers palette. Photoshop automatically assigned the type layer's transparency mask to the pool layer, filling the letters.

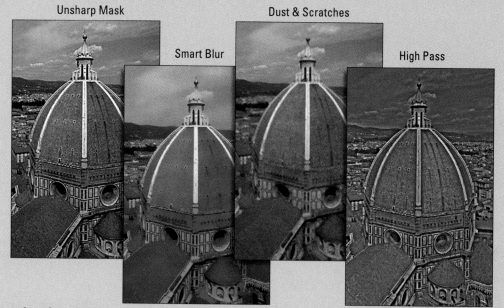

**Color Plate 23-1**

Shown here are the results of four corrective filters, including representatives from the Filter⇨Sharpen, Blur, Noise, and Other submenus. Normally, the High Pass filter takes the saturation out of an image, leaving many areas gray, like an old, sun-bleached slide. To restore the colors, I chose Filter⇨Fade High Pass (⌘/Ctrl+Shift+F) and selected Luminosity from the Mode pop-up menu in the Fade dialog box.

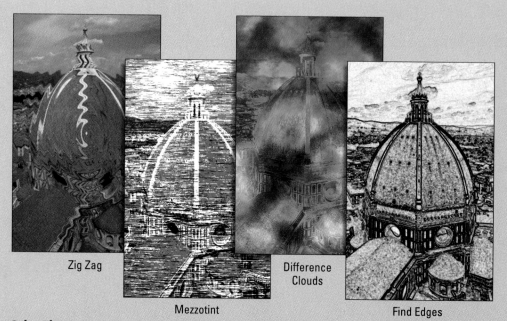

**Color Plate 23-2**

Here are the effects of four destructive filters from the Filter⇨Distort, Pixelate, Render, and Stylize submenus. Every one of these filters has a dramatic impact on the color and detail of an image. From a pixel's perspective, destructive filters are dynamite, so use with care and moderation.

**Color Plate 23-3**
The results of applying the Unsharp Mask filter to independent color channels in an RGB image. In each case, the Amount value was 500, the Radius value was 4.0, and the Threshold was 0.

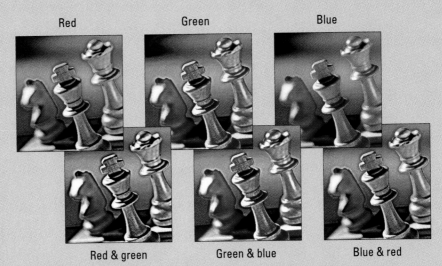

Red Green Blue

Red & green Green & blue Blue & red

**Color Plate 23-4**
Again, I applied Unsharp Mask to the independent color channels, but this time with an exaggerated Radius value, 20.0, a more moderate Amount value, 250, and the default Threshold, 0. Rather than pinpointing the sharpening effect, as in Color Plate 23-3, the high Radius value allows the colors to bleed as they are strengthened by the Amount value.

Red Green Blue

Red & green Green & blue Blue & red

**Color Plate 23-5**
The results of applying Filter ⇨ Other ⇨ High Pass with a Radius value of 5.0 to each channel and pair of channels in an RGB image. To boost the color values in the images slightly, I applied the Auto Levels command (⌘/Ctrl+Shift+L) after each application of High Pass.

Red Green Blue

Red & green Green & blue Blue & red

Normal, 60%

Luminosity, 50%

Darken, 80%

Lighten, 80%

**Color Plate 23-6**
After applying the Gaussian Blur filter with a Radius of 8.0, I used the Fade Gaussian Blur command to mix the filtered image with the original. The labels tell the blend mode and Opacity setting applied to each image.

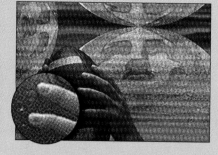

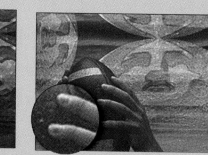

**Color Plate 23-7**
An image scanned from an ancient issue of *Macworld* magazine shown as it appears in the normal RGB mode (top right) and when each channel is viewed separately (top left). The middle images show the affects of the Dust & Scratches filter set to a Radius of 2 and a Threshold of 20. The bottom images show how the channels look after suppressing the moiré patterns with the Gaussian Blur, Median, and Unsharp Mask filters.

**Color Plate 24-1**
The result of applying the Extrude filter to a red rose. If you select the Blocks and Solid Front Faces options, the filter transforms the image into mosaic tiles and shoves the tiles out at you in 3-D space.

**Color Plate 24-2**
Here I applied Filter ➪ Sketch ➪ Charcoal with the foreground color set to dark green and the background color light blue (as demonstrated in the upper left inset). Then I used the Fade Charcoal command to change the blend mode to Overlay.

**Color Plate 24-3**
I applied the Mezzotint filter set to the Long Strokes effect in each of the RGB, Lab, and CMYK color modes (top row). After each application of the filter, I pressed ⌘/Ctrl+Shift+F and faded the filtered image into the original using the Overlay mode and an Opacity setting of 40 percent (bottom row).

RGB          Lab          CMYK

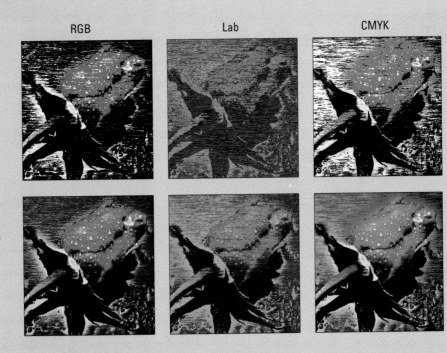

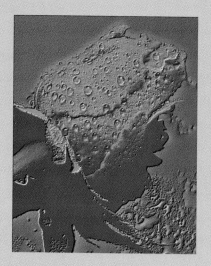

**Color Plate 24-4**
In both examples, I applied the Emboss filter armed with an Angle of 135 degrees, a Height value of 2, and an Amount of 300 percent. To create the left image, I used the Fade command to mix embossed and original images together using the Luminosity blend mode and an Opacity setting of 80 percent. To get the psychedelic effect on right, I selected the Difference mode and reduced the Opacity value to 40 percent.

Original

Blur and Find Edges

Overlay

**Color Plate 24-5**
After selecting an image from the PhotoDisc library (top left), I layered the image, blurred it, applied the Find Edges filter, and darkened it with the Levels command (top middle). I then composited the image using the Overlay mode and an Opacity setting of 80 percent (top right). The bottom row shows the results of applying three effects filters set to the Luminosity mode and 80 percent Opacity settings.

Bas Relief

Plastic Wrap

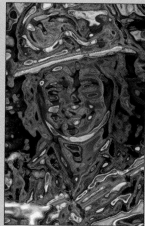

Chrome

**Color Plate 24-6**
These two rows of images show a step-by-step experiment in abstract imagery. Starting with a two-color gradation, I convert it to a spiral with Filter⇨Distort⇨Twirl. Then I copy the spiral to a layer, flip it, rotate it (top right), apply the Difference mode to achieve the orange image (bottom left). I clone the layer again and rotate it, then I clone a third time and rotate and flip the layer. The final image is the result of tweaking each layer with another distortion filter, including Twirl, Spherize, and ZigZag.

Gradation     Twirl x3     Flip Horizontal     Rotate 90° CW

Difference     Rotate 90° CW     Rotate and Flip     and more . . .

**Color Plate 24-7**
In this piece, titled Knowing Risk, distortion expert Mark Collen combines a variety of distortion filtering effects to create a surrealistic landscape. The cat, the book, the mongoose, and the twigs are the only scanned images.

**Color Plate 24-8**
You can force 3D Transform to generate a 3-D shape on an independent layer, as I did when creating this goblet. But 3D Transform provides no control over lighting. The easiest workaround is to apply layer effects. In my case, I used the Drop Shadow and Inner Bevel options. The result is hardly true three-dimensional rendering, but the goblet definitely leaps off the page.

**Color Plate 24-9**
This time, I took my 3-D goblet and set it against a different background. To achieve the more realistic lighting, I applied manual shadow and highlight techniques in combination with a few swipes of the airbrush tool. It took more than 90 minutes to put this image together, but the finished effect is well worth the effort.

**Color Plate 24-10**
The top row shows the results of Shift-choosing the Clouds filter (left), Shift-choosing Difference Clouds (middle), and pressing ⌘/Ctrl+F ten times in a row (right). I then took each of the images from the top row and mixed it with the rose using one of three blend modes (labeled below the bottom row). You can create clouds, haze, and imaginative fill patterns with the Clouds filters.

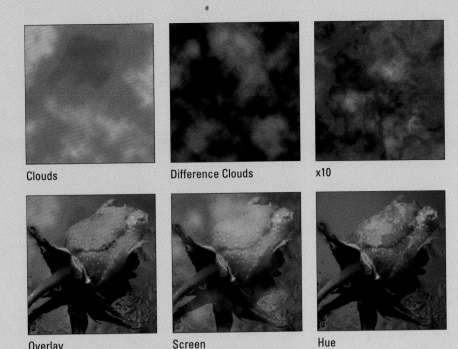

Clouds          Difference Clouds      x10

Overlay          Screen         Hue

**Color Plate 24-11**
Here I used the Lighting Effects filter to assign a total of five white spotlights, two pointing down from above and three pointing up from below. The bumpy surfaces of the second and third images are the results of texture maps. To create the right image, I used the green channel as the texture. In the bottom image, I used a pattern created with the Pointillize filter.

RGB  Lab  CMYK

**Color Plate 30-1**
The results of applying the Invert command to a single image in each of the three color modes. I inverted all channels in the RGB and Lab images and all but the black channel in the CMYK channel.

RGB  Lab  CMYK

**Color Plate 30-2**
Here I administered the High Pass filter with a Radius of 3.0, and then applied Threshold separately to each color channel within the three color modes. To smooth the jagged edges, I resampled each image up to 200 percent and then back down to 50 percent using the Image Size command. Then I repeated the process.

Luminosity  Hard Light  Hue

**Color Plate 30-3**
After cloning the image to a new layer, I applied the High Pass filter and the Posterize command. Then I mixed the layer and the underlying original by choosing each of three overlay modes from the Layers palette. All effects were created with Opacity settings of 100 percent. To make things more colorful, I gave the saturation a healthy boost using the Hue/Saturation command.

**Color Plate 30-4**

You can downplay the colors in selected portions of an image by applying Desaturate to convert the pixels to gray values (top left). You can then use Filter ⇨ Fade to reduce the Opacity setting and bring back some colors (top right). Alternatively, you can Invert the selection, choose Filter ⇨ Fade, select the Color blend mode, and lower the Opacity value to 50 percent (bottom left). Raising the Opacity increases the presence of inverted colors (bottom right).

Desaturate

Fade to 50%

Invert and fade to 50%

Invert and fade to 70%

**Color Plate 30-5**

Starting with the uncorrected pumpkin image (top left), I applied Image ⇨ Adjust ⇨ Auto Levels to it in each of the three color modes. The command is really designed for RGB images and tends to mess up CMYK images (lower right). As you folks who live outside Love Canal are probably aware, few pumpkins are fire-engine red.

Uncorrected

RGB

Lab

CMYK

Master, -40°

Master, +20°

Master, +60°

Cyan only, -40°

Cyan only, +20°

Cyan only, +60°

**Color Plate 30-6**
The results of choosing Image ⇨ Adjust ⇨ Hue/Saturation and applying various Hue values to an entire image (top row) and to only the cyan portions of the image (bottom row).

Master, -50°

Master, +50°

All but cyan and blue, -100

Cyan and blue, -100
All others, +50

**Color Plate 30-7**
The results of applying various Saturation values to an entire image (top row) and to certain colors—namely cyan and blue—independently of others (bottom row). Without creating a selection or mask, you can isolate colored areas using the Hue/Saturation command.

Master, -90°

Master, +90°

Blue areas, 120°
Other, -50°

Blue areas, -60°
Other, 110°

**Color Plate 30-8**
The results of applying various Hue values to an image when the Colorize option is turned off (top row) and on (bottom row). In the bottom images, I selected the blue areas of the horse with the Color Range command and then colorized the blue and non-blue areas as indicated by the labels. Notice that while the top two images continue to possess a variety of differently colored pixels, the bottom images contain only two apiece—pink and green.

**Color Plate 30-9**

These images show the results of correcting images with two of Photoshop's more specialized color commands, Replace Color (top row) and Selective Color (bottom row). The Replace Color command lets you adjust colors while at the same time modifying which pixels are affected and which are not with the help of a Fuzziness option. The Selective Color command adjusts the amount of CMYK ink assigned to predefined color ranges.

Fuzziness, 40

Fuzziness, 200

Red to violet, Relative

Red to violet and black to white, Absolute

**Color Plate 30-10**

The effects of applying each of the thumbnails offered in the Variations dialog box to the familiar pumpkin. In each case, the slider bar was set to its default setting of midway between Fine and Coarse with the Midtones radio button selected.

More Green

Lighter

More Yellow

More Cyan

Original

More Red

More Blue

Darker

More Magenta

Original digital photo

Increase saturation to +80

Median, Gaussian Blur,
and Color mode

Final sharpened image

**Color Plate 30-11**
Starting with a rather typically washed out image that I shot with a Kodak DC50 (top), I copied the image
to a new layer and boosted the saturation with the Hue/Saturation command (second). Then I applied the
Median and Gaussian Blur commands and mixed the layer with the underlying original using the Color
blend mode and an Opacity value of 70 percent (third). Finally, I used Median, Gaussian Blur, and Unsharp
Mask to sharpen the image (bottom).

## Color Plate 30-12

The celebrated Virginia statesman before (left) and after (right) I corrected him with the Levels command. The white histograms superimposed on Jefferson's chest show the original and corrected distribution of brightness values. The colored histograms illustrate the corrections made to the individual red, green, and blue channels.

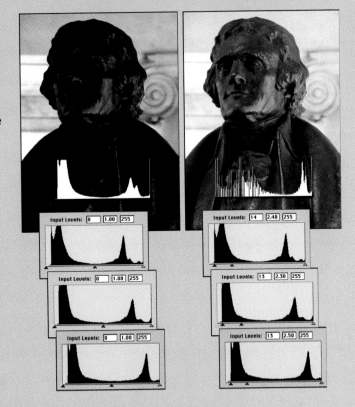

## Color Plate 30-13

You can use the Curves dialog box to apply gradations as color maps. In the top row, I copied the famous Roman to a new layer, blurred him silly, and applied each of three gradients (saved to disk by ⌘/Ctrl+clicking on the Save button in the Gradient Editor dialog box). Then I mixed the images with their underlying originals using the Color blend mode (Shift+Option/Alt+C).

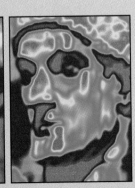

Chrome

Blue, Red, Yellow

Spectrum

Color blend mode

**Color Plate 30-14**
The results of using the Curves command to lighten the colors in the red channel (left), increase the level of contrast in the green channel (middle), and apply an arbitrary color map to the blue channel (right).

**Color Plate 30-15**
These images illustrate one way to use adjustment layers to correct the colors in a flat image. After observing that my original image was way too dark (left), I created a new adjustment layer and used the Curves command to lighten the image (middle). I then added two additional layers to increase the saturation levels with Hue/Saturation and correct the brightness levels of the topiary animal with Levels (right).

**Color Plate 31-1**

Examples of the 17 blend mode options applied to a bright blue Saturn set against the fiery backdrop of Jupiter. I also inserted an 18th Saturn set to the Normal mode and 50 percent Opacity (second down, middle column) just for the sake of comparison. That, and to take up space.

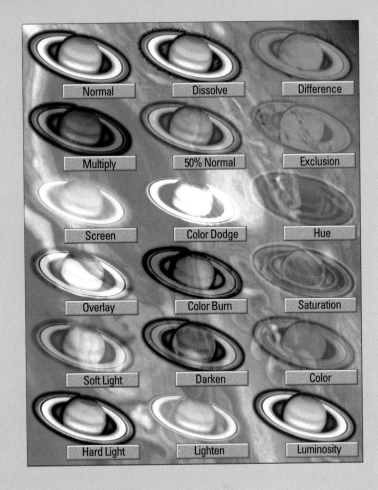

**Color Plate 31-2**

Blend modes change their meaning depending on which layer is in front and which is in back. Here I've taken images of a woman and a leaf and placed them on separate layers. In the top row, the leaf layer is in front, and in the bottom row, the woman is in front. The irony is that every one of these blend modes favors the layer on bottom. Only a few— Normal, Hard Light, and Luminosity—favor the image on top.

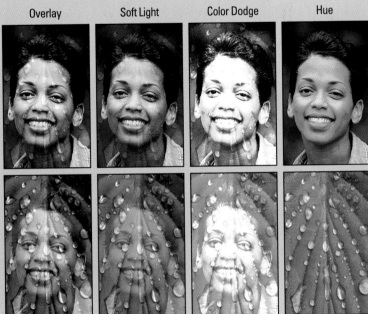

Charcoal    Hard Light    Color    Difference

Original    Soft Light    Color Dodge    Luminosity

Unsharp Mask    Motion Blur    Lens Flare    Find Edges

Difference Sandwich

**Color Plate 31-3**

Each column of images shows a progression in which I sandwiched an image filtered with the Charcoal effect (top left) between two originals (bottom left). Each image in the top row shows the filtered image interacting with the original background layered according to the labeled blend mode. The bottom images show the results of adding the top layer of the sandwich and applying another blend mode. For example, applying Difference to the filtered layer and Luminosity to the top layer creates the bottom right effect.

**Color Plate 31-4**

The top row shows the results of a series of corrective and destructive filters, each of which go a long way toward destroying the detail in my image. But when I insert the filter effect in between two copies of the original image, and then apply the Difference blend mode to the middle and top layers, I bring back much of the detail, as shown in the bottom row. No other technique restores detail quite like a tasty Difference sandwich.

**Color Plate 31-5**
For the sake of comparison, the first image shows the result of compositing an RGB image onto itself using the Hard Light mode. Other examples show the different effects you can achieve by duplicating the image, converting it to the Lab mode, and then mixing the RGB and Lab images together using the Apply Image command, again set to Hard Light.

RGB on RGB

Lightness on RGB

Inverted *b* on RGB

Blue on RGB

**Color Plate 31-6**
After creating a separate mask channel using the Color Range command (shown as a rubylith, top left), I used the mask to protect the background from my Apply Image manipulations. Although I applied some heavy duty blend modes, the blue gray background remained altogether unharmed.

RGB on RGB

Lightness on RGB

Inverted *b* on RGB

Blue on Lab

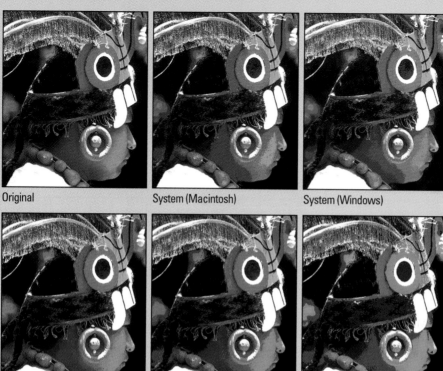

Original

System (Macintosh)

System (Windows)

Adaptive, 8 bits/pixel

Adaptive, 6 bits/pixel

Adaptive, 4 bits/pixel

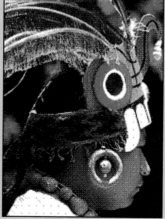

None, 94K

Pattern, 105K

Diffusion, 118K

**Color Plate 32-2**
Here I reduced the image from Color Plate 32-1 using each of three different Dither options—None, Pattern, and Diffusion. Beside each option name is the size of the file when saved in the GIF format. As you can see, GIF is better suited to compressing an image when no dithering is involved.

# Using the CD-ROMs

**A**ttached to the back cover of this book are two CD-ROMs — #1: Images and Utilities and #2: Secrets and Supplementals — packed with artwork, plug-ins, QuickTime movies, bonus chapters, and other goodies. Both CD-ROMs are cross-platform. That is, they work with both Macs and PCs. On the Mac, you need System 7.5 or later. On the PC, you need Windows 95, 98, or NT 4.0 or later. (The CD-ROMs will not function properly under Windows 3.1 or earlier.)

In the following sections, I tell you about the content on each CD-ROM.

## CD-ROM #1: Images and Utilities

This CD-ROM contains an extensive collection of photographs, artwork, and plug-ins that you can use with Photoshop. To view the photographs and artwork, you need Photoshop or some other image editor. You also need Photoshop to take advantage of the filters in the Plug-Ins folder. The remaining files — including artist biographies and documentation — are provided in one of three formats:

+ **Text-only (.txt) files:** Open these in SimpleText, Notepad, or with a word processor.

+ **Acrobat (.pdf) documents:** To open a .pdf file, you need Acrobat Reader or Acrobat Exchange from Adobe. Most folks already have Acrobat Reader, but if you don't, download it from *www.adobe.com*.

+ **Web (.html) pages:** To open these documents, you need access to a Web browser such as Netscape Navigator (*www.netscape.com*) or Microsoft Internet Explorer (*www.microsoft.com*).

The CD-ROM does not contain the software required to read these formats. This shouldn't be a problem because most computers are preconfigured with the software you need.

**Note**

One final note before we get under way: This CD-ROM does not contain the Photoshop 5 application. Photoshop retails for nearly $1,000 (about $600 on the street), so it's unrealistic to expect a copy of the software for the price you paid for this book. This book has just two purposes: (a) to educate digital artists and, more importantly, (b) to prop up youngsters who are too short to reach the table. If you want Photoshop, you have to buy it from Adobe.

## Opening the CD-ROM

To access the images and artwork included on the CD-ROM, start by inserting it into your CD-ROM drive. On a PC, double-click the My Computer icon on your desktop. The CD-ROM drive icon inside the My Computer window changes to Ph5 Bible. On a Mac, the CD-ROM icon, called Ph5 Bible, automatically appears on your desktop. Double-click the Ph5 Bible icon to open the CD-ROM. The window pops open and displays the following items:

+ **AboutThisCD:** This file duplicates some of the text from this appendix. But because I'm the kind of person who would pop the CD-ROM into the drive before ever cracking open the book, I thought it might be a good idea to include a "read me" file for impatient people like me.

+ **Artist Gallery:** This folder contains nearly 150MB of original imagery from 16 of the finest artists working with Photoshop today. The artists cover a broad range of styles and techniques, and you can get some great ideas from looking at their work. Note that these images belong to the artists who created them. Feel free to view them onscreen, but under no condition should you integrate an image from this folder into your own work, post an image on the Internet, or in any way pass it off as your own. Thanks.

+ **Digital Cameras:** Over the years, I've had the opportunity to use virtually every midrange digital camera that's come down the pike. I get a lot of e-mail about cameras, so I figured I'd help you make a decision by giving you the chance to judge the snapshots yourself. This folder contains hundreds of images shot with 27 cameras from 14 different vendors. This time I'm the copyright holder. I don't really care what you do with the photos in the privacy of your own home, but please don't reproduce them or post them online.

+ **DigitalThink:** This folder contains a sample lesson from DigitalThink, a Web-based training company that offers interactive classes in Photoshop and Illustrator written by yours truly. You can check out the entire catalog of courses at *www.digitalthink.com*.

+ **PC MacLAN:** Available to Windows users only, this folder contains a demonstration version of Miramar's PC MacLAN, the easiest solution for networking Macintosh and PC computers. This is the software I use in my office, so I can attest to how great it works. (If you view the CD-ROM on a Mac, you do not see this folder.)

✦ **Plug-Ins:** This folder contains a wide range of Photoshop plug-ins from scads of different vendors, including such luminaries as Alien Skin, Andromeda, and Extensis. Most of the plug-ins are limited demonstration versions that give you ample chance to try out the software before you buy it. Many vendors have graciously shared one or two fully functional plug-ins that are exclusive to this book. You can use them from the CD-ROM without paying another dime. I can proudly say that I know of no other Photoshop book that includes so much free software, and of such excellent caliber.

✦ **Stock Photos:** This folder contains a total of 48 high-resolution images from the titans of digital stock photography, PhotoDisc and Digital Stock. Not coincidentally, every one of these photographs is featured in the figures in this book, so you can follow along with the exercises and techniques exactly as I describe them.

The following sections explain the contents of each of these folders in-depth.

## Artists Gallery

These folders contain images created by 16 of the finest Photoshop artists working today. I'm here to tell you that some of this stuff will knock your socks off. In alphabetical order, the artists include Robert Bowen, Ron Chan, Mark Collen, Katrin Eismann, Helen Golden, Wendy Grossman, Dorothy Krause, Bonny Lhotka, Kent Maske, Judith Moncrieff, Bud Peen, Jeff Schewe, Karin Schminke, Gordon Studer, Richard Tuschman, and Nanette Wylde. All images are provided as inspirational material only; they are not for commercial use and the artists retain all copyrights to their work.

The easiest way to peruse the artwork is to use the Image Database.fdb file included in the Artists Gallery folder. To open this file, you must install Portfolio by double-clicking the Install Portfolio. Provided by Extensis, this demonstration version of Portfolio runs for 60 days. After that you have to either purchase Portfolio from Extensis or do without it.

After you install Portfolio, double-click the Image Database.fdb file to open it. (When Portfolio asks you for a serial number, click the Demo button.) The utility then shows you a long list of thumbnails. To view the thumbnails by artist (Figure 1), press ⌘/Ctrl+K to bring up the Keyword palette and then double-click the name of an artist in the list.

If you like, you can view a full-size image by double-clicking its thumbnail. But for ideal viewing, open the image in Photoshop. Inside Photoshop, choose File ⇨ Color Settings ⇨ RGB Setup and set the RGB pop-up menu to SMPTE-240M (or Adobe RGB if you're using Photoshop 5.0.2). This, of course, assumes that your monitor is properly calibrated or characterized, as explained in Chapter 3. Then open the image you want to view.

Each artist folder contains a short biography of the artist. Open the biography using your favorite word processor.

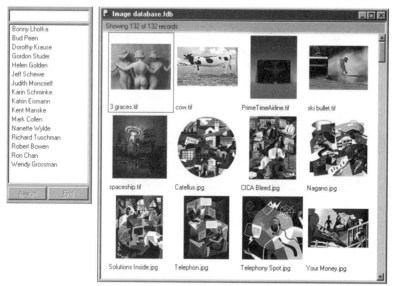

**Figure 1:** Press ⌘/Ctrl+K to bring up the Keyword palette, then double-click an artist's name to view his or her work.

## Digital Cameras

In 1994, Apple introduced the QuickTake 100, the first camera to shoot 24-bit, 640 × 480-pixel digital photographs for less than $1,000. I was fortunate enough to review that camera for *Macworld* magazine, and I have continued to review succeeding midrange cameras, amassing a library of more than 6,000 snapshots to date.

As with any category of hardware, some midrange cameras are great and others are awful. What's unusual is how varied the opinions are from one publication to another. I can't tell you how many times I've felt generous awarding a camera two stars, and then read a four-star review in another trade publication. It's truly bewildering.

It goes without saying that I'm right and other reviewers are raving lunatics. But it occurred to me that you might like the chance to see a few hundred images shot with these cameras to make up your own mind. That's what this folder is all about. The images are grouped by vendor — Kodak, Olympus, Polaroid, and so on — and then divided by camera model. In all, 27 different cameras are represented with four to eight examples from each one.

I corrected the brightness and focus of the images in an effort to make them look their best. After all, Photoshop gives me control over the digital darkroom; I'd be remiss to not take minimal advantage of it. But I didn't do any retouching, nor did I crop the images, so the pixels you see are the ones that the camera captured. You should know that I captured almost all the photographs at the maximum image size permitted by the cameras. (The exceptions are the images shot with the Agfa ePhoto and Polaroid PDC-2000. These are shown at second-to-highest resolution, which yielded sharper results due to unique internal interpolation schemes afforded by the two devices.) The Casio QV-10A squeaks by with the cheesiest and tiniest pictures, measuring just 320 × 240 pixels. The Olympus D-340L weighs in with the biggest and the best picture at 1,280 × 960 pixels. As shown in Figure 2, a D-340L picture is big enough to hold 16 snapshots captured with the QV-10A.

**Figure 2:** An image shot at the San Diego Zoo with the Olympus D-340L compared with one shot in Paris (inset) with the Casio QV-10A. Both images are printed at 300 ppi.

Bear in mind, image quality isn't the only measure of a camera. For example, the Minolta Dimage V takes reasonably good pictures, but it's a pain in the neck to work with. By contrast, the pictures taken with the Fuji DS-7 are fair to average, but the camera is a dream to use. For complete information about each camera — and future models that have come out since the release of this book — see my reviews at *www.macworld.com.* Most of the cameras work the same on Windows, so the reviews should be equally applicable to PC folks.

Again, you can peruse the photographs by opening the Image Database.fdb file in the Digital Cameras folder. (If you haven't yet installed Portfolio, double-click the Install Portfolio icon. When asked for a serial number, click the Demo button.) Then press ⌘/Ctrl+K to view the Keyword palette and double-click the name of the camera you're interested in. For ideal viewing of a full-size photograph, open the image in Photoshop. Be sure the RGB Setup environment is set to SMPTE-240M and that your monitor is properly calibrated with Gamma or some other utility.

# DigitalThink

This folder contains HTML files from DigitalThink, a company that offers online training in Java, C++, and other topics over the World Wide Web. It also has a first-rate course on Photoshop and an even better one on Illustrator, both designed by me. To learn more about these and other training opportunities from DigitalThink, open the index.html document in your favorite Web browser.

# Plug-Ins

The contents of this folder vary depending on whether you're using a Mac or a PC. On the Mac, the Plug-Ins folder contains filters from 12 different vendors. On the Windows side, 11 vendors are represented. This is because two vendors, ImageXpress and Vivid Details, create plug-ins for the Mac only, and another vendor, Ulead, is exclusively Windows. The remaining vendors — Alien Skin, Altamira Group, Andromeda, BoxTop Software, Chroma Graphics, Digital Frontiers, Extensis, Wacom, and Xaos Tools — are cross-platform.

All told, the Plug-Ins folder includes more than 50 pieces of software. Each plug-in includes documentation on the CD-ROM that explains what it does and how it works. Rather than itemize each program, here's a quick summary of the highlights to get you started:

♦ **Alien Skin:** This folder contains a demo version of Eye Candy 3.0, the splendid special effects suite from Alien Skin. As a special gift to *Photoshop 5 Bible* readers, Alien Skin also includes Eye Candy LE 2.1, which includes the fully functioning filters Glass and Swirl, two of my personal favorites. All hail Alien Skin.

♦ **Altamira Group:** Altamira has provided a demonstration version of Genuine Fractals, which rewrites pixels using fractal math to create what amounts to resolution-independent images. For example, you can export a 20MB letter-size image to FIF format, and then import it as a 100MB poster-size image without measurable degradation in quality. Meanwhile, the image takes as little as 1MB of disk space. It's wonderful technology for expert users. To use the filters, add them to Photoshop's Plug-Ins folder, restart Photoshop, and experiment with the commands in the Filter ⇨ Import and File ⇨ Export submenus.

♦ **Andromeda:** Andromeda Software has generously provided samples of six of its special effects and 3-D filter collections. Among these is a fully functioning demo of Series 4, Techtures, an excellent texture creation and manipulation laboratory, which also happens to be available exclusively to *Photoshop 5 Bible* readers. Just double-click the Install utilities to add these plug-ins to Photoshop.

♦ **BoxTop Software:** BoxTop specializes in plug-ins that export and optimize Web graphics. On the Windows side, you'll find three demo plug-ins. Each program is fully functional for 30 days, then, rather than expiring, it merely slows down. Frankly, that's pretty darn generous. On the Mac side you'll find several more demos along with a few freebies, including PhotoGIF Lite, which is available exclusively to *Photoshop 5 Bible* readers.

✦ **Chroma Graphics:** This folder contains three traditional demos but no freebies. I decided to include the filters anyway because they automate one of the most complicated operations in Photoshop: masking. You can't save your work with these demos, but at least you can get a sense of how the filters work.

✦ **Digital Frontiers:** Like BoxTop, Digital Frontiers specializes in plug-ins for exporting and optimizing Web graphics. But unlike BoxTop, all of its filters are cross-platform. As a special service for *Photoshop 5 Bible* readers, Digital Frontiers has provided a free and fully functioning copy of HVS ColorGIF. For more information about this and other Digital Frontiers plug-ins, see Chapter 32.

✦ **Extensis:** This folder includes five Photoshop plug-ins — Mask Pro, PhotoTools, Intellihance, PhotoGraphics, and PhotoFrame — plus two stand-alone applications, PhotoAnimator and Portfolio. Definitely check out Mask Pro, which automates complex masking, and Portfolio, which enables you to assemble catalogs of your images. (If you ever encounter a dialog box that requests a serial number, just click the Demo button and use the software, free, for 30 days.)

✦ **ImageXpress:** Available on the Mac only, this folder contains demonstration versions of Alius and ScanPrepPro. Alius is a first-rate posterization filter; ScanPrepPro is perhaps the most highly rated module for scanning images into Photoshop. Both are worth a look. The installation is a little tricky, so be sure to read the documentation supplied in the folder. Enter **Trial** as the serial number to use either plug-in free for seven days.

✦ **Tormentia:** This is the collection of eight filters that I created using the Filter Factory, as I explain in Chapter D on CD-ROM #2. Each one is fully functional, free, and cross-platform. To install the filters, drag them into Photoshop's Plug-Ins folder. To learn what each of these filters does, read the Torment.txt file included in the Tormentia folder.

✦ **Ulead:** If you Windows folks were starting to get peeved about the absent filters from BoxTop and ImageXpress, here's your chance to get even. This folder contains a grand total of 14 plug-ins and stand-alone utilities from Ulead, and every one of them is available exclusively for Windows. Many of the plug-ins are fully functioning shareware, and one program, Gale10.exe, installs a free version of GIF Animator Lite, available exclusively to *Photoshop 5 Bible* readers.

✦ **Vivid Details:** Available only for Macintosh users, this folder contains a demonstration version of Test Strip. This excellent plug-in is ideal for anyone who owns a color proofing or output device and wants to be able to compare side-by-side color variations. Test Strip eliminates the guesswork of printing reliable color and it's extremely easy to use. What more could you ask for?

✦ **Wacom:** Each one of the eight plug-ins in this folder is free and fully functional. Just drag the filters into Photoshop's Plug-Ins folder, restart Photoshop, and you're ready to go. The catch is that they work only if you own a Wacom drawing tablet. If you have a tablet, you're good to go; if not, visit *www.wacom.com.*

✦ **Xaos Tools:** This folder includes two items. One is a utility that installs Total Xaos (pronounced chaos), which is a collection of three demo plug-ins: the brush laboratory Paint Alchemy, the 3-D type-creation filter Type Caster, and the texture-creation filter Terrazzo. As a special gift to *Photoshop 5 Bible* readers, Xaos has thrown in 32 "luminous texture" images from the company's commercial Fresco collection. If a bunch of textures strikes you as a bit dull, open one or two in Photoshop and you'll quickly change your mind.

Remember, after installing a plug-in from any of the vendors listed above, you must quit Photoshop and relaunch the program in order to load the plug-ins into RAM. Most plug-ins work only if an image is open.

## Stock Photos

The idea behind the Stock Photos folder is to give you access to the original images featured in this book. That way, you can edit the images as you read along. The Stock Photos folder contains two subfolders named after the vendors that contributed photographs to the book, Digital Stock and PhotoDisc. Each subfolder contains another folder called High-rez images. Inside, you'll find 24 high-resolution images from the book.

I've provided an Image Database.fdb file so you can find the file you're looking for without scrambling too much. As I explained in the "Artists Gallery" section, you can open this file with Portfolio from Extensis. If you haven't installed Portfolio, double-click the Install Portfolio icon. When asked for a serial number, click the Demo button. (The demo will last for 60 days.) Then open the Image Database.fdb file and press ⌘/Ctrl+K to view a list of keywords that will help you locate the desired image. Once you've found the image you're looking for, open it up in Photoshop. (These images are too large to open in Portfolio, and besides, Photoshop is where you want to do your editing.)

By way of an endorsement, you can rely on both Digital Stock and PhotoDisc for their vast libraries of high-quality stock photography. If you're looking for an image, one or the other is bound to provide what you need. For more information, or to search for photographs online according to subject, consult the companies' Web sites at *www.digitalstock.com* and *www.photodisc.com*.

# CD-ROM #2: Secrets and Supplementals

This CD-ROM contains bonus chapters and articles, images and QuickTime movies from some of artists featured in the book's color chapters, and artist interviews. The CD-ROM content is divided into eight folders and a loose QuickTime file. The QuickTime files are big — 320 × 240 pixels at 15 frames per second — so they work best on Power Mac and Pentium computers. They will play on 040 and 496 models, but occasional frames may hang and the sound may not properly sync with the video.

Here's a complete rundown of the files:

✦ **Dinotopia.mov:** Run this movie to see Eric Chauvin's vision of Dinotopia live and breathe (Chapter 29). The water comes from Niagara Falls; music and sound effects come from Denver-based musician David Schmal.

If a video plays slowly or unevenly, speed up performance by copying the QuickTime movies to your hard drive. You'll need QuickTime 3 to see all the movies; if you don't have it, run the installer program inside the QuickTime VR folder.

✦ **Bonus Chapters:** Inside this folder are eight bonus chapters. Chapter A contains advice on preparing your system to enable Photoshop to perform at its best. Chapter B takes you on an in-depth tour of the Photoshop 5 desktop, including an introduction to Photoshop's tools, control icons, revised palettes, and more. Chapter C is all about colors. Chapter D shows you how to create custom effects. Chapter E introduces you to Photoshop's shortcuts and walks you through the process of creating scripts. (For a complete list of every shortcut available in Photoshop 5, see Chapter G if you're on a Mac or Chapter H if you're on a PC.) Chapter F identifies the sources of the various photographs that appear in the book.

✦ **Articles and Notes:** Just in case you're hungry for more, this folder includes eight articles and session notes written by yours truly. Many of these articles originally appeared (at least in part) in *Macworld* and *Publish* magazines. Get 21 top Photoshop 5 tips and tricks. Learn more about masking techniques, working with blend modes, creating effects using the history brush and History palette, and using layer effects.

✦ **Reinfeld:** This folder contains four silent QuickTime movies, all of which show moving type effects created by Eric Reinfeld (Chapter 21). If nothing else, check out Trippy.mov. No mind-altering chemicals needed.

✦ **Bowen:** Double-click this folder to access two versions of Robert Bowen's stereoscopic view of New York City (Chapter 14). If you have a monster system with scads of RAM, open the Huge3-D.psd file. Otherwise, open Med3-D.psd instead. Then get yourself a pair of 3-D glasses and put them on with the red lens over your left eye and the blue lens over your right. (You can hear Bowen personally explain the file by running his movie in the Voices folder.)

✦ **Eismann:** This folder contains four QuickTime VR movies created by Katrin Eismann (Chapter 33). All of these movies were created by stitching together pictures from digital cameras.

✦ **Benjamin:** Because Ben Benjamin (Chapter 34) creates his images to be viewed onscreen, I figured you should see them onscreen. Nine of the files are screen shots of his finished Web pages from CNET and E! Online. The tenth file, TalkSoup.gif, is an animated banner ad. You can open it in a Web browser such as Netscape Navigator or a GIF animation utility such as GifBuilder. (Neither of these programs is included on this CD-ROM.)

✦ **Voices:** This folder includes snippets from my phone interviews with the 14 artists featured in the color chapters of this book. Lasting one to two minutes apiece, these QuickTime conversations explore technical topics, personal background, and just plain goofiness. Hear a bit of calming digital camera advice from Katrin Eismann. Find out why Michael Ninness is known to his friends as "Myke with a Y."

Keep in mind that all the conversations in the Voices folder were pieced together from telephone recordings, so the quality is a little choppy. If you have speakers attached to your computer, crank the volume. If you don't, go out and buy some. They're cheap and they make computing much more enjoyable.

## CD-ROM Technical Support

If you have problems getting either of the CD-ROMs to work with your computer, it's very likely that some of your settings files or drivers are not working properly. For assistance, call IDG Books' technical support hotline at 1-800-762-2974. This also is the number to call if a CD-ROM is damaged.

✦    ✦    ✦

# Index

# IDG BOOKS WORLDWIDE, INC. END-USER LICENSE AGREEMENT

<u>READ THIS.</u> You should carefully read these terms and conditions before opening the software packet(s) included with this book ("Book"). This is a license agreement ("Agreement") between you and IDG Books Worldwide, Inc. ("IDGB"). By opening the accompanying software packet(s), you acknowledge that you have read and accept the following terms and conditions. If you do not agree and do not want to be bound by such terms and conditions, promptly return the Book and the unopened software packet(s) to the place you obtained them for a full refund.

1. <u>License Grant.</u> IDGB grants to you (either an individual or entity) a nonexclusive license to use one copy of the enclosed software program(s) (collectively, the "Software") solely for your own personal or business purposes on a single computer (whether a standard computer or a workstation component of a multiuser network). The Software is in use on a computer when it is loaded into temporary memory (RAM) or installed into permanent memory (hard disk, CD-ROM, or other storage device). IDGB reserves all rights not expressly granted herein.

2. <u>Ownership.</u> IDGB is the owner of all right, title, and interest, including copyright, in and to the compilation of the Software recorded on the disk(s) or CD-ROMs ("Software Media"). Copyright to the individual programs recorded on the Software Media is owned by the author or other authorized copyright owner of each program. Ownership of the Software and all proprietary rights relating thereto remain with IDGB and its licensers.

3. <u>Restrictions on Use and Transfer.</u>

   (a) You may only (i) make one copy of the Software for backup or archival purposes, or (ii) transfer the Software to a single hard disk, provided that you keep the original for backup or archival purposes. You may not (i) rent or lease the Software, (ii) copy or reproduce the Software through a LAN or other network system or through any computer subscriber system or bulletin-board system, or (iii) modify, adapt, or create derivative works based on the Software.

   (b) You may not reverse engineer, decompile, or disassemble the Software. You may transfer the Software and user documentation on a permanent basis, provided that the transferee agrees to accept the terms and conditions of this Agreement and you retain no copies. If the Software is an update or has been updated, any transfer must include the most recent update and all prior versions.

4. **Restrictions on Use of Individual Programs.** You must follow the individual requirements and restrictions detailed for each individual program in the "Using the CD-ROMs" appendix of this Book. These limitations are also contained in the individual license agreements recorded on the Software Media. These limitations may include a requirement that after using the program for a specified period of time, the user must pay a registration fee or discontinue use. By opening the Software packet(s), you will be agreeing to abide by the licenses and restrictions for these individual programs that are detailed in the "Using the CD-ROMs" appendix and on the Software Media. None of the material on this Software Media or listed in this Book may ever be redistributed, in original or modified form, for commercial purposes.

5. **Limited Warranty.**

   **(a)** IDGB warrants that the Software and Software Media are free from defects in materials and workmanship under normal use for a period of sixty (60) days from the date of purchase of this Book. If IDGB receives notification within the warranty period of defects in materials or workmanship, IDGB will replace the defective Software Media.

   **(b)** **IDGB AND THE AUTHOR OF THE BOOK DISCLAIM ALL OTHER WARRANTIES, EXPRESS OR IMPLIED, INCLUDING WITHOUT LIMITATION IMPLIED WARRANTIES OF MERCHANTABILITY AND FITNESS FOR A PARTICULAR PURPOSE, WITH RESPECT TO THE SOFTWARE, THE PROGRAMS, THE SOURCE CODE CONTAINED THEREIN, AND/OR THE TECHNIQUES DESCRIBED IN THIS BOOK. IDGB DOES NOT WARRANT THAT THE FUNCTIONS CONTAINED IN THE SOFTWARE WILL MEET YOUR REQUIREMENTS OR THAT THE OPERATION OF THE SOFTWARE WILL BE ERROR-FREE.**

   **(c)** This limited warranty gives you specific legal rights, and you may have other rights that vary from jurisdiction to jurisdiction.

6. **Remedies.**

   **(a)** IDGB's entire liability and your exclusive remedy for defects in materials and workmanship shall be limited to replacement of the Software Media, which may be returned to IDGB with a copy of your receipt at the following address: Software Media Fulfillment Department, Attn.: Photoshop 5 Bible, Gold Edition, IDG Books Worldwide, Inc., 7260 Shadeland Station, Ste. 100, Indianapolis, IN 46256, or call 1-800-762-2974. Please allow three to four weeks for delivery. This Limited Warranty is void if failure of the Software Media has resulted from accident, abuse, or misapplication. Any replacement Software Media will be warranted for the remainder of the original warranty period or thirty (30) days, whichever is longer.

(b) In no event shall IDGB or the authors be liable for any damages whatsoever (including without limitation damages for loss of business profits, business interruption, loss of business information, or any other pecuniary loss) arising from the use of or inability to use the Book or the Software, even if IDGB has been advised of the possibility of such damages.

(c) Because some jurisdictions do not allow the exclusion or limitation of liability for consequential or incidental damages, the above limitation or exclusion may not apply to you.

7. **U.S. Government Restricted Rights.** Use, duplication, or disclosure of the Software by the U.S. Government is subject to restrictions stated in paragraph (c)(1)(ii) of the Rights in Technical Data and Computer Software clause of DFARS 252.227-7013, and in subparagraphs (a) through (d) of the Commercial Computer — Restricted Rights clause at FAR 52.227-19, and in similar clauses in the NASA FAR supplement, when applicable.

8. **General.** This Agreement constitutes the entire understanding of the parties and revokes and supersedes all prior agreements, oral or written, between them and may not be modified or amended except in a writing signed by both parties hereto that specifically refers to this Agreement. This Agreement shall take precedence over any other documents that may be in conflict herewith. If any one or more provisions contained in this Agreement are held by any court or tribunal to be invalid, illegal, or otherwise unenforceable, each and every other provision shall remain in full force and effect.

# my2cents.idgbooks.com

# We're the Best Way to Learn Photoshop.

# Just Ask Deke.

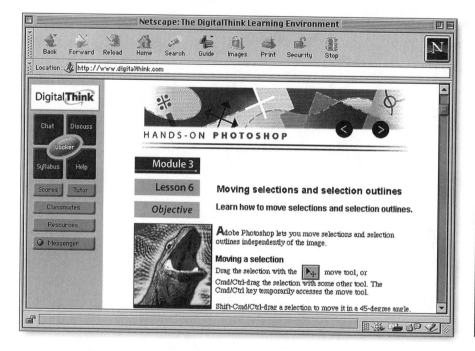

*DigitalThink courses are taught completely over the Web and let you learn what you want, when you want.*

Deke McClelland, author of *The MacWorld Photoshop 5.0 Bible,* is on the World Wide Web with **Hands-On Photoshop,** an all new online course from DigitalThink.

DigitalThink is the only Adobe Authorized Learning Provider (AALP) for online training. Our courses teach you how to get the most out of Adobe Photoshop®, Adobe Illustrator®, Java Programming, the Internet, and more.

Learn anytime you want, from wherever you have a Web connection. DigitalThink courses give you live tutors, chat sessions with experts, interactive quizzes, discussion boards, and more.

If you can't get online, you can still sample DigitalThink's learning environment. Deke has included a lesson from **Hands-On Photoshop** on his CD-ROM in the back of this book.

Not convinced? Come to the DigitalThink site at **http://www.digitalthink.com** to take a FREE demo of a Web-based course. Then sign up for **Hands-On Photoshop** at a 10% discount.

DigitalThink. Simply the best way to learn Adobe Photoshop. Just ask Deke.

**www.digitalthink.com**

# The Biggest Difference In The SpectraView Display System Is There Is No Difference.

Consistency. It's what every graphics professional wants, but seldom achieves. Until now. The SpectraView 1000 color calibrated display system from Mitsubishi Electronics provides monitor-to-monitor color matching throughout the entire prepress process. Unsurpassed color accuracy results in less time and materials needed to complete a job, which improves your productivity and adds more profit to your bottom line. The SpectraView 1000 combines Mitsubishi's award-winning 21" (19.7" diagonal viewable image) DIAMONDTRON™ CRT display with a precise, high-speed SpectraSensor™ colorimeter and custom software to achieve accurate, reliable, repeatable and consistent color performance. Plus, it's available for either PC or Mac, providing a complete cross-platform display-matching solution. To find out how the SpectraView 1000 can make a major difference in your color-critical applications, contact your authorized distributor today: Tekgraf, Inc. at 1-888-321-TKGF.

**SPECTRAVIEW**
COLOR CALIBRATED DISPLAY SYSTEM

**Tekgraf**

MacWEEK
R A T I N G

◆◆◆◆

▲ MITSUBISHI
DISPLAY PRODUCTS
*Innovation On Display*sm

Make something good.

A reminder that DuoScan™ scanners and ePhoto® digital cameras help thousands of people do just that, every day.

# CD-ROM Installation Instructions
## CD #1

Insert the CD in your CD-ROM drive. If you're using a Mac, the CD icon appears on your desktop. If you're using a PC, double-click the My Computer icon on your Desktop and locate your CD-ROM drive. Double-click the CD icon to open the CD-ROM. The window pops open and displays a list of items. To view the photographs and artwork contained on the CD, you will need Photoshop or some other image editor. You will also need Photoshop to take advantage of the filters contained in the Plug-Ins folder. The remaining files are provided in one of three formats:

- ✦ **Text-only (.txt) files:** You can open these in SimpleText, Notepad, or a word processor.

- ✦ **Acrobat (.pdf) documents:** To open a .pdf file, you'll need Adobe's Acrobat Reader. If you don't already have it, you can download the Reader from *www.adobe.com.*

- ✦ **Web (.html) pages:** To open these documents, you need access to a Web browser such as Netscape Navigator (*www.netscape.com*) or Microsoft Internet Explorer (*www.microsoft.com*).

The CD does not contain any of the software required to read these formats, though most computers come preconfigured with the software you need.

## CD #2

Insert the CD in your CD-ROM drive. Locate the CD icon (as described above) and double-click it to display a list of nine folders and two loose QuickTime files. To view the images and artwork in the folders, you will need Photoshop or some other image editor. To play the QuickTime movies, you will need QuickTime 3; if you don't have it, run the installer program inside the QuickTime VR folder. To view the Web pages, you will need a Web browser. And finally, to open the .pdf files, you will need Acrobat Reader.

For a complete rundown on the files included on each CD, see the "Using the CD-ROMs" appendix.